C000217581

STREET ATLAS
West Sussex

Bognor Regis, Brighton, Chichester, Crawley, Horsham, Hove, Worthing

www.philips-maps.co.uk

First published in 1994 by

Philip's, a division of
Octopus Publishing Group Ltd
www.octopusbooks.co.uk
2-4 Heron Quays, London E14 4JP
An Hachette Livre UK Company
www.hachettelivre.co.uk

Fourth colour edition 2008
First impression 2008
WSUDA

ISBN 978-0-540-09271-0 (spiral)

© Philip's 2008

Ordnance Survey®

This product includes mapping data licensed
from Ordnance Survey®, with the permission of
the Controller of Her Majesty's Stationery Office.

© Crown copyright 2008. All rights reserved.
Licence number 100011710

To the best of the Publishers' knowledge, the
information in this atlas was correct at the time
of going to press. No responsibility can be
accepted for any errors or their consequences.

The representation in this atlas of a road, track
or path is no evidence of the existence of a
right of way.

Data for the speed cameras provided by
PocketGPSWorld.com Ltd.

Ordnance Survey and the OS symbol are
registered trademarks of Ordnance Survey, the
national mapping agency of Great Britain

Printed and bound in China by Toppan

Contents

II	**List of mobile speed cameras**	
III	**Key to map symbols**	
IV	**Key to map pages**	
VI	**Route planning**	
VIII	**Administrative and Postcode boundaries**	
1	**Street maps** at 3½ inches to 1 mile	
213	**Street map of Brighton city centre** at 7 inches to 1 mile	
214	**Index** of towns, villages, streets, hospitals, industrial estates, railway stations, schools, shopping centres universities and places of interest	

Digital Data

The exceptionally high-quality mapping found in this atlas is available as digital data in TIFF format, which is easily convertible to other bitmapped (raster) image formats.

The index is also available in digital form as a standard database table. It contains all the details found in the printed index together with the National Grid reference for the map square in which each entry is named.

For further information and to discuss your requirements, please contact james.mann@philips-maps.co.uk

On-line route planner

For detailed driving directions and estimated driving times visit our free route plannner at www.philips-maps.co.uk

Mobile speed cameras

The vast majority of speed cameras used on Britain's roads are operated by safety camera partnerships. These comprise local authorities, the police, Her Majesty's Court Service (HMCS) and the Highways Agency.

This table lists the sites where each safety camera partnership may enforce speed limits through the use of mobile cameras or detectors. These are usually set up on the roadside or a bridge spanning the road and operated by a police or civilian enforcement officer. The speed limit at each site (if available) is shown in red type, followed by the approximate location in black type.

Mike Harrington / Alamy

A27
40 Lancing, near Grand Avenue, Upper Brighton Road

70 Shoreham, Holmbush

70 Angmering, East of Dappers Lane, Hammerpot

A29
30 Aldingbourne, Westergate Street

40 Bognor Regis, Shripney Road

A259
30 Saltdean, Marine Drive

30 Fishbourne, Main Road

30 Lancing, Brighton Road

30 Brighton, Black Rock

30 Bognor Regis, Hotham Way

A280
40 Patching, Long Furlong

A281
30 Horsham, Guildford Road

A283
30 Northchapel, nr Pipers Lane

30 Pulborough, Lower Street (East)

A285
30 Petworth, Station Road

40 Halnaker, Stane Street

A2032
30 Worthing, Littlehampton Road, Poulter's Lane

A2038
30 Hove, Hangleton Road

B2066
30 Hove, New Church Road

B2070
40 Rake, London Road

B2111
30 Lindfield, Lewes Road

B2123
30 Brighton, Woodingdean, Falmer Road

B2138
30 Fittleworth, Lower Street

B2166
30 Bognor Regis, Aldwick Road

UNCLASSIFIED
30 Horsham, Pondtail Road

30 Bognor Regis, Chalcraft Lane

30 Crawley, near Hazlewick Flyover, Gatwick Road

30 Worthing, Marine Parade

30 Worthing, The Boulevard

30 Crawley, Gossops Drive

30 Crawley, Manor Royal

30 Eastbourne, Brodrick Road

30 Brighton, Carden Avenue

30 Hove, Shirley Drive

Motorway with junction number	
Primary route – dual/single carriageway	
A road – dual/single carriageway	
B road – dual/single carriageway	
Minor road – dual/single carriageway	
Other minor road – dual/single carriageway	
Road under construction	
Tunnel, covered road	
Speed cameras - single, multiple	
Rural track, private road or narrow road in urban area	
Gate or obstruction to traffic (restrictions may not apply at all times or to all vehicles)	
Path, bridleway, byway open to all traffic, road used as a public path	
Pedestrianised area	
Postcode boundaries DY7	
County and unitary authority boundaries	
Railway, tunnel, railway under construction	
Tramway, tramway under construction	
Miniature railway	
Railway station Walsall	
Private railway station	
Metro station South Shields	
Tram stop, tram stop under construction	
Bus, coach station	

◆	**Ambulance station**	
◆	**Coastguard station**	
◆	**Fire station**	
◆	**Police station**	
✚	**Accident and Emergency entrance to hospital**	
H	**Hospital**	
+	**Place of worship**	
𝑖	**Information Centre** (open all year)	
🛒	**Shopping Centre**	
P P&R	**Parking, Park and Ride**	
PO	**Post Office**	
🏕 🚐	**Camping site, caravan site**	
⚑ ⨯	**Golf course, picnic site**	
▦ Prim Sch	**Important buildings, schools, colleges, universities and hospitals**	
	Built up area	
	Woods	
River Medway	**Water name**	
	River, weir, stream	
	Canal, lock, tunnel	
	Water	
	Tidal water	
Church	**Non-Roman antiquity**	
ROMAN FORT	**Roman antiquity**	
87	**Adjoining page indicators and overlap bands** The colour of the arrow and the band indicates the scale of the adjoining or overlapping page (see scales below)	
237		

Acad	**Academy**	Inst	**Institute**	Recn Gd	**Recreation Ground**
Allot Gdns	**Allotments**	Ct	**Law Court**		
Cemy	**Cemetery**	L Ctr	**Leisure Centre**	Resr	**Reservoir**
C Ctr	**Civic Centre**	LC	**Level Crossing**	Ret Pk	**Retail Park**
CH	**Club House**	Liby	**Library**	Sch	**School**
Coll	**College**	Mkt	**Market**	Sh Ctr	**Shopping Centre**
Crem	**Crematorium**	Meml	**Memorial**	TH	**Town Hall/House**
Ent	**Enterprise**	Mon	**Monument**	Trad Est	**Trading Estate**
Ex H	**Exhibition Hall**	Mus	**Museum**	Univ	**University**
Ind Est	**Industrial Estate**	Obsy	**Observatory**	W Twr	**Water Tower**
IRB Sta	**Inshore Rescue Boat Station**	Pal	**Royal Palace**	Wks	**Works**
		PH	**Public House**	YH	**Youth Hostel**

Enlarged mapping only

	Railway or bus station building
	Place of interest
	Parkland

■ The small numbers around the edges of the maps identify the 1 kilometre National Grid lines

■ The dark grey border on the inside edge of some pages indicates that the mapping does not continue onto the adjacent page

The scale of the maps on the pages numbered in blue is 5.52 cm to 1 km • 3½ inches to 1 mile • 1: 18103

0   ¼   ½   ¾   1 mile
0   250m   500m   750m   1 kilometre

The scale of the maps on pages numbered in red is 11.04 cm to 1 km • 7 inches to 1 mile • 1: 9051

0   220 yards   440 yards   660 yards   ½ mile
0   125m   250m   375m   ½ kilometre

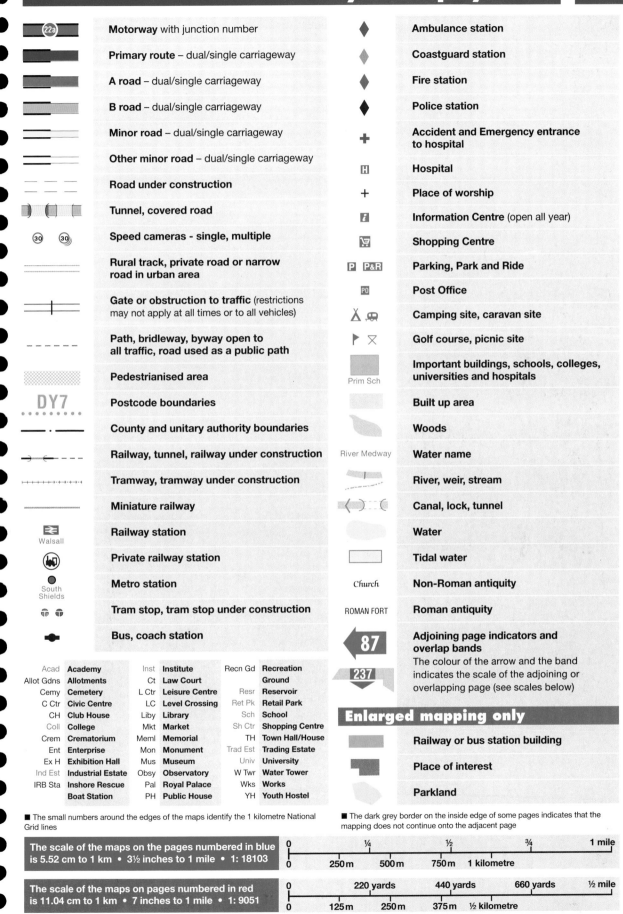

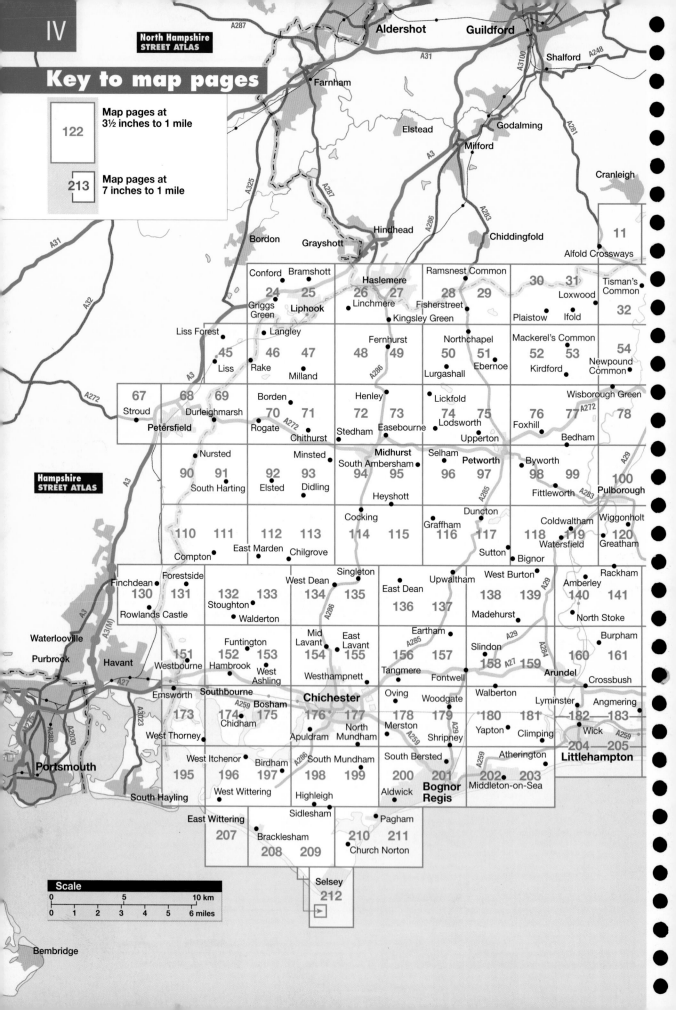

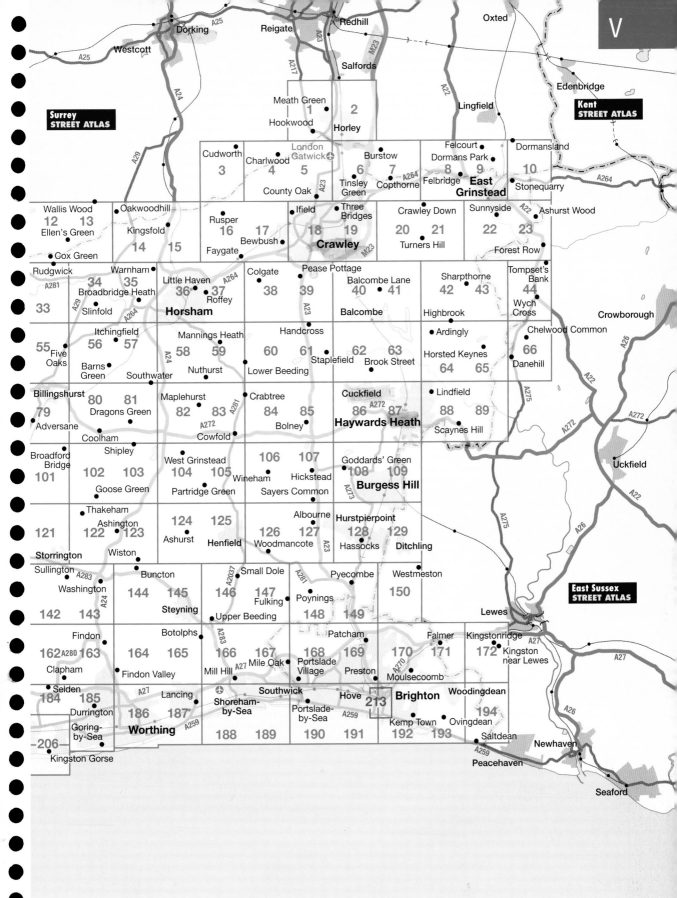

Surrey STREET ATLAS

Kent STREET ATLAS

Dorking
Westcott
A25
Reigate
Redhill
Oxted
Salfords
A217
A23
A22
M23
Edenbridge
Meath Green **1** **2**
Hookwood Horley
Lingfield
A24
A29
Cudworth **3** Charlwood **4** **5** Burstow **6** **7** Felcourt Dormans Park **8** **9** Dormansland **10**
London Gatwick
County Oak A23 Tinsley Green Copthorne A264 Felbridge East Grinstead Stonequarry
Kent
A264
Wallis Wood **12** **13** Oakwoodhill
Ellen's Green
Rusper Ifield Three Bridges Crawley Down Sunnyside Ashurst Wood
Kingsfold **16** **17** **18** **19** **20** **21** **22** **23** A22
Cox Green **14** **15** Faygate Bewbush Crawley Turners Hill Forest Row
Rudgwick Warnham Little Haven Colgate Pease Pottage Balcombe Lane Sharpthorne Tompset's Bank
A281 **34** **35** **36** **37** **38** **39** **40** **41** **42** **43** **44** Crowborough
33 Broadbridge Heath Roffey Balcombe Wych Cross A26
A29 Slinfold Horsham A23 Highbrook
A264 Handcross Ardingly Chelwood Common
Itchingfield **56** **57** Mannings Heath **58** **59** **60** **61** **62** **63** **66**
55 Five Oaks A24 Nuthurst Lower Beeding Staplefield Brook Street Horsted Keynes Danehill
Barns Green Southwater **64** **65**
Billingshurst Maplehurst Crabtree Cuckfield Lindfield
80 **81** **82** **83** A281 **84** **85** A272 **86** **87** **88** **89**
79 Dragons Green Bolney Haywards Heath A272
Adversane A272 Scaynes Hill Uckfield
Coolham Cowfold
Broadford Bridge Shipley West Grinstead **106** **107** Goddards' Green A22 A26
101 **102** **103** **104** **105** Wineham Hicksted **108** **109**
Goose Green Partridge Green Sayers Common Burgess Hill A275
Thakeham Albourne Hurstpierpoint
Ashington **124** **125** **126** **127** **128** **129**
121 **122** **123** Ashurst Henfield Woodmancote A3 Hassocks Ditchling
Storrington Wiston
Sullington A283 Buncton Small Dole Pyecombe Westmeston
Washington **144** **145** **146** **147** **148** **149** **150** Lewes
A24 Fulking Poynings
142 **143** Steyning Upper Beeding East Sussex STREET ATLAS
Findon Botolphs Patcham Falmer Kingstonridge
162 A280 **163** **164** **165** **166** **167** **168** **169** **170** **171** **172** Kingston near Lewes
Clapham A27 Mile Oak Portslade Village Preston A270 Moulsecoomb A27
Findon Valley Mill Hill A27 A27
Selden **184** **185** Lancing Southwick Hove **213** Brighton Woodingdean
Durrington **186** **187** Shoreham-by-Sea **194**
Goring-by-Sea Worthing A259 Portslade-by-Sea A259 Kemp Town Ovingdean A26
-206- **188** **189** **190** **191** **192** **193** Saltdean Newhaven
Kingston Gorse Peacehaven
A259
Seaford

Route Planning

Scale

0   5   10 km

0   1   2   3   4   5   6 miles

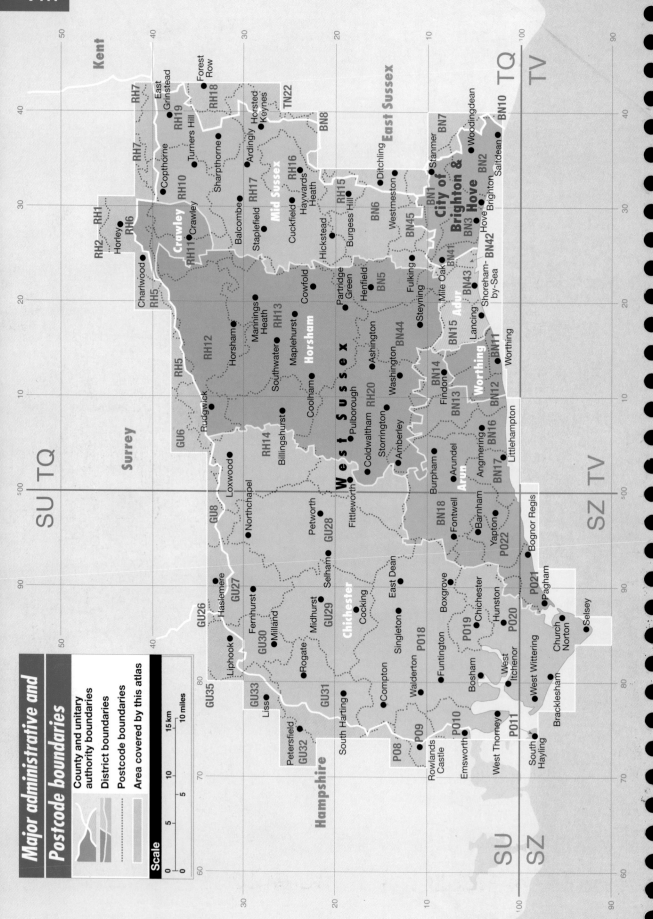

Major administrative and Postcode boundaries

County and unitary authority boundaries

District boundaries

Postcode boundaries

Area covered by this atlas

Scale

0 5 10 15 km

0 5 10 miles

Kent

Surrey

Hampshire

East Sussex

West Sussex

Mid Sussex

Crawley

Horsham

Chichester

Arun

Worthing

Adur

City of Brighton & Hove

SU | TQ

SZ | TV

TV

TQ

Forest Row
East Grinstead
Copthorne
Turners Hill
Sharpthorne
Ardingly
Horsted Keynes
Balcombe
Staplefield
Cuckfield
Haywards Heath
Hickstead
Partridge Green
Henfield
Cowfold
Steyning
Fulking
Washington
Ashington
Storrington
Amberley
Findon
Angmering
Arundel
Barnham
Yapton
Bognor Regis
Pagham
Selsey
Church Norton
West Wittering
Bracklesham
South Hayling
West Thorney
Emsworth
Rowlands Castle
South Harting
Petersfield
Liss
Liphook
Haslemere
Fernhurst
Midhurst
Milland
Rogate
Compton
Walderton
Singleton
East Dean
Cocking
Boxgrove
Chichester
Hunston
West Itchenor
Bosham
Funtington
Petworth
Fittleworth
Northchapel
Loxwood
Billingshurst
Rudgwick
Horsham
Southwater
Maplehurst
Mannings Heath
Coolham
Pulborough
Coldwaltham
Littlehampton
Lancing
Worthing
Shoreham-by-Sea
Mile Oak
Hove
Brighton
Saltdean
Woodingdean
Stanmer
Ditchling
Westmeston
Burgess Hill
Burpham
Fontwell

RH7
RH18
RH19
TN22
BN8
RH17
RH16
RH10
RH11
RH1
RH2
RH6
RH5
RH12
RH13
RH14
RH15
RH20
BN6
BN5
BN45
BN1
BN2
BN3
BN42
BN41
BN43
BN15
BN11
BN14
BN13
BN12
BN16
BN17
BN18
BN7
GU6
GU8
GU26
GU27
GU28
GU29
GU30
GU31
GU32
GU33
GU35
PO8
PO9
PO10
PO11
PO18
PO19
PO20
PO21
PO22
TQ
TV
SU
SZ

Charlwood
Horley
Crawley

30
40
50
60
70
80
90
100
10
20
30
40
50
60
70
80
90
500

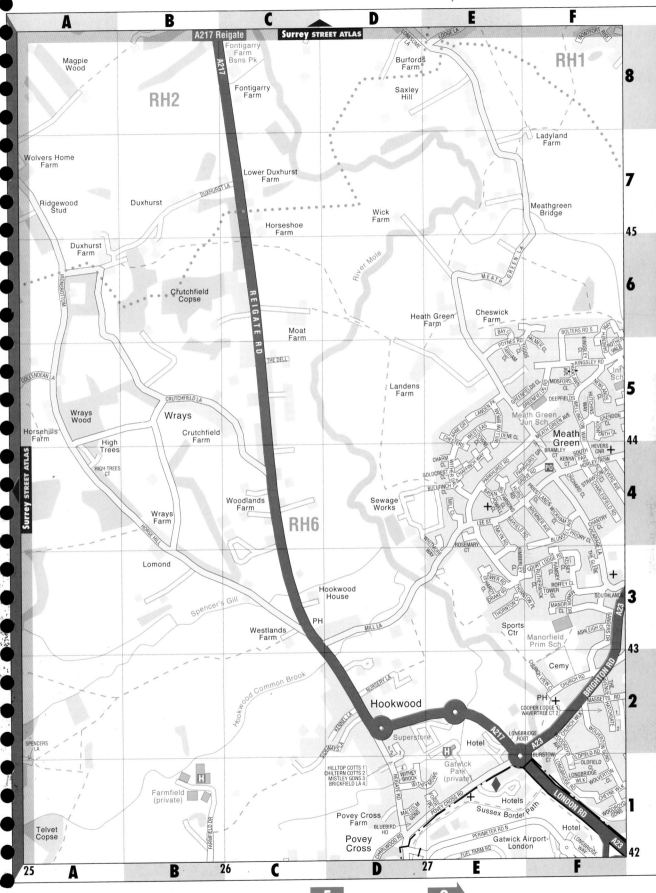

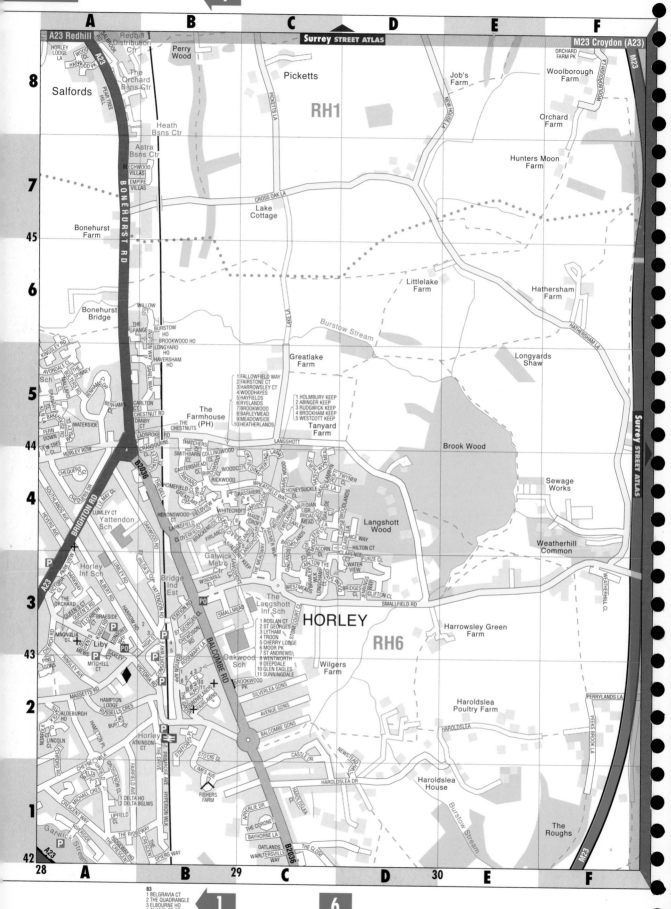

A   B   C   D   E   F

A23 Redhill

M23 Croydon (A23)

8

Salfords

RH1

Pickett's

Job's Farm

Woolborough Farm

Orchard Farm

Hunters Moon Farm

7

45

Bonehurst Farm

Lake Cottage

6

Bonehurst Bridge

Littlelake Farm

Hathersham Farm

Burstow Stream

Longyards Shaw

Greatlake Farm

1 FALLOWFIELD WAY
2 FAIRSTONE CT
3 HARROWSLEY CT
4 WOODHAYES
5 HAYFIELDS
6 RYELANDS
7 BROOKWOOD
8 BARLEYMEAD
9 MEADOWSIDE
10 HEATHERLANDS

1 HOLMBURY KEEP
2 ABINGER KEEP
3 RUDGWICK KEEP
4 BROCKHAM KEEP
5 WESTCOTT KEEP

5

The Farmhouse (PH)

Tanyard Farm

Brook Wood

44

Langshott

Sewage Works

4

Langshott Wood

Weatherhill Common

Gatwick Metro Ctr

Bridge Ind Est

The Langshott Inf Sch

HORLEY

Harrowsley Green Farm

3

RH6

1 ROSLAN CT
2 ST GEORGES
3 LYTHAM
4 TROON
5 CHERRY LODGE
6 MOOR PK
7 ST ANDREWS
8 WENTWORTH
9 DEEPDALE
10 GLEN EAGLES
11 SUNNINGDALE

Wilgers Farm

Oakwood Sch

43

Liby

Haroldslea Poultry Farm

2

Horley

Haroldslea

Haroldslea House

1

1 DELTA HO
2 DELTA BGLWS

FISHERS FARM

The Roughs

42

28   29   30

A   B   C   D   E   F

B3
1 BELGRAVIA CT
2 THE QUADRANGLE
3 ELBOURNE HO
4 CHANDLER CT
5 ROSS CT

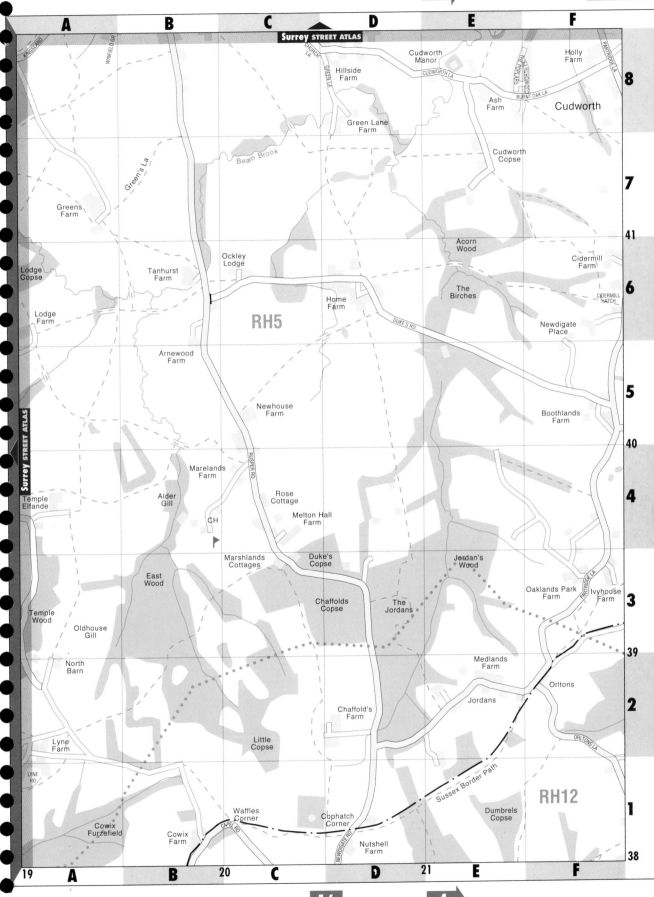

4

Surrey STREET ATLAS

A B C D E F

8

Cudworth Manor
Holly Farm
Hillside Farm
CHURCH LA
GREEN LA
CUDWORTH LA
SHEPHERDS HILL
CUDWORTH RD
BURNT OAK LA
PARTRIDGE LA
Ash Farm
Cudworth

Green Lane Farm

Beam Brook
7
Cudworth Copse

41
Greens Farm
Acorn Wood
Cidermill Farm

Green's La
Ockley Lodge
Tanhurst Farm
The Birches
6
CIDERMILL HATCH

Lodge Copse
Home Farm
DUKE'S RD
Newdigate Place

RH5
Lodge Farm

Arnewood Farm
5

Newhouse Farm
Boothlands Farm

Temple Elfande
40

Marelands Farm
RUSPER RD
Rose Cottage
4

Alder Gill
CH
Melton Hall Farm

Marshlands Cottages
Duke's Copse
Jordan's Wood
Oaklands Park Farm
Ivyhouse Farm
PARTRIDGE LA
3

East Wood
Chaffolds Copse
The Jordans

Temple Wood
Oldhouse Gill
Medlands Farm
39

North Barn
Orltons
2

Chaffold's Farm
Jordans
ORLTONS LA

Lyne Farm
Little Copse
Sussex Border Path
RH12

LYNE HO
1

Cowix Furzefield
Waffles Corner
Cophatch Corner
Dumbrels Copse

Cowix Farm
CAPEL RD
NEWDIGATE RD
Nutshell Farm
38

19 A B 20 C D 21 E F

4

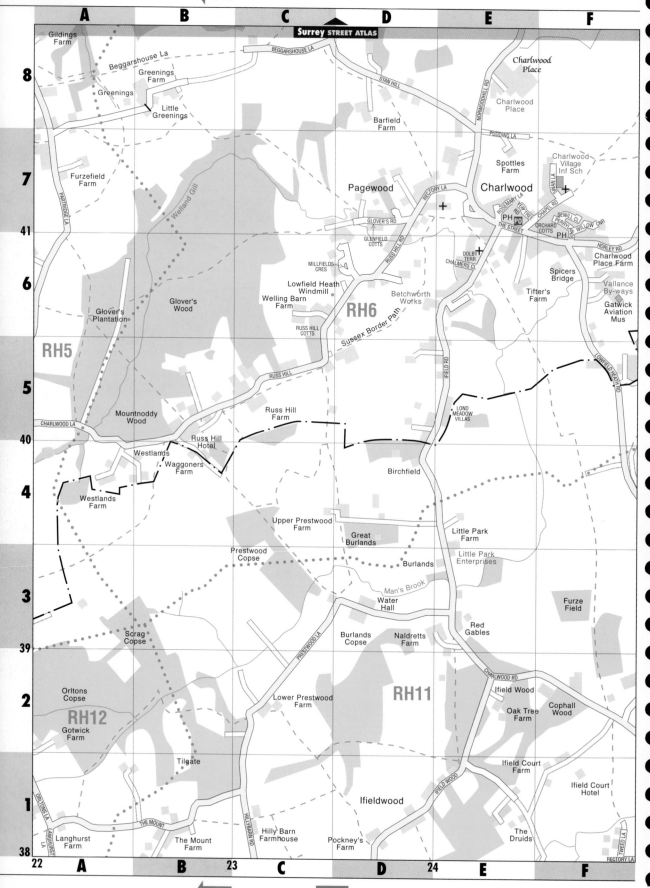

3

Surrey STREET ATLAS

A   B   C   D   E   F

8
Gildings Farm
Beggarshouse La
BEGGARSHOUSE LA
Greenings Farm
Greenings
Little Greenings
STAN HILL
Barfield Farm
Charlwood Place
Charlwood Place
NORWOODHILL RD
PUDDING LA
Charlwood Village Inf Sch

7
Furzefield Farm
PARTRIDGE LA
Welland Gill
Pagewood
RECTORY LA
Spottles Farm
Charlwood
ROSEMARY LA
YEW TREE RD
SWAN LA
CHAPEL RD
SEWILL CL
PERRYLANDS
WILLOW CNR
PH
PO
THE STREET
ORCHARD COTTS
PH
Charlwood Place Farm

41
GLOVER'S RD
GLENFIELD COTTS
RUSS HILL RD
DOLBY TERR
CHALMERS CL
HORLEY RD

6
Glover's Plantation
Glover's Wood
MILLFIELDS CRES
Lowfield Heath Windmill
Welling Barn Farm
RH6
Betchworth Works
Spicers Bridge
Tifter's Farm
Vallance By-ways
Gatwick Aviation Mus
RUSS HILL COTTS
Sussex Border Path
IFIELD RD

RH5

5
Mountnoddy Wood
Russ Hill
RUSS HILL
Russ Hill Farm
LOND MEADOW VILLAS
LOWFIELD HEATH RD

40
CHARLWOOD LA
Russ Hill Hotel
Westlands
Waggoners Farm

4
Westlands Farm
Birchfield
Upper Prestwood Farm
Great Burlands
Little Park Farm
Little Park Enterprises

3
Prestwood Copse
Burlands
Man's Brook
Water Hall
Furze Field

39
Scrag Copse
PRESTWOOD LA
Burlands Copse
Naldretts Farm
Red Gables
CHARLWOOD RD

2
Orltons Copse
RH12
Gotwick Farm
Lower Prestwood Farm
RH11
Ifield Wood
Oak Tree Farm
Cophall Wood

1
ORLTONS LA
LANGHURST LA
Langhurst Farm
Tilgate
THE MOUNT
The Mount Farm
HILLYBARN RD
Hilly Barn Farmhouse
Pockney's Farm
Ifieldwood
IFIELD WOOD
Ifield Court Farm
Ifield Court Hotel
The Druids

38
22   23   24
A   B   C   D   E   F
RECTORY LA
TWEED LA

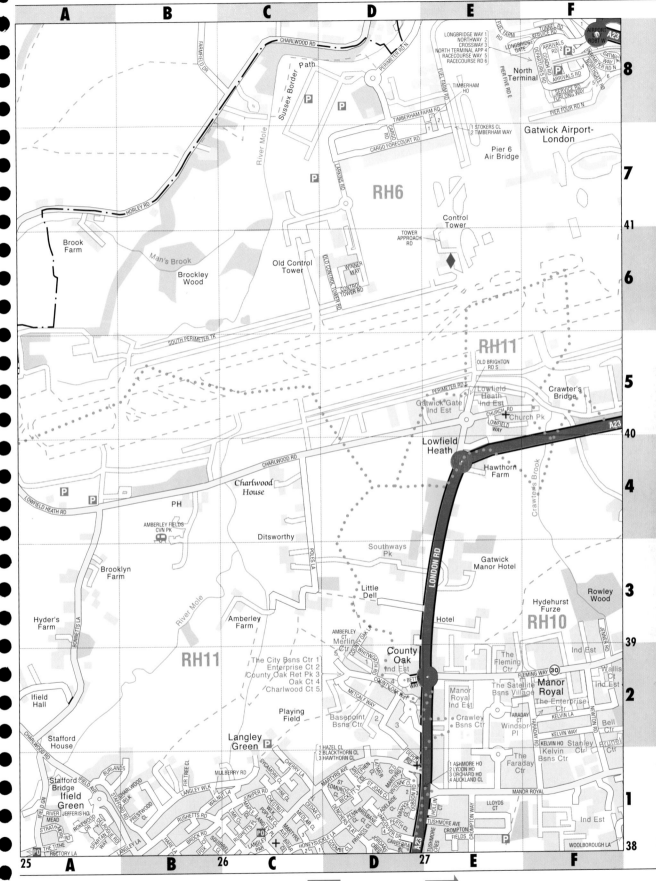

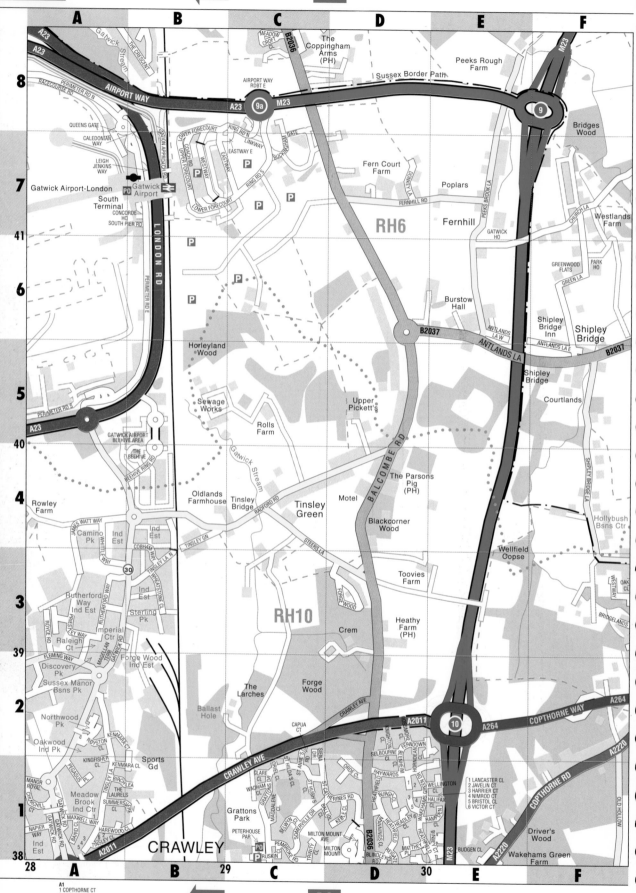

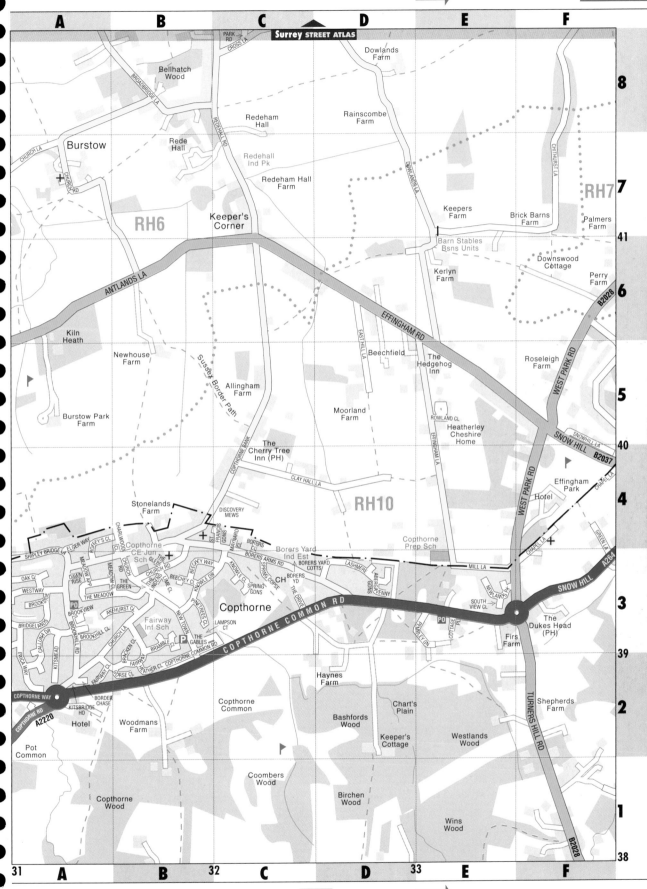

Surrey STREET ATLAS

A B C D E F

A22 Caterham, M25

8 RH6

Nevergood Wood

Leighfurze Field

Eastpark Farm

Quarry Farm

Churchill Stud

Homewood

EAST PARK LA

B2028

Hobbs Ind Est

Wire Mill LA

Wire Mill Lake

THE PLANTATION

WEST PARK RD

Laylands Farm

EASTBOURNE RD

A22

7 West Park

RH7

Woodcock Bridge

The Woodcock (PH)

HEATHERWAY

41 West Park

Stubpond La

STUBPOND LA

Sewage Works

WOODCOCK HILL

Cooper's Moors

B2028

Baker's Wood

Moat Wood

6

Perry Farm

A22

Hedgecourt

P

Park Farm

5 Domewood

Hedgecourt Lake

Park Wood

HERONS CL

MILL LA

40 HERONS LEA

Snow Hill Bsns Ctr

COPTHORNE RD

HEDGECOURT PL

TANGLE OAK

HOUSMAN WAY

B2037 SNOW HILL B2037

Felcot Farm

LYNDHURST FARM CL

Felbridge

4 Snow Hill

Felbridge Prim Sch

A264

A264 SNOW HILL

LAKE VIEW RD

FELCOT RD

CHESTERFIELD CL

Furnace Wood

Michaelmas Farm

ROWPLATT LA

ROWPLATT CL

TWITTEN LA

TITHE ORCH

WARREN CL

EVELYN CL

MC IVER CL

CRAWLEY DOWN RD

LEYBOURNE

Kenward's Farm

Great Frenches Park

WHEELERS WAY

Gibbshaven Farm

FELBRIDGE RD

RH19

3 RH10

FURNACE FARM RD

Nurseries

Felbridge Water

The Birches

39 Furnace Pond

Furnace Wood

Nurseries

+

CUTTINGLYE RD

2 Stubbits Wood

Cuttinglye Wood

HOPHURST HILL

Greenfield Shaw

Gulledge

Down Park Farm

Parkfields Farm

HOPHURST LA

TILTWOOD DR

GAGE RD

AVIARY WR

Hophurst Farm

Sussex Border Path

1

CUTTINGLYE

FERNHURST

HAVEN GDNS

FERN CL

P

The Larches

Railway Shaw

38

34 A 35 B C 36 D E F

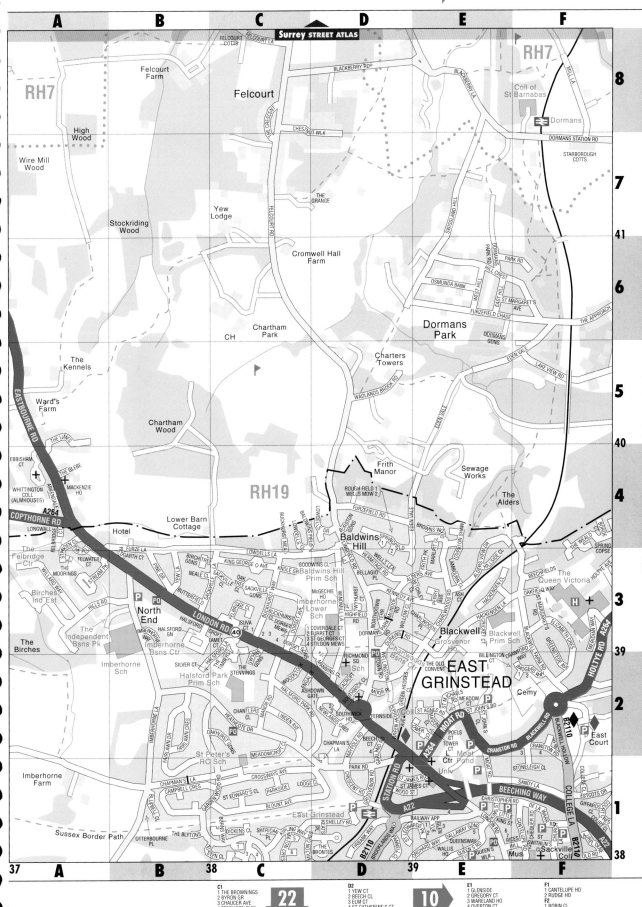

RH7

RH7

Felcourt Farm

High Wood

Wire Mill Wood

Felcourt

Coll of St Barnabas

Dormans

DORMANS STATION RD

STARBOROUGH COTTS

8

Stockriding Wood

Yew Lodge

Cromwell Hall Farm

7

41

6

The Kennels

CH

Chartham Park

Dormans Park

5

Ward's Farm

Chartham Wood

Charters Towers

40

EBBISHAM CT

WHITTINGTON COLL (ALMHOUSES)

A264

COPTHORNE RD

RH19

Frith Manor

ROUGH FIELD 1
WELL'S MDW 2

FURZEFIELD RD

Sewage Works

The Alders

4

LONGWALL

The Felbridge Ctr

Lower Barn Cottage

Hotel

Baldwins Hill

The Weald

SPRING COPSE

Birches Ind Est

North End

LONDON RD
40

Imberhorne Lower Sch

Baldwins Hill Prim Sch

1 COVERDALE CT
2 TURRET CT
3 ST GEORGES CT
4 STILDON MEWS

Blackwell

Blackwell Prim Sch

The Queen Victoria

H

3

The Birches

The Independent Bsns Pk

Imberhorne Bsns Ctr

Imberhorne Sch

SILVER CT

Halsford Park Prim Sch

The Stennings

Charlwoods Bsns Ctr

Grosvenor Ho

The Old Convent

EAST GRINSTEAD

Cemy

A264

HOLTYE RD

39

Imberhorne Farm

St Peter's RC Sch

Chapman's La

Moat Ctr Pond

East Court

B2110

2

Sussex Border Path

East Grinstead

Otterbourne Pl

The Blytons

The Brontes

B2110
BROOKLANDS WAY

A22

STATION RD

Univ

BEECHING WAY

Mus

Sackville Coll

COLLEGE LA
B2110
A22

1

38

C1
1 THE BROWNINGS
2 BYRON GR
3 CHAUCER AVE
4 TENNYSON RISE
5 THE SAYERS
6 WORDSWORTH RISE

D2
1 YEW CT
2 BEECH CL
3 ELM CT
4 ST CATHERINE'S CT

E1
1 GLENSIDE
2 GREGORY CT
3 WARELAND HO
4 OVERTON CT
5 BROOKLAND HO
6 INSTITUTE WLK
7 CANTELUPE MEWS

F1
1 CANTELUPE HO
2 RUDGE HO
F2
1 ROBIN CL
2 EARLE HO
3 EASTCOURT VILLAS
4 THE OLD SURGERY
5 ST JULIAN
6 DRURY LO

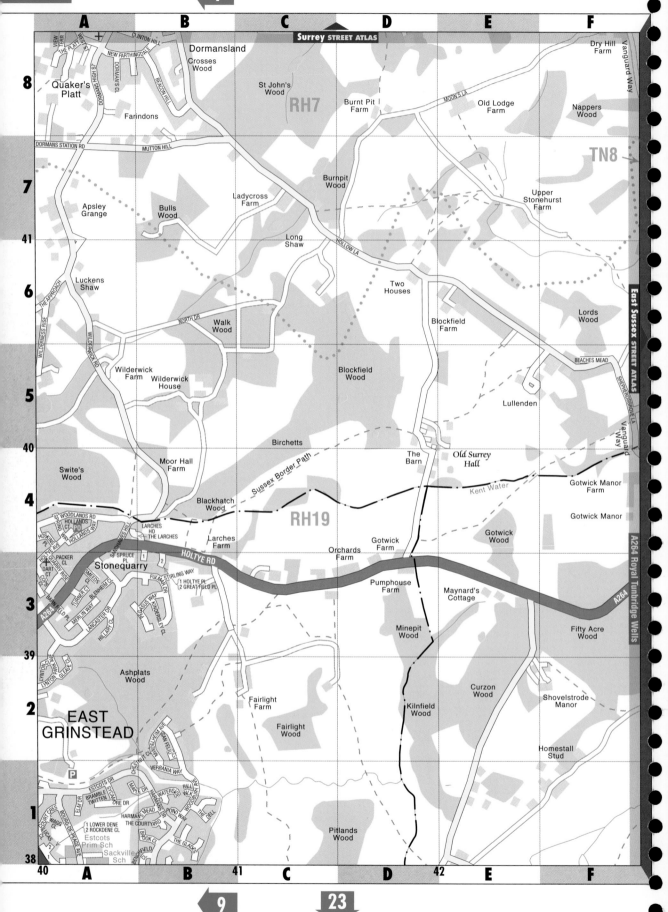

Surrey STREET ATLAS

A   B   C   D   E   F

Dry Hill
Farm

Vanguard Way

Dormansland

Crosses
Wood

8

Quaker's
Platt

St John's
Wood

RH7

Burnt Pit
Farm

MOON'S LA

Old Lodge
Farm

Nappers
Wood

Farindons

DORMANS STATION RD   MUTTON HILL

TN8

7

Apsley
Grange

Bulls
Wood

Ladycross
Farm

Burnpit
Wood

Upper
Stonehurst
Farm

41

Long
Shaw

HOLLOW LA

6

Luckens
Shaw

NORTH DR

Walk
Wood

Two
Houses

Blockfield
Farm

Lords
Wood

East Sussex STREET ATLAS

BEACHES MEAD

SHEPHERDSGROVE LA

5

Wilderwick
Farm

Wilderwick
House

Blockfield
Wood

Lullenden

Vanguard
Way

40

Swite's
Wood

Moor Hall
Farm

Birchetts

Sussex Border Path

The
Barn

Old Surrey
Hall

Gotwick Manor
Farm

4

Blackhatch
Wood

RH19

Kent Water

Gotwick Manor

Larches
Farm

Larches
HO
THE LARCHES

HOLTYE RD

Orchards
Farm

Gotwick
Farm

Gotwick
Wood

A264 Royal Tunbridge Wells

Stonequarry

1 HOLTYE PL
2 GREAT-FIELD PL

Pumphouse
Farm

Maynard's
Cottage

Fifty Acre
Wood

A264

3

A264

39

Ashplats
Wood

Minepit
Wood

Curzon
Wood

Shovelstrode
Manor

2

EAST
GRINSTEAD

Fairlight
Farm

Fairlight
Wood

Kilnfield
Wood

Homestall
Stud

P

VERBANIA WAY

1 LOWER DENE
2 ROCKDENE CL

Estcots
Prim Sch

Sackville
Sch

Pitlands
Wood

38

40   A   B   41   C   D   42   E   F

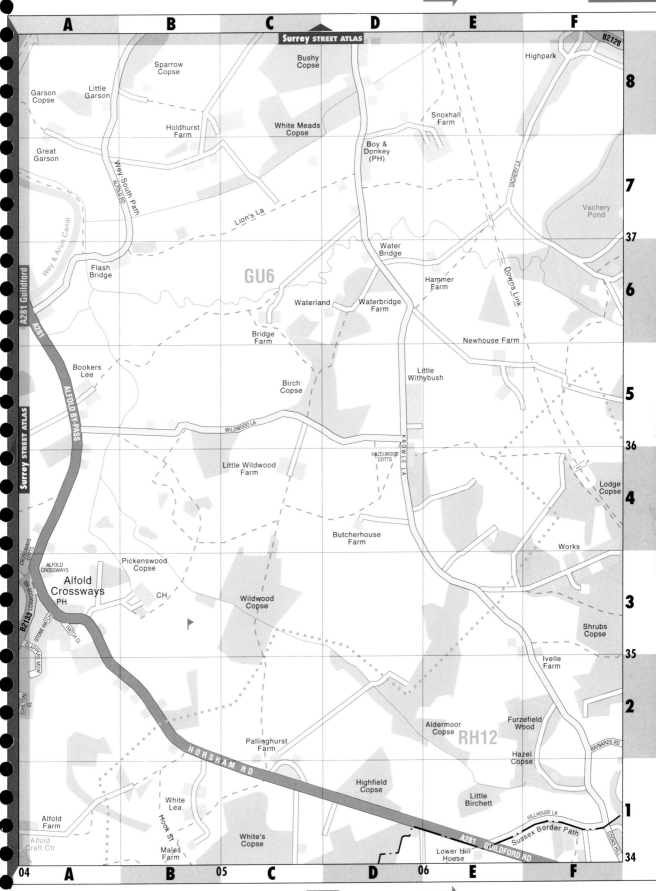

B2128

A   B   C   D   E   F

8

Highpark

Sparrow
Copse

Bushy
Copse

Garson
Copse

Little
Garson

Snoxhall
Farm

Holdhurst
Farm

White Meads
Copse

Boy &
Donkey
(PH)

VACHERY LA

Great
Garson

7

Wey-South Path

ALFOLD RD

Vachery
Pond

Lion's La

37

Water
Bridge

A281 Guildford

A281

Wey & Arun Canal

GU6

Flash
Bridge

Hammer
Farm

6

Downs Link

Waterland

Waterbridge
Farm

Surrey STREET ATLAS

Newhouse Farm

Bridge
Farm

Bookers
Lee

Little
Withybush

Birch
Copse

5

ALFOLD BY-PASS

KNOWLE LA

36

WILDWOOD LA

HAZELWOOD
COTTS

Lodge
Copse

Little Wildwood
Farm

4

Works

Butcherhouse
Farm

CROSSWAYS
COTTS

Pickenswood
Copse

Shrubs
Copse

ALFOLD
CROSSWAYS

OLD LOXWOOD RD

Alfold
Crossways
PH

CH

Wildwood
Copse

3

B2133

STONE HATCH

HATCH CL

35

CLAPPER'S MDW

Ivelle
Farm

CHILTON CL

2

Aldermoor
Copse

Furzefield
Wood

RH12

BAYNARDS RD

HORSHAM RD

Pallinghurst
Farm

Hazel
Copse

Highfield
Copse

1

Little
Birchett

HILLHOUSE LA

White
Lea

Alfold
Farm

Sussex Border Path

COOKS HILL

Hook St

White's
Copse

A281 GUILDFORD RD

Alfold
Craft Ctr

Males
Farm

Lower Hill
House

34

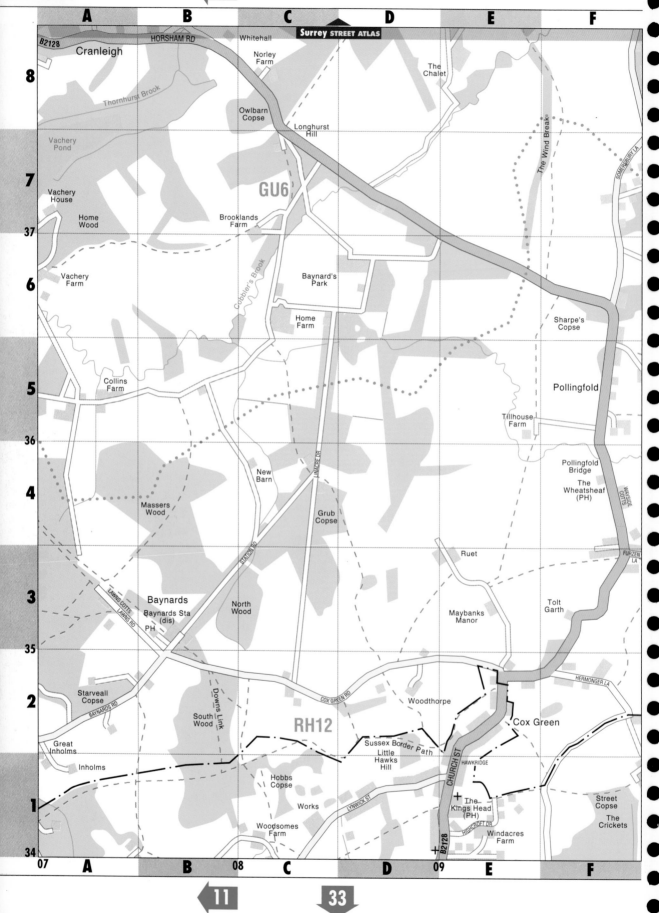

A   B   C   D   E   F

Surrey STREET ATLAS

8

Cranleigh

B2128

HORSHAM RD

Whitehall

Norley
Farm

The
Chalet

Thornhurst Brook

Owlbarn
Copse

Longhurst
Hill

7

GU6

The Wind Break

SOMERSBURY LA

Vachery
Pond

Vachery
House

Home
Wood

Brooklands
Farm

37

6

Vachery
Farm

Baynard's
Park

Cobbler's Brook

Home
Farm

Sharpe's
Copse

5

Collins
Farm

Pollingfold

Tillhouse
Farm

36

New
Barn

LINACRE DR

Pollingfold
Bridge

The
Wheatsheaf
(PH)

WAYSIDE COTTS

4

Massers
Wood

Grub
Copse

Ruet

FURZEN LA

3

Baynards

STATION RD

North
Wood

Maybanks
Manor

Tolt
Garth

LAWNS COTTS

Baynards Sta
(dis)

LAWNS RD

PH

35

Starveall
Copse

BAYNARDS RD

Downs Link

South
Wood

COX GREEN RD

Woodthorpe

HERMONGER LA

2

Cox Green

RH12

Great
Inholms

Inholms

Sussex Border Path

Little
Hawks
Hill

CHURCH ST

HAWKRIDGE

Street
Copse

The
Crickets

1

Hobbs
Copse

Works

LYNWICK ST

The
Kings Head
(PH)

HIGHCROFT DR

Woodsomes
Farm

B2128

Windacres
Farm

34

07   A   08   B   C   08   D   09   E   F

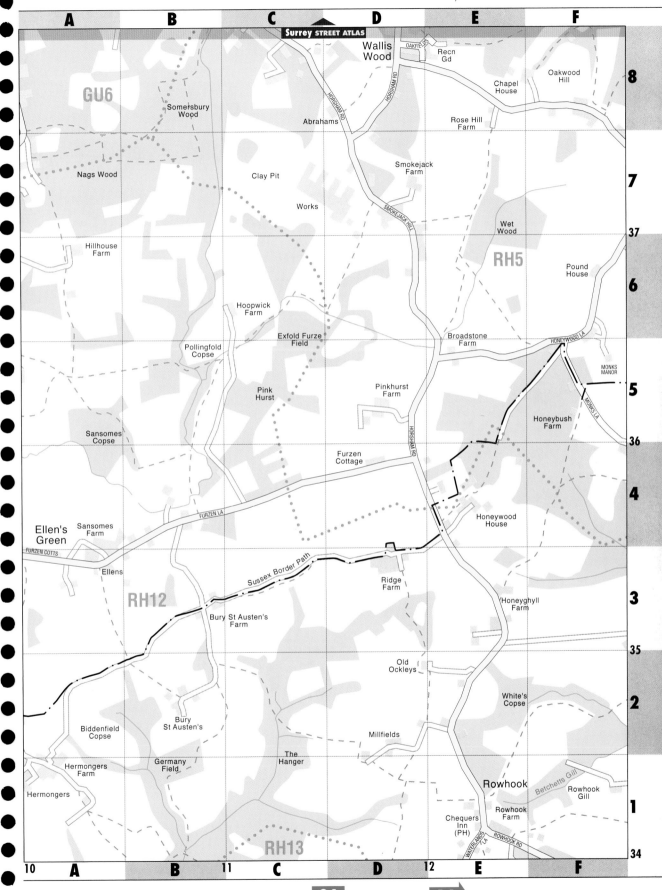

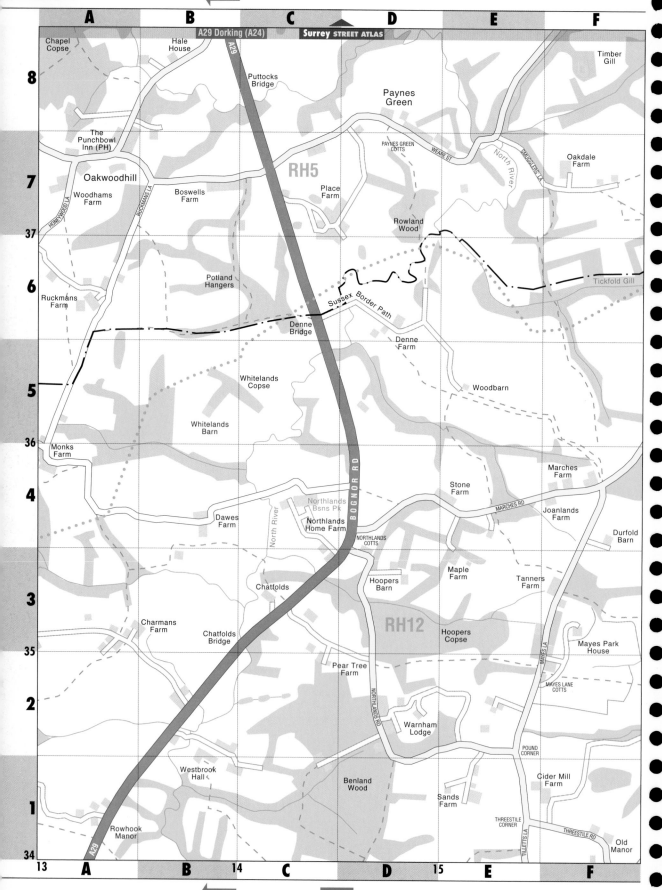

A29 Dorking (A24)
Surrey STREET ATLAS

A   B   C   D   E   F

8

Chapel Copse

Hale House

Timber Gill

Puttocks Bridge

Paynes Green

The Punchbowl Inn (PH)

RH5

PAYNES GREEN COTTS

WEARE ST

North River

SMUGGLERS LA

Oakdale Farm

7

Oakwoodhill

Woodhams Farm

Boswells Farm

Place Farm

Rowland Wood

37

HONEYWOOD LA

RUCKMANS LA

A29

6

Potland Hangers

Sussex Border Path

Tickfold Gill

Ruckmans Farm

Denne Bridge

Denne Farm

5

Whitelands Copse

Woodbarn

Whitelands Barn

36

Monks Farm

Marches Farm

4

Dawes Farm

North River

Northlands Bsns Pk

Northlands Home Farm

NORTHLANDS COTTS

Stone Farm

MARCHES RD

Joanlands Farm

BOGNOR RD

Durfold Barn

3

Charmans Farm

Chatfolds

Hoopers Barn

Maple Farm

Tanners Farm

RH12

Hoopers Copse

35

Chatfolds Bridge

Pear Tree Farm

MAYES LA

Mayes Park House

MAYES LANE COTTS

2

NORTHLANDS RD

Warnham Lodge

POUND CORNER

Cider Mill Farm

1

Westbrook Hall

Benland Wood

Sands Farm

THREESTILE CORNER

TILLETTS LA

THREESTILE RD

Old Manor

34

A29

Rowhook Manor

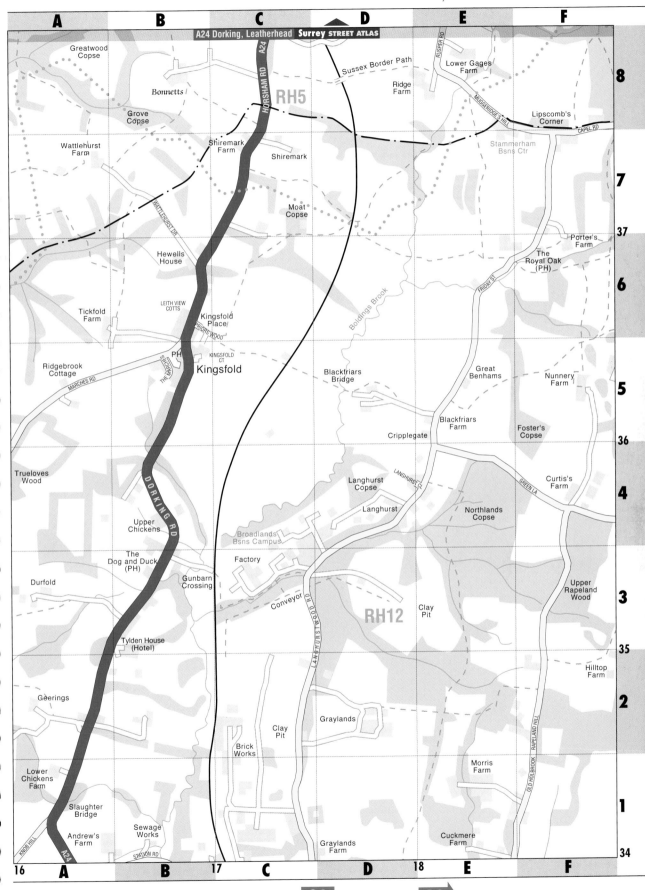

A24 Dorking, Leatherhead | Surrey STREET ATLAS

Greatwood Copse

Bonnetts

RH5

Sussex Border Path

Lower Gages Farm

Ridge Farm

Lipscomb's Corner

Grove Copse

Shiremark Farm

Shiremark

Stammerham Bsns Ctr

8

Wattlehurst Farm

WATTLEHURST DR

Moat Copse

Porter's Farm

7

37

Hewells House

The Royal Oak (PH)

Boldings Brook

FRIDAY ST

6

Tickfold Farm

LEITH VIEW COTTS

Kingsfold Place

PRIORS WOOD

PH

KINGSFOLD CT

Kingsfold

Blackfriars Bridge

Great Benhams

Nunnery Farm

5

Ridgebrook Cottage

MARCHES RD

THE MARCHES

Blackfriars Farm

Foster's Copse

Trueloves Wood

Cripplegate

Blackfriars Farm

36

DORKING RD

Langhurst Copse

LANGHURST CL

Langhurst

Northlands Copse

GREEN LA

Curtis's Farm

4

Upper Chickens

Broadlands Bsns Campus

Factory

The Dog and Duck (PH)

Gunbarn Crossing

Conveyor

LANGHURST WOOD RD

RH12

Clay Pit

Upper Rapeland Wood

3

Durfold

Tylden House (Hotel)

RAPELAND HILL

35

Hilltop Farm

Geerings

Clay Pit

Graylands

2

Brick Works

Morris Farm

OLD HOLBROOK

Lower Chickens Farm

Slaughter Bridge

Andrew's Farm

KNOB HILL

A24

Sewage Works

STATION RD

Graylands Farm

Cuckmere Farm

1

34

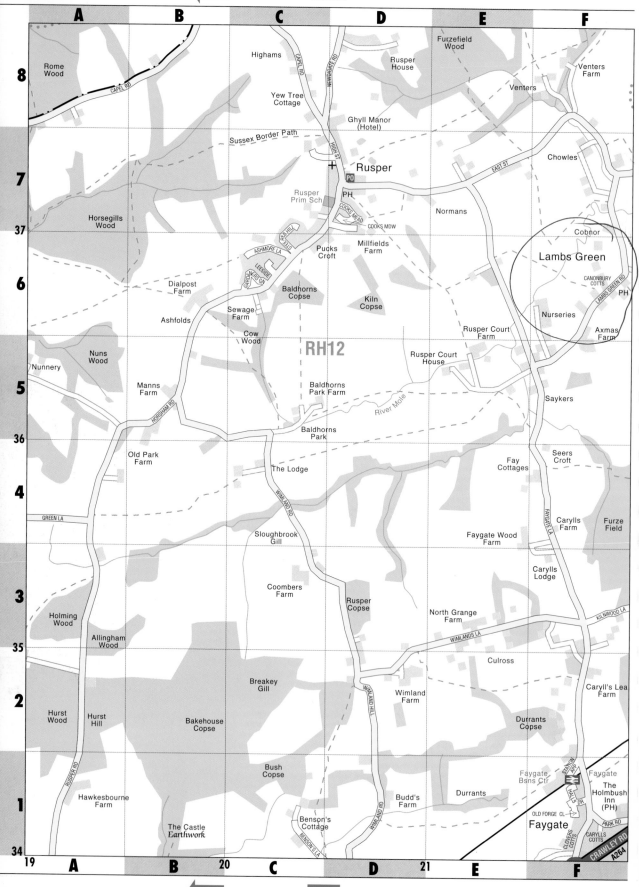

15
3

A B C D E F

8

Rome Wood

Highams

Rusper House

Furzefield Wood

Venters Farm

Venters

Chowles

Yew Tree Cottage

CAPEL RD

Ghyll Manor (Hotel)

EAST ST

Sussex Border Path

7

Rusper
PO
PH

Normans

Cobnor

Horsegills Wood

Rusper Prim Sch

COOKS MEAD

COOKS MDW

37

Lambs Green

STEERS HILL

ASHMORE LA

Pucks Croft

Millfields Farm

CANONBURY COTTS

LAMBS GREEN RD

PH

6

Dialpost Farm

LESSIDE

GARDENERS GN

Baldhorns Copse

Kiln Copse

Nurseries

Ashfolds

Sewage Farm

Cow Wood

RH12

Rusper Court Farm

Axmas Farm

Nuns Wood

Rusper Court House

Nunnery

Manns Farm

Baldhorns Park Farm

River Mole

Saykers

5

HORSHAM RD

36

Old Park Farm

Baldhorns Park

Fay Cottages

Seers Croft

4

The Lodge

WIMLAND RD

FAYGATE LA

Carylls Farm

Furze Field

GREEN LA

Sloughbrook Gill

Faygate Wood Farm

Carylls Lodge

KILNWOOD LA

3

Holming Wood

Coombers Farm

Rusper Copse

North Grange Farm

35

Allingham Wood

WIMLANDS LA

Culross

Caryll's Lea Farm

2

Hurst Wood

Hurst Hill

Breakey Gill

Bakehouse Copse

WIMLAND HILL

Wimland Farm

Durrants Copse

RUSPER RD

Bush Copse

Budd's Farm

Durrants

STATION RD

Faygate Bsns Ctr

HALLS DR

Faygate

1

Hawkesbourne Farm

Benson's Cottage

WIMLAND RD

BENSON'S LA

OLD FORGE CL

The Holmbush Inn (PH)

PARK RD

The Castle Earthwork

Faygate

CLOVERS COTTS

CARYLLS COTTS

34

CRAWLEY RD

A264

19 A B 20 C D 21 E F

15
37

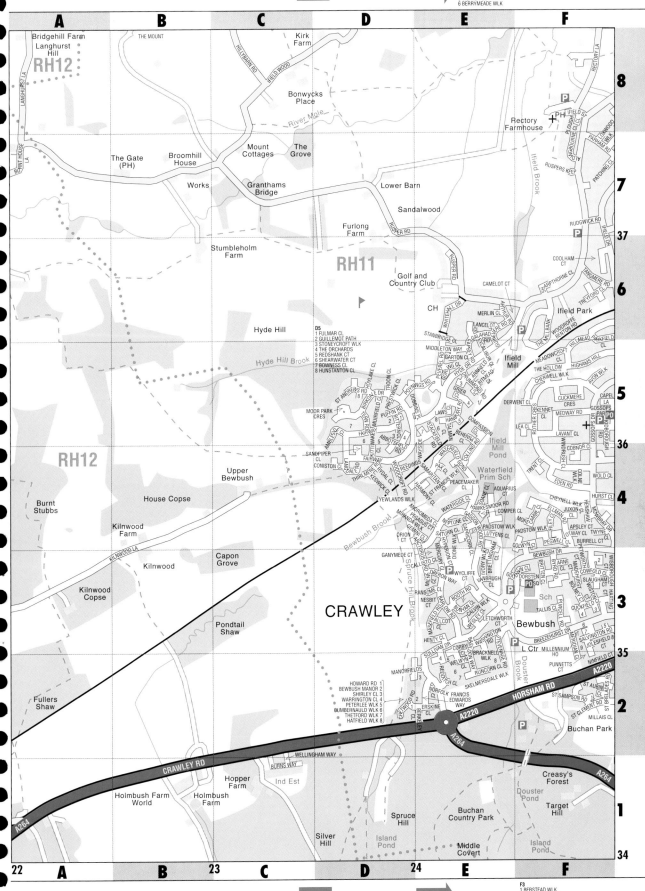

4

18

E5
1 LOVELL PATH
2 DEWAR CL
3 BEAUMONT CL
4 STRICKLAND CL
5 WEAVER CL
6 BERRYMEADE WLK
7 TUNNMEADE
8 HUNTERS LODGE

D5
1 FULMAR CL
2 GUILLEMOT PATH
3 STONEYCROFT WLK
4 THE ORCHARDS
5 REDSHANK CT
6 SHEARWATER CT
7 BOWNESS CL
8 HUNSTANTON CL

HOWARD RD 1
BEWBUSH MANOR 2
SHIRLEY CL 3
WARRINGTON CL 4
PETERLEE WLK 5
CUMBERNAULD WLK 6
THETFORD WLK 7
HATFIELD WLK 8

F3
1 BERSTEAD WLK
2 DONNINGTON CT
3 HASSOCKS CT
4 PYECOMBE CT
5 TELHAM CT
6 WARBLETON HO
7 CALDBECK HO
8 HALNAKER WLK
9 ICKLESHAM HO

18

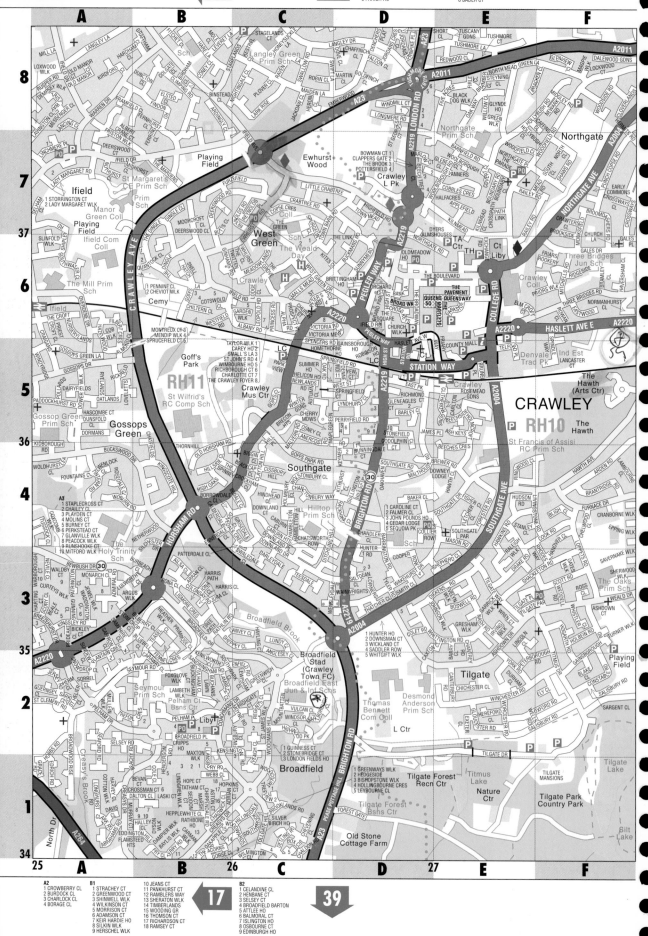

17

5

17

39

D5
1 THE COURTYARD
2 WALSTEAD CT
3 RAVENDENE CT
4 WILLOWFIELD
5 ASHWOOD
6 PARISH HO
7 PERRYFIELD HO
8 HANDSWORTH HO
9 GLENDON HO
10 ALEXANDRA CT
11 SPRING CL

D8
1 CONNAUGHT GDNS
2 ROUNDWAY CT
3 ARCHERS CT
4 CALEDONIAN HO
5 GIBBON PL
6 BADER CT

A2
1 CROWBERRY CL
2 BURDOCK CL
3 CHARLOCK CL
4 BORAGE CL

B1
1 STRACHEY CT
2 GREENWOOD CT
3 SHINWELL WLK
4 WILKINSON CT
5 MORRISON CT
6 ADAMSON CT
7 KEIR HARDIE HO
8 SILKIN WLK
9 HERSCHEL WLK

10 JEANS CT
11 PANKHURST CT
12 RAMBLERS WAY
13 SHERATON WLK
14 TIMBERLANDS
15 WOODING GR
16 THOMSON CT
17 RICHARDSON CT
18 RAMSEY CT

B2
1 CELANDINE CL
2 HENBANE CT
3 SELSEY CT
4 BROADFIELD BARTON
5 ATTLEE HO
6 BALMORAL CT
7 ISLINGTON HO
8 OSBOURNE CT
9 EDINBURGH HO

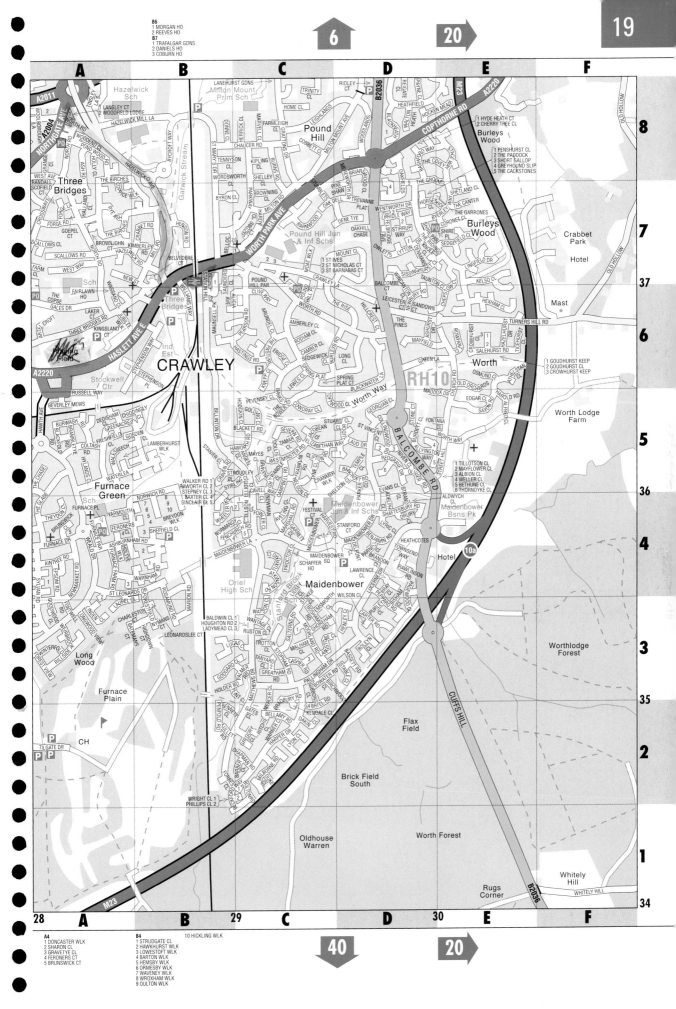

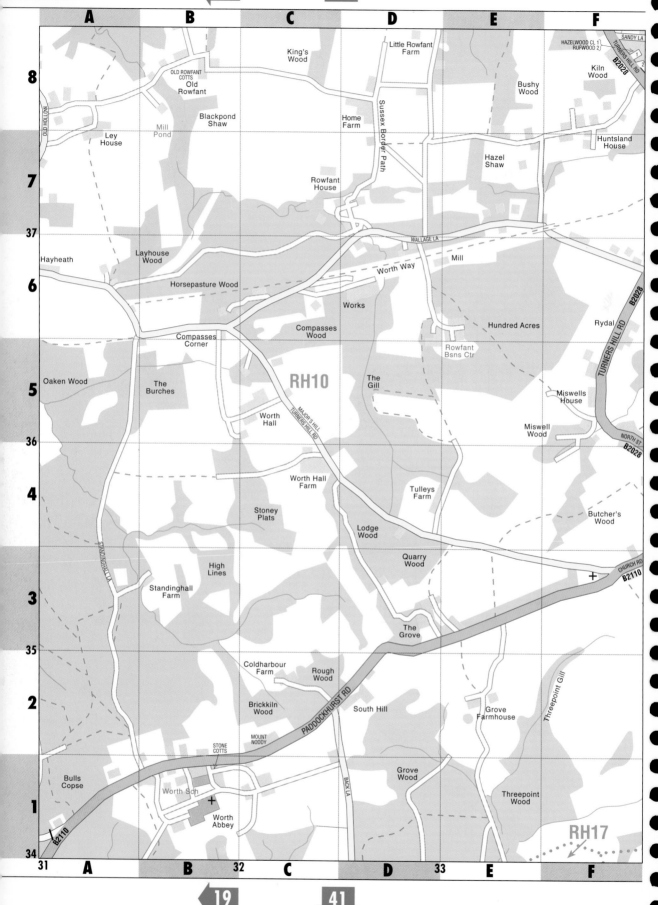

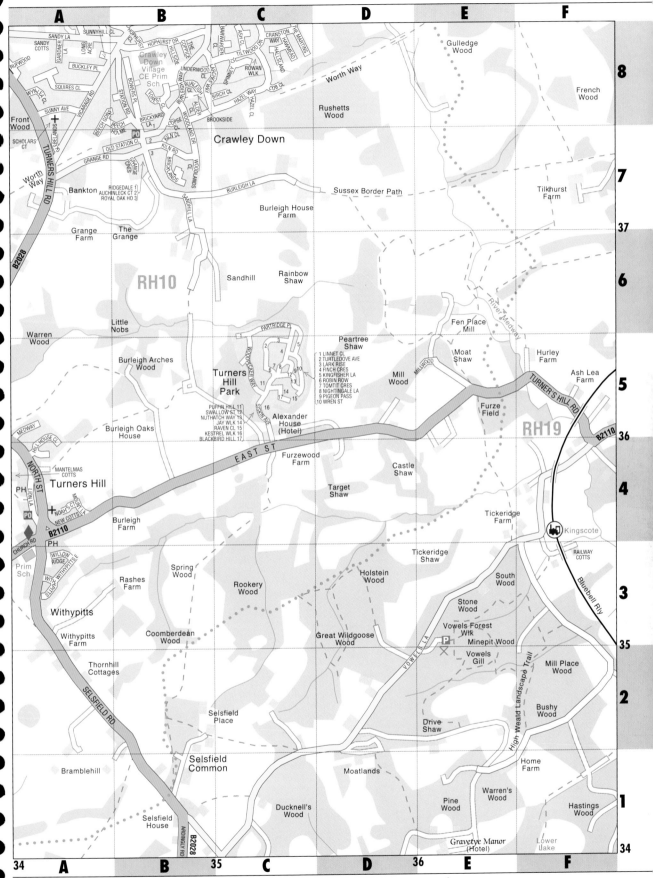

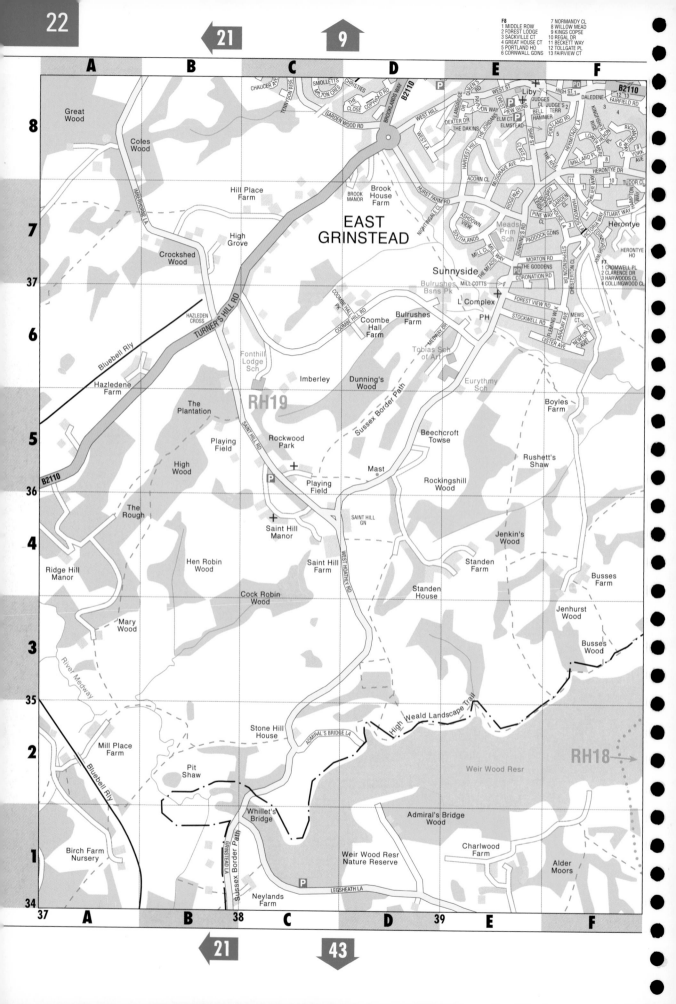

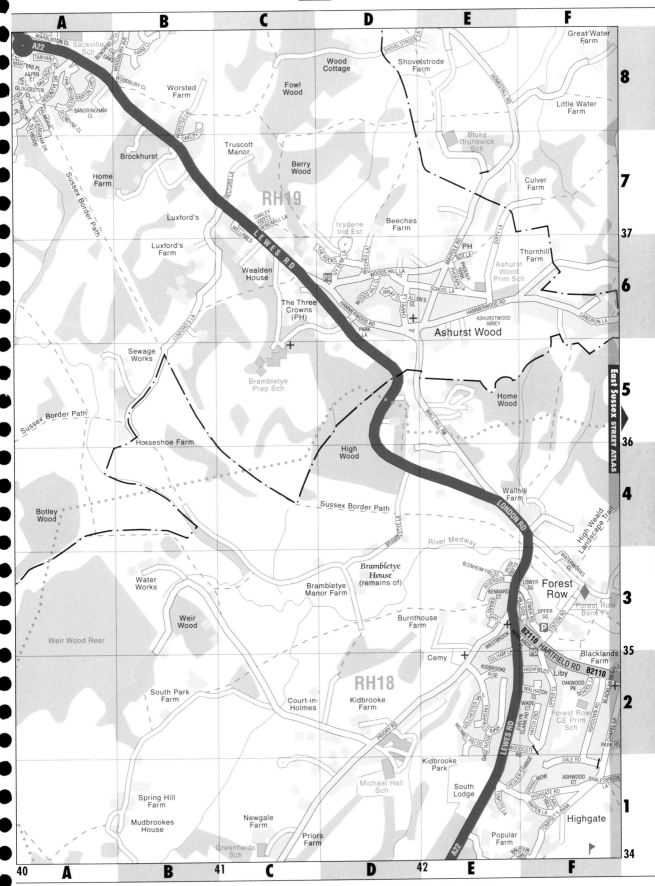

North Hampshire STREET ATLAS

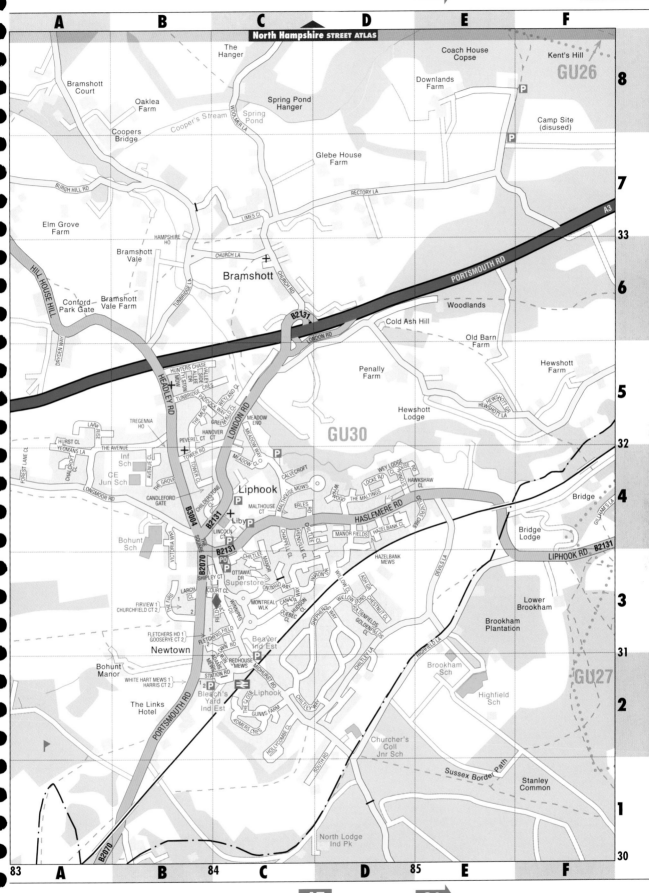

North Hampshire STREET ATLAS

GU26

GU30

GU27

Bramshott

Liphook

Newtown

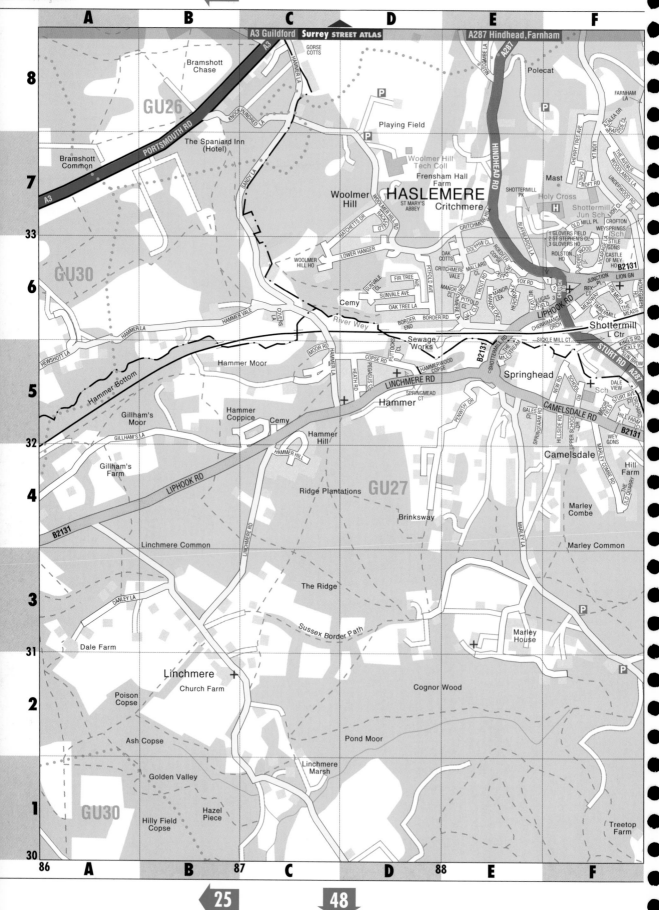

A3 Guildford **Surrey** STREET ATLAS A287 Hindhead, Farnham

A B C D E F

8

GU26

Bramshott
Chase

Bramshott
Common

The Spaniard Inn
(Hotel)

7

Polecat

Playing Field

Woolmer Hill
Tech Coll

Frensham Hall
Farm

Woolmer
Hill

HASLEMERE

St Mary's
Abbey

Critchmere

Mast

Holy Cross

Shottermill
Jun Sch

33

GU30

Woolmer
Hill Ho

Lower Hanger

Oak
Cotts

6

Cemy

Fir Tree

Sunvale Ave

Oak Tree La

Mallard
Cl

Manor
Lea

LIPHOOK RD

Shottermill
L Ctr

River Wey

Border
End

Border Rd

Sewage
Works

STURT RD

5

Hammer Moor

Hammer Bottom

Hammer
Coppice

Cemy

LINCHMERE RD

Hammer

Springhead

CAMELSDALE RD

Camelsdale

Hill
Farm

32

Gillham's
Moor

GILLHAM'S LA

Hammer
Hill

Camelsdale

Hill
Farm

4

Gillham's
Farm

LIPHOOK RD

Ridge Plantations

GU27

Brinksway

Marley
Combe

Marley Common

B2131

Linchmere Common

LINCHMERE RD

3

OXLEY LA

The Ridge

Sussex Border Path

Marley
House

31

Dale Farm

Linchmere

Church Farm

Cognor Wood

2

Poison
Copse

Ash Copse

Pond Moor

Linchmere
Marsh

1

GU30

Golden Valley

Hilly Field
Copse

Hazel
Piece

Treetop
Farm

30

86 A B 87 C D 88 E F

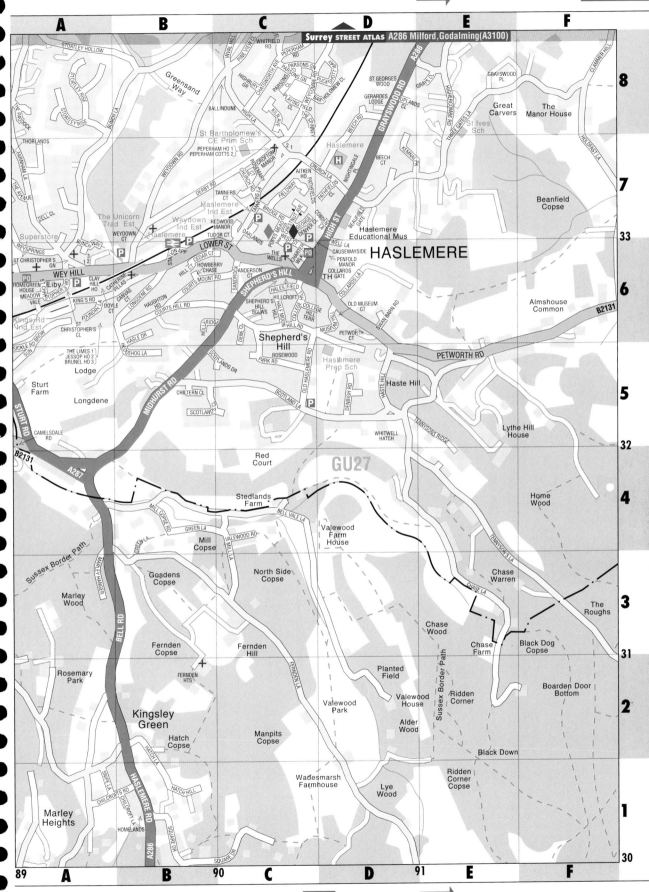

Surrey STREET ATLAS A286 Milford, Godalming(A3100)

HASLEMERE

GU27

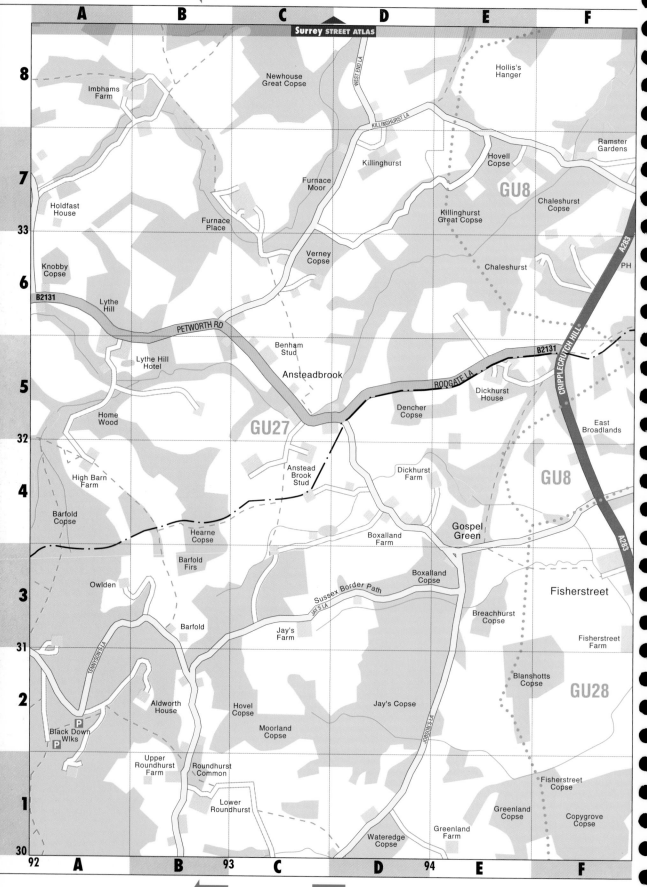

Surrey STREET ATLAS

A   B   C   D   E   F

8   Newhouse Great Copse   Hollis's Hanger
    Imbhams Farm   WEST END LA   Ramster Gardens
7   KILLINGHURST LA   Hovell Copse
    Furnace Moor   Killinghurst   GU8   Chaleshurst Copse
    Holdfast House   Furnace Place   Killinghurst Great Copse   A283
33 Verney Copse   Chaleshurst   PH
6   Knobby Copse
    B2131   Lythe Hill   PETWORTH RD   Benham Stud   B2131   CRIPPLECRUTCH HILL
    Lythe Hill Hotel   Ansteadbrook   RODGATE LA   Dickhurst House
5   GU27   Dencher Copse   East Broadlands
    Home Wood
32 Anstead Brook Stud   Dickhurst Farm   GU8
4   High Barn Farm   Boxalland Farm   Gospel Green   A283
    Barfold Copse   Hearne Copse   Boxalland Copse   Fisherstreet
    Barfold Firs   Sussex Border Path   Breachhurst Copse
3   Owlden   Barfold   JAY'S LA   Fisherstreet Farm
    Jay's Farm
31 TENNYSON'S LA   Blanshotts Copse   GU28
2   Aldworth House   Hovel Copse   Jay's Copse   Fisherstreet Copse
    P   Black Down Wlks   Moorland Copse   JOBSON'S LA
    P
    Upper Roundhurst Farm   Roundhurst Common   Greenland Copse   Copygrove Copse
1   Lower Roundhurst   Greenland Farm
30 Wateredge Copse
    92   A   93   B   C   94   D   E   F

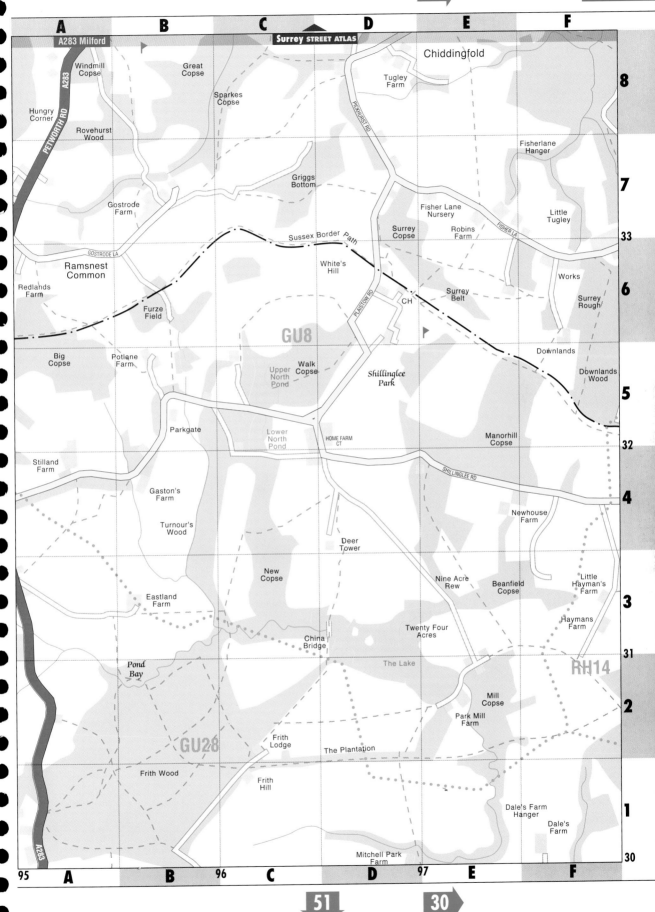

A283 Milford

A

B

C

D

Surrey STREET ATLAS

E

F

Chiddingfold

8

Windmill Copse

Great Copse

Tugley Farm

Sparkes Copse

Fisherlane Hanger

Hungry Corner

Rovehurst Wood

PETWORTH RD

A283

PICKHURST RD

7

Griggs Bottom

Fisher Lane Nursery

Little Tugley

Gostrode Farm

FISHER LA

33

Sussex Border Path

Surrey Copse

Robins Farm

GOSTRODE LA

White's Hill

Works

6

Ramsnest Common

Surrey Rough

Redlands Farm

Furze Field

PLAISTOW RD

CH

Surrey Belt

Downlands

GU8

Big Copse

Potlane Farm

Upper North Pond

Walk Copse

Shillinglee Park

Downlands Wood

5

Parkgate

Lower North Pond

HOME FARM CT

Manorhill Copse

32

Stilland Farm

SHILLINGLEE RD

4

Gaston's Farm

Newhouse Farm

Turnour's Wood

Deer Tower

New Copse

Nine Acre Rew

Beanfield Copse

Little Hayman's Farm

Eastland Farm

Haymans Farm

3

China Bridge

Twenty Four Acres

31

Pond Bay

The Lake

RH14

Mill Copse

2

GU28

Park Mill Farm

Frith Lodge

The Plantation

Frith Wood

Frith Hill

Dale's Farm Hanger

Dale's Farm

1

A283

Mitchell Park Farm

30

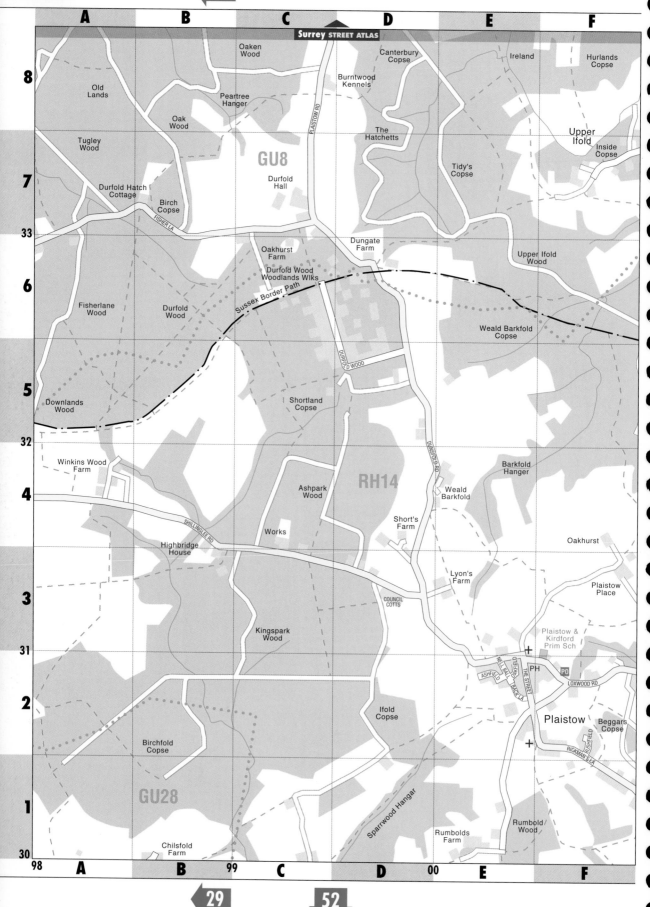

Surrey STREET ATLAS

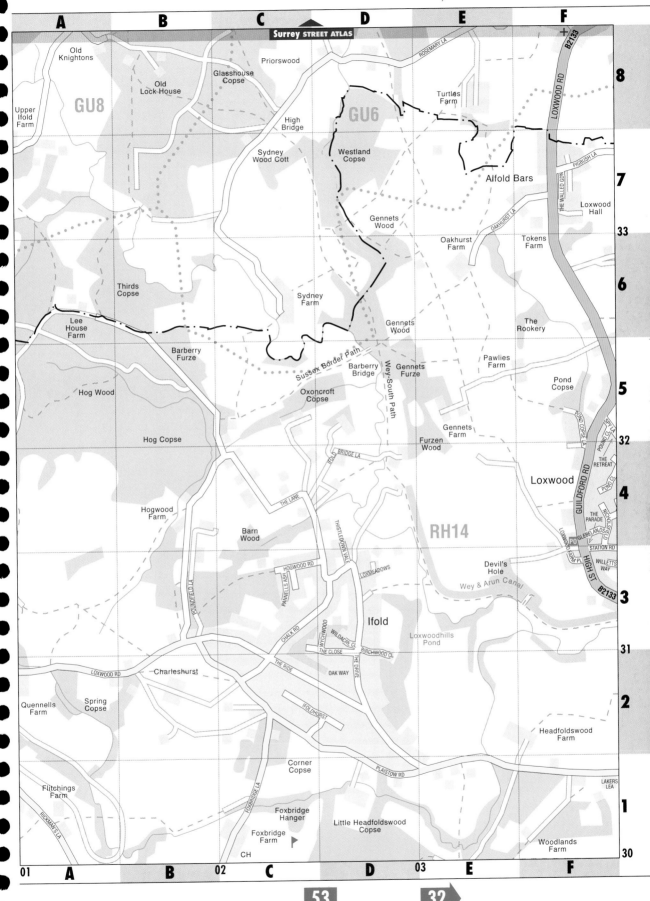

Surrey STREET ATLAS

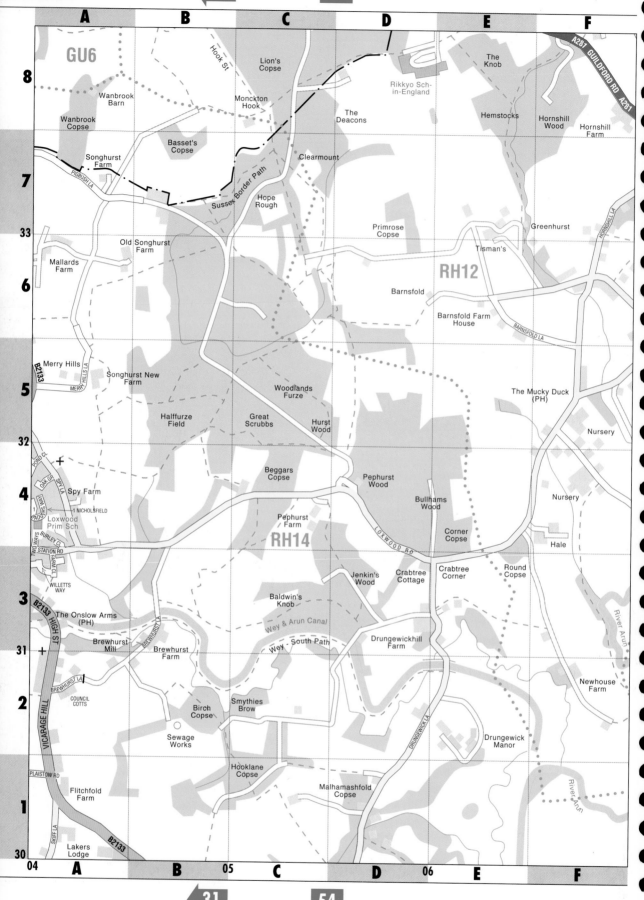

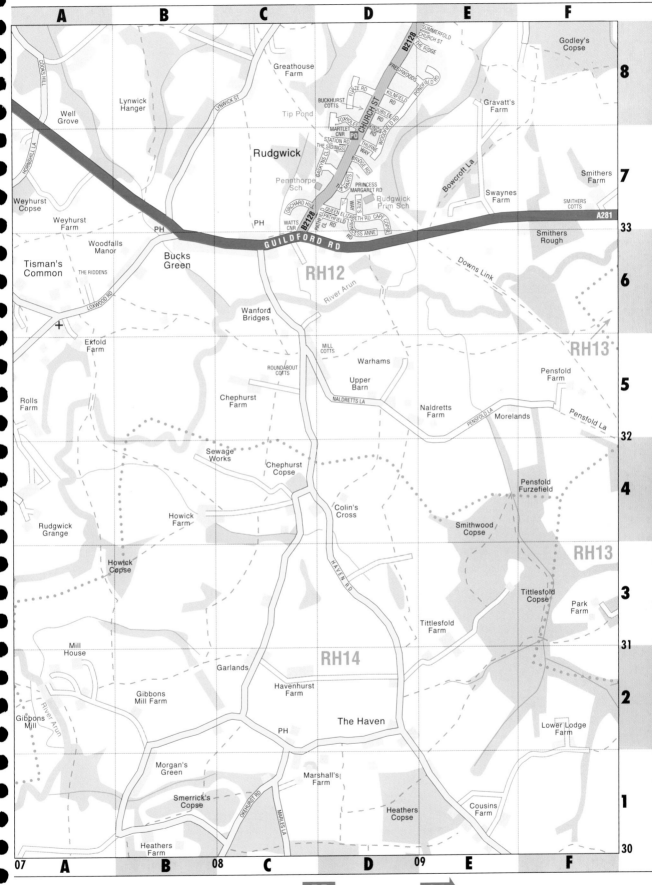

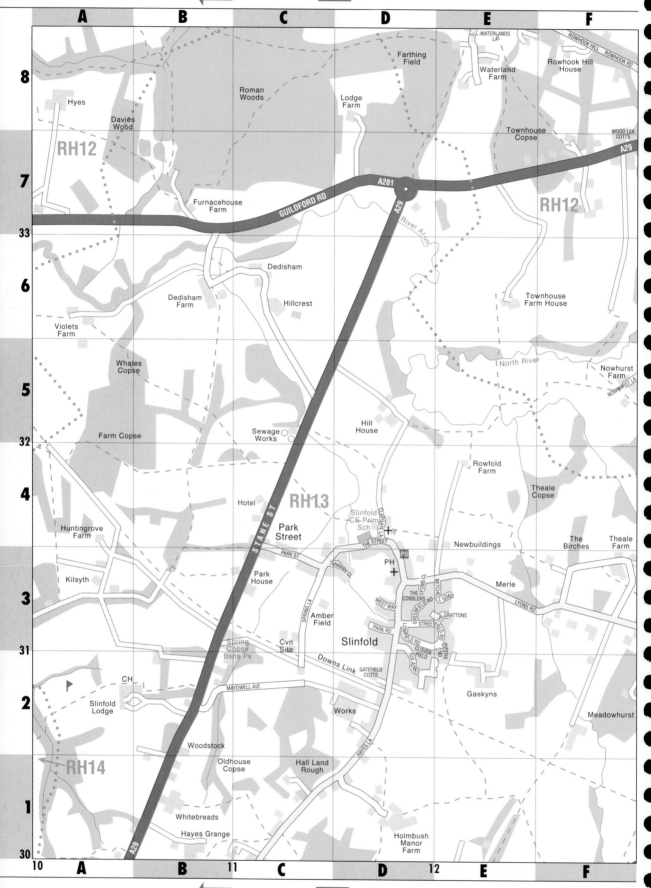

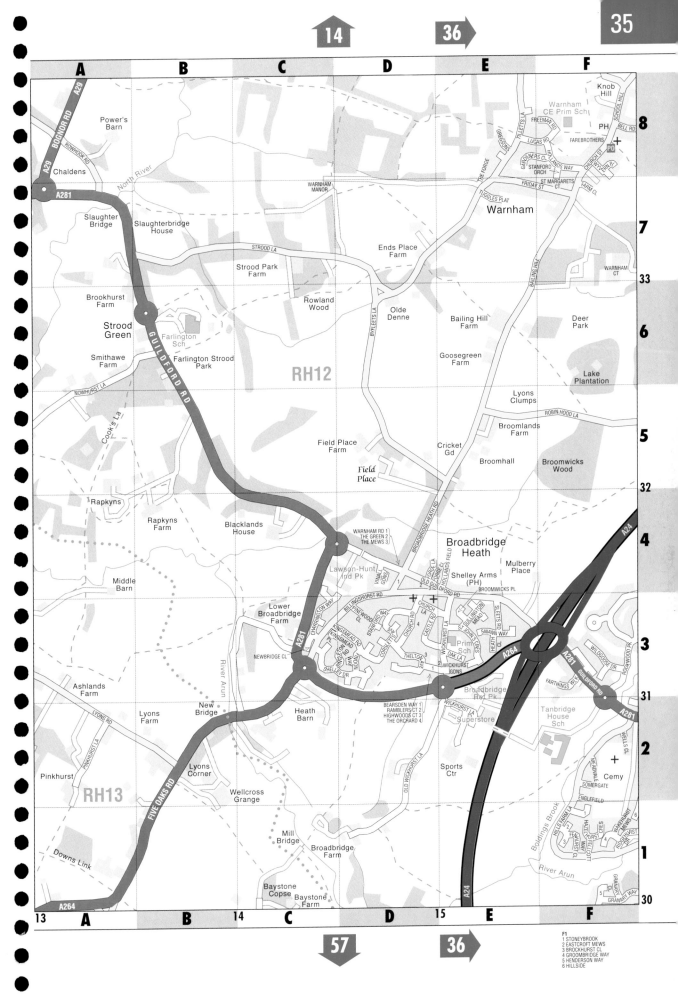

F1
1 STONEYBROOK
2 EASTCROFT MEWS
3 BROCKHURST CL
4 GROOMBRIDGE WAY
5 HENDERSON WAY
6 HILLSIDE

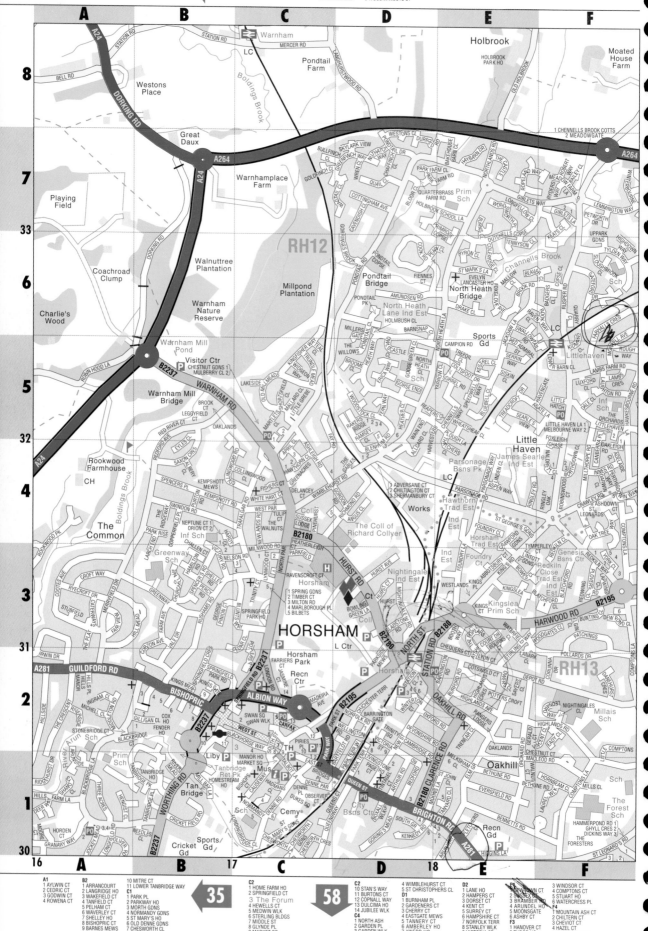

35
15

D5
1 WISTON CT
2 NUTBOURNE CT
3 ASHINGTON CT
4 WARMINGHURST CT
5 MARLBOROUGH CT
6 WOODMANCOTE CT

A1
1 AYLWIN CT
2 CEDRIC CT
3 GODWIN CT
4 ROWENA CT

B2
1 ARRANCOURT
2 LANGRIDGE HO
3 WAKEFIELD CT
4 TANFIELD CT
5 PELHAM CT
6 WAVERLEY CT
7 SHELLEY HO
8 BISHOPRIC CT
9 BARNES MEWS

10 MITRE CT
11 LOWER TANBRIDGE WAY

C1
1 PARK PL
2 PARKWAY HO
3 MORTH GDNS
4 NORMANDY GDNS
5 ST MARY'S HO
6 OLD DENNE GDNS
7 CHESWORTH CL

C2
1 HOME FARM HO
2 SPRINGFIELD CT

3 THE FORUM
4 HEWELLS CT
5 MEDWIN WLK
6 STERLING BLDGS
7 MIDDLE ST
8 GLYNDE PL
9 MARKET SQ

C2
10 STAN'S WAY
11 BURTONS CT
12 COPNALL WAY
13 DULCIMA HO
14 JUBILEE WLK
C4
1 NORTH ASH
2 GARDEN PL
3 GARDEN WLK

4 WIMBLEHURST WAY
5 ST CHRISTOPHERS CL
D1
1 BURNHAM PL
2 GARDENERS CT
3 CHERRY CT
4 EASTGATE MEWS
5 TANNERY CT
6 AMBERLEY HO
7 KNEPP HO

C2
1 LANE HO
2 HAMPERS CT
3 DORSET CT
4 KENT CT
5 SURREY CT
6 HAMPSHIRE CT
7 NORFOLK TERR
8 STANLEY WLK
9 VICTORIA CT

D2
E2
1 BROWN CT
2 SUSSEX HO
3 BRAMBER HO
4 ARUNDEL HO
5 ASHBY CT
F3
1 HANOVER CT
2 TUDOR HO

3 WINDSOR CT
4 COMPTONS CT
5 STUART HO
6 WATERCRESS PL
F4
1 MOUNTAIN ASH CT
2 CHILTERN CT
3 CHEVIOT CT
4 HAZEL CT
5 OSTERLEY HO

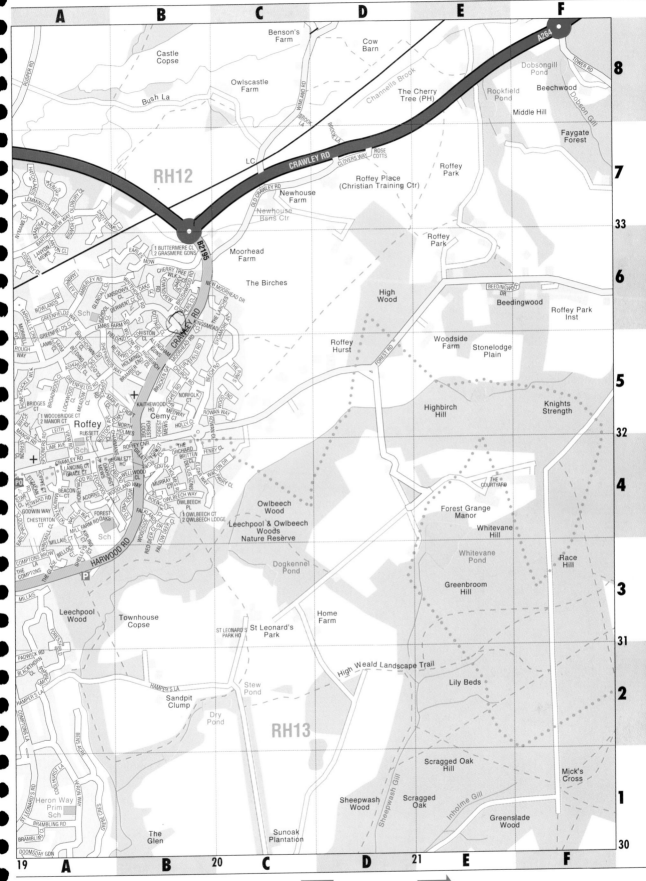

A B C D E F

19 A B 20 C D 21 E F

RH12

RH13

Castle Copse

Benson's Farm

Cow Barn

Channells Brook

Dobsongill Pond

Beechwood

Owlscastle Farm

The Cherry Tree (PH)

Rookfield Pond

Middle Hill

Dobson Gill

Faygate Forest

Bush La

A264

TOWER RD

8

BROOK LA

WIMLAND RD

CRAWLEY RD

LC

CLOVERS WAY

ROSE COTTS

Roffey Park

7

33

Roffey Place (Christian Training Ctr)

Newhouse Farm

OLD CRAWLEY RD

Newhouse Bsns Ctr

Roffey Park

B2195

1 BUTTERMERE CL
2 GRASMERE GDNS

Moorhead Farm

6

The Birches

High Wood

BEEDINGWOOD DR

Beedingwood

Roffey Park Inst

CRAWLEY RD

NEW MOORHEAD DR

Roffey Hurst

FOREST RD

Woodside Farm

Stonelodge Plain

5

Cemy

Roffey

Highbirch Hill

Knights Strength

32

THE COURTYARD

4

Owlbeech Wood

Leechpool & Owlbeech Woods Nature Reserve

Forest Grange Manor

Whitevane Hill

Race Hill

Dogkennel Pond

Greenbroom Hill

Whitevane Pond

HARWOOD RD

3

Leechpool Wood

Townhouse Copse

St Leonard's Park

Home Farm

31

ST LEONARD'S PARK HO

High Weald Landscape Trail

Lily Beds

2

HAMPER'S LA

Stew Pond

Sandpit Clump

Dry Pond

Scragged Oak Hill

Mick's Cross

1

Heron Way Prim Sch

Sheepwash Wood

Scragged Oak

Greenslade Wood

Sheepwash Gill

Inholme Gill

The Glen

Sunoak Plantation

DOOMSDAY GDN

30

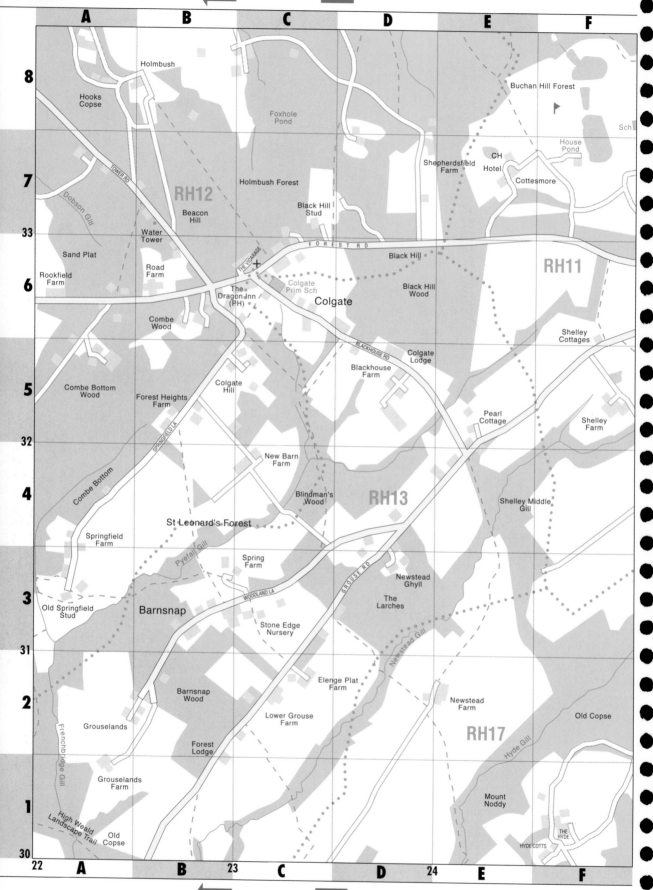

A **B** **C** **D** **E** **F**

M23

Oldhouse Warren

B2036

Bennetts Rough

8

PADDOCKHURST RD

Denches Copse

PH

BALCOMBE RD

B2110

Burnt Place

PARISH LA

7

Cowdray Forest

Forest House

RH10

B2110

LONDON RD

33

Mount Pleasant Farm

Greentrees Farm

Sherlocks

6

Monks Forest Cott

B2036

Stanford Brook

Monks Forest

HIGH ST

5

Forest Lodge

Kings Farm

Brantridge Forest

Balcombe Forest

32

RH17

Sedgy Gill

Burnt Field

4

Brantridge Forest

Highley Manor (Hotel)

CRAWLEY LA

Lodgelands

Scott's Gill

Kelsey House

B2036

Works

Hourglass Wood

3

Brantridge Forest Farm

HANDCROSS RD

Wellgrove Wood

BOUNDARY RD

B2110

31

HIGH BEECHES LA

New England

Balcombe House

Wr Twr

Knoll Wood

Great Cooper's Corner Farm

Red Bridge

LONDON RD

Half Moon Inn

2

Brantridge Wood

Balcombe

HAYWARDS HEATH RD

Brantridge Park Farm

BRANTRIDGE LA

Pond Wood

Casteye Wood

Balcombe CE Prim Sch

BRAMBLE HILL

PO

Alder Wood

THE BROADWAY 1
STOCKPORT RD 2

B BRAMBLE MEAD

Brantridge

Ashen Wood

WESTUP RD

1

Brantridge Park

Banks Wood

Long Shaw

ROCKS LA

Balcombe

NEWLANDS

Westup Farm

Peter's Wood

Balcombe

B2036

JOB-CS

OLDLANDS AVE

30

28 **A** **B** **29** **C** **D** **30** **E** **F**

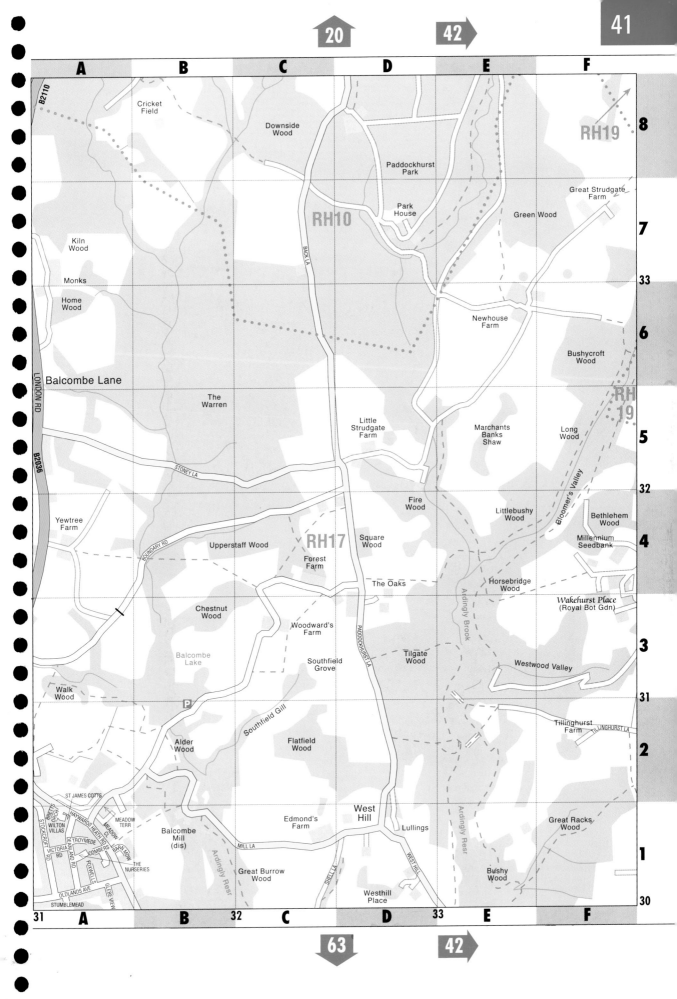

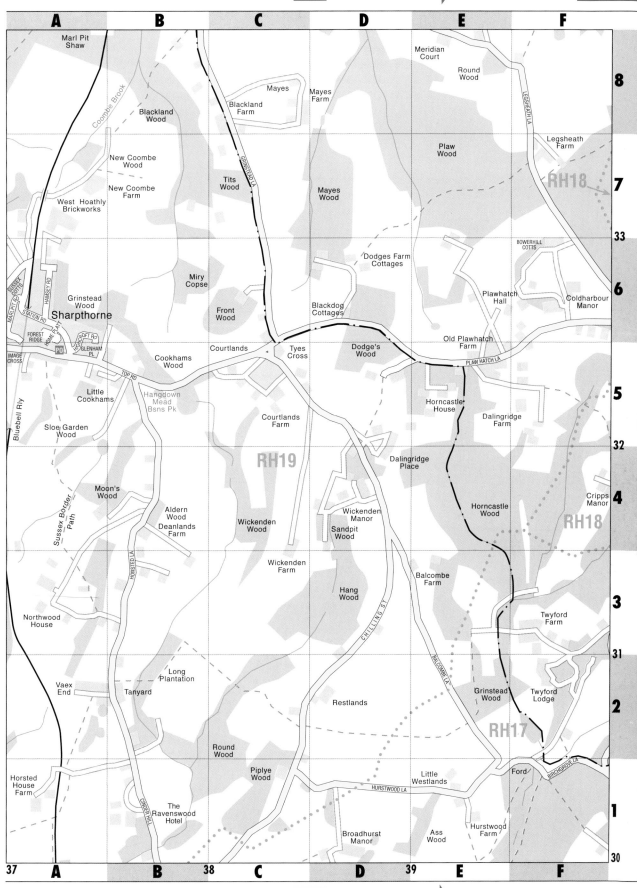

A   B   C   D   E   F

8

7

33

6

5

32

4

3

31

2

1

30

Marl Pit Shaw

Coombe Brook

Blackland Wood

Mayes

Blackland Farm

Mayes Farm

Meridian Court

Round Wood

New Coombe Wood

New Coombe Farm

Tits Wood

GRINSTEAD LA

Mayes Wood

Plaw Wood

Legsheath Farm

RH18

LEGSHEATH LA

West Hoathly Brickworks

Miry Copse

Dodges Farm Cottages

BOWERHILL COTTS

Grinstead Wood

SUSSEX COTTS

HAMSEY RD

Sharpthorne

STATION RD

FOREST RIDGE

HOME PLATT

PO

GLENHAM PL

HIGHCROFT RD

IMAGE CROSS

TOP RD

Front Wood

Blackdog Cottages

Plawhatch Hall

Coldharbour Manor

Courtlands

Tyes Cross

Dodge's Wood

Old Plawhatch Farm

PLAW HATCH LA

Cookhams Wood

Little Cookhams

Hangdown Mead Bsns Pk

Courtlands Farm

Horncastle House

Dalingridge Farm

Bluebell Rly

Sloe Garden Wood

RH19

Dalingridge Place

Cripps Manor

Moon's Wood

Aldern Wood

Deanlands Farm

Wickenden Wood

Wickenden Manor

Sandpit Wood

Horncastle Wood

RH18

HORSTED LA

Sussex Border Path

Wickenden Farm

Hang Wood

CHILLING ST

Balcombe Farm

Northwood House

Twyford Farm

Vaex End

Tanyard

Long Plantation

Restlands

BALCOMBE LA

Grinstead Wood

Twyford Lodge

RH17

Round Wood

Piplye Wood

Little Westlands

Ford

BIRCHGROVE LA

Horsted House Farm

CINDER HILL

The Ravenswood Hotel

HURSTWOOD LA

Broadhurst Manor

Ass Wood

Hurstwood Farm

37   A   B   38   C   D   39   E   F

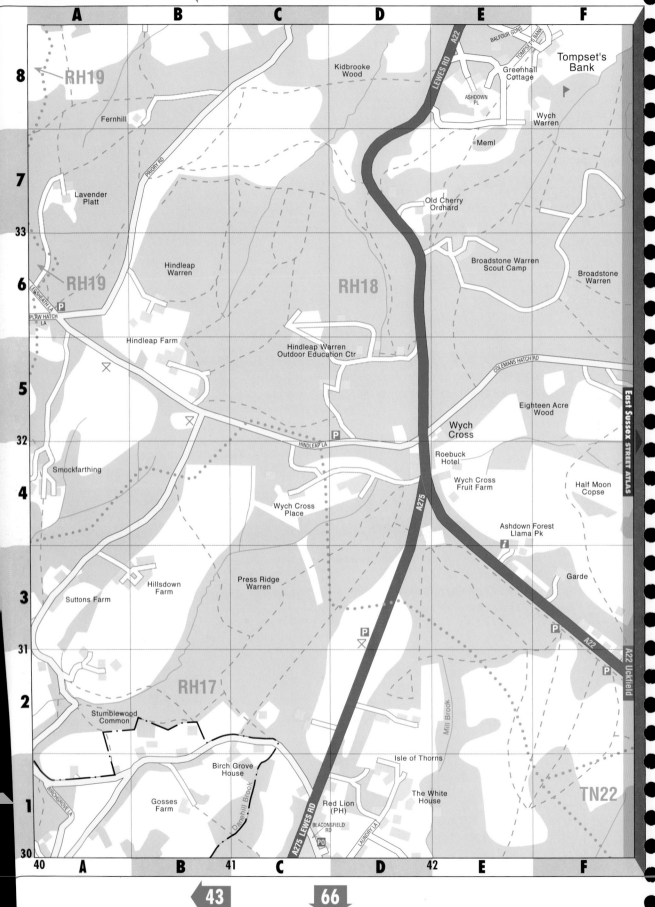

43
23

A B C D E F

8 RH19

Kidbrooke Wood

Fernhill

LEWES RD
A22
BALFOUR GDNS
ASHDOWN PL
Greenhall Cottage
Tompset's Bank
Wych Warren
Meml

7

Lavender Platt

PRIORY RD

Old Cherry Orchard

33

6 RH19

Hindleap Warren

RH18

Broadstone Warren Scout Camp

Broadstone Warren

FOREIGN LA
P
PLAW HATCH LA

Hindleap Farm

Hindleap Warren Outdoor Education Ctr

COLEMANS HATCH RD

5

Eighteen Acre Wood

32

HINDLEAP LA
P

Wych Cross

Roebuck Hotel

Smockfarthing

Wych Cross Fruit Farm

Half Moon Copse

4

Wych Cross Place

A275

Ashdown Forest Llama Pk
i

3 Suttons Farm

Hillsdown Farm

Press Ridge Warren

Garde

P
A22

31

P
A22 Uckfield

RH17

2 Stumblewood Common

P

BIRCHGROVE LA

Birch Grove House

Isle of Thorns

TN22

1 Gosses Farm

Danehill Brook

Red Lion (PH)

The White House

Mill Brook

A275 LEWES RD
BEACONSFIELD RD
PO
LAUNDRY LA

30
40 A B 41 C 42 D E F

East Sussex STREET ATLAS

43
66

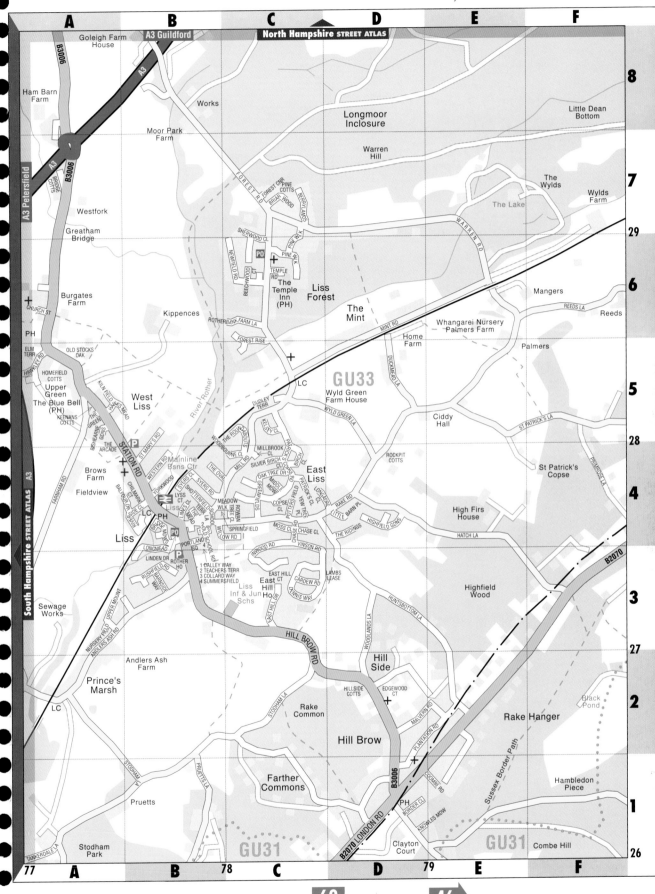

A B C D E F

North Hampshire STREET ATLAS

B3006

A3 Guildford

Goleigh Farm
House

8

Ham Barn
Farm

Works

Longmoor
Inclosure

Little Dean
Bottom

A3 Petersfield

Moor Park
Farm

Warren
Hill

The Wylds

7

A3

BRIDGE COTTS

B3006

Westfork

FOREST RD

FOREST CNR

PINE COTTS

BRIAR WOOD

BERRYLANDS

The Wylds

Wylds
Farm

The Lake

29

Greatham
Bridge

SHERWOOD CL

PINE WLK

PINE WLK

WARREN RD

NEWFIELD RD

BEECHWOOD CT

PO

TEMPLE RD

The Temple Inn
(PH)

Liss
Forest

Mangers

REEDS LA

Reeds

6

CHURCH ST

Burgates
Farm

Kippences

ROTHERBANK FARM LA

The Mint

MINT RD

Whangarei Nursery
Palmers Farm

Palmers

PH

FOREST RISE

Home
Farm

ELM TERR

OLD STOCKS
OAK

DUCKMEAD LA

GU33

HAWKLEY RD

HOMEFIELD COTTS

West
Liss

River Rother

LC

Wyld Green
Farm House

Ciddy
Hall

ST PATRICK'S LA

5

Upper
Green

DUDLEY TERR

The Blue Bell
(PH)

KEENANS COTTS

THE GREEN GDNS

KILN FIELD

MASTHEAD

KELSY CL

WYLD GREEN LA

ROCKPIT
COTTS

St Patrick's
Copse

28

FARNHAM RD

BISHEARNE GDNS

THE ARCADE

STATION RD

ST MARY'S RD

WESTERN RD

WOODBOURNE CL

MILLBROOK CL

MILL RD

SILVER BIRCH CL

THE OVAL

BIRCH RD

East
Liss

PRIMROSE LA

4

Brows
Farm

Fieldview

BALDOUR DR

GLEBE SIDE

CHILMARK CL

YORKWOOD

SYERS RD

SYERS RD

MEADOW WLK

OAK TREE DR

GREENFIELDS

MIDDLE MDW

PATRICK'S CL

YEW TREE

LONGACRE

RAKE RD

LITTLE BARN PL

HIGHFIELD GDNS

High Firs
House

LC

PH

LYSS CT

TIMMS CL

SHOTTERFIELD TERR

SCHOOL LA

OLD SCHOOL RD

ROWAN TREE CL

POTTERS RD

COPSE CL

MOSS CL

CHASE CL

CHASE CL

THE RIDINGS

HATCH LA

Liss

PO

SPRINGFIELD

WILLOW RD

VINSON RD

LONGMEAD

ROTHER HO

LINDEN DR

PORTLAND SQ

1 DALLEY WAY
2 TEACHERS TERR
3 COLLARD WAY
4 SUMMERSFIELD

INNWOOD RD

CARDEW RD

LAMBS LEASE

B2070

3

RUSHFIELD

BARNS CL

WAY

Liss
Inf & Jun
Schs

East
Hill
Ho

EAST HILL RD

EAST HILL DR

DENNIS WAY

HUNTSBOTTOM LA

WOODLANDS LA

Highfield
Wood

Sewage
Works

NURSERY FIELD

UPPER MOUNT

ANDLERS ASH RD

Prince's
Marsh

Andlers Ash
Farm

HILL BROW RD

Hill
Side

27

LC

HILLSIDE COTTS

EDGEWOOD CT

MALVERN RD

2

Black
Pond

Rake
Common

STODHAM LA

Rake Hanger

PLANTATION RD

COOMBE RD

Hambledon
Piece

PRUETTS LA

STODHAM LA

Pruetts

Farther
Commons

Hill Brow

B3006

Sussex Border Path

1

Stodham
Park

TANKERDALE LA

South Hampshire STREET ATLAS

GU31

B2070 LONDON RD

PH

BORDER CL

Clayton
Court

KNOWLES MDW

GU31

Combe Hill

26

45
24

A B C D E F

8

The Broom

Folly Pond

Hilly Fields Copse

Heath Patch

Horse Trials Show Gd

Ram's Horn Copse

7

Langley

The Vineyard

Home Park

Hutfield Copse

Ripsley Farm

Fox Copse

Sussex Border Path

Bishop's Copse

Ripsley House

PH

29

B2070

Langley Bridge Farm

Langley Court

Broad Copse

6

REEDS LA

Brewells Farm

Little Langley Farm

Langley Wood

Heath Patch

GU33

Rake Firs

Chapel Common

Great Hanger

5

Newlands

BREWELLS LA

Rock Field Firs

Maysleith

ST PATRICK'S LA

Rake CE Fst Sch

28

Rake Bsns Pk

Maysleith Hanger

GU30

The Flying Bull (PH)

LONDON RD

FIR TREE COTTS

BULL HILL

Maysleith Wood

4

Rake

Coldharbour Park Farm

PRIMROSE LA

PO

Sun Inn

B2070

SANDY LA

Coldharbour Wood

Hulls Copse

Coldharbour Wood

3

Pot Well

Canhouse Copse

Combeland Farm

CANHOUSE LA

27

Combe Pond

Canhouse Cottage

Great Trippetts Farm

2

Goldring

Lower Common Wood

RAKE RD

GU31

Combe Lodge Farm

Marsh Wood

1

Harting Combe

New Barn Farm

26

80 A B 81 C D 82 E F

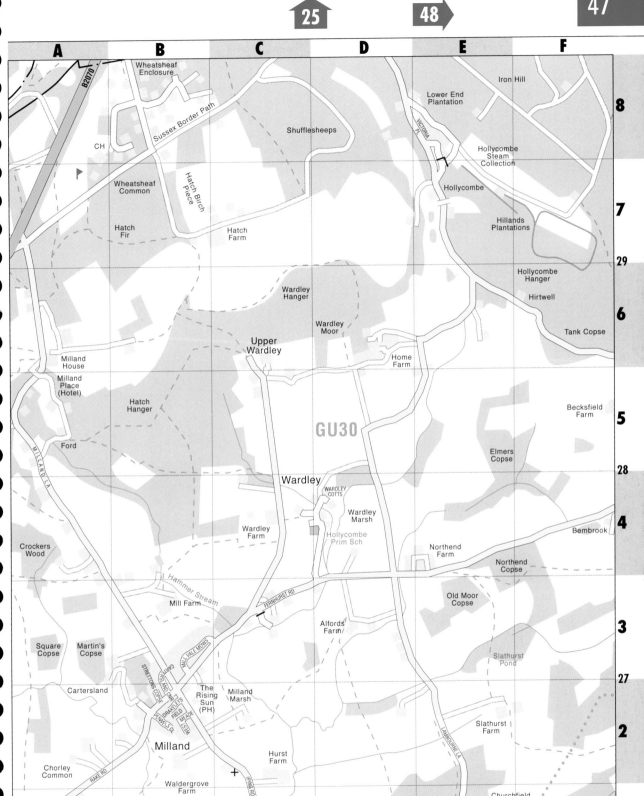

A B C D E F

8

Stanley Farm
The Leithe
Newlands Cottage
The Moor
Shulbrede Priory
Well Copse
West Leithe
Greenhill Wood

Parkgate Copse
Green Hill

7

Parkgate Rough
Bird Piece
Greenhill House
Oakreeds Wood

29

6

GU30
Lower Lodge Farm
Highbuilding Farm

Elmers Marsh

Hawksfold Farm
HAWKSFOLD LA E

5

Minepit Copse
Hartley Green Copse
Furnace Pond
GU27

Luckin's Copse

28

Lower Hawksfold

Taylors Copse

4

Upper North Park Farm

Heathfield Rough
Lower North Park Farm
Amon's Copse

Woodmansgreen
Ward Copse
Whites Lane Gully
Turner's Copse

Butler's Rough
Whitter's Copse

3

Peckham's Copse
WHITES LA

27

Footway Copse
Cavalry Quarters

2

Older Hill Copse
Older Hill
West Copse
Birchhill Copse
Pondfield Copse

LINCH RD
Upper Lodge

Redford Farm
Telegraph Hill
A286

Hookland
GU29
Northpark Copse

1

Redford
Pine Hill House

Henley Common

26
PO
P
A286

86 A B 87 C D 88 E F

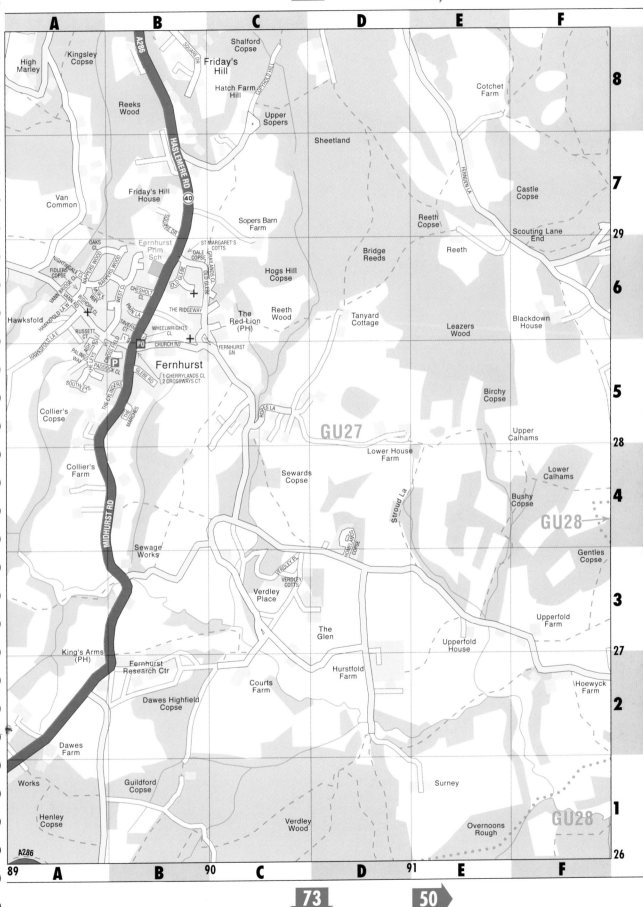

49
28

A B C D E F

8
Abesters Copse
Rickfield Copse
Upper Diddlesford Farm
Fulwick's Copse
Chapel Copse

7
Abesters
Ramsfold Wood
Ramsfold House
New Copse
Bullocks La
Diddlesford Manor Farm

Temple of the Winds
29
FERNDEN LA
GU27
Shopp Hill Farm
Hookhams Farm

6
Quellwood Common
Hillgrove

Blackdown Farm
Hobstevens
Tanland Copse

Upper Barn Hanger

5
Windfall Wood
Sybs Farm
Upper Barn Park Farm

Navant

28
Coochway Ground
Mire Hanger

4
Windfallwood Common
Spring Coppice
Park Farm
GU28
Screechhouse Copse
CROSSWAYS

Little Brockhurst
Northhurst Farm
High La

Great Brockhurst Farm
The Noah's Ark (PH)
Gatehouse Farm

3
Dial Green
Lurgashall
PO

Gentilshurst Farm
Goffs Copse
27
GU27
Greengates Farmhouse
GREENGATES
Bishop's Hanger
Ragham Lodge
Benefold Copse

2
Lower Gentilshurst Farm
HIGHSTEAD LA
Woodfield Row
High Hampstead Farm

Sods Farm
Lickfold Bridge
The Hanger
Chillinghurst Copse

1
The Lickford Inn (PH)
Mill Pond
Old Mill Farm

26
Shotter's Farm
92 A B 93 C D 94 E F

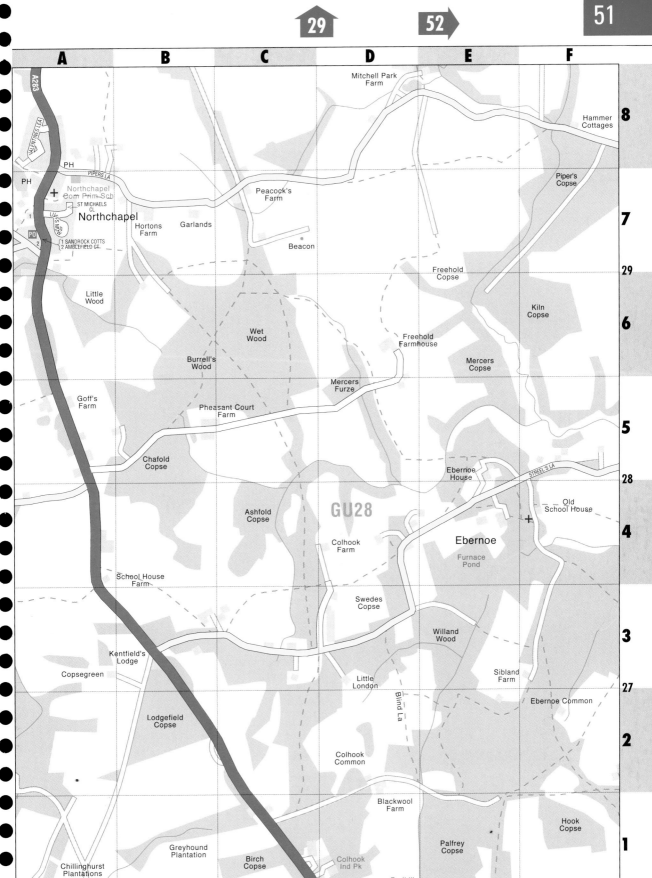

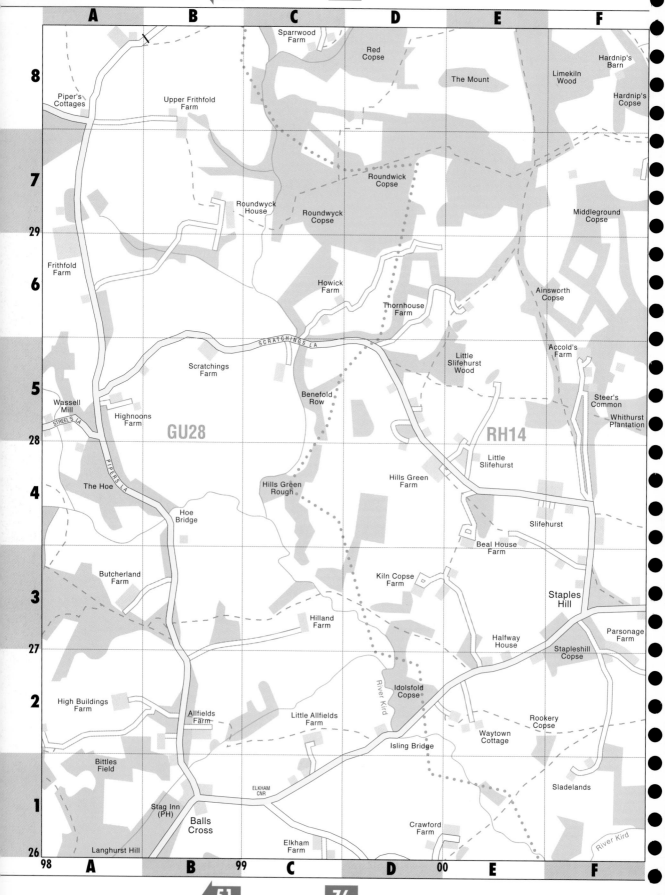

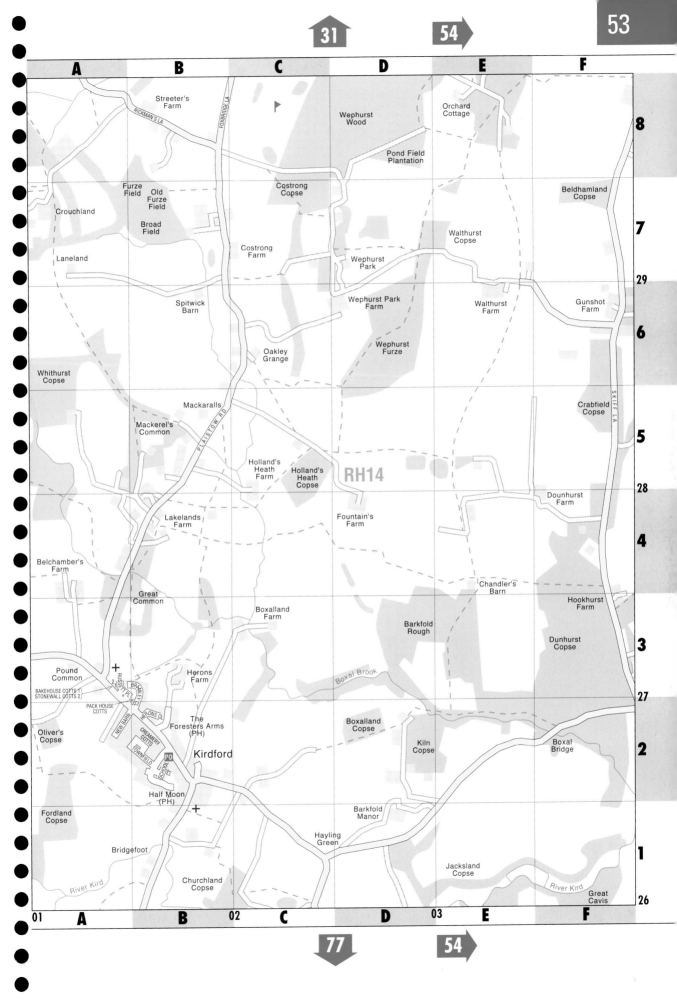

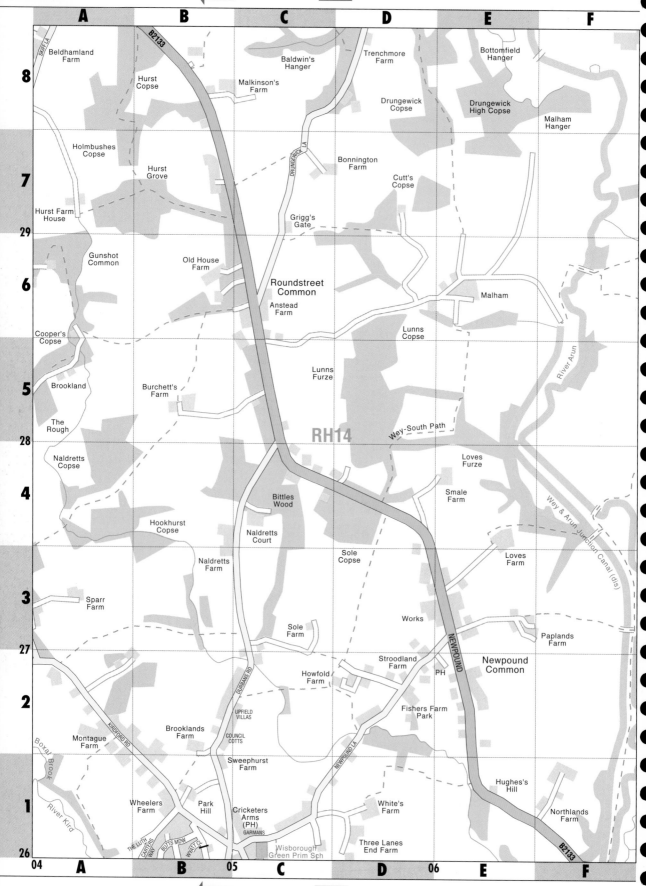

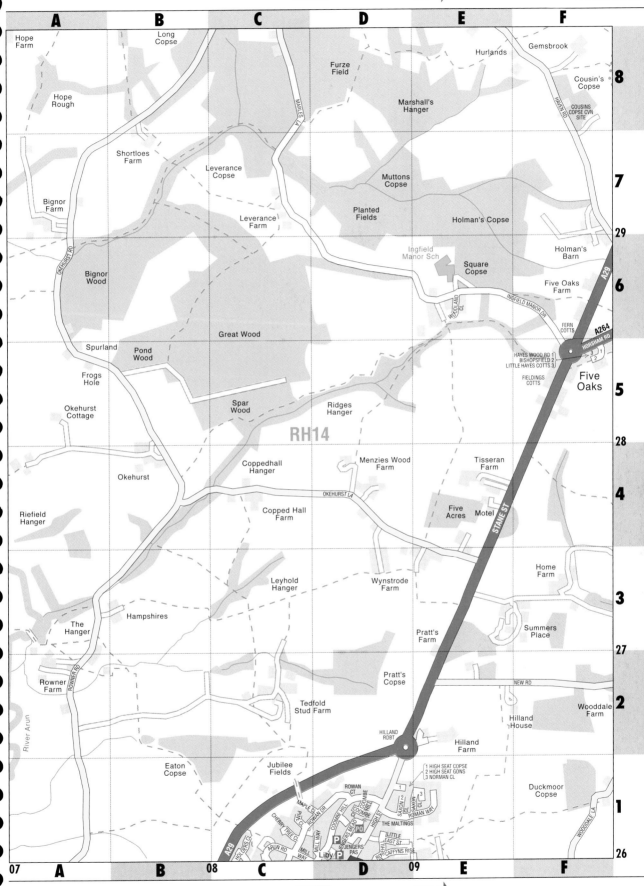

Hope Farm
Long Copse
Furze Field
Hurlands
Gemsbrook
Cousin's Copse
COUSINS COPSE CVN SITE
Hope Rough
Shortloes Farm
Leverance Copse
Marshall's Hanger
Muttons Copse
Bignor Farm
Leverance Farm
Planted Fields
Holman's Copse
Holman's Barn
Ingfield Manor Sch
Square Copse
Five Oaks Farm
Bignor Wood
Great Wood
FERN COTTS
A264
Spurland
Pond Wood
HAYES WOOD RD 1
BISHOPSFIELD 2
LITTLE HAYES COTTS 3
Five Oaks
Frogs Hole
FIELDINGS COTTS
Spar Wood
Ridges Hanger
Okehurst Cottage
RH14
Coppedhall Hanger
Menzies Wood Farm
Tisseran Farm
Okehurst
Riefield Hanger
Copped Hall Farm
OKEHURST LA
Five Acres
Motel
Leyhold Hanger
Wynstrode Farm
Home Farm
Hampshires
The Hanger
Pratt's Farm
Summers Place
NEW RD
Rowner Farm
Pratt's Copse
Wooddale Farm
Tedfold Stud Farm
Hilland House
Hilland Farm
HILLAND RDBT
River Arun
Eaton Copse
Jubilee Fields
1 HIGH SEAT COPSE
2 HIGH SEAT GDNS
3 NORMAN CL
Duckmoor Copse
ROWAN CT
THE MALTINGS
Liby

MARLES LA
OKEHURST RD
ROWNER RD
A29
HORSHAM RD
A29
STANE ST
INGFIELD MANOR DR
WOODLAND CL
HAVEN RD
WOODDALE LA

8
7
29
6
5
28
4
3
27
2
1
26

07
08
09

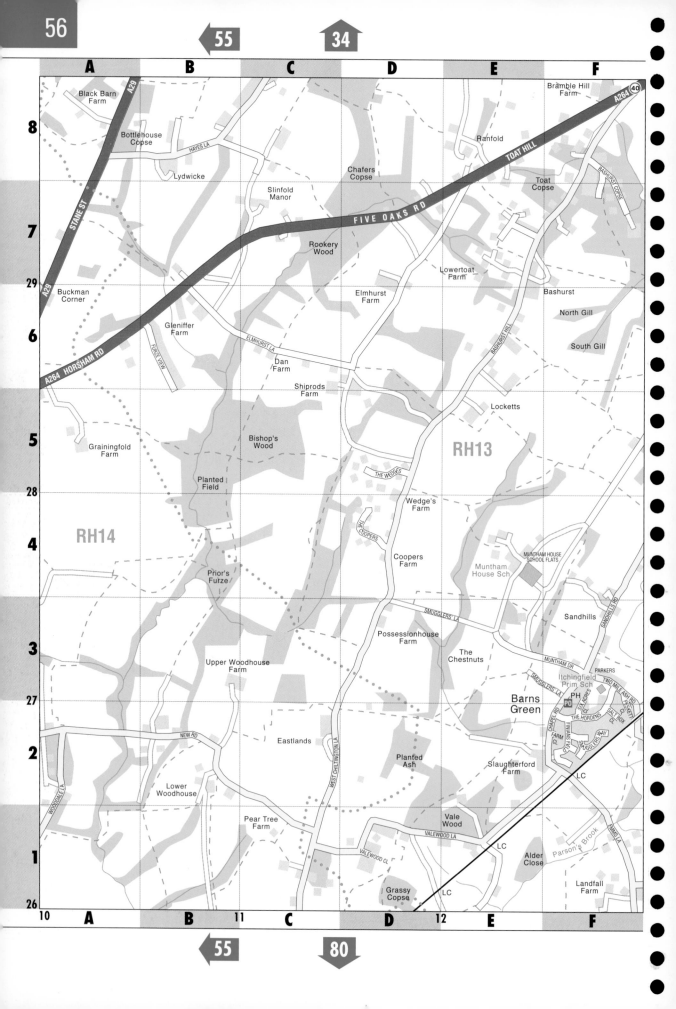

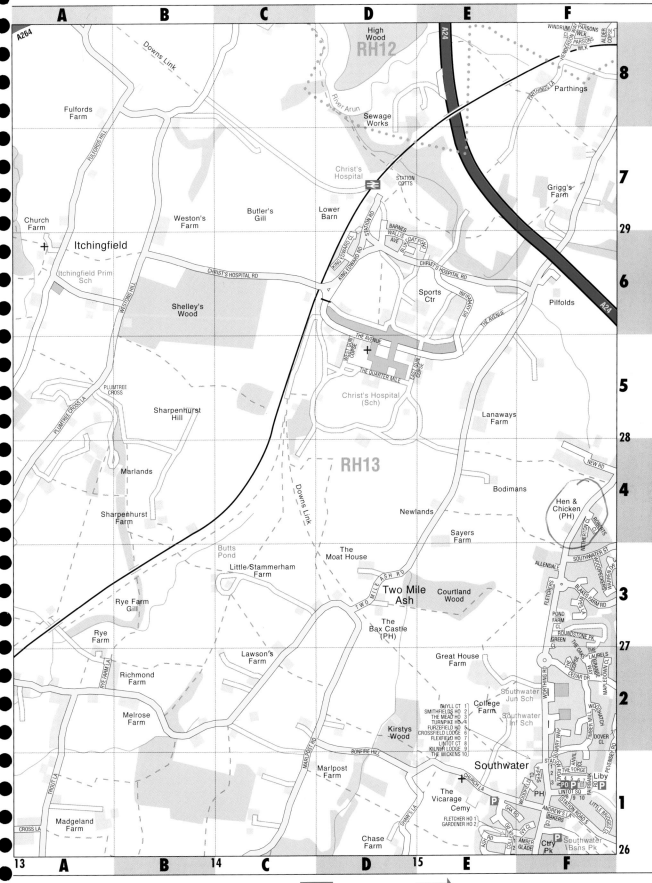

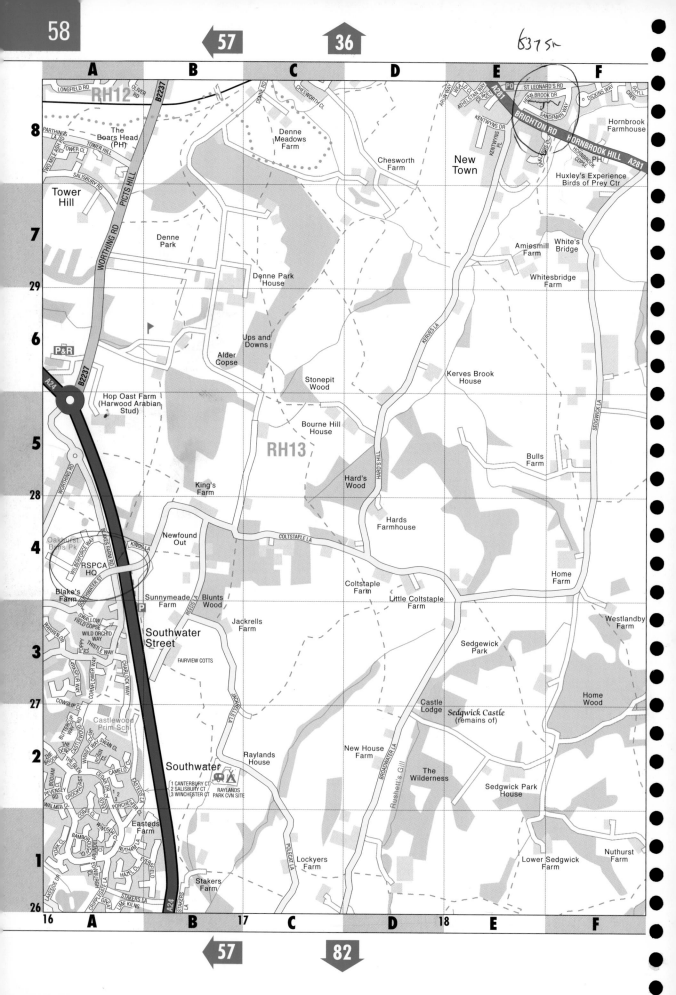

6375

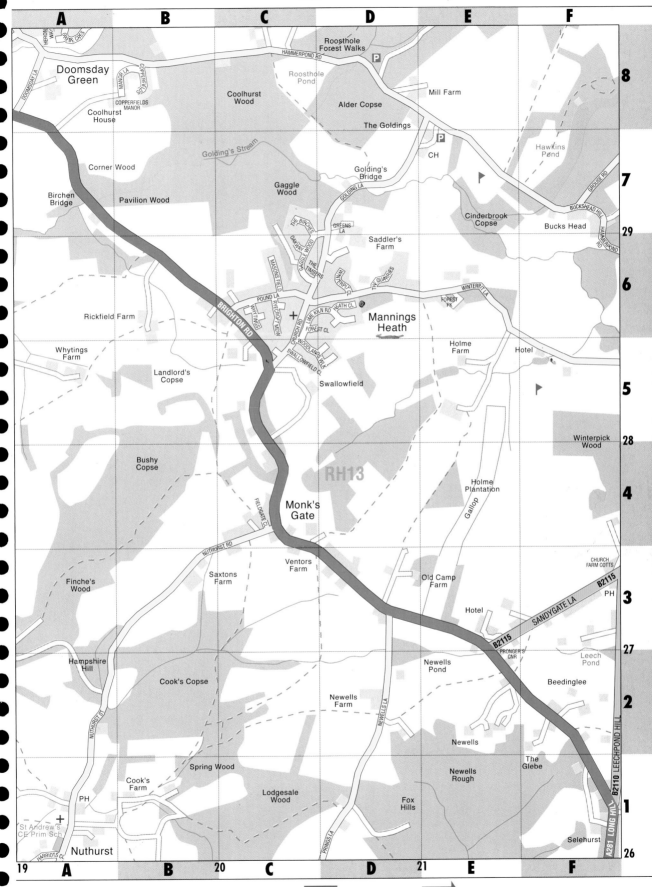

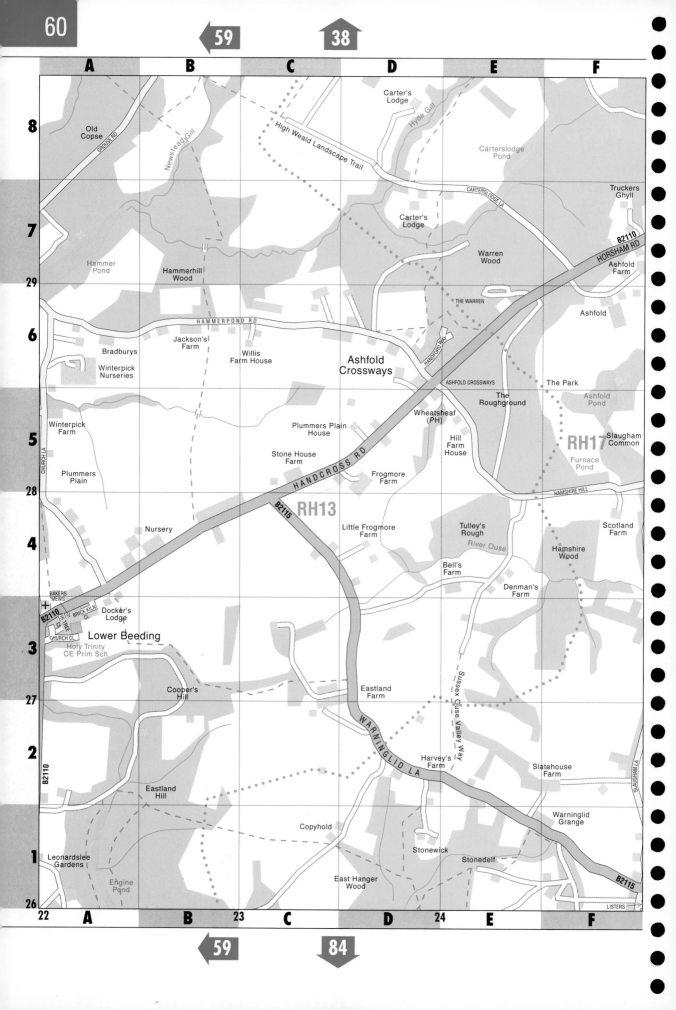

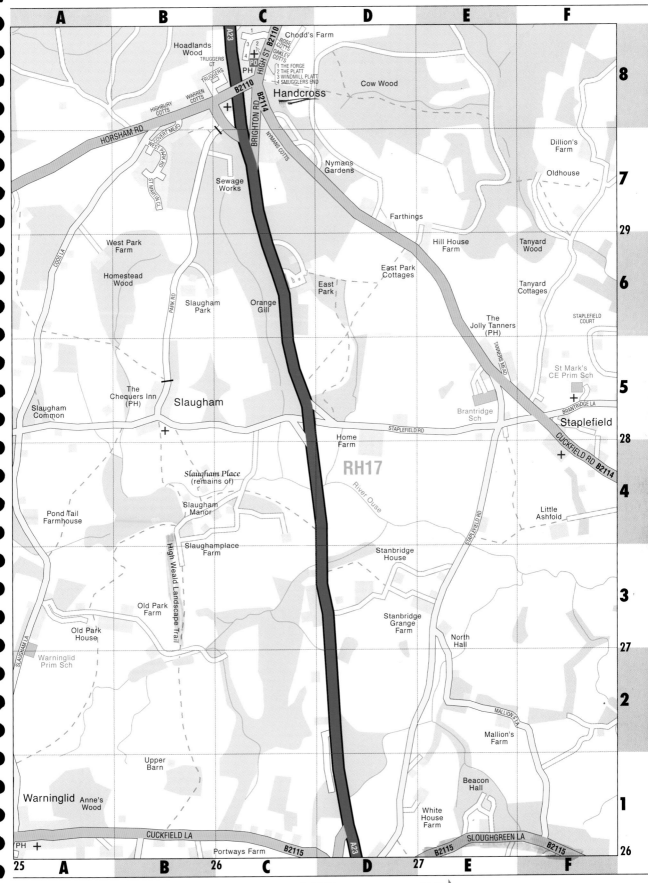

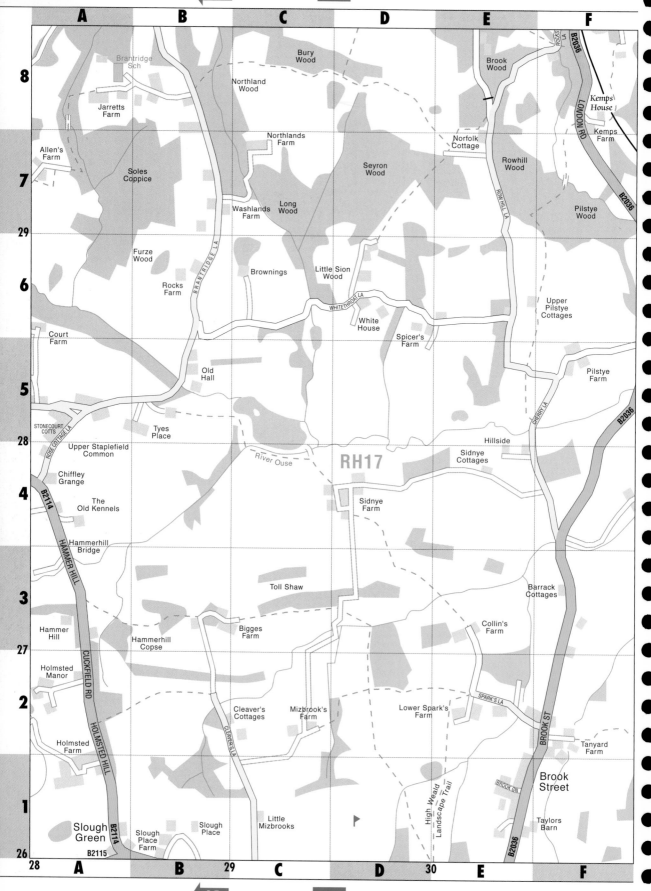

Brantridge Sch

Bury Wood

Northland Wood

Brook Wood

Kemps House

B2036

LONDON RD

Jarretts Farm

Northlands Farm

Norfolk Cottage

Kemps Farm

Allen's Farm

Seyron Wood

Rowhill Wood

Soles Coppice

ROW HILL LA

Pilstye Wood

B2036

Washlands Farm

Long Wood

Furze Wood

BRANTRIDGE LA

Rocks Farm

Brownings

Little Sion Wood

Upper Pilstye Cottages

WHITETHROAT LA

White House

Spicer's Farm

Court Farm

CHERRY LA

Pilstye Farm

Old Hall

Tyes Place

River Ouse

RH17

Hillside

Sidnye Cottages

B2036

STONECOURT COTTS

ROSE COTTAGE LA

Upper Staplefield Common

Sidnye Farm

Chiffley Grange

The Old Kennels

B2114

Hammerhill Bridge

HAMMER HILL

Toll Shaw

Barrack Cottages

Collin's Farm

Hammer Hill

CUCKFIELD RD

HOLMSTED HILL

Hammerhill Copse

Bigges Farm

CLEAVER'S LA

Holmsted Manor

Cleaver's Cottages

Mizbrook's Farm

Lower Spark's Farm

SPARK'S LA

BROOK ST

Holmsted Farm

Tanyard Farm

Brook Street

(BROOK GN)

High Weald Landscape Trail

Slough Green

B2114

Slough Place Farm

Slough Place

Little Mizbrooks

B2036

Taylors Barn

B2115

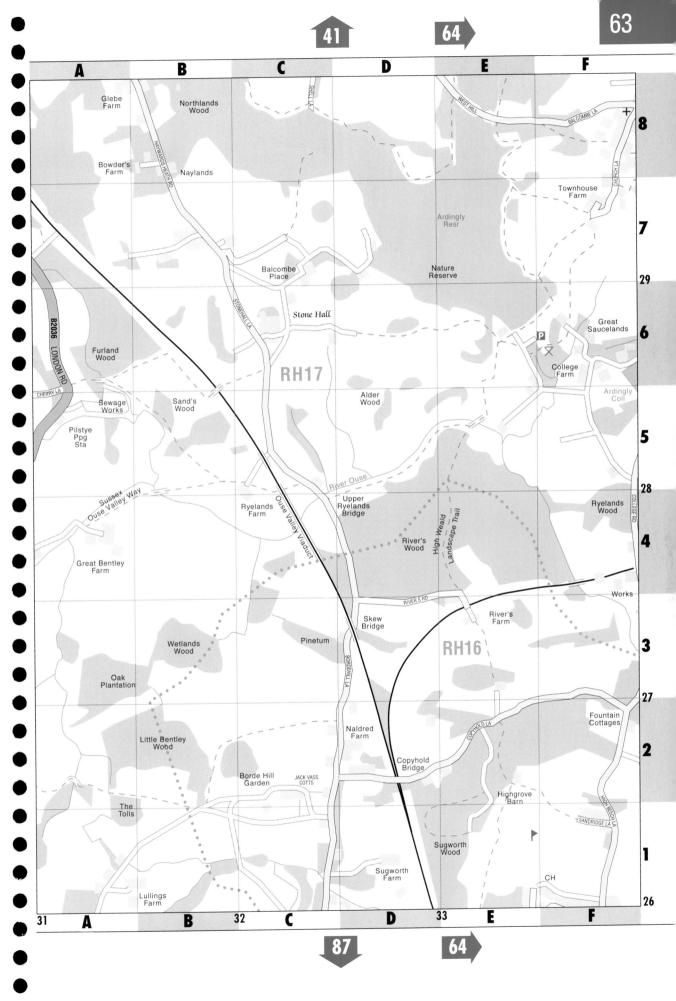

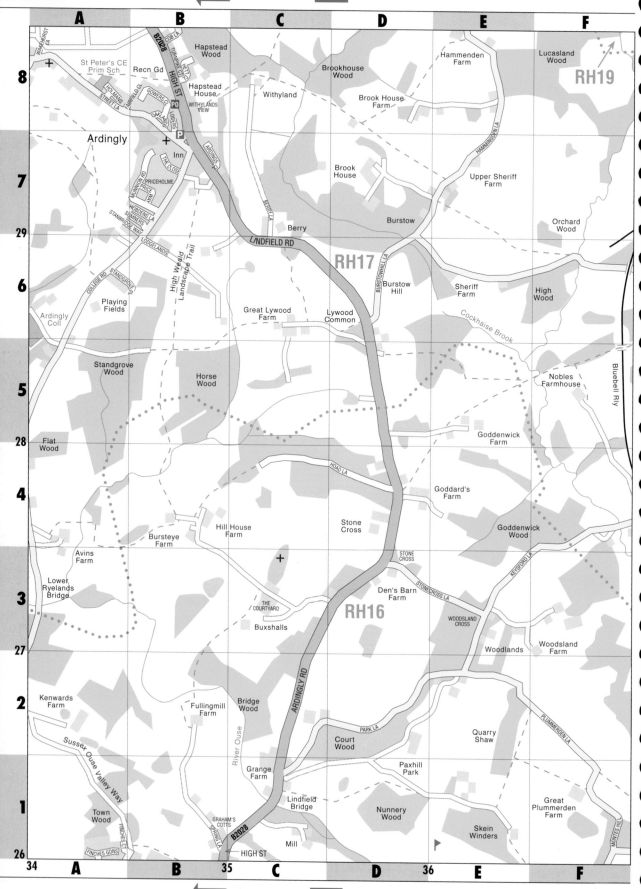

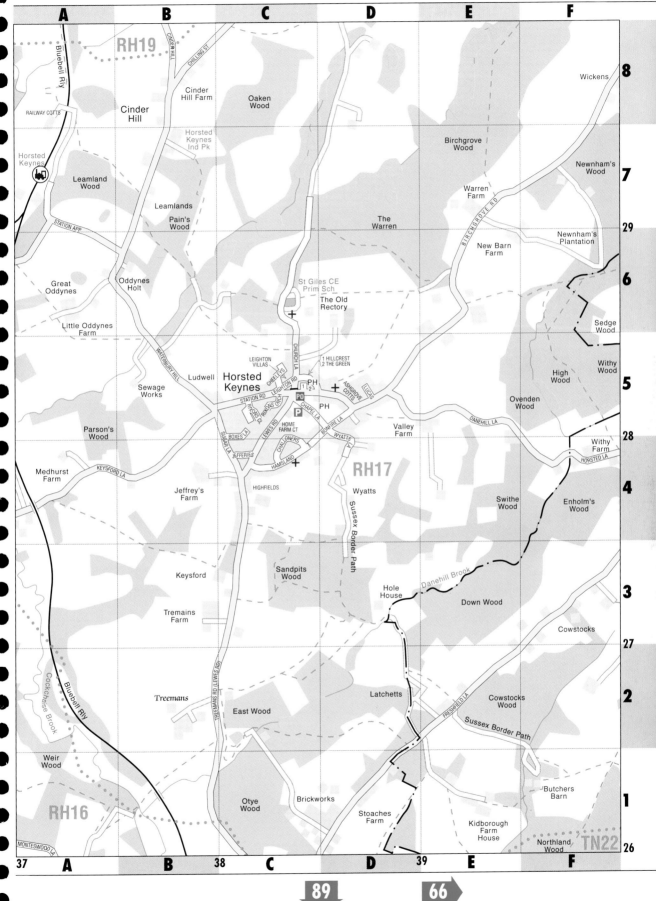

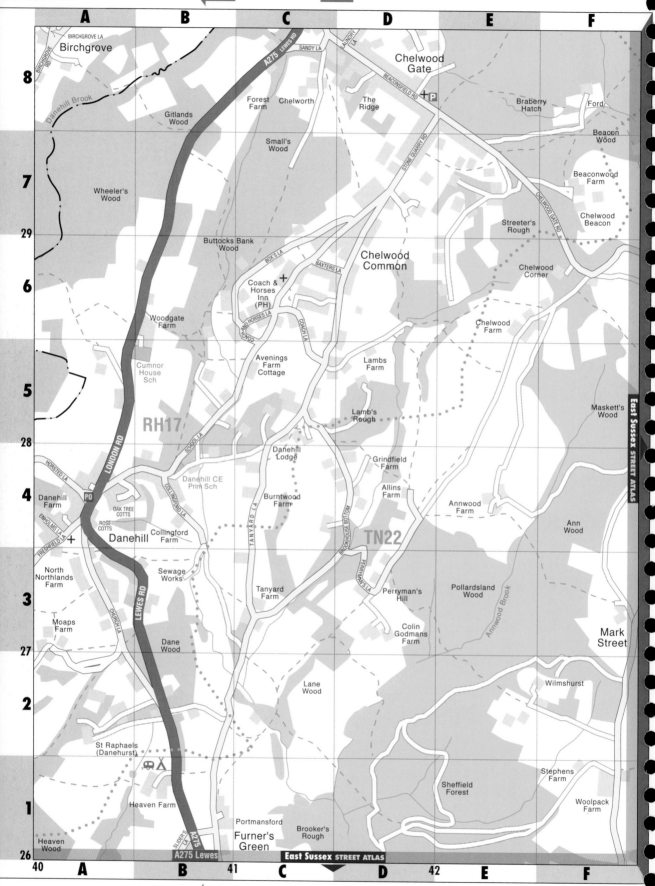

A   B   C   D   E   F

8

Birchgrove
BIRCHGROVE LA
Gitlands Wood
Forest Farm
Chelworth
The Ridge
Chelwood Gate
BEACONSFIELD RD
Braberry Hatch
Ford
Beacon Wood

7
Wheeler's Wood
Small's Wood
Beaconwood Farm
Chelwood Beacon
CHELWOOD GATE RD

29
Buttocks Bank Wood
Streeter's Rough
Chelwood Corner

6
Woodgate Farm
BOX'S LA
Coach & Horses Inn (PH)
BAXTERS LA
Chelwood Common
Chelwood Farm
COACH LA
COACH AND HORSES LA

5
Cumnor House Sch
Avenings Farm Cottage
Lambs Farm
Lamb's Rough
Maskett's Wood
RH17

28
SCHOOL LA
Danehill Lodge
Grindfield Farm
Danehill CE Prim Sch
COLLINGFORD LA

4
Danehill Farm
PO
OAK TREE COTTS
ROSE COTTS
Danehill
Collingford Farm
Burntwood Farm
Allins Farm
Annwood Farm
Ann Wood
HORSTED LA
LONDON RD
ENHOLMS LA
FRESHFIELD LA
TANYARD LA
BROOKHOUSE BOTTOM
TN22

3
North Northlands Farm
Sewage Works
Tanyard Farm
Perryman's Hill
Pollardsland Wood
Annwood Brook
Mark Street
LEWES RD
PERRYMAN'S LA

27
Moaps Farm
CHURCH LA
Dane Wood
Colin Godmans Farm
Wilmshurst

2
Lane Wood

1
St Raphaels (Danehurst)
Heaven Farm
Sheffield Forest
Stephens Farm
Woolpack Farm

26
Heaven Wood
SLIDERS LA
A275
Portmansford
Furner's Green
A275 Lewes
Brooker's Rough
East Sussex STREET ATLAS

40   A   B   41   C   D   42   E   F

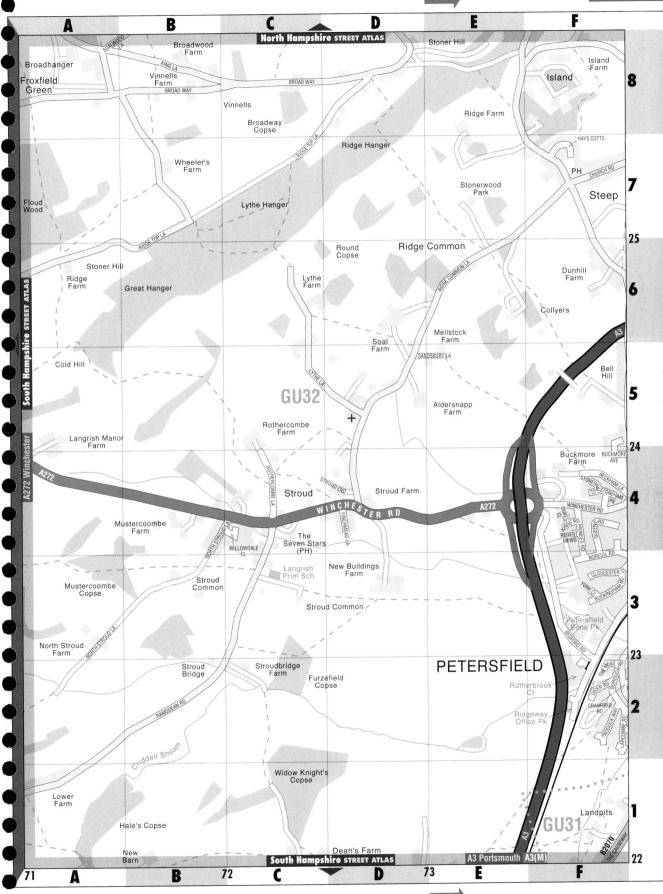

North Hampshire STREET ATLAS

South Hampshire STREET ATLAS

South Hampshire STREET ATLAS

A3 Portsmouth A3(M)

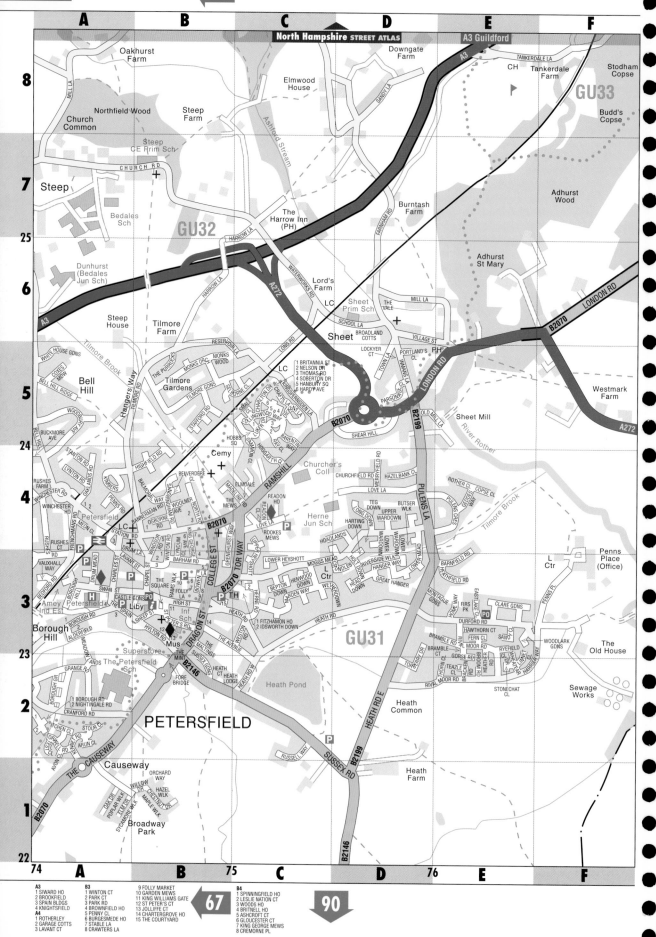

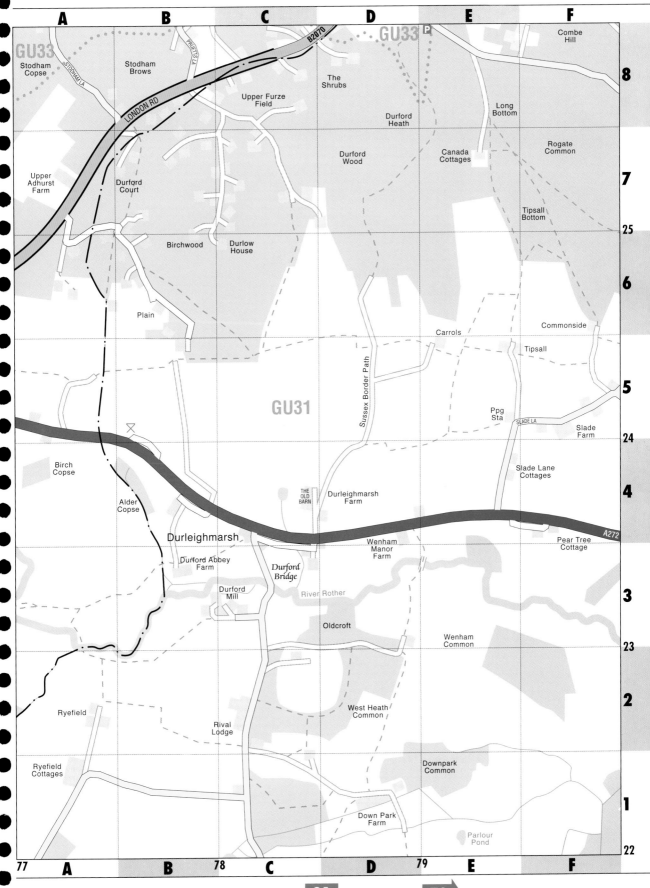

GU33

Combe Hill

Stodham Copse

Stodham Brows

The Shrubs

8

Upper Furze Field

Durford Heath

Long Bottom

Rogate Common

Durford Court

Durford Wood

Canada Cottages

7

Upper Adhurst Farm

Tipsall Bottom

25

Birchwood

Durlow House

6

Plain

Commonside

Carrols

Tipsall

GU31

Sussex Border Path

5

Ppg Sta

SLADE LA

Slade Farm

24

Birch Copse

Slade Lane Cottages

4

Alder Copse

THE OLD BARN

Durleighmarsh Farm

Wenham Manor Farm

Pear Tree Cottage

A272

Durleighmarsh

Durford Abbey Farm

Durford Bridge

Durford Mill

River Rother

Oldcroft

Wenham Common

3

23

Ryefield

Rival Lodge

West Heath Common

2

Ryefield Cottages

Downpark Common

1

Down Park Farm

Parlour Pond

22

77 78 79

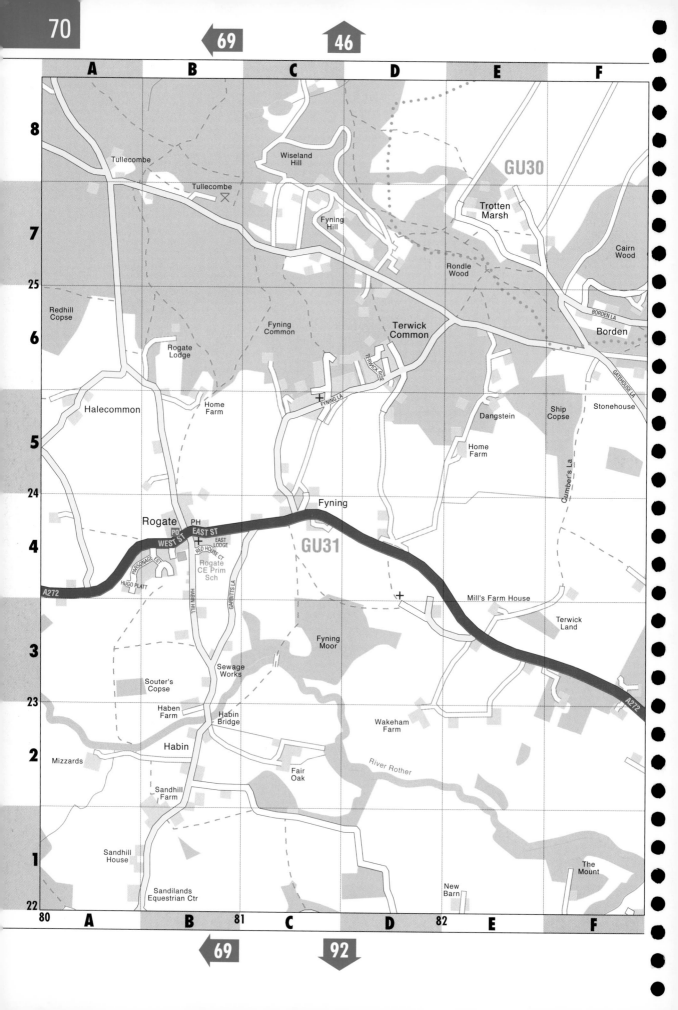

69
46

A B C D E F

8 Tullecombe
Tullecombe
Wiseland Hill
GU30
Trotten Marsh

7 Fyning Hill
Rondle Wood
Cairn Wood

25 Redhill Copse
BORDEN LA
Borden

6 Rogate Lodge
Fyning Common
Terwick Common
GATEHOUSE LA

Home Farm
TERWICK RISE
FYNING LA
Dangstein
Ship Copse
Stonehouse

5 Halecommon
Home Farm

Cumber's La

24 Fyning

4 Rogate
PO PH EAST ST
WEST ST EAST LODGE
RED HOUSE CT
Rogate CE Prim Sch
PARSONAGE ST
HUGO PLATT
A272
GU31
Mill's Farm House
Terwick Land

HABIN HILL
GARBITTS LA

3 Souter's Copse
Fyning Moor
A272

23 Haben Farm
Habin Bridge
Sewage Works
Wakeham Farm

2 Mizzards
Habin
River Rother
Fair Oak

Sandhill Farm

1 Sandhill House
The Mount

22 Sandilands Equestrian Ctr
New Barn

80 A B 81 C D 82 E F

69
92

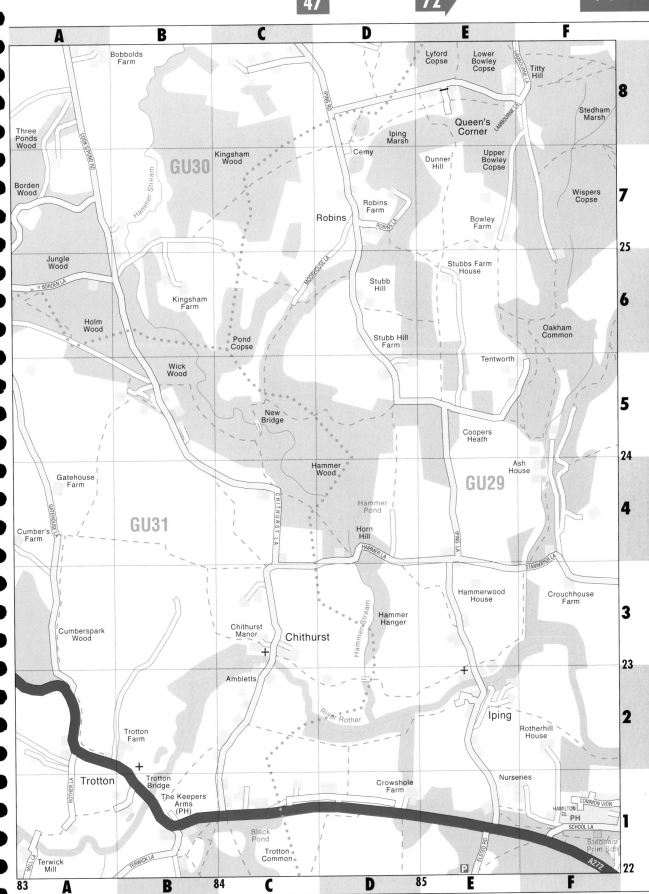

71
48

A286

GU27

	A	B	C	D	E	F

8

Woolbeding Common

Scotland Farmhouse

Little Common

West Heath

Madam's Farm

7

Linch Old Rectory

The Lair

LINCH RD

Lord's Common

HURST PK

KINGS DR

P

25

Woolhouse Farm

Pound Farm

6

Tote Hill

Great Common

Camp Site

Pound Common

Eastshaw Farm

Hollist Common

5

Woodgate Farm

Chapelland Copse

24

Old School

Paylins Copse

Chapelland Buildings

Cherryorchard Cottage

4

TOTE LA

WOOLBEDING LA

EASTSHAW LA

GU29

Lock's Cottages

Whitters Farm

Farthings

OLD BUDDINGTON LA

BUDDINGTON LA

Old Buddington

3

STEDHAM LA

Brambling Farm

Hurst Hills

Stedham Mill Farm

BRAMBLING LA

Buddington Farm

23

MILL LA

Woolbeding

River Rother

Hollist House

HOLLIST LA

UPPERFIELD

WEAVERS CL

DODSLEY GR

2

Bridgefoot

BRIDGEFOOT COTTS

Stedham Bridge

STEDHAM HALL

Woolbeding House

Sewage Works

Midhurst Com

H

A286

DODSLEY LA

QUEENS

YARBOROUGH TERR

LAVENDER ROW

STRATHMOOR GDNS

1

COMMON VIEW

THE ALLEY

THE STREET

Stedham

Great House Farm

Woolbeding Bridge

Midhurst Gram Sch

NORTH ST A272

A286

SCHOOL LA

22

| 86 | A | | 87 | B | C | D | 88 | E | F |

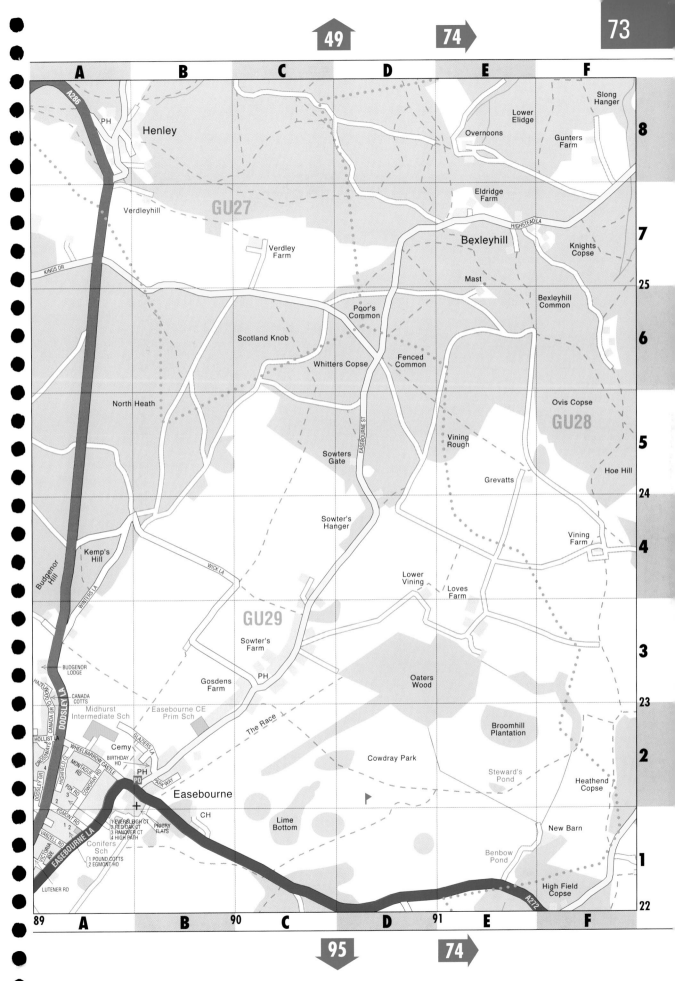

A　B　C　D　E　F

8

Slong Farm
HIGHSTEAD LA
Lickfold
Cobden Farm
Mill Pond
Mill Farm

7

The Plash
COLLYERS COTTS
Close Copse
Dirty Bridge Barn
Dirty Bridge Field
White's Green
Wadlington
Jacksonslake Copse

25

Captains
River Park Farm
Furze Field

6

Lodsworth Common
Outtens Copse

Snapelands Copse
Snapelands
Redens
Lord's Wood
Lodge Farm

5

Leggatt Hill
Limekiln Rough
GU28

24

Redlands Farm
Leggatt Hill Farm
Leggatt Hill
Kimbers Cottage

4

Vining Copse
Smithbrook
Salmonsbridge Farm
WESTLAND'S COPSE LA
River Common

SCHOOL LA
BEECHFIELD
SHEPHERDS LA
Roundabouts Farm

3

Lodsworth
OAKFIELD
Oldpark Copse
River
RIVER LA
JAMES LA
THE CROFT
Hollist Arms (PH)

23

Eel Bridge
Tower
Pitshill
VICARAGE LA
Lodsworth House
CHURCH LA
River Nursery

2

Heathend Copse
River Wood
Standlands
Brookfield Cottage
Dene Dip

Gosdens Heath
Langham Stables
BROOKFIELD LA

1

Gosdensheath Copse
Boughton Dairy Farm

22

Gosdensheath Farm
Path Field
Beggars' Corner
A272

92　A　B　93　C　D　94　E　F

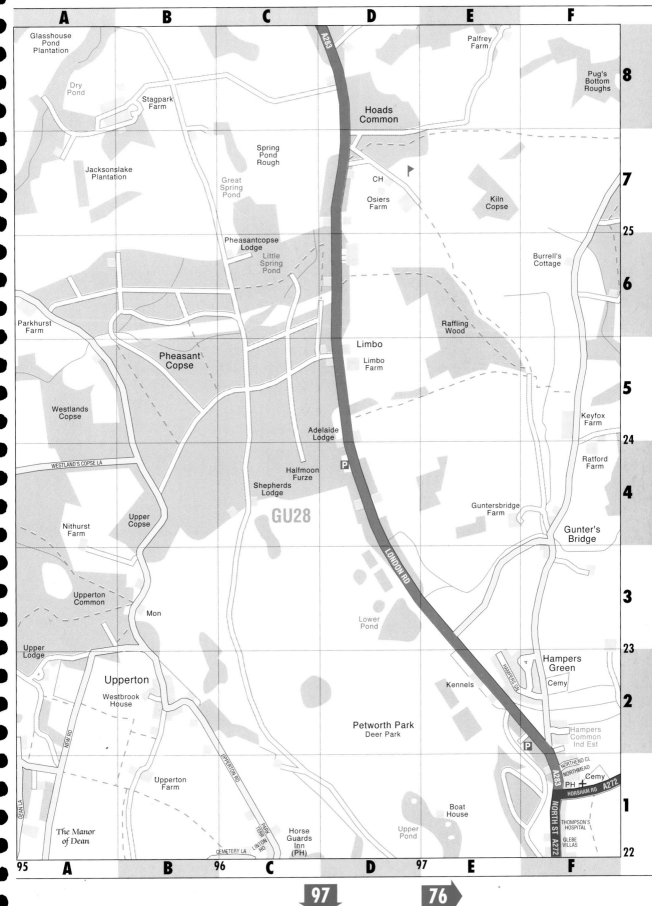

75
52

A B C D E F

8

Pug's Bottom
Langhurst Common
Langhurst Farm

Old Elkham Farm

Crawfold Furze

BANDERSGATE LA

7

Witley Copse

Holland Wood

Old Wood

Medhone Farm

25

6

Holland Wood Cottage

Petsalls Copses

RH14

Stedmans Journey

Medhone Copse

5

Blackbrook Farm

GU28

No Man's Land

Bennyfold Farm House

Bennyfold Copse

Wilderness

BLACKHOUSE LA

24

Warren Wood

4

Rushout Wood

Moor Farm

Pondtail Copse

3

Westland Farm

Buckfold Farm

GLASSHOUSE LA

Beechfield

A272

23

Lower Roxalls

Oldham Copse

2

Upper Roxalls

Oldham Hill

Foxhill

Selscome Farm

HORSHAM RD

Hilliers

Wickhams Hanger

KINGSPIT LA

Dairy

A272

Flexham Park

1

Flathurst Stables

Flathurst

Brinksole Heath

Brinksole Farm

RH20

22

Montpelier Farm

98 A B 99 C D 00 E F

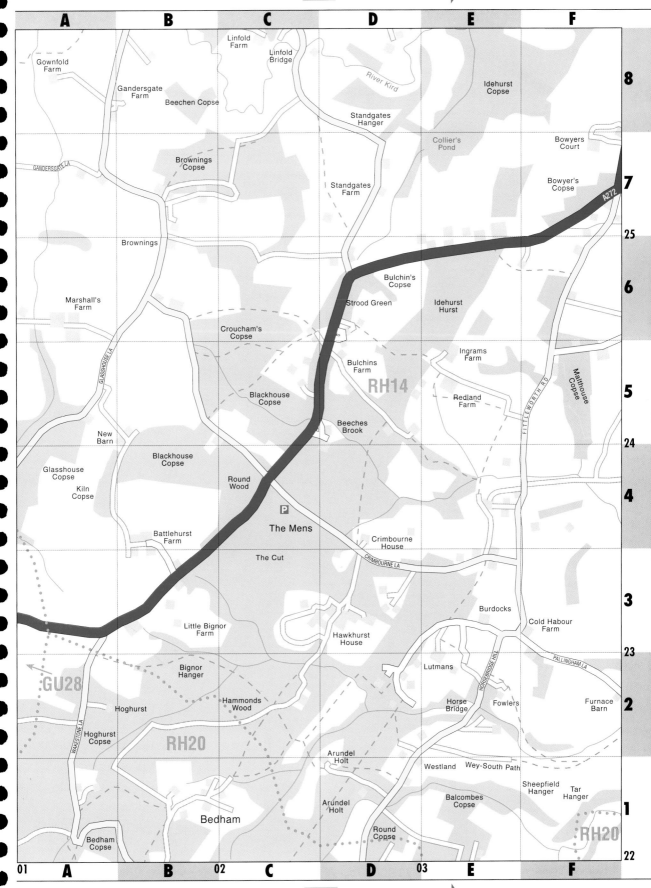

77 54

A B C D E F

8
Olde Farm
CARTERS WAY
MEADOWBANK
1
1 2
SCHOOL RD
PETWORTH RD
PH
P
BUTTS MDW
1
2 THORNTON MDW CL
PO
BALCHINS CL
THE LUTH
Wisborough Green
BILLINGSHURST RD
GLEBE WAY
Green Bridge
A272
River Kird
Sewage Works
WISBOROUGH GDNS
Wharf Farm
A272
New Bridge
Arun Canal (dis)
Guildenhurst Bridge

7
Tanyard Copse
Harsfold Copse
RH14
Orfold Farm
Guildenhurst Manor

25
Harsfold Manor
Harsfold Farm
Streele Farm
Brockhurst Brook

6
Harsfold Hanger
Lording's Lock
Lowfold
River Arun
Tanners Farm
B2133

5
Wey-South Path
Frithwood Farm
Lordings Rough

24
Shipbourne Farm
Woodlands Farm
Knobs Crook

4
Haybarn
Lee Place House
North Wood
Westlands Farm

3
Wabblegate Farm
RH20
Northwood Farm
Bramley Field

23
Haybourne
Snape Farm

2
PALLINGHAM LA
Furnacepond Cottages
Chichester Coll Brinsbury Campus
P P

1
Pallingham Manor Farm
BLACK GATE LA
Rawstick Copse
A29 STANE ST
A29

22
Toat Wood
Stable Barn Farm
The Thimes

04 A 05 B C 06 D E F

77 100

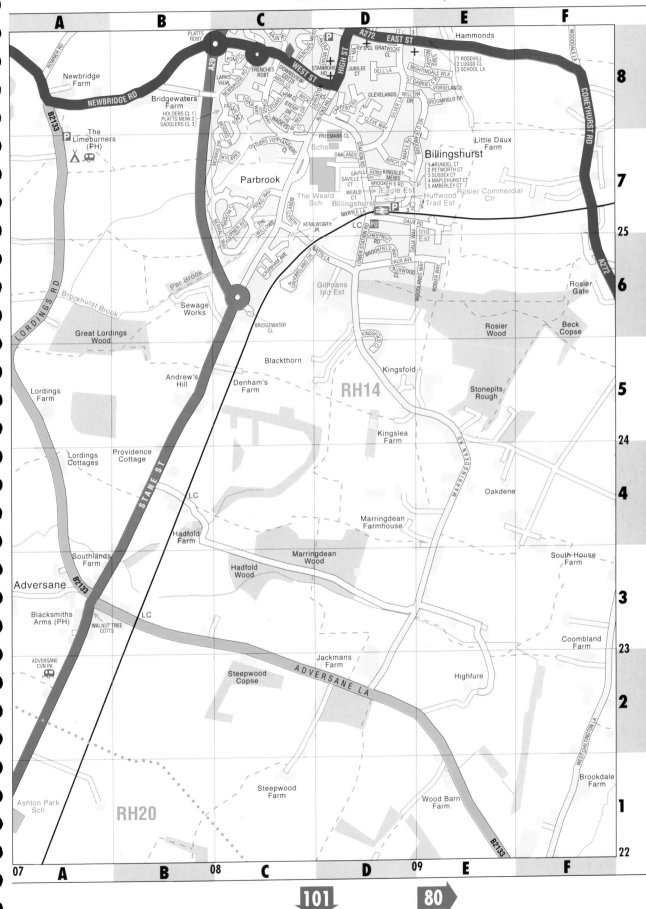

79
56

A B C D E F

8

Rowfold Grange

Woodhouse Copse

Duncan's Farm

Hook Farm

Bullbrook House Farm

Courtland's Farm

7

Rowfold Farm

Ten Acre Copse

Bouges Farm

BROOKS GREEN PK (CVN PK)

EMMS LA

25

Fewhurst Farm

Palmer's Farm

Valelands Farm

Brooks Green

TROUT LA

LACKENHURST LA

6

A272

WEST CHILTINGTON LA

RH14

Emmetts Farm

Chivers Farm

Kettles Bridge

CONEYHURST RD

Court Farm

Court Plantation

Copyhold Farm

5

24

Purveyor's Farm

Coneyhurst

RH13

Rainbow Farm

COOLHAM RD

4

Daniels Farm

Coolham House

Slaughter Bridge Farm

WEST CHILTINGTON LA

Coneyhurst Farm

Balls Green

Thornhill Farm

Lower Barn

River Adur

Hoe's Farm

3

Mast

Snowhill Farm

MILL LA

Bailey's Farm

The Blue Idol

23

WISTERIA PL

William Penn Sch

Hoe's Bridge

A272

Hillside Farm

DORSET HO

2

OLDHOUSE LA

Patman's Farm

Coolham

B2139

The Selsey Arms (PH)

St Cuthmans

Oldhouse Farm

Bridge Hill Farm

1

Goringlee

COOLHAM RD

Oldhouse Gorse

B2139

22

10 A B 11 C D 12 E F

79
102

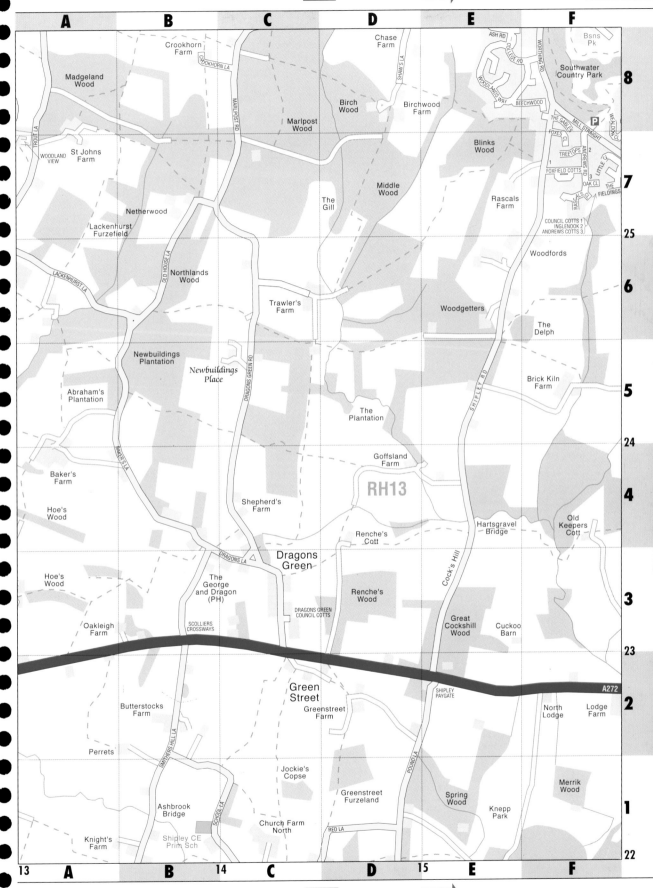

A B C D E F

8

7

25

6

5

24

4

23

2

1

22

13 A B 14 C D 15 E F

Madgeland Wood

Crookhorn Farm

CROOKHORN LA

Chase Farm

SHAW'S LA

Southwater Country Park

Bsns Pk

ASH RD

COLLEGE RD

WORTHING RD

WOODL MID-WAY

BEECHWOOD

MILL STRAIGHT

THE GABLES

FOXES CL

TREE TOPS

FOXFIELD COTTS

OAK CL

ANDREWS RD

LITTLE C'

RASCALS

THE FIELDINGS

WEALDEN CL

P

St Johns Farm

WOODLAND VIEW

TROTT LA

Netherwood

Lackenhurst Furzefield

LACKENHURST LA

OLD HOUSE LA

MARLPOST RD

Marlpost Wood

Birch Wood

Birchwood Farm

Middle Wood

The Gill

Blinks Wood

Rascals Farm

COUNCIL COTTS 1
INGLENOOK 2
ANDREWS COTTS 3

Woodfords

Northlands Wood

Trawler's Farm

Woodgetters

The Delph

Newbuildings Plantation

DRAGONS GREEN RD

Newbuildings Place

Abraham's Plantation

BAKER'S LA

The Plantation

SHIPLEY RD

Brick Kiln Farm

Baker's Farm

Hoe's Wood

Shepherd's Farm

Goffsland Farm

RH13

Hoe's Wood

DRAGONS LA

Dragons Green

Renche's Cott

Hartsgravel Bridge

Old Keepers Cott

Oakleigh Farm

The George and Dragon (PH)

SCOLLIERS CROSSWAYS

DRAGONS GREEN COUNCIL COTTS

Renche's Wood

COCK'S HILL

Great Cockshill Wood

Cuckoo Barn

Butterstocks Farm

SMITHERS HILL LA

Green Street

Greenstreet Farm

SHIPLEY PAYGATE

A272

North Lodge

Lodge Farm

Perrets

Jockie's Copse

POUND LA

Merrik Wood

SCHOOL LA

Ashbrook Bridge

Church Farm North

RED LA

Greenstreet Furzeland

Spring Wood

Knepp Park

Knight's Farm

Shipley CE Prim Sch

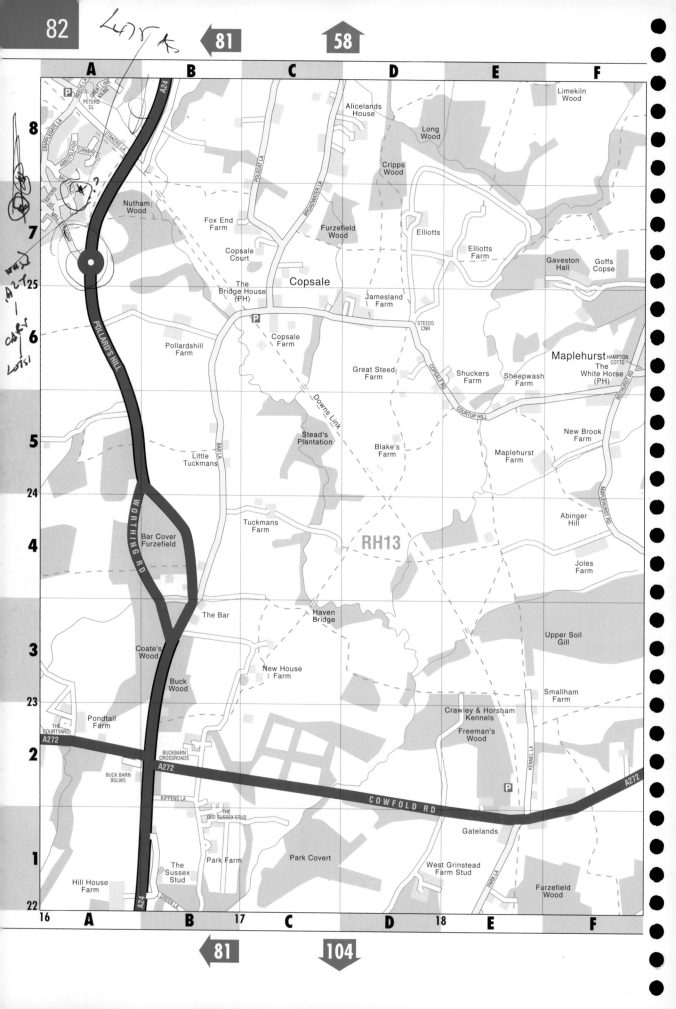

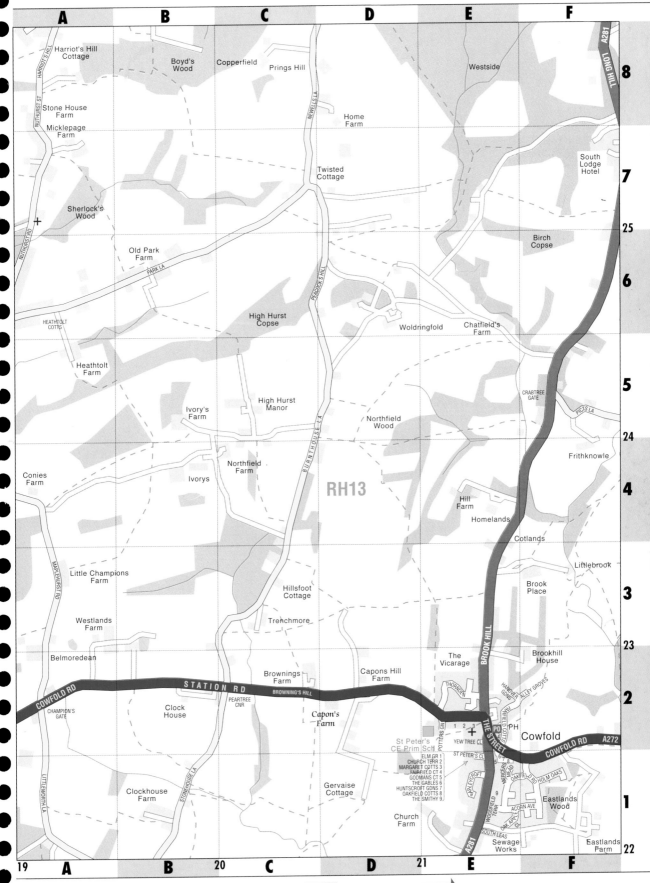

83
60

A B C D E F

8

Lydhurst

Hogstolt
Hill

Leonardslee
Gardens

New
Pond

Rifleman
Inn
(PH)

The Street

Freechase
Hill

Barland's
Farm

7

Crabtree

Free
Chase
Farm

Minepits
Wood

The
Lake

The Crabtree
Inn (PH)

Furnace
Pond

Free
Chase

MILL LA

A281

A281 LOT THING

MILL CL

PEPPERSGATE

25

Steep
Wood

CRABTREE GOLLS

PEPPERSGATE

Peppersgate
Farm

6

Drewitts

RH17

Round
Wood

Den
Wood

PERRYFIELD LA

EARWIG LA

Goodgers

Bushy
Platts

Long
House

Denwood
House

CROSS COLWOOD LA

Chatesgrove

5

Graffields

Hookland
Farm

Bull's
Wood

24

North
Farm

Colwood
Manor
Farm

Chargrove

Westlands

RH13

Barnfield
Wood

PICTS LA

4

Pict's
Farm

Aglands

Spronkett's

Wallhurst
Manor

BULL'S LA

Homefields

SPRONKETT'S LA

3

SMITH'S
CROSS

Kings
Hill

Barnfield
House

Upper
Barn

23

Cooper's
Farm

Six Acre
Shaw

New
Barn

2

Lyelands

Homewood
House

COWFOLD RD

A272

Oakendene
Manor

Southlands
Farm

KENTSTREET LA

Greenacres
Farm

A272

Oakendene
Ind Est

Bugshole
Copse

WINEHAM LA

1

NYE'S HILL

Nye's
Copse

Red
House

22

Taintfield
Wood

22 A 23 B C 23 D 24 E F

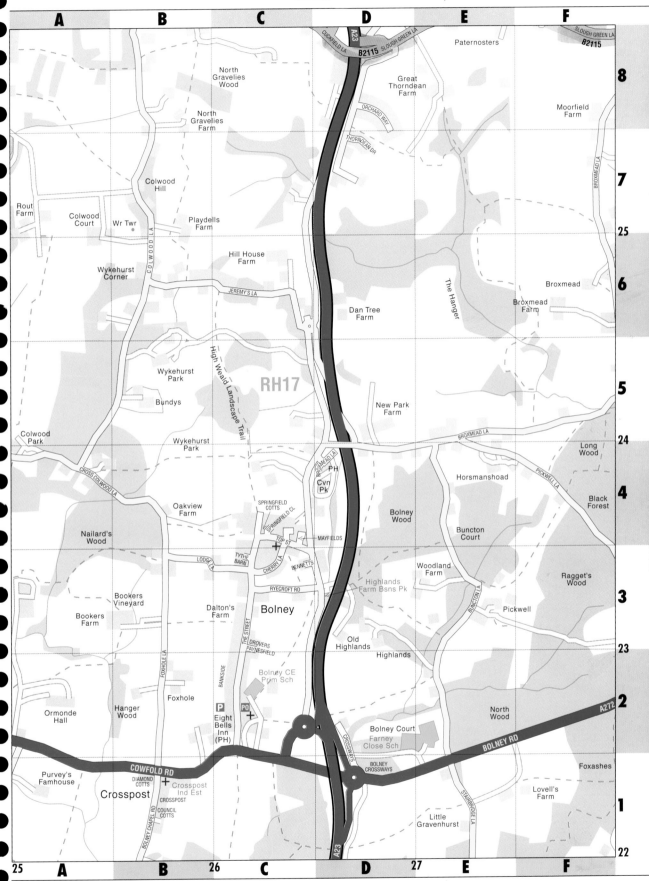

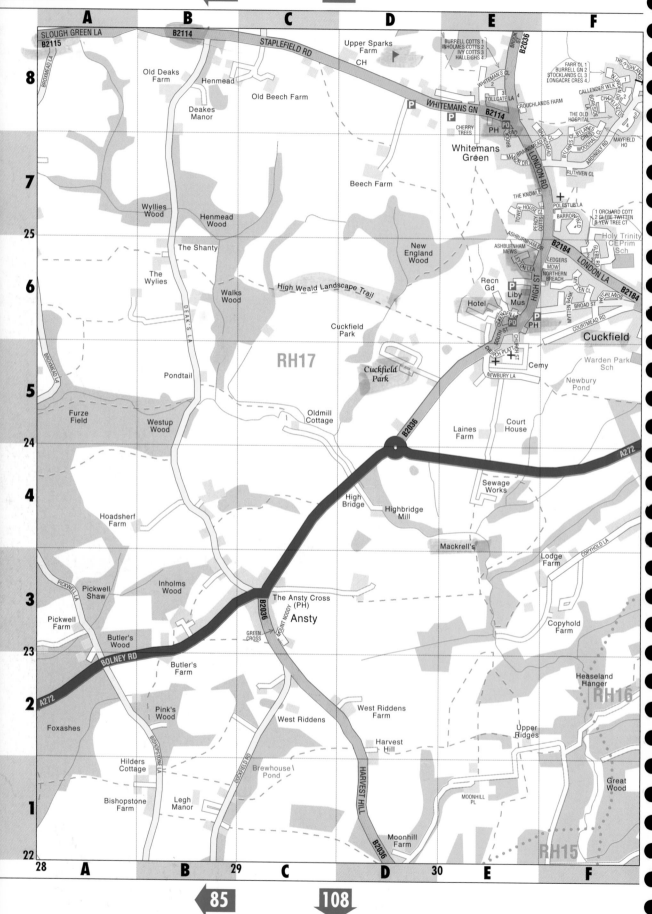

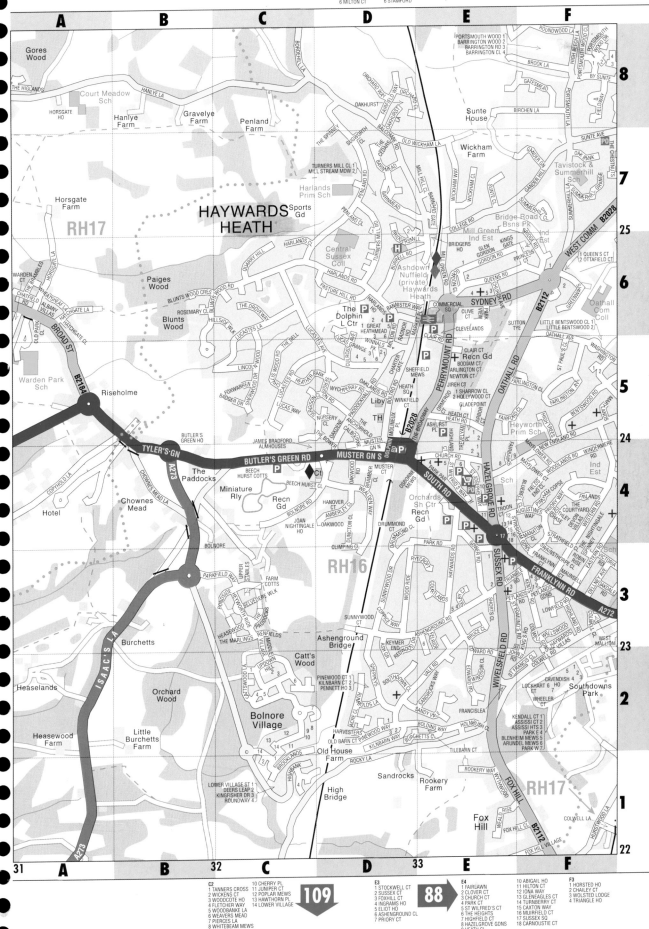

63
D5
1 BYRON CT
2 CHAUCER CT
3 KIPLING CT
4 SHELLEY CT
5 TENNYSON CT
6 MILTON CT

88
D6
1 WILTON
2 LAUREL
3 CANTON
4 PINFOLD
5 ANSCOME
6 STAMFORD

88
E6
1 COPYTHORNE HO
2 KEATON HO
3 GLENFERGUS
4 EMBASSY CT
5 SOUTHLANDS CT

109
C2
1 TANNERS CROSS
2 WICKENS CT
3 WOODCOTE HO
4 FLETCHER WAY
5 WOODBANKE LA
6 WEAVERS MEAD
7 PIERCES LA
8 WHITEBEAM MEWS
9 WHITEBEAM CT
10 CHERRY PL
11 JUNIPER CT
12 POPLAR MEWS
13 HAWTHORN PL
14 LOWER VILLAGE

E3
1 STOCKWELL CT
2 SUSSEX CT
3 FOXHILL CT
4 INGRAMS HO
5 ELIOT HO
6 ASHENGROUND CL
7 PRIORY CT

88
E4
1 FAIRLAWN
2 CLOVER CT
3 CHURCH CT
4 PARK CT
5 ST WILFRED'S CT
6 THE HEIGHTS
7 HIGHFIELD CT
8 HAZELGROVE GDNS
9 HEATH CL
10 ABIGAIL HO
11 HILTON CT
12 IONA WAY
13 GLENEAGLES CT
14 TURNBERRY CT
15 CAXTON WAY
16 MUIRFIELD CT
17 SUSSEX SQ
18 CARNOUSTIE CT

F3
1 HORSTED HO
2 CHAILEY CT
3 WOLSTED LODGE
4 TRIANGLE HO

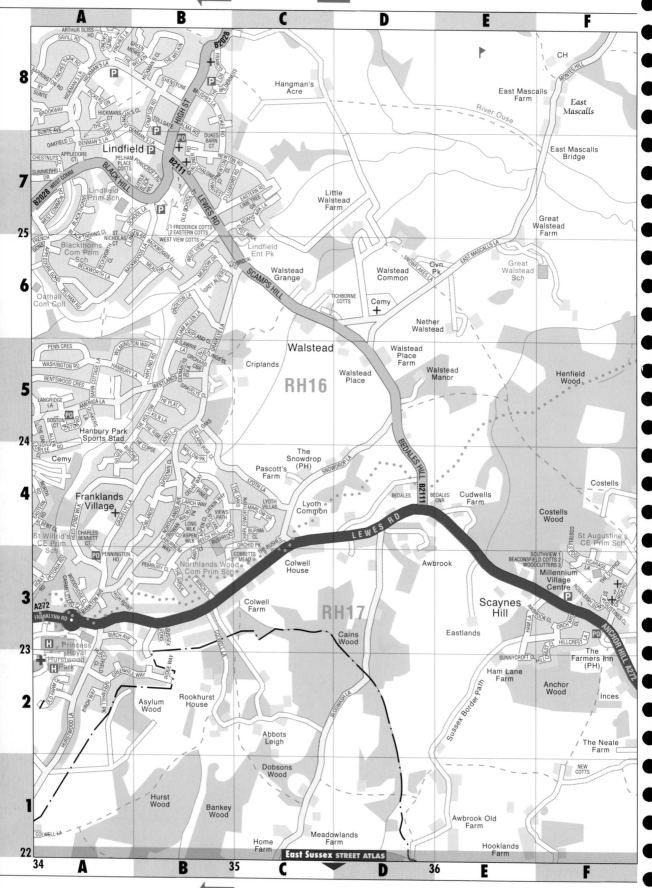

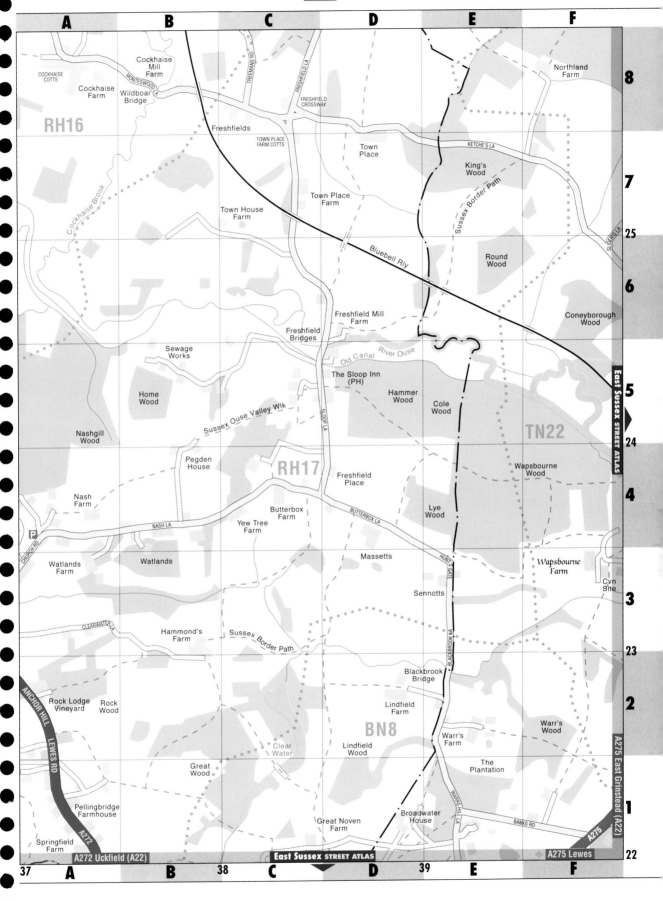

A   B   C   D   E   F

8

COCKHAISE COTTS

Cockhaise Mill Farm

Cockhaise Farm

Wildboar Bridge

MONTESWOOD LA

TREEMANS RD

FRESHFIELD LA

FRESHFIELD CROSSWAY

Northland Farm

KETCHE'S LA

RH16

Freshfields

TOWN PLACE FARM COTTS

Town Place

Town Place Farm

Town House Farm

King's Wood

7

Cockhaise Brook

Sussex Border Path

Bluebell Rly

25

Round Wood

SLUGWASH LA

East Sussex STREET ATLAS

6

Freshfield Mill Farm

Freshfield Bridges

Sewage Works

Old Canal   River Ouse

The Sloop Inn (PH)

Hammer Wood

Cole Wood

Coneyborough Wood

Home Wood

Sussex Ouse Valley Wlk

SLOOP LA

5

24

Nashgill Wood

Pegden House

RH17

Freshfield Place

TN22

Wapsbourne Wood

Nash Farm

NASH LA

Butterbox Farm

Yew Tree Farm

BUTTERBOX LA

Lye Wood

4

Watlands Farm

Watlands

Massetts

HUNT'S GATE

Wapsbourne Farm

Cvn Site

3

CLEARWATER LA

Hammond's Farm

Sussex Border Path

Sennotts

BLACKBROOK LA

23

Blackbrook Bridge

Rock Lodge Vineyard

Rock Wood

Lindfield Farm

Warr's Wood

2

ANCHOR HILL

LEWES RD

Clear Water

Great Wood

Lindfield Wood

BN8

Warr's Farm

The Plantation

A275 East Grinstead (A22)

Pellingbridge Farmhouse

A272

Great Noven Farm

WARKS HILL LA

Broadwater House

BANKS RD

A275

A275

1

Springfield Farm

A272 Uckfield (A22)

East Sussex STREET ATLAS

A275 Lewes

22

37   A   B   38   C   D   39   E   F

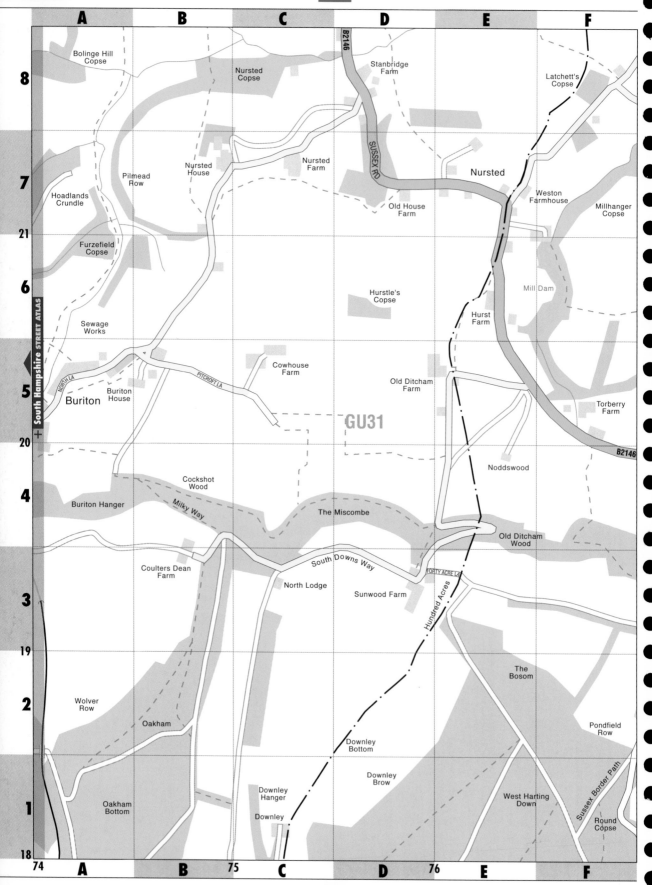

South Hampshire STREET ATLAS

Bolinge Hill Copse

Nursted Copse

Stanbridge Farm

Latchett's Copse

Hoadlands Crundle

Pilmead Row

Nursted House

Nursted Farm

Nursted

SUSSEX RD

B2146

Old House Farm

Weston Farmhouse

Millhanger Copse

Furzefield Copse

Hurstle's Copse

Mill Dam

Sewage Works

Hurst Farm

Buriton

NORTH LA

Buriton House

PITCROFT LA

Cowhouse Farm

Old Ditcham Farm

GU31

Torberry Farm

B2146

Noddswood

Cockshot Wood

Buriton Hanger

Milky Way

The Miscombe

Old Ditcham Wood

Coulters Dean Farm

South Downs Way

North Lodge

Sunwood Farm

FORTY ACRE LA

Hundred Acres

Wolver Row

Oakham

Downley Bottom

The Bosom

Pondfield Row

Oakham Bottom

Downley Hanger

Downley

Downley Brow

West Harting Down

Sussex Border Path

Round Copse

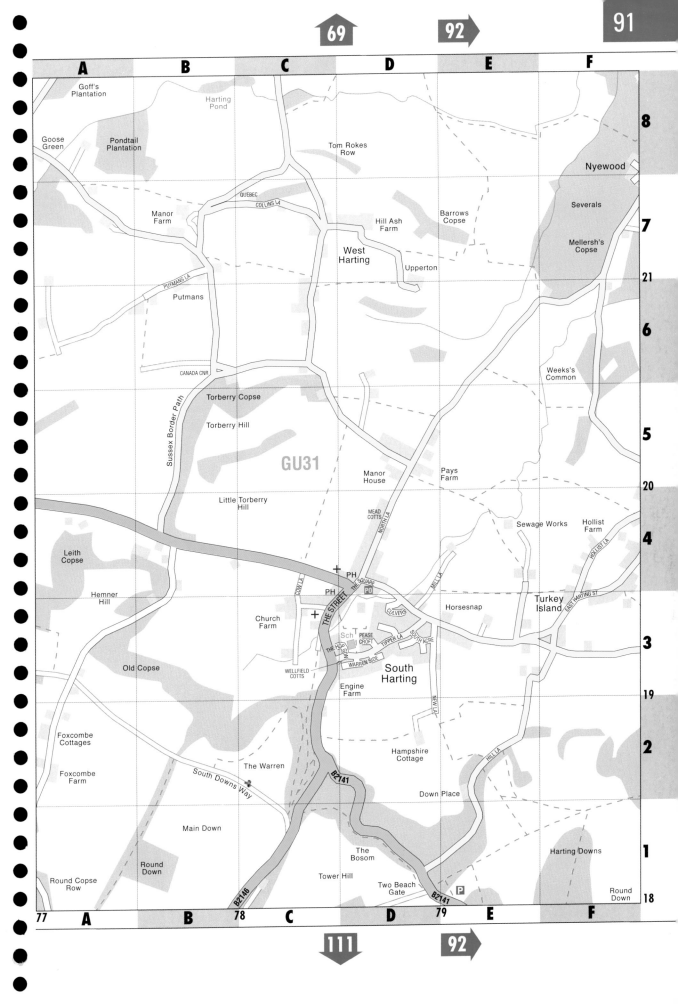

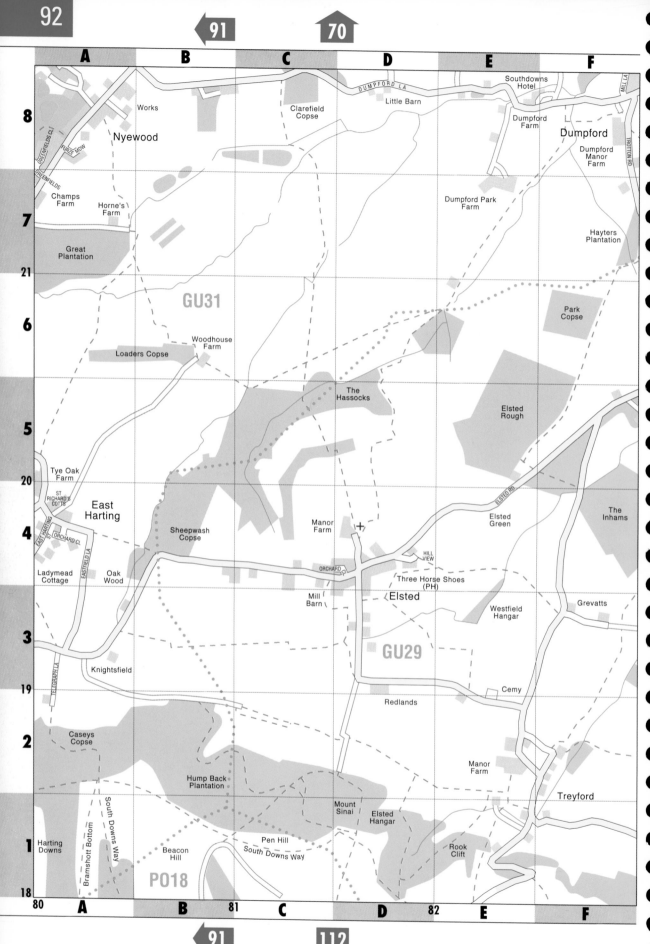

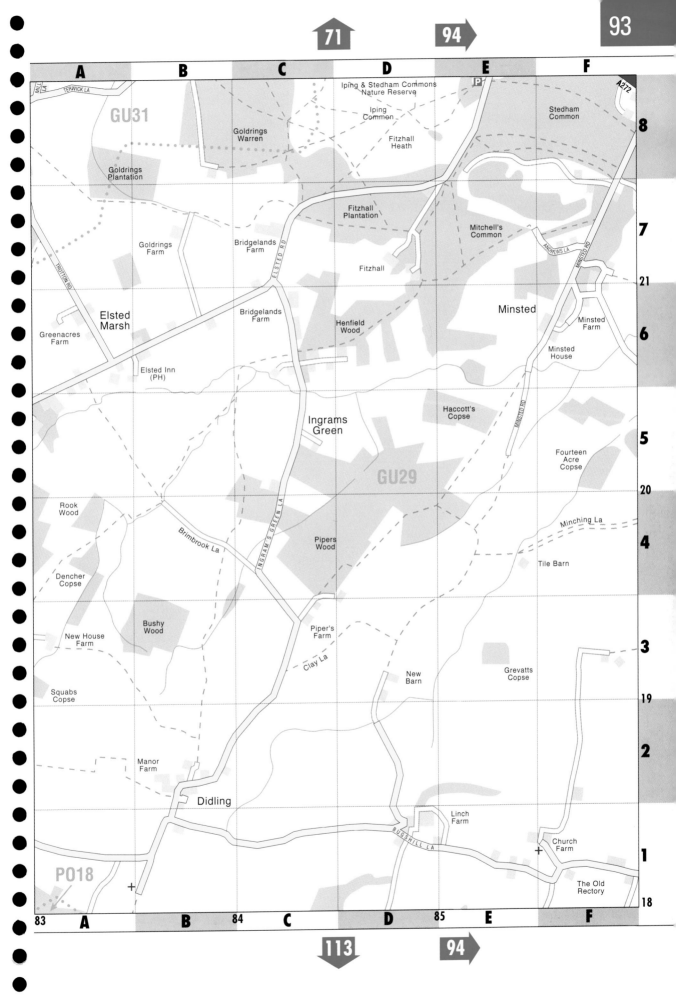

71
94

A   B   C   D   E   F

MILL LA
TERWICK LA

GU31

Goldrings
Warren

Iping & Stedham Commons
Nature Reserve

Iping
Common

Stedham
Common

A272

8

Goldrings
Plantation

Fitzhall
Heath

Fitzhall
Plantation

Mitchell's
Common

7

Goldrings
Farm

Bridgelands
Farm

ELSTED RD

Fitzhall

ANDREWS LA

MINSTED RD

TROTTON RD

Elsted
Marsh

Bridgelands
Farm

Henfield
Wood

Minsted

21

Minsted
Farm

6

Greenacres
Farm

Elsted Inn
(PH)

Minsted
House

Ingrams
Green

Haccott's
Copse

MINSTED RD

Rook
Wood

GU29

Fourteen
Acre
Copse

5

20

Brimbrook La

INGRAM'S GREEN LA

Pipers
Wood

Minching La

4

Dencher
Copse

Tile Barn

Bushy
Wood

Piper's
Farm

3

New House
Farm

Clay La

New
Barn

Grevatts
Copse

19

Squabs
Copse

2

Manor
Farm

Didling

Linch
Farm

1

PO18

BUGSHILL LA

Church
Farm

The Old
Rectory

18

83   A   B   84   C   D   85   E   F

113
94

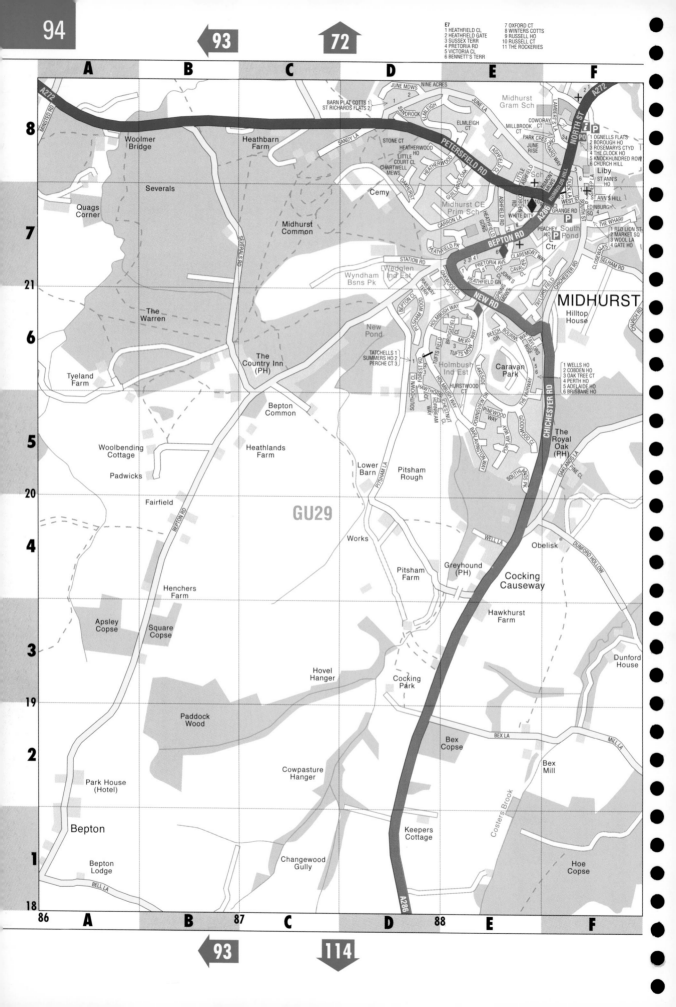

93

72

E7
1 HEATHFIELD CL
2 HEATHFIELD GATE
3 SUSSEX TERR
4 PRETORIA RD
5 VICTORIA CL
6 BENNETT'S TERR

7 OXFORD CT
8 WINTERS COTTS
9 RUSSELL HO
10 RUSSELL CT
11 THE ROCKERIES

A   B   C   D   E   F

8
7
21
6
5
20
4
19
2
3
19
2
1
18

MIDHURST

GU29

Bepton

Woolmer Bridge
Severals
Quags Corner
Heathbarn Farm
Midhurst Common
The Warren
Tyeland Farm
Woolbending Cottage
Padwicks
Fairfield
Henchers Farm
Apsley Copse
Square Copse
Park House (Hotel)
Bepton Lodge
Paddock Wood
The Country Inn (PH)
Bepton Common
Heathlands Farm
Lower Barn
Pitsham Rough
Pitsham Farm
Works
Hovel Hanger
Cowpasture Hanger
Changewood Gully
Cocking Park
Keepers Cottage
New Pond
Greyhound (PH)
Cocking Causeway
Hawkhurst Farm
Obelisk
The Royal Oak (PH)
Caravan Park
Hilltop House
Holmbush Ind Est
Hurstwood Ct
Weddlen Ind Est
Wyndham Bsns Pk
Station Rd
Dunford House
Bex Copse
Bex Mill
Costers Brook
Hoe Copse

1 WELLS HO
2 COBDEN HO
3 OAK TREE CT
4 PERTH HO
5 ADELAIDE HO
6 BRISBANE HO

TATCHELLS 1
SUMMERS HO 2
PERCHE CT 3

1 OGNELLS FLATS
2 BOROUGH HO
3 ROSEMARYS CTYD
4 THE CLOCK HO
5 KNOCKHUNDRED ROW
6 CHURCH HILL

1 RED LION ST
2 MARKET SQ
3 WOOL LA
4 GATE HO

Midhurst Gram Sch
Midhurst CE Prim Sch
St Ann's Hill
South Pond
The Wharf

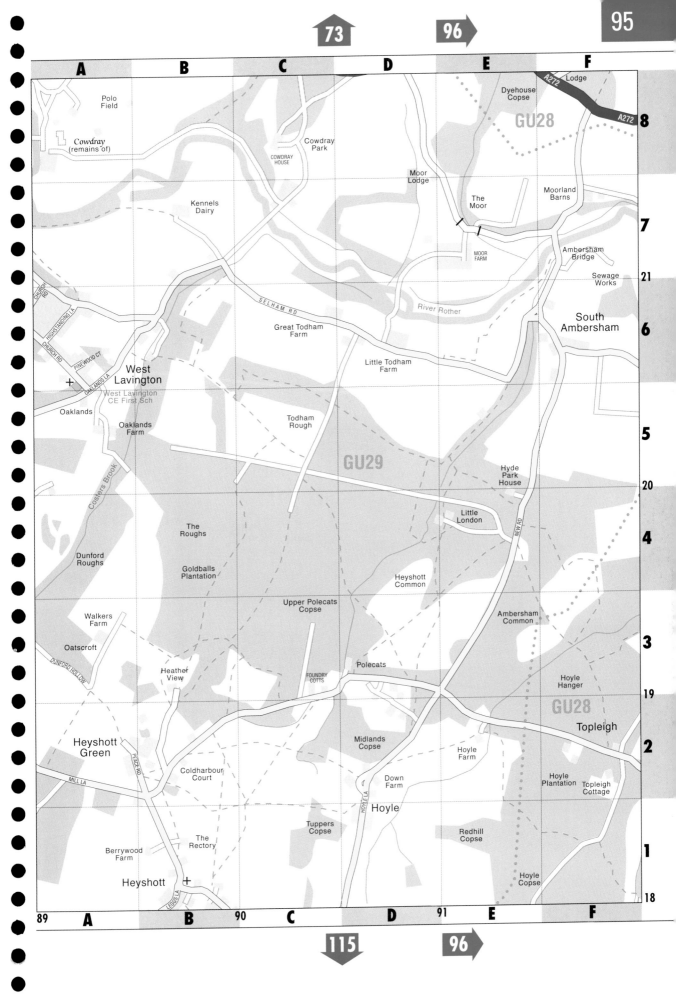

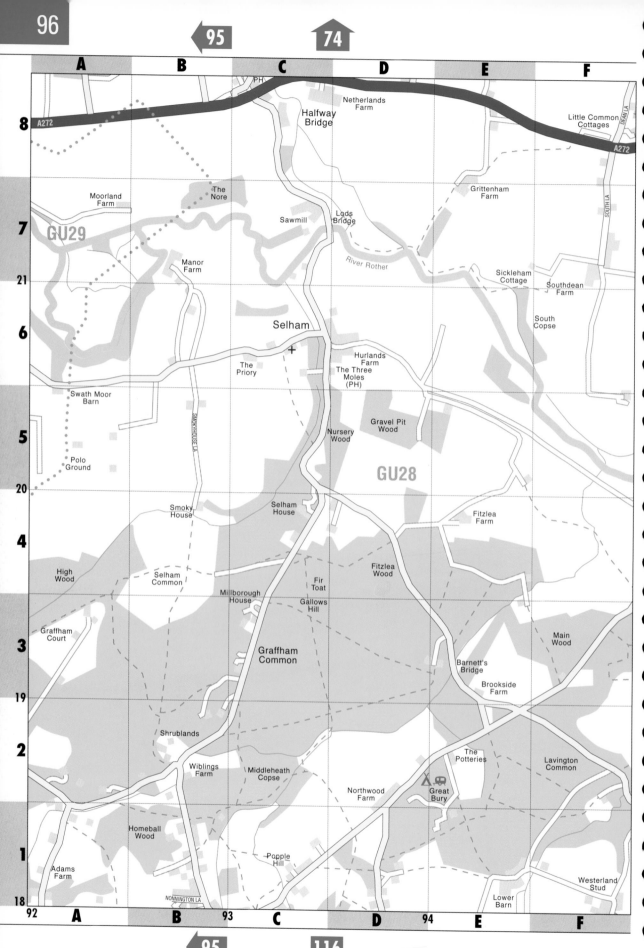

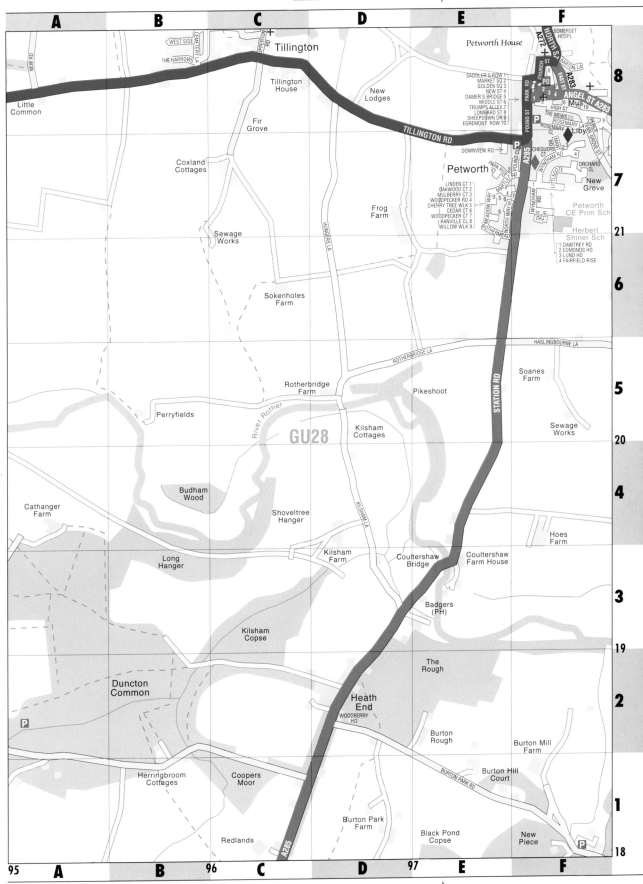

97
76

A **B** **C** **D** **E** **F**

8

Goanah Lodges

SHIMMINGS

Goanah Farm

ANGEL ST A283

SHEEPDOWN DR
SHEEPDOWN CL
ORCHARD CL
GROVE ST
GROVE LA

Sheep Downs

Convalescent Home

Riverhill

Bognor Common

7

Sand Pit

KINGSPIT LA

RIVERHILL LA

Black Horse (PH)

Low Heath

Little Riverhill Copse

21

Barnsgate Farm

Byworth

Welldiggers' Arms (PH)

PLUM PUDDING CNR

6

GROVE LA

Hallgate Farm

Middle Copse

Egdean Common

Little Bognor

5

Haslingbourne

Goft's House

Gorehill House

Edgehill Farm

Froghole House

EGDEAN COTTS

Egdean

RH20

20

GU28

Douglaslake Farm

4

Strood Farm

Egdean Cottage

Douglaslake House

Fittleworth House

A283

3

Pen Copse

Highhoes Copse

Woodruff's Farm

Hesworth Common

B2138

Byworth Hanger

High Hoes

19

Birch Wood

Holly Grove

2

Hesworth Farm

Hesworth Grange

Hammer Moor

Shopham Bridge

Bigenor Farm

PH

1

River Rother

B2138 TRIPP HILL

18

97
118

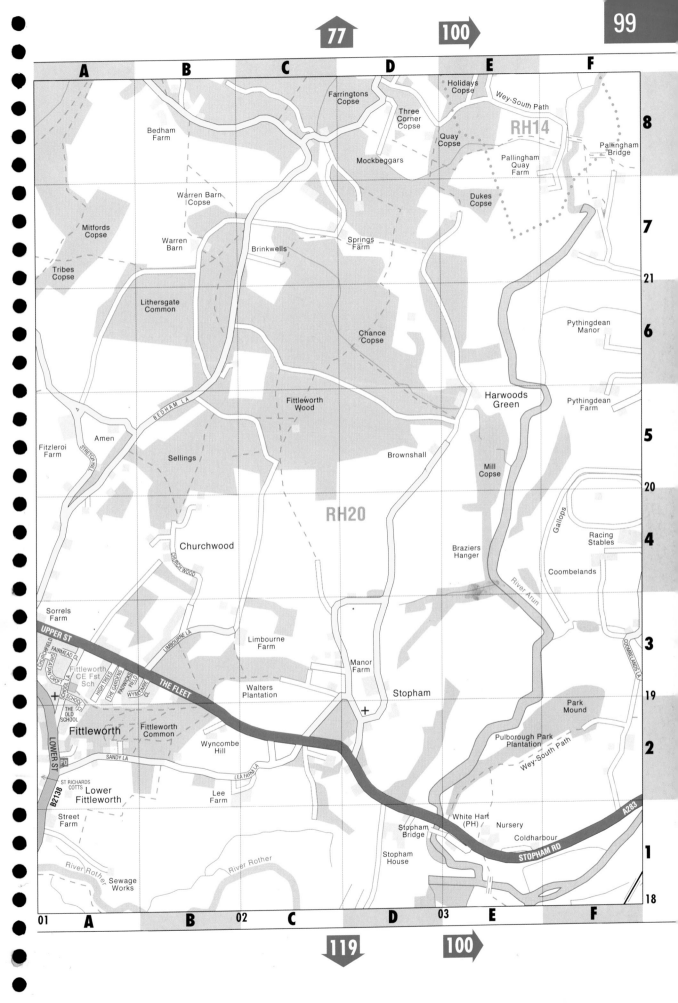

A B C D E F

8

RH14

7

21

6

5

20

4

3

19

2

1

18

Holidays Copse
Wey-South Path
Farringtons Copse
Three Corner Copse
Quay Copse
Mockbeggars
Pallingham Bridge
Pallingham Quay Farm
Bedham Farm
Dukes Copse
Warren Barn Copse
Mitfords Copse
Warren Barn
Brinkwells
Springs Farm
Tribes Copse
Pythingdean Manor
Lithersgate Common
Chance Copse
Pythingdean Farm
BEDHAM LA
Fittleworth Wood
Harwoods Green
Amen
Fitzleroi Farm
STRETCH HILL
Sellings
Brownshall
Mill Copse
RH20
Gallops
Racing Stables
Churchwood
Braziers Hanger
Coombelands
CHURCH WOOD
River Arun
Sorrels Farm
COOMBELANDS LA
UPPER ST
Limbourne Farm
Manor Farm
LIMBOURNE LA
Park Mound
Fittleworth CE Fst Sch
THE FLEET
Walters Plantation
Stopham
FAIRMEAD CL
GREFFEN CROFT
GREYFRIARS CL
HIGH TREES
THE GARDENS
PADWICKS
FIELD
WYNCOMBE CL
Pulborough Park Plantation
SCHOOL LA
THE OLD SCHOOL
Wey-South Path
Fittleworth
Fittleworth Common
Wyncombe Hill
LOWER ST
SANDY LA
LEA FARM LA
White Hart (PH)
Nursery
A283
B2138
ST RICHARDS COTTS
Lower Fittleworth
Lee Farm
Coldharbour
STOPHAM RD
Street Farm
Stopham Bridge
River Rother
Stopham House
River Rother
Sewage Works

99 78

A B C D E F

8

7

21

6

5

20

4

3

19

2

1

18

Mulsey Farm

A29

Stablebarn Farm

Toatwood Farm

Blakewood Stables

Toat House

Ham Copse

Toat Mon

Little Wood

Gay Street La

Thorn Common

Toat La

North Heath Farm

North Heath

Pallingham Lock Farm

Pickhurst

Underley Copse

Pickhurst La

Parson's Field

St Richards Cotts

Wansey's Farm

Wey-South Path

Wiltshire's Farm

Littlehill Copse

Codmore Hill

Broomers Hill Pk

LC

Borough Farm

Coombelands La

Mount

Hill Farm La

Hill Farm

PH

Cray La

Masons Way

RH20

Brook House

Training Gallops

Stane Street Nurseries

Broomers Hill La

Broomershill

Broomershill Farm

Coombelands

Stane Street Cl

The Green

Highfield

New Place Farm

New Place Farm

Brocks Rew Farm

Middle Barn Farm

New Place

St Mary's CE Prim Sch

Holme Street House

The Colonades Superstore

Aston Rise

Orchard Cousins

Strawberry Field

The Spinney

Old Place

Wey Ho

Spiro Cl

New Place Rd

Collingwood Rd

Lum La

Spinney North

Glebelands

Marehill Nurseries

Bell Cl

Wren Cl

Recn Gd

Rectory Cl

Dennis Ct

The Moat

The Mews Southside

Downlands

Hill Barn Farm

Church Pl

Hotel

Old Rectory La

Rectory La

Hillcrest Pk

Pulborough

Church Hill

London Rd

Laurel Mount

Alpha Cotts

Station Approach Ind Est

Station Villas 1 Cobbetts Mews 2 Station App 3

Pulborough

Lyntons

Swan Ct

30

Lower St

PO

Liby

Casper's

A283

Station Rd

Stopham Rd

A29

Swan Cnr

Winers Edge

Poplar Ct

Wharf

Carpenters Mdw

Barn House Cl

Arun View

Rivermead

Mare Hill Rd

PH

Marehill

Kings La

Charters Farm

Pulborough Bridge

River Arun

Arundale Sch

Brook Gate Farm

Old Mill Dr

West Mare La

Batts La

The Willows 1 Riverside Ct 2 Arun Prospect 3

River Stor

1 Wildbrooks Cl 2 Allfrey Plat

Wickford Bridge

West Chillington Rd

Tudor Cl

C2
1 ARUN CT
2 BARCLAYS CT
3 BELGRAVE CT
4 SKEYNE DR
5 BEVERLEY CT
6 BEAUMONT CT
7 BROOK HO
8 BARNHOUSE CL
9 HERON'S RYE
10 KINGFISHER CT
11 CHENE COLLINS CHASE
12 ST MARY'S

A283

99 120

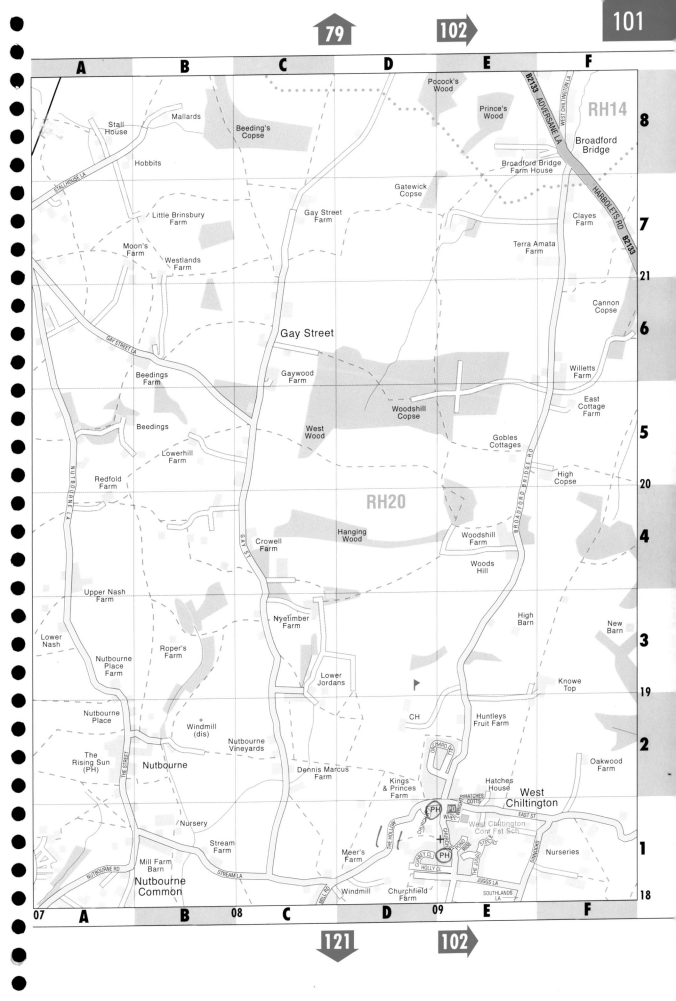

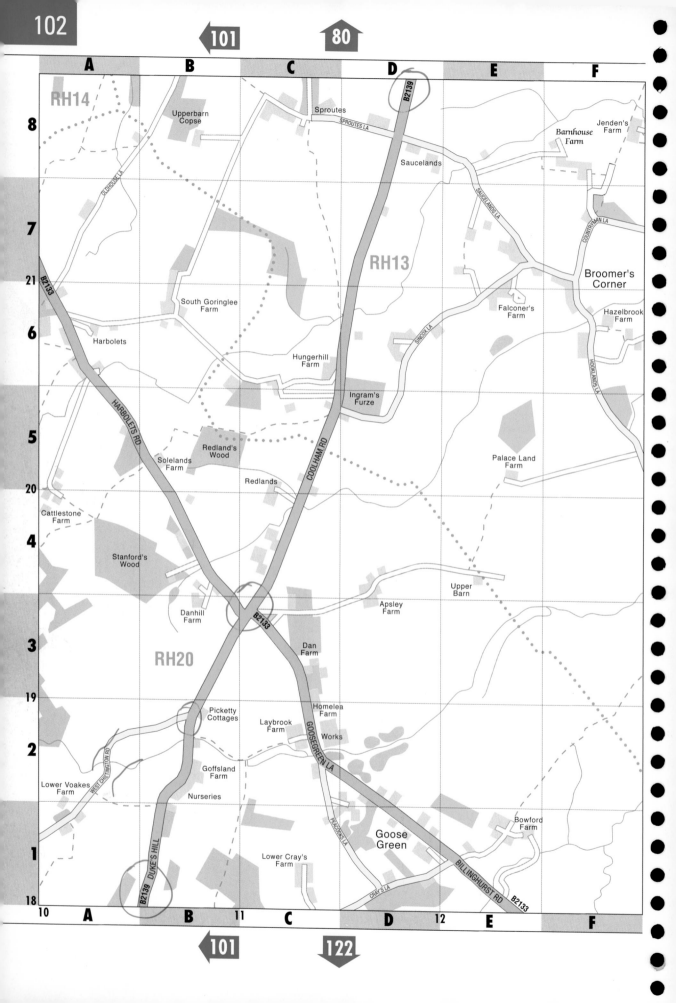

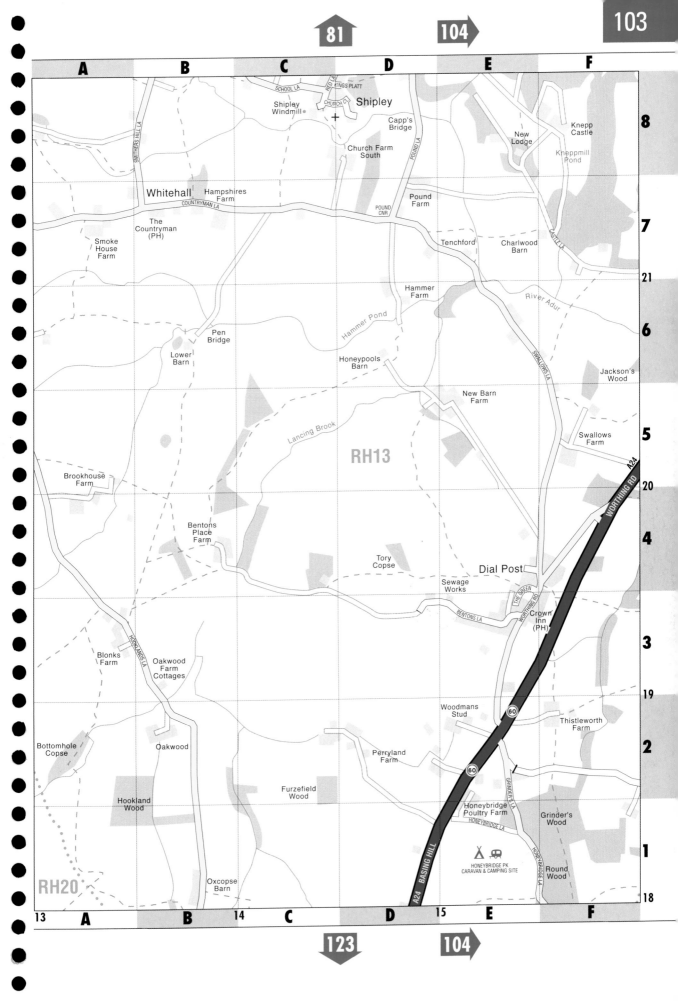

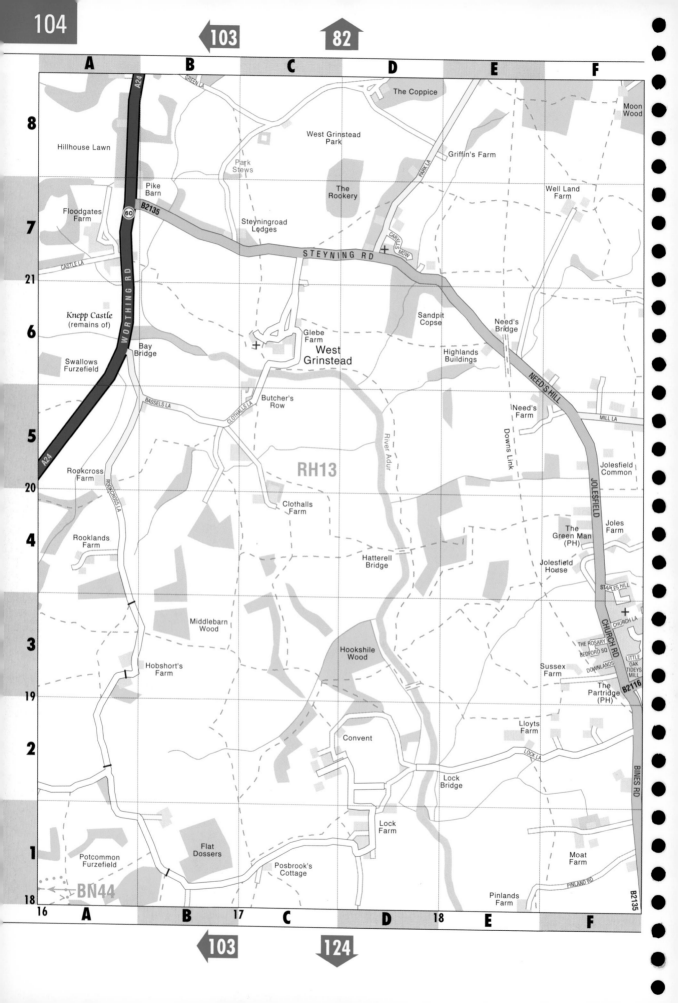

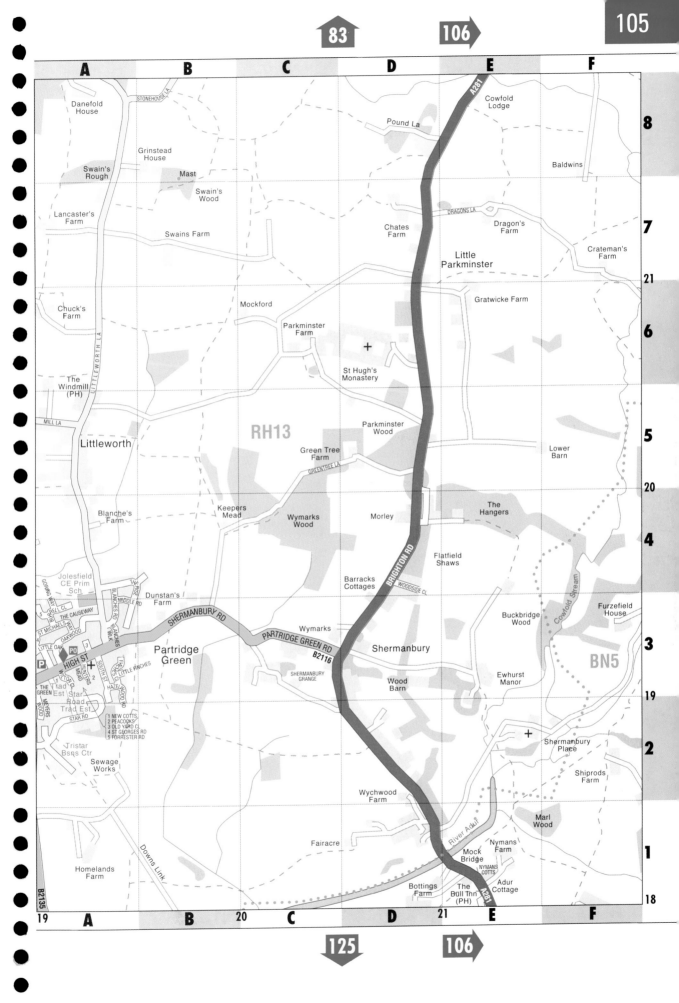

83
106

A B C D E F

8
7
21
6
5
20
4
19
2
18

Danefold House
STONEHOUSE LA
Grinstead House
Swain's Rough
Mast
Swain's Wood
Lancaster's Farm
Swains Farm
LITTLEWORTH LA
Chuck's Farm
Mockford
The Windmill (PH)
MILL LA
Littleworth
RH13
Green Tree Farm
GREENTREE LA
Blanche's Farm
Keepers Mead
Wymarks Wood
Morley
Jolesfield CE Prim Sch
GORING WAY
BELL CL
THE CAUSEWAY
BLANCHES RD
MIDDLE RD
Dunstan's Farm
SHERMANBURY RD
ST MICHAELS
OAKWOOD
BLANCHES WLK
Partridge Green
PARTRIDGE GREEN RD
B2116
Wymarks
Shermanbury
HIGH ST
PO
P
SOUTH ST
LITTLE PINCHES
HUNTERS MEAD
HAZELWOOD RD
THE GREEN
Star Road Trad Est
Trad Est
METERS WOOD
STAR RD
SHERMANBURY GRANGE
1 NEW COTTS
2 PEACOCKS
3 OLD YARD CL
4 ST GEORGES RD
5 FORRESTER RD
Tristar Bsns Ctr
Sewage Works
Wood Barn
Homelands Farm
DOWNS LINK
B2135
Fairacre
Wychwood Farm
River Adur
Bottings Farm
Mock Bridge
The Bull Inn (PH)
NYMANS COTTS
A281
Adur Cottage
Nymans Farm
Marl Wood
Shiprods Farm
Shermanbury Place
BN5
Ewhurst Manor
Buckbridge Wood
Furzefield House
Cowfold Stream
Lower Barn
The Hangers
Flatfield Shaws
BRIGHTON RD
WOODSIDE CL
Barracks Cottages
Parkminster Wood
St Hugh's Monastery
Parkminster Farm
Gratwicke Farm
Little Parkminster
Crateman's Farm
Dragon's Farm
DRAGONS LA
Chates Farm
Pound La
Cowfold Lodge
A281
Baldwins

125
106

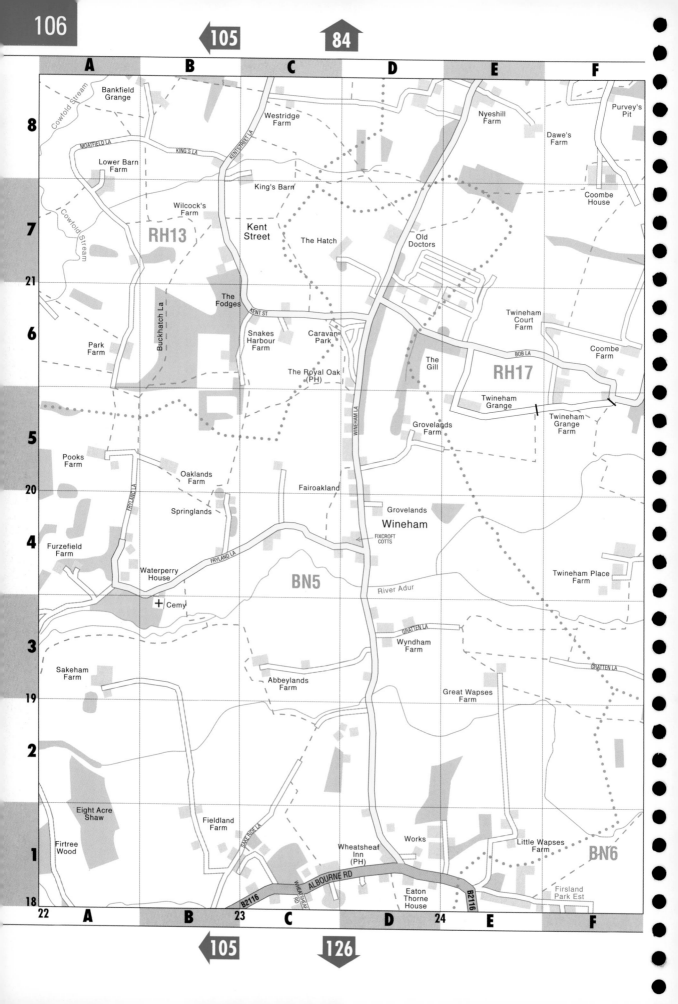

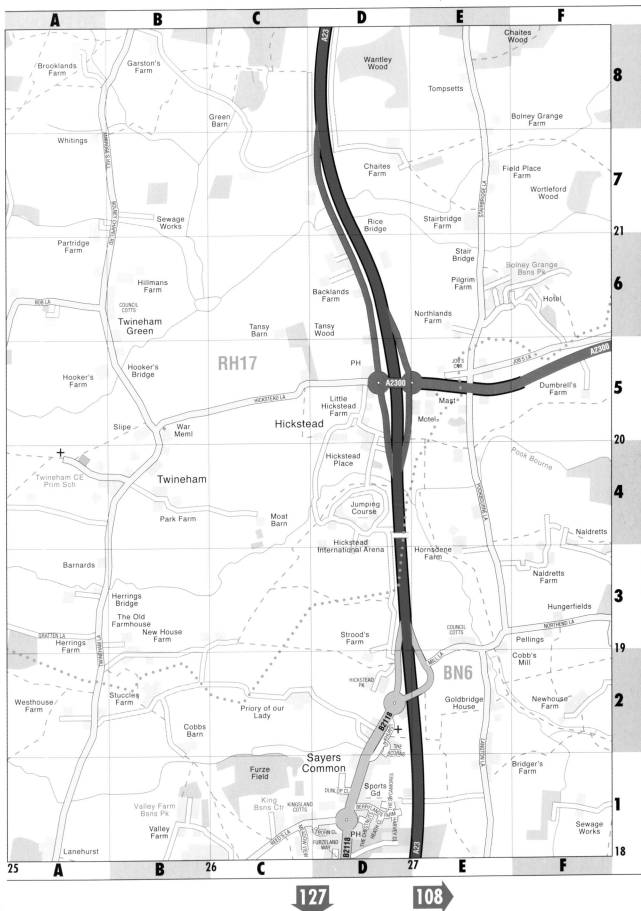

107 86

A B C D E F

8

RH17

Greenacres

Pond Lye

Rushypit Wood

B2036

PAIN'S FLAT

Lower Ridges

Hookhouse Wood

Hookhouse Farm

RH16

7

Streams Farm

Leigh Mill

Paynes Place Farm

Bridge Farm

CUCKFIELD RD

Lye's Farm

Woodfield House

A273

BISHOPSTONE LA

21

Wortleford Bridge

Abbotsford

ISAAC'S LA

6

Sewage Works

Bridge Farm House

Golf Driving Range

CH

Bridge Hall Cottage

B2036

HAMLIN'S CNR

JOB'S LA

A2300

Dean House Farm

RH15

Sheddingdean Bsns Ctr 1
Ashwyn Bsns Ctr 2

FAIRBRIDGE WAY

Fairplace Bridge

A273

5

Goddards' Green

The Dene

The Sportsman (PH)

H

West End Farm

St Paul's RC Coll

A2300

SUSSEX WAY

LANGRIDGE WAY THE SAFFRONS

CLAYTON RD

CORNFORD CL

SEFTON CRES

THE GILLIGANS

MARCHANTS WAY

WOODCROFT

STOKEFIELD

LYWHITE CL

CHILTING LA

THE WICKETS

MAPLE DR

THE POUND

BISHOPSTONE LA

CUCKFIELD RD

GATEHOUSE LA

20

Great Wood

The Acorns

L Ctr

1 THE HORNBEAMS
2 THE ROWANS
3 TRIANGLE WAY

MICARTH CL

WALLIS WAY

SUSSEX WAY

WHEATSHEAF

WITHY BUSH

THE BROOKS

SHEPHERDS MEAD 1
FAIRFIELD GDNS 2

SOUTH LODGE CL

DUNSTAL LAVE

DUNSTAL FARM RD

CHAPEL CL

PACKHAM

TUDOR GDNS

SHEDDINGDEAN CT

LEYLANDS RD

4

Shalford

Jikack Ind Est

BN6

HIGH HATCH LA

The Oaks

BAYLIS WAY

CHAFFINCH CL

PRIMROSE

BLUEBELL WAY

CLOVER CL

BRAMBLE GDN

CULPEPER

CULPEPER CL

HUNNARD CL

TEMPLE GR

BAYLIS WAY

FIELD CL

ST MARY'S RD

ARUNDEL CL

PO

SLIMBRIDGE RD

3

Old House

North End Farm

Oaklands Park

COOPER CL

GATEHOUSE LA

THE MALTINGS

SHELLEY CL

CAULSTOCK RD

SEVENE

MALTHOUSE LA

DENHAM RD

WEST PARK CRES

MAPLE CL

WEST ST

THE JAYS

1 SWALLOW REST
2 STARLING CL
3 WREN CL
4 SWIFT CL

St John's Common

DENHAM CT

POVEYS CL

ROYAL GEORGE RD

COLMER CT CL

CROMWELL RD

Sch

FAIRFIELD PL

NEWPORT RD

PARK CL

ST JOHN'S AVE

Park Rd

PARKSIDE

LOWER CHURCH RD

PO

THE MEADS

NORMAN RD

MILL LA

POMPER LA

19

East Lodge Farm

Eastlands Farm

MALTHOUSE LA

JANE MURRAY WAY

BLACKTHORN

ROBIN CL

SOUTHWAY

POPLARS

MARLBOROUGH

CONDOR WAY

ORCHARD RD

FERRY CL

PORTLAND

ALBION

SCHOOL CL

Sch

2

Pickhams Cottage

Old Mill House

DANWORTH LA

INNOVATION DR

YORK RD

EDWARD WAY

CHARLES AVE

ERICSSON WAY

Sovereign Ctr 1
Victoria Bsns Ctr 2
Sovereign Bsns Pk 3

Teknol House

Victoria Ind Est

Regent Bsns Pk

Braybon Bsns Pk

CONSORT WAY

VICTORIA RD

VICTORIA WAY

VICTORIA CL

QUEEN ELIZABETH AVE

AVOCET

STATION RD

OLD SCHOOL PL

B2113

GRAVETT CT

1

DANWORTH FARM

Kent's Farm

Locks Manor

Maltings Farm

Superstore

ALBERT DR

PAYTON DR

SHOTTERS

MICHELBOURNE

DAINE WAY

HENRY BURT WAY

PANGDENE

PEPPER

COLCHINS

WOODCREST RD

GROVELAND RD

POTTERS

B2036

18

Malthouse Theatre

Scotches

CLAYTON DR 1
NIGHTINGALE LA 2

A273

CHANCTONBURY RD

28 A B 29 C D 30 E F

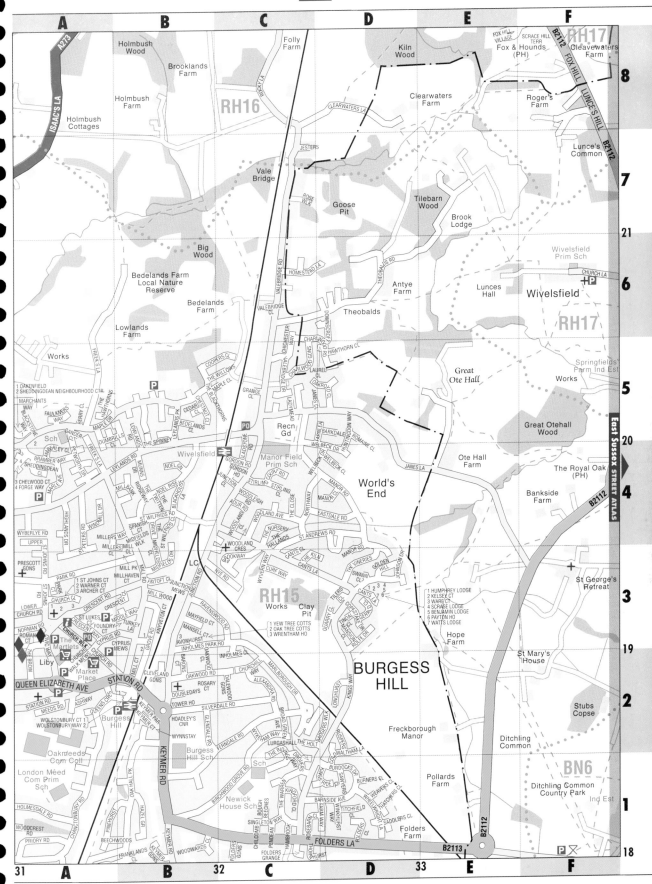

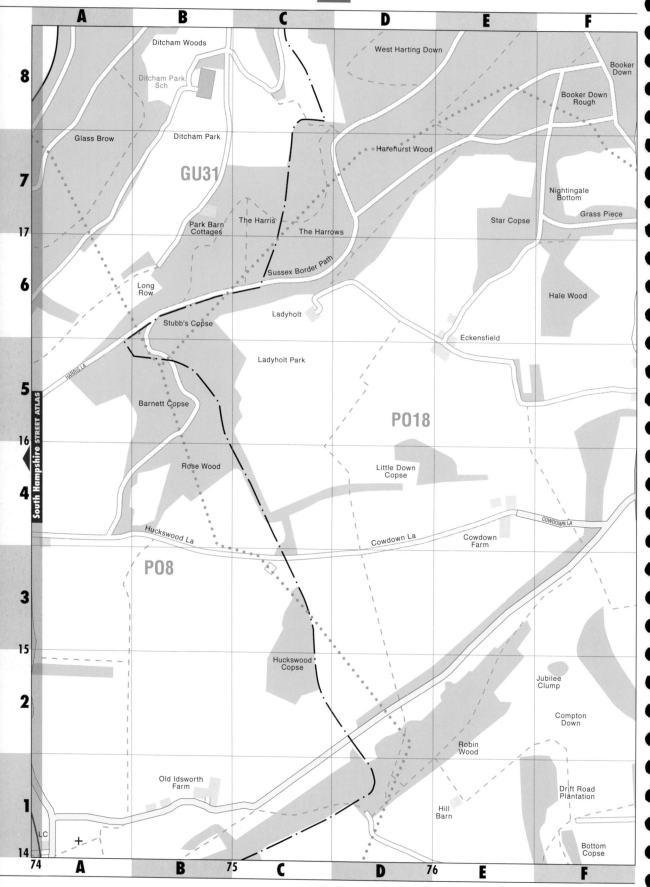

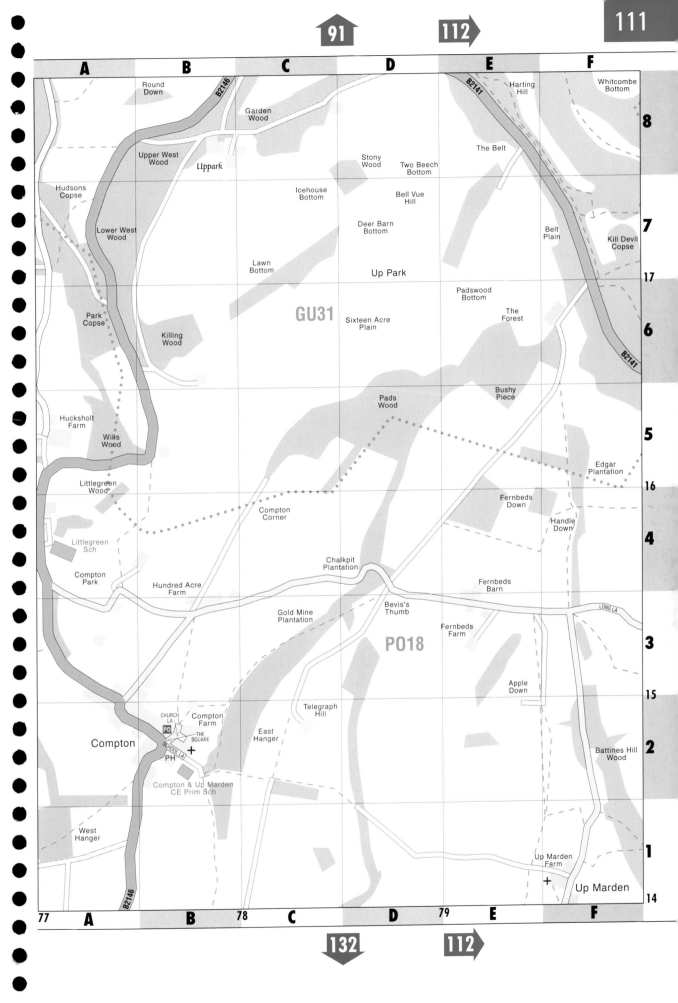

A B C D E F

8

Round Down

B2146

Garden Wood

B2141

Harting Hill

Whitcombe Bottom

Upper West Wood

Uppark

Stony Wood

Two Beech Bottom

The Belt

Hudsons Copse

Icehouse Bottom

Bell Vue Hill

7

Lower West Wood

Deer Barn Bottom

Belt Plain

Kill Devil Copse

Park Copse

Lawn Bottom

Up Park

17

Killing Wood

GU31

Padswood Bottom

B2141

6

Sixteen Acre Plain

The Forest

Hucksholt Farm

Pads Wood

Bushy Piece

5

Wills Wood

Edgar Plantation

Littlegreen Wood

16

Littlegreen Sch

Compton Corner

Fernbeds Down

Handle Down

4

Compton Park

Hundred Acre Farm

Chalkpit Plantation

Fernbeds Barn

LONG LA

Gold Mine Plantation

Bevis's Thumb

Fernbeds Farm

PO18

3

Apple Down

15

CHURCH LA

PO

Compton Farm

THE SQUARE

Telegraph Hill

Compton

SCHOOL LA

East Hanger

Battines Hill Wood

2

PH

Compton & Up Marden CE Prim Sch

West Hanger

Up Marden Farm

1

B2146

Up Marden

14

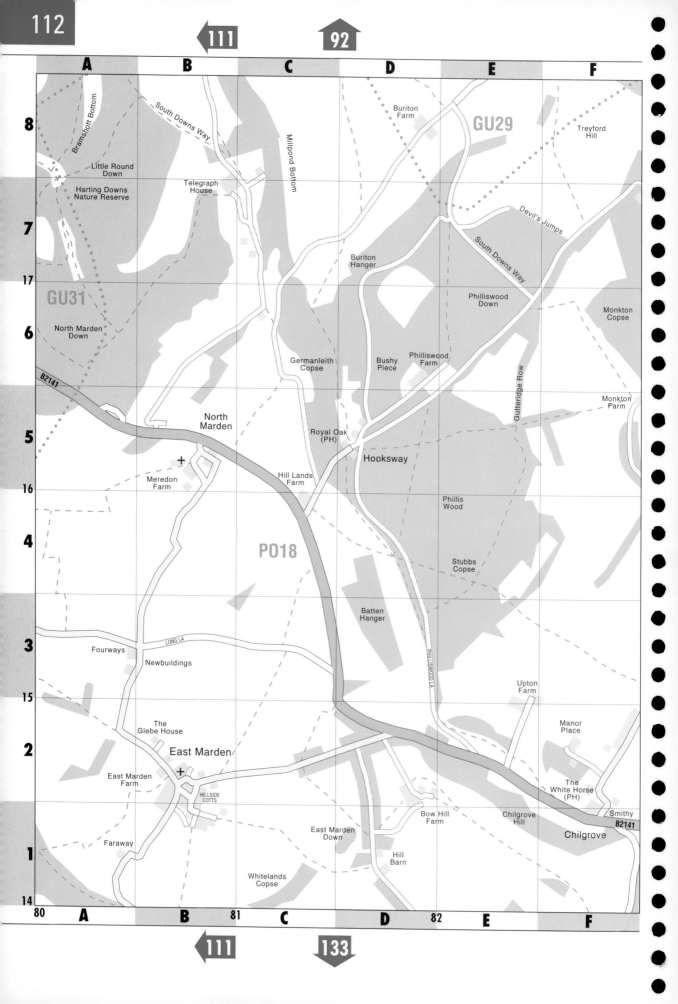

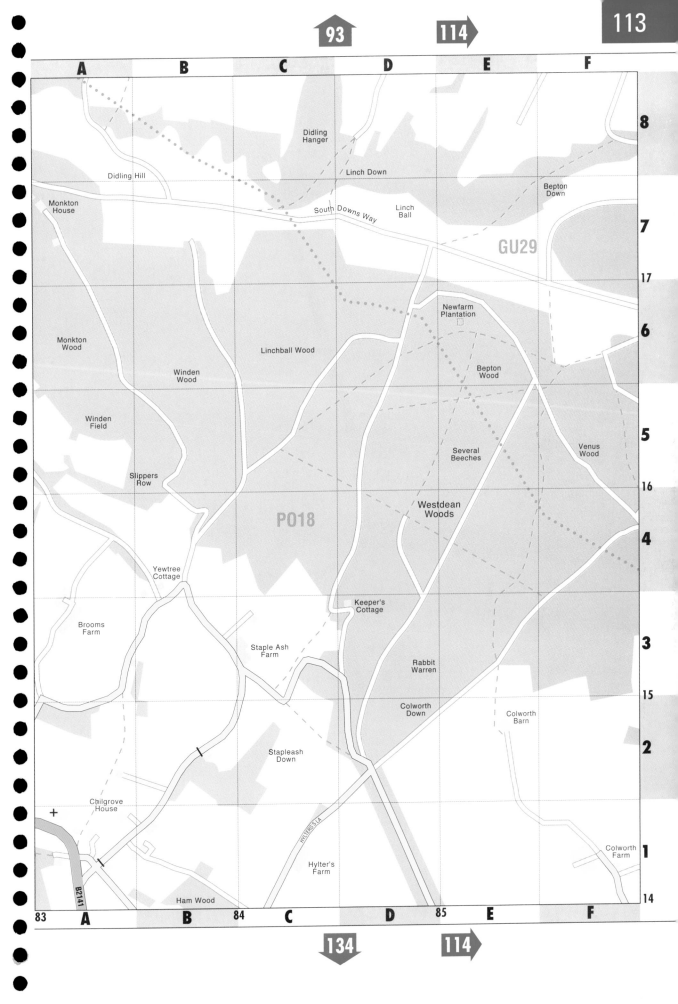

93
114

A B C D E F

8

Didling Hanger

Linch Down

Bepton Down

Didling Hill

7

Monkton House

South Downs Way

Linch Ball

GU29

17

Newfarm Plantation

6

Monkton Wood

Linchball Wood

Bepton Wood

Winden Wood

Venus Wood

5

Winden Field

Several Beeches

Slippers Row

16

Westdean Woods

4

PO18

Yewtree Cottage

Keeper's Cottage

Brooms Farm

3

Staple Ash Farm

Rabbit Warren

Colworth Down

15

Colworth Barn

Stapleash Down

2

Chilgrove House

+

Colworth Farm

1

HYLTERS LA

Hylter's Farm

B2141

14

83 A B 84 C D 85 E F

Ham Wood

134
114

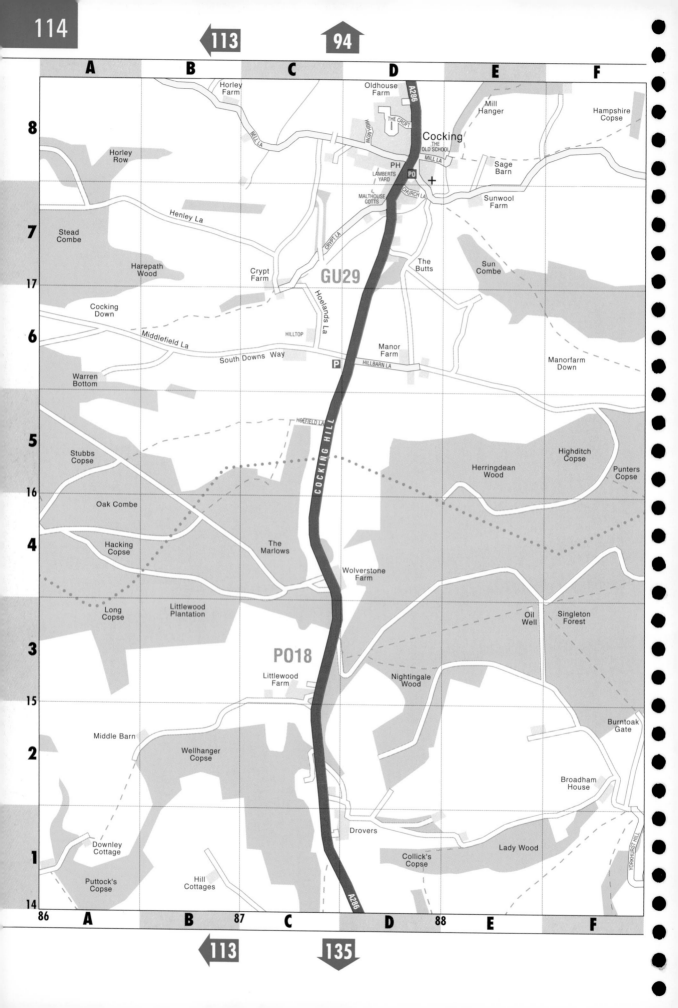

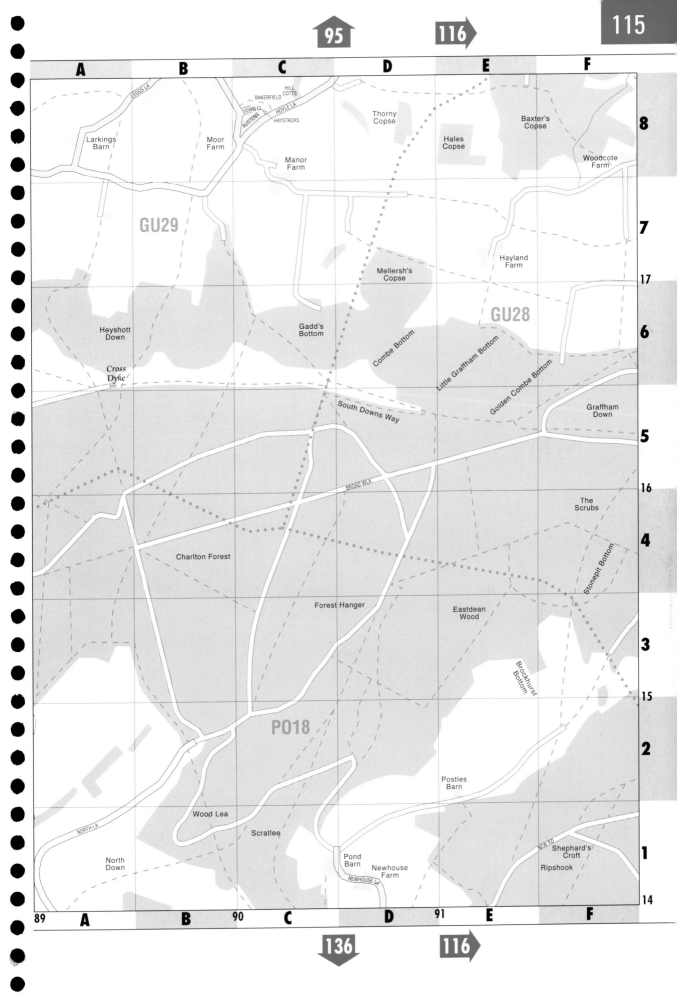

95
116

A B C D E F

8

Larkings Barn

Moor Farm

HILL COTTS
BAKERFIELD
DOWN CL
AUSTENS
HOYLE LA
HAYSTACKS
LEGGS LA

Manor Farm

Thorny Copse

Hales Copse

Baxter's Copse

Woodcote Farm

GU29

7

Hayland Farm

17

Mellersh's Copse

Heyshott Down

Gadd's Bottom

Combe Bottom

Little Graffham Bottom

Golden Combe Bottom

GU28

6

Cross Dyke

South Downs Way

Graffham Down

5

BROAD WLK

The Scrubs

16

Charlton Forest

4

Forest Hanger

Eastdean Wood

Stonepit Bottom

3

Brockhurst Bottom

15

PO18

2

Postles Barn

Wood Lea

Scratlee

NORTH LA

North Down

Pond Barn

Newhouse Farm

NEWHOUSE LA

NEW RD

Shephard's Croft

Ripshook

1

14

89 A B 90 C D 91 E F

115 96

A B C D E F

8

Perrot Farm
Fairacres
Nonnington Farm
STUARTS MDW
The Forester's Arms (PH)
Upper Norwood
Upper Norwood Farm

WOODCOTE GOTTS
White Horse (PH)
Graffham
Old Park Farm

Marsh Farm
GUILLODS GOTTS
PO
7
Parson's Copse
Dominies Wood

ALMSHOUSES
Calloways
Bushy Pieces

17
Dirty La

Tagents Farm
6
Graffham Fst Sch
Lavington Stud

NORWOOD LA

Marlpit Brow
West Lodge
Lavington Park

Limekiln Bottom
Graffham Down
THE DRIVE
Seaford Coll
Lavington House

5
East Lavington
THE GREEN
NORWOOD LA
BEECHWOOD LA
Beechwood House

South Downs Way
GU28
16
Woolavington Down

4
Grass Tegleaze
Furze Field
Barn Tegleaze
Tegleaze Farm
Stickingspit Bottom

Lamb Lea
Tegleaze
Crown Tegleaze
Littleton Down

3
Warren Bottom

15
Limekiln Bottom

2
North Side
Heath Hanger
North Down
Littleton Farm

NEW RD

1
PO18
Malecomb
Waltham Down
A285

WHITE RD

14
92 A B 93 C D 94 E F

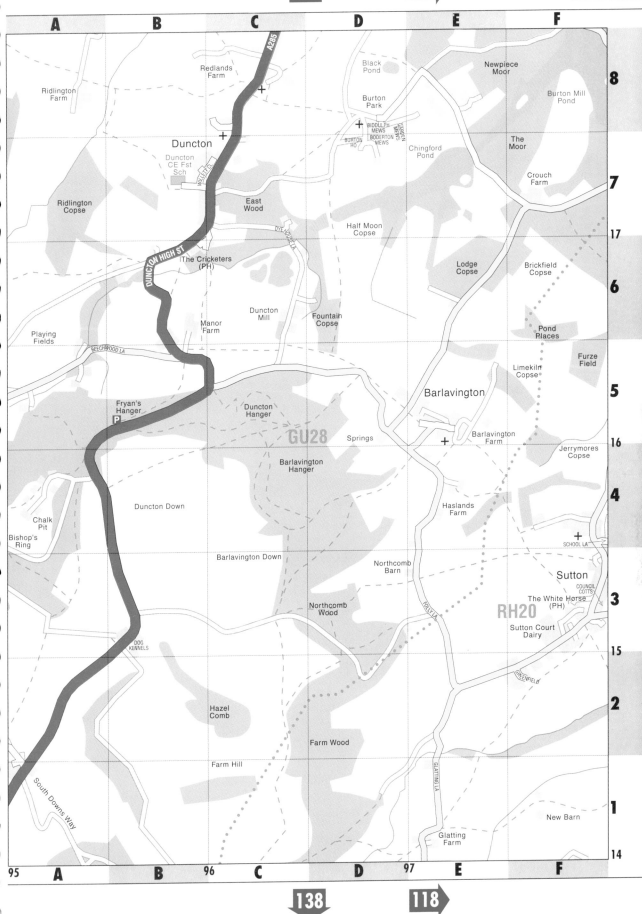

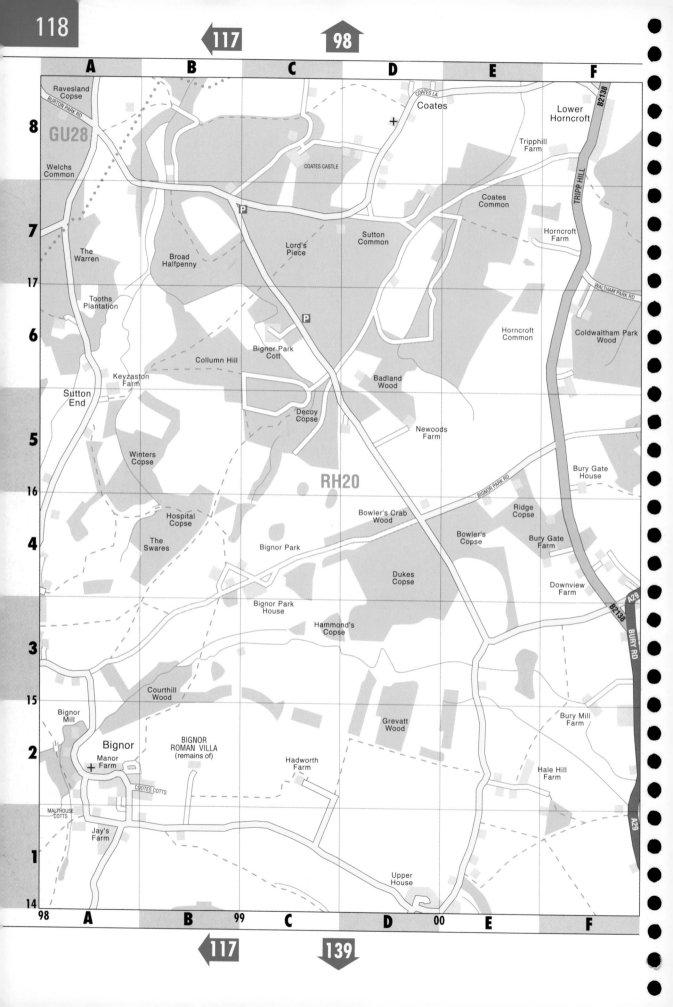

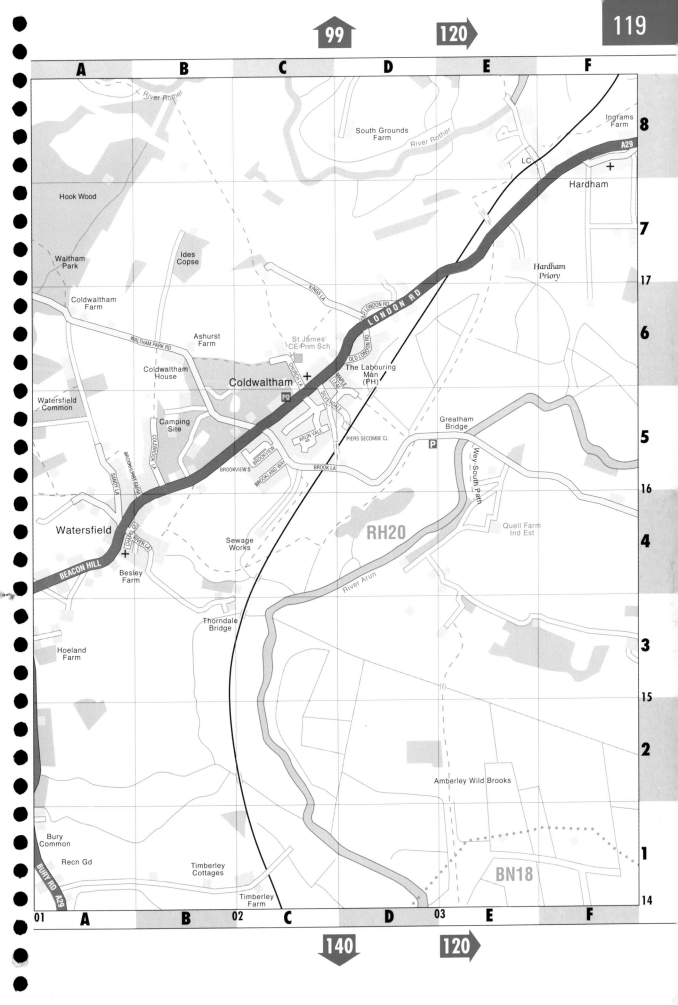

A   B   C   D   E   F

8

LONDON RD A29
A29

Sewage
Works

A283

Winterfields
Farm

River Chilt

7

Pulborough Brooks
Nature Reserve

Banks
Cottage

River Arun

Lickfold
Farm

GOLF CLUB LA

17

Wiggonholt
Farm

6

River Stor

RH20

Wiggonholt

Rush
Brook

Upperton's Barn
Visitors Ctr

P

P

5

Wiggonholt
Common

Redford
House

16

Manor
Farm

Greatham

Washingham

Wassel Pond

4

Greatham
Common

Sparrite
Common

Sparrite
Farm

Northpark
Wood

Bog
Common

Glebe
Farm

The
Sawyard

HURSTON LA

3

Rackham
Common

Bog
Common
Cottages

15

Parham
Farm

2

Rackham
Plantation

Sparrite
Farm

West
Lodges

Fangrove
Hill

Lillywhites
Field

Limekiln
Plat

Douglas's
Lodge

A283

1

RACKHAM ST

Rackham Mill
(disused)

West Plain

Parham House
& Gardens

Parham Park
(Deer Park)

Windmill
Hill

BN18

Rackham
House

14

04   A   B   05   C   D   06   E   F

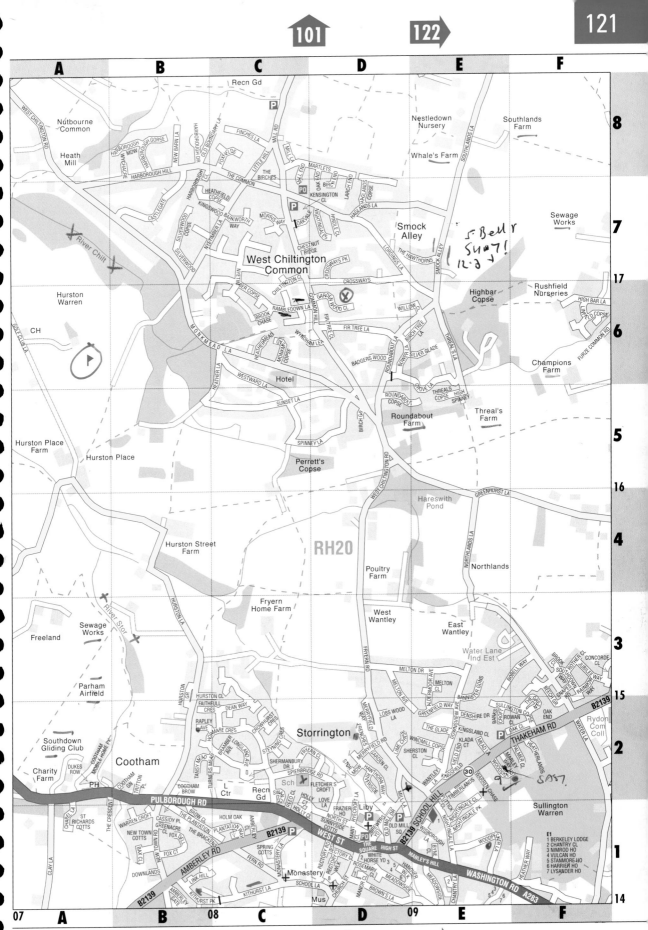

D1
1 RECTORY COTTS
2 WHITE HORSE CT
3 HAMMOND PL
4 MALDEN PL
5 LANGTON PL
6 LINDALE PL
7 MANOR CT
8 CHANCTONBURY WLK

E1
1 BERKELEY LODGE
2 CHANTRY CL
3 NIMROD HO
4 VULCAN HO
5 STANMORE HO
6 HARRIER HO
7 LYSANDER HO

← 121
102

A · B · C · D · E · F

8

Nursery
B2139 DUKE'S HILL

Cray's Farm

Woolvens Farm

B2133

BILLINGSHURST RD

B2133

Town House Farm

Bramblefield

CRAY'S LA

Westlands Farm

THE STREET

Thakeham Fst Sch

7

Chesswood Nursery

White Lion Inn (PH)

Thakeham Place

Thakeham

Mill Copse

West Wolves Farm

Caravan Park

17

WOODLAND COTTS

Warminghurst Farm

HARDBARROW WOODS

Warminghurst

HIGH BAR LA

6

Abingworth

FURZE COMMON RD

Manor House Buildings

RECTORY LA

Meiros Farm

GUYHURST SPINNEY

Nursery

RECTORY PL

PENN GDNS

Nursery

MEIROS WAY

WARMINGHURST CL

VINEY CL

Hotel

STORRINGTON RD

JACKET'S HILL

Lancing Brook

PARK LA

COVERT MEAD

Ashington CE Fst Sch

WILLARD FOSTER LA

THE SANDS

5

Green Dene Farm

Guyhurst Copse

Park Barn

Church Farm

CHURCH LA

16

Meadow Farmhouse

Little Thakeham

STRAWBERRY LA

RH20

Nursery

CHURCH CL

MILL LA

4

The Maples

MERRYWOOD LA

Newhouse Farm

Jinkes Farm

Mitchbourne Farm

A24

MERRYWOOD HO

3

Orchardway Farm

CRESCENT

WOODLANDS LA

SQUIRRELS COPSE

NEWHOUSE LA

MELROSE PL

Lower Barn

Malthouse Farm

LONDON RD

B2139

PINE CL

THAKEHAM COPSE

CHANCTON COPSE

OAK AVE

CHESTNUT CL

TUDOR VILLAGE

GORSE BANK C.

MUTTON'S LA

15

HILLSIDE WK

BIRCH WAY

AZALEA CL

HAZELWOOD CL

ROCK RD

Mutton's Farm

Wiston Bsns Pk

Rydon Com Coll

BUNBURY CL

BRACKEN LA

Longbury Hill

2

HILLSIDE RD

SANDGATE LA

BRINK

FERN CL

HAMPERS LA

Heath Common

GEORGES LA

Nurseries

Nursery

SPRING GDNS

1

Sand Pit

BILBERRY HILL

SANCTUARY LA

VERAS WLK

BADGERS HOLT

SANDY LA

Washington Common

Rock Place Farm

ROCK LA

Castle Farm Estate

A24

14

Sandgate Park

10 · A · B · 11 · C · D · 12 · E · F

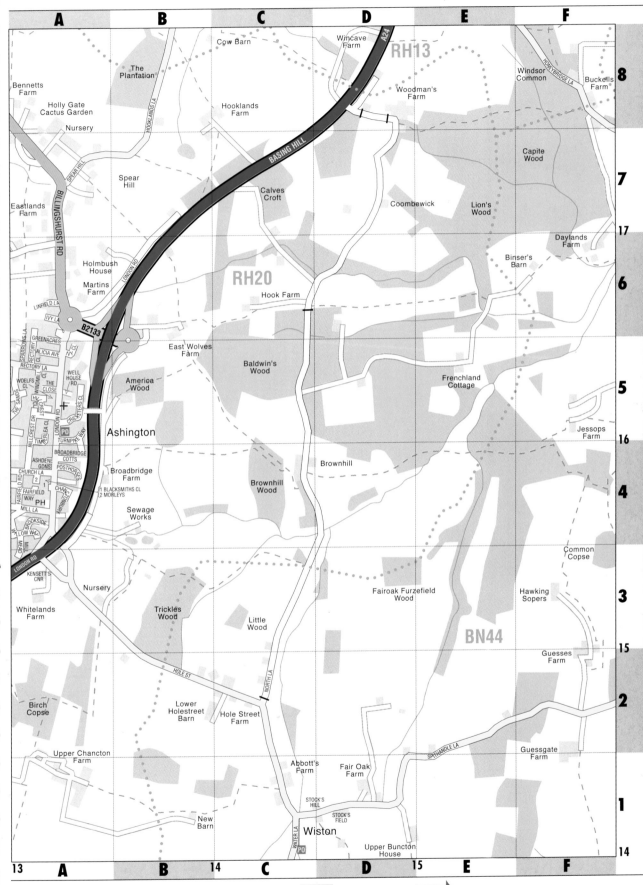

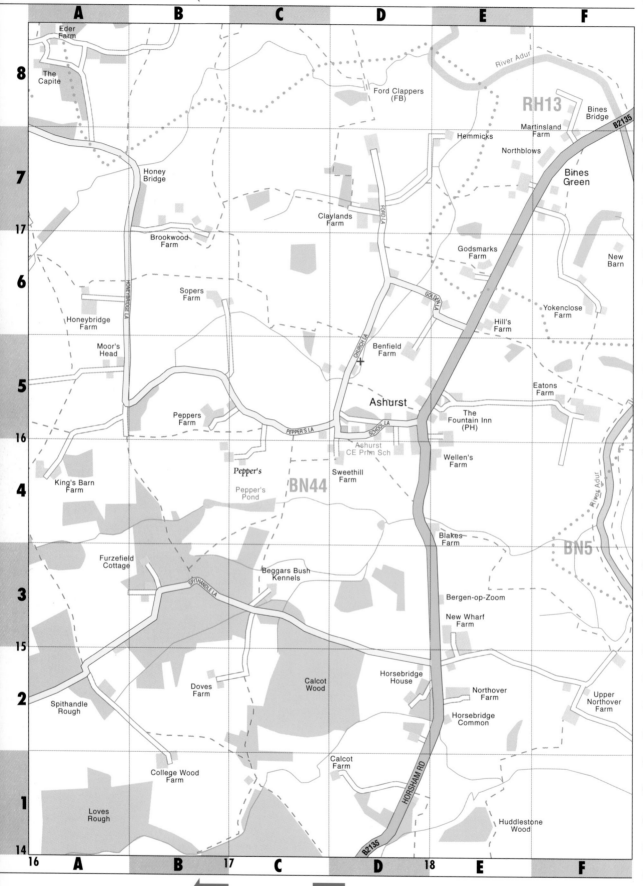

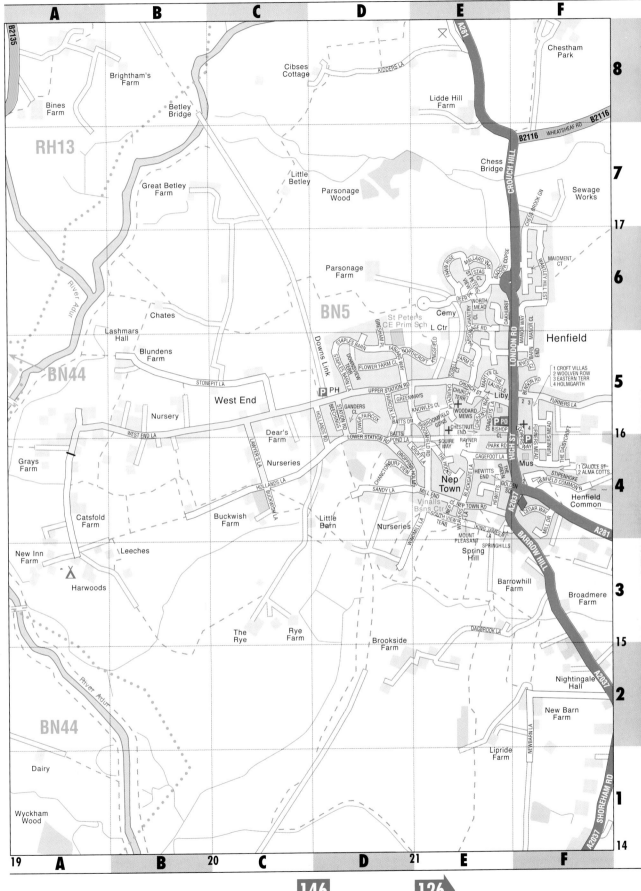

125
106

A B C D E F

8

B2116
WHEATSHEAF RD
B2116

Hollinger

Heatenthorn Farm

Paynesfield North

Firsland Park Est

Morley Farm

Blackstone Gate Wood

B2116

7

Park Farm

Blackstone Gate Farm

High Cross

B2116

17

Woolfly Wood

Woodhouse Wood

6

Woodhouse

Kingsfold

BLACKSTONE LA

Furze Field

Woodhouse Farm

Trusler's Hill Farm

TRUSLER'S HILL LA

5

BN5

Bylsborough Farm

BLACKSTONE RISE

NORTH VIEW

BLACKSTONE ST

BN6

Furners Farm

FURNERS LA

Blackstone Grange

Blackstone

16

Bilsborough Barn

4

Swains Farm

Bassells

Four Elms

Wick Farm

Henfield Common

A281
BRIGHTON RD

BLACKSTONE LA

3

Holedean Farm

West Wood

East Wood

15

Hundred Steddle

Woodmancote Place

Eastout

Kentons Farmhouse

Woodmancote

2

A2037

The Pools

Hole Farm

BRAMWELL LODGE
TERRY'S CROSS

BRAMLANDS LA

Nutknowle Farm

Henfield Bsns Pk

CH

1

Oreham Common

HORN LA

Bramlands

Holmbush Farm

A281

14

22 A B 23 C D 24 E F

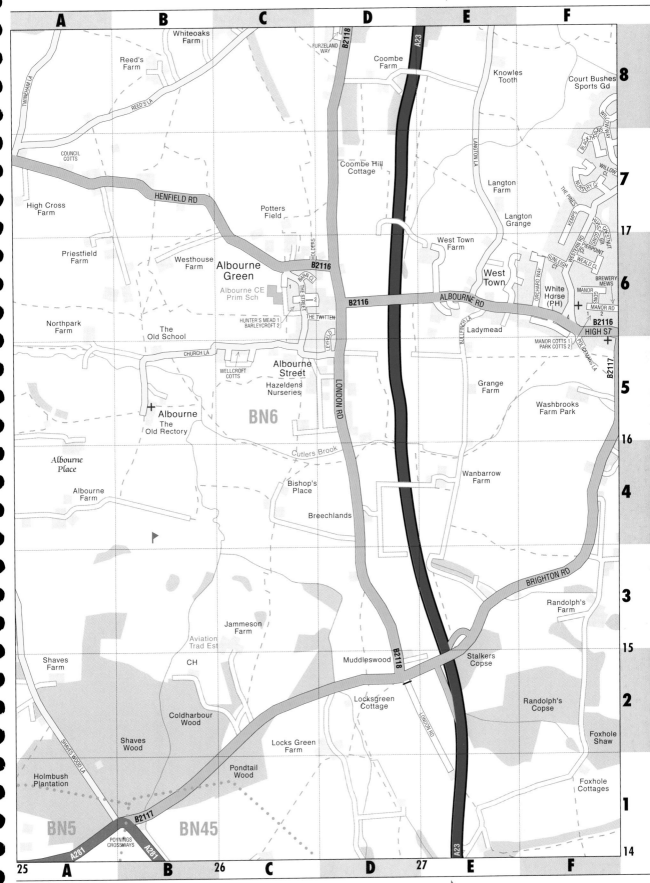

127 108

A B C D E F

8

ARUN BECK
WILLOW WAY
WILLOW GDNS
1 WILLOW WAY
2 WILLOW CL
3 WESTERN RD
4 THE ROWANS
Recn Gd
CUCKFIELD RD
WHITE'S CL
HANNINGTON PL
BISHOPS CL
IDEN HURST
ST LAWRENCE
ICE WAY
FAIRFIELD CRES

Chalkers La
Hurstpierpoint Coll
Dankworth La
Malthouse La
Ruckford House
Highfields Farm

Clayton Priory
Hammond's Mill Farm
MILL RACE
Mill Nursery
New Close Farm
RH15
A273
NIGHTINGALE LA

7

17

WILDERNESS RD
ST CHRISTOPHER'S RD
MARCHANTS CT
MARCHANTS RD
Sch Liby
TRINITY RD
THE GLEBE
P
B2116
HIGH ST
FURLONG CL
PITT LA
WEST FURLONG CT
SOUTH AVE
ALMSHOUSES OF THE HOLY NAME
Cemy
PARKVIEW DOWNSVIEW
Little Park Farm
Big Edgerley
College La
College Pl

Hurst Wickham
Clayton Wickham Farm
Friar's Oak (PH)
CH
LONDON RD
THE BOURNE
Woodside Grange
New Barn Farm

6

Hurstpierpoint
1 RIBBETTS HO
2 TRUMPKINS
3 PITT CT
RIBBETTS COTTS
BROWN TWINS RD
TRINITY CT
ST GEORGE'S HO
ST GEORGE'S LA
CHERINGTON PL
HIGHFIELD DR
WICKHAM DR
HIGHFIELD
ST GEORGES
SPINNEY
HALTON SHAWS
Tott Farm
TOTT HILL
PINE TREE
HASSOCKS RD
RANDIDDLES CL
WICKHAM HILL
THE CROSSWAYS
HURST RD
BELMONT LA
Hurst Wickham Cl
LYNTON CL
WOODSBURY CL
Belmont
WILLOW HO 1
GRACE CT 2
PAVILION LA
MEADOWS
BANKSIDE
BRAMBLES
THE CROFT
PRIORY RD
BELMONT CL
LITTLE COPSE RD
FRIARS OAK RD
KINGS DR
QUEENS DR
THE SPINNEY

5

16

Hassocks
BN6
Ham Farm
Danny Lake
FRIARS CL
STONEPOUND FARM CL
NORTH CT
RAVENSWOOD
SEMLEY RD
STONEPOUND
WOODSLAND RD
CHANCELLORS PK
GRANTHAM PK
THE CLOSE
ORCHARD LA
Hassocks Inf Sch
WILMINGTON CL
B2116
P

4

Bedlam Street
Stanford Cl
Pine Trees
Pine Trees Ct
Stonepound Ridge
Stanford Ave
CHALLOW CL
NORTH BANK
CROWN POINT HO
THE WILLOWS
WOODSLAND CL
THE GENISTOS
SEMLEY LODGE
STATION APP W
STATION APP
Hassocks
SOUTH BANK
KEYMER RD
HASSOCKS LODGE
CLAYTON AVE
PO
WINDMILL AVE
DALE AVE
BROOK AVE
SHANDS
Downlands Com Sch

15

Old Wood
Danny
Little Danny
NEW WAY LA
Furzefield
Ockenden's Wood
Nursery
Stonepound Crossroads
Pound Gate
ROSE CT 1
CLAYTON PARK 2
STANFORD TERR 3
STATION COTTS 4
DUNCTON HO 5
LAGWOOD CL
OCKENDEN WAY
THE ORCHARD
DOWNS VIEW RD
PARKLANDS RD
DANNY WOOD RD
HERON'S TYE 1
SANDBROOK 2
ORION PAR 3
FITZJOHN CT 4
Butcher's Wood

3

2

1

14

Hautboyes
Coldharbour Farm
The Jack & Jill (PH)
BRIGHTON RD
B2112
A273
Lag Wood
Halfway
NEW RD
B2112

Ashen Plantation
The Warrene

28 A 29 B C D 30 E F

127 149

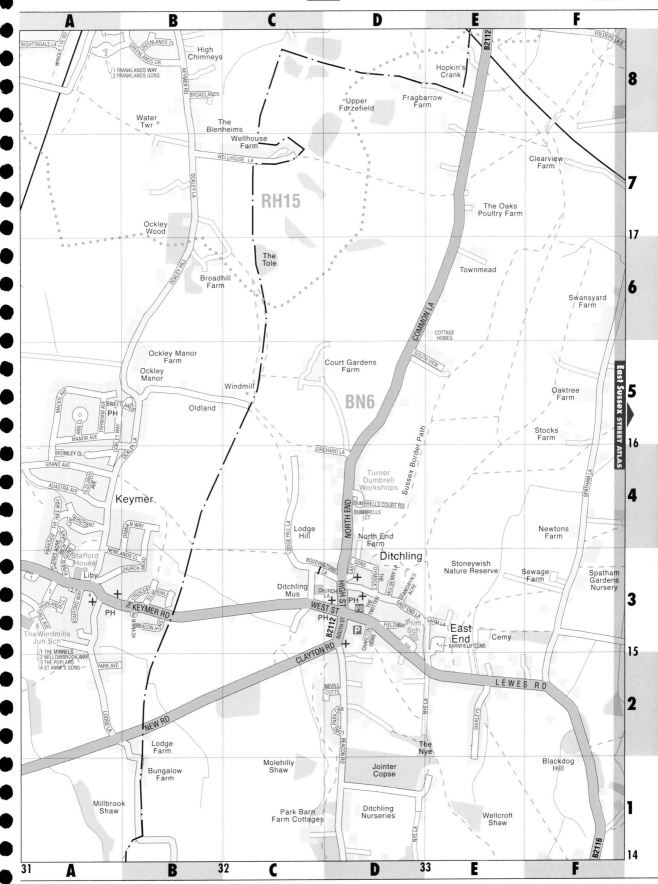

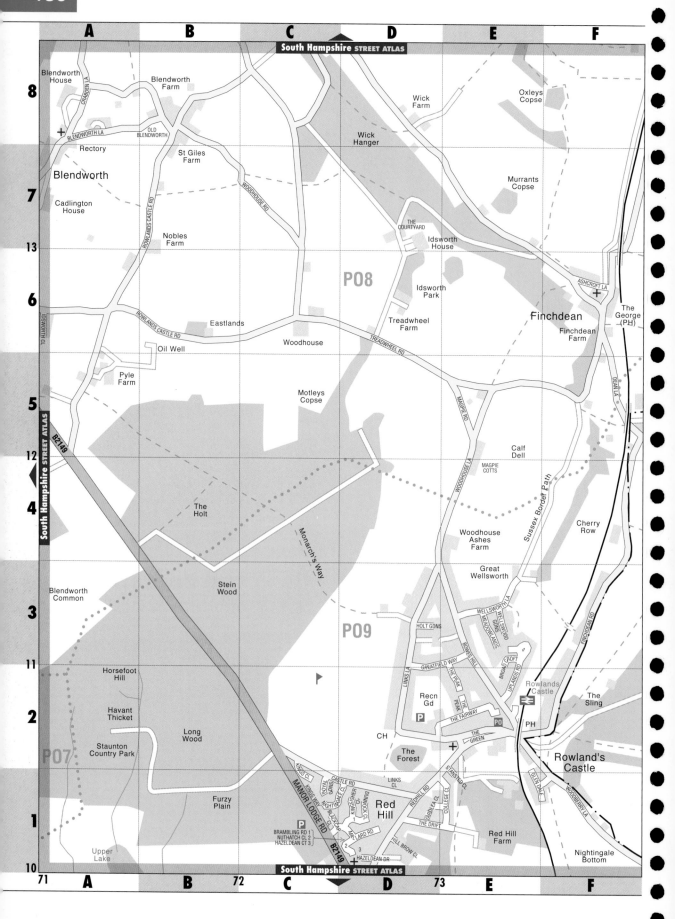

A B C D E F

8

Blendworth
House

CRADDEN LA

Blendworth Farm

+

BLENDWORTH LA

OLD BLENDWORTH

Rectory

Blendworth

7

Cadlington House

St Giles Farm

ROWLANDS CASTLE RD

WOODHOUSE RD

Wick Farm

Wick Hanger

Murrants Copse

Oxleys Copse

13

Nobles Farm

THE COURTYARD

Idsworth House

PO8

6

IDSWORTH CL

ROWLANDS CASTLE RD

Eastlands

Woodhouse

Idsworth Park

TREADWHEEL RD

Treadwheel Farm

ASHCROFT LA

+

Finchdean

Finchdean Farm

The George
(PH)

DEAN LA

Oil Well

Pyle Farm

5

MAGPIE RD

Motleys Copse

Calf Dell

B2149

South Hampshire STREET ATLAS

12

The Holt

WOODHOUSE LA

MAGPIE COTTS

Sussex Border Path

Cherry Row

4

Monarch's Way

Woodhouse Ashes Farm

Great Wellsworth

Stein Wood

PO9

3

Blendworth Common

WELLSWORTH LA

WELLSWORTH GDNS

MEADOWLANDS

HOLT GDNS

BOWES HILL

GREATFIELD WAY

THE PEAK

BROAD CROFT

UPLANDS RD

FINCHDEAN RD

Rowlands Castle

The Sling

11

Horsefoot Hill

LINKS LA

Recn Gd

THE PEAK

THE FAIRWAY

P

PO

PH

2

Havant Thicket

Long Wood

P

CH

THE GREEN

+

Rowland's Castle

GLEN DALE

WOODBERRY LA

PO7

Staunton Country Park

MANOR LODGE RD

The Forest

LINKS CL

STANSTED CL

REDHILL RD

COLLEGE CL

VARDEN CL

Red Hill

1

Furzy Plain

KINGS CL

ROYAL GDNS

CASTLE RD

KINGS WAY

NIGHTINGALE CL

BLACKCAP CL

KINGFISHER CT

BROWNING CL

MALLARD RD

THE DRIFT

HILL BROW CL

Red Hill Farm

Nightingale Bottom

P

BRAMBLING RD 1
NUTHATCH CL 2
HAZELDEAN CT 3

+

HAZELDEAN DR

B2149

Upper Lake

10

71 A B 72 C D 73 E F

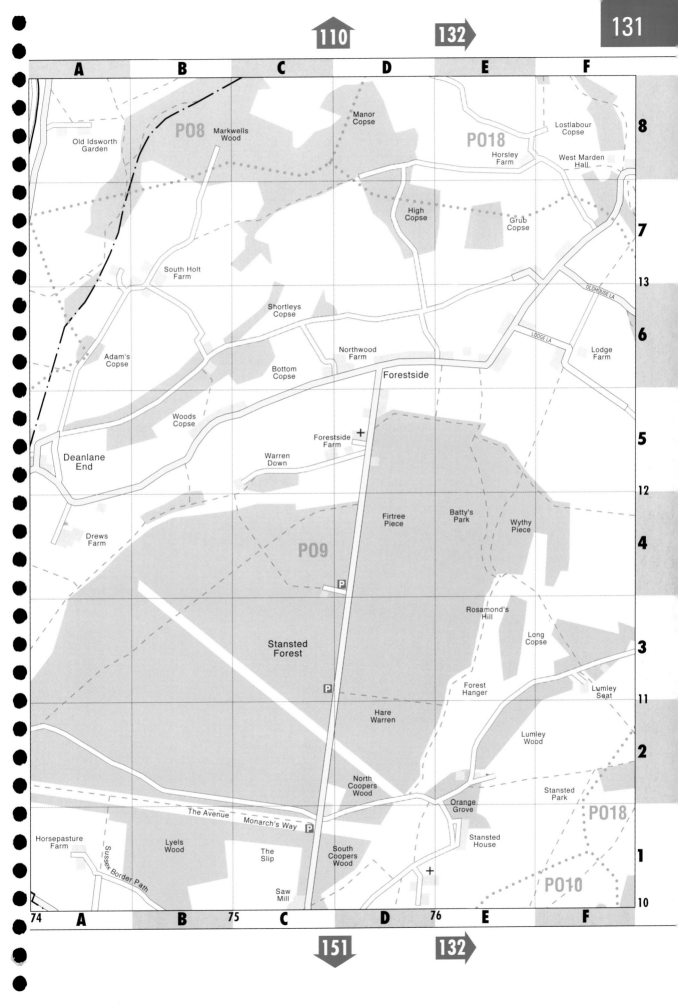

131
111

A **B** **C** **D** **E** **F**

8

DOWN COTTS

Locksash Farm

Hill Farm

Blinkard Copse

Grevitts Copse

PH

West Marden

Sewage Works

7

Malthouse Copse

Dolly's Hanger

Lower Farm

Wheatcroft

NORE DOWN WAY

B2146

13

Nore Down

Lowerfarm Copse

LOCKSASH LA

OLDHOUSE LA

6

Fanny's Row

Lyecommon

Cabragh House

Haslett Copse

Pitlands Farm

5

Birchin Copse

Warren Copse

Woodbarn

Busto Copse

Watergate Farm

PO9

12

Watergate Hanger

Holmes Row

Inholmes Wood

PO18

4

Watergate Park

Piglegged Row

Broadreed Farm

3

Oak Copse

Dundarroch

11

Mitchmere Farm

WOODLANDS LA

Monarch's Way

Manor Farm

MITCHMERE COTTS

2

Woodlands Cottages

Lordington Copse

COOKS LA

The Barley Mow (PH)

BROOKLANDS COTTS

Park Slip

River Ens

Walderton

Walderton Down

1

B2146

Walderton Hill Plantation

10

77 **A** **B** 78 **C** **D** 79 **E** **F**

131
152

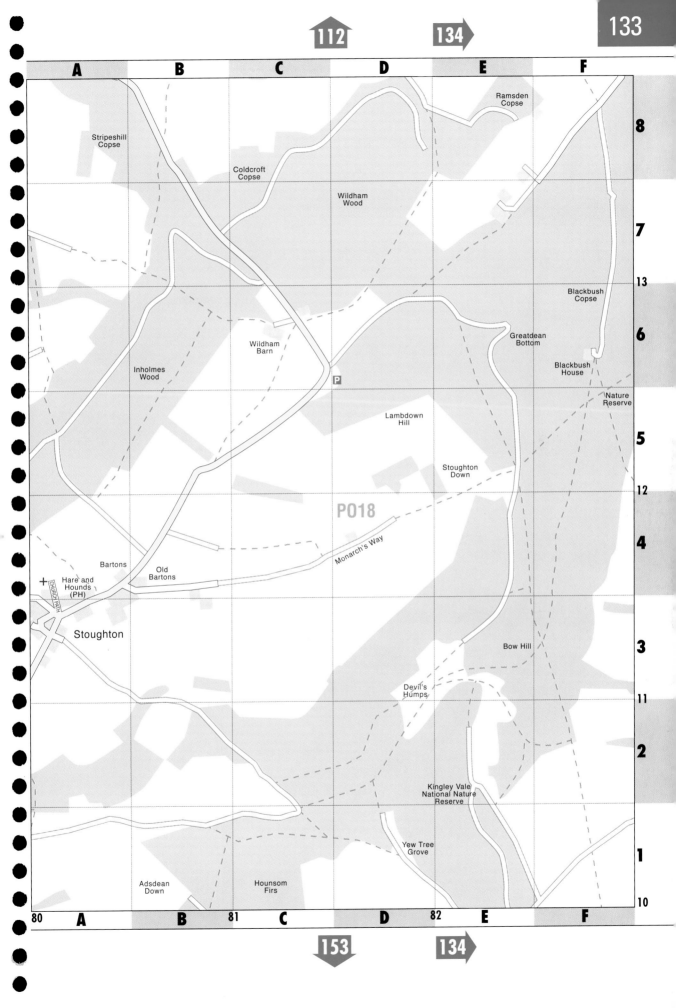

112
134
153
134

133
113

A B C D E F

8

Hylters

Lodge Hill
Farm

Double
Barn

Monarch's Way

Withy Bed

7

Warren Down

Warren
Barn

Warren
Hanger

13

Heathbarn
Down

Whitedown
Plantation

Highdown
Plantation

6

Brickkiln
Farm

THE
WARREN

WARREN
COTTS

Goosehill
Camp

Whiteland
Cottages

Whiteland
Copse

Little
Home
Farm

PHEASANT
COTTS

West Dean
CE Prim Sch

PH
PO

5

Manor
Farm

HASLER'S LA

12

Bottom
Barn

PO18

4

Dean
Cottages

Hensbush
Copse

River Lavant

Lawrence
Copse

Rummages
Barn

Preston
Farm

3

Crows Hall
Copse

Crows Hall
Farm

Binderton La

11

Welldown
Cottages

BINDERTON LA

2

Welldown

Binderton
House

Ox
Barn

1

Slate
Barn

Langford
Farm

10

83 A 84 B C 84 D 85 E F

B2141

HYLTERS LA

A286

CHURCH LA

B2141

A286

STABLE LA

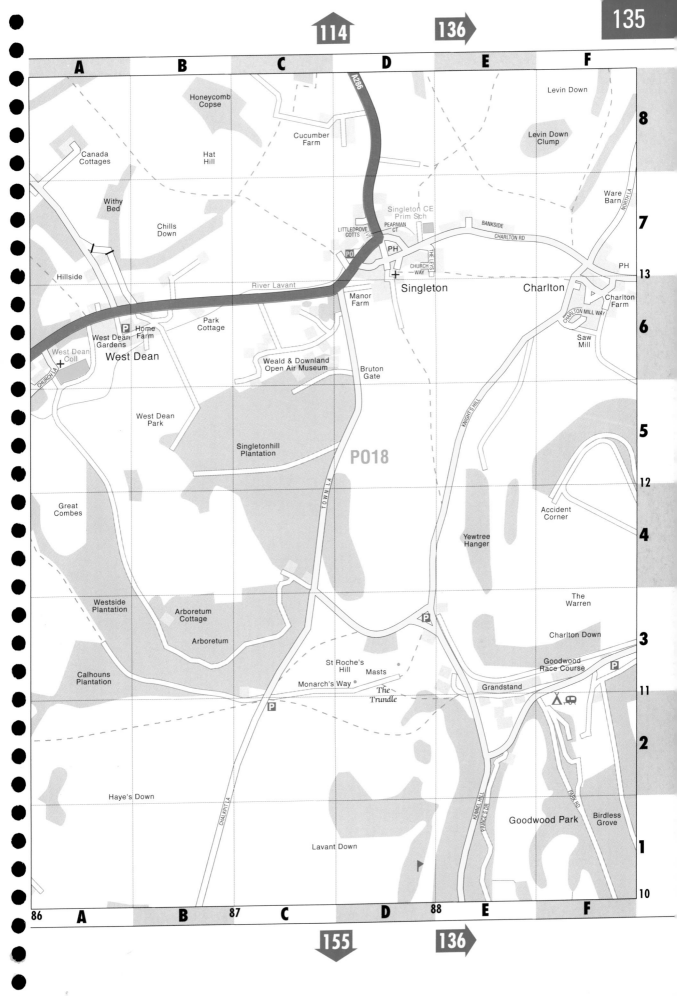

135
115

A B C D E F

8 Court Hill

Halfmoon
Piece

NORTH LA

New Barn

Highdown
Croft High Down

Green Hill

NEWHOUSE LA
NEW RD

7 COURTYARD LA

13 Ide's
Barn

CHARLTON RD DROKE LA

MAIN RD
BUTCHERS LA
P0 CHAPEL ROW

Manor Farm

6 East Dean

Wallerdean
Hill

EASTDEAN HILL

Bubholts

5 Shotter's Ground Chiseldown

Potcomb

12

Charlton
Park

Park
Hill PO18

Monarch's Way

4 Eastdean
Park

Eastdean
Hill

Goodwood
Country Park SELHURSTPARK RD

CHALK RD

Pilleygreen
Lodges

3 P ⚔

Appletree
Bottom

Open
Winkins

11 The
Plantation

Red
Copse

MOLECOMB BROADWALK

2 Molecomb
Peak

Little
Copse

Halnaker Gallop

Ladys
Winkins
Halnaker
Park

1 Hat Hill

Denge
Bottom

10 Molecomb

89 A B 90 C D 91 E F

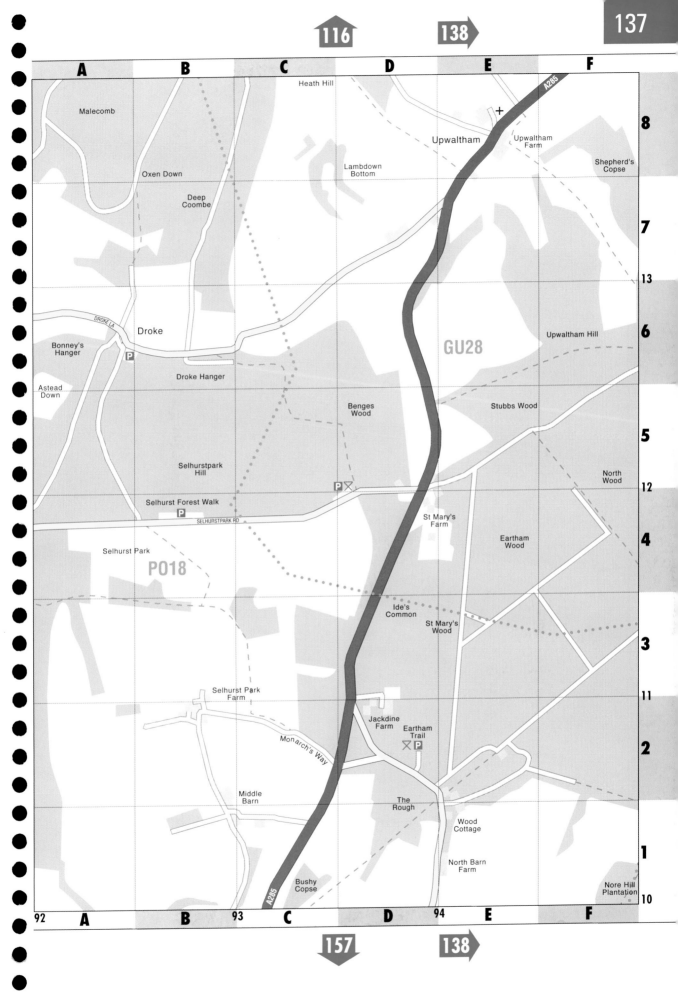

A **B** **C** **D** **E** **F**

8 Littleton End · Scotcher's Bottom · Denture · Glatting Hanger · New Barn

Westwood Bottom · Pitchurst Copse · Coldharbour Farm

Lamb Hanger · GLATTING LA

7 West Wood · Sutton Down · Burton Down · RH20 · Left Hanger

13 · GU28 · Masts · Glatting Beacon · Bignor Hill

6 · South Downs Way · P

Gumber Corner

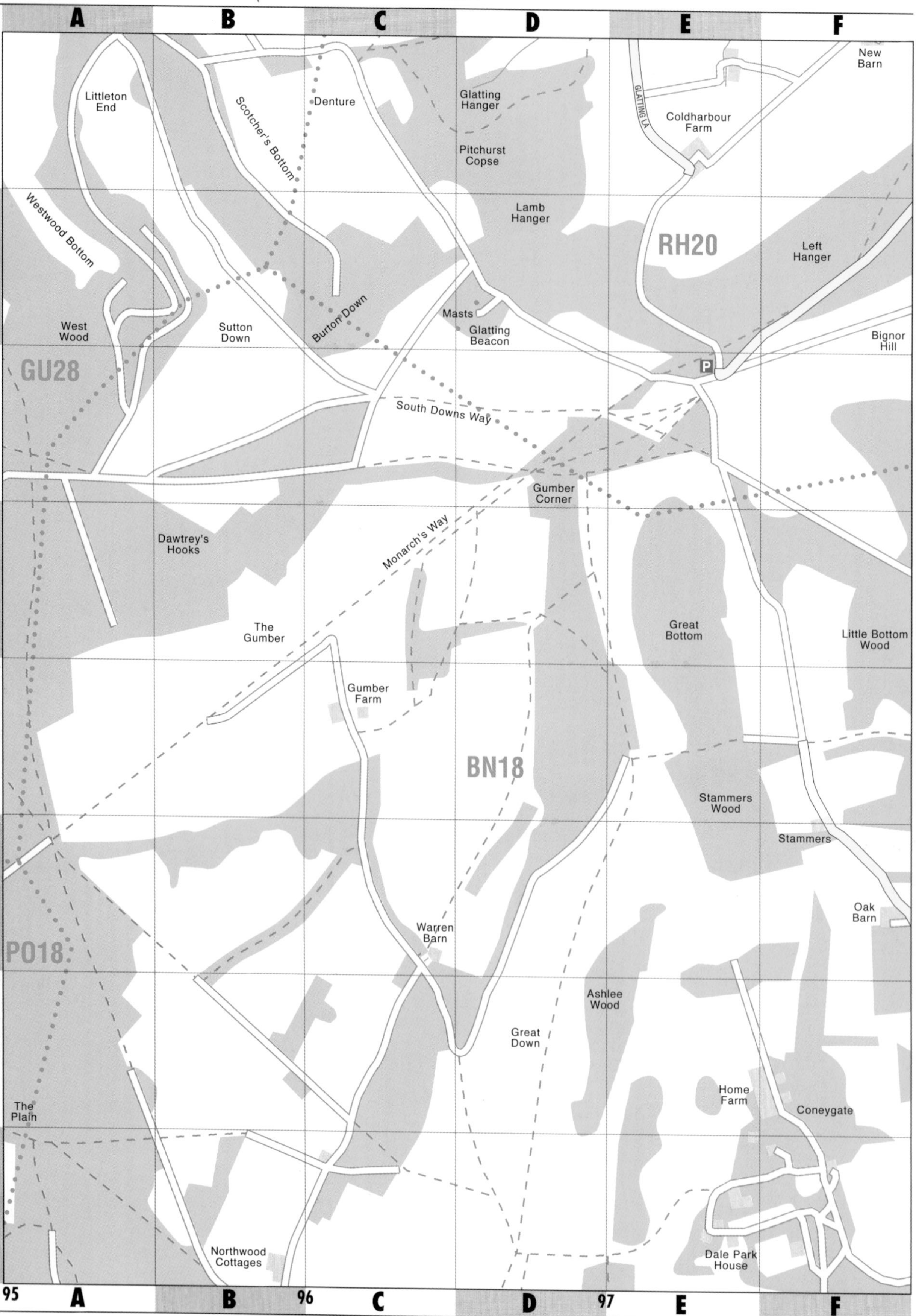

Dawtrey's Hooks · Monarch's Way

5 · The Gumber · Great Bottom · Little Bottom Wood

12 · Gumber Farm

4 · BN18 · Stammers Wood

· Stammers

3 · PO18 · Oak Barn

11 · Warren Barn · Ashlee Wood

2 · Great Down · Home Farm · Coneygate

The Plain

1 · Northwood Cottages · Dale Park House

10

95 **A** **B** 96 **C** **D** 97 **E** **F**

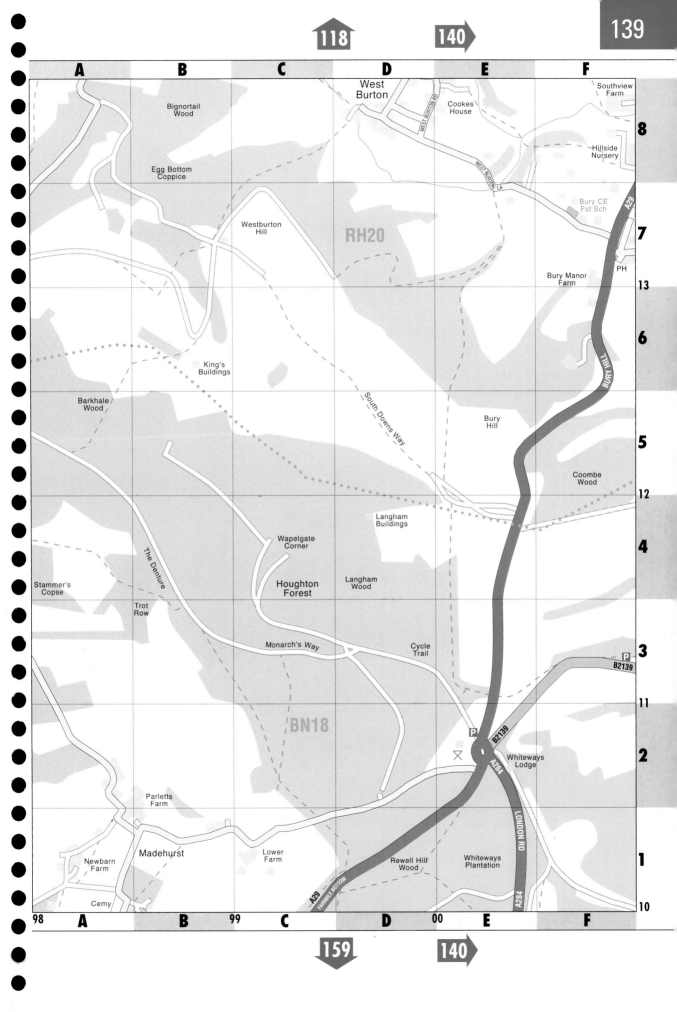

West Burton
Cookes House
Southview Farm
Hillside Nursery
Bignortail Wood
Egg Bottom Coppice
WEST BURTON RD
WEST BURTON LA
Bury CE Fst Sch
8
Westburton Hill
RH20
7
A29
Bury Manor Farm
PH
13
King's Buildings
6
Barkhale Wood
South Downs Way
Bury Hill
BURY HILL
Coombe Wood
5
12
Langham Buildings
Wapelgate Corner
The Denture
Houghton Forest
Langham Wood
4
Stammer's Copse
Trot Row
Monarch's Way
Cycle Trail
3
B2139
P
11
BN18
P
B2139
Whiteways Lodge
2
Parletts Farm
A284
Newbarn Farm
Madehurst
Lower Farm
Rewell Hill Wood
Whiteways Plantation
LONDON RD
1
Cemy
A29 FARMHILL BOTTOM
A284
10

139
119

A B C D E F

8

Timberley Bridge

Hollow Farm

Amberley Swamp

Bury Hollow

Prattendens Farm

Wey-South Path

The Sportsman (PH)

7

NORFOLK COTTS

Bury

Dorset House Sch

The Alley

RACKHAM RD

Castle (Hotel)

HOG LA

EAST ST

ARUN CL

PO

CHURCH ST

HIGH ST

HURST CL

HURST COTTS

13

Castle Farm

Amberley

Amberley CE Fst Sch

TURNPIKE RD

B2139

PH

SCHOOL RD

CHURCH LA

COOMBE CRES

Recn Gd

END COTTS

HANOVER CL

RH20

6

HOUGHTON LA

Sewage Works

Highdown

MILL LA

5

NEW BARN RD

Wysh House

HIGH TITTEN

Amberley Working Mus

Downs Farm

River Arun

12

South Downs Way

Caravan Park

BN18

4

Houghton Bridge

Amberley

HOUGHTON BRIDGE

Bridge Inn (PH)

Houghton

George & Dragon (PH)

SOUTH LA

Houghton Farm

Stoke Hazel Wood

3

B2139

Camp Hill

STOKE RD

Canada

11

Monarch's Way

2

North Stoke Farm

North Stoke

South Wood

1

10

01 A B 02 C D 03 E F

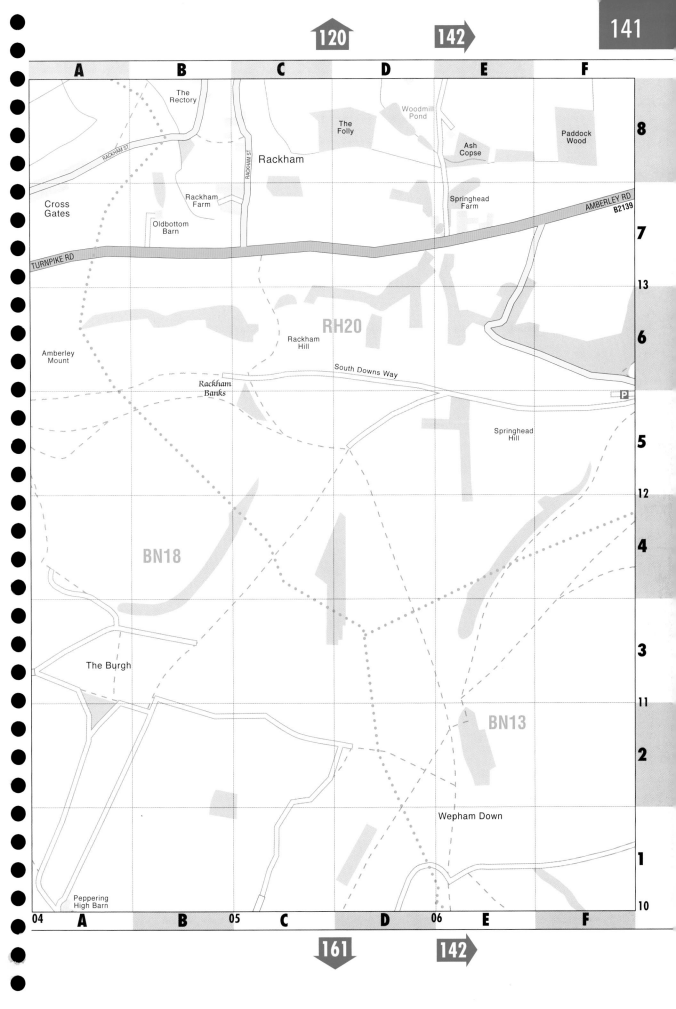

120
142

A B C D E F

8

The Rectory

Woodmill Pond

The Folly

Rackham

Ash Copse

Paddock Wood

RACKHAM ST

RACKHAM ST

Cross Gates

Rackham Farm

Oldbottom Barn

Springhead Farm

AMBERLEY RD

B2139

7

13

TURNPIKE RD

RH20

6

Amberley Mount

Rackham Hill

South Downs Way

Rackham Banks

P

Springhead Hill

5

12

BN18

4

3

The Burgh

11

BN13

2

Wepham Down

1

Peppering High Barn

10

04 A B 05 C D 06 E F

141
121

A B C D E F

8

7

13

6

5

12

4

3

11

2

1

10

B2139

CLAY LA

AMBERLEY RD

B2139

Paygate

KITHURST FARM RD

Kithurst
Farm

Cemy

Gerston
Bsns Pk

Gerston
Farm

GREYFRIARS LA

Coldharbour

Grey Friars
Farm

RH20

Chantry
Hill

South Downs Way

Chantry
Post

BN13

BN14

ST JOSEPHS ABBEY
ST JOSEPH'S MEWS

RAGMSCROFT

ABBEY
HO

BISHOPS
HO

POST VIEW

Chantry
Farm

The Chantry
Est

Chantry
Mill

Sand
Pit

WASHINGTON RD

A283

WATER LA

SULLINGTON LA

Sullington

Sullington
Manor Farm

Waterfall
Cottage

CHANTRY LA

The
Chantry

Sullington
Hill

Hill
Barn

P P

Lee Farm
Copse

Lee
Farm

LEE FARM
COTTS

Old Gray's
Wood

07 A B 08 C D 09 E F

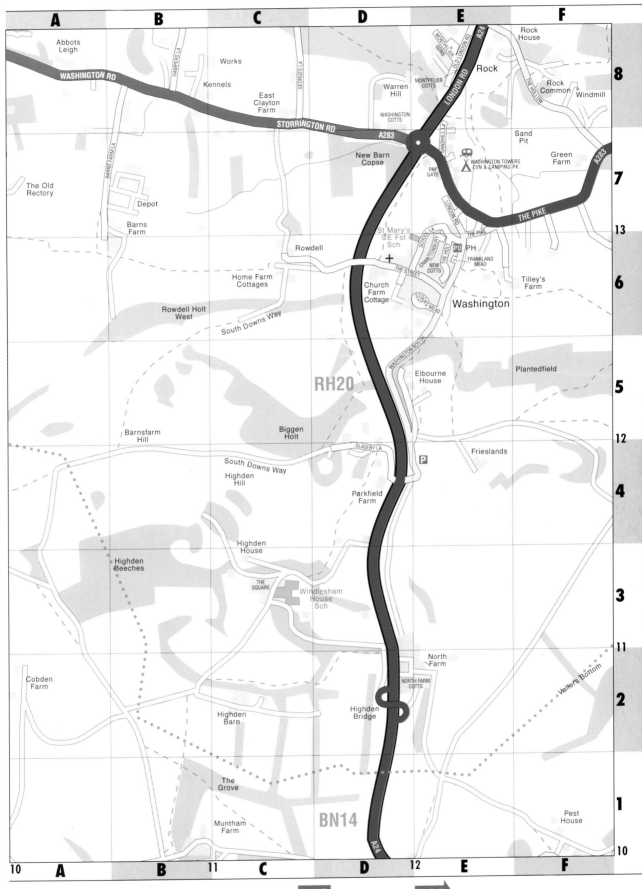

143
123

A   **B**   **C**   **D**   **E**   **F**

8

The Rough

Sevier's Barn

Buncton

Buncton Manor Farm

WATER LA

WASHINGTON RD

A283

THE PIKE

BUNCTON CROSSWAYS

The Falconers

7

Lower Chancton Farm

Model Cottages

A283

13

Newcommon Copse

Copyhold Wood

Bushovel Farm

CHANCTONBURY RING RD

6

Rokers

Lock's Farm

Weppons

MOUSE LA

Wiston Park

RH20

Owlscroft Barn

BN44

Wiston House

5

Combe Holt

Great Barn Farm

12

Chanctonbury Hill

Chanctonbury Ring

4

Chalkpit Wood

Well Bottom

3

Lion's Bank

Court Plantation

South Downs Way

11

Middle Brow

2

Buddington Bottom

BN14

Stump Bottom

Steyning Valley

1

Findon Park House

10

A   13   **B**   14   **C**   **D**   15   **E**   **F**

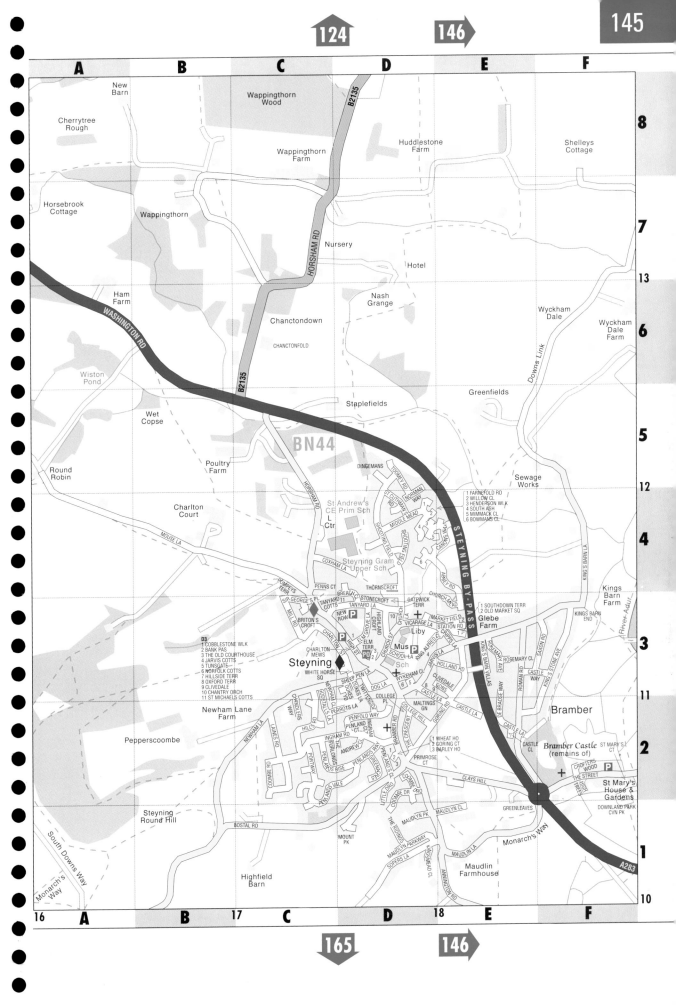

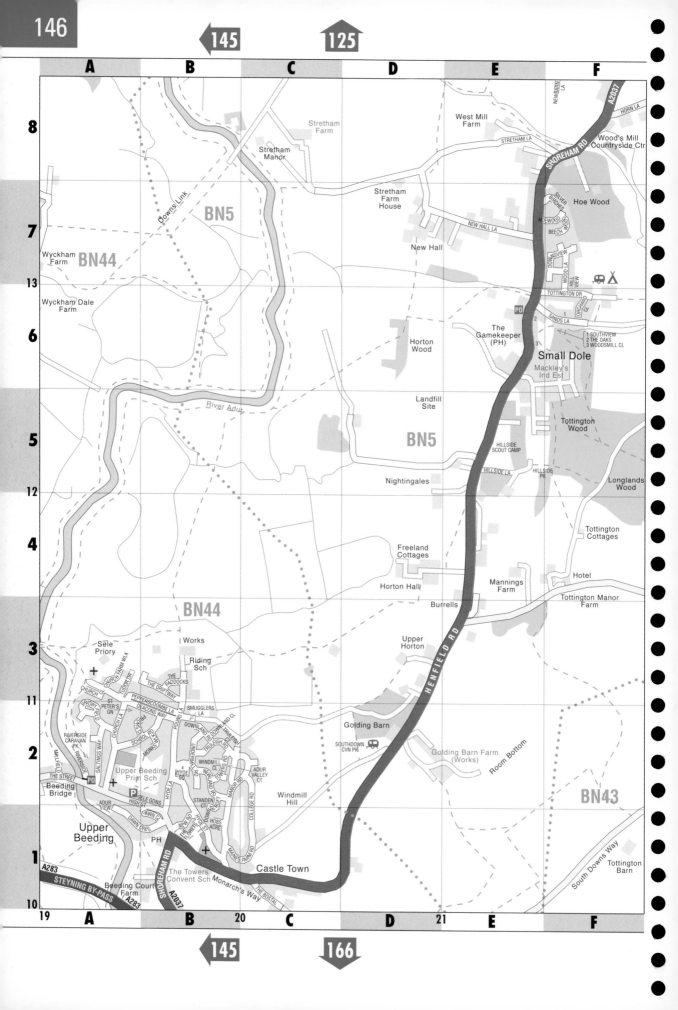

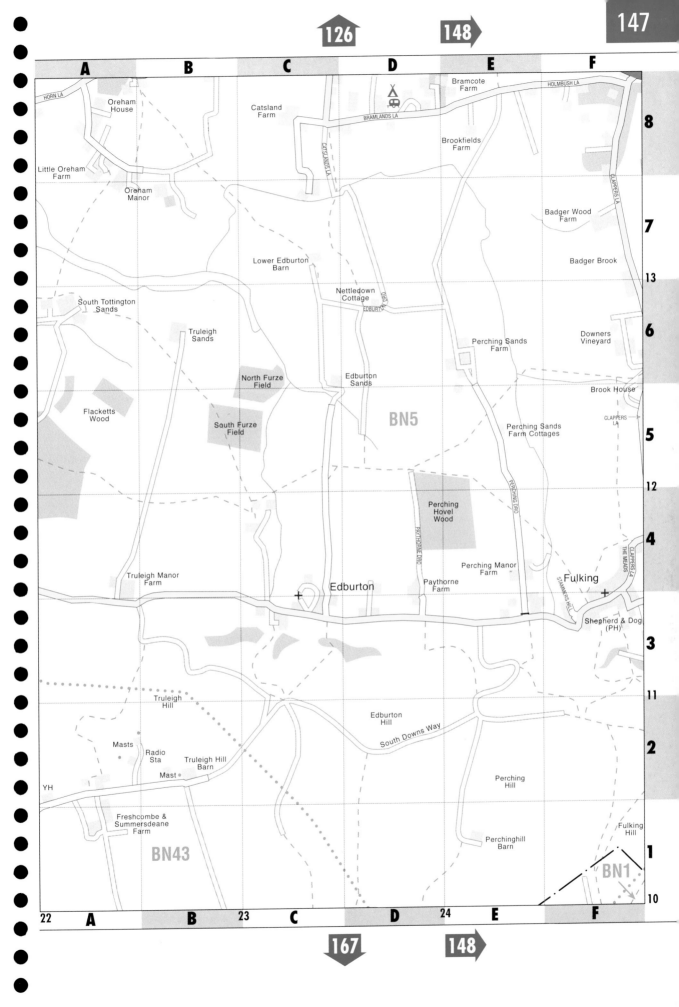

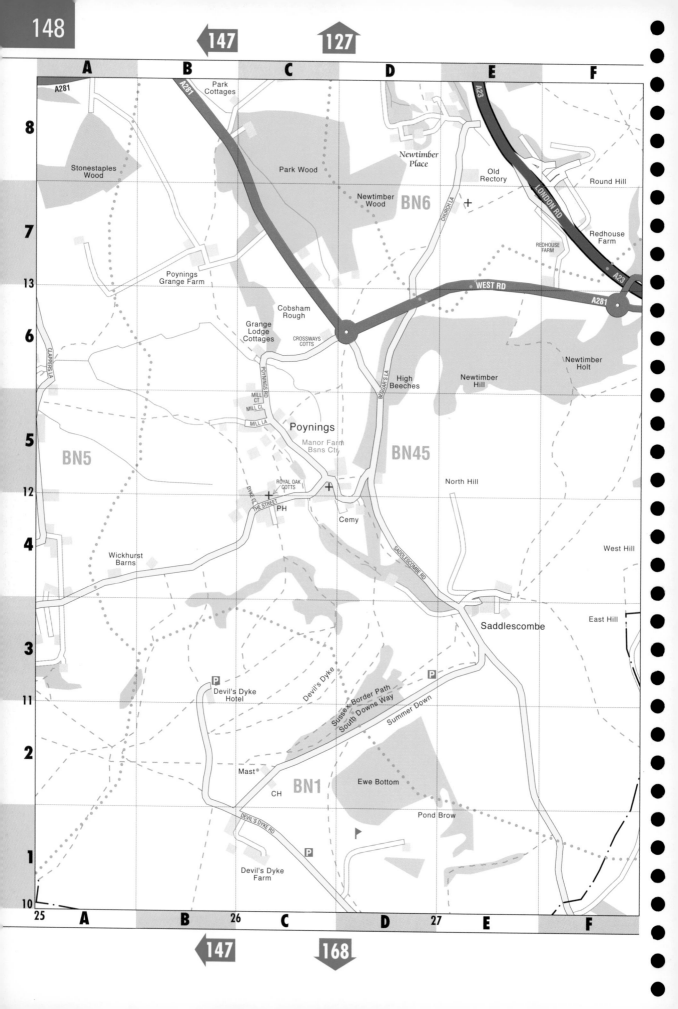

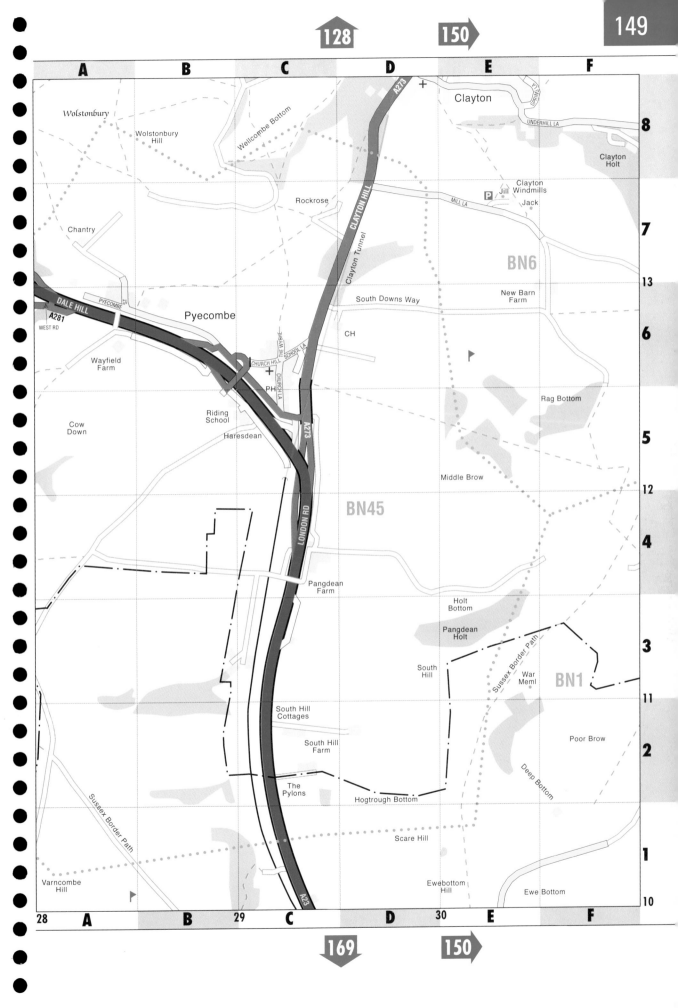

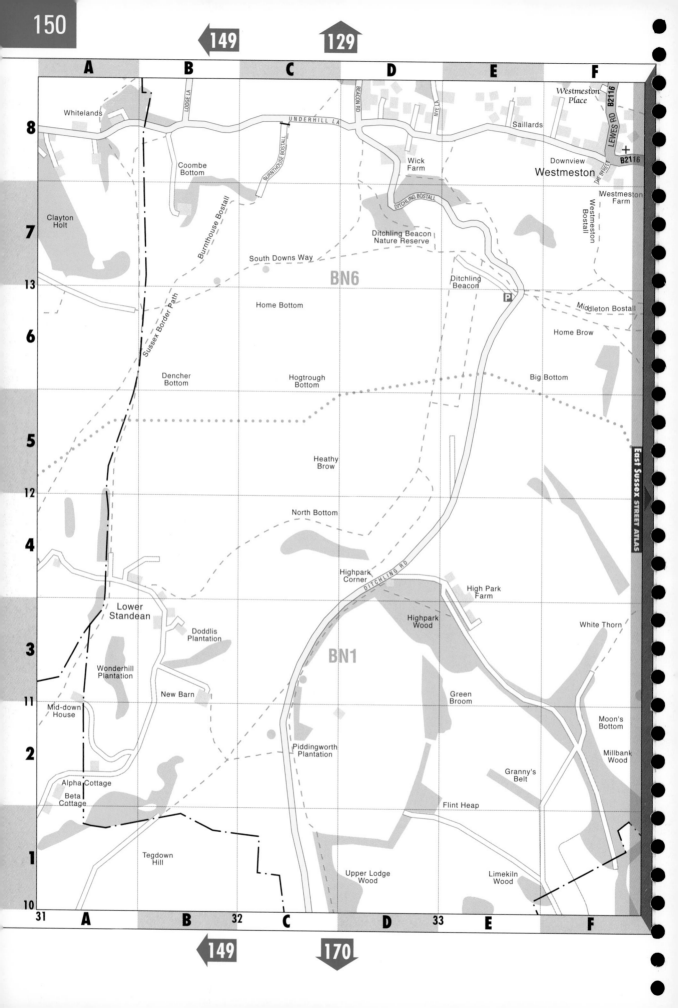

A B C D E F

Whitelands

Coombe
Bottom

LODGE LA

UNDERHILL LA

BEACON RD

NYE LA

Westmeston
Place

LEWES RD B2116

Saillards

Downview
Westmeston

B2116

8

BURNTHOUSE BOSTALL

Wick
Farm

DITCHLING BOSTALL

Westmeston
Farm

Westmeston
Bostall

Clayton
Holt

7

Burnthouse Bostall

Ditchling Beacon
Nature Reserve

South Downs Way

BN6

Ditchling
Beacon

13

Home Bottom

P

Middleton Bostall

6

Sussex Border Path

Home Brow

Dencher
Bottom

Hogtrough
Bottom

Big Bottom

5

Heathy
Brow

12

North Bottom

4

Highpark
Corner

DITCHLING RD

High Park
Farm

Lower
Standean

Doddlis
Plantation

Highpark
Wood

White Thorn

3

Wonderhill
Plantation

BN1

New Barn

Green
Broom

Moon's
Bottom

11

Mid-down
House

Millbank
Wood

2

Piddingworth
Plantation

Granny's
Belt

Alpha Cottage

Beta
Cottage

Flint Heap

Tegdown
Hill

1

Upper Lodge
Wood

Limekiln
Wood

10

31 A B 32 C D 33 E F

East Sussex STREET ATLAS

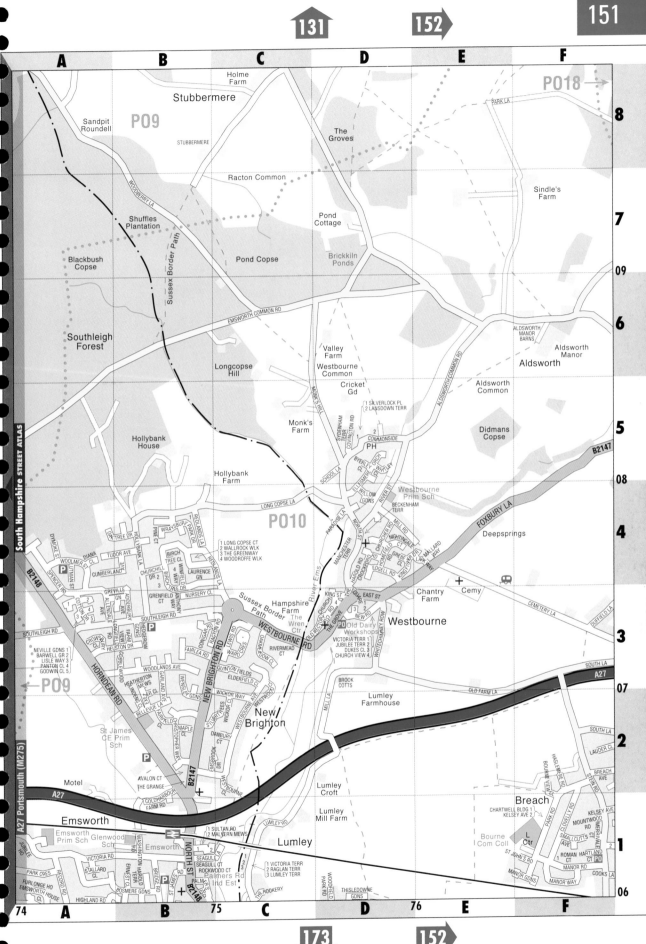

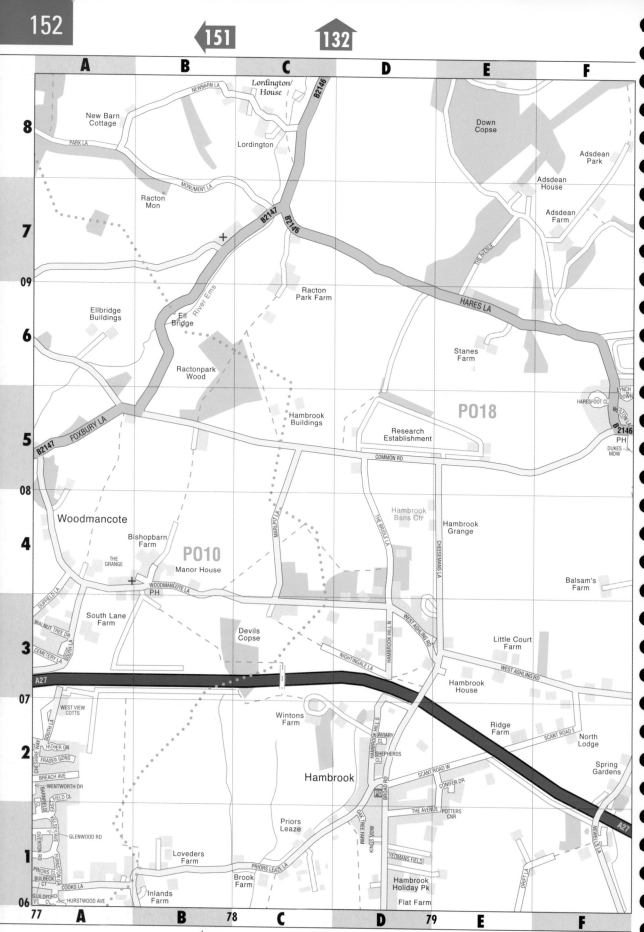

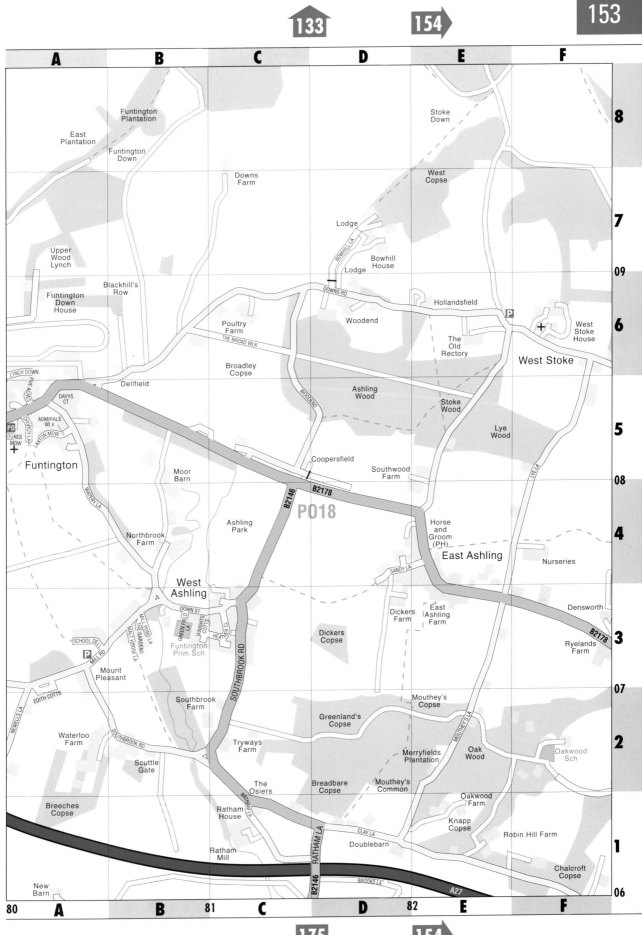

133 154

A B C D E F

8

7

09

6

5

08

4

08

3

07

2

1

06

80 A B 81 C D 82 E F

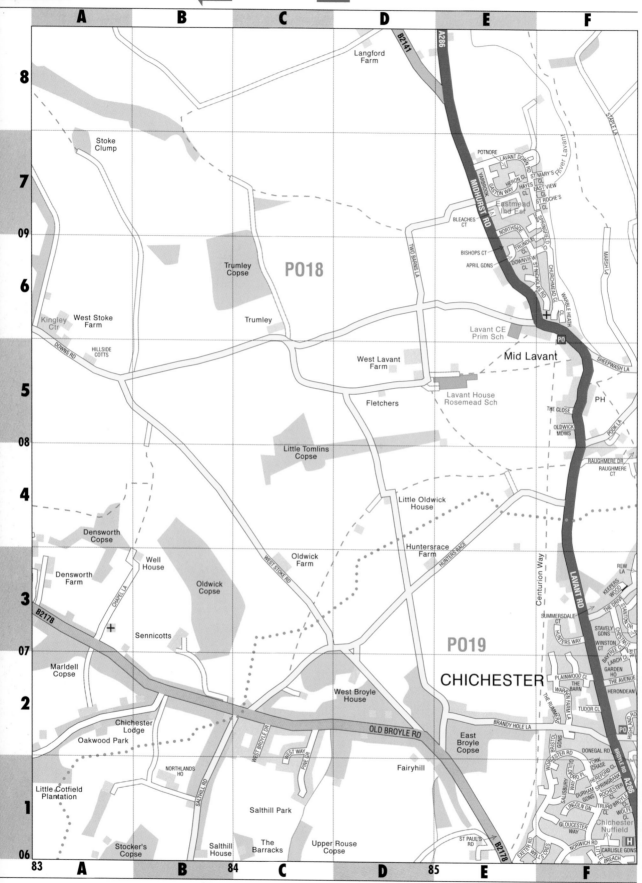

A B C D E F

8

7

09

6

5

08

4

3

07

2

1

06

83 A B 84 C D 85 E F

Langford Farm

Stoke Clump

PO18

Trumley Copse

Kingley Ctr

West Stoke Farm

HILLSIDE COTTS

DOWNS RD

Trumley

West Lavant Farm

Fletchers

Little Tomlins Copse

Densworth Copse

Well House

Oldwick Copse

Densworth Farm

CHAPELLA

SENNICOTTS

B2178

Marldell Copse

Chichester Lodge

Oakwood Park

Little Cotfield Plantation

NORTHLANDS HO

SALTHILL RD

Stocker's Copse

Salthill House

Salthill Park

The Barracks

WEST WAY

PINE GR

WEST BROYLE DR

West Broyle House

Upper Rouse Copse

OLD BROYLE RD

Fairyhill

East Broyle Copse

St Paul's RD

B2178

Oldwick Farm

WEST STOKE RD

Little Oldwick House

Huntersrace Farm

HUNTERS RACE

PO19

CHICHESTER

Centurion Way

BRANDY HOLE LA

LAVANT RD

A286

POTNORE

LAVANT DOWN RD

HERON CL

GASTON WAY

YARBROOK

ST MARY'S CL

HAYES CL

EAST VIEW

ST ROCHE'S CL

MIDHURST RD

Eastmead Ind Est

BLEACHES CT

BISHOPS CT

APRIL GDNS

TWO BARNS LA

NORTHSIDE

SPRINGFIELD

DOWNVIEW CL

TRUNDLE CL

ST NICHOLAS RD

CHURCHMEAD CL

WARBLE HEATH

River Lavant

SHEET LA

MARSH LA

Lavant CE Prim Sch

Mid Lavant

PO

SHEEPWASH LA

PH

THE CLOSE

OLDWICK MDWS

POOK LA

RAUGHMERE DR

RAUGHMERE CT

REW LA

KEEPERS WOOD

THE DRIVE

STANTON DR

SUMMERSDALE CT

HUNTERS WAY

STAVELY GDNS

CHESTNUT

WINSTON CT

BAYTREE CL

LARCH CL

GARDEN HO

THE AVENUE

HERONDEAN

TUDOR CL

THE RUMMERS

PLAINWOOD CL

THE BARN

WARREN FARM LA

PO

DONEGAL RD

BRISTOL

THE SWDS

WORCESTER RD

YORK CHASE

HEREFORD

SPRINGBANK

ROCHESTER

BROYLE RD

SALISBURY

OXFORD PL

DURHAM GDNS

LINCOLN GN

LITTLEFIELD

LICHFIELD CL

TRURO CL

WOLFE CL

GLOUCESTER WAY

Chichester Nuffield

H

EXETER RD

WELL'S CRES

NORWICH RD

CARLISLE GDNS

LINDSEY BREACH

A286

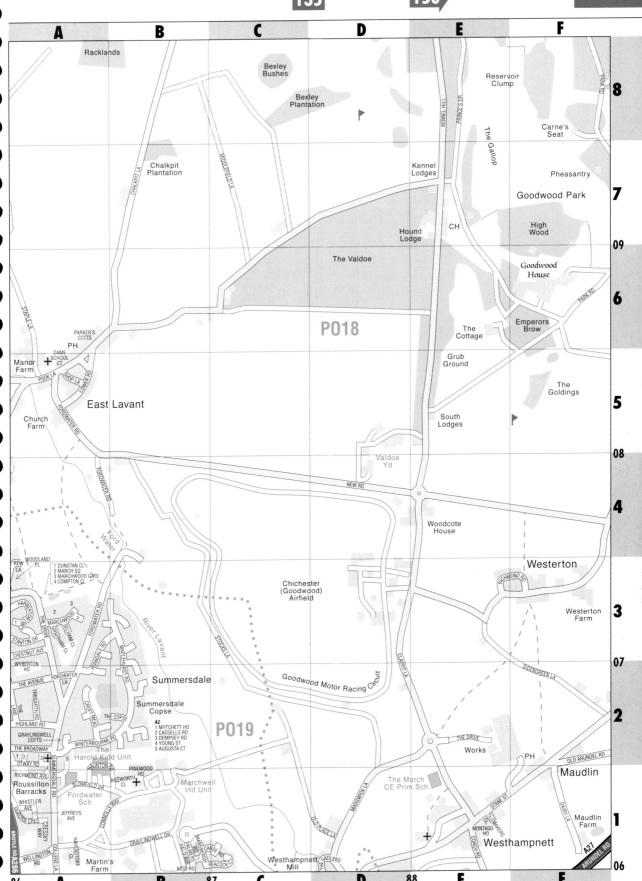

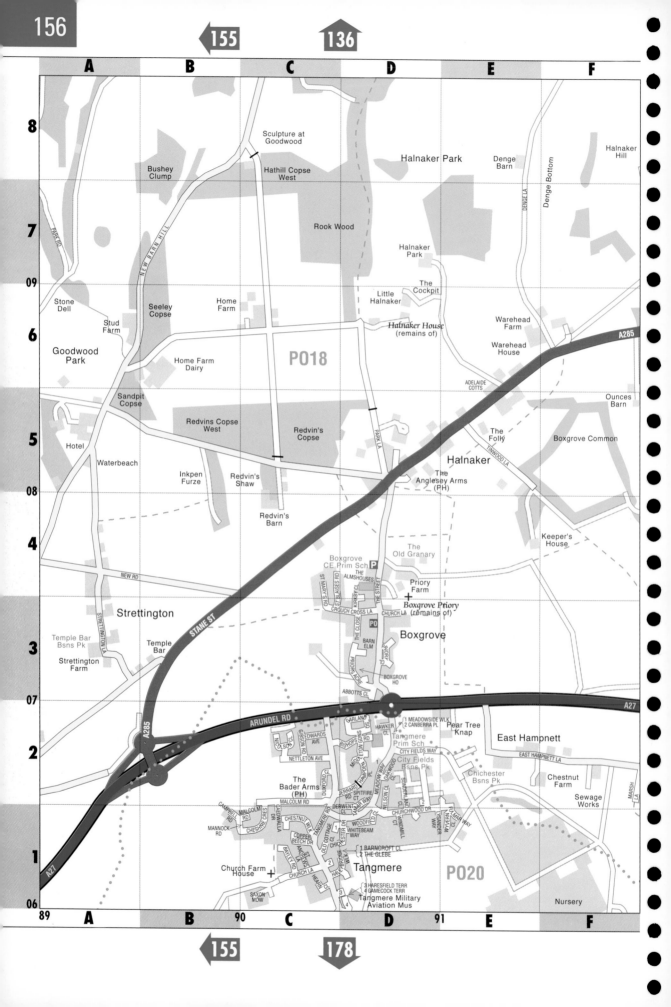

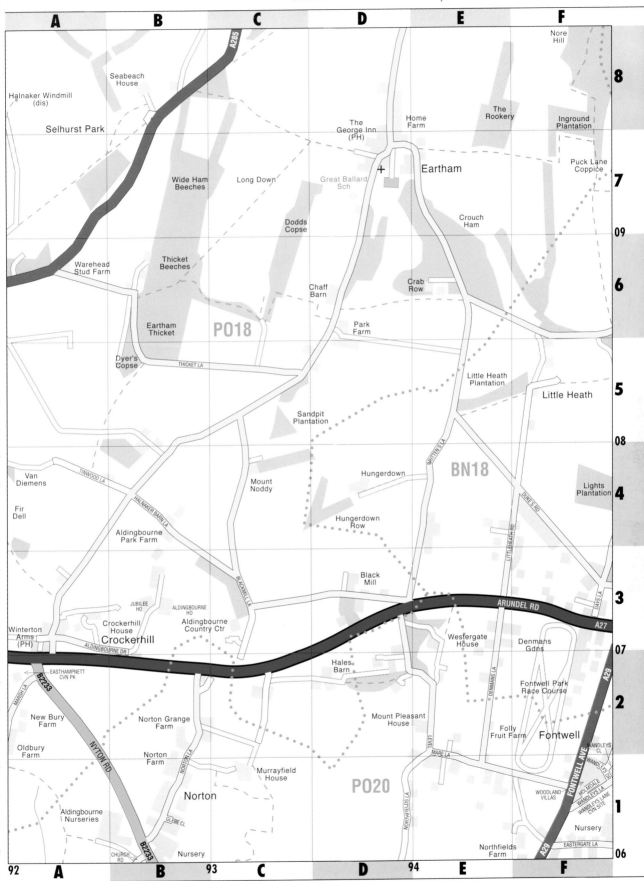

A B C D E F

8

Nore Wood

Dencher Wood

Stag Lodges

The Folly

Little Down

PO18

Dale Park

Steyne

7

Oakfield

09

Courthill Farm

Courthill Cottages

Downe's Barn

NORE WOOD LA

BILL LA

MILL LA

6

Court Hill

Baycombe Wood

Chichester Lodge

A29

Slindon

BAYCOMBE LA

Madehurst Wood

Slindon Coll

TOP RD

DYERS LA

PO

PH

Highfield House

5

Keepers Cottage

Playing Field

CHURCH HILL

Slindon Bottom

Gaston Farm

BN18

The Spur (PH)

The Bellows

TYH TOBAKS

West Stubbs Copse

Slindon Park

MEAD WAY

St Mary's Slindon CE Prim Sch

The Danes

08

REYNOLDS LA

B2132

SLINDON BOTTOM RD

4

Butchers Copse

PARK LA

P

Danes Wood

BRIDLE LA

Slindon Wood

Slindon Common

SUNNYBOX LA

SHELLBRIDGE RD

MILL RD

Mill Farm

3

DUKE'S RD

P

A29

Woodlands Farm

A27

A27

Motel

ORCHARD WAY

Ashbeds

A29

07

LONGON RD

THE CHASE

DEANS CL

HUNTERS MEWS

FURLONG CL

ARUNDEL RD

The Firs

A27

Fontwell

FONTWELL CL

THE RIDINGS

ARUNDEL RD

BARNFIELD COTTS

GOODARCES

Oaks

Little Danes Wood

THE ORCHARD CRES

2

Barn Farm

Works

YAPTON LA

HODGERS HILL

BINSTED LA

WANDLEYS CL

WANDLEYS LA

Wandleys Farm

Wandleys Copse

WEST WALBERTON LA

Potwell Copse

Hoge Farm Ind Est

TYE LA

Hotel

PO20

Nurseries

COPSE LA

Walberton

Avisford

CH

MANSER RD

Nursery

THE DRIVE

FREEMAN LA

EASTERGATE LA

Brookfield Farm

Walberton Green

LONG MEAD

NASH WAY

MILL LA

FIELD CL

NORTH POUND

BAY TREE COTTS

THE STREET

POLING RD

DAIRY LA

Walberton & Binstead CE Prim Sch

The Holly Tree Inn (PH)

AVISFORD PARK RD

B2132

STONEYFIELD COTTS

THE BUNGALOWS 1 HOMEFIELD CRES 2

BARNHAM LA

BIRCH CRS

1

06

95 A B 96 C D 97 E F

139
160

A   B   C   D   E   F

8

Lonebeech
Plantation

Madehurst
Cottage

Duchess
Lodge

Black Barn
Farm

Fairmile Bottom
Nature Trail

Dalesdown
Wood

Horse Shoe
Plantation

Rewell Hill

Park
Rough

Arundel
Park

7

Yewtree
Gate

Punchbowl

Sherwood
Rough

09

Training Gallops

6

The Rough

Rewell Wood

Green Doors
Lodge

5

Screens
Wood

Rewell
House

08

BN18

LONG LA

A284

4

Cricket Hill
Farm

Rough
Copse

Goblestubb's
Copse

Park Farm

PARK FARM
COTTS

The
Arundel
Lodge

The
Waterwoods

3

ARUNDEL RD

HAVENWOOD
PK

Scotland
Barn

CHICHESTER RD

A27

07

Brickkiln
Copse

Winchers
Copse

Paine's
Wood

CANADA RD

ELLIS CL

LANE CL

Barn's
Copse

Singer's
Piece

HILL TERR

DUKES CL

JARVIS RD

PEARSON RD

GREEN

Scotland

HERINGTON RD

Arundel CE
Prim Sch

2

Pedler's
Croft

Binsted Wood

Stewards
Copse

HAZEL GR

OAK END

TORTON HILL RD

BERNARD RD

PRIORY RD

Ash Piece

BINSTED LA

Tortington
Common

BIRCH CL

DALLOWAY RD

HIGH RIDGE CL

STEWARDS RISE

MAXWELL
RD

The
Black Horse
(PH)

Church
Farm

FORD RD

ARUNDEL

1

Binsted

BINSTED LA

06

98   A   B   99   C   00   D   E   F

181
160

Priory Farm

159
140

A · B · C · D · E · F

8

South Stoke Farm
South Stoke
Dry Lodge Plantation
Blue Doors
Fox's Oven

7

Fir Plantation
Peppering Farm
Sewage Works
PH

09

Duke's Plantation
Arundel Park
Herons Wood
Offham Farm
Offham
Jacob's Ladder

6

Offham Preserve
The Black Rabbit Inn

Box Copse
Offham Hanger

5

Hiorne Tower
Mill Hanger
Copyhold
Swanbourne Lake
Arundel Wildfowl & Wetlands Trust
River Arun
BN18

08

The Plantation
London Road Cotts
Monarch's Way
The Woodleighs

4

A284 LONDON RD
Castle Park
ARUNDEL
Woodleighs Hanger
Sefton Place (YH)
South Woodleighs

Trout Fishery

1 CASTLE MEWS
2 BAKERS ARMS HILL
3 KING'S ARMS HILL
4 THE OLD MILL
5 NINEVEH SHIPYARD
6 MAXLETS CT
7 WESTBURY LODGE
8 THE OLD SLIPWAY
9 ARUN ST

MILL RD

3

Arundel & District
H
Tower House Gdns
Cath
Arundel Castle
Mus
Ct
Warningcamp
Common Barn

A27 CHICHESTER RD
A284
Liby
CITY
CROWN YD
RIVER RD

07

Canada Rd
Surrey St
Tarrant St
Wharf
Holmes
Otmers Ind Est
Fitzalan Mews
Queens La
Warningcamp Farm
Council Cotts

2

Warwick Ct
Cemy
PO
Daltons Pl
Fitzalan Rd
ARUNDEL BY-PASS

10 SURREY WHARF
11 SCHOOL LA
12 THE SLIPE
13 WHEELWRIGHTS CL

Batworthpark Plantation
Park Rough
Blackhurst La

Torton Hill Rd
Kirkford Rd
Howard Rd
Wood View
Topro Rd
Arun Terr
Pentfolds Pl
Malthouse Cl
THE CAUSEWAY
Causeway Villas
Arundel Park Inn
Batworthpark Ho
Clay La

1

Arundel P
Priory Farm
Calcetto Priory (remains of)
Convent
Crossbush
The Brocks

BN17
Station Rd
Lyminster Rd
A27
Hotel
Crossbush La
The Terrace

06

01 · A · B · 02 · C · D · 03 · E · F

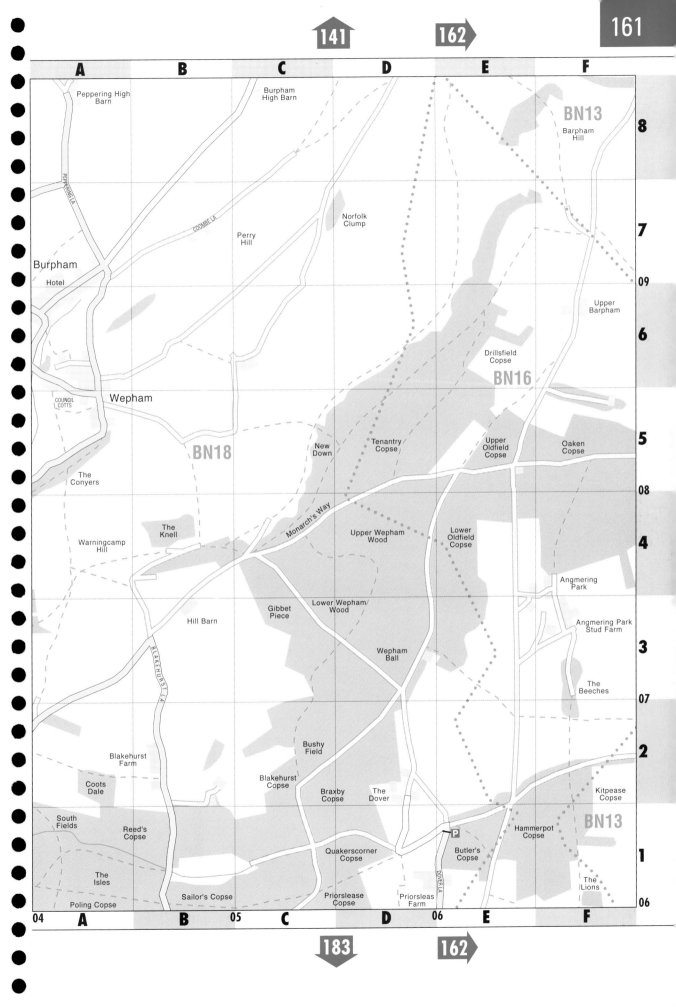

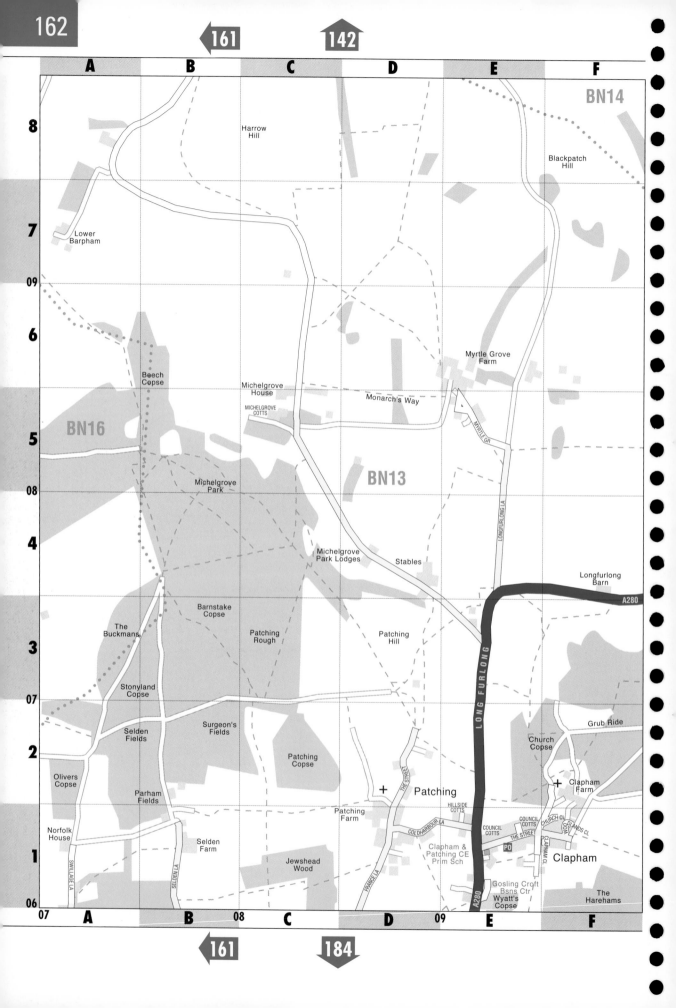

BN14

A   B   C   D   E   F

8

Harrow
Hill

Blackpatch
Hill

7

Lower
Barpham

09

6

Beech
Copse

Myrtle Grove
Farm

Michelgrove
House

Monarch's Way

MICHELGROVE
COTTS

BN16

MYRTLE GR

5

BN13

Michelgrove
Park

LONGFURLONG LA

08

4

Michelgrove
Park Lodges

Stables

Longfurlong
Barn

A280

Barnstake
Copse

Patching
Rough

Patching
Hill

3

LONG FURLONG

The
Buckmans

Stonyland
Copse

07

Grub Ride

Selden
Fields

Surgeon's
Fields

Church
Copse

2

Patching
Copse

Olivers
Copse

Clapham
Farm

Patching

Parham
Fields

HILLSIDE
COTTS

COLDHARBOUR LA

COUNCIL
COTTS

CHURCH CL

OLANDS CL

Norfolk
House

Patching
Farm

THE STREET

COUNCIL
COTTS

THE STREET

CLAPHAM CL

1

Selden
Farm

FRANCE LA

Clapham & Patching CE
Prim Sch

PO

Clapham

SWILLAGE LA

SELDEN LA

Jewshead
Wood

A280

Gosling Croft
Bsns Ctr

Wyatt's
Copse

The
Harehams

06

07   A   B   08   C   D   09   E   F

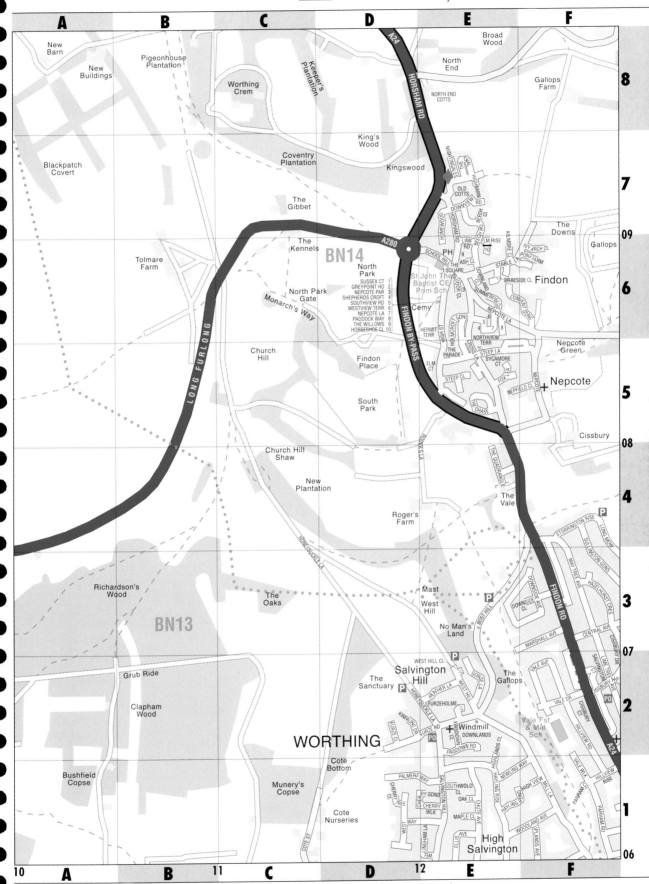

A   B   C   D   E   F

New Barn
New Buildings
Pigeonhouse Plantation
Worthing Crem
Keeper's Plantation

8

Blackpatch Covert

King's Wood

Coventry Plantation

Kingswood

North End

Broad Wood

Gallops Farm

North End Cotts

HORSHAM RD

A24

7

The Gibbet

The Kennels

BN14

A280

Tolmare Farm

North Park

FINDON BY-PASS

Findon

09

The Downs

Gallops

6

Monarch's Way

North Park Gate

1 SUSSEX CT
2 GREYPOINT HO
3 NEPCOTE PAR
4 SHEPHERDS CROFT
5 SOUTHVIEW RD
6 WESTVIEW TERR
7 NEPCOTE LA
8 PADDOCK WAY
9 THE WILLOWS
10 HORSESHOE CL

St John The
Baptist CE
Prim Sch

Cemy

PH

Nepcote Green

Nepcote

LONG FURLONG

Church Hill

Findon Place

South Park

Cissbury

5

Church Hill Shaw

08

New Plantation

The Vale

4

Roger's Farm

STORRINGTON RISE

P

HONEYSUCKLE LA

Richardson's Wood

The Oaks

BN13

Mast
West Hill

No Man's Land

P

Downside Cl

FINDON RD

3

07

Grub Ride

Salvington Hill

West Hill Cl
P

The Sanctuary
P

The Gallops

P

P

2

Clapham Wood

WORTHING

Windmill
DOWNLANDS

Vale Fst
& Mid
Sch

A24

Bushfield Copse

Cote Bottom

Munery's Copse

Cote Nurseries

High Salvington

1

06

163
144

A   B   C   D   E   F

8

New Barn
Church Wood
Findon Park Farm
No Man's Land
BN44
New Hill Barn

7

Monarch's Way
Gallops
Park Brow

09

Lychpole Bottom

6

Canada Bottom

P

5

Cissbury Ring
BN15

08

Cissbury Farm
Hill Barn Covert
BN14

4

Cissbury Plantation
Lychpole Farm

Shipdens Holt
Deep Bottom

Vineyard Hill

3

Sheepcombe Hanger
Lychpole Hill

07

Mount Carvey
Tenants Hill

2

LONG MEADOW
SULLINGTON GDNS
CENTRAL AVE
CISSBURY GDNS
HOLLINGBURY GDNS
SHEPHERD'S MEAD
CISSBURY AVE
LIME TREE AVE

Findon Valley

COOMBE RISE
P

Liby
ALDWICK CRES
THE HEIGHTS
ASHFOLD AVE
KEARSLEY DR
THE HEIGHTS

1

A24
FINDON RD
FRANKLANDS CL
ALLENDALE AVE
GREENTHAM RD
CHANTLEY RD
VALLEY GDNS
FLORAL DENE CT
A24
WISDEN CT
MAYFIELD CL

CH
Lambleys Barn
LAMBLEYS LA

06

13   A   B   14   C   D   15   E   F

163
186

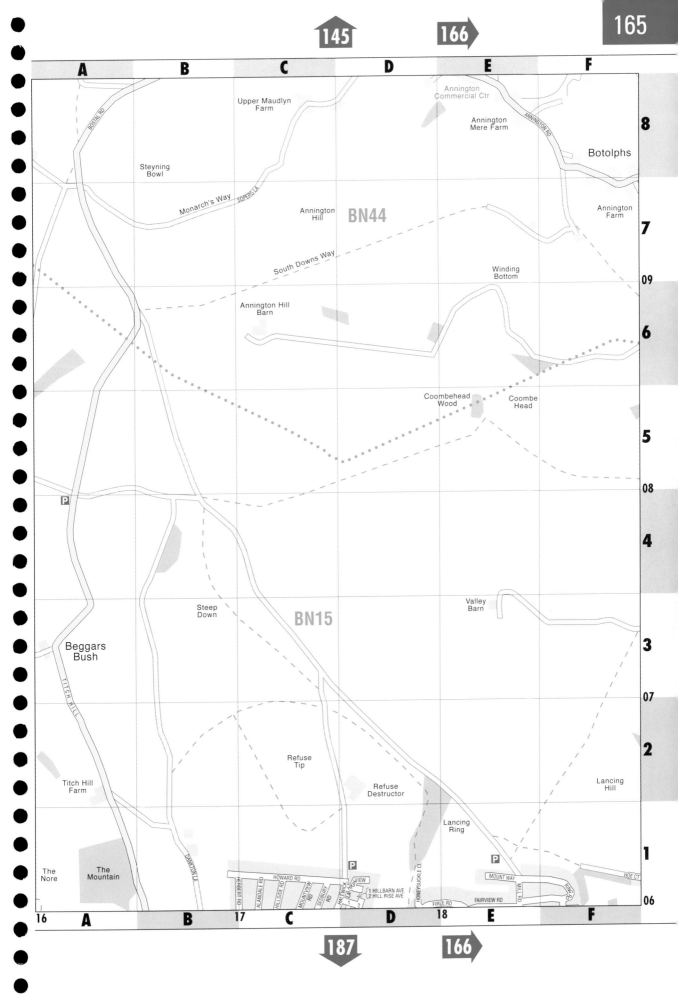

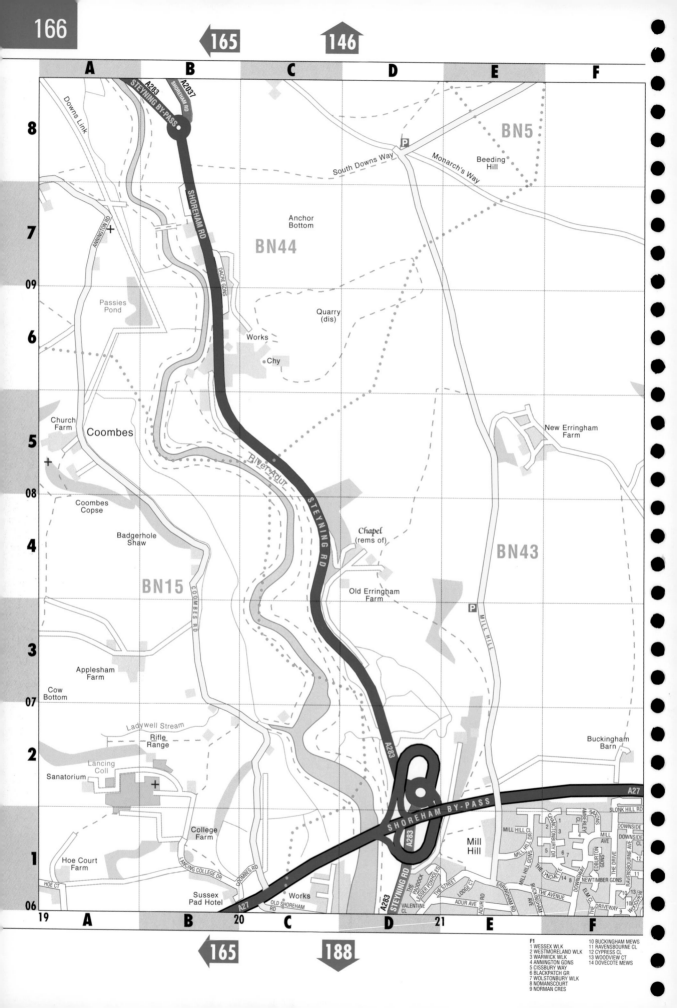

165 146

A   B   C   D   E   F

8

7

09

6

5

08

4

3

07

2

1

06

19   A   B   20   C   D   21   E   F

165 188

Downs Link
A283 STEYNING BY-PASS
A2037 SHOREHAM RD
SHOREHAM RD
ANNINGTON RD
DACRE GDNS
Passies Pond
Church Farm
Coombes
River Adur
Coombes Copse
Badgerhole Shaw
BN15
COOMBES RD
Applesham Farm
Cow Bottom
Ladywell Stream
Rifle Range
Lancing Coll
Sanatorium
College Farm
LANCING COLLEGE DR
COOMBES RD
Hoe Court Farm
HOE CT
Sussex Pad Hotel
A27
OLD SHOREHAM RD
Works

Anchor Bottom
BN44
Quarry (dis)
Works
Chy
STEYNING RD
Chapel (rems of)
Old Erringham Farm

South Downs Way
P
Monarch's Way
BN5
Beeding Hill

New Erringham Farm
BN43
MILL HILL
P
Buckingham Barn

A283
SHOREHAM BY-PASS
A283 STEYNING RD
A27
Mill Hill
SLONK HILL RD
DOWNSIDE
DOWNSIDE CL
MILL AVE
THE DRIVE
NEWTIMBER GDNS
THE AVENUE
THE DRIVEWAY
ERRINGHAM RD
VALENTINE CL
LODGE CT
ADUR AVE
THE STREET
THE PADDOCK
THE LESSER FOXHOLES
CHANCTONBURY DR
MILL HILL CL
MILL HILL GDNS
AMBERLEY CL
WOODVIEW
ELM CL

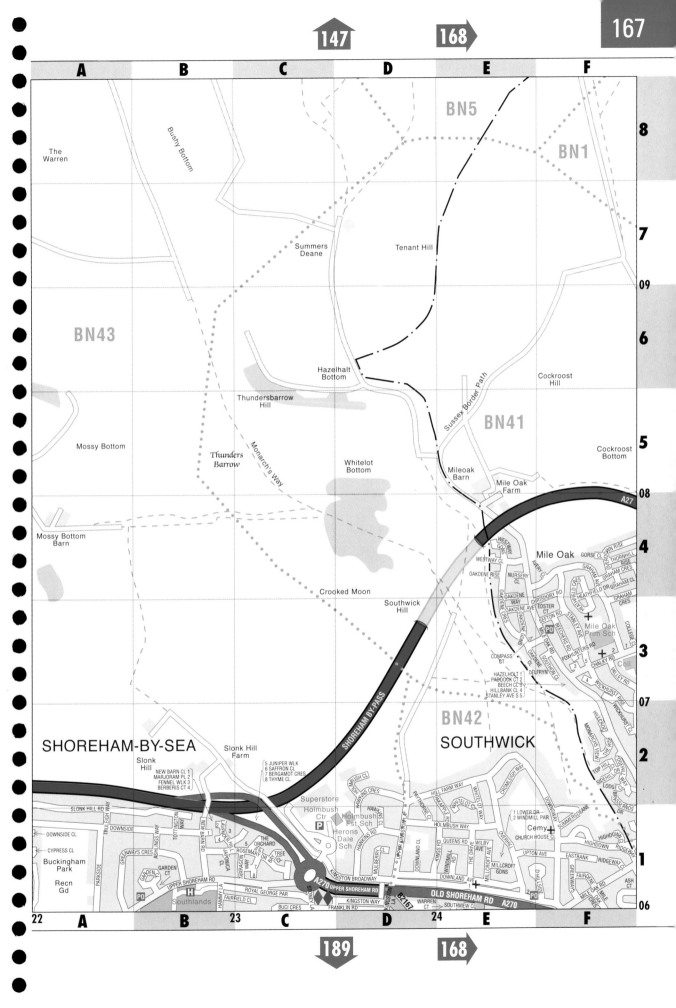

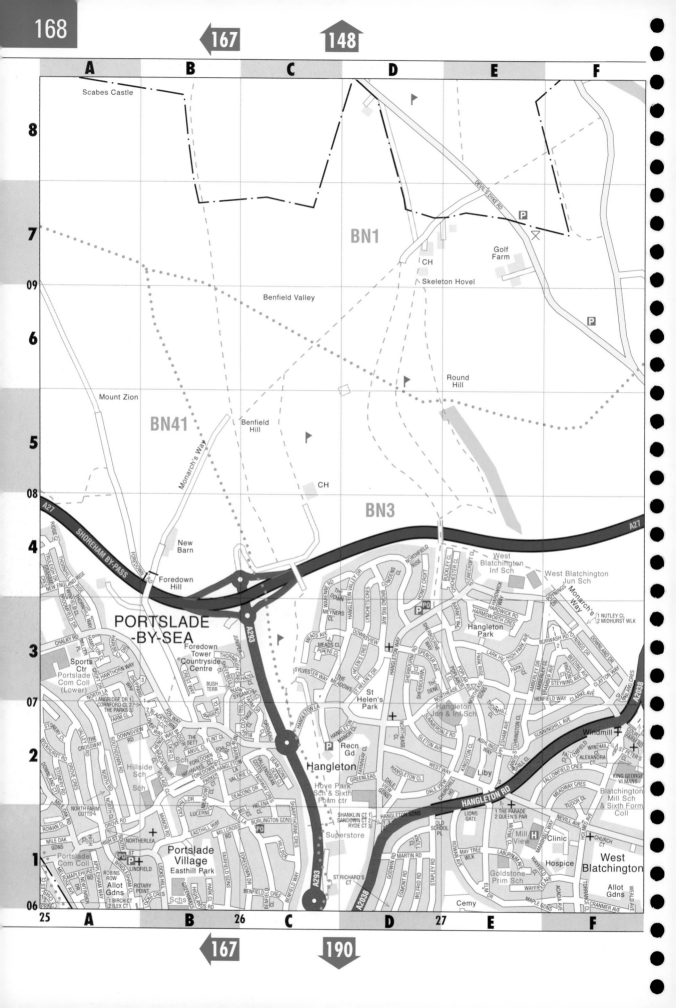

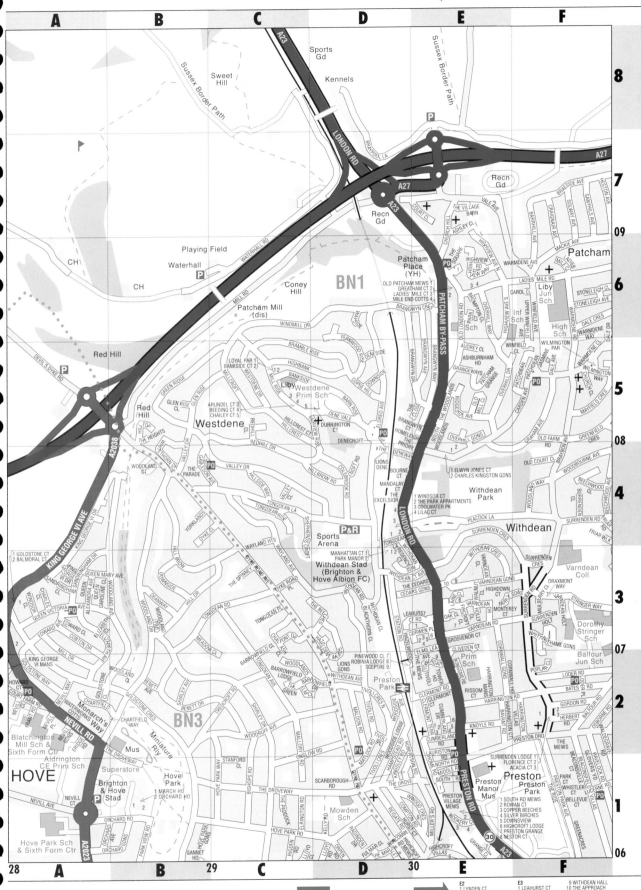

E2
1 LYNDEN CT
2 STAMFORD LODGE
3 CUMBERLAND LODGE
4 CENTENARY HO
5 SHAWCROSS HO
6 CARLTON HO

E3
1 LEAHURST CT
2 CHERRYWOOD
3 CEDARWOOD
4 MAPLEWOOD
5 PINEWOOD
6 BEECHWOOD
7 WITHDEAN CT
8 WELLINGTONIA CT

9 WITHDEAN HALL
10 THE APPROACH

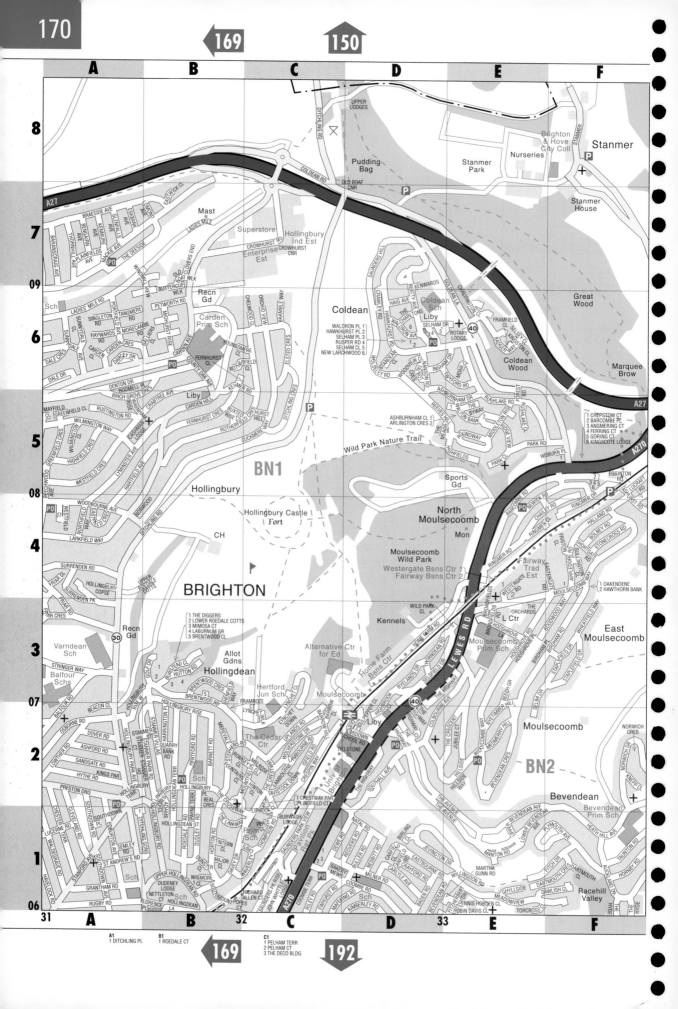

172

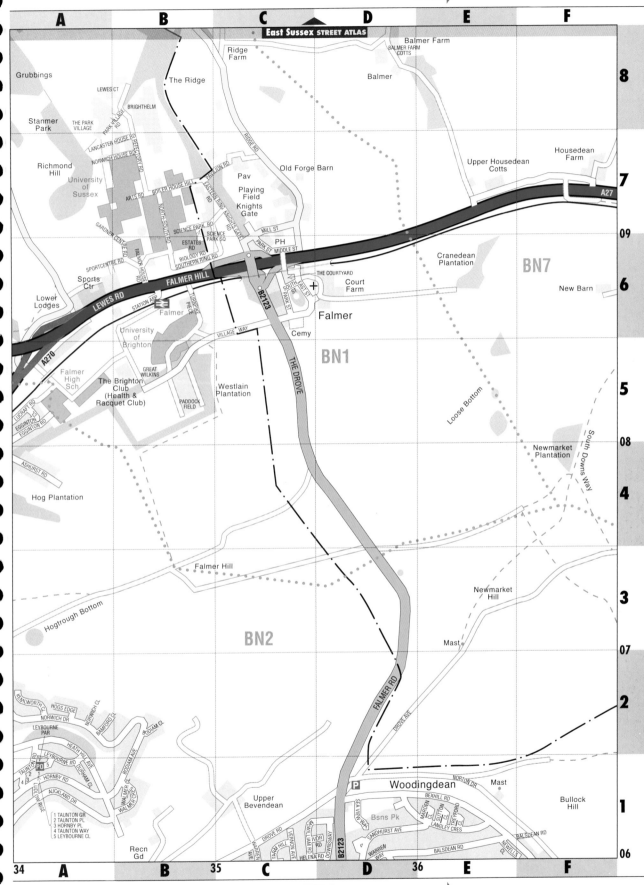

East Sussex STREET ATLAS

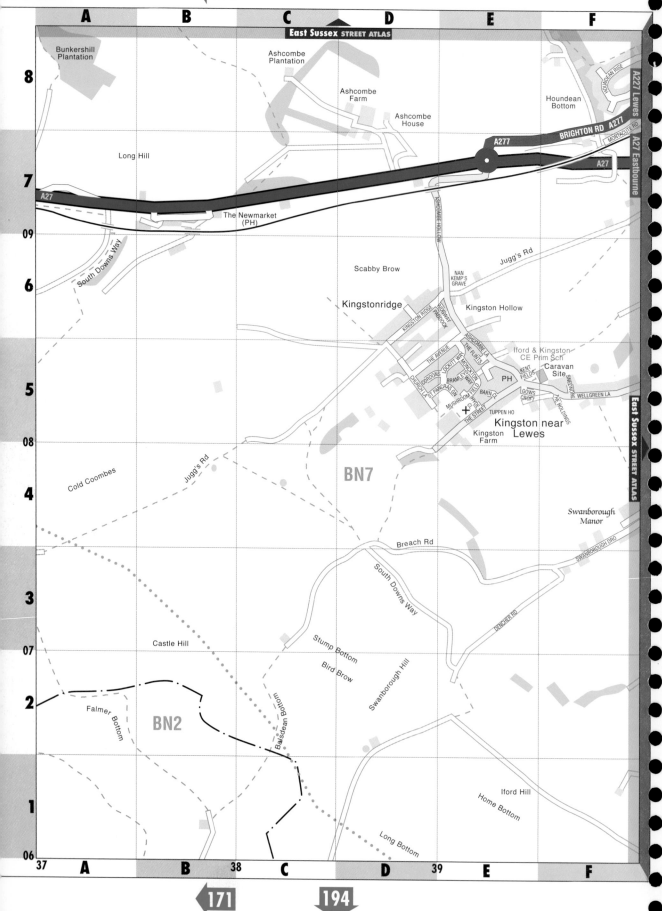

◀ 171

East Sussex STREET ATLAS

	A	B	C	D	E	F

8

Bunkershill
Plantation

Ashcombe
Plantation

Ashcombe
Farm

Ashcombe
House

Houndean
Bottom

HOUNDEAN RISE

A277 Lewes

Long Hill

A277

BRIGHTON RD A277

MONTACUTE RD

A27 Eastbourne

A277

A27

7

A27

The Newmarket
(PH)

ASHCOMBE HOLLOW

Jugg's Rd

09

Scabby Brow

NAN
KEMP'S
GRAVE

Kingston Hollow

6

South Downs Way

Kingstonridge

KINGSTON RIDGE

RIDGWAY

PADDOCK

ASHCOMBE LA

THE FLINTS

Iford & Kingston
CE Prim Sch

Caravan
Site

East Sussex STREET ATLAS

5

THE AVENUE

LOCKITT WK

BRAMLEYS WAY

MONCKTON
WAY

THE TYE

KENT
FIELDS

SNEDMORE

THE HOLDINGS

WELLGREEN LA

CHURCH LA

ST PANCRAS GN

CORDONS

MUSHROOM FIELD

BARN CL

GOWS
CROFT

08

THE STREET

TUPPEN HO

Kingston near
Lewes

4

Cold Coombes

Jugg's Rd

BN7

Kingston
Farm

Swanborough
Manor

Breach Rd

SWANBOROUGH DRO

3

Castle Hill

South Downs Way

DENCHER RD

07

Stump Bottom

Bird Brow

2

Falmer Bottom

BN2

Balsdean Bottom

Swanborough Hill

1

Iford Hill

Home Bottom

Long Bottom

06

37	A		B	38	C		D	39	E		F

◀ 171   194 ▼

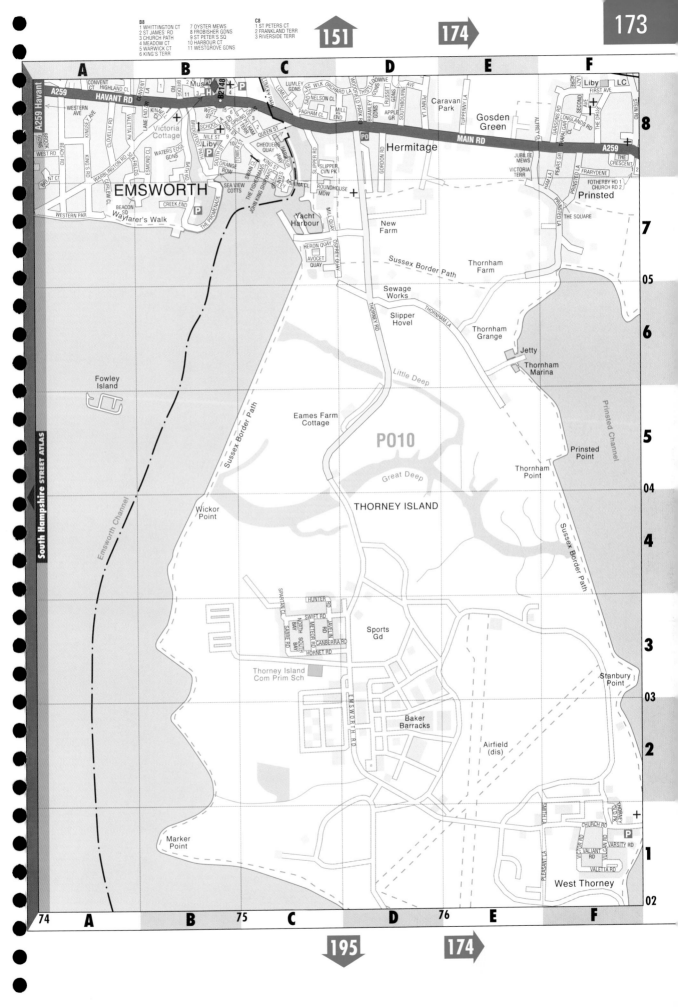

A   B   C   D   E   F

8

Southbourne

Loogebury Cl
NORTHCOTE GDNS
Southbourne Jun & Inf Schs
Cvn Site
INLANDS RD
LC
Works
Nutbourne
LC
Longacres
DRIFT LA
LC
GREEN LA

Southbourne
NEW RD
GOODWD
Cvn Site
PH
MOSDELL RD
A259
30

Ham Brook

PO
Nutbourne Pk
LANGSTONE GDNS
FLAT RD
Flat Farm
BROAD RD
POTTERY LA
BROAD MDW

MAIN RD

The Bosham Inn (PH)

PO10

SCHOOL LA
FARM LA
BELL CT
Nutbourne
Nursery
MANSFIELD COTTS PH
MAYBUSH DR
IVYDENE CRES

7

A259

05

Marsh Farm

COT LA
HAMSTEAD MDW
Chidham Prim Sch

6

CHIDHAM LA
Eastfield Farm

5

Chidham Point

PO18

STEELS LA
Middleton House
Landing Stages
HARBOUR WAY

04

Old House at Home (PH)
MARSH LA
Easton Farm
Chidham
Hard

4

Chidmere Pond

Hovel Barn

3

Thorney Channel

03

New Barn

Cobnor Farm

Bosham Channel

2

Cullimer's Pond

Hard

Cobnor Hard

1

Cobnor House

02

77   A   B   78   C   D   79   E   F

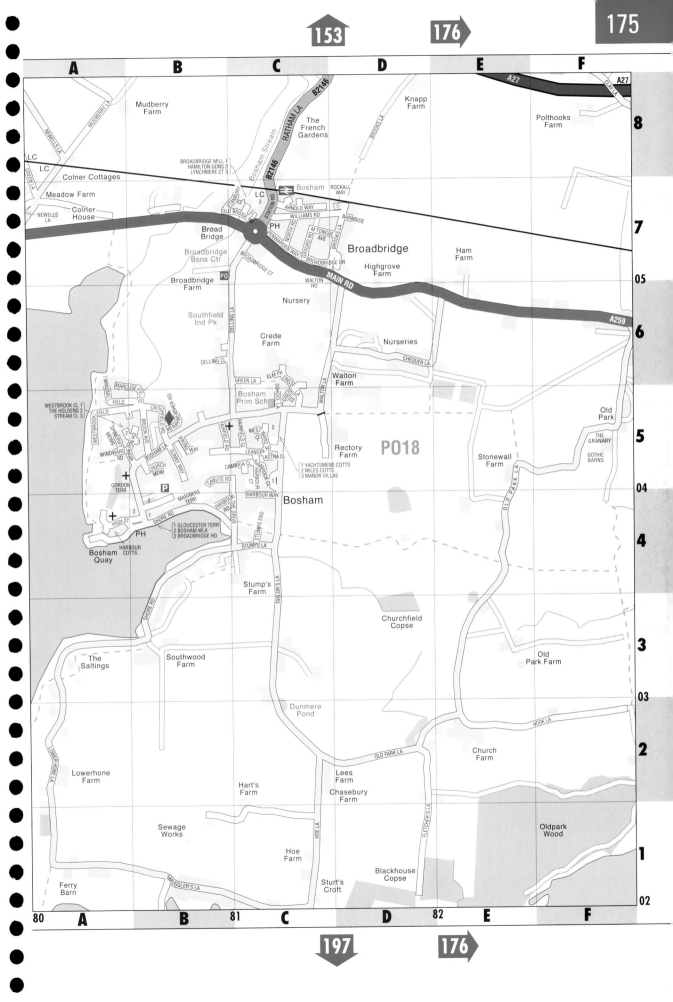

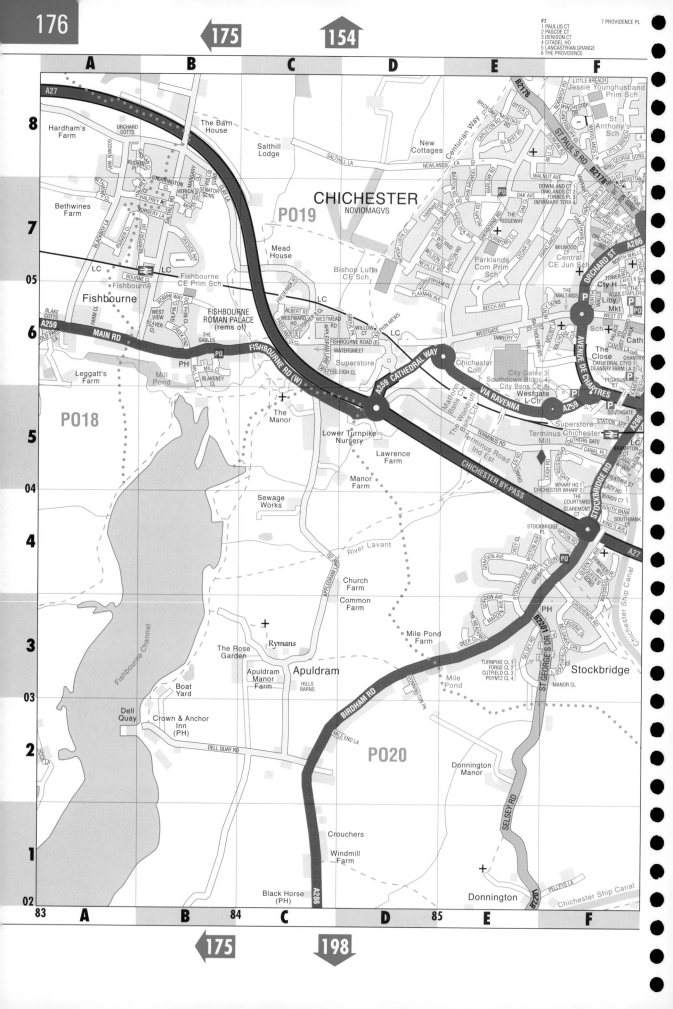

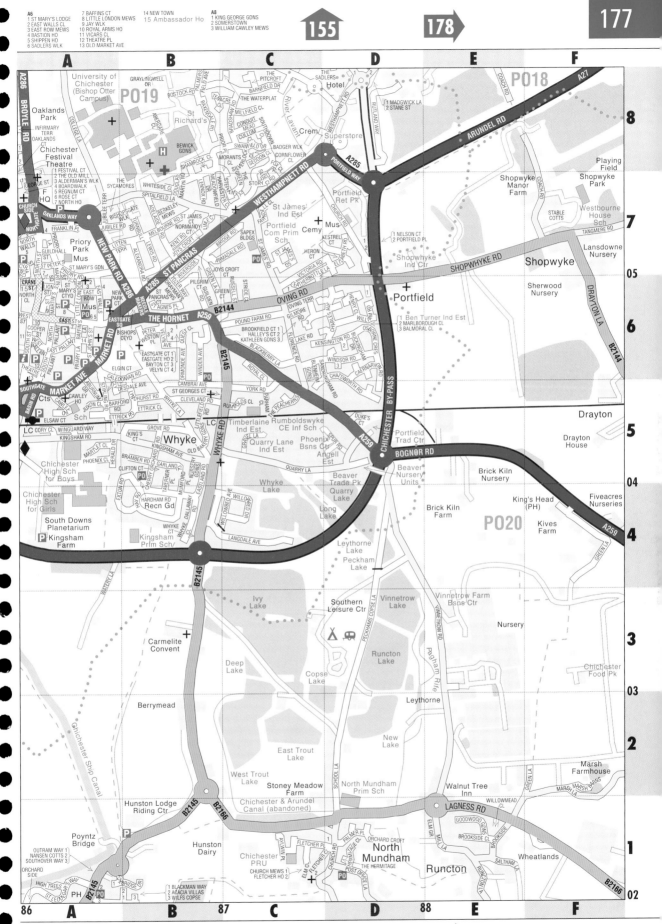

155
178
199
178

A6
1 ST MARY'S LODGE
2 EAST WALLS CL
3 EAST ROW MEWS
4 BASTION HO
5 SHIPPEN HO
6 SADLERS WLK
7 BAFFINS CT
8 LITTLE LONDON MEWS
9 JAY WLK
10 ROYAL ARMS HO
11 VICARS CL
12 THEATRE PL
13 OLD MARKET AVE

14 NEW TOWN
15 Ambassador Ho

A8
1 KING GEORGE GDNS
2 SOMERSTOWN
3 WILLIAM CAWLEY MEWS

← 177
156

PO18

Copse Farm

Shopwyke Park

TANGMERE RD

OVING RD

Ham Farm

HAM LA

Woodfield Farm

MARLPIT LA

GRIBBLE LA
SAMPSONS DRI
WHITAKER PL
DREWITTS MEWS
CHURCH LA
HIGHFIELD LA

Oving

Gribble Inn PH

HIGH ST

BRIAR CL
ST ANDREW'S CL
CHALLEN CL

WOODHORN LA

Madam Green Farm

Woodhorn Cotts

Woodhorn Farm

B2144

Highground Cottage

LC

LC

DRAYTON LA

Withies Farm

Longport Cottage

PO20

04

SILVER LAKES MOBIL HOME PK

DRAYTON PL

Ruffs Cottages

A259

B2144

BOGNOR RD

Downlands Farm

Abelands

Highkettle Farm

Reed's Farm

Merston Common

Colworth Farm

Woodend Farm

Tapner's Barn

Merston

MARSH LA

Manor Farm

Groves Farm

Colworth

Marsh Barn

Hollycroft Farm

Manor Farm

Nurseries

B2166

PO21

Elbridge

Elbridge Farm

A259

← 177
200

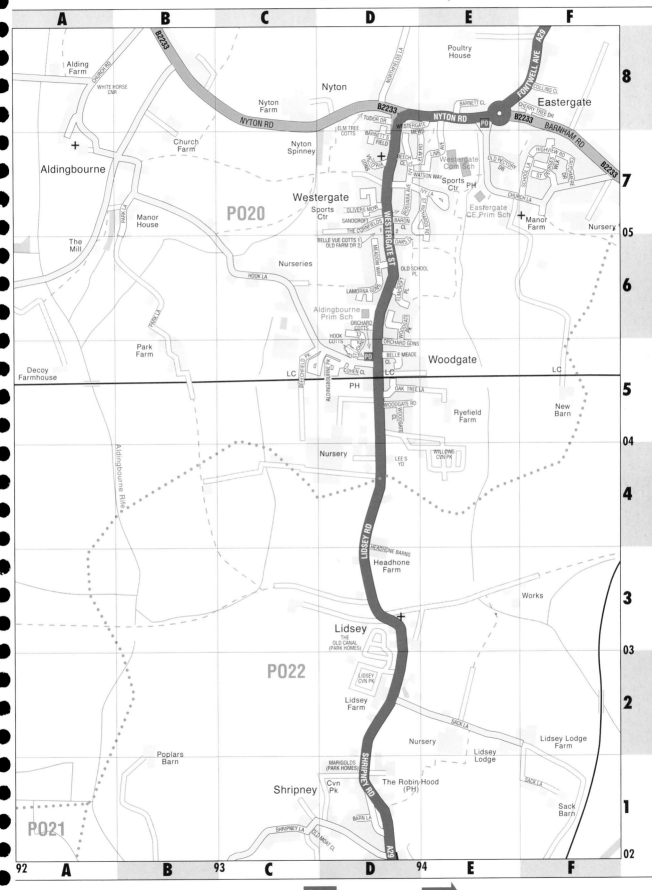

A   B   C   D   E   F

8

Alding
Farm
CHURCH RD
WHITE HORSE
CNR
B2233
Poultry
House
FONTWELL AVE
A29
COLLINS CL
Eastergate
BARNETT CL
Nyton
NYTON RD
B2233
NYTON RD
PO
B2233
CHERRY TREE DR
BARNHAM RD
B2233

Aldingbourne
Church
Farm
Nyton
Farm
Nyton
Spinney
TUDOR DR
ELM TREE
COTTS
BARNETT'S
FIELD
WESTERGATE
MEWS
VICTORIA
GDNS
BEECH CL
IVY CL
ELM RD
LIME AVE
WATSON WAY
Westergate
Com Sch
Sports
Ctr
PH
OLD RECTORY DR
HIGHVIEW RD
SCHOOL LA
ST GEORGES WLK
CRITCHMERE DR
7

Manor
House
PARK LA
Westergate
Sports
Ctr
OLIVERS MDW
SANDCROFT
THE CORNFIELDS
PESVARA AVE
WESTERGATE ST
IVY LA
ST RICHARDS RD
Eastergate
CE Prim Sch
Manor
Farm
CHURCH LA
Nursery
05

The
Mill
PARK LA
Nurseries
BELLE VUE COTTS 1
OLD FARM DR 2
MEADOW WAY
BARON
CL
OAKS CL
Old School
PL
6

HOOK LA
Lamorna Gdns
ELM CROFT
PL
WOODGATE
PK
PARK LA
Aldingbourne
Prim Sch
ORCHARD
COTTS
HOOK
COTTS
ST JOHNS
ORCHARD GDNS
Woodgate
LC

Park
Farm
BEECHFIELD PK
ALDINGBOURNE PK
PO
COHEN CL
BELLE MEADE
CL
LC
LC
5

Decoy
Farmhouse
LC
PH
OAK TREE LA
WOODGATE RD
New
Barn

Aldingbourne Rife
Nursery
LEE'S
YD
WILLOWS
CVN PK
04

4

LIDSEY RD
HEADHONE BARNS
Headhone
Farm
Works

3

Lidsey
THE
OLD CANAL
(PARK HOMES)

03

PO22
LIDSEY
CVN PK
Lidsey
Farm
SACK LA
Lidsey Lodge
Farm
2

Poplars
Barn
MARIGOLDS
(PARK HOMES)
SHRIPNEY RD
Nursery
Lidsey
Lodge
SACK LA

Shripney
Cvn
Pk
The Robin Hood
(PH)
Sack
Barn
1

PO21
SHRIPNEY LA
OLD MOAT CL
BARN LA
A29
02

92   A   93   B   C   94   D   E   F

PO20
Westergate
Nyton

179 158

A B C D E F

8

PO20

Ryburn Farm

North Choller Farm

The Meads

Choller House Farm

Pigeon House Farm

Walberton

ORCHARD VILLAS
PARSONS WLK
MAPLE PAR
PO
THE STREET
CHURCH LA
HENTY CL
THE STREET

BLACKSMITH'S CNR

B2132

Nursery

7

B2233

Fordingbridge Ind Site

Choller Farm

BARNHAM LA

Stemps Wood

Brookside

Nursery

The Lazy W

Walberton Farm

WALBERTON PK

Nursery

YAPTON LA

05

30

Barnham Prim Sch

WENTWORTH CL
SIDNEY WLK
PADDOCKS

Nursery

Nanny Copse

Meadow Farm

Nursery

Resr

Nursery

B2132

6

Nursery

ELM GR
ELM GR S
ELM DALE
THE CEDARS
DOWNVIEW RD
EWENS GDN
SYKE
CLUAN CL
ORIEL CT
TRUNDLE VIEW CL
BENTWORTH
APPLETREE DR
FARNHURST RD
ORCHARD WAY
WOODSIDE
HEDGE END
NURSERY COTTS
STEMPSON DR
KINGSMILL RD
FOX'S CROFT
WARREN WAY
MARDEN HO

Park Rd

LAKE COTTS

Todhurst Farm House

The Sussex Bsns Village

ROSE TERR

LAKE LA

The St Philip Howard RC High Sch

P
PO
WINDMILL CT
THE SQUARE
GOSDEN RD
SAXBY CT
DIAL CL
HALLIFORD DR
BACON RISE
ABBIE CT
GOODACRES
CHURCHILL HO

Nursery

Lake Barn

LC

5

Barnham

MARSHALL CL
GREENBANK
CHERRYTREE COTTS
GARDEN CL
SCHOLAR'S ROW

Barnham

Nursery

LONGACRE PK

Maypole Inn (PH)

MADFLA

04

PO22

PH

CHURCH LA

Nurseries

HILL LA

Tilebarn Farm

YAPTON RD

Parsonage Farm

Windmill (dis)

Nursery

BN18

B2132

4

Highground Barn

HIGHGROUND LA

Barnham Court

Church Farm

BROOK LA

Denges Barn

Yapton CE Prim Sch

Stakers Farm

ORCHARD BSNS PK
CHURCH LA
THE LYCHGATES
THE CROFT
NORTH END RD

Bonhams House

PH

B2132

CHURCH RD

3

Fatting Ground La

MAIN RD

Tillington Cotts

The Pines

TACKLEE RD
WOODLANDS PK
CANAL RD

B2233
PO

03

Fatting Ground Barn

South Barn

Drove La

Drove Lane Farm

Yapton

FOUND PT

COBHAM CL
GILES CL
FIRM RD
BLENHM
LOVEYS RD

2

MILL VIEW RD
MEDWAY COTTS
THE MULBERS
GLADSTONE RD

BILSHAM CT

B2132

Hams

WEST VIEW DR
GRAFTN

BILSHAM RD

The Lamb (PH)

1

WEST VIEW GDNS

Ind Est

Bilsham Farm House

Chapel

BILSHAM LA

Bilsham Manor

B2132

Hobbs Farm

02

95 A B 96 C D 97 E F

159
182

A B C D E F

8

Binsted Park

Lake Copse

Manor House

Meadow Lodge

Priory (remains of)

New Barn

Tortington

TORTINGTON MANOR
THE ARUNDEL WING

7

Oakley Cottages

BINSTED LA

HOE LA

Fairmeads Farm

Slate Barn Farm

Goose Green

THE GOODWOOD WING

THE STABLE CTYD

THE MANOR HQ

FORD RD

THE NEW ENGLAND WING

THE NORFOLK WING

05

Lower Farm

Marsh Farm

Manor Farm

6

YAPTON LA

LAKE LA

LC

Sunnymead Farm

BN18

GAUGEMASTER WAY

THE WILLOWS

Arundel Arms (PH)

5

B2132

NORTH END RD

WEST BANK

EAST BANK

North End

Long Barn

Ford

LC

04

WICKS COTTS

FORD LA

Wicks Farm

Trad Est

Ford Lane Bsns Pk

STATION RD

Marina

River Arun

4

CHURCH LA

1 THE POPLARS
2 THE LIMES

CHURCH RD

1 2

Victorian Bsns Ctr

ROONEY CRES

Ford

3

DOWNVIEW CL

DOWNVIEW WAY

DOWNVIEW CL

P

1 KINGS CL
2 VICTORIA VILLAS
3 BEVERLEY CL
4 HOLKHAM COTTS

Ford Airfield Ind Est

FORD RD

NELSON ROW

ARUN FORD CL

03

MAIN RD

BILSHAM RD

BELMONT

PARK RD

PARK DR

FELLOWS GDNS

FAIR LA

1 3 2 4

GOODWIN CL

Burndell

BURNDELL RD

UPOWA

FLEMING GDNS

DRAKE GR

MOSANG RD

JOHNSON WAY

JUNCTION RD

BERGLE DR

WILLS CL

DOUGLAS CL

SPROULE CL

MILES CL

LEWIS LA

HOLLASTON PK

WILSON CT

HM Prison

HM Prison

Church Farm

2

CHERRY AVE

Ford Aerodrome (disused)

Rudford Ind Est

CHURCH LA

BN17

1

YAPTON RD

Horsemere Green

NINI-HI CVN SITE

MANT CL

WOOLBRIDGE

HORSEMERE GREEN LA

MAY CL

APPLE TREE WLK

WATERFORD GDNS

CROFTHORNE DR

Climping

1 THE BEACHES
2 THE HAMLET

CLIMPING PK

Northwood Farm

B2233

Hall

02

98 A B 99 C D 00 E F

203
182

← 181   ↑ 160

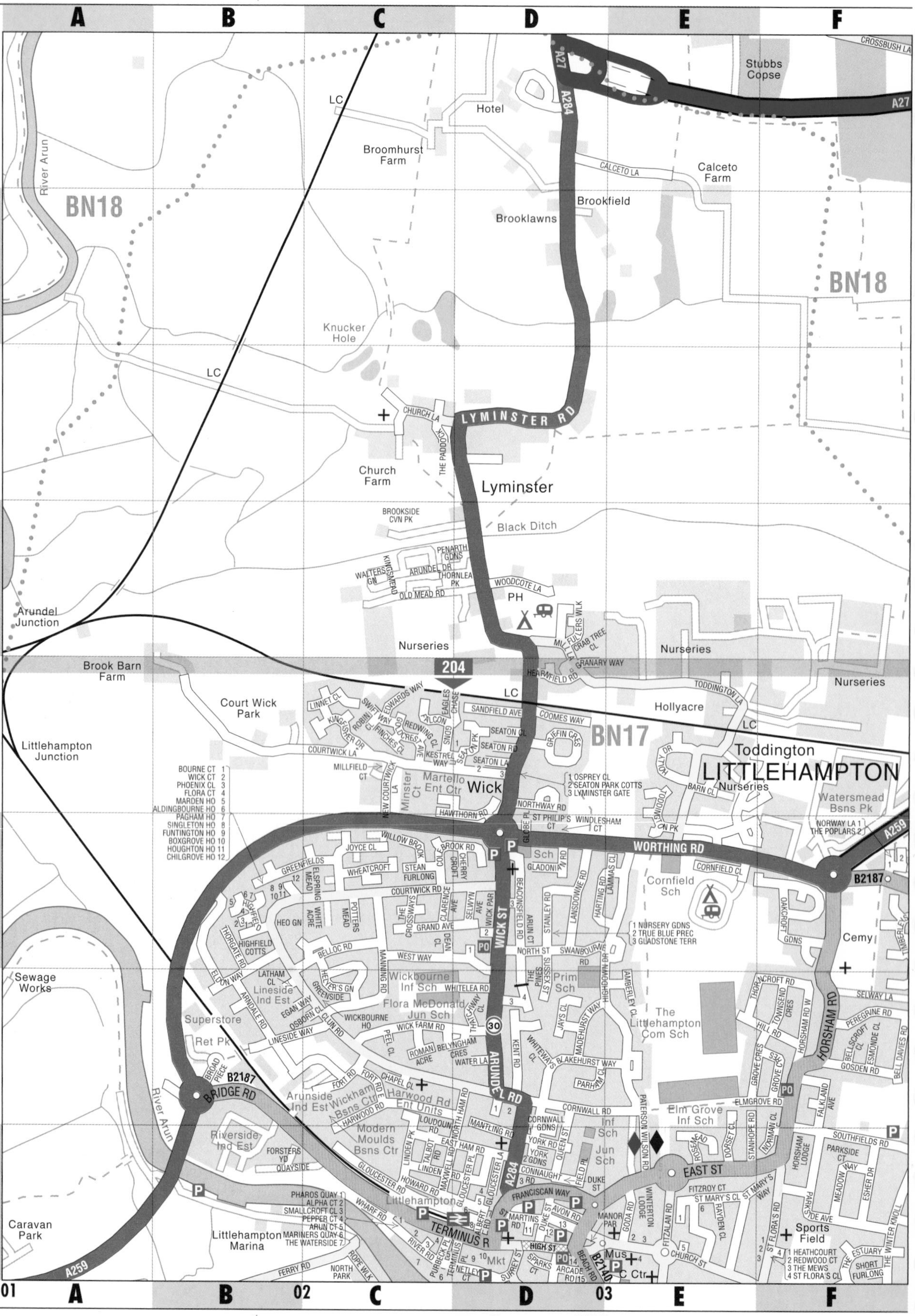

Grid columns: A B C D E F
Grid rows: 8 7 05 6 5 04 4 03 3 2 03 2 1 02

River Arun

BN18

Stubbs Copse

CROSSBUSH LA

A27

A284

Hotel

Broomhurst Farm

CALCETO LA

Calceto Farm

Brookfield

Brooklawns

BN18

LC

Knucker Hole

LYMINSTER RD

CHURCH LA
THE PADDOCKS
Church Farm

Lyminster

BROOKSIDE CVN PK

Black Ditch

PENARTH GDNS
ARUNDEL DR
THORNLEA PK
OLD MEAD RD
WALTERS GN
KINGSMEAD
WOODCOTE LA
PH

Arundel Junction

Brook Barn Farm

Nurseries

MILL FULLERS WLK
CRAB TREE CL
GRANARY WAY

Nurseries

TODDINGTON LA
Hollyacre
Nurseries

HEARTFIELD RD
LC

204

Court Wick Park

Littlehampton Junction

LINNET CL
EDWARDS WAY
SWIFT WAY
REDWING CL
FINCHES CL
KINGFISHER DR
ROBIN CL
ACRES AVE
EAGLES CHASE
FALCON
SANDFIELD AVE
COOMES WAY
SEATON CL
SEATON RD
SEATON LA
KESTREL WAY
HAWTHORN CL
GRAFIN GRS

BN17

LITTLEHAMPTON
Toddington Nurseries
Watersmead Bsns Pk

NORWAY LA 1
THE POPLARS 2

A259

BOURNE CT 1
WICK CT 2
PHOENIX CL 3
FLORA CT 4
MARDEN HO 5
ALDINGBOURNE HO 6
PAGHAM HO 7
SINGLETON HO 8
FUNTINGTON HO 9
BOXGROVE HO 10
HOUGHTON HO 11
CHILGROVE HO 12

MILLFIELD CT
NEW COURTWICK LA
Minster Ct
Martello Ent Ctr
Wick

1 OSPREY CL
2 SEATON PARK COTTS
3 LYMINSTER GATE

NORTHWAY RD
ST PHILIP'S WINDLESHAM CT
NORTHWAY RD

BARN CL
HOLLY DR

KENLY DR

Cornfield Sch
CORNFIELD CL
Cornfield Cl

OAKCROFT GDNS
B2187

Cemy

WORTHING RD

Sewage Works

Superstore
Ret Pk

BROAD PIECE
B2187
BRIDGE RD
River Arun

Riverside Ind Est

FORSTERS YD
QUAYSIDE

GREENFIELDS
ELSING LEAD
WHEATCROFT
COURTWICK RD
THE CROSSWAY
POTTERS MEAD
GRAND AVE
WEST WAY
BELLOC RD
HIGHFIELD COTTS
THORGE HO
HEO GN
WHITE ACRE
HECTOR'S GN
GREENSIDE
EGAN WAY
OSBORN CL
ELM RD
LINESIDE WAY
WICKBOURNE
WICK FARM RD
PEEL CL
ROMAN ACRE
BELYNGHAM CRES
LATHAM CL
LINESIDE IND EST
JOYCE CL
WILLOW BROOK
BROOK RD
COLE RD
CHERRY
CLARENCE AVE
SELWYN RD
WICK ST
BEACONSFIELD RD
GLADONI
Sch

ASHBY WAY
STANLEY RD
LANSDOWNE RD
LAMMAS RD
HARTING RD
NORTH ST
SWANBOURNE

1 NURSERY GDNS
2 TRUE BLUE PREC
3 GLADSTONE TERR

Prim Sch

AMBERLEY RD
THE PARADE

The Littlehampton Com Sch

THORNCROFT RD
TOWNSEND RD
SELWAY LA
SSA

FrankLIN ST
THAKEHAM

30

Flora McDonald Jun Sch

ARUNDEL RD

KENT RD
WHITE WAY
LAWS CL
BLAKEHURST WAY
MADEHURST WAY

GROVE RD
BELLCROFT CL
PEREGRINE PL
ESMONDE CL
GOSDEN RD
BELL DAVIES RD

HORSHAM RD

Arunside Ind Est
Wickham Bsns Ctr
HARWOOD RD
HARWOOD RD Ent Units

Modern Moulds Bsns Ctr

CHAPEL CL
FORT RD
LOUDOUN RD
TALBOT RD

MANTLING RD

CORNWALL RD
CORNWALL GDNS

Inf Sch
Jun Sch

PATERSON WILSON RD
EAST ST

Elm Grove Inf Sch

ELMGROVE RD
STANHOPE RD
INGRAM RD
DORSET RD

Horsham Lodge

FALKLAND AVE
MEADOW WAY
ESHER DR

PARKSIDE

P

GLOUCESTER RD
HOWARD RD
LINDEN RD
EAST HAM RD
YORK RD
YORK RD
CONNAUGHT
REDE PL
DUKE ST

QUEEN ST

ST MARY'S CL

FITZROY CT
ST MARY'S RD
RAYDEN CT

ST FLORA'S RD
ST FLORA'S CL

SOUTHFIELDS RD
THE WINTER KNOLL

Caravan Park

A259

Littlehampton Marina

PHAROS QUAY 1
ALPHA CT 2
SMALLCROFT CL 3
PEPPER CL 4
ARUN CT 5
THE WATERSIDE 7

MARINERS QUAY 6

WHARF RD
RIVER RD
FERRY RD
NORTH PARK

TERMINUS RD

Littlehampton

FRANCISCAN WAY

AVON RD
MARTINS RD

BEACH RD
B2140

SURREY ST
HIGH ST

Mkt

MANOR PAR

WINTERTON
MANOR LODGE
FITZALAN RD
CHURCH ST

Sports Field

THE ESTUARY
SHORT FURLONG

1 HEATHCOURT
2 REDWOOD CT
3 THE MEWS
4 ST FLORA'S CL

Mus
C Ctr

← 181   ↑ 204

D1	D2	E1
1 SCOTT LODGE	8 ROSE CT	1 MERTON DR	1 ST MARY'S GDNS
2 THATCHERS LODGE	9 HAMPTON CT	2 QUANTOCKS	2 TEMPLE CT
3 DEVON CT	10 ANTONIA CT	3 MALTHOUSE PAS	3 AMENIC CT
4 WYCHCROFT	11 ST MARTIN'S LA	4 HAMPTON FIELDS	4 WHITE LODGE
5 HOWARD PL	12 DUKE'S CT		5 SUMMERLEA GDNS
6 MADEHURST CT	13 ANCHOR SPRINGS		6 ST MARY'S CT
7 DRUMMOND CT	14 THE ARCADE		
	15 EVANS GDNS		

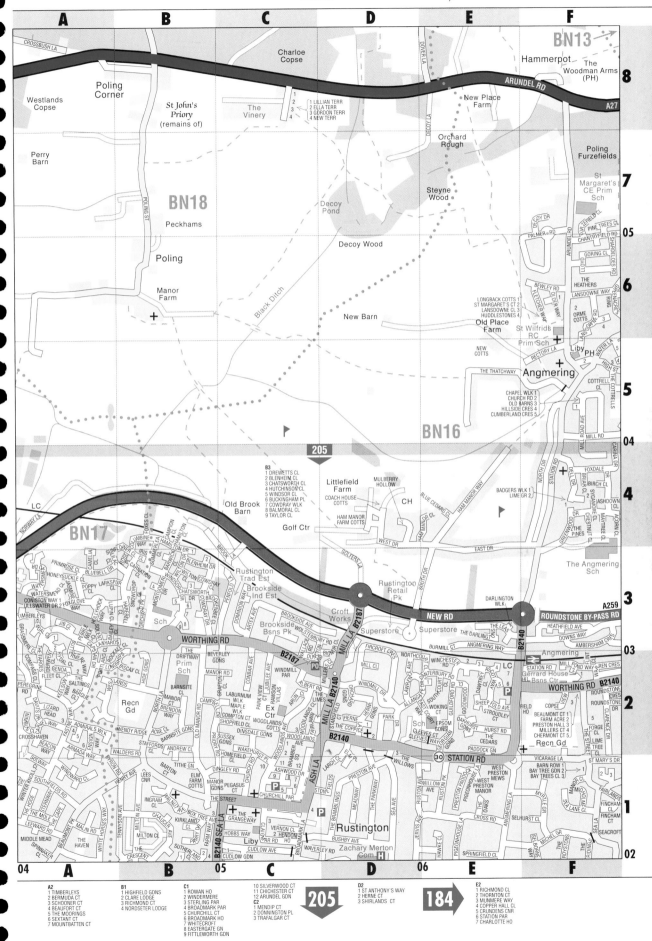

BN13

Hammerpot
The Woodman Arms (PH)

ARUNDEL RD
A27

8

Charloe Copse

1 LILLIAN TERR
2 ELLA TERR
3 GORDON TERR
4 NEW TERR

New Place Farm

Poling Corner

Westlands Copse

St John's Priory (remains of)

The Vinery

Orchard Rough

Poling Furzefields

St Margaret's CE Prim Sch

7

Perry Barn

BN18

Peckhams

Decoy Pond

Steyne Wood

05

Poling

Decoy Wood

LONGBACK COTTS 1
ST MARGARET'S CT 2
LANSDOWNE CL 3
HUDDLESTONES 4

The Heathers

6

Manor Farm

Black Ditch

New Barn

Old Place Farm

St Wilfrids RC Prim Sch

NEW COTTS

ORME COTTS

Liby PH

Angmering

5

BN16

CHAPEL WLK 1
CHURCH RD 2
OLD BARNS 3
HILLSIDE CRES 4
CUMBERLAND CRES 5

04

205

B3
1 DREWETTS CL
2 BLENHEIM CL
3 CHATSWORTH CL
4 HUTCHINSON CL
5 WINDSOR CL
6 BUCKINGHAM PL
7 COWDRAY WLK
8 BALMORAL CL
9 TAYLOR CL

Littlefield Farm

MULBERRY HOLLOW

CH

COACH HOUSE COTTS

BADGERS WLK 1
LIME GR 2

4

Old Brook Barn

Golf Ctr

HAM MANOR FARM COTTS

WEST DR

The Pines

The Angmering Sch

LC

BN17

EAST DR

3

Rustington Trad Est
Brookside Ind Est

Croft Works

Rustington Retail Pk

DARLINGTON WLK

A259
NEW RD   ROUNDSTONE BY-PASS RD

Superstore   Superstore

B2140
Angmering

WORTHING RD

B2187

Brookside Bsns Pk

MILL LA B2187

03

The Driftway Prim Sch

PO

WORTHING RD
B2140

2

Recn Gd

MILL LA B2140

Ex Ctr

B2140

Sch

Recn Gd

30 STATION RD

1

THE STREET

THE GRANGEWAY

Liby

Rustington

Zachary Merton Com H

02

04   A   B   05   C   205   D   184   E   F   06   02

A2
1 TIMBERLEYS
2 BERMUDA CT
3 SCHOONER CT
4 BEAUFORT CT
5 THE MOORINGS
6 SEXTANT CT
7 MOUNTBATTEN CT

B1
1 HIGHFIELD GDNS
2 CLARE LODGE
3 RICHMOND CT
4 NORDSETER LODGE

C1
1 ROWAN HO
2 WINDERMERE
3 STERLING PAR
4 BROADMARK PAR
5 CHURCHILL CT
6 BROADMARK HO
7 WHITECROFT
8 EASTERGATE GN
9 FITTLEWORTH GDN
10 SILVERWOOD CT
11 CHICHESTER CT
12 ARUNDEL GDN

C2
1 MENDIP CT
2 DONNINGTON PL
3 TRAFALGAR CT

D2
1 ST ANTHONY'S WAY
2 HERNE CT
3 SHIRLANDS CT

E2
1 RICHMOND CL
2 THORNTON CT
3 MUNMERE WAY
4 COPPER HALL CL
5 CRUNDENS CNR
6 STATION PAR
7 CHARLOTTE HO

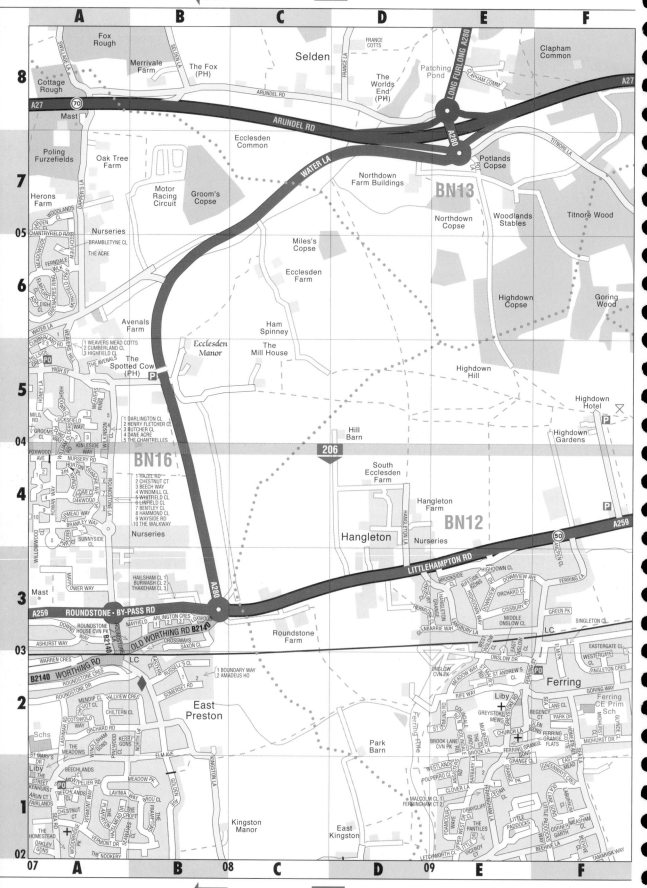

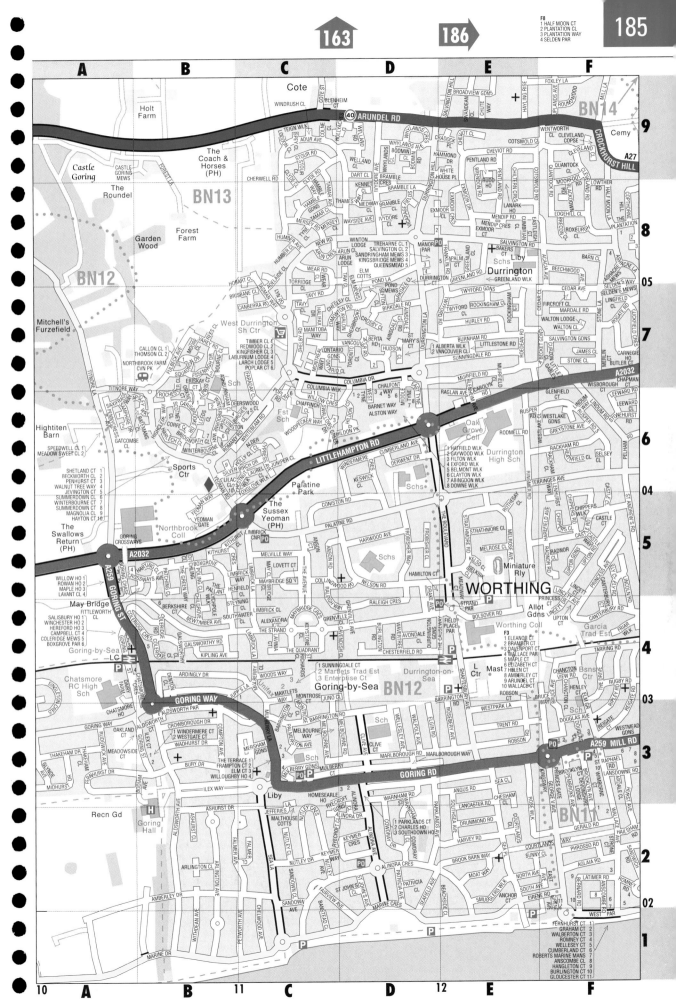

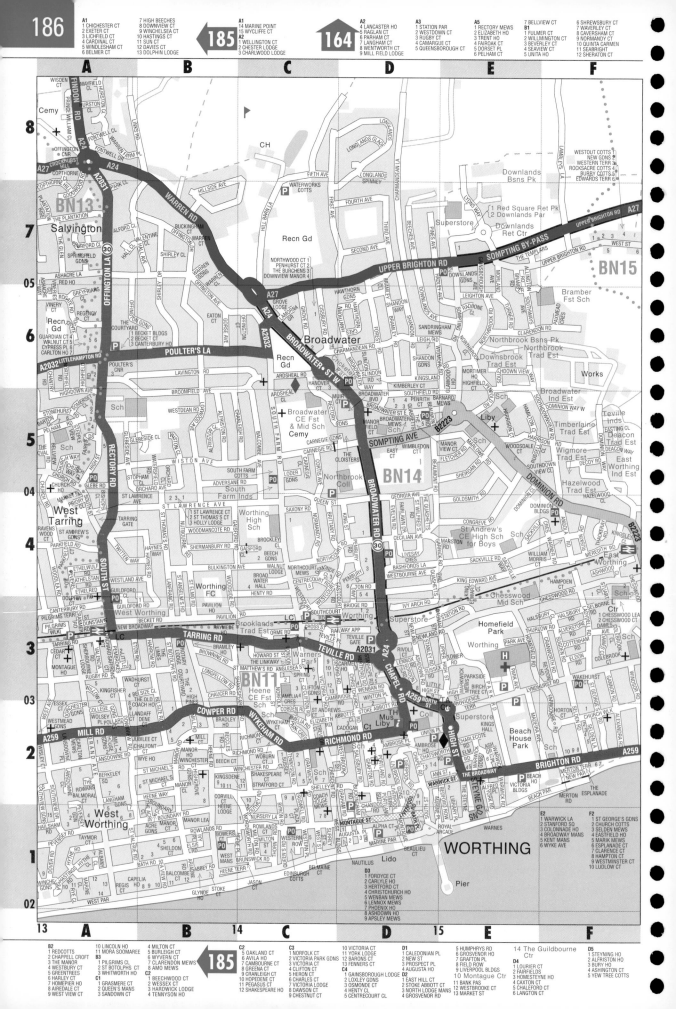

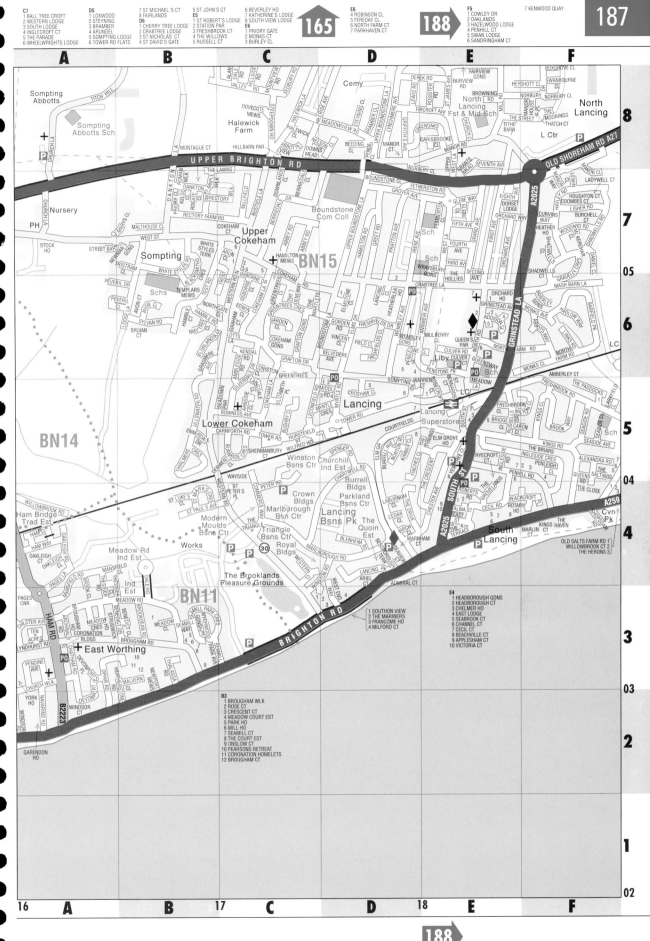

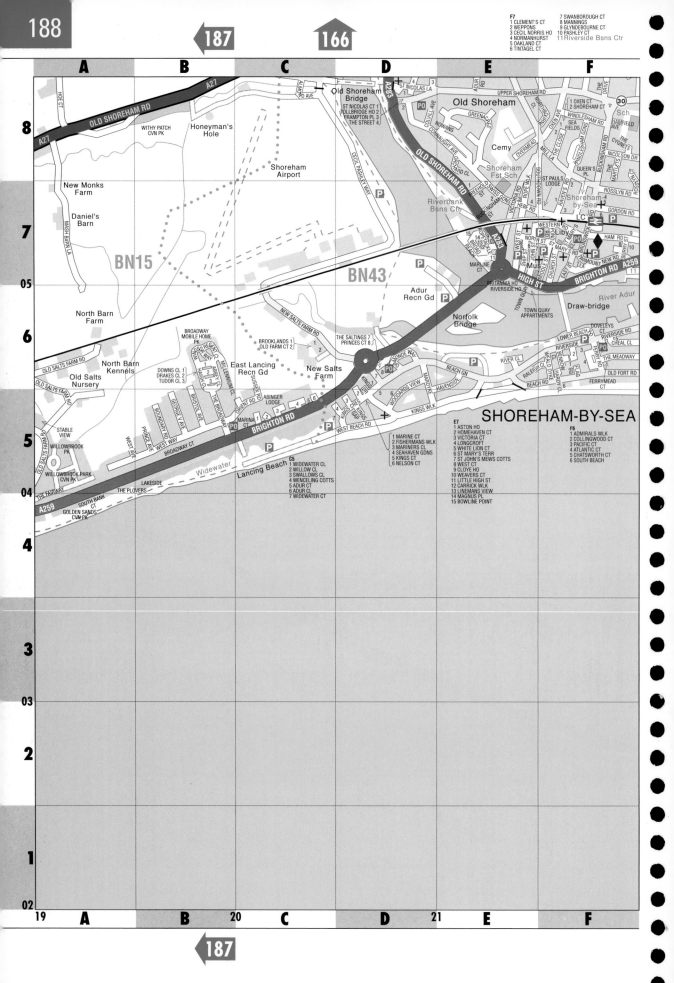

F7
1 CLEMENT'S CT
2 WEPPONS
3 CECIL NORRIS HO
4 NORMANHURST
5 OAKLAND CT
6 TINTAGEL CT
7 SWANBOROUGH CT
8 MANNINGS
9 GLYNDEBOURNE CT
10 PASHLEY CT
11 Riverside Bsns Ctr

A B C D E F

8
7
05
6
5
04
4
3
03
2
1
02

19 A B 20 C D 21 E F

Old Shoreham Bridge
Old Shoreham
Shoreham Airport
New Monks Farm
Daniel's Barn
BN15
North Barn Farm
North Barn Kennels
Old Salts Nursery
Stable View
WILLOWBROOK PK
WILLOWBROOK PARK CVN PK
GOLDEN SANDS CVN PK
THE FAIRWAY
Lancing Beach
Widewater
SHOREHAM-BY-SEA
BN43
East Lancing Recn Gd
New Salts Farm
Adur Recn Gd
Norfolk Bridge
River Adur
Draw-bridge
Town Quay Apartments

C5
1 WIDEWATER CL
2 WILLOW CL
3 SWALLOWS CL
4 WENCELING COTTS
5 ADUR CT
6 ADUR CL
7 WIDEWATER CT

E7
1 ASTON HO
2 HOMEHAVEN CT
3 VICTORIA CT
4 LONGCROFT
5 WHITE LION CT
6 ST MARY'S TERR
7 ST JOHN'S MEWS COTTS
8 WEST CT
9 CLOYE HO
10 WEAVERS CT
11 LITTLE HIGH ST
12 CARRICK WLK
13 LINEMANS VIEW
14 MAGNUS PL
15 BOWLINE POINT

F6
1 ADMIRALS WLK
2 COLLINGWOOD CT
3 PACIFIC CT
4 ATLANTIC CT
5 CHATSWORTH CT
6 SOUTH BEACH

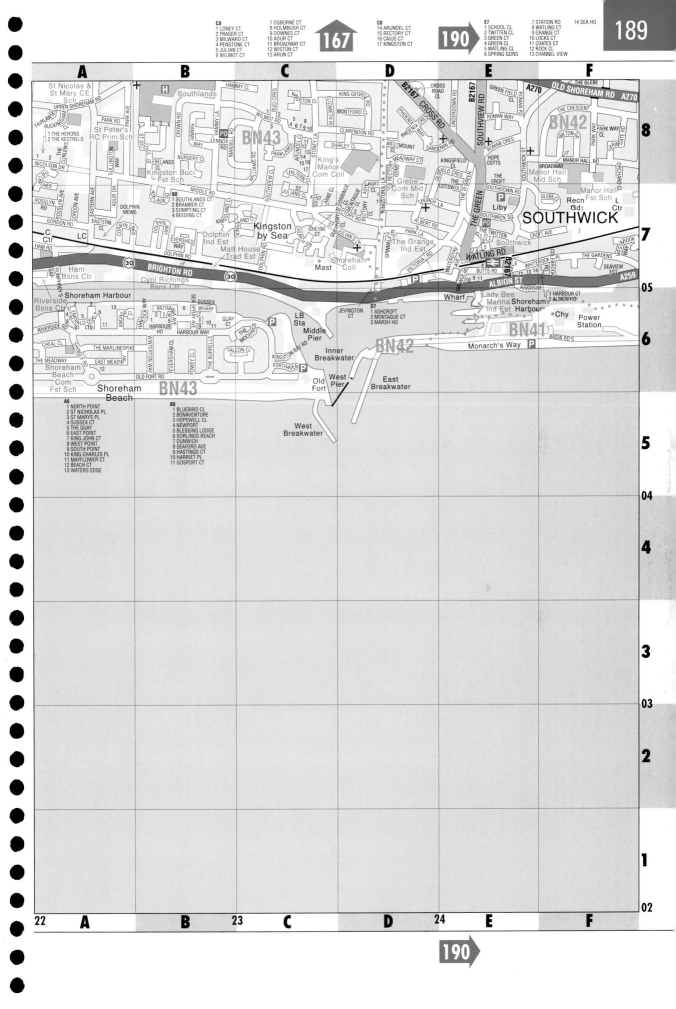

167

190

C8
1 LONEY CT
2 FRASER CT
3 MILWARD CT
4 PENSTONE CT
5 JULIAN CT
6 WILMOT CT
7 OSBORNE CT
8 HOLMBUSH CT
9 DOWNES CT
10 ADUR CT
11 BROADWAY CT
12 WISTON CT
13 ARUN CT

C8
14 ARUNDEL CT
15 RECTORY CT
16 CAIUS CT
17 KINGSTON CT

E7
1 SCHOOL CL
2 TWITTEN CL
3 GREEN CT
4 GREEN CL
5 WATLING CL
6 SPRING GDNS
7 STATION RD
8 WATLING CT
9 GRANGE CT
10 LOCKS CT
11 COATES CT
12 ROCK CL
13 CHANNEL VIEW

14 SEA HO

Southlands

St Nicolas & St Mary CE Sch

BN43

Kingston by Sea

BN42

SOUTHWICK

Shoreham Harbour

Riverside Bsns Ctr

BRIGHTON RD

BN42

Shoreham Harbour

BN41

Monarch's Way

Power Station

Shoreham Beach

BN43

LB Sta
Middle Pier

Inner Breakwater

West Pier

Old Fort

East Breakwater

West Breakwater

A6
1 NORTH POINT
2 ST NICHOLAS PL
3 ST MARYS PL
4 SUSSEX CT
5 THE QUAY
6 EAST POINT
7 KING JOHN CT
8 WEST POINT
9 SOUTH POINT
10 KING CHARLES PL
11 MAYFLOWER CT
12 BEACH CT
13 WATERS EDGE

B6
1 BLUEBIRD CL
2 BONAVENTURE
3 HOPEWELL CL
4 NEWPORT
5 BLESSING LODGE
6 SORLINGS REACH
7 DUNWICH
8 SEAFORD AVE
9 HASTINGS CT
10 HARRIET PL
11 GOSPORT CT

190

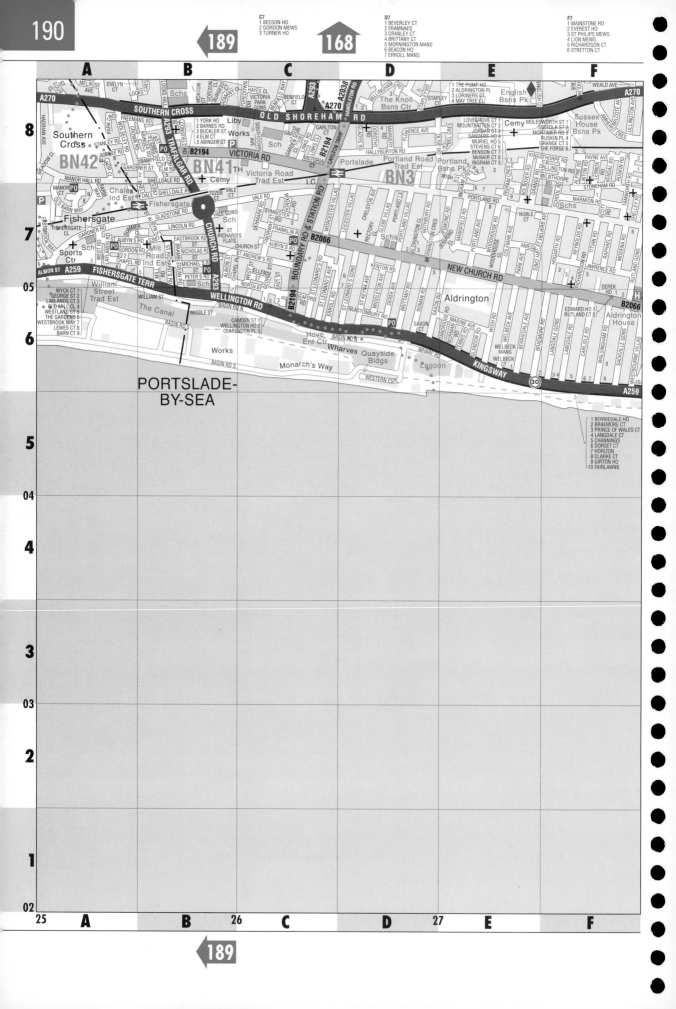

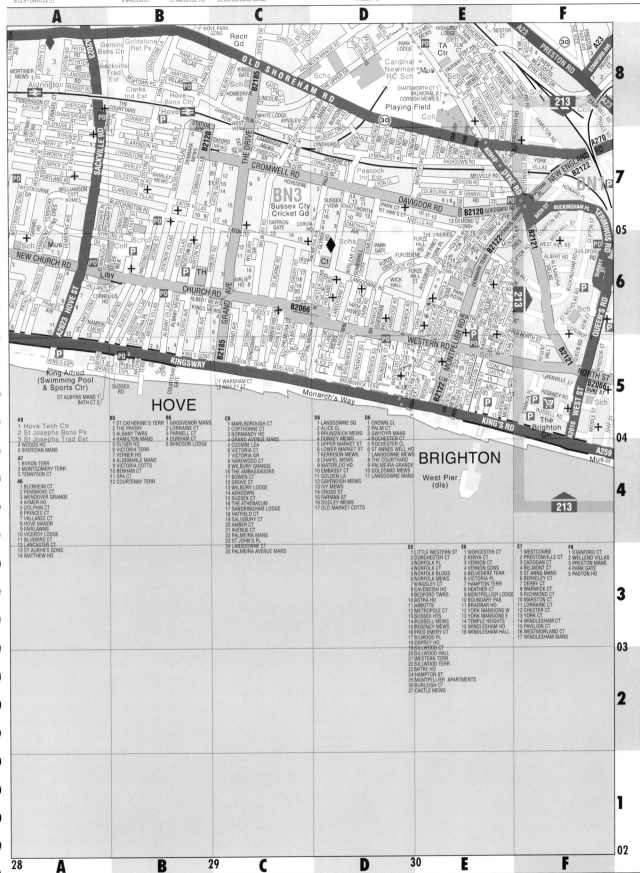

192 For full street detail of the highlighted area see page 213.

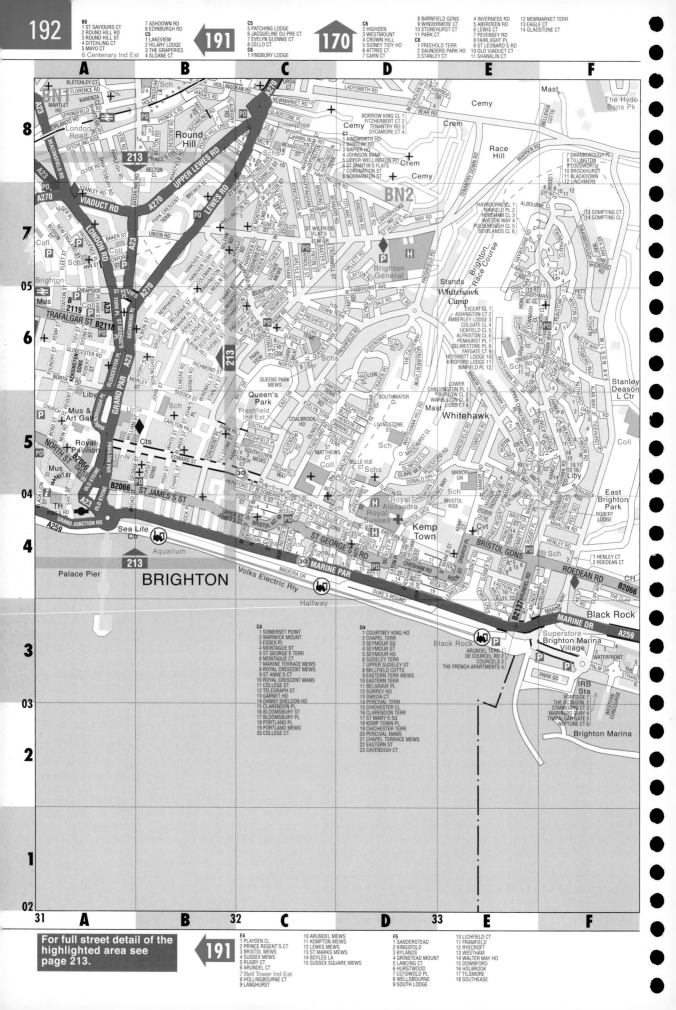

B8
1 ST SAVIOURS CT
2 ROUND HILL RD
3 ROUND HILL ST
4 DITCHLING CT
5 MAYO CT
6 Centenary Ind Est

7 ASHDOWN RD
8 EDINBURGH RD
C5
1 LAKEVIEW
2 HILARY LODGE
3 THE GRAPERIES
4 SLOANE CT

C5
5 PATCHING LODGE
6 JACQUELINE DU PRE CT
7 EVELYN GLENNIE CT
8 CELLO CT
C6
1 FINSBURY LODGE

C6
2 HIGHDEN
3 WESTMOUNT
4 CROWN HILL
5 SIDNEY TIDY HO
6 ATTREE CT
7 CARN CT

C7
1 AINSWORTH HO
2 BARCLAY HO
3 NAPIER HO
4 JOHNSON BANK
5 UPPER WELLINGTON RD
6 ST MARTIN'S FLATS
7 CORONATION ST
8 NORMANTON ST

C8
1 FREEHOLD TERR
2 SAUNDERS PARK HO
3 STANLEY CT

8 BARNFIELD GDNS
9 WINDERMERE CT
10 STONEHURST ST
11 PARK CT

4 INVERNESS RD
5 ABERDEEN RD
6 LEWIS CT
7 PEVENSEY RD
8 FAIRLIGHT PL
9 ST LEONARD'S RD
10 OLD VIADUCT CT
11 SHANKLIN CT

12 NEWMARKET TERR
13 EAGLE CT
14 GLADSTONE CT

7 SWANBOROUGH PL
8 TILLINGTON
9 CODSWORTH
10 BROCKHURST
11 BLACKDOWN
12 LINCHMERE

13 SOMPTING CT
14 SOMPTING CL

← **191**   ↑ **170**

BRIGHTON

C4
1 SOMERSET POINT
2 WARWICK MOUNT
3 ESSEX PL
4 MONTAGUE ST
5 ST GEORGE'S TERR
6 MONTAGUE CT
7 MARINE TERRACE MEWS
8 ROYAL CRESCENT MEWS
9 ST ANNE'S CT
10 ROYAL CRESCENT MANS
11 COLLEGE ST
12 TELEGRAPH ST
13 GARNET HO
14 DANNY SHELDON HO
15 CLARENDON PL
16 BLOOMSBURY ST
17 BLOOMSBURY PL
18 PORTLAND PL
19 PORTLAND MEWS
20 COLLEGE CT

D4
1 COURTNEY KING HO
2 CHAPEL TERR
3 SEYMOUR SQ
4 SEYMOUR ST
5 SEYMOUR HO
6 SUDELEY TERR
7 UPPER SUDELEY ST
8 MILLFIELD COTTS
9 EASTERN TERR MEWS
10 EASTERN TERR
11 BELGRAVE PL
12 SURREY HO
13 SWEDA CT
14 PERCIVAL TERR
15 CHICHESTER CL
16 CLARENDON TERR
17 ST MARY'S SQ
18 KEMP TOWN PL
19 CHICHESTER TERR
20 PERCIVAL MANS
21 CHAPEL TERRACE MEWS
22 EASTERN CT
23 CAVENDISH CT

ARUNDEL TERR 1
DE COURCEL RD 2
COURCELS 3
THE FRENCH APARTMENTS 4

PORTSIDE 1
THE OCTAGON 2
STARBOARD CT 3
MARINERS QUAY 4
TRAFALGAR GATE 5
NEPTUNE CT 6

For full street detail of the highlighted area see page 213.

← **191**

E4
1 PLAYDEN CL
2 PRINCE REGENT'S CT
3 BRISTOL MEWS
4 SUSSEX MEWS
5 RUGBY CT
6 ARUNDEL CT
7 BELL TOWER IND EST
8 HOLLINGBOURNE CT
9 LANGHURST

10 ARUNDEL MEWS
11 KEMPTON MEWS
12 LEWES MEWS
13 ST MARKS MEWS
14 BOYLES LA
15 SUSSEX SQUARE MEWS

F5
1 SANDERSTEAD
2 KINGSFOLD
3 BYLANDS
4 GRINSTEAD MOUNT
5 LANCING CT
6 HURSTWOOD
7 COTSWOLD PL
8 WELLSBOURNE
9 SOUTH LODGE

10 LICHFIELD CT
11 FRAMFIELD
12 RYECROFT
13 WESHAM
14 WALTER MAY HO
15 DOWNFORD
16 HOLBROOK
17 TILSMORE
18 SOUTHEASE

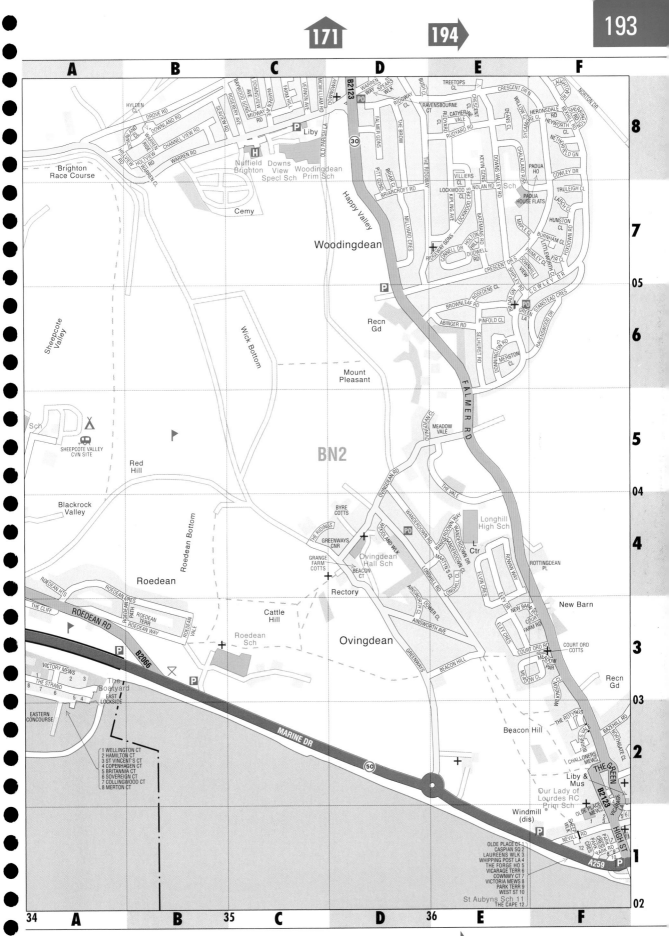

193
172

A B C D E F

8

Standean
Bottom

Whiteway
Bottom

Pickers Hill

Heathy
Brow

7

The
Bostle

Monument

05

BN7

Highdole Hill

Balsdean
Farm

5

Balsdean
Cottages

High Hill

04

Telscombe
Tye

Pickers Hill
Farm

4

BN2

Coombe Bottom

Nursery

Coombe
Farm

Looes
Barn

Coombe Vale

WALDEGRAVE
CT

Westfield
Ave

COOMBE VALE N

COOMBE
MDW

3

WIVELSFIELD RD

Westfield Ave S

WESTFIELD AVE

COOMBE
RISE

HOMEBUSH AVE

VALE RD

STANMER

WESTFIELD RISE

03

BAZEHILL
MANOR

1 CHALLONERS CL
2 TUDOR CL
3 DEAN CL

BAZEHILL RD

WELLESMERE RD

PALMER AVE

PERRY HILL

RIDGEWOOD AVE

HAILSHAM
AVE

LEONARD AVE

HILGROVE RD

HEATHFIELD AVE

BERWICK
RD

SEMPSTEAD RD

Tenant Hill

GORHAM
CL

DEAN COURT RD

LUSTRELLS
RD

BISHOPSTONE DR

SAXON

WINTON AVE

TUMULUS RD

CHILTINGTON N

SALTDEAN VALE

CHILTINGTON

MOUNT DR

Pedlersburgh

COLES
CL

GORHAM AVE

NORTHFIELD
RISE

2

Whiteway La

WESTMESTON AVE

CHORLEY AVE

LINFIELD CL

LUSTRELLS CRES

LUSTRELLS CL

FALMER AVE

CHILTINGTON WAY

GLYNDE
AVE

GREENBANK AVE

Saltdean
Prim Sch

Saltdean

1 SCHOOL LA
2 MAYFIELD CT
3 WESTBROOK
4 SOUTHDOWNS CT

RYE CL

IFIELD CL

Telscombe Tye

Rottingdean

St Margaret's
CE Prim Sch

1 MARINE CT
2 KIPLING CT
3 HIGHCLIFF CT
4 ST MARGARETS
5 OCEAN REACH

CHAILEY AVE

FOUNTHILL RD

ASHDOWN AVE

FOINTHILL RD

ARUNDEL DR W

GLYNDEBOURNE
AVE

SHIPHAM AVE

HOMEBUSH AVE

ROTMELL AVE

ROSSBURY CRES

NORTHWOOD AVE

FENDON AVE

BANNINGS VALE

CHAILEY CL

LEWES CL

ASHURST AVE

1

The
Twitten

ST
AUBYN'S
MEAD

NEWLANDS RD

GP RD

DK PARK

KNOLE
RD

CRANLEIGH AVE

LENHAM
RD

LENHAM AVE

SALTDEAN DR

CHICHESTER
AVE E

ARUNDEL DR E

CHICHESTER
DR E

LINCHMERE
AVE

WITHYHAM
AVE

NUTLEY AVE

LONGRIDGE AVE

BEVENDEAN AVE

HARTFIELD RD

Saltdean
Park

CHICHESTER
CL

OAKLANDS AVE

CROWBOROUGH RD

WICKLANDS AVE

HAMSEY
RD

STEYNING RD

LENHAM RD W

ROMNEY RD

EILEEN AVE

FREDERIC
HO

LEE CRES

MARINE CL

ABBOTSBURY
CL

HOMERIDGE HO

BRAMBLETYNE AVE

BN10

PO

A259

HIGH ST

MARINE DR

A259

A259 Newhaven

Liby

East Sussex STREET ATLAS

GREENWAY CT

37

A

38

B

C

D

39

E

East Sussex STREET ATLAS

193

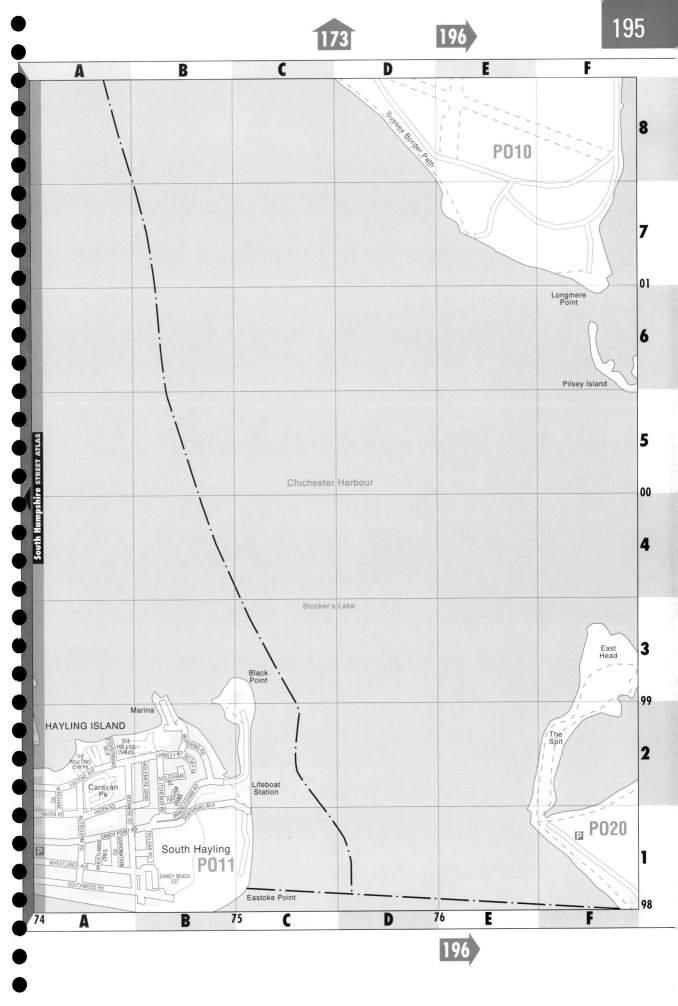

173
196

A   B   C   D   E   F

8

PO10

7

01

Longmere
Point

6

Pilsey Island

5

00

Chichester Harbour

4

Stocker's Lake

3
East
Head

99

The
Spit

2

PO20

Black
Point

Marina

HAYLING ISLAND

THE
HOLLIES
FISHERMANS
CVN PK
WLK
THE
WILLOWS
CVN PK
EASTOKE AVE
WITTERING RD
EARNLEY RD
SELSEY CL
HASLEMERE GDNS
SIDLESHAM
CL
ITCHENOR RD
PAGHAM
GDNS
BRACKLESHAM RD
SEAFARERS WLK
Lifeboat
Station

Caravan
Pk

BIRDHAM
RD
HAVEN RD
HAVEN RD
NUTBOURNE RD
BOSMERE RD
SANDY POINT RD
CORONATION
RD
TRELOAR RD
WHEATLANDS
CRES
South Hayling
PO11
SANDY BEACH
EST
WHEATLANDS AVE
SOUTHWOOD RD

1

Eastoke Point

98

South Hampshire STREET ATLAS

Sussex Border Path

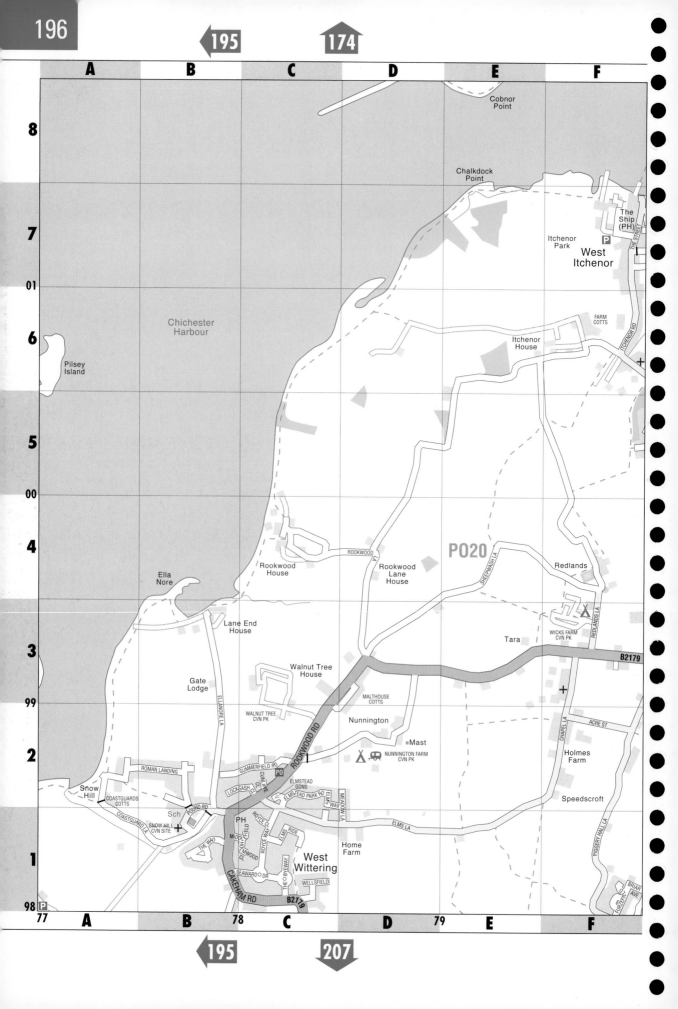

195
174

A B C D E F

8

7

01

6

5

00

4

99

3

2

1

98

77 78 79

A B C D E F

Cobnor Point

Chalkdock Point

Itchenor Park

The Ship (PH)

THE STREET

West Itchenor

ITCHENOR RD

FARM COTTS

Itchenor House

Chichester Harbour

Pilsey Island

Ella Nore

Rookwood House

Rookwood

Rookwood Lane House

PO20

SHEEPWASH LA

Redlands

REDLANDS LA

Wicks Farm CVN PK

Tara

B2179

Lane End House

Gate Lodge

ELLANORE LA

Walnut Tree House

WALNUT TREE CVN PK

MALTHOUSE COTTS

Nunnington

Mast

Nunnington Farm CVN PK

ROOKWOOD RD

CHAPEL LA

ACRE ST

Holmes Farm

Speedscroft

PIGGERY HALL LA

Snow Hill

ROMAN LANDING

COASTGUARDS COTTS

COASTGUARD LA

Snow Hill CVN SITE

Sch

POUND RD

SUMMERFIELD RD

LOCKSASH CL

CUNLIFFE CL

PO

PH

ELMSTEAD GDNS

ELMSTEAD PARK RD

ELMS WAY

MEADOW LA

ELMS LA

Home Farm

ROYCE CL

ROYCE WAY

ELMS RIDE

MIDDLE FIELD

MARSH BARN CL

THE WAD

HOLMWOOD CL

SEAWARD DR

CAKEHAM RD

THE BYEWAY

WELLSFIELD

West Wittering

B2179

BRIAR AVE

FIRST CL

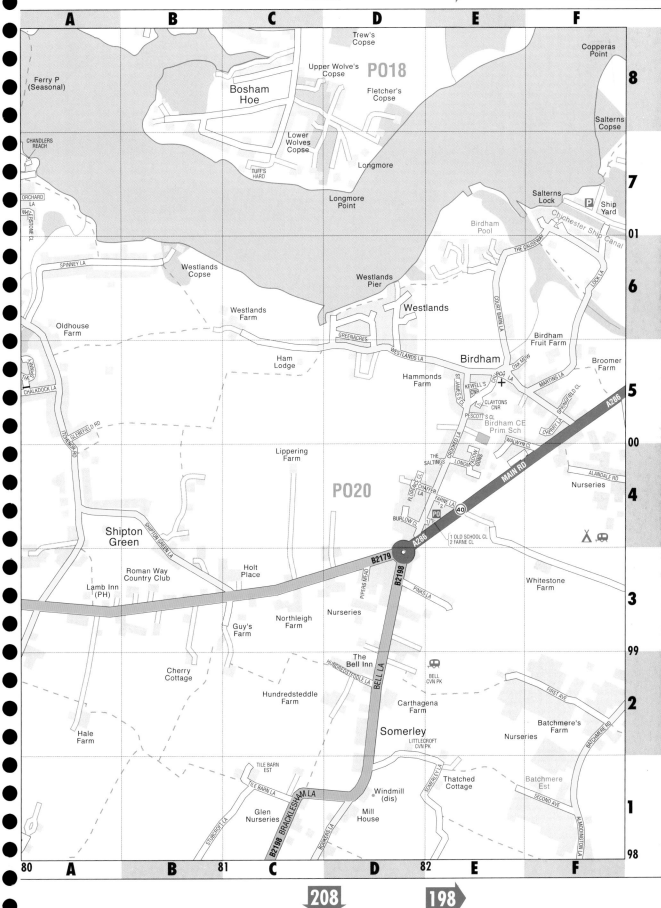

197
176

A **B** **C** **D** **E** **F**

8

Crouchers
Bottom
(Hotel)

New
Barn

ORCHARD SIDE 1
MERLE COURT GDNS 2

Crosbie
Bridge

B2201

Chichester Ship Canal

Bridge
Courtyard

UPHILL WAY
LITTLE
BOULTONS

Salterns
Copse

Pump
Bottom
Farm

The Blacksmith's
Arms (PH)

TRAMWAY
CL

HIGH
BANK

B2145

OAK
VIEW

7

P

Chichester
Marina

Cutfield
Bridge

Price
Cottages

Nurseries

BIRDHAM RD

SELSEY RD

Tennessee
Farm

P

Manhood End
Farm

Sussex
Aquatic &
Falconry Ctr

WOPHAMS LA

Kipson
House

01

Nursery

Kipson Bank
Farm

SELSEY RD

6

Coombers Barn
Farm

Southend
Farm

GREEN LA

White
Walls

Allman
Bsns Pk

Harding's
Farm

5

Birdham
Farm

A286

Cowdray
Farm

PO20

Jury Farm
House

JURY LA

CHICHESTER RD

Sidlesham
Common

B2201

B2145

Hunston
Common

Chichester
Golf Ctr

Driving
Range

The
Piggeries

00

Coneleys
Yd

Jury
Cottage

GORSE
TERR

Marblebridge
Farm

BRIMFAST LA

4

SIDLESHAM LA

Nurseries

COLLINS LA

LOCKGATE RD

Fletchers

STREET
End

STREET END RD

Nurseries

STREET END LA

Woodhorn
Farm

Lockgate
Cottage

FLETCHERS LA

BOXHAM LA

Nurseries

3

Hillands
Farm

MAPSONS LA

Mapsons
Farm

ROTTEN ROW

CHURCH LA

CHALDER LA

CHURCHFIELD
COTTS

BATCHMERE RD

Fletchers
Est

The
Anchor
(PH)

CHURCH FARM LA

99

Church
Farm

2

BRAMER LA

HIGHLEIGH RD

Keynor Rife

SELSEY RD

Fletchers
Est

Nurseries

1

Highleigh

Haise
Farm

Sidlesham

CRITCHEL'S LA

GREEN LA

Littleton
Barn

Nurseries

Willow
Glen

B2145

ROXMER LA

98

83 **A** 84 **B** **C** 84 **D** 85 **E** **F**

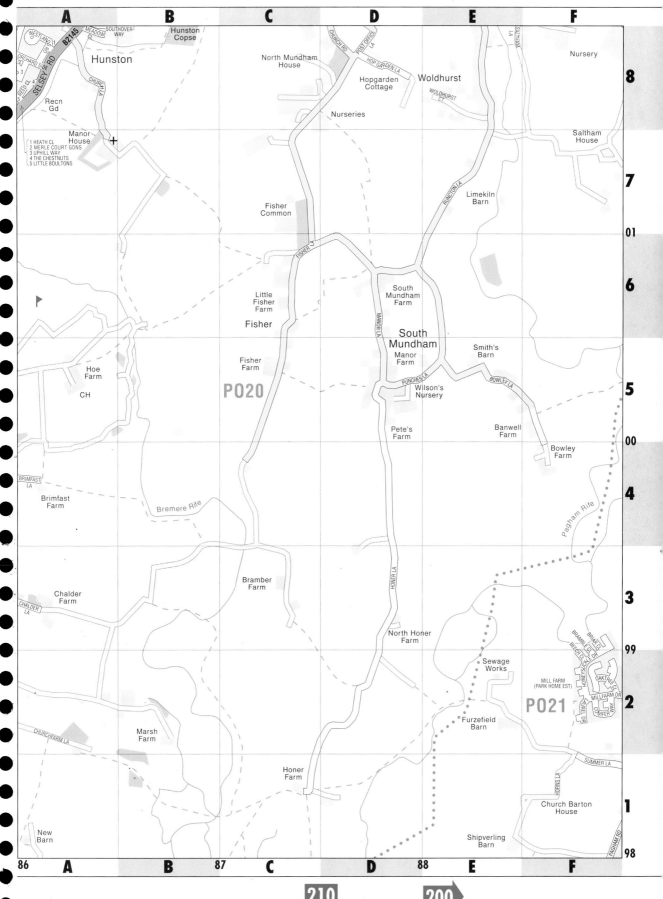

Hunston

Hunston Copse

North Mundham House

Woldhurst

Hopgarden Cottage

Nurseries

Nursery

Saltham House

1 HEATH CL
2 MERLE COURT GDNS
3 UPHILL WAY
4 THE CHESTNUTS
5 LITTLE BOULTONS

Manor House

Recn Gd

Fisher Common

Limekiln Barn

Little Fisher Farm

Fisher

South Mundham Farm

South Mundham

PO20

Fisher Farm

Hoe Farm

CH

Manor Farm

Smith's Barn

Wilson's Nursery

Pete's Farm

Banwell Farm

Bowley Farm

Brimfast Farm

Bremere Rife

Pagham Rife

Chalder Farm

Bramber Farm

North Honer Farm

Sewage Works

MILL FARM (PARK HOME EST)

PO21

Marsh Farm

Furzefield Barn

Honer Farm

Church Barton House

New Barn

Shipverling Barn

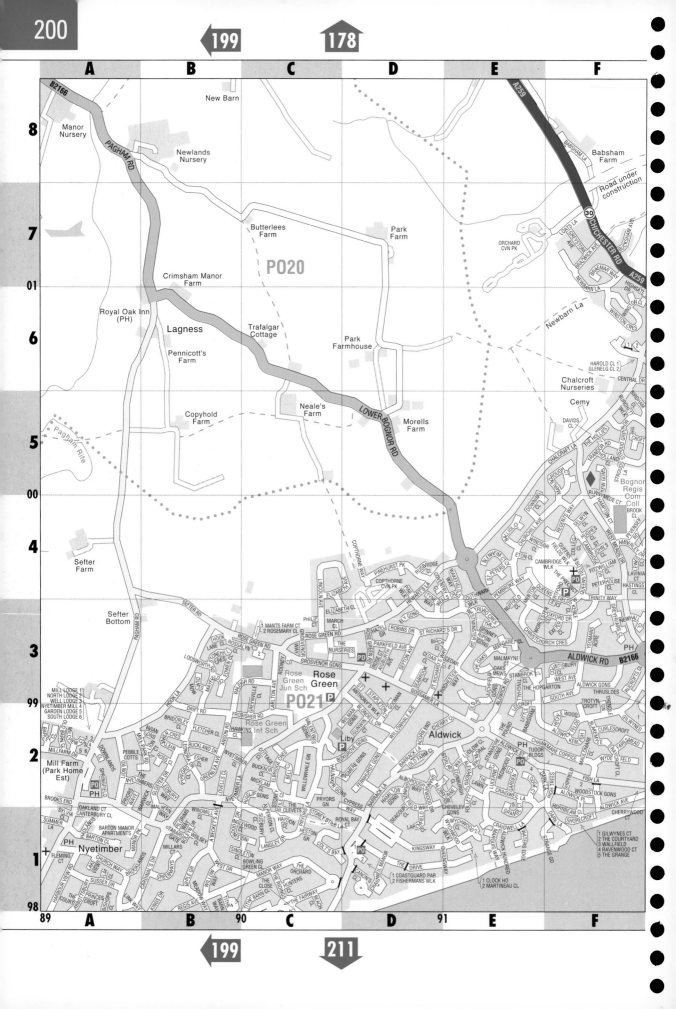

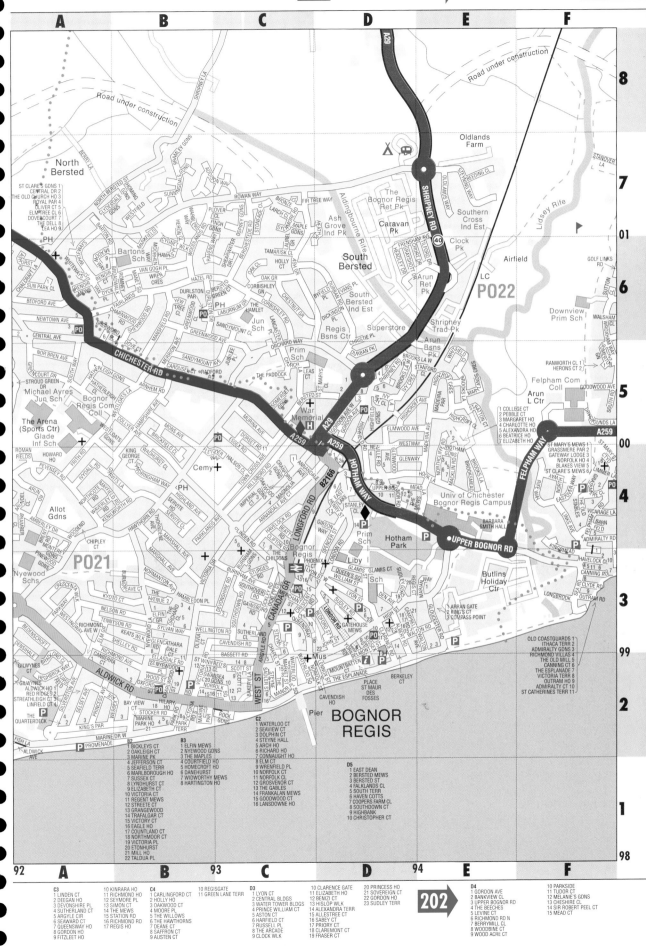

179
202

A B C D E F

8
7
01
6
5
00
4
3
99
2
1
98

North Bersted

St CLARE'S GDNS 1
CENTRAL DR 2
THE OLD CHURCH HO 3
ROYAL PAR 4
OLIVER CT 5
ELMTREE CL 6
DOVER COURT 7
THE DELL 8
LEA HO 9

PH

Road under construction

Road under construction

Oldlands Farm

STANOVER LA

Lidsey Rife

The Bognor Regis Ret Pk

Caravan Pk

Southern Cross Ind Est

Airfield

GOLF LINKS RD

SHRIPNEY RD

A29

Ash Grove Ind Pk

South Bersted

Clock Pk

Arun Ret Pk

PO22

Downview Prim Sch

WALSHAM

Bartons Sch

South Bersted Ind Est

Regis Bsns Ctr

Superstore

Shripney Trad Pk

Arun Bsns Pk

RANWORTH CL 1
HERONS CT 2

Felpham Com Coll

GOODWOOD AVE

CHICHESTER RD

Jun Sch

Prim Sch

War Memorial H

A29

A259

Felpham Com Coll

1 COLLEGE CT
2 PEBBLE CT
3 MARGARET HO
4 CHARLOTTE HO
5 ALEXANDRA HO
6 BEATRICE HO
7 ELIZABETH HO

FELPHAM WAY

A259

Michael Ayres Jun Sch

Bognor Regis Com Coll

The Arena (Sports Ctr)

Glade Inf Sch

ROMAN FIELDS

Allot Gdns

PO21

Nyewood Schs

Cemy

PH

P

P

B2166

LONGFORD RD

HOTHAM WAY

Univ of Chichester Bognor Regis Campus

Barbara Smith Hall

ST MARY'S MEWS 1
GRASSMERE PAR 2
GATEWAY LODGE 3
NORFOLK HO 4
BLAKES VIEW 5
ST CLARE'S MEWS 6

P

VICARAGE LA

P

Prim Sch

Hotham Park

UPPER BOGNOR RD

Bognor Regis

Phoenix

Liby

Glamis Sch

Butlins Holiday Ctr

LONGBROOK

1 ARRAN GATE
2 KING'S CT
3 COMPASS POINT

OLD COASTGUARDS 1
ITHACA TERR 2
ADMIRALTY GDNS 3
RICHMOND VILLAS 4
THE OLD MILL 5
CANNING CT 6
THE ESPLANADE 7
VICTORIA TERR 8
OUTRAM HO 9
ADMIRALTY CT 10
ST CATHERINES TERR 11

ALDWICK RD

P

Mus

i

P

CANADA GR

WEST ST

PLACE ST MAUR DES FOSSES

GILWYNES
GILWYNES
RED RIDGES 1
STREATHLEIGH CT 2
LINFIELD CT 4

THE QUARTERDECK

FISH LA
ALDWICK AVE

P Promenade

Pier

BOGNOR REGIS

MARINE PK

92 A 93 B C 93 D 94 E F

98

202

B2
1 BICKLEYS CT
2 OAKLEIGH CT
3 MARINE PK
4 JEFFERSON CT
5 SEAFIELD TERR
6 MARLBOROUGH HO
7 SUSSEX CT
8 LYNDHURST CT
9 ELIZABETH CT
10 VICTORIA CT
11 REGENT MEWS
12 STREETE CT
13 GRANGEWOOD
14 TRAFALGAR CT
15 VICTORY CT
16 EAGLE HO
17 COUNTLAND CT
18 NORTHMOOR CT
19 VICTORIA PL
20 ETONHURST
21 MILL HO
22 TALDUA PL

B3
1 ELFIN MEWS
2 NYEWOOD GDNS
3 THE MAPLES
4 COURTFIELD HO
5 HOMECROFT HO
6 DANEHURST
7 WIDWORTHY MEWS
8 HARTINGTON HO

C2
1 WATERLOO CT
2 SEAVIEW CT
3 DOLPHIN CT
4 STEYNE HALL
5 ARCH HO
6 RICHARD HO
7 CONNAUGHT HO
8 ELM CT
9 WRENFIELD PL
10 NORFOLK HO
11 NORFOLK CL
12 GROSVENOR CT
13 THE GABLES
14 FRANKALAN MEWS
15 GOODWOOD CT
16 LANSDOWNE HO

D5
1 EAST DEAN
2 BERSTED MEWS
3 BERSTED ST
4 FALKLANDS CL
5 SOUTH TERR
6 HAVEN COTTS
7 COOPERS FARM CL
8 SOUTHDOWN CT
9 HIGHBANK
10 CHRISTOPHER CT

C3
1 LINDEN CT
2 DEEGAN HO
3 DEVONSHIRE PL
4 SUTHERLAND CT
5 ARGYLE CIR
6 SEAWARD CT
7 QUEENSWAY HO
8 GORDON HO
9 FITZLEET HO

10 KINRARA HO
11 RICHMOND HO
12 SEYMORE PL
13 SIMON CT
14 THE MEWS
15 STATION RD
16 RICHMOND RD
17 REGIS HO

C4
1 CARLINGFORD CT
2 HOLLY HO
3 OAKWOOD CT
4 MOORE PL
5 THE WILLOWS
6 THE HAWTHORNS
7 DEANE CT
8 SAFFRON CT
9 AUSTEN CT

10 REGISGATE
11 GREEN LANE TERR

D3
1 LYON CT
2 CENTRAL BLDGS
3 WATER TOWER BLDGS
4 PRINCE WILLIAM CT
5 ASTON CT
6 HARFIELD CT
7 RUSSELL PL
8 THE ARCADE
9 CLOCK WLK

10 CLARENCE GATE
11 ELIZABETH HO
12 BENIZI CT
13 HISLOP WLK
14 ALEXANDRA TERR
15 ALLESTREE CT
16 SABEY CT
17 PRIORY CT
18 CLAREMONT CT
19 FRASER CT

20 PRINCESS HO
21 SOVEREIGN CT
22 GORDON HO
23 SUDLEY TERR

D4
1 GORDON AVE
2 BANKVIEW CL
3 UPPER BOGNOR RD
4 THE BEECHES
5 LEVINE CT
6 RICHMOND RD N
7 BERRYMILL CL
8 WOODBINE CT
9 WOOD ACRE CT

10 PARKSIDE
11 TUDOR CT
12 MELANIE'S GDNS
13 CHESHIRE CL
14 SIR ROBERT PEEL CT
15 MEAD CT

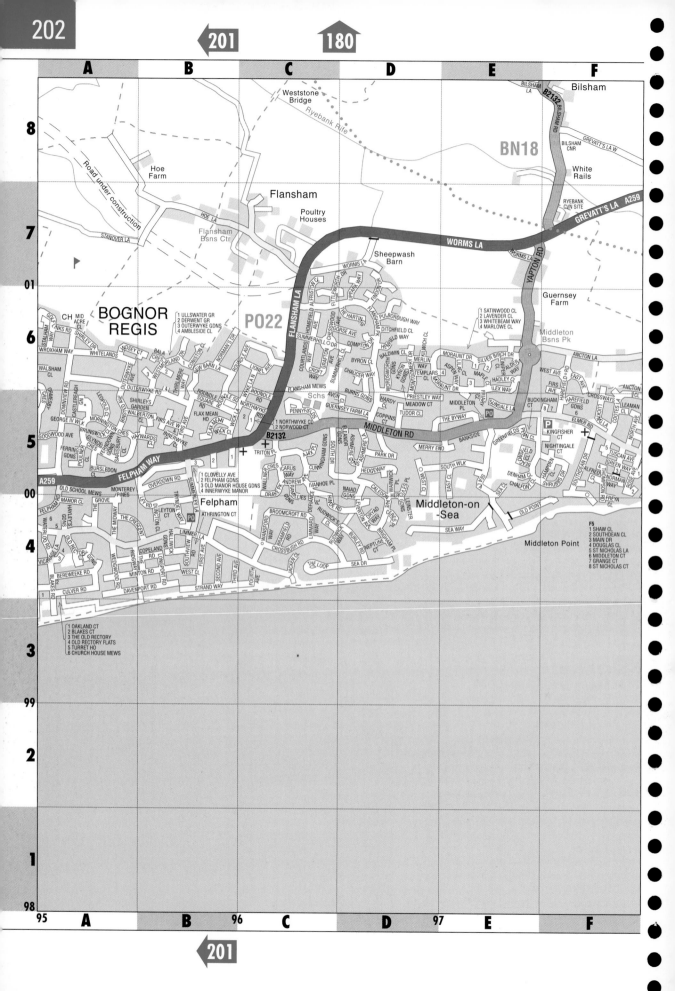

201
180

A B C D E F

8

Weststone
Bridge

Ryebank Rife

BN18

Bilsham

BILSHAM LA

B2132

BILSHAM RD

GREVATT'S LA W

BILSHAM
CNR

White
Rails

Hoe
Farm

Road under construction

Flansham

Poultry
Houses

RYEBANK
CVN SITE

GREVATT'S LA A259

7

HOE LA

STANOVER LA

Flansham
Bsns Ctr

WORMS LA

YAPTON RD

WORMS LA

01

Sheepwash
Barn

WORMS LA

Guernsey
Farm

CH MID
ACRE CL

BOGNOR
REGIS

PO22

1 ULLSWATER GR
2 DERWENT GR
3 OUTERWYKE GDNS
4 AMBLESIDE CL

FLANSHAM LA

UPPARK WAY

FINDON RD

PULBOROUGH WAY

1 SATINWOOD CL
2 LAVENDER CL
3 WHITEBEAM WAY
4 MARLOWE CL

Middleton
Bsns Pk

ANCTON LA

6

GOLF LINKS RD

WROXHAM WAY

SHIRLEY DR

WHITELANDS

LINDSEY CT

BALA
CRES

WESTMORLAND
AVE

CONISTON DR

SW BARN LA

LIONEL AVE

HOE LA

WYKE LA N

ALRISTON

SUMMERFIELD

SUMMERHILL DR

CHESSGROVE

GOSORSE AVE

THE HARTINGS

FITTLEWORTH DR

WORMS LA

DITCHFIELD CL

COMPTON DR

HOPE LD WAY

SILVER BIRCH DR

LILAC CL

MAPLE CL

MORAUNT DR

ASPEN CL

LINDEN
WAY

JUNIPER CL

ALDER
WAY

WEST AVE

FIRS
AVE

HAREFIELD
GDNS

EAST AVE

CROSSWAYS

ANCTON

LEAMAN

WALSHAM
CL

THIRLMERE
AVE

OUTERWYKE
AVE

OUTERWYKE RD

ROUNDLE
SQUARE

ROUNDLE
RD

NORTHWYKE
RD

FLANSHAM MEWS

SUMMERHILL
AVE

GRAFTON
CROFT

COURTLANDS
WAY

CHESSWOOD

BYRON CL

CHAUCER WAY

WORDSWORTH
GDNS

BALDWIN CL

KYNON
GDNS

MONTGOMERY
GDNS

MERLIN
WAY

TEMPLARS

HADLEY CL

FRIARY

ILEX WAY

KILWICH CL

AMAUNT DR

BUCKINGHAM
CT

LUCKING LA

NORTH AVE

5

GEORGE V WLK

GOODWOOD AVE

LEOPOLD CT

BRUNSWICK
CT

MORNINGTON CRES

ELLISON
CL

FERNDOWN

SALISBURY CL

HAYWARDS
CL

SHIRLEYS
GARDEN

WALBERTON

FIRS AVE W

INNERWYKE
CL

FLAX MEAN
HO

FLAX MEN

WYCK CL

1 NORTHWYKE CL
2 NORWOOD CT

AVON CL

BURNS GDNS

GUERNSEY FARM LA

HARDY
CL

COPPINS
CL

MEADOW CT

TUDOR CL

PRIESTLEY WAY

MIDDLETON
PL

THE BYWAY

SUNDALE LA

MIDDLETON RD

MERRY END

BANKSIDE

GREENFIELDS

PENN CL

KINGFISHER
CT

NIGHTINGALE
CT

HAMPDEN
CT

NORMAN
CL

TUSCAN AVE

GREEN WAY

ALFRED
CL

ROSE AVE

FREYA

00

A259

OLD SCHOOL MEWS

FELPHAM WAY

FELPHAM
MANOR CL

MONTEREY
PINES

OVERDOWN RD

DINCTON RD

CLEYTON
CT

TRINDEL WAY

SUMMER LA

PO

Felpham

ATHRINGTON CT

WALNEY
CRES

CARUS
WAY

ANDREW AVE

CUNNINGHAM GDNS

SOUTH DR

PARK DR

HEDGEWAY

KINSWAY

ASHMERE
GDNS

ELEANOR
GDNS

ASHMERE
LA

EAST CT

WEST CT

SOUTH WLK

DENHAM CL

CHALFONT

BEACH
GDNS

FIELD
GDNS

SHRUBBS DR

SOUTHDEAN DR

4

WATERLOO RD

VICARAGE LA

BLAKES RD

HANLEY CT

SINCLAIR
GDNS

MANOR CL

THE GROVE

THE MIDWAY

WENDORE
GDNS

RIDGEWAY

HALLWICK
GDNS

THE CRESCENT

LONGFORD RD

SOUTHVIEW
GDNS

FIRST AVE

WEST CL

SECOND AVE

THIRD AVE

FOURTH AVE

DRAKE PK

DEFIANCE
PL

RALEIGH
WAY

IVANHOE PL

RUDWICK'S
CL

NAIAD
GDNS

HINDE PL

DROAD

BURLEY RD

CALEDON AVE

LEYSTON AVE

LENISTER
CRES

BRIGHAM
CT

NEPTUNE CL

Middleton-on
-Sea

SEA WAY

OLD POINT

Middleton Point

COPELAND
CT

MINTON RD

DAVENPORT RD

BROOMCROFT RD

BRAMFIELD
WAY

CROSSBUSH RD

JACKSON CL

LIMMARD
GDNS

THE LOOP

SEA DR

SEA LA

Felpham
6

BEREWEEKE RD

CULVER RD

OLD RECTORY GDNS

STRAND WAY

BLAKES RD

3

1 OAKLAND CT
2 BLAKES CT
3 THE OLD RECTORY
4 OLD RECTORY FLATS
5 TURRET HO
6 CHURCH HOUSE MEWS

F5
1 SHAW CL
2 SOUTHDEAN CL
3 MAIN DR
4 DOUGLAS CL
5 ST NICHOLAS LA
6 MIDDLETON CT
7 GRANGE CT
8 ST NICHOLAS CT

99

2

1

98

95 A B 96 C D 97 E F

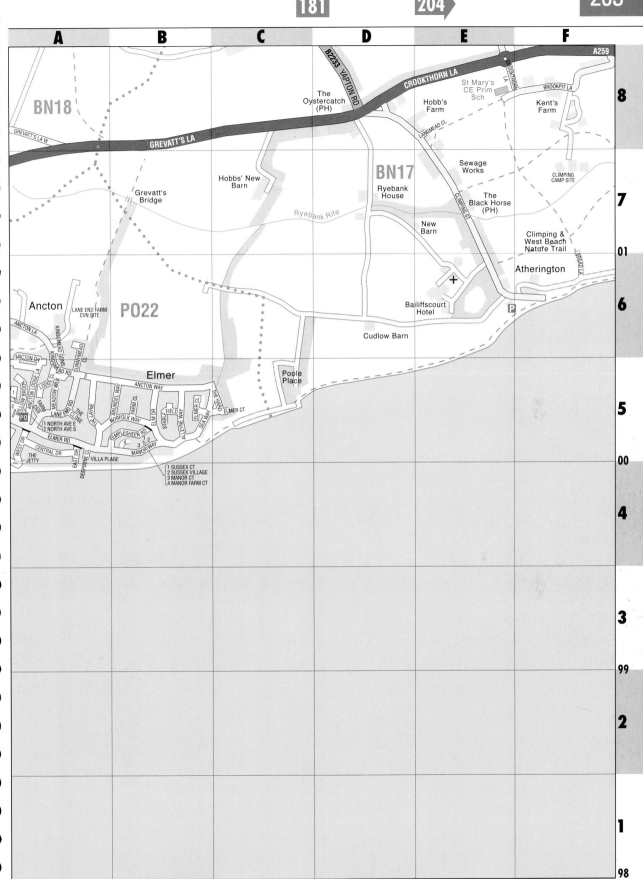

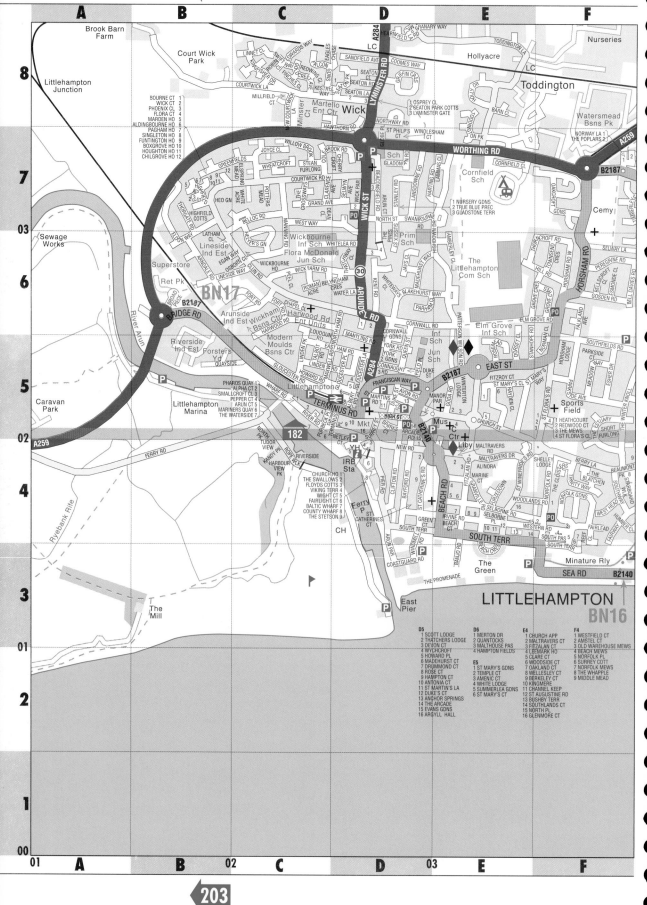

A   B   C   D   E   F

KINLESIDE WAY
FOXWOOD AVE
NURSERY RD
HORTON PL
ASHMORE AVE
OAKWOOD
MEAD WAY
ROWAN WAY
BRAMLEY AV
SUNNYSIDE CL
WILLOWWOOD
MAVI
TOWER WAY

South Ecclesden Farm

Hangleton Farm

1 HAZEL RD
2 CHESTNUT CT
3 BEECH WAY
4 WINDMILL CL
5 WHITFIELD CL
6 LINFIELD CL
7 BENTLEY CL
8 HAMMOND CL
9 WAYSIDE RD
10 THE WALKWAY

Nurseries

Hangleton

Nurseries

HAILSHAM CL 1
BURWASH CL 2
THAKEHAM CL 3

Mast

A259   ROUNDSTONE · BY-PASS RD

LITTLEHAMPTON RD

ROUNDSTONE HOUSE CVN PK
DOWNS WAY
ASHURST WAY

MAYFIELD
ARLINGTON CRES
LOXWOOD
OLD WORTHING RD
B2140
CROSSWAYS
SAXON CL

Roundstone Farm

BROOKSIDE CL
RIFESIDE GDNS
HIGHDOWN CL
DOWNVIEW AVE
ORCHARD CL
CISSBURY
MIDDLE ONSLOW CL
GREEN PK
SINGLETON CL

WARREN CRES
B2140   WORTHING RD
ROUNDSTONE CRES
ROUNDSTONE DR
LC

RUSSELL'S CL
EASTERN
NORTH LA
SOMERSET LA

1 BOUNDARY WAY
2 AMADEUS HO

BN12

ONSLOW CVN PK
MEADOW WAY
ST ANDREW'S CL

EASTERGATE CL
WESTERGATE CL
SINGLETON CRES

MENDIP CL
HILLVIEW CRES
CHEVIOT CL
CHILTERN CL
COTSWOLD WAY
LASMAR RD
ORCHARD RD
THE MEADOWS

East Preston

BN16

ELM AVE
KINGSTON LA

Ferring

RIFE WAY
Liby
GREYSTOKE MEWS
REGENCY CT
GLEN GDNS

Ferring CE Prim Sch

Schs

St Mary's DR
Liby
THE STREET
KENHURST
ARUN CT
FAIRLANDS

BEECHLANDS JCT
MONTPELIER RD
BEECHLANDS CL
CHESTNUT CT
VERMONT DR
WOODBRIDGE
PK

Kingston Manor

East Kingston

BROOK LANE CVN PK
WESTLANDS
POLPERRO CL

MALCOLM CL 1
FERRINGHAM CT 2

DRAYCLIFFE
THE PANTILES
LITTLE PADDOCKS
CORNER MEASHAM
GARTH

THE HOMESTEAD
OAKLEY GDNS

THE NOOKERY
THE SPINNEY
SOUTH VIEW
UPPER DR

184

VICEROY CT

BEEHIVE LA

NORMANDY LA
NORMANDY CL
THE CRESCENT
MANOR RD
WILLOWHAYNE AVE

Kingston Gorse

OCEAN PAR
PH

OCEAN
CHALET CL
HENTY
TELGARTH RD
SARK GDNS
SOMERSET RD

SEAVIEW RD
SEAFIELD CL
WILLOWHAYNE
THE CIRCLE
THE DRIVE
GOLDEN ACRE
SOUTH STRAND

COASTAL RD

PEAK LA
SEA LA
MIDDLE WAY
BROOKSIDE RD
SEAVIEW AVE
GORSE AVE
THE STRAND
SOUTH DR

West Kingston

THE LAWNS
PH

1 WENTWORTH CT
2 CROWN PL
3 CROWN CT
4 WILLOWHAYNE CL
5 WILLOWHAYNE CRES
6 SOUTH STRAND PAR
7 THE PARADE
8 PARADE MANS
9 WILLOWHAYNE CT
10 COASTGUARD COTTS
11 STRAND CT
12 PALM COURT COTTS
13 THE RAMBLERS

F4
1 ST AUBINS CT
2 ST HELIER CT
3 ST AUBINS RD
4 ST MALO CT
5 ELVERLANDS CL
6 DOONE END
7 MILBURY CL
8 FLORIDA GDNS

07   A   B   08   C   D   09   E   F

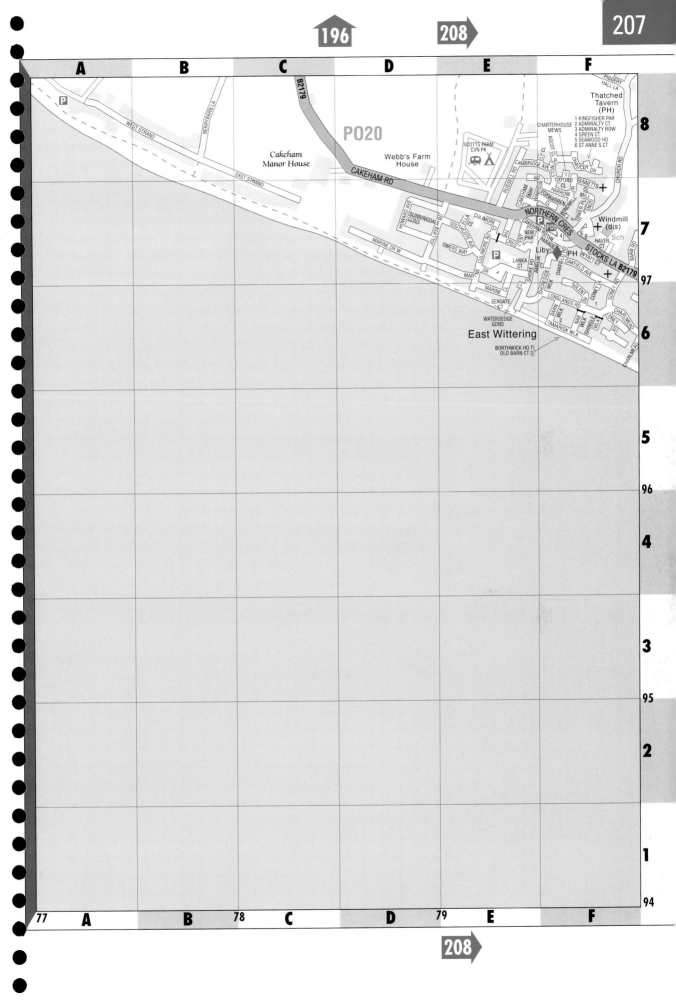

8

PO20

Thatched
Tavern
(PH)

1 KINGFISHER PAR
2 ADMIRALTY CT
3 ADMIRALTY ROW
4 GREEN CT
5 SEAWOOD HO
6 ST ANNE'S CT

CHARTERHOUSE
MEWS

PIGGERY
HALL LA

SCOTTS FARM
CVN PK

Cakeham
Manor House

Webb's Farm
House

WEST STRAND

BERRY BARN LA

B2179

CAKEHAM RD

EAST STRAND

CAMBRIDGE AVE

RUSSELL RD

ELY CL

WINDSOR

FOXWARREN

CHAUCER DR

CHURCH RD

OXFORD
CL

HARROW

BENNETTS
CT

MILL

TOWER PL

Windmill
(dis)

7

NORTHERN CRES

CAKEHAM
ROTHER
NEW
PAR

HAVEN
CT

STOCKS LA B2179

BARN RD

Sch

HOWARD AVE

SUNNINGDALE
GDNS

JOLLIFFE RD

SOUTHCOTE AVE

CULIMORE

CULIMORE RD

ELLA

CENT
CRES

Liby

PH

WYATT CT

97

MARINE DR W

OWERS WAY

LANKA
CT

SHORE RD

AMELIA
CT

SHOREHSIDE

OAKFIELD

OAKFIELD AVE

COMET CL

SOLENT

CANEY

CHARLMEAD

MARINE

SEAGATE
CT

MAR
NE DR

MARINE
CE

LONGLANDS RD

BARN
WLK

SHINGLE
WLK

XISTO

East Wittering

WATERSEDGE
GDNS

TAMARISK W.K.

BORTHWICK HO 1
OLD BARN CT 2

CHARLMEAD

6

5

96

4

3

95

2

1

94

A B C D E F

8

CHURCH FARM LA
CHURCH FARM CT
HILTON PK
Stubcroft Farm
RED HOUSE FARM CAMPING & CVN SITE
SOMERLEY LA
THIRD AVE
Batchmere Est
Almodington

East Wittering Bsns Ctr
B2198
Cherry Tree Farm
BORDERS LA
Somerley Farm
Earnley Gardens
MANHOOD COTTS
EASTON LA

7

FIELD RD
MEADOWS RD
WESSEX AVE
CLAYTON LA
BRACKLESHAM LA
ALMODINGTON LA
Earnley Grange
Grange Farm

97

SOUTHDOWN CT
DOWNVIEW CL
B2179
STOCKS
30
Holiday Centre
Caravan Park
EARNLEY MANOR CL
ON WAY

SEAFIELD WAY
IMAGES LA
KIMBRIDGE LA
ROBINSON WAY
CLAPPERS LA
Earnley
PO20
Grange Rife

6

SEAFIELD WAY
SEAFIELD CL
KIMBRIDGE RD
PEERLEY RD
Camping Site
VALE
INDLEY DR
GRAYSWOOD AVE
ELM CL
BRACKLESHAM CT
BRACKLESHAM CT
PH

WEST BRACKLESHAM DR
PEERLEY CL
ESION WAY
B2179
GARDEN AVE
BEECH AVE
Bracklesham
DROVE LA
Marsh Barn

CORMORANT WAY
SANDOPIPER CT
ROSTOCK
PERE CL
WOODBOROUGH WAY CRES
1 AXFORD CL
2 CHANDLERS LEA
3 HAYWARDS PL
4 CANUTE CL

BOURNE
B2198
PO
ELMODNE CT
ARMADA CT
HARMONY DR
FARM RD
SANDRINGHAM DR
ELCOMBE CL
SHALBOURNE CL
MANTONS CL
WILTON CL
AVEBURY CL

5

WESTERLEY GDNS 1
AZARA PAR 2
P
FIRST AVE
SECOND AVE
THIRD AVE
LADOCK
Marsh Farm

Old Farm Cl
EAST BRACKLESHAM DR
SILVER WAY
WALLINSTEY'S WAY 3
Caravan Park
Sussex Beach Holiday Village

MARINES
SEANELL DR
LEIGH CT
SILVER WAY
STONEY LA

96

4

BYWAVES
Caravan Park

3

Bracklesham Bay

95

2

1

94

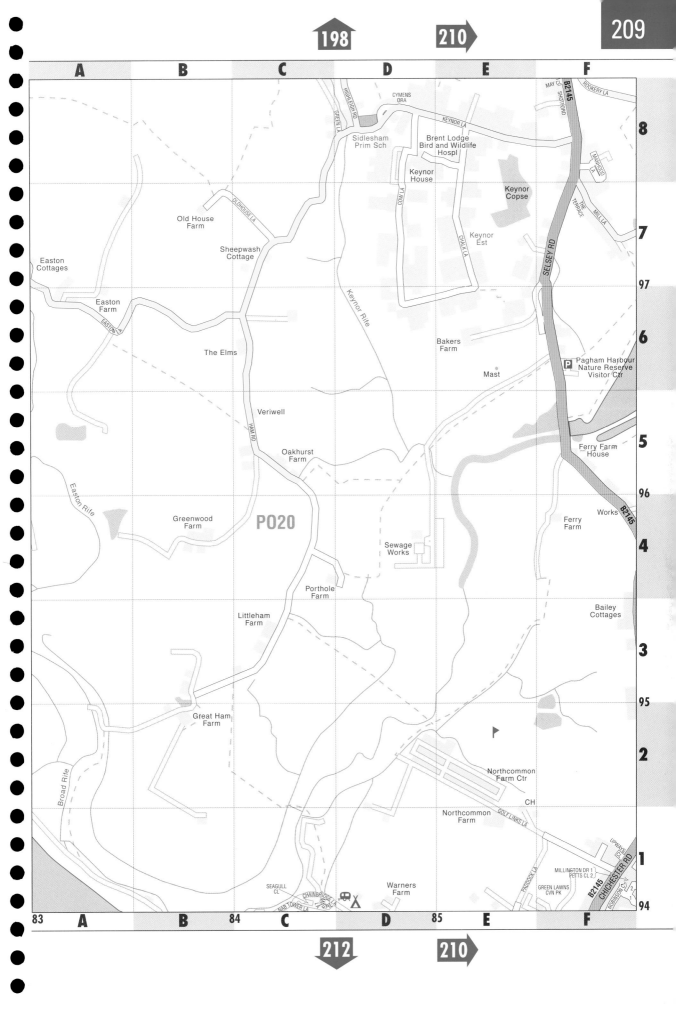

8

CYMENS ORA

KEYNOR LA

Sidlesham Prim Sch

Brent Lodge Bird and Wildlife Hospl

Keynor House

Keynor Copse

HIGHLEIGH RD

GREEN LA

MAY CL

SHOTFORD

B2145

ROOKERY LA

MANHOOD LA

THE TERRACE

MILL A

7

Old House Farm

OLD HOUSE LA

Sheepwash Cottage

COW LA

CHALK LA

Keynor Est

SELSEY RD

Easton Cottages

Easton Farm

EASTON ST

The Elms

Keynor Rife

Bakers Farm

Mast

97

6

Pagham Harbour Nature Reserve Visitor Ctr

P

Veriwell

HAM RD

Oakhurst Farm

5

Ferry Farm House

Easton Rife

Greenwood Farm

PO20

Sewage Works

96

Works

B2145

Ferry Farm

Porthole Farm

Littleham Farm

Bailey Cottages

4

3

Great Ham Farm

95

Northcommon Farm Ctr

CH

2

Broad Rife

Northcommon Farm

GOLF LINKS LA

UPWAYS

MILLINGTON DR 1

PETTS CL 2

GREEN LAWNS CVN PK

PADDOCK LA

B2145

CHICHESTER RD

ROBINSON

1

SEAGULL CL

CHAINBRIDGE LA

NAB TOWER LA

Warners Farm

94

A B C D E F

8 PO20

Rookery Farm

ROOKERY LA

Halsey's Farm

Cumbers

MILL LA

Crab & Lobster (PH)

7

97

6

Pagham Wall

Little Welbourne

Pagham

CHURCH LA

CHURCH CL

VENUS LA

Church Farm Holiday Village

Becket's Barn

PO21

HERON MEAD

MALLARD CRES

MARTLET WAY

SAXON CL

ST. THOMAS DR

SWAN DENE

KESTREL CT

WELL RD

WYTHERING CL

LAGOON RD

HARBOUR RD

WEST FRONT RD

PAGHAM RD

QUEENSMEAD

SEA WAY

JUNE CL

SEA LA

Pagham Lagoon

Pagham Beach Est

P

5

96

4

B2145

Home Farm

Norton

Church Norton

RECTORY LA

GRANGE LA

Norton Priory

P

3

95

1 Trident Bsns Pk
2 The Courtyard

PO20

Pigeonhouse Farm

Lydiate

Greenlease Farm

GRANGE LA

CHICHESTER RD

Coles Farm

2

The Grange

Bird Reserve

1

B2145

Four Ways

MANOR RD

MIN CL

Park Farm

PARK LA

MANOR LA

DRIFT RD

East Beach

EAST BEACH RD

PARK COPSE

1 HARDING CL
2 PETTS CL
3 MILLINGTON DR

94

86 A 87 B C 88 D E F

ELLIS SQ

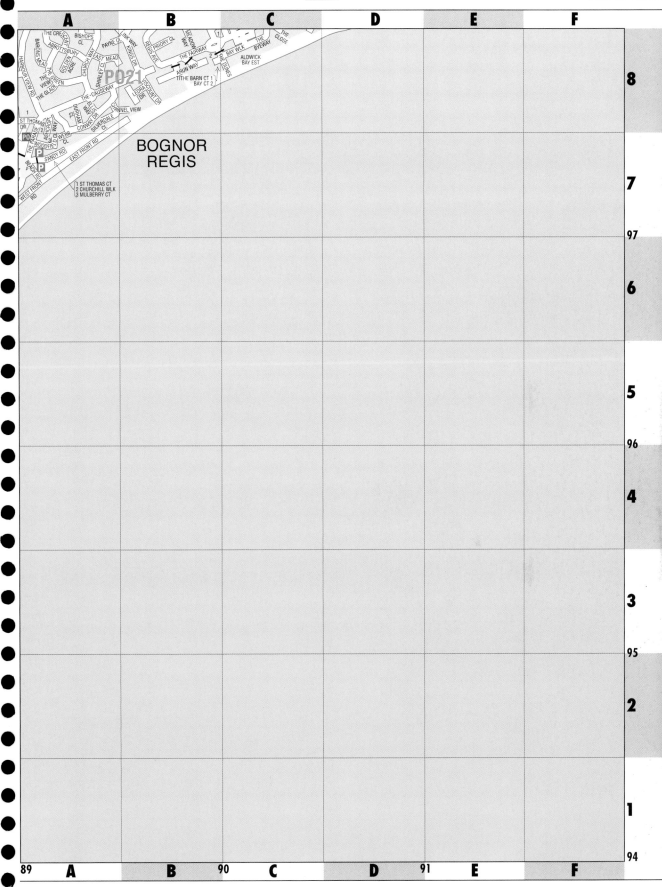

BOGNOR
REGIS

1 ST THOMAS CT
2 CHURCHILL WLK
3 MULBERRY CT

209

D7
1 MEDMERRY CT
2 McRAE CT
3 Selsey Bsns Ctr

F8
1 SHERRINGTON MEWS

210

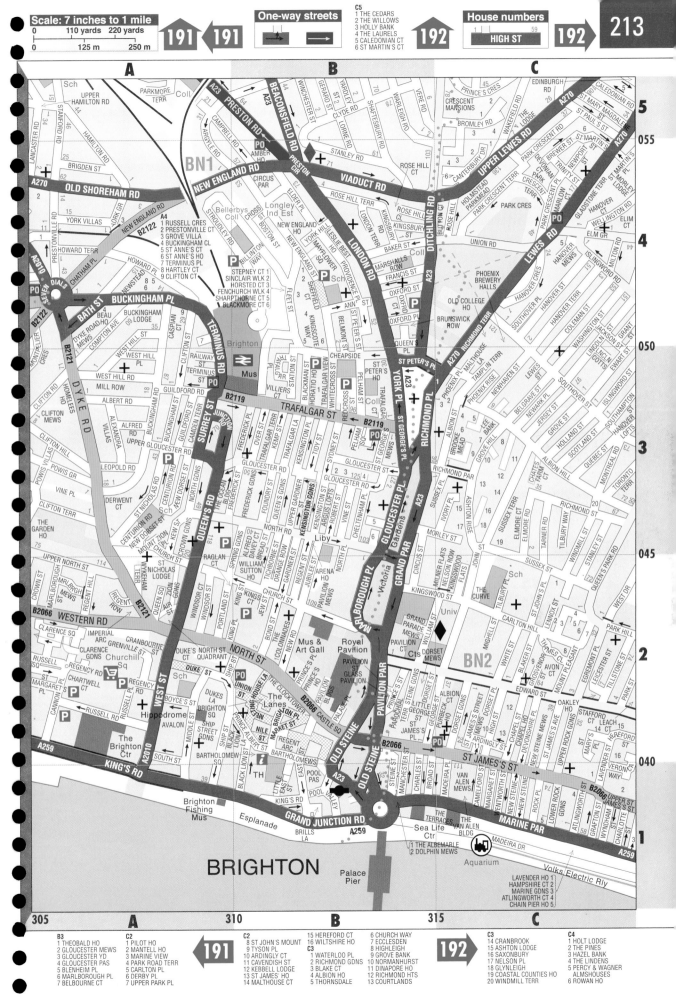

Index

Place name May be abbreviated on the map

Location number Present when a number indicates the place's position in a crowded area of mapping

Locality, town or village Shown when more than one place has the same name

Postcode district District for the indexed place

Page and grid square Page number and grid reference for the standard mapping

Church Rd 6 Beckenham BR2..........53 C6

Cities, towns and villages are listed in CAPITAL LETTERS

Public and commercial buildings are highlighted in magenta   **Places of interest** are highlighted in blue with a star★

Abbreviations used in the index

Acad	Academy	Comm	Common	Gd	Ground	L	Leisure	Prom	Promenade
App	Approach	Cott	Cottage	Gdn	Garden	La	Lane	Rd	Road
Arc	Arcade	Cres	Crescent	Gn	Green	Liby	Library	Recn	Recreation
Ave	Avenue	Cswy	Causeway	Gr	Grove	Mdw	Meadow	Ret	Retail
Bglw	Bungalow	Ct	Court	H	Hall	Meml	Memorial	Sh	Shopping
Bldg	Building	Ctr	Centre	Ho	House	Mkt	Market	Sq	Square
Bsns, Bus	Business	Ctry	Country	Hospl	Hospital	Mus	Museum	St	Street
Bvd	Boulevard	Cty	County	HQ	Headquarters	Orch	Orchard	Sta	Station
Cath	Cathedral	Dr	Drive	Hts	Heights	Pal	Palace	Terr	Terrace
Cir	Circus	Dro	Drove	Ind	Industrial	Par	Parade	TH	Town Hall
Cl	Close	Ed	Education	Inst	Institute	Pas	Passage	Univ	University
Cnr	Corner	Emb	Embankment	Int	International	Pk	Park	Wk, Wlk	Walk
Coll	College	Est	Estate	Intc	Interchange	Pl	Place	Wr	Water
Com	Community	Ex	Exhibition	Junc	Junction	Prec	Precinct	Yd	Yard

Index of towns, villages, streets, hospitals, industrial estates, railway stations, schools, shopping centres, universities and places of interest

214 Abb–Ale

A

Abberton Field BN6..... 128 B5
Abbey Cl BN15........... 188 B6
Abbey Ho RH20......... 142 D8
Abbey Rd
　Brighton BN2...........192 D4
　Lancing BN15...........187 B6
　Steyning BN44.........145 E4
　Worthing BN11.........186 B1
Abbie Ct PO22.........180 C5
Abbotsbury Cl BN2.....194 B1
Abbotsbury Ct RH13... 36 E3
Abbots Cl BN6..........128 E4
Abbotsfield Rd RH11... 17 D4
ABBOTSFORD..........108 E6
Abbotsleigh RH13.......82 A8
Abbots Way BN15.......187 F6
Abbotswood Wlk
　BN16.................205 C4
Abbotts 11 BN1.........191 E5
Abbottsbury PO21......211 A8
Abbotts Cl
　Boxgrove PO18.........156 D3
　Worthing BN11.........186 D2
Abbotts View BN15.....187 C8
A'becket Gdns BN13....185 F7
A'becket's Ave PO21....200 B1
Aberdare Cl PO19.......177 B8
Aberdeen Rd 5 BN2...192 C8
Abergavenny Gdns
　RH10..................... 7 D3
Abigail Ho 10 RH16......87 E4
Abingdon Wlk BN13.....185 D6
Abinger Cl BN41........190 B8
Abinger Keep RH6........2 C4
Abinger Lo BN15........188 C5
Abinger Rd
　Portslade-by-S BN41...190 B8
　Woodingdean BN2.....193 E6
ABINGWORTH..........122 A6
Abrahams Rd RH11..... 18 A1
Acacia Ave
　Hove BN3..............168 F1
　Worthing BN13.........185 F8
Acacia Cl BN1...........169 F2
Acacia Villas PO20.....177 B1
Acorn Ave RH13.........83 F1

Acorn Cl
　Angmering BN16........205 F8
　East Grinstead RH19... 22 E8
　Horley RH6..............2 C4
　Selsey PO20............212 D8
Acorn End PO21........200 D2
Acorns RH13.............37 A4
Acorns The
　Burgess Hill RH15......108 D4
　Crawley RH11..........18 B1
　Sayers Common BN6...107 D2
Acre Cl
　Haywards Heath RH16...87 D2
　Rustington BN16........205 B6
Acre Cl The BN11........186 B1
Acre Gdns BN11.........186 B1
Acre St PO20............196 F2
Acre The BN16..........184 A6
Adams Cl BN1...........170 B2
Adams Mews 6 RH11... 18 B1
Adastra Ave BN6........129 A4
Adderbury Ave PO10...151 B3
Addison Cl BN15........187 E6
Addison Rd BN3.........191 E7
Addison Way PO22.....201 C7
Adelaide Cl
　Crawley RH11...........5 D1
　Horsham RH12..........36 F4
　Worthing BN13.........185 C8
Adelaide Cotts PO18...156 E6
Adelaide Cres BN3......191 C5
Adelaide Rd PO19......177 B7
Adelaide Sq BN43.......189 B7
Adelphi Cl RH10.........19 D4
Admers Cres GU30...... 25 C2
Admiral Cl BN1..........170 B2
Admiral Rd RH11........ 18 A3
Admiral's Bridge La
　RH19...................22 C2
Admirals Wlk
　Funtington PO18........153 A5
　Littlehampton BN17....205 A6
　1 Shoreham-by-S
　BN43.................188 F6
Admiralty Cl
　Bognor Regis PO22.....201 F3
　East Wittering PO20...207 F7
Admiralty Gdns PO22...201 F3
Admiralty Rd PO22.....201 F4
Admiralty Row PO20...207 F7
Adrian Ct RH11.........18 B1

Adur Ave
　Shoreham-by-S BN43...166 E1
　Worthing BN13.........185 C9
Adur Cl 6 BN15.........188 C5
Adur Ct
　5 Lancing BN15........188 C5
　10 Shoreham-by-S
　BN43.................189 C8
Adur Dr BN43...........189 A7
Adur Rd
　Burgess Hill RH15......109 C4
　Shoreham-by-S BN43...188 E8
Adur Valley Ct BN44....146 B2
Adur View BN44.........146 A2
Adversane Ct RH12..... 36 D4
Adversane Cvn Pk
　RH14...................79 A2
Adversane La RH14.....79 D2
Adversane Rd BN44.....186 B5
Aegean Ho 3 BN16.....205 A4
Agate La RH12.........36 F5
Aglaia Rd BN11.........185 F2
Agnes St BN2...........192 C7
Aigburth Ave PO21.....200 D3
Ailsa Cl RH11...........18 B3
Ainsdale Cl BN13.......185 D7
Ainsdale Rd BN13.......185 D7
Ainsworth Ave BN2.....193 D3
Ainsworth Cl BN2.......193 D3
Ainsworth Ho 1 BN2...192 C7
Aintree Rd RH10........19 A4
Airedale Ct 8 BN11.....186 B2
Airlie Ho BN3...........191 C6
Airport Way RH6.........6 B8
Airport Way Rdbt E RH6... 6 C8
Airport Way Rdbt W
　RH6.....................5 F8
Air St BN1...............213 A2
Aitken Ho GU27.........27 C7
Ajax Pl PO22............202 C5
Akehurst Cl RH10........7 B3
Alandale Rd
　Birdham PO20..........197 F4
　Lancing BN15..........165 C1
Alan Way BN3...........192 F5
Albany Cl BN11.........186 A1
Albany Mews BN3.......191 B6
Albany Rd RH11.........18 C6
Albany Terr 3 BN3......191 B5
Albany Villas
　Cuckfield RH17........87 A6
　Hove BN3..............191 B6

Albemarle Mans 8
　BN3....................191 B5
Albemarle The BN2....213 B1
Alberta Rd BN13.......185 D7
Alberta Wlk BN13......185 D7
Albert Cl RH16..........88 A4
Albert Crane Ct RH11... 18 A8
Albert Dr RH15.........108 E2
Albert Mews BN3.......191 C6
Albert Rd
　Bognor Regis PO21....201 D3
　Brighton BN1...........213 A3
　Fishbourne PO19.......176 C6
　Horley RH6..............2 A3
　Littlehampton BN17....204 D5
　Rustington BN16........205 C6
　Southwick BN42.......189 D7
Albery Cl RH12..........36 B4
Albion Cl RH10..........19 D5
Albion Ct
　Brighton BN2...........213 C2
　Burgess Hill RH15......108 F2
Albion Hill BN2.........213 C3
Albion Ho
　4 Brighton BN2........213 C3
　Southwick BN42.......189 F7
Albion Rd PO20.........212 F6
Albion St
　Brighton BN2...........213 C3
　Portslade-by-S BN41...190 B7
　Southwick BN42.......189 E7
Albion Way RH12........36 C2
Albourne CE Prim Sch
　BN6...................127 C6
Albourne Cl BN2.......192 F7
Albourne Rd BN6......127 E6
ALBOURNE STREET...127 C5
Albury Keep RH6.........2 B4
Aldeburgh Ho RH6.......2 A2
Alder Cl
　Crawley Down RH10... 21 B8
　Worthing BN13.........185 C6
Alder Copse RH12...... 57 F8
Alderfield GU32..........68 A3
Alderman's Wlk PO19...177 A7
Aldermoor Ave RH20...121 E3
Alderney Rd BN12......206 F4
Alders Ave RH19.........9 E3
Alders View Dr RH19....9 E3
Alder Way PO22........202 E6
Aldingbourne Cl RH11... 17 F7

Aldingbourne Ctry Ctr★
　PO18.................157 C3
Aldingbourne Dr
　PO18.................157 B3
Aldingbourne Ho
　Crockerhill PO18.......157 B3
　Littlehampton BN17....204 B7
Aldingbourne Pk
　PO20.................179 D5
Aldingbourne Prim Sch
　PO20.................179 D6
Aldrich Cl BN2..........192 F6
ALDRINGTON..........190 E6
Aldrington Ave BN3....191 A8
Aldrington CE Prim Sch
　BN3..................169 A2
Aldrington Cl BN3.....190 D7
Aldrington House Hospl
　BN3..................190 F6
Aldrington Pl BN3.....190 D8
Aldrington Sta BN3.....191 A8
ALDSWORTH..........151 F6
Aldsworth Ave BN12....185 B2
Aldsworth Common Rd
　PO10.................151 E5
Aldsworth Ct BN12.....185 B3
Aldsworth Manor Barns
　PO10.................151 F6
Aldsworth Par BN12....185 B3
ALDWICK..............200 E2
Aldwick Ave PO21......200 F2
Aldwick Bay Est PO21...211 C8
Aldwick Cl 1 BN16.....205 B3
Aldwick Cres BN14.....164 A1
Aldwick Felds PO21....200 F2
Aldwick Gdns PO21.....200 F3
Aldwick Ho PO21......201 A2
Aldwick Hundred
　PO21.................200 E1
Aldwick Pl PO21........200 F2
Aldwick Rd PO21.......201 B2
Aldwick St PO21........200 E2
Aldwych Cl RH10........19 D4
Alexander Cl PO21.....200 E2
Alexandra Ct
　10 Crawley RH10...... 18 D5
　Hove BN3.............168 F2
　Worthing BN12.........185 C4
Alexandra Rd PO21....201 E4
Alexandra Rd
　Burgess Hill RH15......109 C2
　Chichester PO19.......177 B7
　Lancing BN15..........187 F5

Alexandra Rd *continued*
  Worthing BN11 . . . . 186 F2
Alexandra Terr **14**
  PO21 . . . . 201 D3
Alexandra Villas BN1. . . . 213 A3
ALFOLD BARS 31 E7
Alfold By-Pass GU6 . . . . . 11 A5
Alfold Craft Ctr GU6 . . . . . . 11 A1
Alfold Crossways GU6. . . . 11 A5
Alfold Rd GU6 . . . . 11 B7
Alford Cl BN14 . . . . 186 A7
Alfred Cl
  Crawley RH10 . . . . 19 E5
  Middleton-on-S PO22. . . . 202 F5
Alfred Davey Ct BN1 . . . . 213 B5
Alfred Pl BN11 . . . . 186 E2
Alfred Rd BN1 . . . . 213 A3
Alfrey Cl PO10 . . . . 173 E8
Alfriston Cl
  Bognor Regis PO22 . . . . . 202 C6
  Brighton BN2 . . . . 192 F6
  Worthing BN14 . . . . 186 D5
Alfriston Ho **2** BN14 . . . 186 D5
Alfriston Rd BN14. . . . . . . 186 D5
Alice Cl **2** BN3 . . . . 191 D5
Alice St BN3 . . . . 191 D5
Alicia Ave
  Ashington RH20. . . . . 123 A5
  Crawley RH10 . . . . 19 C6
Alicks Hill RH14 . . . . 79 D8
Alinora BN17 . . . . 204 E4
Alinora Ave BN12 . . . . . . 185 D2
Alinora Cl BN12. . . . . 185 D2
Alinora Cres BN12 . . . . . . 185 D2
Alinora Dr BN12 . . . . 185 D2
Allandale Cl PO20 . . . . . . 212 F8
Allangate Dr BN16 . . . . . . 205 D6
Allcard Cl RH12. . . . . 36 D4
Allee Dr GU30 . . . . 25 B5
Allendale RH13 . . . . 57 F3
Allendale Ave
  New Brighton PO10 . . . . . 151 A3
  Worthing BN14 . . . . 164 A1
Allen Rd RH16 . . . . 88 A4
Allen's Cl RH19 . . . . 23 D6
Allestree Ct **15** PO21 . . . 201 D3
Alley Groves RH13 . . . . . . 83 F2
Alleyne Way PO22 . . . . . 203 B5
Alley The
  Amberley RH20 . . . . 140 D7
  Stedham GU29. . . . . 72 A1
Allfrey Plat RH20 . . . . 100 D2
Allfreys Wharf RH20 . . . . 100 B2
Allingham Gdns RH12 . . . . 37 B5
Allington Rd BN14 . . . . . . 186 E7
Allman Bsns Pk PO20 . . . 198 B6
All Saints CE Prim Sch
  RH12. . . . . 36 F6
Allyington Way RH10. . . . . 19 D5
Alma Cotts BN5. . . . . 125 F4
Alma Rd RH16 . . . . 88 B8
Alma St BN15. . . . . 187 E4
Almodington La PO20 . . . 208 E7
Almond Ave BN43 . . . . . . 188 C8
Almond Cl RH11 . . . . 18 A5
Almshouses GU28. . . . . . 116 B7
Almshouses of The Holy
  Name BN6 . . . . 128 A5
Almshouses The
  PO18. . . . . 156 D4
Alperton Cl PO21 . . . . . . 200 C1
Alpha Cotts RH20 . . . . . . 100 D2
Alpha Ct
  Littlehampton BN17. . . . . 204 C5
  Worthing BN11 . . . . 186 D1
Alpha Rd RH11. . . . . 18 C6
Alpine Rd BN3 . . . . 190 F8
Alston Way BN13 . . . . 185 D6
Alternative Ctr for Ed
  BN1. . . . . 170 C3
Alverstone Rd BN11. . . . . 186 F3
Amadeus Ho BN16 . . . . . 206 B6
Ambassador Ho **15**
  PO19. . . . . 177 A6
Ambassadors The **10**
  BN3 . . . . 191 C6
Amber Ct
  20 Hove BN3. . . . . 191 C6
  8 Hove BN3 . . . . 191 D7
Amber Glade RH13. . . . . . 57 F1
Amber Ho
  Brighton BN1. . . . . 213 B4
  Hove BN3. . . . . 191 C6
Amberley CE Fst Sch
  BN18. . . . . 140 E7
Amberley Cl
  Burgess Hill RH15 . . . . . . 109 A4
  Crawley RH10 . . . . 19 C6
  Haywards Heath RH16 . . . 87 D4
  Horsham RH12 . . . . 37 A6
  Hove BN3. . . . . 168 E3
  Littlehampton BN17 . . . . . 204 E6
  Shoreham-by-S BN43. . . 166 F1
  Storrington RH20. . . . . . . 121 C1
Amberley Ct
  Billingshurst RH14 . . . . . . 79 C7
  Lancing BN15. . . . . 187 F6
  8 Worthing BN11 . . . . . 185 F3
Amberley Dr
  Bognor Regis PO21 . . . . . 201 A4
  Hove BN3. . . . . 168 E3
  Worthing BN12 . . . . 185 B2
Amberley Fields Cvn Pk
  RH11. . . . . 5 B4
Amberley Gate BN17. . . . 204 D5
Amberley Ho **6** RH13 . . . 36 D1
Amberley Lo BN2 . . . . . . 192 F6

Amberley Rd
  Horsham RH12 . . . . 37 A6
  Littlehampton BN16. . . . . 205 C4
  Storrington RH20. . . . . . . 142 A8
Amberley Sta BN18. . . . . 140 D4
Amberley Working Mus★
  BN18. . . . . 140 D5
Ambersham Cres
  BN16 . . . . 205 F7
Amblefield Ct GU28 . . . . . 51 A7
Ambleside Cl
  Bognor Regis PO22 . . . . . 202 B6
  Crawley RH11 . . . . 17 D5
Ambleside Rd BN15. . . . . 187 C6
Ambrose Ho BN11 . . . . . . 186 D2
Ambrose Pl BN11 . . . . . . 186 D2
Ambrose's Hill RH17 . . . . 107 B6
Amelia Cres BN11. . . . . . . 186 C2
Amelia Ct PO20. . . . . 207 E7
Amelia Rd BN11 . . . . 186 C2
Amenic Ct **3** BN17. . . . . 204 E5
America La RH16 . . . . 88 A5
Amesbury Cres BN3. . . . . 190 E7
Amey Ind Est GU32. . . . . . 68 C3
Amherst Cres BN3 . . . . . . 190 F8
Amo Mews **8** BN11 . . . . 186 C1
Amstel Ct **2** BN17 . . . . . 204 F4
Amundsen Rd RH12 . . . . . 36 D6
Ancaster Cl BN43 . . . . 189 A6
Anchor Cl BN12. . . . . 185 E2
Anchor Hill RH17 . . . . 88 D3
Anchorhold The RH16 . . . . 87 D5
Anchor Springs **13**
  BN17. . . . . 204 D5
Ancren Cl BN12. . . . . 206 F7
Ancton Cl PO22. . . . . 202 C5
Ancton Dr PO22 . . . . 203 A6
Ancton La PO22 . . . . 202 C5
Ancton Lodge La
  PO22 . . . . 203 A5
Ancton Way PO22 . . . . . . 203 B5
Anderson Ct GU27 . . . . . . 27 C6
Andlers Ash RH13 . . . . 45 A3
Andrew Ave PO22. . . . . . . 202 C5
Andrew Cl
  Rustington BN16 . . . . 205 B6
  Steyning BN44. . . . . 145 D2
Andrews Cotts RH13 . . . . 81 F7
Andrews La GU29. . . . . . . 93 F7
Andrew's La RH13 . . . . 57 F1
Andrews Rd RH13 . . . . . . 81 F7
Andromeda Cl RH11 . . . . . 17 E3
Angell Cl RH10 . . . . 19 C5
Angell Est PO19 . . . . 177 D5
Angel St GU28 . . . . 97 F8
Anglesea St BN11 . . . . . . 186 C3
Anglesey Cl RH11 . . . . 18 C2
Angmering Cl BN1 . . . . . . 170 F5
Angmering La BN16 . . . . . 205 E5
Angmering Sch The
  BN16. . . . . 205 F7
Angmering Sta BN16 . . . . 205 F6
Angmering Way BN16 . . . 205 E7
Angola Rd BN14 . . . . 186 F4
Angus Cl RH12. . . . . 36 D4
Angus Rd BN12 . . . . 185 E3
Annandale Ave PO21 . . . . 201 C4
Ann Cl BN6 . . . . 129 A5
Anne Howard Gdns
  BN18 . . . . 160 A3
Annington Commercial Ctr
  BN44. . . . . 165 E8
Annington Gdns **4**
  BN43 . . . . 166 F1
Annington Rd BN44,
  BN15 . . . . 165 F8
Ann St
  Brighton BN1. . . . . 213 B4
  Worthing BN11 . . . . 186 E2
Annweir Ave BN15 . . . . . . 187 E6
Anscombe Cl BN11. . . . . . 185 F2
Anscombe Rd BN11 . . . . . 185 F2
Anscome **5** RH16. . . . . . 87 D6
Ansisters Rd BN12 . . . . . . 206 E5
Anson Ct BN12. . . . . 185 C5
Anson Rd
  Bognor Regis PO21 . . . . . 200 B2
  Worthing BN12 . . . . 185 C5
Ansty Cl BN2 . . . . 192 E5
Answorth Cl PO19 . . . . . . 155 B1
Anthony Way PO10. . . . . . 151 B3
Antlands La RH6. . . . . .6 C5
Antlands La E RH6. . . . . . . .6 F5
Antlands La W RH6. . . . . . .6 E6
Antonia Ct **10** BN17 . . . 204 D5
Anvil Cl
  Billingshurst RH14. . . . . . 79 C8
  Portslade-by-S BN41. . . . 168 B2
  Southwater RH13 . . . . 57 F1
Aperlie Dr RH6 . . . . 2 C1
Appledore Ct RH16. . . . . . 88 A7
Appledore Gdns RH16. . . . 88 A6
Appledore Rd BN2 . . . . . . 170 F4
Appledram La (N)
  PO19 . . . . 176 C6
Appledram La (S)
  PO20 . . . . 176 C4
Applefield RH10 . . . . 18 E7
Apple Gr
  Bognor Regis PO21 . . . . . 200 B1
  Hermitage PO10 . . . . 173 D8
Applesham Ave BN3 . . . . 168 E2
Applesham Ct **9**
  BN15 . . . . 187 E4
Applesham Way
  BN41 . . . . 168 A1
Appletree Dr PO22. . . . . . 180 B6
Appletrees BN16. . . . . 206 B4

Apple Tree Wlk BN17 . . . 181 D1
Approach The
  10 Brighton BN1. . . . . . 169 E3
  Dormansland RH19 . . . . . . .9 F6
April Cl
  Ferring BN12. . . . . 206 E4
  Horsham RH12 . . . . 36 C4
April Gdns PO18 . . . . 154 E6
Apsley Ct RH11 . . . . 17 F4
Apsley Mews **9**
  BN11 . . . . 186 D3
Apsley Way BN13 . . . . . . 185 B6
Aquarium Sta★ BN2 . . . . 213 C1
Aquarius Ct RH11 . . . . 17 E4
Arbor Ct RH16 . . . . 87 E5
Arcade Rd BN17 . . . . 204 D5
Arcade The
  8 Bognor Regis
    PO21. . . . . 201 D3
  Liss GU33 . . . . 45 A5
  14 Littlehampton BN17 . 204 D5
Archer Ct RH15 . . . . 109 A3
Archers St **3** RH10 . . . . . 18 D8
Arch Ho **5** PO21. . . . . . 201 C2
Archibald Rd BN11. . . . . . 187 A3
Arcturus Rd RH11 . . . . 17 E3
Ardale Cl BN11 . . . . 185 F3
Arden Rd RH10 . . . . 18 F4
Ardingly Cl RH11 . . . . 18 B8
Ardingly Coll Prep Sch
  RH17. . . . . 64 A6
Ardingly Dr **10** BN2. . . . 213 C2
Ardingly Dr BN2 . . . . 185 B4
Ardingly Rd
  Ardingly RH16 . . . . 64 C2
  Cuckfield RH17 . . . . 86 F7
Ardingly St BN2 . . . . 213 C2
Ardingly Cl RH17 . . . . 64 B7
Ardsheal Cl BN14 . . . . . . 186 C5
Ardsheal Rd BN14. . . . . . 186 C6
Arena Ho BN1 . . . . 213 B2
Argus Lofts BN1 . . . . 213 B3
Argus Wlk RH11 . . . . 18 A3
Argyle Cir **5** PO21 . . . . 201 C3
Argyle Rd
  Bognor Regis PO21 . . . . . 201 C3
  Brighton BN1. . . . . 213 A5
Argyll Hall **16** BN17 . . . 204 D5
Ariadne Rd BN11 . . . . . . 186 B1
Ariel Ct BN15 . . . . 187 D4
Arkendale RH19 . . . . 9 A4
Arlington Ave BN12 . . . . . 185 B2
Arlington Cl BN12. . . . . . . 185 B2
Arlington Cres
  Brighton BN1. . . . . 170 E5
  East Preston BN16 . . . . . . 206 B7
Arlington Ct RH16 . . . . 87 E5
Arlington Gdns BN2. . . . . 194 D2
Armada Ho PO19 . . . . . . 177 C7
Armada Way BN17 . . . . . . 205 A6
Arndale Rd BN17 . . . . 204 B6
Arne Cl RH11 . . . . 17 F3
Arne Gr RH6 . . . . .1 E5
Arnell Ave PO20 . . . . 212 E7
Arnfield Cl RH11 . . . . 17 E5
Arnhem Rd PO21 . . . . 201 B5
Arnold St BN2 . . . . 192 C7
Arnold Way PO18 . . . . . . 175 C7
Arnside Cl BN15 . . . . 187 C5
Arran Cl RH11 . . . . 18 B3
Arrancourt **1** RH12. . . . . 36 B2
Arran Gate PO21 . . . . 201 E3
Arrivals Rd RH6. . . . . .5 F8
Artel Croft RH10. . . . . 19 A6
Artex Ave BN16 . . . . 205 C7
Arthur Bliss Ho RH16. . . . 88 A8
Arthur Ct
  Crawley RH11 . . . . 17 E6
  Horsham RH13 . . . . 36 D1
Arthur St BN3 . . . . 191 A8
Arts Rd BN1 . . . . 171 B7
Arun Beck BN6 . . . . 128 A8
Arun Bsns Pk PO22 . . . . . 201 E5
Arun Cl
  Amberley BN18 . . . . 140 E7
  Lancing BN17 . . . . 187 C7
  Petersfield GU31. . . . . 68 A2
  Rustington BN16 . . . . 205 C6
  Worthing BN13 . . . . 185 D8
Arun Cres BN13 . . . . 185 C8
Arun Ct
  East Preston BN16 . . . . . . 206 A5
  Littlehampton BN17. . . . . 204 C5
  Littlehampton, Wick
    BN17. . . . . 204 D7
  1 Pulborough RH20. . . 100 C2
  13 Shoreham-by-S
    BN43. . . . . 189 C8
Arundale Sch RH20 . . . . . 100 D2
Arundel **4** BN15 . . . . . . 187 D5
Arundel By-Pass
  BN18 . . . . 160 B2
Arundel Castle &
  Grounds★ BN18 . . . . . . 160 B3
Arundel CE Prim Sch
  BN18. . . . . 159 F2
Arundel Cl
  Bognor Regis PO21 . . . . . 201 A4
  Conford GU30 . . . . 24 D8
  Crawley RH10 . . . . 19 C6
  Shoreham-by-S BN43. . . 189 C8
  Southwater RH13 . . . . 58 A1
Arundel Ct
  Billingshurst RH14. . . . . . 79 D7
  6 Brighton, Black Rock
    BN2. . . . . 192 E4

Arundel Ct *continued*
  Brighton, Westdene
    BN1. . . . . 169 C5
  Burgess Hill RH15 . . . . . . 108 F4
  Ferring BN12. . . . . 206 F4
  14 Shoreham-by-S
    BN43. . . . . 189 C8
  9 Worthing BN11 . . . . . 185 F3
Arundel & District Hospl
  BN18. . . . . 160 A3
Arundel Dr BN17 . . . . 182 C5
Arundel Dr E BN2 . . . . . . 194 C1
Arundel Dr W BN2 . . . . . . 194 C1
Arundel Gdn **12** BN16 . 205 C5
Arundel Ho **4** RH13. . . . 36 E1
Arundel Mews
  10 Brighton BN2 . . . . . 192 E4
  Haywards Heath RH16 . . . 87 F2
Arundel Mus & Heritage
  Ctr★ BN18 . . . . 160 B3
Arundel Pl BN2 . . . . 192 E3
Arundel RC Cathedral★
  BN18. . . . . 160 B3
Arundel Rd
  Angmering BN16 . . . . 183 F6
  Brighton BN2 . . . . 192 E4
  Chichester PO18, PO19,
    PO20. . . . . 177 E8
  Fontwell BN18 . . . . 157 F3
  Littlehampton BN17 . . . . . 204 C6
  Selden BN16, BN13 . . . . . 184 C8
  Tangmere PO18, PO21 . . 156 C2
  Walberton BN18 . . . . 158 D2
  Worthing BN13 . . . . 185 D9
Arundel St BN2 . . . . 192 E3
Arundel Sta BN18. . . . . . . 160 C1
Arundel Terr BN2 . . . . 192 E3
Arundel Villas GU30 . . . . . 24 D8
Arundel Wildfowl &
  Wetlands Trust★
  BN18. . . . . 160 C5
Arun Ford Cl BN18 . . . . . . 181 E3
Arun Lo BN13. . . . . 185 D8
Arun Par BN17 . . . . 204 D3
Arun Prospect RH20 . . . . 100 A1
Arun Rd
  Billingshurst RH14. . . . . . 55 C1
  Bognor Regis PO21 . . . . . 201 A4
Arun Ret Pk PO22. . . . . . . 201 E6
Arunside RH12. . . . . 36 A1
Arunside Ind Est
  BN17. . . . . 204 C6
Arunside Sch RH12 . . . . . 36 A2
Arun St BN18 . . . . 160 B2
Arun Terr BN18 . . . . 160 A2
Arun Vale RH20 . . . . 119 C5
Arun Vale Inf Sch
  BN17. . . . . 204 D5
Arun Way
  Bognor Regis PO21 . . . . . 211 B8
  Horsham RH13 . . . . 36 E1
Ascot Cl PO20 . . . . 207 F8
Ascot Way BN16 . . . . 205 E6
Ashacre La BN13. . . . . 186 A7
Ashacre Mews BN13 . . . . 185 F8
Ashacre Way BN13. . . . . . 186 A6
Ashburnham Cl
  Brighton BN1. . . . . 170 C5
  Chichester PO19 . . . . 176 D7
  Worthing BN13 . . . . 185 B6
Ashburnham Dr
  Brighton BN1. . . . . 170 C5
  Cuckfield RH17 . . . . 86 E6
Ashburnham Ho BN1. . . . 169 C5
Ashburnham Mews
  RH17 . . . . 86 E6
Ashburnham Rd RH10. . . . 19 A4
Ashby Ct **6** RH13 . . . . . . 36 E1
Ash Cl
  Crawley Down RH10 . . . . . 21 C8
  Findon BN14 . . . . 163 C6
  Hove BN3. . . . . 169 C3
Ash Ct
  East Grinstead RH19 . . . . . 9 E3
  Southwick BN42 . . . . 167 F1
Ashdene Gdns RH20 . . . . 123 A4
Ashdown Ave BN2 . . . . . . 194 C1
Ashdown Cl
  Angmering BN16 . . . . 205 F8
  Haywards Heath RH16 . . . 88 B4
Ashdown Ct
  Crawley RH10 . . . . 18 F3
  Horsham RH13 . . . . 36 E1
Ashdown Dr RH10 . . . . 18 E3
Ashdown Forest Llama
  Pk★ RH18. . . . . 44 E4
Ashdown Gate RH19 . . . . . 9 D2
Ashdown Ho **8** BN11 . . 186 D3
Ashdown Nuffield Hospl
  RH16. . . . . 87 D6
Ashdown Pl RH18. . . . . 44 E4
Ashdown Rd
  7 Brighton BN2 . . . . . . 192 B8
  Forest Row RH18. . . . . 23 F2
  Worthing BN11 . . . . 186 D3
Ashdown View RH19 . . . . . 22 E7
Ashenground Cl **6**
  RH16 . . . . 87 E3

Ashenground Rd RH16 . . . 87 E4
Ashfield RH14 . . . . 30 E2
Ashfield Cl GU29. . . . . 94 E8
Ashfield Rd GU29. . . . . . . 94 E7
Ashfold Ave BN14 . . . . . . 164 A1
Ashfold Crossways
  RH13 . . . . 60 E6
Ashford Rd BN1 . . . . 170 A2
Ash Gr
  Bognor Regis PO22 . . . . . 201 C6
  Fernhurst GU27. . . . . 49 A6
  Haywards Heath RH16 . . . 87 D2
  Liphook GU30 . . . . 25 D3
  Worthing BN11 . . . . 186 A6
Ashgrove Cotts RH17. . . . 65 D5
Ash Grove Ind Pk
  PO22. . . . . 201 D7
Ashington CE Fst Sch
  RH20. . . . . 122 F5
Ashington Ct
  BN2 . . . . 192 F6
  3 Horsham RH12. . . . . . 36 D5
  4 Worthing BN14 . . . . . 186 E6
Ash Keys RH10 . . . . 18 E5
Ash La BN16 . . . . 205 C5
Ashleigh Cl
  Angmering BN16 . . . . 184 A6
  Horley RH6 . . . . 1 F3
Ashleigh Rd RH12. . . . . . . 36 C4
Ashley Cl BN1 . . . . 169 E7
Ashley Ct BN3 . . . . 191 C5
Ashlings Way
  Hove BN3. . . . . 168 E2
  Shoreham-by-S BN43. . . 167 B1
Ashmead Way BN16. . . . . 206 A8
Ashmere Gdns PO22 . . . . 202 B5
Ashmere La PO22 . . . . . . 202 C5
Ashmore Ave BN16 . . . . . 206 A8
Ashmore Ho RH11 . . . . 5 D1
Ashmore La RH12 . . . . . . 16 C6
Ash Rd
  Crawley RH10 . . . . 19 A8
  Southwater RH13 . . . . 57 E1
Ashton Gdns BN16 . . . . . 205 C4
Ashton Lo **15** BN2 . . . . 213 C3
Ashton Park Sch RH14 . . . 79 A1
Ashton Rise BN2 . . . . 213 C3
Ashton Rd BN2 . . . . 194 E1
Ashurst CE Prim Sch
  BN44. . . . . 124 D5
Ashurst Cl
  Bognor Regis PO21 . . . . . 201 A6
  Horsham RH12 . . . . 37 A5
  Worthing BN12 . . . . 185 B2
Ashurst Cotts RH19 . . . . . 42 F4
Ashurst Dr
  Crawley RH10 . . . . 19 D6
  Worthing BN12 . . . . 185 B2
Ashurst Pl RH16 . . . . 87 E5
Ashurst Rd BN2. . . . . 170 F5
Ashurst Way BN16 . . . . . . 206 A7
Ashurstwood Abbey
  RH19 . . . . 23 F6
Ashurst Wood Prim Sch
  RH19 . . . . 23 E6
Ashway RH15 . . . . 109 A2
Ashwood **5** RH11 . . . . . 18 D5
Ashwood Cl BN11 . . . . . . 186 F4
Ashwood Ct RH18. . . . . . . 23 F2
Ashwood Dr BN16 . . . . . . 205 C6
Ashwyn Bsns Ctr
  RH15. . . . . 108 F5
Aspen Cl RH16 . . . . 88 A4
Aspen Ct RH19. . . . . 23 A8
Aspen Way
  Horsham RH12 . . . . 36 E4
  Middleton-on-S PO22. . . 202 A6
Aspen Wlk RH16 . . . . 88 A4
Assisi Ct RH16. . . . . 87 F2
Assisi Hts RH16 . . . . 87 F2
Aston Ct
  5 Bognor Regis
    PO21. . . . . 201 D3
  Crawley RH11 . . . . 18 B1
Aston Lo **1** BN43 . . . . . 188 E7
Aston Rise RH20 . . . . 100 C3
Astra Bsns Ctr RH1 . . . . . . 2 A7
Astra Cl PO18. . . . . 175 C5
Astra Ho **10** BN1 . . . . . 191 E5
Athelstan Cl RH10 . . . . . . 19 E6
Athelstan Rd BN14 . . . . . 186 A4
Athelstan Way RH13 . . . . 58 E8
Athenaeum The **16**
  BN3 . . . . 191 C6
ATHERINGTON 203 F6
Athrington Ct PO22 . . . . . 202 B4
Atkinson Ct RH6 . . . . .2 B1
Atkinson Rd RH10. . . . . . . 19 C4
Atlantic Ct **4** BN43 . . . . 188 F6
Atlantic Ho **12** BN16. . . 205 B4
Atlingworth Ct BN2 . . . . . 213 C1
Atlingworth St BN2 . . . . . 213 C1
Attlee Ho **5** RH11 . . . . . 18 B2
Attree Ct **8** BN2 . . . . . . 192 C6
Attree Dr BN2. . . . . 192 C6
Auchinleck Cl RH10. . . . . . 21 B7
Auckland Cl RH11 . . . . 5 D1
Auckland Dr BN2 . . . . 170 F1
Audrey Cl BN1. . . . . 169 E5
Augusta Ct **5** PO19 . . . 155 A2
Augusta Ho **4** BN11 . . . 186 D1
Augusta Pl BN11 . . . . 186 D1
Augustines Way RH14 . . . 87 F4
Aurum Cl RH6 . . . . .2 B2
Austen Cl RH19 . . . . .9 B1

Austen Ct 9 PO21 ...... 201 C4
Austens GU29 .... 115 C8
Autumn Cl RH11 .... 18 C5
Avalon BN1 .... 213 A2
Avalon Ct PO10 .... 151 B2
Avalon Way BN13 ..... 185 D7
Avebury Cl
  Bracklesham PO20 ..... 208 C5
  Horsham RH12 .... 37 A3
Aveling Cl RH10 ...... 19 C4
Avenals The BN16..... 184 A5
Avenue App PO19...... 176 F7
Avenue Cl GU30 ...... 25 B4
Avenue Ct 21 BN3..... 191 C6
Avenue De Chartres
  PO19 .... 176 F6
Avenue Gdns RH6...... 2 C2
Avenue The
  Bognor Regis PO21 .... 201 B3
  Brighton BN2 .... 170 E1
  Chichester PO19 ..... 155 A2
  Funtington PO18 ..... 152 E7
  Hambrook PO18 ...... 152 D1
  Haslemere GU27 ..... 26 F7
  Horley RH6 ....1 F2
  Horsham RH13 ...... 57 D5
  Kingston near Lewes
    BN7 ....172 D5
  Liphook GU30 ...... 25 B4
  Petersfield GU31 .... 68 B3
  Shoreham-by-S BN43.. 166 F1
  Worthing BN12 ..... 185 C5
Avery Cl BN41 .... 167 F4
Avian Gdns PO21 ..... 200 B2
Aviary Ct PO18 ...... 152 D2
Aviary Way RH11 ..... 8 C1
Aviation Trad Est
  BN6 .... 127 B3
Avila Ho 6 BN11...... 186 C2
Avisford Park Rd
  BN18 .... 158 F1
Avocet Quay PO10 .... 173 C2
Avocet Trad Est RH15 . 108 F2
Avon Cl
  Bognor Regis PO22 ... 202 D5
  Lancing BN15........ 187 B6
  Petersfield GU31...... 68 A3
Avon Ct
  Brighton BN2 .... 213 C2
  Lancing BN15........ 187 B6
Avondale Cl
  Horley RH6 .... 2 A5
  Worthing BN12 ..... 185 D4
Avondale Rd BN3 ..... 191 D7
Avonhurst RH15 ...... 109 B3
Avon Rd BN17 .... 204 D5
Avon Wlk RH11 ...... 17 F5
Awbrook Cl RH17 .... 88 F3
Axford Cl PO20 ...... 208 C5
Aylesbury BN3........ 191 E6
Aylwin Ct 1 RH12 .... 36 A1
Aylwin Pl PO21 ...... 177 C1
Aymer Ho 4 BN3 ..... 191 A6
Aymer Rd BN3 .... 191 A6
Aynsley Ct BN3 ...... 191 C8
Ayshe Court Dr RH13.. 36 E3
Azalea Rd RH20 ...... 122 B2
Azalea Dr GU27 ...... 26 F8
Azara Par PO20 ...... 208 B6

B

Babsham La PO21...... 200 F8
Back La
  Balcombe Lane RH10,
    RH17............. 41 C7
  Crawley RH10 ...... 20 D1
  Plaistow RH14....... 30 E2
Backwoods Cl RH16.... 88 B6
Backwoods La RH16.... 88 B6
Baden Dr RH6 ....1 E4
Baden Rd BN2........ 170 D1
Bader Ct 6 RH11 .... 18 D8
Badger Cl BN41....... 168 B2
Badger Copse BN5..... 125 E6
Badger Dr RH6 .... 87 C5
Badgers Cl RH12...... 36 F6
Badgers Holt RH20.... 122 B1
Badgers Way
  East Grinstead RH19...9 F2
  Loxwood RH14....... 32 A4
Badgers Wlk
  Angmering BN16...... 205 F8
  Burgess Hill RH15..... 109 D2
Badgers Wood RH20... 121 D6
Badger Way BN1...... 170 E6
Badger Wlk PO19 .... 177 C8
Baffins Ct 7 PO19 .... 177 A6
Baffin's La PO19 ..... 177 A6
Bailey Cl
  Horsham RH12 ...... 36 F7
  Littlehampton BN17... 205 A7
Bailing Hill RH12..... 35 E7
Baird Cl RH10 .... 6 A1
Bakehouse Barn Cl
  RH12 .... 36 E7
Bakehouse Cotts RH14 . 53 A3
Bakehouse Rd RH6 ... 2 A5
Baker Cl RH10 ...... 18 D4
Bakerfield GU28 ..... 115 C8
Bakers Arms Hill
  BN18 .... 160 B3
Bakers Cl RH13...... 57 F1
Bakers Ct BN13...... 185 E8

Baker's La RH13 ...... 81 B4
Bakers Mews RH13 .... 60 A3
Baker St BN1 .... 213 B4
Bakery La PO21....... 201 C2
Bakery Mews BN1..... 170 C1
Balchins Cl RH14 .... 78 B8
Balcombe CE Prim Sch
  RH17............... 40 F2
Balcombe Ct
  Crawley RH10 ...... 19 D7
  Worthing BN11 ..... 186 B1
Balcombe Gdns RH6 .. 2 C2
Balcombe La
  Ardingly RH17 ...... 63 F8
  Sharpthorne RH17, RH19 . 43 E2
Balcombe Rd
  Balcombe Lane RH17... 40 F8
  Crawley, Tinsley Green RH6,
    RH10.............. 6 D5
  Crawley, Worth RH10... 19 D5
  Haywards Heath RH16 . 87 D7
  Horley RH6 .... 2 B2
  Balcombe Sta RH17... 40 F1
Baldwin Cl
  Crawley RH10 ...... 19 C3
  Middleton-on-S PO22...202 D6
Baldwins Field RH19 .. 9 C4
BALDWINS HILL 9 D4
Baldwins Hill Prim Sch
  RH19.............. 9 D3
Balfour Dr GU33 .... 45 B4
Balfour Gdns BN18.... 23 E1
Balfour Inf Sch BN1... 170 A3
Balfour Jun Sch BN1... 170 A3
Balfour Rd BN1....... 170 A2
Ballindune GU27 ..... 27 C8
Balliol Cl
  Bognor Regis PO21 ... 200 E4
  Crawley RH10 ...... 6 D1
Ball Tree Croft 1
  BN15 .... 187 C7
Balmer Farm Cotts
  BN7 .... 171 D8
Balmoral
  Brighton BN1........ 191 E8
  East Grinstead RH19... 23 A8
Balmoral Cl
  Bognor Regis PO21 ... 200 E2
  Chichester PO19 .... 177 D6
  8 Rustington BN16... 205 B7
Balmoral Ct
  6 Crawley RH11 .... 18 B2
  Hove BN3........... 169 A3
  Worthing BN11 ..... 186 A2
Balmoral Way GU32... 68 B4
Balsdean Rd BN2 .... 171 F1
Baltic Wharf BN17 ... 204 D4
Baltimore Ct 9 BN3 .. 191 C7
Bamborough Cl RH13 . 58 A1
Bamford Cl BN2...... 171 A2
Bampfield St BN41.... 190 B8
Bancroft Rd RH10 ... 19 D5
Banjo Rd BN17....... 204 E3
Bank La RH10........ 18 D6
Bank Pas
  2 Steyning BN44.... 145 D3
  11 Worthing BN11.... 186 D2
Banks Croft RH20..... 121 E2
Bankside
  Bolney RH17 .... 85 C2
  Brighton BN1........ 169 D5
  Hassocks BN6 ...... 128 F5
  Middleton-on-S PO22...202 E5
  Singleton PO18 ..... 135 E7
Bankside Ct BN1..... 169 C5
Banks Rd
  Crawley RH10 ...... 19 C5
  Scaynes Hill BN8..... 89 F1
Bankview Cl 2 PO22...201 D4
Bannerman Rd GU32... 68 B4
Bannings Vale BN2 ... 194 E1
Bannister Gdns RH20.. 121 E3
Bannister Way RH16... 87 D6
Banstead Cl RH10 ... 185 C1
Baranscraig Ave BN1.. 170 A7
Barbara Smith Hall
  PO21 .... 201 E4
Barbary La BN12...... 206 E5
Barber Cl RH10 ..... 19 C2
Barclay Ho 2 BN2.... 192 C7
Barclays Ct 2 RH20... 100 C2
Barcombe Pl BN1..... 170 F5
Barcombe Rd BN1.... 170 E4
Barentin Way GU31... 68 C5
Barfield Pk BN15 .... 187 F6
Barford Rd PO19 .... 177 A5
Barham Rd GU32 .... 68 B3
Barkdale RH15........ 109 D5
Barker Cl PO18 ..... 176 A7
Barkworth Way RH20.. 121 C7
Bar La RH13......... 82 B5
BARLAVINGTON 117 C2
Barlavington Way
  GU29 .... 94 E5
Barley Cl
  Bognor Regis PO21 ... 200 A2
  Crawley RH10 ...... 18 D5
Barleycroft
  Albourne Green BN6... 127 C6
  Cowfold RH13 ...... 83 E1
Barley Dr RH15....... 108 D4
Barley Ho RH44...... 145 D2
Barleymead RH6.......2 B4
Barlow Rd
  Chichester PO19 .... 176 E8
  Crawley RH11 ...... 17 E3

Barnard Gate RH16 ... 87 E7
Barnard Mews BN14... 186 E5
Barn Cl
  Albourne Green BN6... 127 C6
  Kingston near Lewes
    BN7............... 172 E5
  Littlehampton BN17...204 E8
  Pease Pottage RH11 .. 39 B7
  Worthing BN13 ..... 185 F8
Barn Cottage La RH16.. 88 A5
Barncroft Cl PO20 ... 156 C1
Barn Ct BN42 .... 190 F4
Barn Elm PO18 ...... 156 D3
Barn End BN5........ 125 F5
Barnes Cl PO20 ..... 212 E5
Barnes Mews 9 RH12... 36 B2
Barnes Rd BN41...... 190 B8
Barnes Wallis Ave
  RH13 .... 57 D6
Barnett Cl PO20 .... 179 E8
Barnett Rd BN1...... 170 B2
Barnett's Field PO20 .. 179 D7
Barnet Way
  Hove BN3........... 168 E3
  Worthing BN13 ..... 185 D6
Barn Feld PO22....... 201 F4
Barnfield Cl PO10.... 152 A1
Barnfield Cotts RH10 . 19 A3
Barnfield Dr PO18,
  PO19 .... 177 C8
Barnfield Gdns
  8 Brighton BN2 .... 192 C6
  Ditchling BN6........ 129 E3
Barn Field Pl RH19 ... 10 A3
Barnfield Rd
  Crawley RH10 ...... 18 E7
  Petersfield GU31 .... 68 E3
Barnham La BN18,
  PO22 .... 180 C7
Barnham Prim Sch
  PO22 .... 180 B6
Barnham Rd PO20,
  PO22 .... 180 A6
Barnham Sta PO22 ... 180 B5
Barnhouse Cl 8
  RH20 .... 100 C2
Barn House La RH20... 100 C3
Barn La PO22........ 179 D1
Barn Mdw RH17 ..... 41 A1
Barnmead RH16 ..... 87 D7
Barn Plat Cotts GU29.. 94 D8
Barn Rd PO20........ 207 F7
Barn Rise
  Barnham PO22....... 180 C5
  Brighton BN1........ 169 D5
Barn Row BN5 ...... 205 F5
Barns Farm La RH20... 143 B7
Barnsfold La RH12 ... 32 E6
Barnside PO18........ 175 D7
Barnside Ave RH15.... 109 D1
Barnsite Cl BN16..... 205 B6
Barnside Way GU33... 45 B3
Barnsite Gdns BN16... 205 B6
Barnsnap Cl RH12..... 36 D6
Barn Stables Bsns Units
  RH10...............7 E6
Barn The PO19 ...... 154 F2
Barn Wlk PO20 ..... 207 F6
Barnwood RH10 ..... 19 C7
Baron Cl PO20 ...... 179 D7
Barons Ct
  Burgess Hill RH15..... 109 B2
  12 Worthing BN11.... 186 D2
Barons Mead PO21.... 211 A8
Barque Cl BN17...... 205 A6
Barrack La PO21 .... 200 D2
Barrhill Ave BN1..... 169 F7
Barrington Cl
  Haywards Heath RH16 . 87 F8
  Worthing BN12 ..... 185 C3
Barrington Gate RH12... 36 D2
Barrington Rd
  Crawley RH10 ...... 18 D3
  Horsham RH13 ...... 36 B2
  Lindfield RH16...... 88 A8
  Worthing BN12 ..... 185 E4
  Worthing, Goring-by-Sea
    BN12............. 185 C3
Barrington Wood RH16.. 87 F8
Barrow Cl
  Billingshurst RH14.... 79 C7
  Brighton BN1........ 170 C2
Barrowfield Cl BN3 .. 169 C3
Barrowfield Dr BN3... 169 D2
Barrowfield Lo BN3... 169 C2
Barrow Hill
  Brighton BN1........ 170 C2
  Henfield BN5........ 125 F3
Barry Cl RH10 ...... 18 E3
Barry Wlk BN2....... 192 C6
Bartholomew Cl GU27... 27 D8
Bartholmews BN1 ... 213 B2
Bartholomew Sq BN1.. 213 B2
Bartholomew Way
  RH12 .... 37 A7
Barton Cl
  Bognor Regis PO21 ... 200 A1
  Worthing BN13 ..... 186 A5
Barton Cres RH19..... 23 A8
Barton Ct BN16...... 205 B5
Barton La GU28...... 97 F8
Barton Manor Apartments
  PO21 .... 200 A1
Barton Rd
  Bognor Regis PO22 ... 201 A4
  Chichester PO19 .... 176 A5
Bartons Inf Sch PO22.. 201 B6

Barton Way PO20 .... 208 B6
Barton Wlk 4 RH10... 19 B4
Barttelot Rd RH12 ... 36 D2
Barwell Gr PO10 .... 151 A3
Barwick Cl BN16..... 205 B7
Basepoint Bsns Ctr
  RH11...............5 D2
Bashfords La BN14.... 186 D4
Bashford Way RH10... 19 B4
Bashurst Copse RH13.. 56 F8
Bashurst Hill RH13 ... 56 E6
Basildon Way RH11 .. 17 C2
Basing Hill RH20,
  RH13 .... 123 C7
Basin Rd PO19....... 177 A5
Basin Rd N BN41..... 190 B6
Basin Rd S BN3, BN41.. 190 B6
Bassels La RH13 .... 104 B5
Bassett Rd
  Bognor Regis PO21 ... 201 C3
  Crawley RH10 ...... 19 D3
Bastion Ho 4 PO19 .. 177 A6
Batchmere Est
  Almodington PO20 ... 197 F1
  Bracklesham PO20 ... 208 B5
Batchmere Rd PO20... 198 A2
Batemans Cl BN13 ... 185 B6
Batemans Ct RH10 ... 19 A3
Batemans Rd BN2.... 193 E7
Bates Rd BN1........ 169 F2
Bath Ct BN3......... 191 A5
Bath Pl BN11........ 186 D1
Bath Rd
  Emsworth PO10..... 173 B8
  Worthing BN11 ..... 186 B1
Bath St BN1......... 213 A4
Batts Dr BN5 .... 125 D5
Batts La RH20 ...... 100 C1
Batts Pond La BN5 ... 125 D4
Batworthpark Ho
  BN18 .... 160 E1
Bavant Rd BN1....... 169 E2
Bax Cl RH20......... 121 B1
Baxendale Rd PO19... 177 B8
Baxter Cl RH10 ..... 19 B4
Baxters La RH17 .... 66 C6
Baxter St BN2 ...... 192 C7
Bay Cl RH6..........1 E6
Baycombe La BN18 ... 158 D6
Bay Ct PO21 .... 211 B8
Bayfield Rd RH6 ....1 E4
Bayford Rd BN17..... 204 D4
Bayhams Field RH19... 42 F6
Bayhorne La RH6 .... 2 C1
Bayley Rd PO20...... 156 C1
Baylis Cres RH15..... 108 D4
Baylis Wlk RH11 .... 18 B1
Baynards Rd RH12 ... 12 A2
Bayton Ct PO19 ..... 177 B6
Baytree Cl PO19 .... 154 F3
Bay Tree Cotts BN18.. 158 D1
Bay Tree Gdn BN16... 205 F5
Bay Trees Cl BN16... 205 F5
Bay View Ct PO21.... 201 B2
Bay Wlk PO21 ...... 211 C8
Baywood Gdns BN2... 193 C8
Bazehill Manor BN2... 194 A3
Bazehill Rd BN2 .... 193 F2
Beach Cl PO21....... 200 C1
Beachcroft Pl BN15... 187 F4
Beach Ct
  Littlehampton BN17... 204 E4
  6 Rustington BN16... 205 B4
  12 Shoreham-by-S
    BN43............. 189 A6
Beaches The BN17.... 181 D1
Beach Gdns PO20..... 212 D5
Beach Gn BN43 ..... 188 E6
Beach Ho BN11...... 186 E2
Beach Mews 4 BN17.. 204 F4
Beach Par BN11 .... 186 F2
Beach Rd
  Emsworth PO10..... 173 A8
  Littlehampton BN17... 204 E4
  Pagham PO21....... 211 A7
  Selsey PO20........ 212 F8
  Shoreham-by-S BN43.. 188 E6
Beachside Cl BN12.... 185 C2
Beachville Ct 8 BN15.. 187 E4
Beachy Rd RH11 .... 18 A1
Beacon Cl BN1....... 170 A2
Beacon Ct
  Horsham RH13 ...... 37 A4
  Ovingdean BN2...... 193 D4
Beacon Dr PO20 .... 212 E6
Beacon Hill
  Dormansland RH7.... 10 B8
  Ovingdean BN2...... 193 E3
  Watersfield RH20 ... 119 A4
Beacon Ho 6 BN2 ... 190 D7
Beacon Hurst BN6 ... 129 B3
Beacon Rd BN6 ..... 129 D2
Beaconsfield Cl PO22.. 202 E5
Beaconsfield Cotts
  RH17 .... 88 F3
Beaconsfield Rd
  Brighton BN1........ 192 A8
  Chelwood Gate RH17... 66 D8
  Littlehampton BN17... 204 D7
  Portslade-by-S BN41... 190 B8
Beaconsfield Villas
  BN1 .... 169 F1
Beacon Sq PO10 .... 173 A7
Beaconsville Ct BN1 .. 169 F1
Beacon The RH19..... 42 E7
Beacon Way BN17 ... 205 A6

Beagle Dr BN18....... 181 B2
Beal Cres BN1 ...... 170 B2
Beale Cl RH11 ...... 18 A3
Beale St RH15 ...... 108 F1
Bearsden Way RH12... 35 D3
Beatrice Ho PO22 ... 201 E4
Beatty Ave BN1...... 170 D6
Beatty Rd PO21...... 201 C4
Beaufield Cl PO20 ... 212 D5
Beaufield Gate GU27... 27 D7
Beaufort Ct 4 RH17... 205 A6
Beaufort Terr BN2.... 192 C6
Beau Ho BN1........ 213 A4
Beaulieu Ct BN11 ... 186 D1
Beaumont Cl 3 RH11.. 17 E5
Beaumont Ct
  East Preston BN16 ... 205 F6
  6 Pulborough RH20... 100 C2
Beaumont Pk BN17 .. 205 A5
Beaumont Rd BN14... 186 D5
Beaver Cl
  Fishbourne PO19..... 176 B6
  Horsham RH12 ...... 36 F6
Beaver Ind Est GU30 .. 25 C4
Beaver Nursery Units
  PO19...............177 D5
Beaver Trade Pk
  PO19...............177 D5
Beccles Rd BN11..... 186 B2
Beckenham Terr
  PO10 .... 151 D4
Becket Bldgs BN14... 186 A6
Becket Ct BN14 .... 186 A6
Becket Rd BN14 ..... 186 B3
Beckett La RH11 ....5 D1
Beckett Way 11 RH19... 22 F8
Beckford Way RH10... 19 B2
Beckham La GU32 ... 67 F4
Beckley Cl BN2 ..... 192 E5
Beckworth Cl
  Lindfield RH16...... 88 A6
  Worthing BN13 ..... 185 B6
Beckworth La RH16... 88 A6
Bedale Cl RH11 ..... 18 C4
Bedales RH17........ 88 D4
Bedales Cnr RH17.... 88 D4
Bedales Hill RH16,
  RH17 .... 88 D4
Bedales Sch GU32 ... 68 A7
Bedelands Cl RH15.... 109 B5
Bedenscroft PO21 ... 201 A3
Bedford Ave PO21.... 201 A6
Bedford Pl BN1...... 191 E5
Bedford Rd
  Horsham RH13 ...... 36 D1
  Petersfield GU32..... 67 F3
Bedford Row RH11 .. 186 E2
Bedford Sq
  Brighton BN1........ 191 E5
  Partridge Green RH13.. 104 F3
Bedford St
  Bognor Regis PO21 ... 201 D3
  Brighton BN2........ 192 C4
Bedford Twrs 9 BN1.. 191 E5
Bedham La RH20 .... 99 B5
Beech Ave
  Bracklesham PO20 ... 208 B6
  Chichester PO19 .... 176 E6
Beech Cl
  Bognor Regis PO21 ... 199 F2
  2 East Grinstead RH19... 9 D2
  Findon BN14........ 163 E7
  Portslade-by-S BN41... 167 F3
  Westergate PO20 ... 179 D7
Beechcroft Cl GU30 .. 24 D3
Beech Ct
  East Grinstead RH19... 9 D2
  Haslemere GU27 .... 27 D7
  Worthing BN11 ..... 186 B2
Beechers Rd BN41.... 167 F3
Beeches Ave BN14.... 186 D7
Beeches Cres RH10... 18 E4
Beeches La RH19 .... 23 D6
Beeches Mead RH19... 10 F5
Beeches The
  4 Bognor Regis
    PO22............. 201 D4
  Brighton BN1........ 169 D3
Beechey Cl RH10 ....7 B3
Beechey Way RH10 ...7 B3
Beechfield GU28 .... 74 B3
Beechfield Pk PO20... 179 C5
Beechfields RH19.....9 F3
Beech Gdns
  Crawley Down RH10... 21 A8
  Worthing BN14 ..... 186 C5
Beech Gr
  Brighton BN2........ 170 E3
  Midhurst GU29 ..... 94 E6
  Storrington RH20..... 121 C3
Beech Hill RH16 .... 88 B4
Beech Holme RH10 .. 21 B8
Beech Hurst Cl RH16.. 87 C4
Beech Hurst Cotts
  RH16 .... 87 C4
Beechings BN5 ..... 125 D5
Beeching Way RH19...9 E1
Beechlands Cl BN16... 206 A5
Beechlands Ct BN16.. 206 A5
Beech Rd
  Findon BN14........ 163 E7
  Haslemere GU27 .... 27 D8
  Horsham RH13 ...... 37 B5
Beechside RH10 .... 18 E5
Beech Tree Cl RH10... 18 D7
Beech View BN16..... 184 A6
Beech Way BN16..... 206 A8

Bee–Bon 217

Beechwood
6 Brighton BN1 169 E3
Southwater RH13 81 F8
Beech Wood BN5 146 F7
Beechwood Ave
Brighton BN1 169 F4
Worthing BN13 185 F8
Beechwood Cl BN1 169 F4
Beechwood Ct
Liss GU33 45 C6
1 Worthing BN11 186 C2
Beechwood La GU28 117 B5
Beechwoods RH15 109 A1
Beechwood Villas RH1 2 A7
Beeding Ave BN3 168 F3
Beeding Cl
Bognor Regis PO22 201 E7
Horsham RH12 37 A5
Lancing BN15 187 D8
Beeding Ct
Brighton BN1 169 C5
4 Shoreham-by-S BN43 189 B8
Beedingwood Dr RH12 37 E6
Beehive Cl BN12 206 F5
Beehive La BN12 206 F5
Beehive Ring Rd RH6 6 B4
Beehive The RH6 6 B4
Beeson Ho 1 BN41 190 C7
Beggarshouse La RH6 4 C8
Beggar's La BN45 148 D6
Behenna Cl RH11 17 E5
Belbourne Ct 7 BN1 213 B3
Belfast St BN3 191 B7
Belgrave Cres PO19 176 F3
Belgrave Ct 3 RH20 100 C2
Belgrave Pl 11 BN2 192 D4
Belgrave St BN2 213 C3
Belgravia Ct 1 RH6 2 B3
Belinus Dr RH14 79 C8
Bellagio Pl RH19 9 D3
Bellamy Rd RH10 19 C2
Bell Cl
Chichester PO19 176 F8
Pulborough RH20 100 B2
Bell Ct
Bognor Regis PO21 200 C2
Nutbourne PO18 174 B7
Bell Ctr RH10 5 F2
Bell Cvn Pk PO20 197 E2
Bell Davies Rd BN17 204 F6
Belle Meade Cl PO20 179 D5
Bellerbys Coll BN1 213 B4
Bellevue Cotts BN2 192 F8
Belle Vue Cotts PO20 179 D7
Bellevue Ct BN1 169 F1
Belle Vue Ct BN2 192 D5
Belle Vue Gdns BN2 192 D4
Bellevue La PO10 151 B2
Bell Hammer RH19 22 E8
BELL HILL 68 A5
Bell Hill GU32 68 A5
Bell Hill Ridge GU32 68 A5
Bellingham Cres BN3 190 D8
Bell La
Cocking GU29 114 C8
Somerley PO20 197 D2
Bellmead 7 BN3 191 D7
Belloc Cl RH10 19 C7
Belloc Ct RH13 37 A3
Belloc Rd BN17 204 C7
Bell Rd
Kingsley Green GU27 27 B3
Warnham RH12 36 A8
Bellscroft Cl BN17 204 F6
Bell Tower Ind Est 7 BN2 192 E4
Bell Vale La GU27 27 C4
Bellview Ct 7 BN13 186 A5
Bellview Rd BN13 186 A5
Belmaine Ct BN11 186 C1
Belmer Ct 6 BN11 186 A1
Belmont BN1, BN3 191 E7
Belmont Cl BN6 128 E5
Belmont Ct 4 BN1 191 E7
Belmont La BN6 128 C5
Belmont St
Bognor Regis PO21 201 D3
Brighton BN1 213 B3
Belmont Terr BN18 181 A2
Belmont Wlk BN13 185 D6
Belsize Cl BN11 186 B3
Belsize Rd BN11 186 B2
Belton Cl BN2 192 B8
Belton Rd BN2 192 B8
Belvedere BN1 191 E8
Belvedere Ave BN15 187 D6
Belvedere Ct RH10 19 B7
Belvedere Terr 5 BN1 191 E6
Belvedere Wlk RH16 87 C3
Belverdere Cl GU32 68 B4
Belyngham Cres BN17 204 D6
Bembridge St BN2 192 C8
Benbow Cl BN43 188 F6
Benchfield Cl RH19 10 B1
Benedict Cl BN11 187 B3
Benedict Dr BN11 187 A3
Benett Ave BN3 169 B2
Benett Dr BN3 169 B2
Benfield Cl BN41 168 C1
Benfield Cres BN41 168 C1
Benfield Ct BN41 190 C8
Benfield Jun Sch BN41 190 C8
Benfield Way BN41 168 C1
Bengairn Ave BN1 170 A7
Benham Ct 10 BN3 191 B5
Benhams Cl RH6 2 A5
Benhams Dr RH6 2 A5
Benizi Ct 12 PO21 201 D3
Benjamin Lo RH15 109 D3
Benjamin Rd RH10 19 D4
Bennett Cl RH10 19 B2
Bennett Rd BN2 192 E4
Bennetts RH17 85 C3
Bennetts Cl PO20 207 F7
Bennetts Rd RH13 36 E1
Bennett's Terr 6 GU29 94 E7
Bens Acre RH13 37 A2
Benson Ct BN3 190 E7
Benson Rd BN5 125 F5
Benson's La RH12 16 C1
Bentham Rd BN2 192 C7
Bentley Cl BN16 206 A8
Bentons La RH13 103 E3
Bentswood Cres RH16 88 A5
Bentswood Rd RH16 87 F5
Ben Turner Ind Est PO19 177 D6
Bentworth PO22 180 B6
BEPTON 94 A1
Bepton Cl GU29 94 D6
Bepton Down GU31 68 C3
Bepton Rd GU29 94 B4
Berberis Ct BN43 167 B1
Beresford Ct 12 BN3 191 D7
Beresford Rd BN2 192 D5
Bereweeke Rd PO22 202 A4
Bergamot Cres BN43 167 C1
Berghestede Rd PO22 201 C6
Berkeley Cl RH11 17 E2
Berkeley Ct
Bognor Regis PO21 201 D2
6 Hove BN3 191 E7
9 Littlehampton BN17 204 E4
Berkeley Lo 1 RH20 121 E1
Berkeley Mews PO19 177 B7
Berkeley Sq BN11 186 A2
Berkshire Ct BN12 185 B4
Bermuda Ct 2 BN17 205 A6
Bernard Pl BN2 192 C7
Bernard Rd
Arundel BN18 159 F2
Brighton BN2 192 C7
Worthing BN11 185 F2
Berrall Way RH14 79 C7
Berriedale Ave BN3 190 E6
Berriedale Cl BN15 187 C7
Berriedale Dr BN15 187 C7
Berriedale Ho BN3 190 E6
Berrybarn La PO20 207 B8
Berry Cl RH15 109 A5
Berry La
Ardingly RH17 64 C7
Bognor Regis PO22 201 A7
Littlehampton BN17 204 F4
Berrylands GU33 45 C7
Berrylands Farm BN6 107 D1
Berrymeade Wlk 6 RH11 17 E5
Berrymill Cl 7 PO21 201 D4
Berstead Wlk 1 RH11 17 F3
Bersted Green Ct PO22 201 C6
Bersted Mews 2 PO22 201 D5
Bersted St
Bognor Regis PO22 201 C5
3 Bognor Regis PO22 201 D5
Berwick Rd BN2 194 D3
Bessborough Terr BN15 187 D4
Betchley Cl RH19 9 E3
Betchworth Works RH6 4 D6
Bethune Cl RH10 19 D5
Bethune Rd RH13 36 E1
Bethwines Cl PO18 176 A7
Betts Way RH10 5 D2
Bevan Ct RH11 18 B1
BEVENDEAN 170 F2
Bevendean Ave BN2 194 D1
Bevendean Cres BN2 170 E2
Bevendean Prim Sch BN2 170 F1
Bevendean Rd BN2 170 D1
Beverley Cl
Selsey PO20 212 F7
Yapton BN18 181 A3
Beverley Ct
1 Hove BN3 190 D7
5 Pulborough RH20 100 C2
3 Worthing BN11 186 B1
Beverley Gdns BN16 205 C7
Beverley Ho 6 BN15 187 E5
Beverley Mews RH10 19 A5
BEWBUSH 17 F3
Bewbush Com Prim Sch RH11 17 F3
Bewbush Dr RH11 17 F3
Bewbush Manor RH11 17 E2
Bewick Gdns PO19 177 B8
Bewley Rd BN16 183 F6
Bexhill Rd BN2 171 E1
Bex La GU29 94 E2
BEXLEYHILL 73 E7
Bickley Ct RH11 18 A3
Bickleys Ct 1 PO21 201 B2
Biddulph Mews GU28 117 D8
Biggin Cl RH11 18 C4
Bignor Cl
Horsham RH12 37 A7
Rustington BN16 205 D6
Bignor Park Rd RH20 118 E5
Bignor Roman Villa (remains of)* RH20 118 B2
Bigwood Ave BN3 191 D8
Bilberry Cl RH11 18 B3
Bilbets RH12 36 C3
Billingshurst Inf Sch RH14 79 B7
Billingshurst Jun Sch RH14 79 D7
Billingshurst Rd
Ashington RH20 122 F8
Broadbridge Heath RH12 35 D3
Wisborough Green RH14 78 C8
Billingshurst Sta RH14 79 D7
Billington Ct RH19 9 E2
Billinton Dr RH10 19 B5
Billinton Way BN1 213 B4
BILSHAM 202 F8
Bilsham Cnr BN18 202 F8
Bilsham Ct BN18 180 F2
Bilsham La BN18 180 E1
Bilsham Rd BN18 180 F1
Binderton La PO18 134 D2
BINES GREEN 124 F7
Bines Rd RH13 104 F2
Binney Ct RH10 6 E1
Binstead Cl RH11 18 B8
Binsted Ave PO22 202 A5
Binsted Cl BN16 205 B4
Binsted La BN18 181 B7
Biology Rd BN1 171 B6
Birch Ave RH17 88 A3
Birch Cl
Angmering BN16 205 F8
Arundel BN18 159 E1
Bognor Regis PO21 200 D3
Crawley Down RH10 21 C8
Haywards Heath RH17 88 B3
Lancing BN15 187 D4
Liss GU33 45 C4
Birch Ct BN42 168 A1
Birch Dr RH14 79 D7
Birch End RH20 121 D7
Birchen La RH16 87 F8
Birches Cl
Selsey PO20 212 C7
Worthing BN13 185 C6
Birches Ind Est RH19 9 A3
Birches Rd RH12 37 B5
Birches The
Crawley RH10 19 A7
Mannings Heath RH13 59 C7
West Chiltington Common RH20 121 C8
Birch Gr RH20 121 D5
Birch Grove Cres BN1 170 A5
Birchgrove La RH17 44 A1
Birchgrove Rd RH17 65 E7
Birch Lea RH10 6 A1
Bircholt Rd GU30 24 D4
Birch Tree Cl PO10 151 B4
Birch Tree Ct BN11 186 E3
Birch Tree Dr PO10 151 B4
Birch Tree Gdns RH19 9 B3
Birch Tree La RH20 121 E6
Birch Way
Haywards Heath RH17 88 A2
Heath Common RH20 122 B3
Birchwood Cl
Crawley RH10 19 C3
Horley RH6 2 B4
Ifold RH14 31 D3
Birchwood Grove Com Prim Sch RH15 109 C1
Birchwood Grove Rd RH15 109 C1
Birdham CE Prim Sch PO20 197 E5
Birdham Cl
Bognor Regis PO21 200 F5
Crawley RH11 18 B8
Birdham Pl BN2 170 E3
Birdham Rd
Apuldram PO19, PO20 176 D2
Brighton BN2 170 F3
South Hayling PO11 195 A2
Birkdale Cl BN13 185 D7
Birkdale Dr RH11 17 D5
Birkdale Rd BN13 185 D7
Birling Cl BN2 170 D1
Birthday Ho GU29 73 B2
Biscay Cl BN16 205 B6
Bisham Cl RH10 19 D3
Bishearne Gdns GU33 45 A5
Bishop Cl BN5 125 E5
Bishop Luffa CE Sch PO19 176 D7
Bishop Luffa Cl PO19 176 D7
Bishopric RH12 36 B2
Bishopric Ct 8 RH12 36 B2
Bishops Cl
Bognor Regis PO21 211 A8
Fernhurst GU27 49 A6
Worthing BN13 186 A4
Bishop's Cl BN6 128 A7
Bishops Ct
Horsham RH12 36 C1
Mid Lavant PO18 154 E6
Bishops Ctyd PO19 177 B6
Bishopsfield RH14 55 F5
Bishopsgate Wlk PO19 177 B7
Bishops Ho RH20 142 D8
Bishops Rd
Hove BN3 169 C1
Tangmere PO20 156 D2
Bishopstone Dr BN2 194 B2
Bishopstone La
Goddards' Green BN6 108 A5
Goddards' Green BN6, RH17 108 A7
Bishopstone Wlk RH11 18 C1
Bishop Tufnell CE Inf Sch PO22 202 C5
Bishop Tufnell CE Jun Sch PO22 202 C5
Bitmead Cl RH11 17 E5
Bittern Cl RH11 17 D5
Blackberry La
Chichester PO19 177 C6
Felcourt RH7 9 E8
Selsey PO20 212 C7
Blackberry Rd RH19, RH7 9 D8
Blackbird Cl RH15 108 D3
Blackbird Hill RH10 21 C5
Blackboy La PO18 176 A7
Blackbridge Ct RH12 36 A2
Blackbridge La RH12 36 A1
Blackbrook La BN8, RH17 89 E2
Blackcap Cl
Crawley RH11 18 C4
Red Hill PO9 130 C1
Black Cnr RH10 6 D4
Black Dog Wlk RH10 18 E8
Blackdown BN2 192 F7
Blackdown Rd BN13 185 F8
Black Down Wlks* GU27 28 A2
Blackett Rd RH10 19 C5
Blackfold Rd RH10 19 A5
Blackgate La BN5 125 E4
Black Gate La RH20 100 D7
Blackheath RH10 19 D8
Black Hill RH16 88 A7
Black Horse Cvn Pk PO20 212 C8
Black Horse Way RH12 36 C2
Blackhouse La
Burgess Hill RH15 109 B4
Foxhill GU28 76 D5
Blackhouse Rd RH13 38 D5
Blacklands Cres RH18 23 F2
Black Lion La BN1 213 A2
Black Lion St BN1 213 B1
Blackman St BN1 213 B3
Blackman Way PO20 177 B1
Blackmill La PO18 157 C3
Blackmore Ct BN1 213 B4
Blackpatch Gr 6 BN43 166 F1
BLACK ROCK 192 F3
Black Rock (for Marina) Sta* BN2 192 E3
Blacksmiths Cl RH20 123 A4
Blacksmith's Cnr BN18 180 F8
Blacksmiths Cres BN15 187 B6
Blackstone La
Blackstone BN5, BN6 126 E6
Woodmancote BN5 126 D3
Blackstone Rise BN5 126 E5
Blackstone St BN5 126 E5
Blackstone Way RH15 109 A5
Black Swan Cl RH11 39 B7
Blackthorn Cl
Brighton BN1 169 D3
Crawley RH11 5 C1
Horsham RH13 37 A2
Portslade-by-S BN41 168 B2
Blackthorns
Hurstpierpoint BN6 127 F7
Lindfield RH16 88 A7
Blackthorns Cl RH16 88 A6
Blackthorns Com Prim Sch RH16 88 A6
Blackthorns The RH15 109 B5
Blackwater La RH10 19 D6
BLACKWELL 9 E3
Blackwell Farm Rd RH19 9 F3
Blackwell Hollow RH19 9 F2
Blackwell Prim Sch RH19 9 E3
Blackwell Rd RH19 9 F2
Blake Cl RH10 18 F2
Blake Cotts PO18 176 A6
Blake Ct 3 BN2 213 C3
Blakehurst La BN18 161 B3
Blakehurst Way BN17 204 D6
Blakemyle PO21 200 F2
Blakeney Cl PO19 176 B6
Blaker St BN2 213 C2
Blakes Ct PO22 202 A4
Blakes Farm Rd RH13 58 A4
Blakes Rd PO22 202 A4
Blakes View PO22 201 F4
Blanches Rd RH13 105 A3
Blanches Wlk RH13 105 A3
Blatchen The BN17 204 F4
Blatchford Cl RH13 36 F3
Blatchford Rd RH13 36 F3
Blatchington Mill Sch & Sixth Form Coll BN3 169 A2
Blatchington Rd BN3 191 B7
Bleaches Ct PO18 154 E7
Bleach's Yard Ind Est GU30 25 B2
Blendworth La PO8 130 A8
Blenheim Ave BN13 185 E6
Blenheim Cl
Crawley RH10 6 D1
East Grinstead RH19 10 A3
2 Rustington BN16 205 B7
Blenheim Ct
Bognor Regis PO21 200 E4
1 Hove BN3 191 A6
Worthing BN13 185 C9
Blenheim Dr BN16 205 B7
Blenheim Fields RH18 23 E3
Blenheim Gdns PO19 177 C6
Blenheim Mews RH16 87 F2
Blenheim Pl 5 BN1 213 B3
Blenheim Rd
Horsham RH12 36 D4
Lancing BN15 187 D4
Yapton BN18 180 F2
Blessing Lo 5 BN43 189 B6
Bletchley Ct BN1 192 A8
Bligh Cl RH10 18 F4
Blindley Rd RH10 6 D1
Blomfield Dr PO19 155 A1
Blondell Dr PO21 200 D2
Bloomsbury Pl 17 BN2 192 C4
Bloomsbury St 16 BN2 192 C4
Bloor Cl RH12 36 D7
Blount Ave RH19 9 C1
Bluebell Cl
Crawley RH11 18 B3
East Grinstead RH19 9 B1
Haywards Heath RH16 87 F4
Horsham RH12 36 E5
Bluebell Dr BN17 205 A7
Bluebell Rly* RH17, RH19, TN22 43 A5
Bluebell Way RH15 108 D4
Blueberry Hill RH20 122 B1
Bluebird Cl 1 BN43 189 B6
Bluebird Ct 11 BN3 191 A6
Bluebird Ho RH6 1 D1
Blue Cedars Cl BN16 205 E8
Bluecoat Pond RH13 57 D6
Blue Idol The* RH13 80 B3
Blundell Ave RH6 1 F4
Blunden Dr RH17 86 F8
Blunts Way RH12 36 C3
Blunts Wood Cres RH16 87 B6
Blunts Wood Rd RH16 87 C6
Blytons The RH19 9 B1
Boardwalk PO19 177 A7
Boatyard The BN2 193 A3
Bob La BN5, RH17 106 E6
Boddingtons La BN6 129 D3
Boderton Mews GU28 117 D7
Bodiam Ave
Brighton BN2 171 B1
Worthing BN12 185 B3
Bodiam Cl
Brighton BN2 171 B2
Crawley RH10 19 C6
Southwater RH13 58 A2
Bodiam Ct RH16 87 E5
Bodiham Ho 15 BN3 191 D7
Bodmin Cl BN13 185 D9
Bodmin Rd BN13 185 D9
Bognor Rd
Chichester PO19, PO20 177 D5
Warnham RH12, RH5 14 D4
Bognor Regis Com Coll
Bognor Regis PO21 200 F4
Bognor Regis PO21 201 A5
Bognor Regis Mus* PO21 201 D2
Bognor Regis Ret Pk The PO22 201 D7
Bognor Regis Sta PO21 201 C3
Bohunt Sch GU30 25 B4
Boiler House Hill BN1 171 B7
Bolding Way RH16 87 E2
Boleyn Cl RH10 19 D3
Boleyn Dr PO21 200 B1
Bolney CE Prim Sch RH17 85 C2
Bolney Chapel Rd RH17 107 B7
Bolney Crossways RH17 85 D1
Bolney Ct RH11 17 F3
Bolney Grange Bsns Pk RH17 107 F6
Bolney Rd
Ansty RH17 86 A2
Bolney RH17 85 E2
Brighton BN2 170 F4
Bolnore RH16 87 B4
Bolnore Rd RH16 87 C4
BOLNORE VILLAGE 87 C2
Bolsover Rd
Hove BN3 190 E8
Worthing BN13 185 E4
Bolters Rd RH6 2 A5
Bolters Rd S RH6 1 F6
Bolton Rd RH10 19 C2
Boltro Rd RH16 87 D5
Bonaventure 2 BN43 189 B6
Bonchurch Rd BN2 192 C7
Bond St
Arundel BN18 160 A3

Bond St continued
Brighton BN1 . . . . 213 B2
Bonehurst Rd RH1, RH6 . . . . . . 2 A7
Bonfire Hill RH13 . . . . 57 D1
Bonfire La RH17 . . . . 65 D5
Bonnar Cl PO20 . . . . 212 D6
Bonnar Rd PO20 . . . . 212 D6
Bonnetts La RH11 . . . . 5 A3
Bonny Wood Rd BN6 . . . . . . 128 E3
Bookers La PO20 . . . . 208 C8
Bookers Vineyard★
RH17 . . . . 85 B3
Booth Mus of Natural
History★ BN1 . . . . 191 E8
Booth Rd RH11 . . . . 17 E3
Booth Way RH13 . . . . 36 E3
Borage Cl 4 RH11 . . . . 18 A2
Borde Hill Gdn★ RH16 . . . . 63 C2
Bordehill La RH16,
RH17 . . . . 63 D3
Borden La GU30 . . . . 71 A6
Border Chase RH10 . . . . 7 A2
Border Ct GU33 . . . . 45 D1
Border Ct RH19 . . . . 9 F4
Border End GU27 . . . . 26 D6
Border Rd GU27 . . . . 26 D6
Borers Arms Rd RH10 . . . . . . 7 C3
Borers Ct RH10 . . . . 7 C4
Borers Yard Cotts RH10 . . . . 7 C3
Borers Yard Ind Est
RH10 . . . . 7 C3
Borers Yd RH10 . . . . 7 D3
Borough Gr GU32 . . . . 68 A2
BOROUGH HILL 68 A3
Borough Hill GU32 . . . . 68 A3
Borough Ho GU29 . . . . 94 F8
Borough Rd GU32 . . . . 68 A3
Borough St BN1 . . . . 191 E6
Borrowdale Cl RH11 . . . . 18 B4
Borrow King Cl BN2 . . . . . . 192 D8
Borthwick Ho PO20 . . . . 207 F6
Bosham La PO18 . . . . 175 B5
Bosham Prim Sch
PO18 . . . . 175 C5
Bosham Rd RH10 . . . . 19 C3
Bosham Sta PO18 . . . . 175 C7
Bosham Wlk PO18 . . . . 175 B4
Bosmere Gdns PO10 . . . . . . 151 B1
Bosmere Rd PO11 . . . . 195 A2
Bostal Rd BN44 . . . . 145 C1
Bostal The BN44 . . . . 146 C1
Bost Hill BN13, BN14 . . . . . . 163 E3
Bostock Ave RH12 . . . . 37 A5
Bostock Rd PO19 . . . . 177 B8
Boston Ct RH16 . . . . 88 A5
Boston Rd RH16 . . . . 88 A5
Boston St BN1 . . . . 213 B4
Boswell Rd RH10 . . . . 18 A5
Botany Cl BN16 . . . . 205 E4
Bough Beeches RH15 . . . . . 109 C1
Boulevard The
Crawley RH10 . . . . 18 E6
Worthing BN12, BN13 . . . . 185 E5
Boundary Cl
Crawley RH10 . . . . 18 E7
Worthing BN11 . . . . 186 B1
Boundary Pas 10 BN3 . . . . . 191 E6
Boundary Rd
Balcombe Lane RH17 . . . . . . 41 B4
Brighton BN2 . . . . 192 F4
Crawley RH10 . . . . 18 E7
Lancing BN15 . . . . 188 B5
Portslade-by-S BN3,
BN41 . . . . 190 C7
Worthing BN11 . . . . 186 B1
Boundary Way BN16 . . . . . . 206 B6
Boundstone Cl BN15 . . . . . . 187 D7
Boundstone Com Coll
BN15 . . . . 187 D7
Boundstone La BN15 . . . . . . 187 D6
Bourg-de-Peage Ave
RH19 . . . . 10 A1
Bourne Cl
Fishbourne PO19 . . . . 176 A7
Worthing BN13 . . . . 185 B7
Bourne Com Coll
PO10 . . . . 151 F1
Bourne Ct
Bracklesham PO20 . . . . . . 208 A5
Brighton BN1 . . . . 169 D4
Littlehampton BN17 . . . . . 204 B7
Bourne The BN6 . . . . 128 E5
Bourne View Cl PO10 . . . . . 151 F2
Bourne Way GU29 . . . . 94 E6
Bourns Ct RH13 . . . . 36 E3
Bowater Rd RH10 . . . . 19 C3
Bowen Ct 11 BN3 . . . . 191 C6
Bowen La GU31 . . . . 68 B3
Bowerhill Cotts RH19 . . . . . . 43 F6
Bower La RH20 . . . . 121 D6
Bowers Ct BN11 . . . . 186 B1
Bowers Pl RH10 . . . . 21 B8
Bower The
Crawley RH10 . . . . 19 C5
Haywards Heath RH16 . . . . . 87 D5
Bowes Cl RH13 . . . . 36 E3
Bowes Hill PO9 . . . . 130 E3
Bowhill La PO18 . . . . 153 D7
Bowley La PO20 . . . . 199 E5
Bowline Point 15
BN43 . . . . 188 E7
Bowling Green Cl
PO21 . . . . 200 B1
Bowling Green La
RH12 . . . . 36 D3

Bowman Ct RH10 . . . . 18 D7
Bowmans Cl BN44 . . . . 145 D4
Bowness Ave BN15 . . . . 187 C5
Bowness Cl 7 RH11 . . . . 17 D5
Bowring Way BN2 . . . . 192 D4
Boxall Wlk RH13 . . . . 36 D1
Boxes La RH17 . . . . 65 C5
Boxgrove CE Prim Sch
PO18 . . . . 156 D4
Boxgrove Cl BN15 . . . . 187 F8
Boxgrove Gdns PO21 . . . . . 200 D2
Boxgrove Ho
Boxgrove PO18 . . . . 156 D3
Littlehampton BN17 . . . . . 204 B7
Boxgrove Par BN12 . . . . 185 B4
Boxgrove Priory★
PO18 . . . . 156 D3
Boxham La PO20 . . . . 198 D3
Box La RH19 . . . . 23 E6
Box's La RH17 . . . . 66 C6
Box Tree Ave BN16 . . . . 205 B5
Boyce's St BN1 . . . . 213 A2
Boyles La 14 BN2 . . . . 192 E4
Brackenbury Ct BN41 . . . . . 168 B2
Bracken Cl
Copthorne RH10 . . . . 7 B2
Crawley RH10 . . . . 18 F8
Heath Common RH20 . . . . 122 B2
Bracken Gr RH12 . . . . 37 B5
Bracken La RH20 . . . . 122 B2
Bracken Rd GU31 . . . . 68 E2
Brackenside RH6 . . . . 2 B4
Brackenthe RH20 . . . . 121 B1
Brackla Cl RH10 . . . . 18 F8
Bradbury Rd RH10 . . . . 19 C3
Brading Rd BN2 . . . . 192 C7
Bradley Ho RH11 . . . . 186 B2
Bradlond Cl PO21 . . . . 201 A3
Bradshaw Rd PO19 . . . . 177 C8
Braemar Ho 11 BN1 . . . . . . 191 E6
Braemar Way PO21 . . . . 200 F7
Braemore Ct BN3 . . . . 190 E6
Braemore Rd BN3 . . . . 190 E6
Braeside RH6 . . . . 2 A3
Braeside Ave BN1 . . . . 170 A7
Braeside Cl
Findon BN14 . . . . 163 E6
Haslemere GU27 . . . . 26 F8
Brainsmead RH17 . . . . 86 F7
Brainsmead Cl RH17 . . . . . . 86 E7
Bramber 3 BN15 . . . . 187 D5
Bramber Ave
Hove BN3 . . . . 168 F3
Storrington RH20 . . . . 121 C2
Bramber Castle★
BN44 . . . . 145 F2
Bramber Cl
Bognor Regis PO21 . . . . . 201 A4
Crawley RH10 . . . . 18 E8
Haywards Heath RH16 . . . . 87 D4
Horsham RH12 . . . . 37 B5
Lancing BN15 . . . . 187 D8
Bramber Ct
8 Hove BN3 . . . . 191 B7
2 Shoreham-by-S
BN43 . . . . 189 B8
7 Worthing BN11 . . . . . . 185 C1
Bramber Fst Sch
BN14 . . . . 186 F6
Bramber Ho 8 RH13 . . . . . . 36 E1
Bramber Rd
Chichester PO19 . . . . 177 B5
Steyning BN44 . . . . 145 D2
Worthing BN14 . . . . 186 E6
Bramber Sq BN16 . . . . 205 C6
Bramber Way RH15 . . . . 109 A4
Bramble Cl
Bognor Regis PO21 . . . . . 199 F2
Copthorne RH10 . . . . 7 B3
Worthing BN13 . . . . 185 D8
Bramble Cres BN15 . . . . 185 D9
Bramble Ct GU31 . . . . 68 E3
Brambledean Rd
BN41 . . . . 190 B7
Bramble Gdns RH15 . . . . . . 108 D4
Bramble Hill RH17 . . . . 40 F2
Bramble La BN13 . . . . 185 D8
Bramble Mead RH17 . . . . . . 40 F1
Bramble Rd GU31 . . . . 68 E3
Bramble Rise BN1 . . . . 169 C5
Brambles BN6 . . . . 128 F5
Brambles The RH17 . . . . 87 A6
Bramble Twitten RH19 . . . . . 10 A1
Brambletye La RH18 . . . . 23 D4
Brambletye Prep Sch
RH19 . . . . 23 C5
Brambletye Rd RH10 . . . . . . 19 A5
Brambletyne Ave
BN2 . . . . 194 D1
Brambletyne Cl BN14 . . . . . 184 A6
Bramble Way BN1 . . . . 170 C6
Brambling Cl RH13 . . . . 37 A1
Brambling La GU29 . . . . 72 C3
Brambling Rd
Horsham RH13 . . . . 37 A1
Red Hill PO9 . . . . 130 D1
Bramblings The
BN16 . . . . 205 D5
Bramfield Rd PO22 . . . . 202 C4
Bramlands Cl BN5 . . . . 147 D8

Bramley Cl
Crawley RH10 . . . . 18 F6
Kirdford RH14 . . . . 53 B3
Worthing BN14 . . . . 186 D6
Bramley Ct RH13 . . . . 1 F4
Bramley Gdns
Bognor Regis PO22 . . . . . 201 B7
Hermitage PO10 . . . . 173 D8
Bramley Ho BN11 . . . . 186 B3
Bramley Rd BN14 . . . . 186 D6
Bramleys BN7 . . . . 172 E5
Bramley Way BN16 . . . . 206 A8
Bramley Wlk RH6 . . . . 2 C3
Brampton Cl PO20 . . . . 212 D7
Brampton Ct PO19 . . . . 176 F5
Bramwell Lo BN5 . . . . 126 C2
Brandon Cl RH10 . . . . 19 D4
Brandy Hole La PO19 . . . . . 154 E2
Brangwyn Ave BN1 . . . . 169 E5
Brangwyn Cres BN1 . . . . 169 E6
Brangwyn Ct BN1 . . . . 169 E5
Brangwyn Dr BN1 . . . . 169 E5
Brangwyn's Acre BN6 . . . . . 129 D3
Brangwyn Way BN1 . . . . 169 E5
BRANTRIDGE 40 B1
Brantridge La RH17 . . . . 62 B6
Brantridge Rd RH10 . . . . 18 F4
Brantridge Sch
Staplefield, Brantridge
RH17 . . . . 62 A8
Staplefield RH17 . . . . 61 E5
Brasslands Dr BN41 . . . . . . 167 F1
Braybon Ave BN1 . . . . 169 F4
Braybon Bsns Pk
RH15 . . . . 108 E2
Bray Cl RH10 . . . . 19 D4
Braypool La BN1 . . . . 169 D7
Brazwick Ave PO21 . . . . 200 F7
Breach Ave PO10 . . . . 152 A2
Breach Cl BN44 . . . . 145 D4
Bread La BN17 . . . . 203 F6
Bread St BN1 . . . . 213 B3
Bream Cl PO20 . . . . 212 B8
Brecon Cl RH13 . . . . 185 F8
Brecon Ct 6 BN3 . . . . 191 C7
Brecon Hts RH11 . . . . 18 C5
Brede Cl BN2 . . . . 192 F5
Breezehurst Dr RH11 . . . . . . 17 F3
Bremere La PO20 . . . . 198 C2
Bremer Ave RH6 . . . . 1 F4
Brendon Rd BN13 . . . . 185 E8
Brendon Way BN16 . . . . 205 B6
Brent Ct PO20 . . . . 173 A8
Brent Lodge Bird &
Wildlife Hospl★
PO20 . . . . 209 E8
Brent Rd PO21 . . . . 201 A4
Brentwood Cl BN1 . . . . 170 B3
Brentwood Cres BN1 . . . . . . 170 B3
Brentwood Rd BN1 . . . . 170 B3
Brettingham Cl RH11 . . . . . . 17 E3
Bretton RH15 . . . . 108 E5
Bretts Orch RH17 . . . . 41 A1
Brewell Rd RH10 . . . . 18 E4
Brewells La GU33 . . . . 46 A5
Brewer St BN2 . . . . 213 C4
Brewers Yd RH20 . . . . 121 D1
Brewery Hill BN18 . . . . 160 B2
Brewery Mews BN6 . . . . 127 F6
Brewhurst La RH14 . . . . 32 A2
Breydon Wlk RH10 . . . . 19 B4
Briar Ave PO20 . . . . 196 F1
Briar Cl
Angmering BN16 . . . . 205 F8
Bognor Regis PO21 . . . . . 199 F3
Crawley RH11 . . . . 5 C1
Oving PO20 . . . . 178 C6
Woodingdean BN2 . . . . . . 193 D7
Yapton BN18 . . . . 180 F3
Briarcroft Rd BN2 . . . . 193 D7
Briars The BN15 . . . . 187 F5
Briars Wood RH6 . . . . 2 C4
Briar Wood GU33 . . . . 45 C7
Brickfield Cl PO21 . . . . 201 B5
Brickfield La RH11 . . . . 1 D1
Brick Kiln Cl RH13 . . . . 60 A3
Bricklands RH10 . . . . 21 B7
Brickyard La RH10 . . . . 21 B8
Brideake Cl RH11 . . . . 18 A3
Brideoake Cl PO19 . . . . 176 E8
Bridge Cl
Burgess Hill RH15 . . . . . . 108 F4
Lancing BN15 . . . . 187 E5
Worthing BN12 . . . . 185 C5
Bridge Cotts GU33 . . . . 45 A7
Bridgefield Cl GU29 . . . . 94 E6
Bridgefoot Cotts GU29 . . . . . 72 A2
Bridgefoot Path PO10 . . . . . 173 B8
Bridge Ind Est RH6 . . . . 2 B3
Bridgelands RH10 . . . . 7 A3
Bridge Mdws GU33 . . . . 45 B4
Bridge Rd
Chichester PO19 . . . . 177 C7
Emsworth PO10 . . . . 151 B1
Haslemere GU27 . . . . 27 C7
Haywards Heath RH16 . . . . 87 F6
Littlehampton BN17 . . . . . 204 B6
Rudgwick RH12 . . . . 33 D7
Worthing BN14 . . . . 186 D3
Bridge Road Bsns Pk
RH16 . . . . 87 F7
Bridgers Ho RH16 . . . . 87 E6
Bridgersmill RH16 . . . . 87 D6
Bridges Cl RH6 . . . . 2 D3
Bridges Ct RH12 . . . . 37 A5
Bridges Pl RH12 . . . . 36 C1
Bridgewater Cl BN14 . . . . . . 79 C6

Bridgeway The PO20 . . . . . . 212 D6
Bridgnorth Cl BN13 . . . . 185 B6
Bridle La BN18 . . . . 158 D4
Bridle La The PO18 . . . . 152 D4
Bridle Way RH10 . . . . 19 D7
Bridle Way The PO20 . . . . . 212 D7
Bridorley Cl PO21 . . . . 200 B2
Brierley Gdns BN15 . . . . 187 F6
Brigden St BN1 . . . . 213 A4
Brigham Pl PO22 . . . . 202 D4
Brighthelm BN1 . . . . 171 B8
Brighton & Hove High
Sch Jun Dept BN3 . . . . . 191 D8
Brighton Coll BN2 . . . . 192 C4
Brighton College Prep Sch
BN2 . . . . 192 C4
Brighton Fishing Mus★
BN1 . . . . 213 A1
Brighton General Hospl
BN2 . . . . 192 D7
Brighton & Hove City Coll
BN1 . . . . 170 F8
Brighton & Hove High Sch
BN1 . . . . 191 E6
Brighton & Hove Stad
BN3 . . . . 169 B1
Brighton, Hove & Sussex
Sixth Form Coll BN3 . . . . 191 E8
Brighton Marina BN2 . . . . . 192 F2
Brighton Marina Village
BN2 . . . . 192 F3
Brighton Mus & Art Gall★
BN1 . . . . 213 B2
Brighton Pl BN1 . . . . 213 B2
Brighton Race Course
BN2 . . . . 193 A8
Brighton Rd
Crawley RH11 . . . . 18 D4
Handcross RH17 . . . . 61 C8
Hassocks BN6 . . . . 128 D2
Horley RH6 . . . . 1 F2
Horsham RH13 . . . . 36 E1
Horsham RH13 . . . . 58 F8
Hurstpierpoint BN6 . . . . . 127 F3
Kingston near Lewes
BN7 . . . . 172 F6
Mannings Heath RH13 . . . . 59 C6
Partridge Green RH13 . . . 105 D4
Pease Pottage RH11 . . . . . 39 B5
Shoreham-by-S BN43 . . . . 189 B7
Woodmancote BN5 . . . . . 126 A3
Worthing BN11, BN15,
BN43 . . . . 187 C3
Brighton Sea Life Ctr★
BN1 . . . . 213 B1
Brighton Sq BN1 . . . . 213 B2
Brighton Sta BN1 . . . . 213 B3
Brighton Steiner Sch Ltd
BN2 . . . . 192 F4
Brighton Toy & Model Mus
The★ BN1 . . . . 213 B3
Brills La BN1 . . . . 213 B1
Brimfast La PO20 . . . . 198 F4
Brisbane Cl
Crawley RH11 . . . . 5 D1
Worthing BN13 . . . . 185 C7
Brisbane Ho GU29 . . . . 94 E6
Bristol Ave BN15 . . . . 188 B5
Bristol Cl RH10 . . . . 6 D1
Bristol Gate BN2 . . . . 192 D4
Bristol Gdns
Brighton BN2 . . . . 192 E4
Chichester PO19 . . . . 154 F2
Bristol Mews 3 BN2 . . . . . . 192 E4
Bristol Pl BN2 . . . . 192 E4
Bristol Rd BN2 . . . . 192 C4
Bristol Rise BN2 . . . . 192 E4
Bristol St BN2 . . . . 192 E4
Britannia Ave BN43 . . . . 189 B6
Britannia Ct BN3 . . . . 193 A3
Britannia Ho BN43 . . . . 188 E7
Britannia St GU31 . . . . 68 C5
British Engineerium Mus★
BN3 . . . . 169 B2
Britnell Ho 4 GU31 . . . . 68 B4
Briton's Croft BN44 . . . . . . 145 C3
Brittany Ct 4 BN2 . . . . 190 D7
Brittany Rd
Hove BN3 . . . . 190 D6
Worthing BN14 . . . . 186 C4
Britten Cl
Crawley RH11 . . . . 17 F3
Horsham RH13 . . . . 37 B4
Britten's La BN18 . . . . 157 E4
Brittingham Ho RH11 . . . . . . 18 D6
Broadbridge Bsns Ctr
PO18 . . . . 175 B7
Broadbridge Cotts
RH20 . . . . 123 A4
Broadbridge Ct PO18 . . . . . 175 C7
Broadbridge Dr PO18 . . . . . 175 C7
Broadbridge Heath Rd
RH12 . . . . 35 D4
Broadbridge Ho PO18 . . . . . 175 B4
Broadbridge La RH6 . . . . 7 B8
Broadbridge Mill
PO18 . . . . 175 C7
Broadbridge Ret Pk
RH12 . . . . 35 E3
Broad Croft PO9 . . . . 130 D3
BROADFIELD 18 C1
Broadfield Barton 4
RH11 . . . . 18 B2
Broadfield Dr RH11 . . . . 18 B3
Broadfield East Jun & Inf
Schs RH11 . . . . 18 C2
Broadfield Pl RH11 . . . . 18 B2

Broadfields BN2 . . . . 170 E3
Broadfields Rd BN2 . . . . 170 E3
Broadford Bridge Rd RH20,
RH14 . . . . 101 E4
Broad Gn BN2 . . . . 193 E6
Broad Green Ave
RH15 . . . . 109 C2
Broadland Cotts GU32 . . . . . 68 D6
Broadlands
Burgess Hill RH15 . . . . . . 129 B8
Horley RH6 . . . . 2 C4
Broadlands Bsns Campus
RH12 . . . . 15 C4
Broadmark Ave BN16 . . . . . 205 C4
Broadmark Beach
BN16 . . . . 205 C3
Broadmark Ho 6
BN16 . . . . 205 C5
Broadmark La BN16 . . . . . . 205 C5
Broadmark Par 4
BN16 . . . . 205 C5
Broadmark Way
BN16 . . . . 205 C4
Broad Mdw PO18 . . . . 174 D8
Broadmead RH6 . . . . 2 C4
Broad Piece BN17 . . . . 204 B6
Broad Rd PO18 . . . . 152 D2
Broad Reach BN43 . . . . 188 E7
Broad Rig Ave BN3 . . . . 168 D3
Broad St
Brighton BN2 . . . . 213 B1
Cuckfield RH17 . . . . 87 A6
Broad Strand BN16 . . . . 205 D3
Broad View PO20 . . . . 212 F7
Broadview Gdns
BN13 . . . . 185 E9
BROADWATER 186 C6
Broadwater Bvd
BN14 . . . . 186 D5
Broadwater CE Fst & Mid
Sch BN14 . . . . 186 C5
Broadwater Hall
BN14 . . . . 186 C4
Broadwater Ind Est
BN14 . . . . 186 F5
Broadwater La RH13 . . . . . . 58 D2
Broadwater Manor Sch
BN14 . . . . 186 D5
Broadwater Mews
BN14 . . . . 186 D5
Broadwater Rd BN11,
BN14 . . . . 186 D4
Broadwater St E
BN14 . . . . 186 D5
Broadwater St W
BN14 . . . . 186 C6
Broadwater Way
BN14 . . . . 186 D6
Broadway
Selsey PO20 . . . . 212 C8
Southwick BN42 . . . . 189 F8
Broad Way GU32 . . . . 67 B8
Broadway Ct
Lancing BN15 . . . . 188 B5
11 Shoreham-by-S
BN43 . . . . 189 C8
Broadway Mans 4
BN11 . . . . 186 E2
Broadway Mobile Home
Pk BN15 . . . . 188 B6
Broadway The
Balcombe RH17 . . . . 40 F2
Brighton BN2 . . . . 192 F4
Chichester PO19 . . . . 155 A2
Crawley RH10 . . . . 18 D6
Haywards Heath RH16 . . . . 87 E5
Lancing BN15 . . . . 188 B5
Worthing BN11 . . . . 186 E2
Broad Wlk
Crawley RH10 . . . . 18 D6
Heyshott GU28, GU29,
PO18 . . . . 115 D5
Broad Wlk The PO18 . . . . . 153 C6
Broadwood Cl RH12 . . . . 37 A5
Broadwood Rise RH11 . . . . . 18 A2
Brock End RH17 . . . . 86 E8
Brockham Keep RH6 . . . . 2 C4
Brockhurst BN2 . . . . 192 F7
Brockhurst Cl 3 RH12 . . . . . 35 F1
Brockhurst Farm
RH20 . . . . 119 B5
Brockley Cl BN14 . . . . 186 C4
Brock Rd RH11 . . . . 5 B1
Bromley Cl BN6 . . . . 129 A4
Bromley Rd BN2 . . . . 213 C5
Brompton Cl BN1 . . . . 169 E6
Brontes The RH19 . . . . 9 D1
Bronze Cl PO22 . . . . 201 C7
Brook Ave
Bosham PO18 . . . . 175 B5
Hassocks BN6 . . . . 128 F3
Brook Barn Way
BN12 . . . . 185 E2
Brook Chase RH20 . . . . 121 C6
Brook Cl
Bognor Regis PO21 . . . . . 200 F4
East Grinstead RH19 . . . . . 10 B1
Storrington RH20 . . . . 121 F3
Worthing BN11 . . . . 187 A4
Brook Cotts PO10 . . . . 151 D3
Brook Ct RH12 . . . . 36 B5
Brookdean Rd BN11 . . . . . . 187 B3
Brooke Mead BN2 . . . . 213 C3
Brookenbee Cl BN16 . . . . . . 205 B7
Brooker Pl BN3 . . . . 191 A7
Brooker's Rd RH14 . . . . 79 D7
Brooker St BN3 . . . . 191 A7
Brookfield 2 GU32 . . . . 68 A3

Brookfield Ct PO19 . . . . 177 C6
Brookfield Way RH14 . . . 79 D6
Brook Gdns PO10 . . . . 173 A8
Brook Gn RH17 . . . . 62 E1
Brookham Sch GU30 . . . 25 E2
Brook Hill RH13 . . . . . . 83 E3
Brookhill Cl RH10 . . . . . . 7 A3
Brookhill Rd RH10 . . . . . 7 A3
Brook Ho 7 RH20 . . . . 100 C2
Brookhouse Bottom
  TN22 . . . . 66 D4
Brook La
  Coldwaltham RH20 . . . 119 C5
  Faygate RH12 . . . . . . 37 C8
  Ferring BN12 . . . . . . 206 E6
  Haywards Heath RH16 . 87 F8
  Rustington BN16 . . . . 205 C7
Brookland Ho 5 RH19 . . 9 E1
Brooklands
  Bognor Regis PO21 . . . 200 A1
  Haywards Heath RH16 . 87 C1
  Shoreham-by-S BN43 . . 188 C6
Brooklands Cotts
  PO18 . . . . 132 E2
Brooklands Rd RH11 . . . 18 C1
Brooklands Trad Est
  BN14 . . . . 186 C3
Brooklands Way RH19 . . 22 D8
Brookland Way RH20 . . 119 C5
Brook Lane Cvn Pk
  BN12 . . . . 206 E6
Brooklyn Ave BN11 . . . 185 F3
Brooklyn Ct BN11 . . . . 185 F3
Brook Manor RH19 . . . . 22 D7
Brookpit La BN17 . . . . 203 F8
Brook Rd RH12 . . . . . . 36 E6
Brook Sch The RH10 . . . 19 C3
Brooks End PO21 . . . . 200 A4
Brooks Green Pk (Cvn Pk)
  RH13 . . . . 80 F7
Brookside
  Ashington RH20 . . . . 123 A4
  Copthorne RH10 . . . . . 7 A3
  Crawley Down RH10 . . 21 B8
  Crawley RH10 . . . . . . 18 F7
  Runcton PO20 . . . . . 177 E1
Brookside Ave BN16 . . 205 C7
Brookside Bsns Pk
  BN16 . . . . 205 C7
Brookside Cl
  Ferring BN12 . . . . . . 206 E7
  Runcton PO20 . . . . . 177 E1
Brookside Cvn Pk
  BN17 . . . . 182 C5
Brookside Ind Est
  BN16 . . . . 205 C7
Brookside Rd BN16 . . . 206 D4
Brooks La
  Bognor Regis PO22 . . . 201 E4
  Bognor Regis PO22 . . . 201 E5
  Broadbridge PO18 . . . 175 D7
Brooks La W PO22 . . . 201 D5
Brooksmead PO22 . . . 201 E4
Brook St RH17 . . . . . . 62 F2
Brooks The RH15 . . . . 108 E5
Brooks Way RH20 . . . . 100 C2
Brook The
  Crawley RH10 . . . . . . 18 D7
  Southwater RH13 . . . . 58 A2
Brookview
  Coldwaltham RH20 . . . 119 C5
  Copthorne RH10 . . . . . 7 A3
Brookview S RH20 . . . 119 C5
Brookway
  Burgess Hill RH15 . . . 109 C3
  Lindfield RH16 . . . . . 88 A4
Brook Way BN15 . . . . 187 F5
Brookwood RH6 . . . . . . 2 B4
Brookwood Ho RH6 . . . . 2 B6
Brookwood Pk RH6 . . . . 2 B2
Broomcroft Rd PO22 . . 202 C4
Broomdashers Rd
  RH10 . . . . 18 F7
Broome Cl RH12 . . . . . 36 D5
BROOMERSHILL 100 E4
Broomers Hill La
  RH20 . . . . 100 E4
Broomers Hill Pk
  RH20 . . . . 100 D5
Broomfield RH BN14 . . 186 B5
Broomfield Dr
  Billingshurst RH14 . . . 79 E8
  Portslade-by-S BN41 . . 168 A3
Broomfield Gdns BN5 . 125 E5
Broomfield Rd
  Henfield BN5 . . . . . . 125 E5
  Selsey PO20 . . . . . . 212 F8
Broom Rd GU31 . . . . . 68 E2
Broomwicks Pl RH12 . . 35 E3
Brou Cl BN16 . . . . . . 206 B5
Brougham Ct 12
  BN11 . . . . 187 B3
Brougham Ho BN11 . . . 187 A3
Brougham Rd BN11 . . . 187 B3
Brougham Wlk 1
  BN11 . . . . 187 B3
Brow Cl RH20 . . . . . . 121 B1
Brownfield Ho 4
  GU31 . . . . 68 B3
Browning Cl RH10 . . . 19 C7
Browning Rd
  Lancing BN15 . . . . . . 187 E8
  Worthing BN11 . . . . . 186 B3
Browning's Hill RH13 . . 83 C2
Brownings The 1 RH19 . 9 C1
Brownjohn Cl RH10 . . . 19 A7
Brownleaf Rd BN2 . . . 193 E6
Brown's La RH20 . . . . 121 D1

Browns Wood RH19 . . . . 9 E4
Brown Twins Rd BN6 . . 128 B5
Brow The
  Burgess Hill RH15 . . . 109 A2
  Woodingdean BN2 . . . 193 D8
Broxmead La
  Bolney RH17 . . . . . . 85 D4
  Cuckfield RH17 . . . . . 86 A5
Broyle Cl PO19 . . . . . 154 F1
Broyle Rd PO19 . . . . . 177 A8
Bruce Ave BN11 . . . . 185 F4
Bruce Cl RH16 . . . . . . 87 F3
Bruce Way BN11 . . . . 185 F4
Brunel Ctr RH10 . . . . . . 5 F4
Brunel Ho GU27 . . . . . 27 A6
Brunswick Cl
  Bognor Regis PO22 . . . 202 A5
  Crawley RH10 . . . . . . 19 A4
Brunswick Ct 5 RH10 . . 19 A4
Brunswick Mews 3
  BN3 . . . . 191 D5
Brunswick Pl BN3 . . . 191 D6
Brunswick Rd
  Hove BN3 . . . . 191 D6
  Shoreham-by-S BN43 . . 188 F4
  Worthing BN11 . . . . . 186 C1
Brunswick Row BN1 . . 213 B4
Brunswick St E BN3 . . 191 D5
Brunswick St W BN3 . . 191 D5
Brunswick Sq BN3 . . . 191 D5
Brunswick Terr BN1,
  BN3 . . . . 191 D5
Brushes Lawn RH16 . . . 88 B8
Brushwood Rd RH12 . . . 37 B6
Bryce Cl RH12 . . . . . . 37 A5
Buchan Ctry Pk*
  RH11 . . . . 17 E1
Buchans Lawn RH11 . . . 18 B2
Buci Cres BN43 . . . . . 167 C1
Buck Barn Bglws RH3 . . 82 A2
Buckbarn Crossroads
  RH13 . . . . 82 B2
Buckhurst Cl RH19 . . . . 9 C3
Buckhurst Cotts RH12 . . 33 D8
Buckhurst Mead RH19 . . 9 C4
Buckhurst Way RH19 . . . 9 C3
Buckingham Ave
  BN43 . . . . 166 C3
Buckingham Cl
  4 Brighton BN1 . . . . 213 A4
  Shoreham-by-S BN43 . . 189 A8
Buckingham Com Mid Sch
  BN43 . . . . 188 F8
Buckingham Ct
  Crawley RH11 . . . . . . 18 B2
  Middleton-on-S PO22 . . 202 E5
  Worthing BN14 . . . . . 186 B7
Buckingham Dr
  Chichester PO19 . . . . 177 D6
  East Grinstead RH19 . . 23 D8
Buckingham Gate RH6 . . 6 C7
Buckingham Lo BN1 . . 213 A4
Buckingham Mews 10
  BN43 . . . . 166 F1
Buckingham Pl
  Brighton BN1 . . . . . . 213 A4
  6 Rustington BN16 . . 205 B7
Buckingham Rd
  Brighton BN1 . . . . . . 213 A3
  Petersfield GU32 . . . . 67 F3
  Shoreham-by-S BN43 . . 188 F8
  Worthing BN11 . . . . . 186 D2
Buckingham St
  Brighton BN1 . . . . . . 213 A3
  Shoreham-by-S BN43 . . 188 E7
Buckland Dr PO21 . . . 200 B2
Buckler St BN41 . . . . 190 B8
Buckley Cl BN3 . . . . . 168 E4
Buckley Pl RH10 . . . . . 21 A8
Buckmans Rd RH11 . . . 18 D6
Buckmore Ave GU32 . . . 67 F4
Bucknor Cl PO21 . . . . 200 C2
BUCKS GREEN 33 B6
Bucksham Ave PO21 . . 200 F7
Buckshead Hill RH13 . . 59 F7
Buckswood Dr RH11 . . . 18 A4
Buckwish La BN5 . . . . 125 C4
Buddington La GU29 . . 72 F3
Budgen Cl RH10 . . . . . . 6 D1
Budgenor Lo GU29 . . . 73 A3
Buffbeards La GU27 . . . 26 E6
Bugshill La GU29 . . . . 93 D1
Bulbeck Cl RH15 . . . . 108 E1
Bulbeck Cft PO10 . . . . 152 A1
Bulkington Ave BN14 . . 186 B4
Bulldogs Bank RH19 . . 42 F5
Buller Rd BN2 . . . . . . 170 D1
Bullfinch Cl
  Horley RH6 . . . . 1 E4
  Horsham RH12 . . . . . 36 C7
Bullfinch La BN6 . . . . 127 E6
Bull Hill GU33 . . . . . . 46 A4
Bull's La RH13, RH17 . . 84 D4
Bulrushes Bsns Pk
  RH19 . . . . 22 D6
Bunbury Cl RH20 . . . . 122 D2
Bunch La GU27 . . . . . 27 B8
Bunch Way GU27 . . . . 27 A6
Buncton Crossways
  BN44 . . . . 144 C2
Buncton La RH17 . . . . 85 D3
Bungalows The BN18 . . 158 D1
Bunting Cl RH13 . . . . . 36 B5
Bunyan Cl RH11 . . . . . 17 E3
Burbeach Cl RH11 . . . . 18 B3
Burchell Rd BN15 . . . . 187 F7
Burchens The BN14 . . . 186 C6

Burchetts Cl RH16 . . . . 87 E2
Burchett Wlk PO21 . . . 200 F5
Burch Gr BN18 . . . . . 158 D1
Burdett Cl RH10 . . . . . 19 D5
Burdett Rd RH10 . . . . . 19 D5
Burdock Cl 2 RH11 . . . 18 A2
Burdocks Dr RH15 . . . 109 D1
Burford Cl BN14 . . . . 186 A7
Burford Rd RH13 . . . . . 36 C2
Burgesmede Ho 6
  GU32 . . . . 68 B3
Burgess Cl BN41 . . . . 190 B8
Burgess Hill Sch
  RH15 . . . . 109 B2
Burgess Hill Sta
  RH15 . . . . 109 B2
Burgh Cl RH10 . . . . 6 D1
Burgh Hill Rd GU30 . . . 25 A7
Burlands RH11 . . . . 5 A1
Burleigh Cl RH10 . . . . . 21 B8
Burleigh Ct
  26 Brighton BN1 . . . . 191 E5
  5 Worthing BN11 . . . 186 C1
Burleigh La RH10 . . . . 21 C7
Burleigh Way RH10 . . . 21 B8
Burley Cl
  3 Lancing BN15 . . . . 187 E6
  Loxwood RH14 . . . . . 32 A4
Burley Rd PO22 . . . . . 202 D4
Burleys Rd RH10 . . . . . 19 C6
BURLEYS WOOD 19 E7
Burlington Ct BN11 . . . 185 F2
Burlington Gdns
  Portslade-by-S BN41 . . 168 C1
  Selsey PO20 . . . . . . 212 F6
Burlington Rd BN12 . . 185 D4
Burlington St BN2 . . . 192 C4
Burlow Cl
  Birdham PO20 . . . . . 197 D4
  Brighton BN2 . . . . . . 192 E5
Burma Cl RH16 . . . . . . 88 C4
Burmill St BN16 . . . . 205 E7
BURNDELL 181 B3
Burndell Rd BN18 . . . 181 A2
Burners Cl RH15 . . . . 109 D1
Burnes Vale BN2 . . . . 193 F2
Burney Ct 5 RH11 . . . . 18 A3
Burngreave Ct PO21 . . 201 B3
Burnham Ave PO21 . . . 201 C3
Burnham Cl BN2 . . . . 193 F7
Burnham Gdns PO21 . . 201 C3
Burnham Pl 1 RH13 . . . 36 D1
Burnham Rd BN13 . . . 185 E7
Burns Cl RH12 . . . . . . 36 E7
Burns Gdns PO22 . . . 202 D5
Burnside Cres BN15 . . . 187 C5
Burns Rd RH10 . . . . . . 19 C8
Burns Way
  Crawley RH12 . . . . . . 17 C1
  East Grinstead RH19 . . 9 C1
Burnthouse Bostall
  BN6 . . . . 150 C8
Burntcross La RH13 . . . 83 C4
Burnt House La RH12 . . 17 A7
Burnt Oak La RH5 . . . . . 3 F1
Burrell Ave BN15 . . . . 187 D5
Burrell Bldgs BN15 . . . 187 D5
Burrell Cl RH13 . . . . . 105 A3
Burrell Cotts RH17 . . . 86 E8
Burrell Ct RH11 . . . . . 17 F4
Burrell Gn RH17 . . . . . 86 F8
Burrell Rd RH10 . . . . . 87 D6
Burrells The BN43 . . . 189 B6
Burry Cotts BN15 . . . . 186 F7
Bursledon Cl PO22 . . . 202 A5
Burstead Cl BN1 . . . . 170 B3
Burston Gdns RH19 . . . 9 D4
Burstow Cl RH6 . . . . . . 1 F1
Burstowhill La RH17 . . 64 D6
Burstow Ho RH6 . . . . . . 2 B6
Burton Cl RH6 . . . . 2 A2
Burton Ho GU28 . . . . 117 D7
Burton Park Rd GU28 . . 97 E1
Burton St 11 RH12 . . . . 36 C2
Burton Villas BN3 . . . 191 D8
Burwash Cl BN16 . . . . 206 B7
Burwash Lo BN1 . . . . 170 C1
Burwash Rd
  Crawley RH10 . . . . . . 19 A5
  Hove BN3 . . . . 168 F3
Bury CE Inf Sch RH20 . . 139 F7
Bury Dr BN12 . . . . . . 185 B3
Bury Hill BN18, RH20 . . 139 F6
Bury Ho
  Bury RH20 . . . . 140 A7
  3 Worthing BN14 . . . 186 D5
BURY HOLLOW 140 A8
Bury Rd RH20 . . . . . . 118 F3
Bushby Ave BN16 . . . . 205 D5
Bushby Cl BN15 . . . . . 187 C5
Bushby Terr 13 BN17 . . 204 E4
Bush Cl BN2 . . . . 193 D8
Bush Cottage Cl
  BN41 . . . . 168 C2
Bush Farm Dr BN41 . . 168 C3
Bushfield RH14 . . . . . 30 F2
Bush Terr RH14 . . . . . 168 B3
Busticle La BN15 . . . . 187 C7
Butcher Cl BN16 . . . . 184 A5
Butchers Lo PO18 . . . 136 C6
Bute St BN2 . . . . 192 D5
Butler's Green Ho
  RH16 . . . . 87 B5
Butler's Green Rd
  RH16 . . . . 87 C4
Butlers Rd RH13 . . . . . 37 B4
Butlins Holiday Ctr*
  PO21 . . . . 201 E3

Butser Wlk GU31 . . . . . 68 D4
Butterbox La RH17 . . . . 89 D4
Buttercup Way RH13 . . . 58 A4
Buttercup Wlk BN1 . . . 170 B7
Butterfield RH19 . . . . . . 9 B1
Buttermere Cl RH12 . . . 37 B6
Buttermere Way
  BN17 . . . . 205 A4
Butt La BN18 . . . . . . 158 C6
Button Ct BN2 . . . . . 213 C4
Butts Cl RH11 . . . . . . 18 B7
Butts Mdw RH14 . . . . . 54 E6
Butts Rd BN42 . . . . . 189 E7
Buxted Rise BN1 . . . . 170 B5
Buxton Rd BN1 . . . . . 191 E7
Bycroft Way RH10 . . . . 19 B8
Byerley Cl PO10 . . . . 151 D5
Byerley Way RH10 . . . . 19 E7
Byeway The
  Bognor Regis PO21 . . . 211 C8
  West Wittering PO20 . . 196 C1
Byfield Pl PO21 . . . . . 201 D6
Byfleets La RH12 . . . . . 35 D6
Bylands 3 BN2 . . . . . 192 F5
Bylanes Cl RH17 . . . . . 86 F7
Bylanes Cres RH17 . . . 86 F8
Byne Cl RH20 . . . . . . 121 C1
Byrd Rd RH11 . . . . . . 17 F3
Byre Cotts BN2 . . . . . 193 D4
Byron Cl
  Bognor Regis PO22 . . . 202 D6
  Crawley RH10 . . . . . . 19 B7
  Horsham RH12 . . . . . 36 E6
Byron Ct
  1 Haywards Heath
  RH16 . . . . 87 D5
  Stockbridge PO19 . . . 176 F4
Byron Gr 2 RH19 . . . . . 9 C1
Byron Rd
  Littlehampton BN16 . . 205 A5
  Worthing BN11 . . . . . 186 C1
Byron St BN3 . . . . . . 191 A7
Byron Terr 1 BN3 . . . . 191 A7
By Sunte RH16 . . . . . . 87 F8
Bywater Way PO19 . . . 176 F4
Bywaves PO20 . . . . . 208 C4
Byways PO20 . . . . . . 212 C5
Byway The
  Brighton BN1 . . . . . . 170 E5
  Middleton-on-S PO22 . . 202 E5
BYWORTH 98 B6
Byworth Cl BN2 . . . . . 192 F6

C

Caburn Ct RH11 . . . . . 18 C4
Caburn Hts RH11 . . . . . 18 C4
Caburn Rd BN3 . . . . . 191 E7
Cackstones The RH10 . . 19 D7
Cadogan Ct
  3 Brighton BN1 . . . . 191 E7
  Worthing BN11 . . . . . 186 D2
Caedwalla Dr PO20 . . . 156 C1
Caernarvon Rd PO19 . . 177 D6
Caffins Cl RH10 . . . . . 18 E8
Caffyns Rise RH14 . . . . 55 D1
Cagefoot La BN5 . . . . 125 E4
Caister's Cl BN16 . . . . 191 C8
Caius Ct 16 BN43 . . . . 189 C8
Cakeham Rd PO20 . . . 207 D8
Cakeham Way PO20 . . 207 E7
Calbourne RH16 . . . . . 87 D5
Calceto La RH17 . . . . 182 E8
Caldbeck Ho 7 RH11 . . 17 F3
Calderdale Cl RH11 . . . 18 B4
Caledon Ave PO22 . . . 202 D5
Caledonian Ct 5
  BN2 . . . . 213 C5
Caledonian Ho 4
  RH10 . . . . 18 D8
Caledonian Pl 1
  BN11 . . . . 186 D1
Caledonian Rd
  Brighton BN2 . . . . . . 213 C5
  Chichester PO19 . . . . 177 B6
Caledonian Way RH6 . . . 6 D7
Callender Wlk RH17 . . . 86 F8
Callisto Cl RH11 . . . . . 17 E3
Callon Cl RH13 . . . . . 185 B7
Calluna Dr RH10 . . . . . 7 A3
Calvecroft GU30 . . . . . 25 C4
Calvin Wlk RH11 . . . . . 17 E3
Camargue Ct 4 BN11 . . 186 A3
Camber Cl
  Brighton BN2 . . . . . . 192 F5
  Crawley RH10 . . . . . . 19 C6
Cambourne Ct 7
  BN11 . . . . 186 C2
Cambrai Ave PO19 . . . 177 B5
Cambria Cl PO18 . . . . 175 C5
Cambridge Ave PO20 . . 207 E8
Cambridge Dr PO21 . . 200 F4
Cambridge Gr BN3 . . . 191 C7
Cambridge Mews
  BN3 . . . . 191 C7
Cambridge Rd
  Horsham RH13 . . . . . 36 D2
  Hove BN3 . . . . 191 D6
  Worthing BN11 . . . . . 186 D3
Cambridge Wlk PO21 . . 200 F4
Camden Ho BN41 . . . . 190 D6
Camden Terr BN1 . . . . 213 A3
Camelford St BN2 . . . 213 C1
Camelia Cl RH13 . . . . . 58 A2
Camelot Cl RH13 . . . . . 58 A2
Camelot Ct RH11 . . . . . 17 E6
CAMELSDALE 26 F4

Camelsdale Fst Sch
  GU27 . . . . 26 F5
Camelsdale Rd GU27 . . 26 F5
Camino Pk RH10 . . . . . 6 A4
Campbell Cres RH19 . . . 9 B1
Campbell Ct BN12 . . . 185 A4
Campbell Dr BN16 . . . 205 B6
Campbell Rd
  Bognor Regis PO21 . . . 201 D3
  Brighton BN1 . . . . . . 213 A6
  Crawley RH10 . . . . . . 19 C5
  Tangmere PO20 . . . . 156 B1
Campion Cl BN16 . . . . 205 B8
Campion Rd RH12 . . . . 36 E5
Canada Cnr GU31 . . . . 91 B6
Canada Cotts GU29 . . . 73 A3
Canada Gr
  Bognor Regis PO21 . . . 201 C3
  Midhurst GU29 . . . . . 73 A2
Canada Rd BN18 . . . . 159 F3
Canada Way GU30 . . . 25 C3
Canadian Cres PO20 . . 212 C5
Canal Pl PO19 . . . . . 176 F5
Canal Rd BN18 . . . . . 180 F3
Canal Wharf PO19 . . . 176 F5
Canberra Cl RH11 . . . . . 5 D1
Canberra Ct PO21 . . . 201 A2
Canberra Pl
  Horsham RH12 . . . . . 36 F4
  Tangmere PO20 . . . . 156 D2
Canberra Rd
  Thorney Island PO10 . . 173 C3
  Worthing BN13 . . . . . 185 C7
Candleford Gate GU30 . 25 B4
Canfield Cl BN2 . . . . . 170 D1
Canfield Rd BN2 . . . . 170 D1
Canhouse La GU31,
  GU33 . . . . 46 C3
Canning Ct PO22 . . . . 201 F3
Canning Rd PO22 . . . . 201 F3
Canning St BN2 . . . . . 192 D5
Cannon Pl BN1 . . . . . 213 A2
Canonbury Cotts RH12 . 16 F6
Canon La PO19 . . . . . 176 F6
Canon's Cl PO21 . . . . 200 D1
Canons Way BN44 . . . 145 E4
Cansiron La RH19 . . . . 23 F6
Cantelupe Ho 1 RH19 . . 9 F1
Cantelupe Mews 7
  RH19 . . . . 9 F1
Cantelupe Rd RH19 . . . 9 F1
Canterbury Cl
  Bognor Regis PO21 . . . 200 A1
  Chichester PO19 . . . . 176 F8
Canterbury Ct
  Southwater RH13 . . . . 58 A2
  Worthing BN13 . . . . . 185 F4
Canterbury Dr 5
  BN2 . . . . 213 C4
Canterbury Ho BN14 . . 186 A6
Canterbury Rd
  Crawley RH10 . . . . . . 18 E2
  Rustington BN16 . . . . 205 E6
  Worthing BN13 . . . . . 186 A3
Canter The RH10 . . . . . 19 E7
Canton 3 RH16 . . . . . 87 D6
Cants Cl RH15 . . . . . 109 C3
Cants La RH15 . . . . . 109 C3
Canute Cl PO20 . . . . . 208 C5
Canute Rd PO18 . . . . 175 B5
Canvas St GU27 . . . . . 27 B6
Canvey Cl RH11 . . . . . 18 C3
Cape Copse RH12 . . . . 33 D7
Capelia Ho BN11 . . . . 186 A1
Capel La RH11 . . . . . . 17 F5
Capel Rd RH12 . . . . . 16 A8
Capenors RH15 . . . . . 108 F1
Cape The
  Littlehampton BN17 . . 205 A5
  Rottingdean BN2 . . . . 193 F1
Capricorn Cl RH11 . . . 17 E4
Capsey Rd RH11 . . . . . 17 E5
Capstan Dr BN17 . . . . 205 A7
Capua Ct RH10 . . . . . . 6 C2
Caraway Cl RH11 . . . . 18 B2
Carden Ave
  Brighton BN1 . . . . . . 169 F5
  Brighton BN1 . . . . . . 170 B6
Carden Cl BN1 . . . . . 170 A6
Carden Cres BN1 . . . . 170 A6
Carden Hill BN1 . . . . . 170 B5
Carden Prim Sch BN1 . . 170 B6
Cardew Rd GU33 . . . . 45 C3
Card Hill RH18 . . . . . . 23 F1
Cardinal Ct 4 BN11 . . . 186 A1
Cardinal Newman RC Sch
  BN3 . . . . 191 D8
Cardinal's Dr PO21 . . . 200 B1
Carey Ho RH11 . . . . . 18 C6
Carfax RH12 . . . . 36 C2
Cargo Forecourt Rd
  RH6 . . . . 5 D7
Cargo Rd RH6 . . . . 5 D7
Carina Dr BN16 . . . . . 205 F8
Carisbrooke Cl BN15 . . 187 E8
Carisbrooke Dr BN13 . . 185 B6
Carisbrooke Rd BN2 . . 192 D7
Carlford Ct PO19 . . . . 176 E8
Carlingford Ct 1
  PO21 . . . . 201 C4
Carlisle Gdns PO19 . . . 154 F2
Carlisle Rd BN3 . . . . . 190 F6
Carlton Ave PO21 . . . . 200 C3
Carlton Cl RH10 . . . . . 18 E5

Carlton Ct
Horley RH6 . . . . 2 A5
Portslade-by-S BN41 . . . . . 190 C8
Carlton Hill BN2 . . . . 213 C2
Carlton Hill Prim Sch
BN2 . . . . 213 C2
Carlton Ho
⬛6 Brighton BN1 . . . . 169 E2
Worthing BN13 . . . . 186 A6
Carlton Mews BN11 . . . . . 186 A2
Carlton Pl ⬛5 BN2 . . . . . . 213 C2
Carlton Terr BN3,
BN41 . . . . 190 C8
Carlton Tye RH6 . . . . 2 C3
Carlyle Ho BN2 . . . . 170 D1
Carlyle Ho ⬛2 BN14 . . . . . 186 D3
Carlyle St BN2 . . . . 192 C7
Carman Wlk RH11 . . . . 18 B1
Carmel Ho
Hove BN3 . . . . 191 A7
Worthing BN11 . . . . 186 A6
Carmelstead Cl RH16 . . . . 88 A3
Carnation Cl BN17 . . . . . . 205 B7
Carn Ct ⬛7 BN2 . . . . 192 C6
Carnegie Cl BN14 . . . . . . 186 C5
Carnegie Gdns BN14 . . . . 186 D5
Carnegie Ho BN13 . . . . . . 185 F7
Carnegie Rd BN14 . . . . . . 186 C5
Carnforth Rd BN15 . . . . . . 187 C5
Carnoustie Ct ⬛18 RH16 . . 87 E4
Carol Cl BN1 . . . . 169 F6
Caroline Ct RH11 . . . . 18 D4
Carolyn Ho BN13 . . . . 185 E6
Caron Cl BN17 . . . . 187 E5
Carousel Ct PO21,
PO22 . . . . 201 B5
Carpenters Mdw
RH20 . . . . 100 C2
Carrick Wlk ⬛12 BN43 . . . 188 E7
Carron La GU29 . . . . 94 E7
Carse Rd PO19 . . . . 155 C1
Carter Rd RH10 . . . . 19 D3
Cartersland Cnr GU30 . . . . 47 B3
Carterslodge La RH17 . . . . 60 E7
Cartersmead Cl RH6 . . . . . . 2 B4
Carters Way RH14 . . . . 78 B8
Carvel Way RH20 . . . . 205 A6
Carylls Cotts RH12 . . . . . . 16 F1
Carylls Mdw RH13 . . . . . . 104 D7
Casher Rd RH10 . . . . 19 C3
Cashman Lo BN1 . . . . 170 A5
Caspian Cl PO19 . . . . 176 B3
Caspian Ct BN1 . . . . 213 A4
Caspian Ho ⬛4 BN16 . . . . 205 A4
Caspian Sq BN2 . . . . 193 F1
Cassells Rd ⬛2 PO19 . . . . 155 A2
Cassidy Pl RH20 . . . . 121 B1
Castle Cl
Bramber BN44 . . . . 145 E2
Worthing BN13 . . . . 185 F5
Castle Ct BN13 . . . . 185 F5
Castle Dr RH6 . . . . 2 C2
Castlegate RH20 . . . . 121 B7
Castle Gdns
Arundel BN18 . . . . 160 A3
Petersfield GU32 . . . . 68 A3
Castle Goring Mews
BN13 . . . . 185 A9
Castle La
Bramber BN44 . . . . 145 E2
West Grinstead RH13 . . . 103 F7
Castle Mews
Arundel BN18 . . . . 160 B3
⬛27 Brighton BN1 . . . . . . 191 E5
Castle Of Mey Ho
GU27 . . . . 26 F6
Castle Rd
Broadbridge Heath
RH12 . . . . 35 D3
Red Hill PO9 . . . . 130 D1
Worthing BN13 . . . . 185 F5
Castlereagh Gn PO22 . . . . 202 A5
Castle Sq BN1 . . . . 213 B2
Castle St BN1 . . . . 191 E5
Castle The RH12 . . . . 36 E7
CASTLE TOWN 146 C1
Castle Way
Bramber BN44 . . . . 145 E3
Worthing BN13 . . . . 185 F5
Castlewood Prim Sch
RH13 . . . . 58 A2
Castlewood Rd RH13 . . . . . 58 A2
Caterways RH12 . . . . 36 A3
Cathedral Ctyd PO19 . . . . 176 F6
Cathedral Way PO19 . . . . 176 D6
Catherine Vale BN13 . . . . 193 E8
Catherine Villas GU27 . . . . 27 B6
Catkin Way RH16 . . . . 88 B4
Catslands La BN5 . . . . 147 C8
Cattswood La RH16 . . . . . . 87 C2
Caudle St BN5 . . . . 125 F4
CAUSEWAY 68 A1
Causeway RH16 . . . . 36 C1
Causeway Ct BN18 . . . . . . 160 C2
Causewayside GU27 . . . . . . 27 D6
Causeway The
Arundel BN18 . . . . 160 C2
Birdham PO20 . . . . 197 F6
Bognor Regis PO21 . . . . . 211 A8
Brighton BN2 . . . . 192 D6
Partridge Green RH13 . . . 105 A3
Petersfield GU31 . . . . 68 A1
Selsey PO20 . . . . 212 C6
Worthing BN12 . . . . 185 E4

Causeway Villas
BN18 . . . . 160 C2
Cavalier Cl GU29 . . . . 94 E7
Cavalier Way RH19 . . . . . . 22 F7
Cavell Way RH10 . . . . 19 C5
Cavendish Cl
Horsham RH12 . . . . 36 D7
Worthing BN12 . . . . 185 D4
Cavendish Ct ⬛23 BN2 . . . 192 D4
Cavendish Ho
Bognor Regis PO21 . . . . . 201 D2
⬛8 Brighton BN1 . . . . . . 191 E5
Haywards Heath RH16 . . . 87 F2
Cavendish Mews ⬛12
BN1 . . . . 191 D5
Cavendish Pl BN1 . . . . 191 E5
Cavendish Rd PO21 . . . . . 201 C3
Cavendish St
⬛11 Brighton BN2 . . . . . . 213 C2
Chichester PO19 . . . . 176 F7
Caversham Ct ⬛8
BN11 . . . . 186 B1
Cawley Ho PO19 . . . . 177 A5
Cawley Rd PO19 . . . . 177 A5
Caxton Ct RH10 . . . . 18 E3
Caxton Ct ⬛4 BN14 . . . . . 186 D4
Caxton Way ⬛15 RH16 . . . 87 E4
Cecil Ct ⬛7 BN15 . . . . 187 E4
Cecilian Ave BN14 . . . . . . 186 D4
Cecil Norris Ho ⬛3
BN43 . . . . 188 F7
Cecil Pashley Way
BN43 . . . . 188 D8
Cecil Rd BN15 . . . . 187 E4
Cedar Ave BN13 . . . . 185 F7
Cedar Cl
Angmering BN16 . . . . 206 A8
Bognor Regis PO21 . . . . . 200 D3
Burgess Hill RH15 . . . . . 109 B5
Crawley RH11 . . . . 5 C1
Ferring BN12 . . . . 206 E5
Horsham RH12 . . . . 36 C3
Lancing BN15 . . . . 187 D4
Worthing BN13 . . . . 185 F7
Cedar Cl E PO21 . . . . 200 E3
Cedar Ct
Haslemere GU27 . . . . 27 B6
Petworth GU28 . . . . 97 E7
Worthing BN13 . . . . 186 A3
Cedar Ctr The BN1 . . . . . . 170 C2
Cedar Dr
Chichester PO19 . . . . 176 E7
Southwater RH13 . . . . . . 58 A1
Cedar Lo RH11 . . . . 18 D4
Cedars Farm Cl RH14 . . . . 79 C8
Cedars Gdns BN1 . . . . 169 E3
Cedars The
Barnham PO22 . . . . 180 B6
⬛1 Brighton BN2 . . . . . . 213 C5
Brighton, Withdean
BN1 . . . . 169 E3
Haywards Heath RH16 . . . 87 D7
Rustington BN16 . . . . 205 E6
Cedar Way
Haywards Heath RH16 . . . 88 B4
Henfield BN5 . . . . 125 F4
Cedarwood ⬛3 BN1 . . . . . 169 E3
Cedric Ct ⬛2 RH12 . . . . . . 36 A1
Celandine Ct ⬛1 RH11 . . . 18 B2
Cello Ct ⬛8 BN2 . . . . 192 C5
Cemetery La
Tillington GU28 . . . . 75 C1
Westbourne PO10 . . . . . . 151 F3
Centenary Ho ⬛4 BN1 . . . 169 E2
Centenary Ind Est ⬛6
BN2 . . . . 192 B8
Central Ave
Bognor Regis PO21 . . . . . 201 A6
Littlehampton BN16 . . . . 205 C4
Worthing BN14 . . . . 163 F3
Central Bldgs ⬛2
PO21 . . . . 201 D3
Central CE Jun Sch
PO19 . . . . 176 F7
Central Dr
Bognor Regis PO21 . . . . . 201 A6
Middleton-on-S PO22 . . . 203 A5
Central Sussex Coll
RH12 . . . . 36 D3
Central Sussex Coll
(Haywards Heath
Campus) RH16 . . . . 87 D6
Centrecourt Cl ⬛5
BN14 . . . . 186 C4
Centrecourt Rd BN14 . . . . 186 C4
Centurion Rd BN1 . . . . 213 A3
Ceres Pl PO22 . . . . 202 D4
Chadborn Cl BN2 . . . . 192 D5
Chadwick Cl RH11 . . . . 18 B1
Chaffer La PO20 . . . . 197 D4
Chaffinch Cl
Burgess Hill RH15 . . . . . 108 D4
Crawley RH11 . . . . 18 D8
Horsham RH12 . . . . 36 D7
Worthing BN13 . . . . 185 C6
Chaffinch Way RH6 . . . . . . 1 E4
Chailey Ave BN2 . . . . 194 A1
Chailey Cl ⬛2 RH11 . . . . . 18 A3
Chailey Cres BN2 . . . . 194 A1
Chailey Ct
Brighton BN1 . . . . 169 C1
⬛2 Haywards Heath
RH16 . . . . 87 F3
Chailey Rd BN1 . . . . 170 E4
Chainbridge La PO20 . . . . 209 C1
Chain Pier Ho BN2 . . . . . . 213 C1
Chalcraft La PO21 . . . . . . 200 F5
Chalcroft Cl GU30 . . . . 25 A4

Chalder La PO20 . . . . 198 F3
Chaldon Rd RH11 . . . . 18 C1
Chaleford Ct ⬛5 BN14 . . . 186 D4
Chalet Cl BN12 . . . . 206 E4
Chalet Gdns BN12 . . . . . . 206 E4
Chalet Rd BN12 . . . . 206 E4
Chalex Ind Est BN42 . . . . 190 A7
Chalfont Cl PO22 . . . . 202 E5
Chalfont Ct BN11 . . . . 186 B2
Chalfont Dr BN3 . . . . 169 C3
Chalfont Way BN13 . . . . . 185 D7
Chalkdock La PO20 . . . . . 197 A5
Chalkers La BN6 . . . . 128 B8
Chalk La PO20 . . . . 209 E7
Chalkland Rise BN2 . . . . . 193 E8
Chalkpit La PO18 . . . . 155 B7
Chalk Rd
Goodwood Park PO18 . . . 136 A4
Ifold RH14 . . . . 31 C3
Chalky Rd BN41 . . . . 168 A3
Challen Cl PO20 . . . . 178 C6
Challen Ct RH12 . . . . 36 B3
Challoners RH17 . . . . 65 C4
Challoners Cl BN2 . . . . . . 194 A2
Challoners Mews
BN2 . . . . 193 F2
Challow Cl BN6 . . . . 128 E4
Chalmers Cl RH6 . . . . 4 E6
Chaloner Cl RH16 . . . . 88 B7
Chaloner Rd RH16 . . . . 88 B7
Chalvington Cl BN1 . . . . . 170 E6
Champion's Gate RH13 . . . 83 A2
Champions Row BN3 . . . . 191 C8
Chancellors Pk BN6 . . . . . 128 F4
Chanctonbury RH20 . . . . . 123 A4
Chanctonbury Cl
Rustington BN16 . . . . 205 B4
Washington BN20 . . . . . . 143 E6
Chanctonbury Dr
BN43 . . . . 166 F1
Chanctonbury Rd
Burgess Hill RH15 . . . . . 109 A1
Hove BN3 . . . . 191 E7
Rustington BN16 . . . . 205 B4
Chanctonbury Ring Rd
BN44 . . . . 144 D6
Chanctonbury View
BN5 . . . . 125 D4
Chanctonbury Way
RH11 . . . . 18 C4
Chanctonbury Wlk ⬛8
RH20 . . . . 121 D1
Chancton Cl BN11 . . . . . . 185 F4
Chancton Copse
RH20 . . . . 122 B3
Chanctonfold BN44 . . . . . 145 C4
Chancton View Rd
BN11 . . . . 185 F4
Chandler Cl RH10 . . . . 18 D4
Chandler Ct ⬛4 RH6 . . . . . 2 B3
Chandler Rd PO19 . . . . . . 176 E5
Chandlers Lea PO20 . . . . . 208 C5
Chandlers Reach
PO20 . . . . 197 A7
Chandlers Way BN44 . . . . 145 C2
Chandos Rd BN11 . . . . . . 186 D2
Channel Ct ⬛6 BN15 . . . . 187 E4
Channel Keep ⬛11
BN17 . . . . 204 E4
Channel View
Bognor Regis PO21 . . . . . 211 A8
⬛13 Southwick BN42 . . . 189 E7
Channel View Rd BN2 . . . 193 B8
Chantlers Cl RH19 . . . . 9 C2
Chantrelles The BN16 . . . 184 A5
Chantrey Rd RH10 . . . . 18 E3
Chantry Cl
Henfield BN5 . . . . 125 E6
Horley RH6 . . . . 1 F4
⬛2 Storrington RH20 . . . 121 E1
Chantry Est The RH20 . . . 142 E8
Chantryfield Rd BN16 . . . 183 F6
Chantry La RH20 . . . . 142 E6
Chantry Orch ⬛10
BN44 . . . . 145 D3
Chantry Rd BN13 . . . . 186 A6
Chantry The PO19 . . . . . . 176 F6
Chapel Cl
Burgess Hill RH15 . . . . . 108 F4
Littlehampton BN17 . . . . 204 C6
Watersfield RH20 . . . . . . 119 A4
Chapelfields RH17 . . . . 86 F8
Chapel Ho BN2 . . . . 213 C2
Chapel La
Ashurst Wood RH19 . . . . . 23 D6
Cootham RH20 . . . . 121 A1
Copthorne RH10 . . . . 7 F4
East Ashling PO18 . . . . . 154 A3
Forest Row RH18 . . . . 23 F2
Horsted Keynes RH17 . . . 65 C5
West Wittering PO20 . . . . 196 F2
Chapel Mews BN3 . . . . . . 191 D5
Chapel Pl BN41 . . . . 190 B7
Chapel Rd
Barns Green RH13 . . . . . . 56 F2
Charlwood RH6 . . . . 4 F7
Portslade-by-S BN41 . . . . 190 A7
Worthing BN11 . . . . 186 D3
Chapel Row
East Dean PO18 . . . . 136 C6
West Hoathly RH19 . . . . . 42 E7
Chapel St
Bognor Regis PO21 . . . . . 201 C2
Brighton BN2 . . . . 213 C2
Chichester PO19 . . . . 176 F6
Petersfield GU32 . . . . 68 B3
Chapel Terr ⬛2 BN2 . . . . 192 D4

Chapel Terrace Mews ⬛21
BN2 . . . . 192 D4
Chapel Wlk BN16 . . . . 183 F5
Chapman Ct BN13 . . . . . . 185 F7
Chapman Rd RH10 . . . . 19 C2
Chapman's La
East Grinstead RH19 . . . . . 9 B1
East Grinstead RH19 . . . . . 9 D1
Chappell Cl GU30 . . . . 25 C4
Chappell Croft ⬛2
BN11 . . . . 186 B2
Charis Ct ⬛18 BN3 . . . . . 191 C7
Charlecote Rd BN11 . . . . . 186 E2
Charles Ave
Burgess Hill RH15 . . . . . 108 D2
Chichester PO19 . . . . 177 D6
Charles Bennett Ct
RH16 . . . . 88 A4
Charles Cl BN3 . . . . 169 A3
Charles Ct ⬛6 BN11 . . . . . 186 C3
Charlesfield Rd RH6 . . . . . . 1 F4
Charles Ho
Selsey PO20 . . . . 212 E8
Worthing BN12 . . . . 185 D3
Charles Kingston Gdns
BN1 . . . . 169 E4
Charles St
Brighton BN2 . . . . 213 B1
Petersfield GU32 . . . . 68 A3
Charleston Ct RH10 . . . . . . 19 B3
Charlesworth Pk RH16 . . . 88 C4
Charlmead PO20 . . . . 207 F6
Charlock Cl ⬛3 RH11 . . . . 18 A2
Charlock Way RH13 . . . . . . 58 A3
Charlotte Ct RH11 . . . . 18 C6
Charlotte Ho
Bognor Regis PO21 . . . . . 201 E4
⬛7 Rustington BN16 . . . 205 E6
Charlotte St BN2 . . . . 213 C1
Charlton Dr GU31 . . . . 68 C5
Charlton Gdns BN6 . . . . . 129 D3
Charlton Mews BN44 . . . . 145 D3
Charlton Mill Way
PO18 . . . . 135 F6
Charlton Rd PO18 . . . . 136 B6
Charlton St BN44 . . . . 145 C3
Charltons The BN1 . . . . . . 170 D6
Charlwood Cl RH10 . . . . 7 B4
Charlwood Ct RH11 . . . . 5 D2
Charlwood Gdns
RH15 . . . . 109 C5
Charlwood La RH5 . . . . 4 A5
Charlwood Lo ⬛3
BN11 . . . . 186 A2
Charlwood Pl RH6 . . . . 4 E8
Charlwood Rd
Burgess Hill RH15 . . . . . 109 D6
Crawley RH6, RH11 . . . . . . 5 C4
Hookwood RH6, RH11 . . . . 5 C8
Rusper RH11, RH6 . . . . 4 E2
Charlwoods Bsns Ctr
RH19 . . . . 9 D2
Charlwoods Pl RH19 . . . . . . 9 E3
Charlwoods Rd RH19 . . . . . 9 E3
Charlwood St PO21 . . . . . . 201 B2
Charlwood Village Inf Sch
RH6 . . . . 4 F7
Charlwood Wlk RH11 . . . . . 5 B1
Charmandean La
BN14 . . . . 186 D8
Charmandean Rd
BN14 . . . . 186 D6
Charmans Cl RH12 . . . . . . 37 B5
Charm Cl RH6 . . . . 1 E4
Charnwood Rd PO22 . . . . . 201 B6
Charrington Way RH12 . . . 35 C3
Charter Gate RH16 . . . . . . 87 D5
Chartergrove Ho ⬛14
GU31 . . . . 68 B3
Charterhouse Mews
PO20 . . . . 207 F8
Charter Wlk GU27 . . . . 27 C6
Chartfield BN3 . . . . 169 A2
Chartfield Way BN3 . . . . . 169 B2
Chartwell Bldg PO10 . . . . 151 F1
Chartwell Ct BN1 . . . . 213 A2
Chartwell Mews GU29 . . . . 94 D8
Chartwell Rd BN15 . . . . . . 187 D5
Chase Cl GU33 . . . . 45 C4
Chase La GU27 . . . . 27 E3
Chase Rd GU33 . . . . 45 C4
Chase The
Crawley RH10 . . . . 19 A5
Fontwell BN18 . . . . 158 A3
Nepcote BN14 . . . . 163 E5
Chatelet Cl RH6 . . . . 2 B4
Chates Farm Ct BN2 . . . . . 213 C3
Chatfield Rd RH17 . . . . 87 A6
Chatfields RH11 . . . . 18 B4
Chatham Pl BN1 . . . . 213 A4
Chatham Rd BN11 . . . . 187 A3
Chatsmore Cres BN12 . . . 185 A4
Chatsmore Ho BN12 . . . . . 185 A3
Chatsmore RC High Sch
BN12 . . . . 185 A4
Chatsworth Ave GU27 . . . . 27 C8
Chatsworth Cl ⬛3
BN16 . . . . 205 B7
Chatsworth Ct
Brighton BN1 . . . . 191 E8
⬛5 Shoreham-by-S
BN43 . . . . 188 F6
Chatsworth Dr BN16 . . . . . 205 B7
Chatsworth Rd
Brighton BN1 . . . . 191 E8
Chichester PO19 . . . . 177 D6
Worthing BN11 . . . . 186 D2
Chatsworth Row RH11 . . . . 18 C4

Chatsworth Sq BN3 . . . . . 191 D7
Chaucer Ave
⬛3 East Grinstead RH19 . . 9 C1
Rustington BN16 . . . . 205 B5
Chaucer Ct ⬛2 RH16 . . . . 87 D5
Chaucer Dr PO20 . . . . 207 F8
Chaucer Rd
Crawley RH10 . . . . 19 C8
Worthing BN13 . . . . 186 B3
Chaucer Way PO22 . . . . . . 202 D6
Chawkmare Coppice
PO20 . . . . 200 F2
Chayle Gdns PO20 . . . . . . 212 E6
Cheal Cl BN43 . . . . 188 F6
Cheam Rd BN16 . . . . 205 D4
Cheapside BN1 . . . . 213 B3
Cheeleys RH17 . . . . 65 C5
Cheesemans La PO18 . . . . 152 E4
Chelmer Ho ⬛3 BN15 . . . 187 E4
Chelston Ave BN3 . . . . 190 D7
Cheltenham Pl BN1 . . . . . 213 B3
Chelwood Ave BN12 . . . . . 185 C1
Chelwood Cl
Brighton BN1 . . . . 170 C6
Crawley RH10 . . . . 18 F4
Chelwood Ct RH15 . . . . . . 109 A4
Chelwood Gate Rd RH17,
TN22 . . . . 66 F7
Chene Collins Chase ⬛11
RH20 . . . . 100 C2
Chennells Brook Cotts
RH12 . . . . 36 F7
Chennells Way RH12 . . . . . 36 E5
Chepstow Ct RH10 . . . . 19 E6
Chepstow Ct BN1 . . . . 170 F5
Chequer Grange RH18 . . . . 23 E1
Chequer La PO18 . . . . 175 D6
Chequer Rd RH19 . . . . 9 F1
Chequers Cl RH6 . . . . 2 A4
Chequers Ct
Horsham RH13 . . . . 36 E2
Petworth GU28 . . . . 97 F7
Chequers Dr RH6 . . . . 2 A4
Chequers Quay PO10 . . . . 173 C8
Cherington Cl BN6 . . . . . . 128 B5
Chermont Cl RH16 . . . . . . 205 F6
Cherrimans Orch GU27 . . . 26 F6
Cherry Ave BN18 . . . . 181 A2
Cherry Cl
Bognor Regis PO21 . . . . . 200 E2
Burgess Hill RH15 . . . . . 108 E3
Cherry Croft BN17 . . . . . . 204 D7
Cherry Ct ⬛3 RH13 . . . . . . 36 E1
Cherry Gdns
Selsey PO20 . . . . 212 D5
Worthing BN13 . . . . 163 D1
Cherry La
Birdham PO20 . . . . 197 F5
Bolney RH17 . . . . 85 C3
Brook Street RH17 . . . . . . 62 F5
Crawley RH11 . . . . 5 C1
Cherrylands Cl GU27 . . . . . 49 B6
Cherry Lo RH6 . . . . 2 B2
Cherry Mdws RH11 . . . . . . 18 C5
Cherry Orchard Rd
PO19 . . . . 177 B5
Cherry Pl ⬛10 RH16 . . . . . 87 C2
Cherry Tree Ave GU27 . . . . 26 F7
Cherry Tree Cl
Billingshurst RH14 . . . . . . 55 C1
Crawley RH10 . . . . 19 D8
Worthing BN13 . . . . 163 D1
Cherrytree Cotts
PO22 . . . . 180 C5
Cherry Tree Dr PO20 . . . . . 179 F8
Cherry Tree Lo ⬛1
BN15 . . . . 187 D6
Cherry Trees RH17 . . . . . . 86 E8
Cherry Tree Wlk
Horsham RH12 . . . . 37 B6
Petworth GU28 . . . . 97 E7
Cherry Wlk BN13 . . . . 163 E1
Cherrywood ⬛2 BN1 . . . . 169 E3
Cherrywood Ct PO21 . . . . . 200 F2
Cherwell Rd BN13 . . . . . . 185 C9
Cherwell Wlk RH11 . . . . . . 17 F5
Chesham Cl BN12 . . . . 185 E3
Chesham Pl BN2 . . . . 192 D4
Chesham Rd BN2 . . . . 192 D4
Chesham St BN2 . . . . 192 D4
Cheshire Cl ⬛13 PO21 . . . 201 D4
Cheshire Cres PO20 . . . . . 156 C1
Cheshire Way PO10 . . . . . 152 A2
Chesholt Cl GU27 . . . . 49 B6
Chesley Cl BN13 . . . . 185 C7
Chess Brook Gn BN5 . . . . 125 F7
Chesswood Ave PO22 . . . . 202 C6
Chesswood Cl BN11 . . . . . 186 F4
Chesswood Ct BN11 . . . . . 186 F4
Chesswood Lea BN11 . . . . 186 F4
Chesswood Mid Sch
BN11 . . . . 186 F4
Chesswood Rd BN11 . . . . . 186 F4
Chester Ave
Lancing BN15 . . . . 187 E4
Worthing BN11 . . . . 187 A3
Chester Ct ⬛12 BN3 . . . . 191 E7
Chesterfield Cl RH19 . . . . . 8 C4
Chesterfield Rd BN12 . . . . 185 D4
Chester Lo ⬛2 BN11 . . . . 186 A2
Chesters RH6 . . . . 1 E5
Chester Terr BN1 . . . . 170 A1
Chesterton Cl RH19 . . . . . 22 F7
Chesterton Ct RH13 . . . . . 37 A4
Chestnut Ave
Chichester PO19 . . . . 154 F3
Haslemere GU27 . . . . 27 C7

Chestnut Cl
Angmering BN16 . . . . **205** F8
Burgess Hill RH15 . . . . . . **109** B5
East Grinstead RH19 . . . . . . **10** A1
Heath Common RH20 . . . . **122** B3
Liphook GU30 . . . . **25** D3
Midhurst GU29 . . . . **94** E5
Chestnut Ct
Angmering BN16 . . . . **206** A8
East Preston BN16 . . . . . . **206** A5
Horsham RH13 . . . . **36** E2
9 Worthing BN11. . . . . . . **186** C3
Chestnut Dr GU31. . . . . . . **68** B1
Chestnut End BN5 . . . . . **125** E5
Chestnut Gdns RH12 . . . **36** C5
Chestnut Gr
Bognor Regis PO22 . . . . . **201** C6
Hurstpierpoint BN6 . . . . . **127** F7
Chestnut Rd
Billingshurst RH14. . . . . . **79** D7
Horley RH6 . . . . **2** B5
Chestnut Ridge RH20 . . **121** C7
Chestnuts Cl RH16 . . . . . **88** A7
Chestnuts The
Haywards Heath RH16 . . . **87** F7
Horley RH6 . . . . **2** A5
Hunston PO20 . . . . **199** A8
Sayers Common RH16 . . . **107** D1
Chestnut Way BN5. . . . . **125** E5
Chestnut Wlk
Crawley RH11 . . . . **5** C1
Felcourt RH19 . . . . **9** C8
Pulborough RH20. . . . . . . **100** B2
Tangmere PO20 . . . . **156** C1
Worthing BN13 . . . . **185** C6
Chesworth Cl
7 Horsham RH13 . . . . . . **36** C1
Tower Hill RH13. . . . . **58** C8
Chesworth Cres RH13 . . **36** C1
Chesworth Gdns RH13 . . **36** C1
Chesworth La RH12,
RH13 . . . . **36** C1
Chetwood Rd RH11 . . . . . **17** D2
Cheveley Gdns PO21 . . . **200** E2
Chevening Cl RH11 . . . . . **18** C1
Cheviot Cl
East Preston BN16 . . . . . . **206** A6
Worthing BN13 . . . . **185** E9
Cheviot Ct 3 RH12. . . . . **36** F4
Cheviot Rd BN13. . . . . . . **185** E9
Cheviot Wlk RH11. . . . . . **18** B6
Cheyne BN43 . . . . **189** C7
Cheynell Wlk RH11. . . . . **17** F4
Cheyne Wlk RH6. . . . . **2** A1
Chichester Bsns Pk
PO20. . . . . **156** E2
Chichester By-Pass
Chichester PO20 . . . . **177** D5
Stockbridge PO19 . . . . . . **176** F4
Chichester Cath PO19. . . **176** F6
Chichester Cl
15 Brighton BN2 . . . . . . **192** D4
Crawley RH10 . . . . **18** E2
Hove BN3. . . . . **168** E4
Saltdean BN2. . . . . **194** C1
Chichester Coll PO19 . . . **176** E6
Chichester Coll Brinsbury
Campus RH20 . . . . **78** F1
Chichester Ct
11 Rustington BN16 . . . . **205** C5
1 Worthing BN11. . . . . **186** A1
Chichester District Mus★
PO19. . . . . **177** A6
Chichester Dr PO20 . . . . **156** D1
Chichester Dr E BN2 . . . **194** C1
Chichester Dr W BN2 . . . **194** B1
Chichester Festival
Theatre PO19. . . . . **177** A8
Chichester Food Pk
PO20. . . . . **177** F3
Chichester Gate PO19 . . **176** F5
Chichester High Sch for
Boys PO19. . . . . **177** A5
Chichester High Sch for
Girls PO19. . . . . **177** A4
Chichester Nuffield Hospl
PO19. . . . . **154** F1
Chichester Pl BN2 . . . . . **192** D4
Chichester PRU PO20 . . . **177** C1
Chichester Rd
Arundel BN18 . . . . **159** E3
Bognor Regis PO21,
PO22. . . . . **201** B5
Midhurst GU29 . . . . **94** F5
Selsey PO20. . . . . **212** G8
Street End PO20 . . . . **198** E4
Chichester Sta PO19 . . . **176** F5
Chichester Terr
19 Brighton BN2. . . . . . **192** D4
Horsham RH12 . . . . **36** D2
Chichester Way
Burgess Hill RH15 . . . . . . **109** C5
Selsey PO20. . . . . **212** G8
Chichester Wharf
PO19 . . . . **176** F5
Chiddingly Cl
Brighton BN2. . . . . **192** F5
Crawley RH10 . . . . **19** B5
Chiddingly Ho 11
BN3. . . . . **191** D7
Chidham La PO18. . . . . . **174** E6
Chidham Prim Sch
PO18. . . . . **174** E6
Chilcomb RH15 . . . . **109** C1
Chilcroft La GU27. . . . . . . **27** B1
Chilcroft Rd GU27. . . . . . . **26** F7
Chilcrofts Rd GU27. . . . . . **27** A1
Childerstone Cl GU30 . . . **25** B4

CHILGROVE **112** F1
Chilgrove Cl PO20 . . . . . **185** B4
Chilgrove Ho BN17. . . . . **204** B7
Chilling St RH19 . . . . **43** D3
Chillis Wood Rd RH16 . . . **87** C5
Chilmark Ct GU33 . . . . . . **45** B4
Chiltern Cl
Crawley RH11 . . . . **18** B6
East Preston BN16 . . . . . . **206** A6
Haslemere GU27 . . . . **27** B5
Shoreham-by-S BN43. . . . **189** C8
Chiltern Cotts RH6. . . . . . . **1** D2
Chiltern Cres BN13 . . . . **185** E8
Chiltern Ct 2 RH12 . . . . . **36** F4
Chiltons The PO21 . . . . . **201** C3
Chine The BN17 . . . . **205** A4
Chipley Ct PO21 . . . . **201** A4
Chippendale Rd RH11 . . . **18** B1
Chippers Cl BN13 . . . . . . **185** F5
Chippers Rd BN13 . . . . . **185** F5
Chippers Wlk BN13 . . . . **185** F5
Chithurst La GU31,
GU30 . . . . **71** C4
Chodds Cotts RH17 . . . . . **39** C1
Chorley Ave BN2. . . . . . . **194** B2
Chownes Mead La
RH16 . . . . **87** B4
Chrisdory Rd BN41. . . . . **167** F3
Christchurch Cres
PO21 . . . . **200** E3
Christchurch Ho 4
BN11 . . . . **186** D3
Christchurch Rd
BN11 . . . . **186** D3
Christie Pl PO22 . . . . **201** D6
Christies RH19. . . . . **22** D8
Christopher Ct 10
PO21 . . . . **201** D5
Christopher Rd RH19. . . . . **9** E1
Christopher Way
PO10 . . . . **151** B2
Christ's Hospital Rd
Horsham RH13 . . . . **57** E6
Itchingfield RH13. . . . . **57** C6
Christ's Hospital (Sch)
RH13. . . . . **57** D5
Christ's Hospital Sta
RH13. . . . . **57** D7
Church App 1 BN17 . . . . **204** E4
Church Ave RH16 . . . . **87** E6
Church Cl
Ashington RH20 . . . . **122** F4
Brighton BN1. . . . . **169** F5
Burgess Hill RH15 . . . . . . **109** A3
Clapham BN13. . . . . **162** F1
Lancing BN15. . . . . **187** E8
Lower Beeding RH13. . . . . **60** A3
Pagham PO21 . . . . **210** E7
Shipley RH13 . . . . **103** D8
Upper Beeding BN44. . . . . **146** A3
Church Cotts 2 BN11. . . **186** F2
Church Ct
3 Haywards Heath
RH16. . . . . **87** E4
Hove BN3. . . . . **168** F1
Churcher Rd PO10 . . . . . **151** D4
Churcher's Coll GU31. . . . **68** C4
Churcher's Coll Jnr Sch
GU30. . . . . **25** D2
Church Farm Cotts
RH13 . . . . **59** F3
Church Farm Ct PO20 . . **208** A8
Church Farm Holiday
Village PO21. . . . . **210** E7
Church Farm La
East Wittering PO20 . . . . **208** A8
Street End PO20 . . . . **198** E4
Church Farm Wlk
BN44 . . . . **146** A3
Churchfield RH20 . . . . **99** A3
Churchfield Cotts
PO20 . . . . **198** F3
Churchfield Cl PO18 . . . . . **25** B3
Churchfield Rd GU31. . . . . **68** D4
Church Gn BN43 . . . . **189** C7
Church Gr RH20 . . . . **101** D1
Church Hill
Brighton BN1. . . . . **169** E2
Midhurst GU29 . . . . **94** F4
Pulborough RH20. . . . . . . **100** B2
Pyecombe BN45. . . . . **149** C6
Slindon BN18. . . . . **158** C5
West Hoathly RH19. . . . . . **42** F6
Church Ho
Littlehampton BN17. . . . . **204** D4
Worthing BN14 . . . . **186** A5
Church House Cl
BN42 . . . . **167** F1
Church House Mews
PO22 . . . . **202** A4
Churchill Ave
Bognor Regis PO21 . . . . . **200** E4
Horsham RH12 . . . . **36** B3
Churchill Ct
Crawley RH10 . . . . **6** A1
5 Rustington BN16 . . . . **205** C5

Church St continued
Liss GU33 . . . . **45** A6
Littlehampton BN17. . . . . **204** E5
Petworth GU28 . . . . **97** F8
Portslade-by-S BN41. . . . **190** B7
Rudgwick, Cox Green
RH12. . . . . **12** E1
Rudgwick RH12 . . . . **33** E8
Shoreham-by-S BN43. . . . **188** F7
Steyning BN44. . . . . **145** D3
Storrington RH20 . . . . **121** D1
Warnham RH12 . . . . **35** F8
West Chiltington RH20 . . . **101** E1
Church Terr
Cowfold RH13 . . . . **83** E2
Henfield BN5. . . . . **125** E5
Church View PO10 . . . . . **151** B3
Church View Cl RH6 . . . . . **1** C1
Church Walk Mews
RH15 . . . . **109** A3
Church Way
Bognor Regis PO21 . . . . . **200** A1
6 Brighton BN2 . . . . . . **213** C3
Singleton PO18 . . . . **135** D7
Worthing BN13 . . . . **186** A5
Church Way Cl BN13 . . . **186** A5
Church Wlk
Burgess Hill RH15 . . . . . . **109** A3
Crawley RH10 . . . . **18** D6
Horley RH6 . . . . **1** F2
Worthing BN11 . . . . **186** F2
CHURCHWOOD **99** B4
Church Wood RH20 . . . . . **99** B4
Churchwood Dr PO20 . . **156** D1
Churt Dr PO22 . . . . **201** D6
Chute Ave BN13 . . . . **163** E1
Chute Way BN13 . . . . . . **185** E9
Cidermill Hatch RH5 . . . . . **3** F6
Cinder Hill RH19 . . . . **43** B1
Circle The BN16 . . . . **206** A4
Circus Par BN1 . . . . **213** B2
Circus St BN2 . . . . **213** B2
Cissbury Ave BN14 . . . . . **163** F2
Cissbury Cl RH12 . . . . **37** A6
Cissbury Cres BN2 . . . . . **194** A1
Cissbury Ct BN14 . . . . . . **163** F2
Cissbury Dr BN14 . . . . . . **163** F3
Cissbury Gdns BN14. . . . **164** A1
Cissbury Hill RH11 . . . . . **18** C4
Cissbury Rd
Burgess Hill RH15 . . . . . . **108** E4
Ferring BN12. . . . . **206** E7
Hove BN3. . . . . **191** E7
Worthing BN14 . . . . **186** C6
Cissbury Ring★ BN14 . . **164** B5
Cissbury Way 5
BN43 . . . . **166** F1
Citadel Ho 4 PO19 . . . . . **176** F7
City Bsns Ctr
Chichester PO19 . . . . **176** F5
Horsham RH13 . . . . **36** D1
City Bsns Ctr The RH11. . . **5** D2
City Coll Brighton & Hove
Brighton BN1. . . . . **213** A5
Brighton BN1. . . . . **213** B3
Brighton, Whitehawk
BN2. . . . . **192** F5
Hove BN3. . . . . **191** A6
City Fields Bsns Pk
PO20. . . . . **156** D2
City Fields Way PO20 . . **156** D2
City Gates PO19 . . . . **176** F5
Civic Way RH15 . . . . **109** A3
Claigmar Rd BN16 . . . . . **205** C5
Clair Ct RH16 . . . . **87** E5
Clair Rd RH16 . . . . **87** E5
Clammer Hill GU27 . . . . . **27** F8
Clapgate La RH13 . . . . . . **34** D4
Clapham Cl BN13 . . . . . . **162** F1
Clapham Comm BN13 . . **184** E8
Clapham & Patching CE
Prim Sch BN13 . . . . **162** E1
Clappers Gate RH10. . . . . **18** D7
Clappers La
Bracklesham PO20 . . . . . **208** C6
Fulking BN5 . . . . **147** F5
Clappers Mdw GU6 . . . . . **11** A3
Clare Cl RH10. . . . . **6** C1
Clare Ct 5 BN17. . . . . . . **204** E4
Clare Gdns GU31. . . . . **68** E3
Clare Lo 2 BN16. . . . . . . **205** B5
Claremont Ct
18 Bognor Regis
PO21. . . . . **201** D3
Chichester PO19 . . . . **176** F4
Claremont Way GU29 . . . **94** E7
Clarence Ave BN17. . . . . **204** C7
Clarence Ct
Horley RH6 . . . . **2** D4
7 Worthing BN11. . . . . **186** F2
Clarence Dr
2 East Grinstead
RH19. . . . . **22** F7
East Preston BN16 . . . . . **205** F6
Clarence Gate 10
PO21 . . . . **201** D3
Clarence Gdns BN1 . . . . **213** A2
Clarence Rd
Bognor Regis PO21. . . . . **201** D3
Horsham RH13 . . . . **36** E1
Clarence Sq BN1. . . . . . . **213** A2
Clarence Way RH6. . . . . . . **2** D4
Clarendon Ho 2 BN3 . . **191** D7
Clarendon Mews 7
BN11 . . . . **186** C1

Clarendon Rd
Hove BN3. . . . . **191** B7
Shoreham-by-S BN42,
BN43. . . . . **189** D8
Worthing BN14 . . . . **186** E6
Clarendon Terr 16
BN2 . . . . **192** D4
Clarendon Villas BN3 . . **191** B7
Clare Wlk BN2. . . . . **192** D5
Clarke Ave BN3. . . . . **168** F3
Clarke Ct BN3 . . . . **190** F6
Clark Rd RH11. . . . . **18** A1
Clarks Ind Est BN3. . . . . **191** B8
Clay Hall La RH10 . . . . **7** C4
Clay Hill Ho GU27. . . . . . . **27** A6
Clay La
Cootham RH20. . . . . **121** A1
Crossbush BN18 . . . . **160** F1
Fishbourne PO18, PO19 . . **176** D3
West Ashling PO18 . . . . . **153** D1
Claypit La PO18. . . . . **155** D2
Clays Cl RH19. . . . . **22** E8
Clays Hill BN44. . . . . **145** E2
Clayton Ave BN6. . . . . . . **128** F3
Clayton Cl PO20 . . . . **212** C6
Clayton Dr RH15 . . . . **108** F1
Clayton Hill
Clayton BN6, BN45 . . . . . **149** D7
Crawley RH11 . . . . **18** C4
Clayton La PO20 . . . . **208** B7
Clayton Pk BN6. . . . . **128** E4
Clayton Rd
Brighton BN2. . . . . **192** D7
Ditchling BN6. . . . . **129** C3
Selsey PO20. . . . . **212** C6
Claytons Cnr PO20 . . . . . **197** E5
Clayton Way BN3 . . . . . . **168** F3
Clayton Windmills★
BN6. . . . . **149** E7
Clayton Wlk BN13. . . . . . **185** D6
Clearwater La RH17. . . . . **89** A3
Clearwaters La RH16 . . . **109** D8
Cleaver's La RH17 . . . . . . **62** B2
Cleeves Ct BN16 . . . . **205** E6
Cleeves Way BN16 . . . . . **205** E6
Clement's Ct 1 BN43 . . **188** F7
Clerks Acre BN6. . . . . . . **129** A4
Clermont Ct BN1. . . . . . . **169** E2
Clermont Rd BN1 . . . . . . **169** E2
Clermont Terr BN1. . . . . . **169** E2
Cleveland Cl BN13 . . . . . **185** F9
Cleveland Copse
BN13 . . . . **185** F9
Cleveland Gdns RH15 . . **109** B2
Cleveland Rd
Brighton BN1. . . . . **170** A1
Chichester PO19 . . . . **177** B5
Worthing BN13 . . . . **185** F8
Clevelands
Billingshurst RH14. . . . . . **79** D8
Haywards Heath RH16 . . . **87** E6
Clevets The PO21 . . . . . . **200** C1
Cleve Way RH14 . . . . **79** D8
Cliff App BN2 . . . . **192** F4
Cliff Rd BN2 . . . . **192** F4
Cliff The BN2 . . . . **192** F4
Clifton Cl RH6 . . . . **2** D3
Clifton Ct
9 Brighton BN1 . . . . . . **213** A4
Chichester PO19 . . . . **177** B5
4 Littlehampton BN11. . **186** C3
Clifton Gdns BN11 . . . . . **186** C3
Clifton Hill BN1. . . . . **213** A3
Clifton Mews BN1. . . . . . **213** A3
Clifton Pl BN1 . . . . **191** E6
Clifton Rd
Bognor Regis PO21 . . . . . **201** C4
Brighton BN1. . . . . **213** A3
Burgess Hill RH15 . . . . . . **108** D5
Crawley RH10 . . . . **19** C5
Littlehampton BN17. . . . . **204** D4
Worthing BN11 . . . . **186** C3
Clifton St BN1 . . . . **213** A4
Clifton Terr BN1. . . . . **213** A3
Cliftonville Ct 6 BN3 . . **191** B7
Climping Camp Site
BN17 . . . . **203** F7
Climping Cl RH16 . . . . **87** D3
Climping Ct 2 BN16 . . . . **205** B3
Climping Pk BN17 . . . . . . **181** F1
Climping Rd RH11 . . . . . . **18** B8
Climping St BN17. . . . . . . **203** E7
Climping & West Beach
Nature Trail★ BN17 . . . **203** F7
Clinton Hill RH7 . . . . **10** A8
Clitherow Gdns RH10 . . . **18** E5
Clive Ave BN12 . . . . **185** D3
Clive Ct
Haywards Heath RH16 . . . **87** E6
Worthing BN12 . . . . **185** E4
Clivedale 9 BN44. . . . . . **145** D3
Clivedale Gdns BN44. . . . **145** E3
Cliveden Ct BN1 . . . . **169** E3
Clive Way RH10. . . . . **19** C6
Clock Ho PO21. . . . . **200** E1
Clock Ho The GU29 . . . . . **94** F8
Clock Pk PO22. . . . . **201** D3
Clocktower The BN1. . . . **213** B2
Clock Wlk 9 PO21 . . . . . **201** D3
Cloisters The
Littlehampton BN17. . . . . **204** F4
Worthing BN14 . . . . **186** D5
Close The
Ardingly RH17 . . . . **64** B7
Ashington RH20. . . . . **123** A5

Church St
Amberley BN18 . . . . **140** D7
Brighton BN1. . . . . **213** B2
Crawley RH11 . . . . **18** C6
Cuckfield RH17 . . . . **86** E6
Henfield BN5 . . . . **125** E5

Church Ho
Littlehampton BN17. . . . . **204** D4
Worthing BN14 . . . . **186** A5

Churchill Ho
Barnham PO22. . . . . **180** C5
Hove BN3. . . . . **168** E2
Churchill Ind Est
BN15. . . . . **187** D5
Churchill Par BN16 . . . . . **205** C5
Churchill Sq BN1 . . . . . . **213** A2
Churchill Way RH15. . . . . **109** C2
Churchill Wlk PO21 . . . . . **211** A8
Church La
Albourne Green BN6 . . . . **127** B5
Ardingly RH17 . . . . **63** F8
Ashington RH20. . . . . **123** A4
Ashurst BN44 . . . . **124** D5
Barnham PO22. . . . . **180** B4
Birdham PO20 . . . . **197** E5
Bognor Regis PO22 . . . . . **201** C5
Boxgrove PO18 . . . . **156** D3
Bramshott GU30 . . . . **25** C6
Broadbridge Heath RH12 . . **35** D3
Burgess Hill RH17 . . . . . . **109** F6
Burstow RH6 . . . . **6** F7
Bury RH20 . . . . **140** A7
Climping BN17, BN18 . . . **181** E1
Cocking GU29 . . . . **114** D7
Coldwaltham RH20 . . . . . **119** C6
Compton PO18. . . . . **111** B2
Copthorne RH10 . . . . **7** B3
Crawley RH10 . . . . **18** F6
Danehill RH17 . . . . **66** A3
Ditchling BN6. . . . . **129** D3
Eastergate PO20 . . . . **179** E8
East Grinstead RH19. . . . . **9** F1
Ferring BN12. . . . . **206** E6
Funtington PO18 . . . . **153** A5
Haslemere GU27 . . . . **27** D7
Henfield BN5 . . . . **125** E5
Horsted Keynes RH17 . . . . **65** C5
Hunston PO20 . . . . **199** A8
Kingston near Lewes
BN7. . . . . **172** D5
Lancing BN15. . . . . **187** A8
Littlehampton BN17. . . . . **182** C6
Lodsworth GU28 . . . . **74** C2
Lower Beeding RH13. . . . . **60** A5
Oving PO20 . . . . **178** C7
Pagham PO21 . . . . **210** E8
Partridge Green RH13. . . . **104** F3
Poynings BN45, BN6 . . . . **148** E7
Pyecombe BN45. . . . . **149** C6
Southwater RH13 . . . . **57** E1
Southwick BN42 . . . . **189** D7
Steyning BN44 . . . . **145** D3
Street End PO20 . . . . **198** E3
Tangmere PO20 . . . . **156** C1
Upper Beeding BN44. . . . **146** A2
Walberton BN18 . . . . **180** E8
West Dean PO18. . . . . **134** F5
Yapton BN18 . . . . **180** F4
Church Mdw PO18 . . . . . **175** B5
Church Mead
Keymer BN6. . . . . **129** B3
Steyning BN44. . . . . **145** E3
Churchmead Cl PO18 . . **154** F6
Church Mews PO20 . . . . **177** D1
Church Path
3 Emsworth PO10 . . . . **173** B8
Stoughton PO18. . . . . **133** A4
Walberton PO21 . . . . **5** E5
Church Pl
Brighton BN2. . . . . **192** E4
Pulborough BN20. . . . . . . **100** B2
Church Platt RH17 . . . . . . **86** E5
Church Rd
Aldingbourne PO20 . . . . . **179** A8
Angmering BN16 . . . . **183** F5
Bramshott GU30 . . . . **25** C6
Broadbridge Heath RH12 . . **35** D3
Burgess Hill RH15 . . . . . . **109** A3
Burstow RH6 . . . . **7** A7
Chichester PO19 . . . . **177** D7
Copthorne RH10 . . . . **7** B3
Crawley, Lowfield Heath
RH11. . . . . **5** E5
Crawley, Worth RH10. . . . . **19** E6
East Wittering PO20 . . . . **207** F8
Fernhurst GU27. . . . . **49** B5
Haslemere GU27 . . . . **27** C7
Haslemere, Shottermill
GU27. . . . . **26** F6
Haywards Heath RH16 . . . **87** E4
Horley RH6 . . . . **1** F2
Horley RH6 . . . . **2** A3
Horsham RH12 . . . . **37** B5
Hove BN3. . . . . **191** B6
Mannings Heath RH13. . . . **59** C6
North Mundham PO20. . . . **177** D1
Partridge Green RH13. . . . **104** F3
Portslade-by-S BN41. . . . **190** B7
Rustington BN16 . . . . **205** C5
Scaynes Hill RH17 . . . . **88** F3
Selsey PO20. . . . . **212** E8
Southbourne PO10 . . . . . **173** F8
Steep GU32 . . . . **68** B7
Turners Hill RH10 . . . . **21** A3
Westbourne PO10 . . . . . . **151** D3
West Lavington GU29 . . . . **95** A6
West Thorney PO10. . . . . **173** F1
Worthing BN13 . . . . **186** A4
Yapton BN18 . . . . **180** F3
Churchside PO19 . . . . . . **177** C1

Close The continued
Bognor Regis PO21 . . . . . . **200** C1
Boxgrove PO18 . . . . **156** D3
Brighton BN1 . . . . **169** E5
Burgess Hill RH15 . . . . **109** E4
East Grinstead RH19 . . . . . . **22** D8
Hassocks BN6 . . . . **128** F4
Horley RH6 . . . . **2** C1
Ifold RH14 . . . . **31** D3
Lancing BN15. . . . . **187** F4
Liphook GU30 . . . . **25** C2
Middleton-on-S PO22. . . . . **203** A5
Mid Lavant PO18 . . . . **154** F5
Rustington BN16 . . . . **205** A4
Selsey PO20. . . . . **212** G8
Shoreham-by-S BN43. . . . . **188** F8
Closewalks GU29 . . . . **94** F7
Clothalls La RH13 . . . . **104** B5
Clovelly Ave PO22. . . . . . . **202** B5
Clovelly Rd
Breach PO10 . . . . **151** F1
Emsworth PO10. . . . . **173** A8
Clover Ct 2 RH16. . . . . **87** E4
Clover Field RH13. . . . . **34** D3
Cloverfields RH6. . . . . **2** B4
Clover La BN12. . . . . **206** E5
Cloverlands RH16. . . . . **18** F8
Clovers Cotts RH12. . . . . . . **16** F1
Clovers End
Brighton BN1. . . . . **170** B7
Horsham RH12 . . . . **37** A5
Clovers Way RH12 . . . . **37** D7
Clover Way BN41 . . . . **168** B2
Cloye Ho 9 BN43. . . . . **188** E7
Club Wlk BN16. . . . . **206** A4
Clun Rd BN17. . . . . **204** C6
Clyde Cl BN13 . . . . **185** C9
Clyde Rd
Bognor Regis PO22 . . . . . . **201** F3
Brighton BN1. . . . . **213** A4
Worthing BN13 . . . . **185** C9
Clydesdale Ave PO19. . . . . **177** B5
Clydesdale Gdns
PO22. . . . . **201** A7
Coach & Horses La
RH17. . . . . **66** C6
Coach House Cl PO20. . . . . **212** E7
Coach House Cotts
BN16 . . . . **205** D8
Coach House Mews
BN11 . . . . **186** C2
Coach La RH17. . . . . **66** C6
Coachmans Dr RH11 . . . . . . **18** B2
Coach Rd
Crawley, Gatwick Airport
RH6. **5** F8
Crawley, Gatwick Airport
RH6. **6** B7
Shopwyke PO20. . . . . **177** F7
Westhampnett PO18. . . . . . **155** E1
Coalbrook Ho BN2. . . . . . . **192** C5
Coast 13 BN16 . . . . **205** B4
Coastal Counties Ho 19
BN2. . . . . **213** C3
Coastal Rd BN16. . . . . **206** C4
Coastguard Cotts 10
BN16. . . . . **206** A4
Coastguard La PO20. . . . . . **196** A1
Coastguard Par PO20 . . . . . **200** D1
Coastguard Rd BN17. . . . . **204** D3
Coastguards Cotts
PO20. . . . . **196** A2
COATES. **118** D8
Coates Castle RH20. . . . . . **118** C8
Coates Ct 11 BN42 . . . . **189** E7
Coates La RH20. . . . . **118** D8
Cobbett Cl RH10. . . . . **19** C8
Cobbetts Mead RH16. . . . . . **88** B3
Cobbetts Mews RH20. . . . . **100** A2
Cobblers The RH13. . . . . **34** D3
Cobbles Cres RH10. . . . . . . **18** E7
Cobblestone Wlk 1
BN44. . . . . **145** D3
Cobblewood PO10. . . . . . . **151** B3
Cob Cl RH10. . . . . **21** C8
Cobden Ho GU29 . . . . **94** E6
Cobden La GU27 . . . . **27** D7
Cobden Rd
Brighton BN2. . . . . **192** C7
Midhurst GU29 . . . . **94** E2
Worthing BN11 . . . . **186** C2
Cobham Cl BN15. . . . . **180** F2
Cobham Way RH10. . . . . **6** B4
Cob La RH17. . . . . **42** B1
Cobnor Cl RH11. . . . . **17** F4
Cobton Dr BN3. . . . . **169** A3
Coburn Ho 3 RH10 . . . . **19** B7
Cob Wlk RH11 . . . . **18** A6
Cockhaise Cotts RH16. . . . . **89** A8
COCKING CAUSEWAY **94** E4
Cocking Hill GU29,
PO18. . . . . **114** C5
Cohen Cl PO20. . . . . **179** C5
Cokeham Ct BN15. . . . . **187** C6
Cokeham Gdns BN15. . . . . **187** C6
Cokeham La BN15 . . . . **187** C6
Cokeham Rd BN15. . . . . . . **187** C6
Colbourne Ave BN2. . . . . . **170** D2
Colbourne Rd BN3. . . . . . . **191** E7
Colchester Vale RH18 . . . . . **23** E2
Colchins RH15. . . . . **108** F1
COLDEAN. **170** D6
Coldean La BN1 . . . . **170** E6
Coldean Prim Sch
BN1. . . . . **170** D6

Coldean Rd BN1 . . . . **170** C8
Coldharbour Farm Rd
PO10. . . . . **151** B2
Coldharbour La BN13 . . . . . **162** D1
Coldwaltham La
RH15. . . . . **109** D2
Colebrook Cl BN11. . . . . . . **186** F3
Colebrook Ct BN11. . . . . . . **186** F3
Colebrook La RH20 . . . . . . **119** B5
Colebrook Rd
Brighton BN1. . . . . **169** D4
Littlehampton BN17. . . . . . **204** C7
Southwick BN42 . . . . **189** F7
Cole Ct RH11 . . . . **18** B1
Coleman Ave BN3. . . . . **190** E7
Colemans Hatch Rd
RH18. . . . . **44** E5
Coleman St BN2 . . . . **213** C4
Coleridge Cl
Horsham RH12 . . . . **36** E6
Worthing BN13 . . . . **185** B4
Coleridge Cres BN12. . . . . **185** A4
Coleridge Mews
BN12. . . . . **185** B4
Coleridge Rd BN12. . . . . . . **185** B4
Coleridge St BN3 . . . . **191** A8
Colet Rd RH10 . . . . **18** D3
Colgate Cl
Brighton BN2. . . . . **192** F6
Crawley RH11 . . . . **18** B8
Colgate Prim Sch
RH13. . . . . **38** C6
Colhook Ind Pk GU28 . . . . . **51** D1
Colindale Rd RH20. . . . . . . **206** E6
Colindale Rd N BN12. . . . . **206** E6
Collards Gate GU27. . . . . . . **27** D6
Collards La GU27 . . . . **27** D6
Collard Way GU33. . . . . **45** B4
College Cl
Bognor Regis PO21 . . . . . . **200** F4
East Grinstead RH19 . . . . **9** F1
Handcross RH17 . . . . **39** C2
Portslade-by-S BN41. . . . . **167** F3
Red Hill PO9 . . . . **130** E1
College Ct
Bognor Regis PO22 . . . . . . **201** E5
Brighton BN2 . . . . **192** C4
College Gdns
Brighton BN2. . . . . **192** C4
Worthing BN11 . . . . **186** A2
College Hill
Haslemere GU27 . . . . **27** C6
Steyning BN44. . . . . **145** D2
College Hill Terr GU27 . . . . . **27** C6
College La
Chichester PO19 . . . . **177** A8
East Grinstead RH19 . . . . **9** F1
Hurst Wickham BN6. . . . . . **128** C6
College Pl
Brighton BN2. . . . . **192** C4
Hurst Wickham BN6. . . . . . **128** C6
Steyning BN44. . . . . **145** D2
College Rd
Ardingly RH16, RH17. . . . . . **64** A6
Brighton BN2. . . . . **192** C4
Crawley RH10 . . . . **18** E6
Haywards Heath RH16 . . . . . **87** E7
Southwater RH13 . . . . **57** E1
Upper Beeding BN44. . . . . **146** C1
College St
11 Brighton BN2. . . . . **192** C4
Petersfield GU31, GU31. . . . **68** B3
College Terr BN2 . . . . **192** D5
Collendean La RH6. . . . . **1** A5
Collier Row RH10. . . . . **18** D4
Collingford La RH17. . . . . . . **66** B4
Collingwood Rd RH20. . . . . **100** C3
Collingwood Cl
4 East Grinstead
RH19. . . . . **22** F7
Horley RH6 . . . . **2** B4
Horsham RH12 . . . . **36** C4
Collingwood Ct
Brighton BN2. . . . . **193** A3
2 Shoreham-by-S
BN43. . . . . **188** F6
Collingwood Rd
Crawley RH10 . . . . **19** D5
Horsham RH12 . . . . **36** B4
Worthing BN12 . . . . **185** C5
Collingwood Way
GU31. . . . . **68** C5
Collins Cl PO20 . . . . **179** F8
Collins La GU31. . . . . **91** C7
Collins Rd RH11 . . . . **17** E4
Collins's La PO20 . . . . **198** C4
Coll of Richard Collyer
The RH12 . . . . **36** D4
Coll of St Barnabas RH7 . . . **9** F8
Collyer Ave PO21 . . . . **201** B5
Collyers Cotts GU28 . . . . . . **74** B7
Collyers Cres GU30 . . . . **25** E4
Colmer Ct RH15. . . . . **108** E3
Colmer Pl RH15. . . . . **108** E3
Colne Cl BN13 . . . . **185** C9
Colne Wlk RH11 . . . . **17** F4
Colonades The RH20. . . . . **100** B3
Colonnade Ho 3
BN11 . . . . **186** E2
Colonnades The BN1. . . . . **213** B2
Colonsay Rd RH11 . . . . **18** B3
Coltash Rd RH10. . . . . **19** A5
Colt's Bay PO21. . . . . **200** C1
Coltsfoot Dr RH12 . . . . **36** E5
Colt St PO20. . . . . **212** D8
Coltstaple La RH13. . . . . **58** C4
Columbia Dr BN13. . . . . . . **185** D7
Columbia Wlk BN13. . . . . . **185** C7

Columbine Way BN17 . . . . **205** B8
Colvill Ave BN43 . . . . **188** D8
Colwell Cl RH16. . . . . **87** F3
Colwell Gdns RH16. . . . . . . **87** F3
Colwell La
Haywards Heath, Fox Hill
RH17. . . . . **87** F1
Haywards Heath, Franklands
Village RH17. . . . . **88** B3
Colwell Rd RH16. . . . . **87** F2
Colwood La RH17. . . . . **85** B6
COLWORTH. **178** E2
Colwyn Cl RH11. . . . . **17** F4
Combers RH17. . . . . **41** A1
Commerce Way BN15. . . . . **187** C4
Commercial Rd RH15. . . . . **108** F3
Commercial Sq BN2 . . . . . . **87** E6
Common Hill RH20. . . . . . . **121** D6
Common La BN2. . . . . **129** D6
Common Rd PO10,
PO18. . . . . **152** D5
Commonside PO10. . . . . . . **151** D5
COMMON THE. **36** A4
Common The RH20. . . . . . . **121** C8
Common View GU29 . . . . . . **71** F1
Compass Cl BN17. . . . . **205** A6
Compass Dr BN41. . . . . **167** E3
Compassion Cl RH11 . . . . . . **17** E5
Compass Point PO21 . . . . . **201** E3
Comper Cl RH11. . . . . **17** E4
Compton Ave
Brighton BN1. . . . . **213** A4
Worthing BN12 . . . . **185** B3
Compton Cl PO19 . . . . **155** A3
Compton Ct BN16. . . . . **205** C6
Compton Dr PO22. . . . . **202** D6
Compton Rd
Brighton BN1. . . . . **169** D1
Lindfield RH16. . . . . **88** B8
Comptons Brow La
RH13. . . . . **37** A3
Comptons Ct 4 RH13. . . . . . **36** F3
Comptons La RH13. . . . . **36** F3
Comptons The RH13. . . . . . . **37** A3
Compton & Up Marden CE
Prim Sch PO18. . . . . **111** B2
Conbar Ho BN16. . . . . **205** C6
Concorde Cl RH20. . . . . **121** F3
Concorde Ho RH6. . . . . **6** B7
Condor Way RH15. . . . . **108** E3
Conduit Mead PO19. . . . . . **177** C8
Coneleys Yd PO20. . . . . **198** D5
Coney Cl
Crawley RH11 . . . . **18** B8
East Wittering PO20. . . . . . **207** F6
Coney Croft RH12. . . . . **37** B5
Coneyhurst Rd RH14. . . . . . . **79** F8
Coney Rd RH20 . . . . **207** F6
Coney Six PO20. . . . . **207** F6
Congreve Rd BN14. . . . . . . **186** E4
Conifer Dr PO18 . . . . **152** E2
Conifers Cl RH12. . . . . **37** B6
Conifers Sch GU29. . . . . **73** A1
Conifer Way PO21 . . . . **199** F2
Conigar Rd PO10 . . . . **151** B3
Coniston Cl
Bognor Regis PO22 . . . . . . **202** B6
Crawley RH11 . . . . **17** D4
Horsham RH12 . . . . **37** B6
Lancing BN15. . . . . **187** C6
Coniston Ct 9 BN3. . . . . . . **191** D7
Coniston Rd BN12 . . . . **185** C5
Coniston Way BN17. . . . . . **205** A4
Connaught Ave BN43. . . . . **188** E8
Connaught Gdns 1
RH10. . . . . **18** D8
Connaught Ho 7
PO21. . . . . **201** C2
Connaught Jun Sch
BN17. . . . . **204** D5
Connaught Rd
Hove BN3. . . . . **191** A6
Littlehampton BN17. . . . . . **204** D5
Connaught Terr BN3. . . . . . **191** B7
Connell Dr BN2. . . . . **193** E7
Connolly Way PO19 . . . . . . **155** A1
Consort Way
Burgess Hill RH15. . . . . . . **108** E2
Horley RH6 . . . . **2** A3
Consort Way E RH6. . . . . **2** B2
Constable Dr PO20. . . . . . . **212** F7
Constable Rd RH10. . . . . **18** F2
Control Tower Rd RH6 . . . . . **5** D6
Convent Ct PO10. . . . . **173** A4
Convent Gdns BN14. . . . . . **163** F6
Convent La PO10 . . . . **173** B8
Conway Ct 1 BN3 . . . . **191** B8
Conway Dr PO21. . . . . **211** A8
Conway Pl BN3 . . . . **191** A8
Conway St BN3 . . . . **191** B8
Cook Rd
Crawley RH10 . . . . **18** F4
Horsham RH12 . . . . **36** D6
Cooksbridge Rd BN2. . . . . **192** D4
Cooks Hill RH12 . . . . **33** A8
Cooks La
Breach PO10 . . . . **152** A1
Walderton PO18 . . . . **132** C2
Cooks Mdw RH12 . . . . **16** D7
Cooks Mead RH12 . . . . **16** D7
Cook's Pond Rd GU30. . . . . **71** A7
Coolham Ct RH11 . . . . **17** F6
Coolham Dr BN2 . . . . **192** E7
Coolham Rd
Brooks Green RH13. . . . . . . **80** E4
Goose Green RH13,
RH20. . . . . **100** C5
Coolhurst La RH13. . . . . **37** A1

Coolwater Pk BN1 . . . . **169** D4
Coombe Cl
Billingshurst RH14. . . . . **55** D1
Crawley RH11 . . . . **5** D1
Coombe Cotts RH19. . . . . . . **42** F6
Coombe Cres RH20 . . . . . . **140** A7
Coombe Dr BN44. . . . . **145** D2
Coombe Dro BN44. . . . . . . **145** D2
Coombe Hall Pk RH19. . . . . **22** D6
Coombe Hill Rd RH19. . . . . . **22** D6
Coombe La BN18 . . . . **161** B7
Coombelands La
Codmore Hill RH20. . . . . . **100** A5
Pulborough RH20. . . . . **100** A3
Coombe Lea 5 BN3. . . . . . **191** C6
Coombe Mdw BN2. . . . . . . **194** E3
Coombe Rd
Brighton BN2. . . . . **170** D1
Hill Brow GU33 . . . . **45** E1
Steyning BN44. . . . . **145** C2
Coombe Rise
Saltdean BN2. . . . . **194** D3
Worthing BN14 . . . . **164** A2
Coombe Road Prim Sch
BN2. . . . . **170** D1
Coombers La RH16. . . . . **88** B5
COOMBES. **166** A5
Coombes Ct BN15. . . . . **187** F7
Coombes Rd BN15. . . . . . . **166** B3
Coombe Terr BN2. . . . . **170** C1
Coombe Vale BN2 . . . . **194** D3
Coomes Way BN17. . . . . . . **204** D8
Cooper Lo RH6 . . . . **1** F2
Coopers Cl RH15. . . . . **109** B5
Coopers Farm Cl 7
PO22. . . . . **201** D5
Cooper St PO19 . . . . **177** A6
Coopers The RH13. . . . . **56** D4
Coopers Way BN5. . . . . **125** F4
Coopers Wood RH17 . . . . . . **39** C3
Coos La RH17. . . . . **61** A6
Cootes Ave RH12 . . . . **36** A3
Cootes Cotts RH20. . . . . . . **118** B2
Cootes La PO22. . . . . **202** F5
Cootham Brow RH20. . . . . . **121** B1
Cootham Gn RH20. . . . . . . **121** B2
Cootham Mobile Home Pk
RH20. . . . . **121** A2
Copeland Rd PO22. . . . . . . **202** B4
Copenhagen Ct BN2 . . . . . **193** A3
Copestake Dr RH15. . . . . . . **109** D3
Copnall Way 12 RH12. . . . . **36** C2
Copper Beech Dr
PO20. . . . . **156** C1
Copper Beeches BN1 . . . . . **169** E1
Copper Cl RH15. . . . . **108** C4
Copperfield Pl RH12. . . . . . . **36** B4
Copperfields RH13. . . . . **59** B8
Copperfields Manor
RH13. . . . . **59** B8
Copper Hall Cl 4
BN16. . . . . **205** E6
Coppets Wood 8
BN16. . . . . **205** B4
Coppice La PO20. . . . . **212** D8
Coppice Rd RH12 . . . . **37** A5
Coppice The
Crawley Down RH10 . . . . . . **21** B8
Rustington BN16 . . . . **205** D6
Scaynes Hill RH17 . . . . **88** F3
Coppice Way RH16. . . . . **87** D3
Coppice Wlk RH10 . . . . **19** A7
Coppins Ct PO22. . . . . **202** D5
Copsale Rd RH13. . . . . **82** D6
Copse Cl
Crawley Down RH10 . . . . . . **21** B8
East Grinstead RH19. . . . . . **10** A3
Horsham RH12 . . . . **36** F6
Liss GU33 . . . . **45** C4
Petersfield GU31. . . . . **68** E4
Copse Cres RH11. . . . . **18** C7
Copse Hill BN1 . . . . **169** D5
Copse La
Horley RH6 . . . . **2** C4
Walberton BN18 . . . . **158** D2
Copse Rd GU27 . . . . **26** D5
Copse The
Chichester PO19 . . . . **155** B2
Crawley RH10 . . . . **19** A6
Haywards Heath RH16 . . . . . **88** B5
Southwater RH13 . . . . **57** F2
Copse View BN16. . . . . **205** F6
Copthorne Bank RH10,
RH6. **7** C4
Copthorne CE Jun Sch
RH10. . . . . **7** C3
Copthorne Cl BN13. . . . . . . **186** A8
Copthorne Common Rd
RH10. . . . . **7** C3
Copthorne Ct
1 Crawley RH10 . . . . **6** A1
2 Hove BN3. . . . . **191** C6
Copthorne Cvn Pk
PO21. . . . . **200** D4
Copthorne Hill PO13. . . . . . **185** F8
Copthorne Prep Sch
RH10. . . . . **7** E3
Copthorne Rd
Copthorne RH10 . . . . **6** F1
Crawley RH10 . . . . **19** E8
Domewood RH19. . . . . **8** D4
Copthorne Way
Bognor Regis PO21. . . . . . **200** D4
Copthorne RH10 . . . . **6** F2
Copyhold Hill GU27 . . . . **49** C8

Copyhold La
Cuckfield RH17 . . . . **87** A4
Haywards Heath RH16 . . . . . **63** E2
Copyhold Rd RH19 . . . . **22** D8
Copythorne Ho 1
RH16. . . . . **87** E6
Coral Cl PO20. . . . . **212** B8
Coral La PO20. . . . . **212** B8
Corbishley Gn PO22. . . . . . **201** C6
Corbishley Rd PO22. . . . . . **201** C6
Corby Cl RH11 . . . . **17** E3
Corbyn Cres BN43 . . . . **189** A7
Cordal Cl BN16. . . . . **205** B4
Cordons BN7 . . . . **172** D5
Corfe Cl
Southwater RH13 . . . . **58** A1
Worthing BN13 . . . . **185** B6
Cormorant Way PO20 . . . . . **208** A6
Cornelius Ho BN3. . . . . **191** A6
Corner Garth BN12. . . . . . . **206** F5
Cornfield Cl BN17. . . . . **204** E7
Cornfield Sch BN17 . . . . . . **204** E7
Cornfields The PO20 . . . . . **179** D7
Cornflower Cl PO19 . . . . . . **177** C8
Cornflower Way RH13. . . . . . **58** A3
Cornford Cl
Burgess Hill RH15. . . . . . . **108** E5
Portslade-by-S BN41. . . . . **168** B2
Cornish Mews BN1. . . . . . . **191** E8
Cornwall Ct 2 BN3 . . . . **191** C7
Cornwall Gdns
Brighton BN1. . . . . **169** E2
6 East Grinstead RH19 . . . **22** F8
Littlehampton BN17. . . . . . **204** D6
Cornwall Ho BN1 . . . . **169** E2
Cornwall Rd BN17. . . . . **204** D6
Coronation Bldgs
BN11 . . . . **187** A3
Coronation Homelets 11
BN11 . . . . **187** B3
Coronation Rd
East Grinstead RH19 . . . . . . **22** E7
South Hayling PO11. . . . . . **195** A1
Coronation St 7 BN2 . . . . . **192** C7
Coronet Cl RH10. . . . . **19** E7
Coronet The RH6. . . . . **2** C1
Corselts Ave RH12 . . . . **35** D3
Cortis Ave BN14. . . . . **186** C5
Corunna Dr RH13 . . . . **36** F2
Corvill Ct BN11 . . . . **186** B2
Cory Cl PO19 . . . . **177** A5
Costells Edge RH17. . . . . . . **88** F3
COTE. **185** C9
Cote St BN13 . . . . **163** C1
Cot La PO18 . . . . **174** D6
Cotland Rd PO20. . . . . **212** F6
Cotsford RH11. . . . . **39** B7
Cotswold Cl
Crawley RH11 . . . . **18** B6
Worthing BN13 . . . . **185** E9
Cotswold Ct RH13. . . . . **36** F2
Cotswold Pl 7 BN2 . . . . **192** F5
Cotswold Rd BN13 . . . . **185** E8
Cotswolds The BN42. . . . . **189** E7
Cotswold Way BN16. . . . . . **206** A6
Cottage Cl
Bognor Regis PO21 . . . . . . **200** C2
Horsham RH12 . . . . **37** B6
Cottage Homes BN6 . . . . . **129** E6
Cottage Pl RH10. . . . . **7** E3
Cottenham Rd BN11. . . . . . **186** F3
Cottesmore St Mary's RC
Prim Sch BN3. . . . . **191** D8
Cottesmore Sch RH11. . . . . . **39** A8
Cottingham Ave RH12. . . . . . **36** D7
Cotton Dr PO10. . . . . **151** A3
Cotton Wlk RH11 . . . . **18** A1
Cottrell Cl BN16. . . . . **183** F5
Cottrells The BN16. . . . . . . **183** F5
Coulstock Rd RH15. . . . . . . **108** C3
Council Cotts
Albourne Green BN6 . . . . . **127** A7
Clapham BN13. . . . . **162** E1
Crosspost RH17. . . . . **85** B1
Loxwood RH14. . . . . **32** A2
Plaistow RH14. . . . . **30** D3
Sayers Common BN6 . . . . . **107** E3
Southwater RH13 . . . . **81** F7
Sutton RH20 . . . . **117** F3
Twineham RH17. . . . . **107** B6
Warningcamp BN18. . . . . . **160** F2
Wepham BN18. . . . . **161** A5
Wisborough Green RH14. . . **54** B2
Countisbury Cl PO21. . . . . . **200** F3
Countland Ct 17 PO21 . . . **201** B2
Countryman La RH13. . . . . . **103** B7
County Mall RH10. . . . . **18** E5
COUNTY OAK. **5** D2
County Oak Ave BN1. . . . . . **170** B6
County Oak Ind Est
RH10. . . . . **5** D2
County Oak La RH11 . . . . **5** D3
County Oak Ret Pk
RH11. . . . . **5** D2
County Oak Way RH10,
RH11. . . . . **5** D2
County Wharf BN17. . . . . . **204** D4
Courcels BN2. . . . . **192** E3
Court Barn La PO20. . . . . . **197** E6
Court Cl
Brighton BN1. . . . . **169** E7
East Grinstead RH19. . . . . . . **9** F1
Liphook GU30 . . . . **25** B3
Court Cres RH19 . . . . **9** F1
Courtenay Gate BN3 . . . . . **191** B5
Courtenay Terr 12
BN3 . . . . **191** B5

Court Est The [8]
BN11 . . . . 187 B3
Court Farm Rd
Hove BN3. . . . . 169 A2
Rottingdean BN2 . . . . 193 F3
Courtfield Ho [4]
PO21 . . . . 201 B3
Courtfields BN15 . . . . 187 D5
Courtlands
[13] Brighton BN2 . . . . . . 213 C3
Haywards Heath RH16 . . 87 E3
Courtlands CI BN12 . . . 185 E2
Courtlands Way
Bognor Regis PO22 . . . . 202 C6
Worthing BN11, BN12 . . 185 F2
Court Lodge Rd RH6 . . . . 1 F3
Court Meadow Sch
RH17. . . . . 87 A8
Courtmead Rd RH17 . . . 86 F6
Courtney King Ho [1]
BN2 . . . . 192 D4
Court Ord Cotts BN2 . . 193 F3
Court Ord Rd BN2. . . . . 193 F3
Courts Hill Rd GU27. . . . 27 B6
Courts Mount Rd GU27 . . 27 B6
Court The PO21. . . . . . . 200 A1
Courtup Hill RH13 . . . . . 82 E5
Courtwick La BN17. . . . 204 C8
Courtwick Rd BN17 . . . 204 C7
Courtyard La PO18. . . . 136 C7
Courtyard The
Bognor Regis PO21 . . . . 200 F2
Chichester PO19. . . . . . 176 F4
[1] Crawley RH10 . . . . . . 18 D5
East Grinstead RH19. . . . 10 B1
Falmer BN1 . . . . 171 C6
Faygate RH12 . . . . 37 E4
Finchdean PO8. . . . . . . 130 D7
Haywards Heath RH16 . . 87 F4
Hove BN3. . . . . 191 B8
[8] Hove BN3. . . . . 191 D6
Lindfield RH16 . . . . 64 C3
[15] Petersfield GU31. . . . 68 B3
Selsey PO20. . . . . 210 A3
West Grinstead RH13 . . . 82 A2
Worthing BN11 . . . . . . 186 B3
Worthing, Salvington
BN14. . . . . 186 A6
Cousins Copse Cvn Site
RH14 . . . . 55 F8
Cousins Way RH20 . . . . 100 C3
Coventry CI PO21 . . . . . 200 D4
Coventry St BN1 . . . . . . 191 E8
Cove Rd BN16 . . . . 205 B4
Coverdale Ct RH19. . . . . . 9 C3
Covers La GU27. . . . . . . 26 C6
Covert CI RH10 . . . . 18 E7
Covert Mead
Ashington RH20. . . . . . 122 F5
Handcross RH17 . . . . . . 61 B7
Covey The RH10 . . . . . . 19 E8
Covington Rd PO10 . . . 151 D5
Cowdens CI BN3. . . . . . 168 D4
Cowdown La PO18 . . . . 110 F4
Cowdray* GU29 . . . . 95 A8
Cowdray Ct
Crawley RH10 . . . . 19 C5
Rustington BN16 . . . . . 205 B7
Worthing BN12 . . . . . . 185 D2
Cowdray Ct
[1] Hove BN3. . . . . 191 D7
Midhurst GU29 . . . . 94 F8
Cowdray Dr
Rustington BN16 . . . . . 205 B7
Worthing BN12 . . . . . . 185 D2
Cowdray Ho GU29 . . . . . 95 C8
Cowdray Rd GU29 . . . . . 73 A2
Cowdray Wlk [7] BN16 . . 205 B7
Cowfold CI RH11. . . . . . . 17 F3
Cowfold Rd
Brighton BN2 . . . . 192 E5
Cowfold RH13 . . . . 82 D2
Crosspost RH13, RH17 . . 84 C2
Cow La
Sidlesham PO20. . . . . . 209 D7
South Harting GU31 . . . . 91 C4
Cowley Dr
[1] Lancing BN15. . . . . 187 F5
Woodingdean BN2 . . . . 193 F7
Cownwy Ct BN2. . . . . . . 193 F1
Cowper Rd BN11. . . . . . 186 B2
Cowper St BN3 . . . . 191 A7
Cowslip CI RH13 . . . . . . 58 A2
Coxcomb Wlk RH11 . . . . 18 A4
Coxes Mdw GU32 . . . . . 68 A5
Coxes Rd PO20 . . . . . . 212 D6
Cox Gr RH15. . . . . 108 E5
COX GREEN 12 E2
Cox Green Rd RH12 . . . . 12 C2
Coxham La BN44. . . . . . 145 C4
Cox Ho RH12 . . . . 36 B2
Coxswain Way PO20 . . . 212 E5
Crabbet Rd RH10 . . . . . . 19 B7
Crabden La PO8 . . . . . . 130 A8
Crablands PO20 . . . . . . 212 D7
Crablands CI PO20 . . . . 212 C7
Crabtree Ave BN1. . . . . 170 B5
Crab Tree CI BN17 . . . . 182 D5
Crabtree Cotts RH13 . . . 84 A7
Crabtree Gate RH13. . . . 83 F5
Crabtree La BN15 . . . . . 187 E6
Crabtree Lo [2] BN15 . . . 187 D6
Crabtree Rd RH11. . . . . . 18 C7
Cradock PI BN13. . . . . . 185 E9
Crafts La GU31. . . . . 68 C5
Craggits La BN5 . . . . 68 E5
Craigans RH11. . . . . 18 A5
Craignair Ave BN1 . . . . 169 F7

Craigweil La PO21 . . . . . 200 E2
Craigweil Manor
PO21. . . . . 200 D1
Cranborne Wlk RH10 . . . 18 F4
Cranbourne CI RH6 . . . . . 2 B5
Cranbourne St BN1 . . . . 213 A2
Cranbrook [14] BN2 . . . . 213 C3
Crane St PO19 . . . . 177 A6
Cranford Gdns PO21 . . . 201 C4
Cranford Rd GU31 . . . . . 68 A2
Cranham Ave RH14 . . . . 79 C6
Cranleigh Ave BN2. . . . 194 B1
Cranleigh Ct [9] BN11 . . 186 C2
Cranleigh Rd BN14. . . . 186 C5
Cranley Ct [3] BN3. . . . 190 D7
Cranmer Ave BN3. . . . . 168 F1
Cranmer Rd BN13. . . . . 186 A3
Cranmer Wlk RH10 . . . . 19 C5
Cranston CI RH19 . . . . . . 9 F2
Cranston Way RH10 . . . 21 C8
Cranworth Rd BN11. . . . 186 F3
Craven Rd
Brighton BN2. . . . . 192 D6
Crawley RH10 . . . . 19 B5
Crawford Gdns RH10 . . . 36 E4
Crawford Way RH19. . . . . 9 F3
Crawley Ave
Crawley, Ifield RH10,
RH11. . . . . 18 A6
Crawley RH10 . . . . 6 C1
Crawley Bsns Ctr RH10. . . 5 E2
Crawley Coll RH10 . . . . 18 E6
Crawley Coll (West Green
Annexe) RH11 . . . . . . 18 C7
Crawley Down Rd RH10 . . 8 F4
Crawley Down Village CE
Prim Sch RH10 . . . . . 21 B8
Crawley Foyer The
RH11 . . . . 18 C6
Crawley Hospl RH11 . . . 18 C6
Crawley La
Balcombe RH17. . . . . . 40 E4
Crawley RH10 . . . . 19 C7
Crawley Mus Ctr*
RH11. . . . . 18 C5
Crawley Rd
Brighton BN2. . . . . 170 D6
Crawley RH12 . . . . 17 B1
Faygate RH12 . . . . 37 D7
Horsham RH12 . . . . . . 37 B5
Crawley Sta RH10. . . . . 18 E5
Crawters CI RH10 . . . . . 18 F7
Crawters La [6] GU31 . . 68 B3
Crayford Rd BN2. . . . . . 170 D1
Cray La RH20 . . . . 100 D5
Cray's La RH20 . . . . . . 122 C8
Creamery Cotts RH14 . . 53 B2
Creasys Dr RH11. . . . . . 18 A1
Crede CI PO18 . . . . 175 C5
Crede La PO18. . . . . . . 175 C5
Creek End
Emsworth PO10. . . . . . 173 B7
Fishbourne PO19. . . . . 176 B6
Cremorne PI [8] GU32 . . 68 B4
Crescenta Wlk PO21 . . . 201 A3
Crescent CI
Burgess Hill RH15 . . . . 109 B3
Woodingdean BN2 . . . . 193 E8
Crescent Ct [3] BN11 . . 187 B3
Crescent Dr N BN2. . . . 193 E8
Crescent Dr S BN2. . . . 193 E7
Crescent Mans BN2 . . . 213 C5
Crescent PI BN2. . . . . . 192 C4
Crescent Rd
Bognor Regis PO21 . . . 201 C3
Brighton BN2. . . . . 192 B8
Burgess Hill RH15 . . . . 109 A3
East Grinstead RH19. . . . 9 D1
Worthing BN11 . . . . . . 186 C2
Crescent Rise RH20 . . . 122 A3
Crescent The
Bognor Regis, Felpham
PO22. . . . . 202 A4
Bognor Regis PO21 . . . 211 A8
Brighton BN2. . . . . 170 E2
Cootham RH20. . . . . . . 121 A2
East Wittering PO20 . . . 207 E7
Felcourt RH19 . . . . 9 C8
Horley RH6 . . . . 6 B8
Horsham RH12 . . . . . . 36 A2
Keymer BN6. . . . . 129 B3
Lancing BN15. . . . . 187 E5
Rustington BN16 . . . . . 205 B6
Southbourne PO10 . . . . 173 F8
Southwick BN42 . . . . . 189 F8
Steyning BN44. . . . . . . 145 D2
West Kingston BN16 . . . 206 A4
Crescent Way
Burgess Hill RH15 . . . . 109 A3
Horley RH6 . . . . 2 A1
Crespin Way BN1 . . . . . 170 C2
Cressey Way PO19 . . . . 155 A1
Crest Way BN41. . . . . . . 168 B3
Crestway Par BN1 . . . . . 170 C2
Crestway The BN1 . . . . . 170 C2
Crewdson Rd RH6 . . . . . . 2 B3
Cricket Ct RH19. . . . . 9 E3
Cricketers CI RH20. . . . 123 A5
Cricketers Par BN14 . . . 186 D6
Cricket Hill RH16 . . . . . . 64 C2
Cricket Field Rd RH12. . . 36 B1
Crimbourne La RH14. . . . 77 D3
Cripland CI RH16 . . . . . . 88 B6
Cripplecrutch Hill
GU27. . . . . 28 F5
Cripplegate La RH13 . . . 82 A8
Cripps Ho RH11. . . . . . . 18 B2
Cripps La BN44 . . . . . . 145 E3
Critchel's La PO20 . . . . 198 C1

Critchfield Rd PO18. . . . 175 B5
CRITCHMERE 26 E7
Critchmere Dr PO20 . . . 179 F7
Critchmere Hill GU27 . . . 26 E7
Critchmere La GU27 . . . . 26 E6
Critchmere Vale GU27 . . 26 E6
Crockford Rd PO10 . . . . 151 D4
Crockham CI RH11. . . . . 18 C4
Crockhurst Rd BN2. . . . 192 C7
Crockhurst Hill BN13. . . 185 F9
Croft Ave BN42 . . . . 189 F7
Croft Dr BN41. . . . . 168 A3
Crofters Wood BN44. . . 145 F2
Croft La BN5 . . . . 125 E4
Croft Mead PO19 . . . . . 155 A2
Crofton GU27 . . . . 27 C7
Crofton Manor GU27 . . . 27 C7
Croft Rd
Brighton BN1. . . . . 169 D4
Selsey PO20. . . . . 212 D7
Croft The
Bognor Regis PO21 . . . . 200 F5
Cocking GU29 . . . . 114 D8
Crawley RH11 . . . . 18 A6
East Preston BN16 . . . . 206 A5
Hassocks BN6 . . . . 128 F5
Lodsworth GU28 . . . . . . 74 B3
Southwick BN42 . . . . . 189 E8
Yapton BN18 . . . . 180 F4
Croft Villas BN5 . . . . . . 125 E5
Croft Way
Bognor Regis PO22 . . . . 202 C6
Horsham RH12 . . . . 36 A3
Selsey PO20. . . . . 212 D7
Croft Works BN16. . . . . 205 D7
Cromleigh Way BN42 . . 167 E2
Crompton Fields RH10 . . . 5 E1
Crompton Way RH10. . . . . 5 E1
Cromwell Ct [3] BN3. . . 191 D7
Cromwell Mews RH15 . . 108 F4
Cromwell PI [1] RH19 . . . 22 F7
Cromwell Rd
Burgess Hill RH15 . . . . 108 F3
Hove BN3. . . . . 191 C7
Cromwell St BN2 . . . . . 192 C7
Crooked La PO20 . . . . . 197 E4
Crookhorn La RH13 . . . . 81 B8
Crookthorn La BN17 . . . 203 E8
Cropthorne Dr BN17 . . . 181 E1
Crosbie CI PO19 . . . . . . 176 F3
Crosby CI BN13 . . . . . . 185 D7
Croshaw Dr BN15 . . . . . 187 D5
Crossbush La BN18 . . . . 160 E1
Crossbush Rd
Bognor Regis PO22 . . . . 202 C4
Brighton BN2. . . . . 192 E6
Cross Colwood La
RH17 . . . . 84 F5
Crossfield GU27 . . . . 49 B5
Crossfield RH13. . . . . . . 57 F1
CROSS GATES 141 A2
Crosshaven BN17 . . . . . 205 A6
Cross Keys RH10 . . . . . . 18 D6
Cross La
Barns Green RH13. . . . . 57 A1
Burstow RH9 . . . . 7 C8
Nepcote BN2 . . . . 163 E5
Crossman Ct RH11 . . . . . 18 B1
Cross Oak La RH1. . . . . . 2 C7
Crosspath RH10 . . . . . . 18 E7
Crosspost RH17. . . . . . . 85 B1
Crosspost Ind Est
RH17. . . . . 85 B1
Cross Rd
Rustington BN16 . . . . . 205 E5
Southwick BN42 . . . . . 189 D8
Cross Road CI BN42. . . 189 D8
Cross St
Brighton BN1. . . . . 213 B4
[14] Hove BN1, BN3 . . . . 191 D5
Worthing BN11 . . . . . . 186 C3
Crossway RH6 . . . . 5 B1
Crossways
Bolney RH17. . . . . 85 D2
Crawley RH10 . . . . 19 A7
East Preston BN16 . . . . 206 B7
Middleton-on-S PO22. . . 202 F5
Midhurst GU29 . . . . 73 A2
Navant Hill GU28 . . . . . 50 E4
West Chiltington Common
RH20. . . . . 121 D7
Crossways Ave
East Grinstead RH19. . . . 9 C1
Worthing BN12 . . . . . . 185 B5
Crossways CI RH10. . . . . 18 F7
Crossways Cotts
Alfold Crossways GU6. . . 11 A3
Poynings BN45 . . . . . . 148 A5
Crossways Ct GU27 . . . . 49 B6
Crossways Pk RH20 . . . 121 D7
Crossways The
Hassocks BN6 . . . . 128 C4
Littlehampton BN17. . . . 204 C7
Crossway The
Brighton BN1. . . . . 170 B2
Portslade-by-S BN41. . . 168 A2
Crouch Cross La
PO18 . . . . 156 D3
Crouch Hill BN5 . . . . . . 125 F7
Crouchlands Farm
RH17 . . . . 86 E8
Crowberry CI [1] RH11. . . 18 A2
Crowborough Dr
BN12 . . . . 185 B3
Crowhurst CI RH10. . . . . 19 E6
Crowhurst Cnr BN1 . . . . 170 C7
Crowhurst Cres RH20 . . 121 C2
Crowhurst Keep RH10. . . 19 E6

Crowhurst Rd BN1 . . . . . 170 C7
Crown Bldgs BN15. . . . . 187 C4
Crown CI [1] BN3. . . . . . 191 D6
Crown Ct [3] BN16. . . . . 206 A4
Crown Gdns BN1 . . . . . . 213 A2
Crown Hill [4] BN2 . . . . . 192 C6
Crown PI [2] BN16. . . . . 206 A4
Crown Point Ho BN6 . . . 128 F4
Crown Rd
Portslade-by-S BN41. . . . 190 A8
Shoreham-by-S BN43. . . 189 B8
Crown St BN1 . . . . 213 A4
Crown Yd BN18. . . . . . . 160 B3
Crowsbury CI PO10 . . . . 151 A3
Croxton La RH16. . . . . . . 88 B6
Croy CI PO19 . . . . 176 E4
Crundens Cnr [5]
BN16 . . . . 205 E6
Crundles GU31 . . . . 68 D3
Crutchfield La RH6. . . . . . 1 B5
Crypt La GU29 . . . . 114 C7
Cuckfield CI RH11 . . . . . 17 F3
Cuckfield Cres RH13 . . . 185 F7
Cuckfield La RH17 . . . . . 61 B1
Cuckfield Mus* RH17. . . 86 E6
Cuckfield Rd
Ansty RH17 . . . . 86 C3
Burgess Hill RH15 . . . . 108 E7
Goddards' Green BN6,
RH17. . . . . 108 A4
Hurstpierpoint BN6 . . . . 128 A7
Slough Green RH17 . . . . 62 A2
Cuckmere Cres RH11 . . . 17 F5
Cuckmere Way BN1. . . . 170 C5
Cudlow Ave BN16. . . . . 205 C5
Cudlow Gdn BN16. . . . . 205 C4
Cudworth La RH5 . . . . 3 E8
Cudworth Pk RH5. . . . . . . 3 F8
Cuffs Hill RH10 . . . . 19 E2
Culimore CI PO20 . . . . . 207 E7
Culimore Rd PO20 . . . . 207 E7
Cullum Ct PO19 . . . . . . 177 C8
Culpepper RH15 . . . . . . 108 E4
Culpepper CI BN2. . . . . 170 D2
Culross Ave RH16 . . . . . . 87 D5
Culver Ct BN15 . . . . 187 E6
Culver Rd
Bognor Regis PO22 . . . . 202 A4
Lancing BN15. . . . . 187 E6
Culvers GU31 . . . . 91 D3
Cumberland Ave
New Brighton PO10. . . . 151 B4
Worthing BN12 . . . . . . 185 D6
Cumberland CI BN16. . . 184 A5
Cumberland Cres
BN16 . . . . 183 F5
Cumberland Ct BN11. . . 185 F2
Cumberland Dr BN1 . . . 169 E2
Cumberland Lo [3]
BN1 . . . . 169 E2
Cumberland Rd
Angmering BN16 . . . . . 184 A5
Brighton BN1. . . . . 169 E2
Cumbernauld Wlk
RH11 . . . . 17 E2
Cumbrian CI BN13 . . . . 185 E8
Cumnor House Sch
RH17. . . . . 66 B5
Cunliffe Ct [3] BN11 . . . 185 F3
Cunningham Gdns
PO22 . . . . 202 C5
Curbey CI RH20 . . . . . . 101 D1
Curf Way RH15. . . . . . . 109 C3
Curlescroft PO21 . . . . . 200 F2
Curlew CI PO10 . . . . . . 173 A7
Curlews The RH43 . . . . . 189 A8
Curteys Wlk RH11. . . . . . 18 A3
Curve The BN2 . . . . 213 C2
Curvins Way BN15 . . . . 187 F7
Curwen PI BN1 . . . . 169 E3
Curzon Ave RH12 . . . . . . 36 B3
Curzon CI BN13 . . . . . . 185 F7
Cutfield CI PO19. . . . . . 176 F3
Cuthbert Rd BN2. . . . . . 192 C5
Cuttinglea La RH10 . . . . . 8 A1
Cuttinglye Rd RH10 . . . . . 8 C2
Cygnets The BN43 . . . . 188 F8
Cygnet Wlk PO22 . . . . . 201 B6
Cylinders The GU27. . . . 49 B5
Cymens Ora PO20. . . . . 209 D8
Cypress Ave BN13. . . . . 185 C6
Cypress CI [12] BN43 . . . 166 F1
Cypress PI BN14 . . . . . . 186 A6
Cypress Way PO21 . . . . 200 D1
Cyprus Mews RH15 . . . . 109 B3
Cyprus Rd RH15 . . . . . . 109 A3
Cyril Richings Bsns Ctr
BN43. . . . . 189 B7

D

Dacre Gdns BN44 . . . . . 166 B7
Dagbrook La BN5. . . . . . 125 C3
Dagmar St BN11 . . . . . . 186 E3
Dairy Farm BN12. . . . . . 185 A4
Dairyfields RH11. . . . . . . 18 A5
Dairy La
Maudlin PO18 . . . . 155 F1
Walberton BN18 . . . . . . 158 D1
Daisycroft The BN5 . . . . 125 F4
Dakin CI BN15 . . . . 19 C2
Dakins Rd RH19 . . . . 22 E8
Dale Ave
Brighton BN1. . . . . 169 F5
Keymer BN6. . . . . 129 A3
Dale CI RH12 . . . . 36 F5
Dale Copse GU27 . . . . . . 49 B6

Dale Cres BN1 . . . . 169 F6
Dale Ct PO21 . . . . 201 B3
Daledene RH19 . . . . 22 F8
Dale Dr BN1 . . . . 170 A6
Dale Hill BN45 . . . . 149 A6
Dale Rd
Forest Row RH18. . . . . . 23 F1
Worthing BN11 . . . . . . 187 B4
Dale View
Haslemere GU27 . . . . . . 26 F5
Hove BN3. . . . . 168 D2
Dale View Gdns BN3 . . . 168 D2
Dalewood Gdns
Burgess Hill RH15 . . . . 109 C2
Crawley RH10 . . . . 18 F8
Dallaway Gdns RH19 . . . . 9 E1
Dallaway Rd PO19 . . . . 177 B4
Dalley Way GU33 . . . . . . 45 B4
Dallington Rd BN3 . . . . 190 F8
Dalloway Rd BN18 . . . . 159 F1
Dalton CI RH11 . . . . 18 B1
Daltons PI BN18 . . . . . . 160 A2
Damer's Bridge GU28 . . . 97 F8
Dame School Ct
PO18 . . . . 155 A5
Damian Way BN6. . . . . . 129 B4
Dampier Wlk RH11. . . . . . 18 B1
Danbury Ct PO10 . . . . . 151 C2
Danby Ct RH6 . . . . 2 B5
Dane Acre BN16 . . . . . . 184 A5
Danefield Rd PO20. . . . . 212 C6
Danehill CE Prim Sch
RH17. . . . . 66 B4
Danehill La RH17 . . . . . . 65 E5
Danehill Rd BN2 . . . . . . 192 F5
Danehurst [6] PO21. . . . 201 B3
Danehurst Cres RH13 . . . 36 F2
Daniel CI BN15 . . . . 187 F7
Daniels Ho [2] RH10 . . . . 19 B7
Dankton Gdns BN15. . . . 187 B7
Dankton La BN15 . . . . . 187 B7
Danley La GU27. . . . . . . 26 A3
Danny Sheldon Ho [14]
BN2 . . . . 192 C4
Danworth Farm BN6 . . . 108 A1
Danworth La BN6. . . . . . 108 B2
Dapper's La BN16. . . . . 184 A7
Darcey Dr BN1. . . . . 170 A6
Darenth Way RH6. . . . . . . 1 F6
Dark La PO21. . . . . 200 F1
Darleydale RH11 . . . . . . 18 C3
Darlington CI BN13 . . . . 184 A5
Darlingtons The
BN16 . . . . 205 E6
Darlington Wlk BN16. . . 205 E7
Dart CI BN13 . . . . 185 D9
Dart Ct RH19 . . . . 10 A3
Dartmouth CI BN2 . . . . 170 F1
Dartmouth Cres BN2. . . 170 F1
Darwin CI RH12 . . . . 36 F4
D'aubigny Rd BN2 . . . . 192 B8
Daux Ave RH14 . . . . 79 D6
Daux Rd RH14 . . . . 79 D6
Daux Way RH14 . . . . 79 D6
Dauxwood CI RH14. . . . . 79 D6
Davenport CI [3] BN11 . . 185 F3
Davenport Rd PO22 . . . . 202 B4
Davey Dr BN1 . . . . 170 B1
Davids CI PO21 . . . . 200 F5
Davies Ct [12] BN11. . . . 186 A1
Davigdor Inf Sch BN3 . . 191 D6
Davigdor Rd BN3 . . . . . 191 E7
Davis CI RH11 . . . . 18 A1
Davison CE High Sch for
Girls BN11. . . . . 186 F4
Davits Dr BN17 . . . . 205 A6
Davits Ct PO18 . . . . 153 A5
Dawes Ave BN11. . . . . . 186 F3
Dawes CI BN11 . . . . 186 F3
Dawlish CI BN2. . . . . . . 170 F1
Dawn CI BN44 . . . . 146 B1
Dawn Cres BN44 . . . . . 146 A1
Dawn Rise RH10 . . . . 7 A3
Dawson Ct [8] BN11 . . . 186 C3
Dawson Terr BN2 . . . . . 192 C6
Dawtrey CI BN16. . . . . . 205 E6
Dawtrey Rd GU28 . . . . . . 97 F7
Daynes Way RH15. . . . . 108 E1
Days Lo PO18 . . . . 157 F3
Deacons Dr BN41. . . . . . 168 C2
Deacons Way BN44 . . . . 146 B2
Deacon Trad Est
BN14. . . . . 186 F5
Deacon Way BN14 . . . . 186 F5
Deak's La RH17 . . . . 86 B6
Dean CI
Littlehampton BN17. . . . 204 C7
Portslade-by-S BN41. . . 168 C2
Rottingdean BN2 . . . . . 194 A2
Dean Court Rd BN2. . . . 194 A2
Deane Ct [7] PO21. . . . . 201 C4
Deanery CI PO19. . . . . . 176 F6
Deanery Farm La
PO19 . . . . 176 F6
Dean Gdns BN41. . . . . . 168 C2
Dean La
Finchdean PO8, PO9 . . . 130 F5
Upperton GU28 . . . . 75 A1
Deanland Rd RH17. . . . . 41 A1
DEANLAND END 131 A5
Deans CI
Fontwell BN18. . . . . . . 158 A3
Woodingdean BN2 . . . . 193 E8
Dean St BN1. . . . . 191 E5
Deanway BN3 . . . . 169 B3

Dean Way RH20. . . . . .121 C2
De Braose Way BN44. . . . 145 E2
Deco Bldg The **3**
BN2. . . . . .170 C1
De Courcel Rd BN2 . . . . . . 192 E3
Decoy Dr BN16 . . . . 183 F7
Decoy La BN18 . . . . 183 B8
Decoy Rd BN14. . . . . 186 F5
Dedisham Cl RH10 . . . . 19 A5
Deegan Ho **2** PO21 . . . . 201 C3
Deepdale RH6. . . . . .2 B2
Deepdene GU27 . . . . 26 E6
Deepdene Ct PO22. . . . . . 203 A5
Deepdene Sch BN3 . . . . . . 190 D7
Deepfields RH6. . . . . .1 F5
Deer Cl PO19 . . . . 176 E3
Deer Park Cl PO20 . . . . . . 212 B8
Deer Park Dr PO20 . . . . . . 212 B8
Deer Park La PO20. . . . . . 212 B8
Deer Pk BN5 . . . . 125 E6
Deers Leap RH16 . . . . 87 C3
Deerswood Cl
Crawley RH11. . . . . 18 B7
Worthing BN13 . . . . 185 B6
Deerswood Ct RH11. . . . . . 18 A7
Deerswood Rd RH11 . . . . . 18 B7
Deer Way RH12 . . . . 36 A1
Deeside Ave PO19 . . . . . . 176 B7
Deeside The BN1 . . . . 170 A7
Defiance Pl PO22 . . . . 202 C4
Delancey Ct RH12. . . . . . . 36 C4
De La Warr Rd RH19 . . . . . .9 F1
Delfont Cl RH10 . . . . 19 D4
Delfryn BN41 . . . . 167 F3
Delius Gdns RH12 . . . . 37 B4
Dell Cl GU27 . . . . 27 A7
Dell Dr BN16 . . . . 205 F8
Delling Cl PO18. . . . . 175 B6
Delling La PO18 . . . . 175 C6
Dell La RH14. . . . . 79 D8
Dellney Ave RH16 . . . . 87 F3
Dell Quay Rd PO20 . . . . . 176 B2
Dell The
Bognor Regis PO22 . . . . . 201 A6
East Grinstead RH19 . . . . 10 B1
Haywards Heath RH16 . . 87 C5
Horley RH6 . . . . 2 B4
Sidlow RH6 . . . . 1 C5
Delrogue Rd RH11 . . . . 5 A1
Delta Bglws RH6. . . . . 2 A1
Delta Dr RH6 . . . . 2 A1
Delta Ho RH6. . . . . 2 A1
De Montfort Rd BN2 . . . . . 192 C7
Dempsey Rd **3** PO19 . . . . 155 A2
Dempsey Wlk RH11 . . . . . . 18 A8
Den Ave PO21 . . . . 201 D3
Denbigh Rd GU27 . . . . 27 D5
Dencher Rd BN7. . . . . 172 E3
Denchers Plat RH11. . . . . . . 5 D1
Dene Cl
Haslemere GU27 . . . . 27 C6
Horley RH6 . . . . 1 E5
Denecroft BN1 . . . . 169 D5
Dene Ct BN1. . . . . 186 B2
Dene Hospl The BN6 . . . . . 108 B5
Deneside BN1 . . . . 169 D5
Dene The
Hove BN3. . . . . 168 D3
Southwater RH13 . . . . . . 58 A2
Dene Tye RH10 . . . . 19 D7
Dene Vale BN1 . . . . 169 D5
Deneway The
Brighton BN1 . . . . 169 D4
Lancing BN15. . . . . 187 C6
Denge La PO18 . . . . 156 E7
Denham Cl PO22 . . . . 202 E5
Denham Ct RH15 . . . . 108 D3
Denham Rd RH15 . . . . 108 D3
Denison Ct **3** PO19 . . . . . 176 F7
Denman's Cl RH16 . . . . 88 A8
Denmans Gdns*
BN18. . . . . 157 F3
Denmans La BN18,
PO20 . . . . 157 G2
Denman's La RH16. . . . . . . 88 A7
Denmark Mews BN3 . . . . . 191 B7
Denmark Rd BN41 . . . . . . 190 C7
Denmark Terr BN1. . . . . . . 191 E6
Denmark Villas BN3 . . . . . 191 B7
Denne Par RH12, RH13. . . . 36 C1
Denne Pl RH12 . . . . 36 C1
Denne Rd
Crawley RH11. . . . . 18 D5
Horsham RH12 . . . . 36 C1
Dennis Ct RH20 . . . . 100 C2
Dennis Hobden Cl
BN2. . . . . 170 E1
Dennis Way GU33 . . . . 45 C3
Denny's Cl PO20 . . . . 212 E7
Denshare Rd PO20 . . . . . . 212 E8
Denshire Dr RH20. . . . . . . 121 E2
Densihale PO21. . . . . 201 A3
Denton Cl BN12. . . . . 185 B4
Denton Dr BN1 . . . . 170 A6
Denvale Trad Pk RH6 . . . . . 18 E5
Departures Rd RH6 . . . . . . .5 F8
Depot Rd
Crawley RH11. . . . . 5 D1
Horsham RH13 . . . . 36 E2
Derby Ct **2** BN3 . . . . 191 E7
Derby Pl **6** BN2 . . . . 213 C2
Derby Rd PO22 . . . . 27 B7
Derek Ave BN3 . . . . 190 D6
Derek Ho BN3 . . . . 190 F6

Derek Rd BN15 . . . . 187 E8
Dervia Ho BN3. . . . . 191 C7
Derwent Cl
Crawley RH11. . . . . 17 F5
Horsham RH12 . . . . 37 B6
Lancing BN15. . . . . 187 C5
Littlehampton BN17. . . . . 205 A7
Tangmere PO20. . . . . . . 156 D2
Derwent Ct BN1 . . . . 213 A3
Derwent Dr BN12,
BN13 . . . . 185 D6
Derwent Gr PO22 . . . . . . 202 B6
Desmond Anderson Prim
Sch RH10 . . . . 18 D2
Desmond Way BN2 . . . . . 192 F6
Detling Rd RH11 . . . . 18 C1
Devil's Dyke* BN1. . . . . . 148 C3
Devil's Dyke Rd BN1 . . . . 168 E7
Devils La GU30 . . . . 25 E3
Devon Ct **3** BN17. . . . . . 204 D5
Devonian Ct BN2 . . . . . . 213 C4
Devonport Pl BN11. . . . . . 187 A3
Devonport Rd BN11. . . . . 187 A2
Devonshire Ct **1**
BN3. . . . . 191 C7
Devonshire Lo BN11 . . . . . 185 F3
Devonshire Pl
3 Bognor Regis
PO21. . . . . 201 C3
Brighton BN2 . . . . 213 C2
Devonshire Rd
Bognor Regis PO21. . . . . 201 C3
Horsham RH13 . . . . 36 D2
Devon Villas RH16 . . . . . . 87 F4
Dewar Cl **2** RH11. . . . . . 17 E5
Dewe Rd BN2 . . . . 170 C1
Dew Pond Cl RH13. . . . . . 36 F3
Dexter Dr RH19 . . . . 22 E8
Dharma Sch The BN1 . . . . 170 A6
Dial Cl PO22. . . . . 180 C5
DIAL GREEN 50 B3
Diamond Cotts RH17. . . . . 85 B1
Diana Cl PO10 . . . . 151 A4
Dickens Cl RH19 . . . . 9 C1
Dickens La GU31. . . . . 68 C5
Dickens Rd BN16. . . . . . . 18 E3
Dickinson Pl PO22. . . . . . 201 D6
Dickins Way RH13 . . . . . . 58 F8
Diggers The BN1 . . . . 170 B3
Dinapore Ho **11** BN2 . . . . 213 C3
Dingemans BN44 . . . . 145 D5
Dingle Cl RH11 . . . . 18 B7
Dingle The RH11 . . . . 18 B6
Dingley Rd BN16. . . . . . . 205 C5
Dinsdale Gdns BN16 . . . . 205 C6
Dione Wlk RH11 . . . . 17 E4
Dirty La RH19 . . . . 23 E7
Discovery Mews RH10. . . . . 7 C4
Discovery Pk RH10. . . . . . . 6 A2
Ditcham Park Sch
GU31. . . . . 110 B8
Ditchfield Cl PO22 . . . . . . 202 D6
Ditchling Beacon Nature
Reserve* BN6 . . . . 150 D7
Ditchling Bostall BN6 . . . . 150 D7
Ditchling Cl BN12. . . . . . . 185 B5
Ditchling Common Ctry
Pk* BN6. . . . . 109 F1
Ditchling Cres BN1 . . . . . . 170 C5
Ditchling Ct **4** BN1 . . . . . 192 B8
Ditchling Gdns BN1 . . . . . 170 B1
Ditchling Hill RH11 . . . . . . 18 C4
Ditchling Mus* BN1 . . . . . 129 C3
Ditchling Pl **1** BN1 . . . . . 170 A1
Ditchling Rd
Brighton BN1, BN2 . . . . . 170 B4
Westmeston BN1, BN6 . . 150 D4
Ditchling Rise BN1. . . . . . 192 A8
Ditchling St Margaret's CE
Prim Sch BN6 . . . . 129 D3
Dobbins Pl RH11. . . . . . . 17 E5
Dobson Rd RH11. . . . . 5 D1
Dodsley Gr GU29. . . . . . . 72 F2
Dodsley La GU29. . . . . . . 73 A2
Dog Kennels GU28 . . . . . 117 B3
Dog La BN44 . . . . 145 D3
Dolby Terr RH11 . . . . .4 E6
Dollis Cl RH10 . . . . 19 C5
Dolphin Cl
Fishbourne PO19. . . . . . 176 B6
Haslemere GU27 . . . . . . 26 E6
Dolphin Ct
3 Bognor Regis
PO21. . . . . 201 C2
5 Hove BN3. . . . . 191 A6
Rustington BN16 . . . . . . 205 D4
Worthing BN13 . . . . 186 A3
Dolphin Ind Est BN43 . . . . 189 B7
Dolphin Lo **13** BN11 . . . . . 186 A1
Dolphin Mews
Brighton BN2. . . . . 213 B1
Chichester PO19 . . . . . . 176 D6
Shoreham-by-S BN43. . . 189 A7
Dolphin Rd
Haywards Heath RH16 . . 87 D4
Shoreham-by-S BN43. . . 189 B7
Dolphin Way
Rustington BN16 . . . . . . 205 D4
Shoreham-by-S BN43. . . 189 B7
Domehouse Cl PO20 . . . . 212 E5
Dominion Bldgs BN14. . . . 186 F4
Dominion Cl BN14. . . . . . 186 E5
Dominion Ct BN14. . . . . . 186 F5
Dominion Way
Rustington BN16 . . . . . . 205 C7
Worthing BN14 . . . . 186 F5

Dominion Way W
BN14. . . . . 186 F5
Donald Hall Rd BN2. . . . . 192 D5
Donaldson Cl PO20 . . . . . 212 C8
Doncaster Wlk **1**
RH10. . . . . 19 A4
Donegal Rd PO19 . . . . . . 154 F1
Donkey La RH6 . . . . 6 D7
Donkey Mews **4** BN3 . . . . 191 D5
Donne Cl RH10 . . . . 19 B8
DONNINGTON 176 E1
Donnington Ct **2**
RH11. . . . . 17 F3
Donnington Pk PO20. . . . . 176 D3
Donnington Pl **2**
BN16 . . . . 205 C6
Donnington Rd BN2 . . . . . 193 E6
Doomsday Gdn RH13. . . . 37 A1
Doomsday La RH13 . . . . . 59 A8
Doone End **6** BN12 . . . . 206 F4
Dorchester Ct **2** BN1 . . . 191 E5
Dorchester Gdns
BN11 . . . . 186 A2
Dorking Rd
Kingsfold RH12, RH5 . . . 15 B4
Warnham RH12 . . . . 36 B6
Dormans RH11 . . . . 18 A5
Dorman's Cl RH7 . . . . 10 A8
Dormans Gdns RH19 . . . . .9 E6
Dormans High St RH7 . . . . 10 A8
Dormans Park Rd
Dormans Park RH19 . . . . .9 E6
East Grinstead RH19 . . . . 9 D3
Dormans Sta RH7. . . . . . . .9 F8
Dormans Station Rd
RH7 . . . . .9 F7
Dorothy Rd BN3 . . . . 190 D8
Dorothy Stringer High Sch
BN1. . . . . 169 F3
Dorset Ave RH19 . . . . .9 C3
Dorset Cl BN17 . . . . 204 C5
Dorset Ct
3 Horsham RH12 . . . . 36 D2
Hove BN3. . . . . 190 F6
Dorset Gdns
Brighton BN2. . . . . 213 C2
East Grinstead RH19 . . . . 9 C3
Dorset Ho RH13. . . . . 80 D7
Dorset House Sch
RH20. . . . . 140 B7
Dorset Lo BN15 . . . . 187 E7
Dorset Mews
Brighton BN2. . . . . 213 B2
East Grinstead RH19 . . . . 9 C3
Dorset Pl
Brighton BN2. . . . . 213 C2
5 Worthing BN14 . . . . 186 A5
Dorset Rd PO21. . . . . 201 C5
Dorset St BN2 . . . . 213 B2
Dorsten Sq RH11 . . . . 17 F3
Doubledays RH15. . . . . . . 109 B2
Douglas Ave BN11 . . . . . . 185 F3
Douglas Cl
4 Middleton-on-S
PO22. . . . . 202 F5
Worthing BN11 . . . . 185 F3
Yapton BN18 . . . . 181 B2
Douglas Martin Rd
PO19. . . . . 177 B7
Dove Cl RH11 . . . . 18 D8
Dovecote Mews
Lancing BN15. . . . . 187 C8
14 Shoreham-by-S
BN43. . . . . 166 F1
Dove Ct PO22. . . . . 201 B5
Dovedale Cres RH11 . . . . . 18 B4
Doveleys Ct BN43 . . . . . . 188 F6
Dover Cl RH13 . . . . 57 F2
Dovercourt PO22 . . . . 201 A6
Dover La BN16, BN18 . . . . 183 E8
Dover Rd
Brighton BN1. . . . . 170 A2
Worthing BN11 . . . . 186 A1
Dower Cl BN2 . . . . 193 D3
Dower Wlk RH11 . . . . 18 A5
Dowlands La RH10, RH6. . . .7 D7
Downash Cl BN2. . . . . . . 192 E6
Down Cl GU29 . . . . 115 C8
Down Cotts PO18 . . . . . . 132 A8
Downe Cl RH6 . . . . .1 E5
Downes Ct **9** BN43 . . . . . 189 C8
Downe Wlk BN13 . . . . . . 185 D6
Downey Lo RH11. . . . . . . 18 E4
Downford **15** BN2 . . . . . 192 F5
Downhill View BN2 . . . . . 193 E7
Downing Cl PO21 . . . . . . 200 E4
Downland Ave BN42 . . . . 167 E1
Downland Cl
Findon BN14 . . . . 163 E6
Southwick BN42 . . . . . . 167 D1
Upper Beeding BN44. . . . 146 B2
Woodingdean BN2. . . . . 193 B8
Downland Cres BN3. . . . . 168 F3
Downland Ct
Chichester PO19 . . . . . . 176 F8
Crawley RH11 . . . . 18 C4
Portslade-by-S BN41. . . . 168 A2
Downland Dr
Crawley RH11 . . . . 18 C3
Hove BN3. . . . . 168 F3
Downland Park Cvn Pk
BN44 . . . . 145 F1
Downland Pl RH11 . . . . . . 18 C4
Downland Rd
Upper Beeding BN44. . . . 146 B2
Woodingdean BN2. . . . . 193 B8
Downlands
Cootham RH20. . . . . 121 B1

Downlands continued
Partridge Green RH13 . . . 104 F3
Pulborough RH20. . . . . . 100 D2
Worthing BN13 . . . . 163 E2
Downlands Ave BN14 . . . . 186 D6
Downlands Bsns Pk
BN14 . . . . 186 E8
Downlands Cl
Bognor Regis PO21. . . . . 200 A2
Lancing BN15. . . . . 187 C7
Downlands Com Sch
BN6. . . . . 128 F3
Downlands Gdns
BN14 . . . . 186 E7
Downlands Par BN14. . . . . 186 E7
Downlands Ret Ctr
BN14. . . . . 186 E7
Downsbrook Mid Sch
BN14 . . . . 186 E5
Downsbrook Trad Est
BN14. . . . . 186 E6
Downs Cl BN15 . . . . 188 B6
Downscroft
Burgess Hill RH15 . . . . . 109 D6
Upper Beeding BN44. . . . 146 B1
Downside
Brighton BN1. . . . . 169 D5
Hove BN3. . . . . 169 B3
Downside Ave BN14. . . . . 163 F3
Downside Cl
Shoreham-by-S BN43. . . 166 F1
Worthing BN14 . . . . 163 F3
Downside Ct **6** BN16 . . . 205 B3
Downs Inf Sch BN1 . . . . . 192 B8
Downs Jun Sch BN1 . . . . . 170 A1
Downsman Ct RH10 . . . . . 18 D3
Downs Mead BN15 . . . . . 187 C8
Downs Park Sch
BN41. . . . . 168 B2
Downs Rd
Burgess Hill RH15 . . . . . 108 E4
West Stoke PO18. . . . . . 153 D6
Down St PO18 . . . . 153 B3
Downs Valley Rd BN2 . . . . 193 E8
Downsview
Brighton BN1. . . . . 169 E1
Hove BN3. . . . . 168 D3
Hurstpierpoint BN6 . . . . 128 A3
Small Dole BN5 . . . . 146 F7
Downsview Ave
Storrington BN20 . . . . . . 121 E2
Woodingdean BN2. . . . . 193 C8
Downsview Cotts RH14. . . 79 D8
Downsview Dr GU29 . . . . . 94 E5
Downsview Rd
Horsham RH12 . . . . 37 B6
Kingston Gorse BN16 . . . 206 D4
Portslade-by-S BN41. . . . 168 D4
Downs View Rd BN6 . . . . 128 F3
Downs View Specl Sch
BN2. . . . . 193 C8
Downsview Terr BN5. . . . . 125 D5
Downsway
Shoreham-by-S BN43. . . 166 F1
Southwick BN42 . . . . . . 167 F1
Woodingdean BN2. . . . . 171 D1
Downs Way BN16 . . . . . . 205 F7
Down Terr BN2 . . . . 192 C6
Down The BN3 . . . . 168 D4
Downview Ave BN12 . . . . 206 E7
Downview Cl
East Wittering PO20 . . . . 208 A6
Mid Lavant PO18 . . . . . . 154 E6
Yapton BN18 . . . . 181 B2
Downview Ct **8**
BN11 . . . . 186 A1
Downview Manor
BN14 . . . . 186 C6
Downview Prim Sch
PO22. . . . . 201 F6
Downview Rd
Barnham PO22. . . . . 180 A7
Bognor Regis PO22 . . . . 202 A5
Ferring BN12. . . . . 206 E7
Findon BN14 . . . . 163 E7
Petworth GU28 . . . . 97 E7
Worthing BN11 . . . . 186 A2
Yapton BN18 . . . . 181 A3
Downview Way BN18. . . . . 181 A3
Doyle Ct GU27 . . . . 27 A6
Dragons Green Council
Cotts RH13. . . . . 81 C3
Dragons Green Rd
RH13 . . . . 81 C5
Dragons La
Dragons Green RH13. . . . 81 C3
Partridge Green RH13. . . 105 E7
Dragon St GU31, GU32 . . . 68 B3
Drake Ave BN12 . . . . 185 D5
Drake Cl RH12 . . . . 36 E6
Drake Gr BN16 . . . . 181 B2
Drakeleys Field GU30 . . . . 47 B2
Drake Pk PO22 . . . . 202 C5
Drake Rd
Crawley RH10 . . . . 18 E3
Horley RH6 . . . . 1 E3
Drakes Cl BN15 . . . . 188 B6
Draxmont Way BN1 . . . . . 169 F3
Draycliff Cl BN12 . . . . 206 E5
Drayman's Mews
PO19. . . . . 177 B6
DRAYTON 177 F5
Drayton La PO20 . . . . 178 A5
Drayton Pk PO20. . . . . . . 178 A4
Drewetts Cl **1** BN16 . . . . 205 B7
Drewitts Mews PO20 . . . . 178 C7

Drift La
Nutbourne PO18 . . . . . . 174 E8
Selsey PO20. . . . . 212 C7
Drift Rd
Bognor Regis PO21. . . . . 200 B2
Selsey PO20. . . . . 212 G8
Drift The PO9. . . . . 130 D1
Driftway The
Littlehampton BN16. . . . . 205 B7
Upper Beeding BN44. . . . 146 B3
Drive Lo **10** BN3. . . . . . . 191 C7
Drive Prep Sch The
BN3. . . . . 191 C8
Drive The
Bognor Regis PO21. . . . . 200 D1
Bosham PO18 . . . . 175 C4
Burgess Hill RH15 . . . . . 109 B4
Chichester PO19 . . . . . . 155 A3
Copthorne RH10 . . . . 7 C3
East Lavington GU28 . . . 116 E5
Fontwell PO20 . . . . 158 A1
Horley RH6 . . . . 2 B1
Hove BN3. . . . . 191 C7
Ifold RH14 . . . . 31 D2
Lancing BN15. . . . . 187 D4
Shoreham-by-S BN43. . . 166 F1
Southbourne PO10 . . . . 173 F8
Southwick BN42 . . . . . . 167 E1
Westhampnett PO18 . . . 155 E2
West Kingston BN16 . . . 206 B4
Worthing BN11 . . . . 185 F4
Driveway The BN43 . . . . . 166 F1
DROKE 137 B6
Droke La PO18. . . . . 136 E6
Dropping Holms BN5 . . . . 125 D4
Drove Ave BN2 . . . . 171 D2
Drove Cres BN41. . . . . . . 168 C2
Drove La
Earnley PO20. . . . . 208 D5
Yapton BN18 . . . . 180 D2
Drove Rd
Portslade-by-S BN41. . . . 168 A1
Woodingdean BN2. . . . . 193 B8
Drovers RH17. . . . . 85 C3
Drovers Cl BN41 . . . . 168 C2
Drovers Way RH15 . . . . . . 109 C1
Drove The
Brighton BN1. . . . . 169 D1
Falmer BN1. . . . . 171 C5
Droveway The
Haywards Heath RH16 . . 87 C6
Hove BN3. . . . . 169 B1
Hove BN3. . . . . 169 C1
Drum La GU32 . . . . 68 B3
Drum Mead GU32 . . . . . . 68 A3
Drummond Cl RH16. . . . . . 87 D4
Drummond Ct
Haywards Heath RH16 . . 87 D4
7 Littlehampton BN17 . . . 204 D5
Drummond Rd
Crawley RH11. . . . . 17 E5
Worthing BN12 . . . . 185 E2
Drungewick La RH14 . . . . . 32 D2
Drury Cl RH10 . . . . 19 D4
Drury Lo **6** RH19 . . . . . . .9 F2
Dryad Way PO22 . . . . 202 D2
Dryden Way GU30 . . . . . . 25 A5
Drygrounds La PO22 . . . . 201 F5
Duck La
Midhurst GU29 . . . . 94 F7
Selsey PO20. . . . . 212 B8
Duckmead La GU33 . . . . . 45 D5
Duckyls Cotts RH19 . . . . . 42 D7
Dudeney Lo BN1. . . . . . . 170 B1
Dudley Mews **16** BN3. . . . 191 D5
Dudley Rd BN1 . . . . 170 B1
Dudley Terr GU33. . . . . . . 45 C5
Dudwell Rd BN2 . . . . 193 E7
Duffield La PO10. . . . . . . 152 A3
Duke Cl RH10. . . . . 19 C2
Dukes Barn Ct RH16 . . . . . 88 B7
Dukes Cl
Arundel BN18 . . . . 159 F2
Petersfield GU32 . . . . . . 67 F4
Westbourne PO10 . . . . . 151 D3
Duke's Cl BN1 . . . . 213 A2
Duke's Ct
Chichester PO19 . . . . . . 177 D5
12 Littlehampton BN17 . . . 204 D5
Duke's Hill RH20. . . . . . . 122 A8
Dukes La
Brighton BN1. . . . . 213 A2
Steyning BN44 . . . . 145 D3
Dukes Mdw
Bognor Regis PO21. . . . . 200 B3
Funtington PO18 . . . . . . 152 F5
Duke's Mound BN2 . . . . . 192 D4
Dukes Rd RH16 . . . . 88 B8
Duke's Rd
Fontwell BN18 . . . . 157 F4
Newdigate RH5 . . . . 3 D6
Dukes Row RH20 . . . . . . 121 A2
Dukes Sq RH12 . . . . 36 C1
Duke St
Brighton BN1. . . . . 213 A2
Littlehampton BN17. . . . . 204 D5
Dukes Yd BN44 . . . . 145 D3
Dulcima Ho **18** RH12 . . . . 36 C2
Dumbrells Court Rd
BN6. . . . . 129 D4
Dumbrells Ct BN6. . . . . . 129 D4
Dumbrills Cl RH15 . . . . . . 109 A5
Dumpford La GU31. . . . . . 92 D8
Duncan Rd PO19 . . . . 176 F8
Dunctan CE Fst Sch
GU28. . . . . 117 B7
Dunctan Cl
Bognor Regis PO22 . . . . 202 B4

Duncton Cl continued
Crawley RH11 . . . . 18 B8
Haywards Heath RH16 . . 87 D4
Duncton High St
GU28 . . . . 117 B6
Duncton Ho BN6 . . . . . . 128 E4
Duncton Rd BN16 . . . . . 205 C6
Dunes The PO21 . . . . . . 211 C8
Dunford Hollow GU31 . . . 94 F4
Dunhurst (Bedales Jun
Sch) GU32 . . . . 68 A6
Dunlop Cl BN6 . . . . 107 D1
Dunn's Rd RH19 . . . . . . 22 E7
Dunnock Cl PO21 . . . . . 130 D1
Dunsfold Cl RH11 . . . . . . 18 A5
Dunsfold Rd GU8, RH14 . . 30 D4
Dunstall Ave RH15 . . . . 108 E4
Dunstall Farm Rd
RH15 . . . . 108 F4
Dunstan Cl PO19 . . . . . 155 A3
Dunster Cl BN1 . . . . . . 170 B1
Dunwich 7 BN43 . . . . . 189 B6
Durban Pk PO22 . . . . . . 201 D5
Durban Rd PO22 . . . . . . 201 D6
Durbans Rd RH14 . . . . . . 54 C2
Durfold Rd RH12 . . . . . . 36 D7
Durfold Wood RH14 . . . . 30 D5
Durfold Wood Woodlands
Wlks★ GU8 . . . . 30 C6
Durford Rd GU31 . . . . . . 68 E3
Durham Cl
Bognor Regis PO21 . . . . 211 A8
Brighton BN2 . . . . 171 A1
Crawley RH10 . . . . 18 E2
Durham Cl 4 BN3 . . . . . 191 B6
Durham Gdns PO19 . . . . 154 F1
Durkins Rd RH19 . . . . 9 D3
Durlston Dr PO22 . . . . . 201 B6
Durlston Par PO22 . . . . . 201 B6
Durnford Cl PO19 . . . . . 176 E7
DURRINGTON 185 E8
Durrington Ct
Brighton BN1 . . . . 169 D5
Worthing BN13 . . . . 185 D8
Durrington Fst Sch
BN13 . . . . 185 E8
Durrington Gdns
BN12 . . . . 185 D4
Durrington High Sch
BN13 . . . . 185 E6
Durrington Hill BN13 . . . 185 D8
Durrington La BN13 . . . . 185 D7
Durrington Mid Sch
BN13 . . . . 185 E8
Durrington-on-Sea Sta
BN12 . . . . 185 E4
Dutchells Copse RH12 . . . 36 E7
Duxford Cl PO20 . . . . . 156 C2
Duxhurst La RH2 . . . . 1 B7
Dyall Cl RH15 . . . . 108 E4
Dye House La GU28 . . . . 117 C7
Dyers Almshouses
RH10 . . . . 18 D7
Dyers La BN18 . . . . 158 C5
Dyke Cl
Hove BN3 . . . . 169 B4
Poynings BN45 . . . . . . 148 C4
Dyke Rd BN1, BN3 . . . . . 191 E7
Dyke Road Ave BN1,
BN3 . . . . 169 C3
Dyke Road Dr BN1 . . . . . 191 F8
Dyke Road Mews
BN1 . . . . 213 A4
Dyke Road Pl BN1 . . . . . 169 C3
Dymock's The BN6 . . . . 129 D3
Dymoke St PO10 . . . . . 151 A4
Dyson Wlk RH11 . . . . . . 18 B1

E

Eady Cl RH13 . . . . 36 F2
Eagle Ct 13 BN2 . . . . . . 192 C8
Eagle Est RH14 . . . . 79 D7
Eagle Ho 16 PO21 . . . . . 201 B2
Eagles Chase BN17 . . . . 204 D8
Earle Ho 2 RH19 . . . . 9 F2
Earles Mdw RH12 . . . . . . 37 B6
Earlswood Rd RH13 . . . . . 37 A4
Early Commons RH10 . . . . 18 F7
Earnley Gdns★ PO20 . . . 208 E7
Earnley Manor Cl
PO20 . . . . 208 D7
Earnley Rd PO11 . . . . . . 195 B2
Eartham Trail★ PO18 . . . 137 D2
Earwig La RH17 . . . . 84 E6
EASEBOURNE 73 B2
Easebourne CE Prim Sch
GU29 . . . . 73 B2
Easebourne La GU29 . . . . 73 A1
Easebourne St GU28,
GU29 . . . . 73 D5
East Ave
Middleton-on-S PO22 . . . 202 F6
Worthing BN12 . . . . 185 F2
Eastbank BN42 . . . . 167 F1
East Bank
Selsey PO20 . . . . 212 F7
Yapton BN18 . . . . 181 A5
East Bank Wlk 2
BN17 . . . . 205 A4
EAST BEACH 212 F8
East Beach Rd PO20 . . . . 212 G8
Eastbourne Rd
Brighton BN2 . . . . 170 D1
Felbridge RH7 . . . . 8 E8
East Bracklesham Dr
PO20 . . . . 208 B5

Eastbrook Rd BN41 . . . . 190 B7
Eastbrook Way BN42 . . . 190 A7
East Cl PO22 . . . . 202 E5
Eastcourt Rd BN14 . . . . 186 D4
Eastcourt Villas 3 RH19 . . . 9 F2
East Court Way BN16 . . . 205 E6
Eastcroft Mews 2
RH12 . . . . 35 F1
East Ct BN14 . . . . 186 D5
Eastdale Rd RH15 . . . . . 109 D4
East Dean 1 PO22 . . . . . 201 D5
Eastdean Hill PO18 . . . . 136 C5
East Dr
Angmering BN16 . . . . . . 205 E7
Brighton BN2 . . . . 192 C5
Middleton-on-S PO22 . . . 203 A5
Easteds La RH13 . . . . 58 A2
EAST END 129 E3
East End La BN6 . . . . . . 129 D3
Eastergate CE Prim Sch
PO20 . . . . 179 E7
Eastergate Cl BN12 . . . . 206 F7
Eastergate Gn 8
BN16 . . . . 205 C5
Eastergate La BN18,
PO20 . . . . 158 B1
Eastergate Rd BN2 . . . . . 170 F4
Eastern Ave BN43 . . . . . 189 A7
Eastern Cl
East Preston BN16 . . . . . 206 B6
Shoreham-by-S BN43 . . . 189 A7
Eastern Concourse
BN2 . . . . 193 A2
Eastern Cotts RH16 . . . . . 88 B7
Eastern Pl BN2 . . . . 192 E4
Eastern Rd
Brighton BN2 . . . . 192 D4
Haywards Heath RH16 . . . 87 F3
Lindfield RH16 . . . . 88 C7
Eastern Ring Rd BN1 . . . 171 C7
Eastern St 22 BN2 . . . . . 192 D4
Eastern Terr
10 Brighton BN2 . . . . . 192 D4
Henfield BN5 . . . . 125 F5
Eastern Terrace Mews 9
BN2 . . . . 192 D4
East Field Cl PO10 . . . . . 152 A1
Eastfield Cres BN1 . . . . . 170 A4
Eastfield Ho 4 BN11 . . . . 186 F2
Eastfield La GU31 . . . . . . 92 A4
East Front Rd PO21 . . . . 211 A4
Eastgate Ct PO19 . . . . . 177 B6
Eastgate Ho PO19 . . . . . 177 B6
Eastgate Mews 4
RH13 . . . . 36 D1
Eastgate Sq PO19 . . . . . 177 A6
East Gdns BN6 . . . . 129 D3
East Grinstead Sta
RH19 . . . . 9 D1
East Grinstead Town
Mus★ RH19 . . . . 9 F1
East Gun Copse RH13 . . . 57 D5
EAST HAMPNETT 156 E2
Easthampnett Cvn Pk
PO18 . . . . 157 A2
East Hampnett La
PO18 . . . . 156 F2
East Ham Rd BN17 . . . . . 204 D5
East Harting St GU31 . . . . 91 F3
East Hill RH19 . . . . 9 E6
East Hill Ct
Liss GU33 . . . . 45 C3
1 Worthing BN11 . . . . . 186 D2
Easthill Dr BN41 . . . . . . 168 B2
East Hill Dr GU33 . . . . . . 45 C3
East Hill La RH10 . . . . 7 D5
Easthill Way BN41 . . . . . 168 B1
Easting Cl BN14 . . . . . . 186 F5
East Lake PO21 . . . . 201 D4
Eastlake Cl GU31 . . . . . . 68 E3
Eastland Rd PO19 . . . . . 177 B5
Eastleigh Ct BN13 . . . . . 185 E8
EAST LISS 45 C4
East Lo
4 Lancing BN15 . . . . . 187 E4
Rogate GU31 . . . . 70 B4
East Lockside BN2 . . . . . 193 A3
East Mascalls La RH16 . . . 88 E6
East Mead
Bognor Regis PO21 . . . . 211 A4
Ferring BN12 . . . . 206 F5
Eastmead Ind Est
PO18 . . . . 154 E7
East Meadway BN43 . . . . 189 A6
EAST MOULSECOOMB
. . . . 170 F3
Eastoke Ave PO11 . . . . . 195 A2
Easton Cres RH14 . . . . . . 79 E8
Easton La PO20 . . . . 209 A6
East Onslow Cl BN12 . . . 206 E6
Eastover Way PO22 . . . . 201 F4
East Pallant PO19 . . . . . 177 A6
East Park La RH7 . . . . 8 C8
East Pk RH10 . . . . 18 D5
Eastpoint PO20 . . . . 212 E7
East Point 6 BN43 . . . . . 189 A6
East Preston Inf Sch
BN16 . . . . 206 A6
East Preston Jun Sch
BN16 . . . . 206 A6
East Row PO19 . . . . 177 A6
East Row Mews 3
PO19 . . . . 177 A6
Eastshaw La GU29 . . . . . . 72 C4
East St
Amberley BN18 . . . . 140 E4
Billingshurst RH14 . . . . . 79 D8
Brighton BN1 . . . . 213 B1

East St continued
Chichester PO19 . . . . . . 177 A6
Falmer BN1 . . . . 171 C6
Horsham RH12 . . . . 36 C1
Lancing BN15 . . . . 187 E4
Littlehampton BN17 . . . . 204 E5
Petworth GU28 . . . . 97 F8
Portslade-by-S BN41 . . . 190 C7
Rogate GU31 . . . . 70 B4
Rusper RH12 . . . . 16 E7
Selsey PO20 . . . . 212 E7
Shoreham-by-S BN43 . . . 188 F7
Turners Hill RH10, RH19 . . 21 C4
Westbourne PO10 . . . . . 151 D3
West Chiltington RH20 . . 101 E1
East Strand PO20 . . . . . . 207 C8
East Tyne BN13 . . . . 185 D7
East View PO18 . . . . 154 F7
East Walls PO19 . . . . . . 177 A6
East Walls Cl 2 PO19 . . . 177 A6
Eastway RH6 . . . . 6 B7
East Way PO20 . . . . 212 F7
Eastway E RH6 . . . . 6 C7
East Wick RH16 . . . . 88 C7
Eastwick Cl BN1 . . . . . . 170 B7
Eastwood Rd BN14 . . . . 186 F5
EAST WORTHING 187 A3
East Worthing Ind Est
BN14 . . . . 186 F5
East Worthing Sta
BN11 . . . . 186 F4
Eaton Ct
9 Hove BN3 . . . . 191 B7
Worthing BN14 . . . . 186 B6
Eaton Gardens Mans 20
BN3 . . . . 191 C7
Eaton Gate 17 BN3 . . . . . 191 C7
Eaton Gdns BN3 . . . . . . 191 C7
Eaton Gr BN3 . . . . 191 C7
Eaton Hall 18 BN3 . . . . . 191 C7
Eaton Manor 11 BN3 . . . 191 C7
Eaton Pl BN2 . . . . 192 D4
Eaton Rd BN3 . . . . 191 C7
Eaton Villas BN3 . . . . . . 191 B7
Ebbisham Ct RH19 . . . . . . 9 A4
Ecclesden 7 BN2 . . . . . . 213 C3
Edburton Ave BN1 . . . . . 170 A1
Edburton Dro BN5 . . . . . 147 D6
Edburton Gdns BN43 . . . 166 F1
Eddington Hill RH11 . . . . 18 B1
Eden Rd RH10 . . . . 17 F4
Eden Vale
Dormans Park RH19 . . . . . 9 F5
East Grinstead RH19 . . . . . 9 D4
Edgar Cl RH10 . . . . 19 E5
Edgehill Cl BN13 . . . . . . 185 F8
Edgehill Way BN41 . . . . . 167 F2
Edgell Rd PO10 . . . . 151 D4
Edgewood Ct GU33 . . . . . 45 D2
Edinburgh Cl
Bognor Regis PO21 . . . . 200 E2
Southwater RH13 . . . . . . 58 A1
Edinburgh Cotts
BN11 . . . . 186 C1
Edinburgh Ho 9 RH11 . . . 18 B2
Edinburgh Rd 8 BN2 . . . 192 B8
Edinburgh Sq GU29 . . . . . 94 F7
Edinburgh Way RH19 . . . . 22 F7
Edith Cotts PO18 . . . . . . 153 A2
Edmonds Ho GU28 . . . . . . 97 F7
Edmonton Rd BN13 . . . . 185 D7
Edrich Rd RH11 . . . . 18 A1
Edster Ct BN41 . . . . 167 F3
Edward Ave
Hove BN3 . . . . 169 A3
Saltdean BN2 . . . . 194 D3
Edward Bryant Prim Sch
PO21 . . . . 201 D4
Edward Cl BN3 . . . . 169 A3
Edward Ho
Hove BN3 . . . . 190 F6
Selsey PO20 . . . . 212 E8
Edward Rd RH16 . . . . 87 D4
Edwards Ave PO20 . . . . . 156 C2
Edward St BN2 . . . . 213 C2
Edwards Terr BN15 . . . . . 186 F7
Edwards Way BN17 . . . . 204 C8
Edward Way RH15 . . . . . 108 D2
Edwen Cl PO21 . . . . 200 B3
Edwin Cl BN15 . . . . 187 C6
Eels Cross PO20 . . . . . . 212 B8
Effingham Cl BN2 . . . . . 194 C2
Effingham La 4 RH11 . . . . 7 E4
Effingham Rd RH10, RH6 . . 7 D6
Egan Way BN17 . . . . 204 C6
EGDEAN 98 D4
Egdean Cotts RH20 . . . . . 98 D5
Egginton Cl BN1 . . . . . . 171 A5
Egginton Rd BN2 . . . . . . 170 F5
Egmont Ho GU29 . . . . . . 73 A1
Egmont Mews GU29 . . . . 94 F8
Egmont Rd
Hove BN3 . . . . 168 D1
Midhurst GU29 . . . . 73 A1
Egremont Pl BN2 . . . . . . 213 C2
Egremont Row GU28 . . . . 97 F8
Eighth Ave BN15 . . . . . . 187 E7
Eileen Ave BN2 . . . . 194 B1
Eirene Ave BN12 . . . . . . 185 F2
Eirene Rd BN11, BN12 . . . 185 F2
Elbourne Ho 3 RH6 . . . . . 2 B3
ELBRIDGE 178 E1
Elbridge Cres PO21 . . . . 200 C4
Elcombe Cl PO20 . . . . . . 208 C5

Elder Cl BN41 . . . . 168 B2
Elderfield Cl PO10 . . . . . 151 C3
Elder Pl BN1 . . . . 213 B4
Eldon Rd BN1 . . . . 186 F3
Eldon Way BN17 . . . . . . 204 B6
Eldred Ave BN1 . . . . 169 D5
Eleanor Cl GU30 . . . . 24 D8
Eleanor Ct 1 BN11 . . . . . 185 F3
Eleanor Gdns PO22 . . . . 202 D5
Eley Cres BN2 . . . . 193 B3
Eley Dr BN2 . . . . 193 B3
Elfin Gr PO21 . . . . 201 B3
Elfin Mews 1 PO21 . . . . . 201 B3
Elgar Way RH10 . . . . 37 B4
Elger Way RH10 . . . . 7 A4
Elgin Cl RH13 . . . . 36 F3
Elgin Ct PO19 . . . . 177 A5
Elgin Rd BN12 . . . . 185 D3
Elim Ct BN2 . . . . 213 C4
Eliot Dr GU27 . . . . 26 E6
Eliot Ho 5 RH16 . . . . 87 E3
Elizabethan Way RH10 . . . 19 C5
Elizabeth Ave
Bognor Regis PO21 . . . . 200 D4
Hove BN3 . . . . 169 A3
Elizabeth Cl
Bognor Regis PO21 . . . . 200 C3
Hove BN3 . . . . 169 A3
Elizabeth Cres RH19 . . . . . 9 F3
Elizabeth Ct
9 Bognor Regis
PO21 . . . . 201 B2
Horley RH6 . . . . 2 A3
7 Hove BN3 . . . . 191 C7
6 Worthing BN11 . . . . . 185 F3
Elizabeth Ho
11 Bognor Regis
PO21 . . . . 201 D3
Bognor Regis PO21 . . . . 201 E4
2 Worthing BN13 . . . . . 186 A5
Elizabeth Pl BN15 . . . . . 187 C5
Elizabeth Rd
Chichester PO19 . . . . . . 177 D7
Shoreham-by-S BN43 . . . 189 C8
Worthing BN11 . . . . 186 C2
Elkham Cnr GU28 . . . . . . 52 C1
Ella Cl PO20 . . . . 207 E7
Ellanore La PO20 . . . . . . 196 B2
Ellasdale Rd PO21 . . . . . 201 B2
Ella Terr BN18 . . . . 183 C8
Ellen Ho 3 BN3 . . . . 191 B7
Ellen St
Hove BN3 . . . . 191 B7
Portslade-by-S BN41 . . . 190 C7
Ellesmere Orch PO10 . . . 151 D5
Elliot Cl RH10 . . . . 19 C4
Ellis Ave BN13 . . . . 163 E6
Ellis Ct BN18 . . . . 159 F2
Ellis Sq PO20 . . . . 212 F8
Ellis Way PO21 . . . . 211 A8
Ellman Rd RH11 . . . . 17 F4
Ellson Cl RH11 . . . . 19 C4
Elm Ave BN16 . . . . 206 B6
Elm Cl
Bognor Regis PO21 . . . . 200 A1
Bracklesham PO20 . . . . 208 B6
Hove BN3 . . . . 169 C2
North Mundham PO20 . . 177 C1
Shoreham-by-S BN43 . . . 166 F1
Elm Cotts BN13 . . . . 185 D7
Elm Croft Ct RH10 . . . . . 18 E6
Elmcroft Pl PO20 . . . . . . 179 D6
Elm Ct
8 Bognor Regis
PO21 . . . . 201 C2
Brighton BN1 . . . . 191 E8
3 East Grinstead RH19 . . . 9 D2
East Grinstead, Sunnyside
RH19 . . . . 22 E8
Nepcote BN14 . . . . 163 E5
Portslade-by-S BN41 . . . 190 B8
Worthing BN12 . . . . 185 C3
Elmdale GU31 . . . . 68 C4
Elm Dale PO22 . . . . 180 A6
Elmdene Ct PO20 . . . . . 208 B5
Elm Dr
East Grinstead RH19 . . . . 10 A1
Elmer PO22 . . . . 203 B5
Hove BN3 . . . . 168 E1
Petersfield GU31 . . . . . . 68 A1
Elmer Cl PO22 . . . . 203 B5
Elmer Ct PO22 . . . . 203 C5
Elmer Rd PO22 . . . . 202 F5
Elm Farm Cotts BN16 . . . 205 B5
Elm Gr
Barnham PO22 . . . . 180 B7
Bognor Regis PO21 . . . . 201 A3
Brighton BN2 . . . . 192 C5
Cowfold RH13 . . . . 83 E2
Horsham RH13 . . . . 36 E1
Lancing BN15 . . . . 187 D5
Runcton PO20 . . . . 177 E1
Selsey PO20 . . . . 212 D7
Worthing BN11 . . . . 185 E6
Elm Grove Fst Sch
BN11 . . . . 185 F3
Elm Grove Ho BN15 . . . . 187 E5
Elm Grove Inf Sch
BN17 . . . . 204 E6
Elm Grove La BN44 . . . . 145 D3
Elm Grove Prim Sch
BN2 . . . . 192 C7
Elm Grove Rd BN17 . . . . 204 F6
Elm Gr S PO22 . . . . 180 A6
Elmhurst Cl BN16 . . . . . 184 A6
Elmhurst La RH13 . . . . . . 56 C6
Elmleigh GU29 . . . . 94 D8
Elmleigh Ct GU29 . . . . . . 94 E8

Elm Mews BN13 . . . . . . 185 D7
Elmore Ct BN2 . . . . 213 C3
Elmore Rd BN2 . . . . 213 C3
Elm Pk
Bosham PO18 . . . . 175 C6
Ferring BN12 . . . . 206 F7
Elm Pl BN16 . . . . 205 D6
Elm Rd
Portslade-by-S BN41 . . . 190 B8
Westergate PO20 . . . . . 179 E7
Worthing BN11 . . . . 186 E2
Elm Rise BN14 . . . . 163 E6
Elms Dr BN15 . . . . 187 D6
Elmsfield PO20 . . . . 212 E7
Elms La PO20 . . . . 196 D1
Elms Lea Ave BN1 . . . . . 169 E3
Elms Ride PO20 . . . . 196 C1
Elmstead RH19 . . . . 22 E8
Elmstead Gdns PO20 . . . 196 C2
Elmstead Park Rd
PO20 . . . . 196 C2
Elmstone Cl BN15 . . . . . 187 D6
Elms Way PO20 . . . . 196 C2
Elm Terr
Liss GU33 . . . . 45 A5
Steyning BN44 . . . . 145 D3
Elm Tree Cl
Bognor Regis PO21 . . . . 201 A6
Selsey PO20 . . . . 212 E8
Elm Tree Cotts PO20 . . . 179 D8
Elmwood Ave PO22 . . . . 201 D5
Elrington Rd BN3 . . . . . . 169 C1
Elsaw Ct PO19 . . . . 177 A5
Elsie Rd BN11 . . . . 186 B1
Elspring Mead BN17 . . . . 204 C7
Elsted Cl RH11 . . . . 18 B8
Elsted Cres BN1 . . . . . . 170 C6
Elsted Rd GU29 . . . . 93 C7
Elverlands Cl 5 BN12 . . . 206 F4
Elvin Cres BN2 . . . . 193 C4
Elwood Cl RH15 . . . . . . 108 F1
Elwyn Jones Ct BN1 . . . . 169 E4
Ely Cl
Crawley RH10 . . . . 18 F2
East Wittering PO20 . . . . 207 F8
Worthing BN13 . . . . 185 F5
Ely Gdns PO21 . . . . 200 D3
Ely Rd BN13 . . . . 185 F5
Embassy Ct
10 Brighton BN1 . . . . . 191 D5
4 Haywards Heath
RH16 . . . . 87 E6
Emberwood RH11 . . . . . . 18 D8
Emerald Quay BN43 . . . . 189 A6
Emlyn Rd RH6 . . . . 1 E4
Emmabrook Ct BN16 . . . 205 A3
Emms La RH13 . . . . 80 F7
Empire Villas RH1 . . . . . . 2 A7
Emsbrook Dr PO10 . . . . 151 B2
Emsworth Cl RH10 . . . . . 19 C3
Emsworth Common Rd
PO10, PO9 . . . . 151 C6
Emsworth House Cl
PO10 . . . . 151 A1
Emsworth Mus★
PO10 . . . . 173 B8
Emsworth Prim Sch
PO10 . . . . 151 A1
Emsworth Rd PO10 . . . . 173 D2
Emsworth Sta PO10 . . . . 151 B1
End Cotts BN18 . . . . 140 E6
Enfield Rd RH11 . . . . 18 C2
Engalee RH19 . . . . 9 C2
Englefield RH12 . . . . 35 F2
English Bsns Pk BN3 . . . 190 E8
English Cl BN3 . . . . 190 E8
English Martyrs RC Prim
Sch BN12 . . . . 185 D6
Enholms La RH17 . . . . . . 66 A4
Ennerdale Cl RH11 . . . . . 18 B4
Ennerdale Dr BN15 . . . . 187 B5
Ensign Way BN17 . . . . . 205 A6
Enterprise Ct
Crawley RH10 . . . . 5 D2
Worthing BN12 . . . . 185 C4
Enterprise Ctr The RH10 . . . 5 F2
Enterprise Est BN1 . . . . 170 C2
Enterprise Point BN2 . . . 192 C8
Epping Wlk RH10 . . . . . . 18 F4
Epsom Gdns BN16 . . . . . 205 E6
Epsom Rd RH10 . . . . 19 A4
Erica Way
Copthorne RH10 . . . . 7 A2
Horsham RH12 . . . . 36 D5
Ericsson Way RH15 . . . . 108 D2
Eridge Cl RH10 . . . . 19 C6
Eridge Rd BN3 . . . . 169 A2
Erin Way RH15 . . . . 108 E3
Eriskay Ct BN13 . . . . . . 185 B7
Eriswell Rd BN11 . . . . . . 186 C1
Erles Rd GU30 . . . . 25 C4
Ernest Cl PO10 . . . . 151 B1
Erringham Rd BN43 . . . . 166 E1
Erroll Mans 7 BN3 . . . . . 190 D7
Erroll Rd BN3 . . . . 190 C6
Erskine Cl RH11 . . . . 17 E2
Esher Cl PO21 . . . . 200 B2
Esher Dr BN17 . . . . 204 F6
Eskbank Ave BN1 . . . . . 170 A7
Esmond Cl PO10 . . . . . . 173 B8
Esmonde Cl BN17 . . . . . 204 F6
Esplanade Ct 6 BN11 . . . 186 F2
Esplanade The
Bognor Regis, Felpham
PO22 . . . . 201 F3

Esplanade The continued
Bognor Regis PO21 . . . . . . **201** D2
Worthing BN11 . . . . **186** F2
Essenhigh Dr BN13 . . . . . **185** B7
Essex Ct BN11 . . . . **186** A2
Essex Pl 3 BN2 . . . . **192** C4
Essex Rd PO21 . . . . **201** C5
Essex St BN2 . . . . **192** C4
Estates Rd BN1 . . . . **171** B7
Estcots Dr RH19 . . . . **10** A1
Estcots Prim Sch RH19 . . . **10** A1
Estuary The BN17 . . . . . **204** F5
Ethelred Rd BN14 . . . . . . **186** A4
Ethel St BN3 . . . . **191** B7
Ethelwulf Rd BN14 . . . . . . **186** A4
Eton Cl PO21 . . . . **200** E4
Eton Dr PO20 . . . . **207** F8
Etonhurst 20 PO21 . . . . . **201** B2
Eton Rd BN11 . . . . **186** A3
Ettrick Cl PO19 . . . . **177** B5
Ettrick Rd PO19 . . . . **177** B5
Eurythmy Sch RH19 . . . . . . **22** E6
Evans Cl RH10 . . . . **19** D5
Evans Gdns 15 BN17 . . . . **204** D5
Evans Pl PO22 . . . . **201** D6
Evelyn Ave BN16 . . . . . . **205** D4
Evelyn Cl RH19 . . . . **8** F4
Evelyn Clark Ho RH18 . . . . **23** F2
Evelyn Cl BN41 . . . . **190** A8
Evelyn Glennie Ct 7
BN2 . . . . **192** C5
Evelyn Lancaster Ho
RH12 . . . . **36** E6
Evelyn Rd BN14 . . . . **186** D4
Evelyn Terr BN2 . . . . **192** C5
Evelyn Wlk RH10 . . . . **18** E3
Everest Ho 2 BN3 . . . . . **190** F7
Eversfield RH13 . . . . **58** B1
Eversfield Rd RH13 . . . . . . **36** E1
Evershed Way BN43 . . . . **189** B7
Eversleigh Ct GU29 . . . . . . **73** A2
Ewart St BN2 . . . . **213** C3
Ewelands RH6 . . . . **2** C4
Ewens Gdns PO22 . . . . . . **180** A7
Ewhurst Cl RH11 . . . . **18** C6
Ewhurst Rd
Brighton BN2 . . . . **170** C1
Crawley RH11 . . . . **18** C7
Excalibur Cl RH11 . . . . **17** E5
Exceat Cl PO22 . . . . **192** E6
Excelsior The BN1 . . . . . . **169** D4
Exchange Rd RH10 . . . . . . **18** E6
Exeter Cl
Bognor Regis PO21 . . . . . **200** F3
Crawley RH10 . . . . **18** E2
New Brighton PO10 . . . . . **151** B2
Exeter Ct 2 BN11 . . . . . **186** A1
Exeter Rd PO19 . . . . **154** E1
Exeter St BN1 . . . . **191** E8
Exford Wlk BN13 . . . . **185** D6
Exmoor Cl BN13 . . . . **185** E8
Exmoor Cres BN13 . . . . . . **185** E8
Exmoor Ct BN13 . . . . **185** E8
Exmoor Dr BN13 . . . . **185** E8
Exton Rd PO19 . . . . **177** A4
Eyles Cl RH12 . . . . **36** B4

F

Fabians Way BN5 . . . . **125** D5
Fairbank Rd RH13 . . . . **57** F1
Fairbanks RH16 . . . . **87** E4
Fairbridge Way RH15 . . . . **108** F5
Faircox La BN5 . . . . **125** D5
Fairdene BN42 . . . . **167** F1
Fairfield Ave RH6 . . . . **2** A1
Fairfield Cl
Ardingly RH17 . . . . **64** A8
Bosham PO18 . . . . **175** C5
Burgess Hill RH15 . . . . . **108** F4
New Brighton PO10 . . . . . **151** B2
Shoreham-by-S BN43 . . . **167** C1
Fairfield Cotts RH13 . . . . . **83** E2
Fairfield Cres BN6 . . . . . . **128** A6
Fairfield Ct RH13 . . . . **83** E2
Fairfield Gdns
Burgess Hill RH15 . . . . . **108** F4
Portslade-by-S BN41 . . . . **168** B1
Fairfield Rd
Ashington RH20 . . . . **123** A4
Bosham PO18 . . . . **175** B5
Burgess Hill RH15 . . . . . **108** F4
East Grinstead RH19 . . . . . **22** F8
Fairfield Rise GU28 . . . . . . **97** F7
Fairfields
2 Worthing BN14 . . . . . **186** D4
Worthing, West Tarring
BN14 . . . . **186** A5
Fairfield Way
Ashington RH20 . . . . **123** A4
Haywards Heath RH16 . . . . **87** D8
Fairford Cl RH16 . . . . **87** E5
Fairholme Dr BN18 . . . . . . **181** A2
Fairlands
Bognor Regis PO22 . . . . . **201** B6
East Preston BN16 . . . . . **206** A5
8 Lancing BN15 . . . . **187** D5
Fairlawn
1 Haywards Heath
RH16 . . . . **87** E4
Rustington BN16 . . . . . . **205** C6
Fairlawn Cres RH19 . . . . **9** B2
Fairlawn Dr
East Grinstead RH19 . . . . . . **9** B2

Fairlawn Dr continued
Worthing BN14 . . . . **186** D4
Fairlawn Ho RH10 . . . . **19** A6
Fairlawns
Horley RH6 . . . . **2** B2
9 Hove BN3 . . . . **191** A6
Shoreham-by-S BN43 . . . **189** A8
Fairlea Cl RH15 . . . . **108** F4
Fairlead BN17 . . . . **204** F4
Fairlea Rd PO10 . . . . **151** B3
Fairlie Gdns BN13 . . . . . . **169** E3
Fairlight Ct BN17 . . . . **204** D4
Fairlight Pl 8 BN2 . . . . . **192** C8
Fairlight Prim Sch
BN2 . . . . **192** C8
Fairmead Cl RH10 . . . . **99** A3
Fairmile Bottom
BN18 . . . . **159** B7
Fairmile Bottom Nature
Trail★ BN18 . . . . **159** C8
Fairoak Ct 4 BN13 . . . . . **186** A5
Fairstone Ct RH6 . . . . **2** B4
Fair View RH12 . . . . **36** A3
Fairview Ave BN12 . . . . . . **185** C2
Fairview Cotts RH13 . . . . . **58** B3
Fairview Ct 13 RH19 . . . . . **22** F8
Fairview Gdns BN15 . . . . . **187** E8
Fairview Rd BN15 . . . . **187** E8
Fairview Rise BN1 . . . . . . **169** D5
Fairway
Copthorne RH10 . . . . **7** B2
Crawley RH11 . . . . **17** D4
Littlehampton BN17 . . . . . **205** A4
Fairway Bsns Ctr BN2 . . . **170** E4
Fairway Cres BN41 . . . . . . **168** C2
Fairway Inf Sch RH10 . . . . . **7** B3
Fairways BN1 . . . . **191** E8
Fairway The
Bognor Regis PO21 . . . . . **211** B8
Lancing BN15 . . . . **188** A5
Midhurst GU29 . . . . **94** E6
Rowland's Castle PO9 . . . **130** A4
Fairway Trad Est BN17 . . . **170** E4
Faithfull Cres RH20 . . . . . **121** B2
Falcon Cl
Crawley RH11 . . . . **18** D8
Shoreham-by-S BN43 . . . **189** C6
Falcon Gdns BN17 . . . . . . **204** C8
Falkland Ave BN17 . . . . . . **204** F4
Falklands Cl 4 PO22 . . . . **201** D5
Falklands Dr RH13 . . . . **37** B4
Fallow Deer Cl RH13 . . . . . **37** B4
Fallowfield Cl BN3 . . . . . . **168** F2
Fallowfield Cres BN3 . . . **168** F2
Fallowfield Way RH6 . . . . . . **2** B4
Falmer Ave
Rottingdean BN2 . . . . . . **194** B2
Worthing BN12 . . . . **185** B2
Falmer Cl
Crawley RH11 . . . . **18** D4
Worthing BN12 . . . . **185** C2
Falmer Gdns BN12 . . . . . . **193** D8
Falmer High Sch BN1 . . . . **171** A5
Falmer Hill BN1 . . . . **171** B6
Falmer House Rd
BN1 . . . . **171** B6
Falmer Rd BN2 . . . . **193** E5
Falmer Sta BN1 . . . . **171** B6
Famet Ct RH19 . . . . **9** C3
Faraday Ave RH19 . . . . **22** F6
Faraday Cl BN13 . . . . **185** C6
Faraday Ct RH10 . . . . **5** F1
Faraday Ctr The RH10 . . . . . **5** F1
Faraday Rd RH10 . . . . **5** F2
Farebrothers RH12 . . . . . . **35** F8
Faresmead PO21 . . . . **200** F2
Farhalls Cres RH12 . . . . . . **36** F6
Farlington Ave RH16 . . . . . **87** F5
Farlington Cl RH16 . . . . **87** F5
Farlington Sch RH12 . . . . . **35** B6
Farm Acre BN16 . . . . **205** F6
Farman St 15 BN3 . . . . . . **191** D5
Farm Ave RH12 . . . . **36** B3
Farm Cl
Barns Green RH13 . . . . . . **56** F2
Crawley RH10 . . . . **19** A7
East Grinstead RH19 . . . . . **23** B8
Elmer PO22 . . . . **203** B6
Fishbourne PO18 . . . . . . **176** A6
Hassocks BN6 . . . . **128** E4
Henfield BN5 . . . . **125** C5
Loxwood RH14 . . . . **32** A3
Portslade-by-S BN41 . . . . **168** A2
Warnham RH12 . . . . **35** F7
Farm Cnr PO22 . . . . **203** A5
Farm Cotts
Haywards Heath RH16 . . . . **87** C3
West Itchenor PO20 . . . . **196** F6
Farmfield Cl RH6 . . . . **5** B8
Farmfield Hospl (private)
RH6 . . . . **1** B1
Farm Hill BN2 . . . . **193** C8
Farm La
Ditchling BN6 . . . . **129** E3
Nutbourne PO18 . . . . . . **174** B7
Farmleigh Cl RH10 . . . . **18** C8
Farm Mews BN3 . . . . **191** D6
Farm Rd
Bracklesham PO20 . . . . . **208** B5
Hove BN3 . . . . **191** D6
Farm View PO10 . . . . **151** B3
Farm Way
Burgess Hill RH15 . . . . . **109** D1
Rustington BN16 . . . . . . **205** B5
Southwick BN42 . . . . **190** A7

Farmway Cl BN3 . . . . **168** D2
Farncombe Rd BN11 . . . . . **186** F2
Farndell Cl PO19 . . . . **177** C2
Farne Cl PO20 . . . . **197** E4
Farnefold Rd BN44 . . . . . . **145** D4
Farne La PO20 . . . . **197** E4
Farney Close Sch
RH17 . . . . **85** D2
Farnham Ave BN6 . . . . . . **129** A5
Farnham Cl RH11 . . . . **39** C8
Farnham La GU27 . . . . **27** A7
Farnham Rd
Liss GU33 . . . . **45** A4
Steep GU32 . . . . **68** D7
Farnhurst Rd PO22 . . . . . . **180** B6
Farnlea RH15 . . . . **109** D5
Faroes The BN17 . . . . **205** A6
Farr Cl RH17 . . . . **86** F8
Farriers Cl RH14 . . . . **79** C7
Farriers Ct RH12 . . . . **36** C2
FARTHER COMMONS **45** C1
Farthings Wlk RH12 . . . . . . **35** F3
Fastnet Way BN17 . . . . . . **205** A6
Faulkner Cl RH11 . . . . **39** C8
Faulkners Way RH15 . . . . . **109** A5
Fawn Rise BN5 . . . . **125** C6
Faygate Bsns Ctr RH12 . . . **16** F1
Faygate Cl BN2 . . . . **192** E6
Faygate La RH12 . . . . **16** F4
Faygate Sta RH12 . . . . **16** F1
Fay Rd RH12 . . . . **36** C5
Felbridge Ave RH10 . . . . . . **19** D7
Felbridge Cl RH19 . . . . **9** C3
Felbridge Ct RH19 . . . . **9** A3
Felbridge Ctr The RH19 . . . . **9** A3
Felbridge Prim Sch
RH19 . . . . **8** F4
Felbridge Rd RH19 . . . . **8** D3
Felcot Rd RH19 . . . . **8** C4
Felcourt Cotts RH19 . . . . . . **9** C8
Felcourt La RH19 . . . . **9** C8
Felcourt Rd RH19, RH7 . . . . **9** C7
Feld The RH19 . . . . **9** A4
Fellcott Way RH12 . . . . **35** F1
Fellows Gdns BN18 . . . . . . **181** A2
FELPHAM **202** B4
Felpham Com Coll
PO22 . . . . **201** F5
Felpham Gdns PO22 . . . . . **202** B5
Felpham Rd PO22 . . . . **201** F4
Felpham Way PO22 . . . . . . **202** A5
Felride RH16 . . . . **87** E3
Felwater Ct RH19 . . . . **9** A3
Fenby Cl RH13 . . . . **37** C4
Fenchurch Rd RH10 . . . . . . **19** B4
Fenchurch Wlk BN1 . . . . . **213** B4
Fender Ho RH12 . . . . **36** B2
Fenhurst Cl RH12 . . . . **35** F1
Fennel Cres RH11 . . . . **18** B2
Fennel Wlk BN43 . . . . **167** B1
Fenners Ct 13 BN11 . . . . . **186** C3
Fereday Cl 5 BN15 . . . . . . **187** E6
Fermandy La RH10 . . . . **8** A1
Fern Cl GU31 . . . . **68** E3
Fern Cotts RH14 . . . . **55** F6
Ferndale Rd
Burgess Hill RH15 . . . . . **109** C3
Chichester PO19 . . . . **155** A3
Hove BN3 . . . . **191** D7
Ferndale Wlk BN16 . . . . . . **184** A6
Fernden Hts GU27 . . . . **27** B2
Fernden La GU27 . . . . **27** C2
Ferndown
Crawley RH10 . . . . **6** D2
Horley RH6 . . . . **2** A5
Ferndown Gdns PO22 . . . . **202** A5
FERNHILL **6** F7
Fernhill Cl RH10 . . . . **8** B1
Fernhill Rd RH6 . . . . **6** D7
Fernhurst Cl
Brighton BN1 . . . . **170** B6
Crawley RH11 . . . . **18** B8
Fernhurst Cres BN1 . . . . . . **170** B5
Fernhurst Ct BN11 . . . . **185** F2
Fernhurst Dr BN12 . . . . . . **185** A3
Fernhurst Gdns PO21 . . . . . **200** D2
Fernhurst Gn GU27 . . . . **49** B6
Fernhurst Prim Sch
GU27 . . . . **49** B6
Fernhurst Rd GU30 . . . . **47** C3
Fernleigh Cl PO19 . . . . **176** C6
Fern Rd RH20 . . . . **121** C1
Fernside RH19 . . . . **9** D2
Fern Way RH12 . . . . **36** D5
Fernwood Rise BN1 . . . . . . **169** D5
Feroners Cl RH10 . . . . **19** A4
Feroners Ct 4 RH10 . . . . . . **19** A4
Ferring CE Prim Sch
BN12 . . . . **206** F6
Ferring Cl
Crawley RH11 . . . . **18** B8
Ferring BN12 . . . . **206** E4
Lancing BN15 . . . . **187** E7
Ferring Ct BN1 . . . . **170** F5
Ferring Gdns PO22 . . . . . . **202** A5
Ferring Grange Flats
BN12 . . . . **206** E6
Ferring Grange Gdns
BN12 . . . . **206** E6
Ferringham La BN12 . . . . . **206** E5
Ferringham Way
BN12 . . . . **206** E4
Ferring La BN12 . . . . **206** F7
Ferring Marine BN12 . . . . . **206** E4
Ferring St BN12 . . . . **206** E6
Ferrymead BN43 . . . . **188** F6
Ferry Rd
Littlehampton BN17 . . . . **204** B4

Ferry Rd continued
Shoreham-by-S BN43 . . . . **188** F6
Festival Ct
Chichester PO19 . . . . **177** A7
Crawley RH10 . . . . **19** C4
Fetherston Rd BN15 . . . . . **187** E7
Feversham Cl BN43 . . . . . . **189** B6
Fidler Cl PO20 . . . . **210** A1
Fidlers Copse GU27 . . . . . . **49** A6
Field Cl
Burgess Hill RH15 . . . . . **108** E4
Lancing BN15 . . . . **187** D6
Walberton BN18 . . . . **158** D1
Field End RH20 . . . . **121** E2
Fieldgate Cl RH13 . . . . **59** C4
Field Ho BN16 . . . . **205** F6
Fieldings Cotts RH14 . . . . . **55** F5
Fieldings The
Horley RH6 . . . . **2** C4
Southwater RH13 . . . . . . **81** F7
Field Pl
Liphook GU30 . . . . **25** C3
Littlehampton BN17 . . . . **204** D5
Field Place Fst Sch
BN12 . . . . **185** D5
Field Place Par BN12 . . . . **185** E4
Field Rd PO20 . . . . **208** A2
Field Row 8 BN11 . . . . . . **186** D2
Fields End Cl RH16 . . . . **87** F4
Fieldview RH6 . . . . **2** B4
Fieldway
Ditchling BN6 . . . . **129** D3
Haslemere GU27 . . . . **27** C7
Haywards Heath RH16 . . . . **87** F8
Fiennes Ct RH12 . . . . **36** D6
Fifth Ave
Lancing BN15 . . . . **187** E7
Worthing BN14 . . . . **186** C8
Filbert Cres RH11 . . . . **18** A6
Filey Cl RH11 . . . . **17** F4
Filton Wlk BN13 . . . . **185** D6
Fincham Cl BN16 . . . . **205** F5
Fincham Ct BN16 . . . . **205** F5
Finch Cres RH10 . . . . **21** C5
Finchdean Rd PO9 . . . . . . **130** F7
Finches Cl
Lancing BN15 . . . . **187** D5
Littlehampton BN17 . . . . **204** C8
Partridge Green RH13 . . . **105** A3
Finches Ct RH16 . . . . **64** A1
Finches Gdns RH16 . . . . . . **88** A8
Finches La
Lindfield RH16 . . . . **88** A8
West Chiltington Common
RH20 . . . . **121** C8
Finches Park Rd RH16 . . . . **88** A8
Finches The BN43 . . . . . . **189** A8
Finch Gdns PO22 . . . . **201** B7
Findon Ave BN2 . . . . **194** C3
Findon By-Pass BN14 . . . . **163** D6
Findon Cl BN3 . . . . **168** F3
Findon Dr PO22 . . . . **202** D6
Findon Rd
Brighton BN2 . . . . **192** F5
Crawley RH11 . . . . **18** B8
Worthing BN14 . . . . **163** F3
FINDON VALLEY **164** A2
Findon Way BN12 . . . . **35** D3
Finians Field RH13 . . . . **56** F7
Finisterre Way BN17 . . . . . **205** A4
Finsbury Cl RH11 . . . . **18** C2
Finsbury Lo 1 BN2 . . . . . . **192** C6
Finsbury Rd BN2 . . . . **192** C6
Firbank Way RH19 . . . . **9** D1
Fir Cl BN2 . . . . **193** F7
Fircroft Ave BN15 . . . . **187** F8
Fircroft Cl
Brighton BN1 . . . . **169** E3
Worthing BN13 . . . . **185** F7
Fircroft Cres BN16 . . . . . . **205** D7
Firlands
Haywards Heath RH16 . . . . **87** F4
Horley RH6 . . . . **2** B4
Firle Cl RH10 . . . . **18** E8
Firle Rd
Brighton BN2 . . . . **192** D6
North Lancing BN15 . . . . **165** E1
Firs Ave PO22 . . . . **202** B5
Firs Ave W PO22 . . . . **202** B5
Firsdown Cl BN13 . . . . **163** E2
Firsdown Rd BN13 . . . . . . **163** E2
Firsland Park Ind Est
BN6 . . . . **126** F8
Firs Pk GU31 . . . . **68** E3
First Ave
Almodington PO20 . . . . . **197** F2
Bognor Regis PO22 . . . . . **202** B4
Bracklesham PO20 . . . . . **208** B5
Hove BN3 . . . . **191** C6
Lancing BN15 . . . . **187** E7
Middleton-on-S PO22 . . . . **202** F6
Southbourne PO10 . . . . . **173** F8
Worthing BN14 . . . . **186** C7
Firs The GU30 . . . . **25** B3
Firtoft Cl RH15 . . . . **109** B3
Fir Tree Cl
Crawley RH11 . . . . **5** B1
Lower Beeding RH13 . . . . **60** A3
West Chiltington Common
RH20 . . . . **121** D6
Fir Tree Cotts RH14 . . . . . . **55** F5
Fir Tree La RH20 . . . . **121** D6
Fir Tree Way
Bognor Regis PO22 . . . . . **201** C7
Keymer BN6 . . . . **129** A4

Firview GU30 . . . . **25** B3
Fishbourne CE Prim Sch
PO19 . . . . **176** B6
Fishbourne Rd (E)
PO19 . . . . **176** D6
Fishbourne Rd (W) PO19,
PO20 . . . . **176** C6
Fishbourne Roman Pal★
PO19 . . . . **176** B6
Fishbourne Sta PO19 . . . . **176** B7
FISHER **199** C6
Fisher Cl RH10 . . . . **18** E4
Fisher La
Chiddingfold GU8 . . . . **29** E7
Dunsfold GU8 . . . . **30** B7
South Mundham PO20 . . . **199** C6
Fishermans The
PO10 . . . . **173** C8
Fishermans Wlk
Bognor Regis PO21 . . . . . **200** D1
Selsey PO20 . . . . **212** F7
Shoreham-by-S BN43 . . . **188** D5
South Hayling PO11 . . . . **195** A2
Fishers Cl BN17 . . . . **205** A4
Fishers Ct RH12 . . . . **36** C4
Fishers Farm RH6 . . . . **2** B1
Fishers Farm Pk★
RH14 . . . . **54** D2
FISHERSGATE **190** A7
Fishersgate Cl BN41 . . . . . **190** A7
Fishersgate Fst Sch
BN41 . . . . **190** A7
Fishersgate Sta BN41 . . . . **190** B7
Fishersgate Terr
BN41 . . . . **190** A7
Fish La
Bognor Regis PO21 . . . . . **200** F2
Selsey PO20 . . . . **212** B8
Fitch Dr BN2 . . . . **170** F1
Fitchet Cl RH11 . . . . **17** F4
Fittleworth CE Fst Sch
RH20 . . . . **99** A3
Fittleworth Cl BN12 . . . . . . **185** B5
Fittleworth Dr PO22 . . . . . . **202** C6
Fittleworth Gdn 9
BN16 . . . . **205** C5
Fittleworth Rd RH14 . . . . . . **77** F5
Fitzalan Ct
3 Littlehampton
BN17 . . . . **204** E4
4 Rustington BN16 . . . . **205** B3
Fitzalan Mews BN18 . . . . . **160** B2
Fitzalan Rd
Arundel BN18 . . . . **160** B2
Horsham RH12, RH13 . . . . **37** A4
Littlehampton BN17 . . . . **204** E4
Fitzhamon Ho GU31 . . . . . . **68** C3
Fitzherbert Ct BN2 . . . . . . **192** D8
Fitzherbert Dr BN2 . . . . . . **192** D8
Fitzjohn St BN6 . . . . **128** F3
Fitzleet Ho 9 PO21 . . . . . **201** C3
Fitzroy Ct BN17 . . . . **204** E5
Fitzwilliam Cl PO21 . . . . . . **200** F4
Five Acres
Crawley RH10 . . . . **18** E8
Funtington PO18 . . . . . . **153** A5
Five Oaks Rd
Broadbridge Heath RH12,
RH13 . . . . **35** B2
Itchingfield RH13 . . . . **56** D7
Fixcroft Cotts BN5 . . . . . . **106** D4
Flag Ct BN3 . . . . **191** B5
Flag Sq BN43 . . . . **188** F6
Flamsteed Hts RH11 . . . . . . **18** B1
Flansham Bsns Ctr
PO22 . . . . **202** B6
Flansham La PO22 . . . . . . **202** C6
Flansham Mews
PO22 . . . . **202** D6
Flansham Pk PO22 . . . . . . **202** D6
FLATHURST **76** A1
Flatt Rd PO18 . . . . **174** D8
Flaxman Ave PO19 . . . . . . **176** D6
Flax Mean PO22 . . . . **202** B5
Flax Mean Ho PO22 . . . . . . **202** B5
Fleet Cl BN17 . . . . **205** A6
Fleet St BN1 . . . . **213** B4
Fleet The RH20 . . . . **99** B3
Fleming Ct PO21 . . . . **200** A1
Fleming Ctr The RH10 . . . . . **5** E2
Fleming Way RH10, RH11 . . . **5** F2
Fleming Wlk RH19 . . . . **22** F6
Fletcher Cl
Bognor Regis PO21 . . . . . **200** B2
Crawley RH10 . . . . **18** E4
North Mundham PO20 . . . **177** D1
Fletcher Ho
North Mundham
PO20 . . . . **177** C1
Southwater RH13 . . . . . . **57** E1
Fletcher Pl PO20 . . . . **177** C1
Fletcher Rd BN14 . . . . **186** E5
FLETCHERS **198** D4
Fletchers RH13 . . . . **57** F3
Fletchers Cl RH13 . . . . **36** E1
Fletchers Est
Highleigh PO20 . . . . **198** C2
Sidlesham PO20 . . . . **198** E2
Fletchers Field GU30 . . . . . **25** C3
Fletchers Ho GU30 . . . . **25** B3
Fletcher's La PO18 . . . . . . **175** D7
Fletchers Way PO20 . . . . . **198** D3
Fletcher Way
Angmering BN16 . . . . . . **183** F6
Bognor Regis PO21 . . . . . **201** B4
4 Haywards Heath
RH16 . . . . **87** C2

Fletching Cl BN2........ 192 F6
Flexfield Ho RH13........ 57 F1
Flimwell Cl BN2 .... 192 E5
Flint Cl
  Crawley RH10 .... 19 B3
  East Preston BN16 ...... 205 F6
  Portslade-by-S BN41 .... 168 B2
Flint Cotts BN18........ 160 A3
Flint Ho 2 BN16 .... 205 C4
Flints The BN7........... 172 E5
Flora Ct BN17........... 204 B7
Floral Dene Ct BN14 .... 164 A1
Flora McDonald Jun Sch
  BN17................... 204 C6
Florence Ave BN3....... 190 D8
Florence Ct PO20 .... 197 D4
Florence Ct BN1 .... 169 F2
Florence Pl BN1 .... 170 B1
Florence Rd
  Brighton BN1........... 192 A8
  Chichester PO19 .... 177 C6
Florets The BN44....... 146 B1
Florida Cl BN12......... 206 F4
Florida Gdns 8 BN12 ... 206 F4
Florida Rd BN12 .... 206 F4
Florlandia Cl BN15...... 187 B6
Flower Farm Cl BN5 .... 125 D5
Floyds Cotts BN17...... 204 D4
Foamcourt Waye
  BN12................... 206 E5
Folders Cl RH15 .... 109 C1
Folders Gdns RH15...... 109 C1
Folders Grange RH15 ... 109 C1
Folders La RH15......... 109 D1
Folders La E BN6 .... 129 F8
Fold Sch The BN3........ 190 D7
Follett Cl PO21 .... 200 E2
Follis Gdns PO19........ 176 B8
Folly La
  Petersfield GU32........ 68 B3
  Sutton GU28, RH20 ..... 117 E3
Folly Market 9 GU31 .... 68 B3
Fontana Cl RH10........ 19 E5
Fonthill Lodge Sch
  RH19.................... 22 C6
Fonthill Rd BN3......... 191 B8
Fontigarry Farm Bsns Pk
  RH2..................... 1 C8
Fontwell Ave BN18,
  PO20................... 157 F1
Fontwell Cl
  Rustington BN16........ 158 A2
  Worthing BN14 .... 205 B4
Fontwell Dr BN14....... 186 A8
Fontwell Park Race
  Course★ BN18......... 157 F2
Fontwell Rd
  Crawley RH10 .... 19 A3
  Selsey PO20............ 212 G8
Forbes Cl RH10......... 19 B2
Forbes Pl PO19......... 176 F8
Ford Airfield Ind Est
  BN18................... 181 C3
Fordingbridge Ct RH12... 36 C1
Fordingbridge Ind Site
  PO22................... 180 A7
Ford La
  Ashurst BN44 .... 124 D7
  Ford BN18.............. 181 C4
Ford Lane Bsns Pk
  BN18................... 181 D4
Ford Rd
  Arundel BN18 .... 160 A2
  Ford BN18.............. 181 E3
  Tortington BN18........ 181 F7
Ford Sta BN18.......... 181 E5
Fordwater Gdns
  BN18................... 181 B2
Fordwater La PO19 ..... 155 A2
Fordwater Rd
  Chichester PO18,
    PO19................. 155 A3
  East Lavant PO18 ...... 155 A5
Fordwater Sch PO19.... 155 A1
Fordyce Ct 1 BN14 .... 186 D3
Fore Bridge GU31....... 68 B2
Foredown Cl BN41...... 168 B2
Foredown Dr BN41...... 168 C1
Foredown Rd
  Portslade-by-S BN41 ... 168 B3
  Portslade Village BN41 . 168 B4
Foredown Tower
  Countryside Ctr★
  Portslade-by-S BN41 ... 168 B3
  Portslade-by-S BN41 ... 168 B3
Forest Cl
  Crawley Down RH10 .... 21 B8
  Horsham RH12 .... 37 B4
  Mannings Heath RH13... 59 C6
Forest Cnr GU33 .... 45 C7
Forester Rd RH10 ...... 18 E4
Foresters The RH13..... 36 F1
Forestfield
  Crawley RH10 .... 19 B3
  Horsham RH13 .... 37 A3
Forest Gate RH11 ...... 18 D1
Forest La BN13......... 185 B9
Forest Lane Cl GU30 ... 25 A4
Forest Lo
  2 East Grinstead
    RH19................. 22 F8
  Horsham RH12 .... 37 B5
Forest Mews RH12 ..... 37 B5
Forest Oaks RH13...... 37 B4
Forest Pk RH13 .... 59 E6
Forest Rd
  Brighton BN1........... 170 E6

Forest Rd continued
  Colgate RH11, RH12,
    RH13................. 38 C6
  Faygate RH12, RH13 .... 37 D5
  Liss GU33 .... 45 C7
  Midhurst GU29 .... 94 D6
  Worthing BN14 .... 186 D6
Forest Ridge RH19...... 43 A6
Forest Rise GU33 ...... 45 C6
Forest Row Bsns Pk
  RH18.................... 23 F3
Forest Row CE Prim Sch
  RH18.................... 23 F2
Forest Sch The RH13.... 36 F1
FORESTSIDE 131 D6
Forestside PO9 .... 131 D6
Forest View RH10....... 19 A3
Forest View Rd RH19.... 22 E6
Forge Cl
  Broadbridge Heath
    RH12................. 35 D4
  East Preston BN16 ..... 205 F6
  Portslade-by-S BN41 ... 168 B2
  Stockbridge PO19 ...... 176 F3
Forge Ho The BN2....... 193 F1
Forge La
  Broadbridge Heath
    RH12................. 35 D4
  Crawley RH10 .... 19 A7
Forge Pl RH6........... 1 E1
Forge Rd RH10 .... 19 A7
Forge The
  Handcross RH17........ 61 C8
  Hove BN3............... 190 F8
  Selsey PO20............ 212 D7
  Southwater RH13 .... 57 F1
  Warnham RH12 .... 35 E7
Forge Way
  Billingshurst RH14...... 79 C8
  Burgess Hill RH15 ...... 109 A4
Forge Wood RH10 ..... 6 D3
Forge Wood Ind Est
  RH10.................... 6 B2
Forrester Rd RH13...... 105 A3
Forsters Yd BN17....... 204 B5
Forthaven BN43 .... 189 C6
Fort Rd BN17........... 204 C6
Fort Rd E BN17......... 204 C6
Forty Acre La GU31 .... 90 E3
Forum The 3 RH12 .... 36 C2
Foster Ct BN3 .... 191 E6
Foster La RH20 .... 122 F5
Fosters BN16 .... 205 E4
Fosters Cl BN16........ 205 E4
Fotherby Ho PO10 ..... 173 F8
Foundry Cl RH13....... 36 E4
Foundry Cotts GU29.... 95 C3
Foundry Ct RH15....... 109 B3
Foundry Ct RH13 ...... 36 E3
Foundry La
  Haslemere GU27....... 27 A6
  Horsham RH13 .... 36 E3
Foundry Rd RH18 ...... 180 F2
Foundry St BN1......... 213 B3
Fountains Cl
  Brighton BN1........... 170 B2
  Crawley RH11 .... 18 A4
Founthill Ave BN2 ...... 194 B1
Founthill Rd BN2 .... 194 B1
Fourth Ave
  Bognor Regis PO22..... 202 C4
  Hove BN3............... 191 B6
  Lancing BN15........... 187 E7
  Worthing BN14 .... 186 D7
Fowey Cl BN43......... 189 B6
Fowler Cl RH10 .... 19 C4
Foxbridge Dr PO20..... 177 A1
Foxbridge La RH14..... 31 C1
Foxbury La PO10....... 151 E4
Fox Cl
  Burgess Hill RH15...... 108 F1
  Chichester PO19 .... 177 C8
  Crawley RH11 .... 5 B1
Fox Ct RH20 .... 121 B1
Foxdale Dr BN16....... 205 F8
Fox Dell RH20 .... 121 B1
Foxdown Rd BN2 ...... 193 F7
Foxes Cl
  Rustington BN16....... 205 B8
  Southwater RH13 ...... 81 F7
Foxes Croft PO22 ...... 180 C6
Foxfield Cotts RH13.... 81 F7
Foxfields RH20 .... 121 C8
Foxglove Ave RH12 .... 36 E6
Foxglove Cl RH15...... 108 D4
Foxglove Way BN17 ... 205 A7
Foxglove Wlk
  Crawley RH11 .... 18 B3
  Worthing BN13 .... 185 C6
FOX HILL 87 E1
Fox Hill RH16.......... 87 E1
Fox Hill Cl RH16....... 87 F1
Foxhill Ct 3 RH16 ..... 87 E3
Fox Hill Village RH16... 87 F1
Foxhole La RH17....... 85 B2
Foxholes RH12......... 33 D8
Foxhunters Rd BN41 ... 167 F3
Fox Lea BN14.......... 163 E5
Foxleigh Chase RH12... 36 F5
Foxley La BN13........ 185 F9
Fox Rd
  Haslemere GU27....... 26 E6
  Midhurst GU29 .... 73 A2
Foxwarren RH16....... 87 C5
Foxwarren Cl PO20..... 207 F7
Fox Way BN41......... 168 B2
Foxwells RH17......... 41 A1
Foxwood Ave BN16.... 206 A8

Framfield 11 BN2 .... 192 F5
Framfield Cl
  Brighton BN1........... 170 E6
  Crawley RH11 .... 18 A8
Framnaes 2 BN3 .... 190 D7
Frampton Ct BN12 ..... 185 C3
Frampton Pl BN43 ..... 188 D8
Framptons The BN16.... 206 B5
Framroze Ct BN1 ...... 170 B2
France Cotts BN13..... 184 D8
France La BN13........ 162 D1
Franciscan Way
  BN17................... 204 D5
Francis Edwards Way
  RH11................... 17 E2
Francislea RH16 .... 87 E2
Francis Rd RH16 ...... 88 B8
Francis St BN1 .... 213 B4
Francome Ho BN15..... 187 D3
Frandor Rd PO21 ...... 200 F5
Frankalan Mews 14
  PO21................... 201 C2
Frankland Mead
  RH20................... 143 E6
Franklands Cl
  Burgess Hill RH15...... 109 B1
  Worthing BN14 .... 164 A1
Franklands Gdns
  RH15................... 129 A8
FRANKLANDS VILLAGE
  .... 88 A4
Franklands Way
  RH15................... 129 A8
Frankland Terr 2
  PO10................... 173 C8
Franklin Pl PO19....... 177 A7
Franklin Rd
  Brighton BN2........... 192 C7
  Crawley RH10 .... 19 C5
  Portslade-by-S BN41 ... 190 C7
  Shoreham-by-S BN43... 167 D1
  Worthing BN13 .... 185 E8
Franklin St BN2........ 192 C8
Franklynn Ct RH16 .... 87 F3
Franklynn Rd RH16 .... 87 F3
Frankton Ave RH16 .... 88 A3
Frant Rd BN3.......... 169 A2
Frarydene PO10 .... 173 F8
Fraser Ct PO20 .... 212 F6
Fraser Ct
  19 Bognor Regis
    PO21................. 201 D3
  2 Shoreham-by-S
    BN43................. 189 C8
Fraser Gdns PO10...... 152 A2
Frazier Ho RH20 .... 121 D1
Fred Emery Ct 16
  BN1................... 191 E5
Frederic Ho BN2....... 194 B1
Frederick Cotts RH16... 88 B7
Frederick Gdns BN1 ... 213 B3
Frederick Pl BN1 ...... 213 B3
Frederick Rd PO19..... 176 C7
Frederick St BN1 ...... 213 B3
Freehold St BN43 ..... 188 E7
Freehold Terr 1 BN2 ... 192 C8
Freek's La RH15 .... 109 A5
Freeland Cl PO19 ...... 176 C6
Freeman Cl BN18 ...... 158 B1
Freeman Rd RH12...... 35 F8
Freemans Cl RH14 .... 79 C8
Freemans Rd BN41..... 190 A8
Freeways PO20 .... 212 C8
French Apartments The
  BN2................... 192 E3
Frenches RH20 .... 121 D2
Frenches Mead RH14 .. 79 C8
Frenches Rdbt RH14 ... 79 C8
French Gdns RH16 ..... 88 A6
Frenchmans Rd GU32... 68 A4
Frensham Ave PO22.... 201 D6
Freshbrook Cl BN15.... 187 E5
Freshbrook Ct 3
  BN15................... 187 E6
Freshbrook Fst Sch
  BN15................... 187 E6
Freshbrook Rd BN15... 187 E5
Freshfield Bank RH18 .. 23 E2
Freshfield Cl RH10..... 19 A5
Freshfield Crossway
  RH17................... 89 C8
Freshfield Ind Est
  BN2................... 192 C5
Freshfield La RH17..... 65 E2
Freshfield Pl BN2 ...... 192 C5
Freshfield Rd BN2 ..... 192 D6
Freshfields BN15....... 187 D6
Freshfields Dr BN15.... 187 D6
Freshfield St BN2...... 192 C6
Freshfield Way BN2.... 192 C5
Freshlands RH14....... 79 C8
Freshwoods RH12...... 33 D8
Freya Cl PO22 .... 202 F4
Friar Cl BN1 .... 170 A4
Friar Cres BN1 .... 170 A3
Friar Rd BN1 .... 170 A3
Friars Cl BN6.......... 128 E4
Friars Oak Rd BN6..... 128 E5
Friars Rookery RH10 ... 18 F6
Friar Wlk
  Brighton BN1........... 169 F4
  Worthing BN13 .... 185 F4
Friary Cl PO22 .... 202 E5
Friary La PO19......... 177 A6
Friary Way RH10 ...... 18 E5
Friday St
  Faygate RH12 .... 15 E6
  Warnham RH12 .... 35 E7

Friends Cl RH11 .... 5 D1
Frimley Cl BN2 .... 193 F7
Friston Cl BN2......... 170 F4
Friston Wlk RH11 ..... 18 A7
Frith Pk RH19.......... 9 E3
Frith Rd
  Bognor Regis PO21..... 201 A4
  Hove BN3............... 191 A8
Frobisher Ct BN12 ..... 185 D5
Frobisher Gdns 8
  PO10................... 173 B8
Frobisher Rd PO21..... 200 C2
Frobisher Way
  Littlehampton BN16..... 205 E4
  Worthing BN12 .... 185 D5
Fry Cl RH11............ 18 B1
Fry Cres RH15 .... 108 E5
Fryern Cl RH20 .... 121 C2
Fryern Rd RH20 .... 121 D3
Fryland La BN5 .... 106 B4
Fuel Farm Rd
  Crawley RH6........... 5 E8
  Hookwood RH6......... 1 E1
Fulbeck Ave BN13 ..... 185 B7
Fulfords Hill RH13 ..... 57 A7
Fulham Cl RH11 .... 18 B2
Fullers Wlk BN17 ...... 182 D5
Fulmar Cl
  1 Crawley RH11 .... 17 D5
  Hove BN3.............. 169 D1
Fulmar Dr RH19 .... 10 B3
Fulmar Way PO20...... 156 E1
Fulmer Ct 1 BN11 ..... 186 B1
Funtington Ho BN17.... 204 B7
Funtington Prim Sch
  PO18................... 153 B3
Furlong Cl BN18 .... 158 B3
Furlonge Ho PO10 ..... 151 A1
Furlongs The BN44 .... 145 D2
Furlong Way RH6....... 5 F8
Furnace Dr RH10 ...... 18 F4
Furnace Farm Rd
  RH10.................... 19 A4
FURNACE GREEN 19 A5
Furnace Par RH10 ..... 19 A4
Furnace Pl RH10....... 19 A4
FURNACE WOOD 8 C4
Furnance Farm Rd
  RH19................... 8 C3
Furners La BN5........ 126 A5
Furners Mead BN5 .... 125 F4
Furnston Gr PO10...... 152 A1
Furse Feld PO21 ...... 201 A2
Furze Cl
  Horley RH6............ 2 D3
  Worthing BN13 .... 163 D6
Furze Common Rd
  RH20................... 122 A6
Furze Croft BN3........ 191 D6
Furzedene BN3 .... 191 D6
Furzedown BN17 ...... 204 E4
Furzefield
  Crawley RH11 .... 18 C7
  East Wittering PO20 .... 196 F1
Furzefield Chase RH19... 9 E6
Furzefield Cl BN16..... 183 F7
Furzefield Ho RH13.... 57 F1
Furzefield Rd
  East Grinstead RH19.... 9 D4
  Horsham RH12 .... 37 B5
Furze Hill BN3......... 191 D6
Furze Hill Ct BN3...... 191 E6
Furze Hill Ho BN3...... 191 E6
Furzeholme BN13...... 163 E2
Furze La RH19......... 9 B4
Furzeland Way BN6.... 127 D8
Furze Mdw GU31...... 92 A8
Furze Cotts RH12...... 13 A3
Furze La RH12, RH5 ... 13 B4
Furze Rd
  Rudgwick RH12 .... 33 D8
  Worthing BN13 .... 163 E2
Furze View RH13 ...... 56 B6
FYNING 70 C4
Fyning La GU31........ 70 C5

G

Gableson Ave BN1 ..... 169 B4
Gables The
  13 Bognor Regis
    PO21................. 201 C2
  Copthorne RH10 .... 7 B3
  Cowfold RH13 .... 83 E1
  Fishbourne PO19....... 176 B6
  Horsham RH12 .... 36 D4
  Southwater RH13 ...... 81 F8
Gabriel Rd RH10....... 19 C2
Gage Cl RH10.......... 8 C1
Gage Ridge RH18 ..... 23 E2
Gaggle Wood RH13 ... 59 C6
Gainsboro Rd PO21.... 201 C3
Gainsborough Ave
  BN14................... 186 E7
Gainsborough Dr
  PO20................... 212 F7
Gainsborough Ho
  Crawley RH10 .... 18 D6
  16 Hove BN3........... 191 C7
Gainsborough Lo 1
  BN14................... 186 C4
Gainsborough Rd RH10.. 18 F3
Gaisford Cl BN14 ..... 186 C4
Gaisford Rd BN14...... 186 B4
Galahad Rd RH11 ..... 17 E6
Gales Cl GU27 .... 26 E5
Gales Dr RH10......... 18 F6

Gales Pl RH10 .... 18 F6
Galleries The 16 BN3... 191 D7
Galliers Cl BN1 .... 170 B6
Galsworthy Cl BN3..... 185 B4
Galsworthy Rd BN12 ... 185 B4
Gamecock Terr PO20 ... 156 D1
Gammon Cl GU31...... 68 C5
Gander Cl RH15........ 109 A5
Gander Gn RH16 ...... 87 F7
Gander Hill RH16 ...... 87 F7
Ganders Cl BN5........ 125 D5
Gandersgate La RH14... 77 A7
Gannet Ho BN3 .... 169 B1
Gannon Rd BN11....... 186 F3
Ganymede Ct RH11 ... 17 E3
Garage Cotts 2 GU32... 68 A4
Garbitts La GU31....... 70 B4
Garcia Trad Est BN13... 185 F4
Garden Ave PO20 ..... 208 B6
Garden Cl
  Angmering BN16........ 184 A7
  East Grinstead RH19.... 22 F7
  Lancing BN15........... 187 C6
  Portslade-by-S BN43.... 190 C8
  Shoreham-by-S BN43.... 167 B1
  Storrington RH20....... 121 D2
Garden Cres PO22 .... 180 C5
Garden Ct
  Bognor Regis PO20..... 200 E2
  Shoreham-by-S BN43.... 167 B1
Gardener Ho RH13 .... 57 E1
Gardeners Cl RH12..... 35 E8
Gardeners Ct 2 RH13... 36 D1
Gardeners Gn RH12 ... 16 C6
Gardener St BN41...... 190 B8
Garden Ho PO19 ...... 154 F2
Garden Ho The BN1.... 213 A3
Garden House La RH19.. 22 F7
Garden Lo PO21 .... 200 A2
Garden Mead RH19 ... 42 E6
Garden Mews
  Duncton GU28......... 117 D8
  10 Petersfield GU32.... 68 B3
Garden Pl 2 RH12 .... 36 C4
Gardens The
  Fittleworth RH20....... 99 A3
  Southwick BN42 .... 189 F7
  West Ashling PO18 .... 153 B3
Garden Wlk
  Crawley RH11 .... 18 C5
  3 Horsham RH12....... 36 C4
Garden Wood Cl
  RH20................... 121 D6
Garden Wood Rd RH19... 22 C8
Gardner Centre Rd
  BN1................... 171 B6
Gardner La RH10 ...... 21 A8
Gardner Rd BN41...... 190 A7
Gardner St BN1........ 213 B2
Garendon Ho BN11 ... 187 A2
Garland Ave PO10..... 151 B3
Garland Cl PO19 ...... 177 B5
Garland Rd RH19 ..... 9 D2
Garland Sq PO20...... 156 D2
Garmans RH14........ 54 C1
Garnet Ho 13 BN2 .... 192 C4
Garrett Cl RH10....... 19 C4
Garrick Rd BN14 ...... 186 E4
Garrick Wlk RH10 ..... 18 E3
Garrones The RH10 ... 19 E7
Garsons Rd PO10 ..... 173 F8
Garton Cl RH11....... 17 E5
Gaskyns Cl RH12...... 33 D7
Gasson Wood Rd RH11... 17 E4
Gaston Way PO18...... 154 E7
Gatcombe Cl BN13..... 185 B6
Gateford Cotts RH13... 34 D2
Gateford Dr RH12...... 36 F6
Gate Ho GU29 .... 94 F7
Gatehouse La
  Goddards' Green BN6,
    RH15................. 108 C4
  Trotton GU31.......... 71 A4
Gatehouse Mews
  PO21................... 201 D3
Gates Cl RH10......... 19 C2
Gatesmead RH16 ..... 87 F8
Gateway Lo PO22...... 201 F4
Gateway Terr BN44.... 145 D3
Gattons Inf Sch The
  RH15................... 108 E3
Gattons The RH15..... 108 E3
Gatwick Airport Beehive
  Area RH6.............. 6 B5
Gatwick Airport-London
  RH6................... 5 F7
Gatwick Airport Sta
  RH6................... 6 B7
Gatwick Aviation Mus★
  RH6................... 4 F6
Gatwick Gate Ind Est
  RH11................... 5 E5
Gatwick Ho RH6....... 6 E7
Gatwick Metro Ctr RH6 .. 2 B3
Gatwick Park Hospl
  (private) RH6.......... 1 E2
Gatwick Rd RH6, RH10... 6 A3
Gatwick Way RH6...... 5 F8
Gaugemaster Way
  BN18................... 181 E4
Gay St RH20 .... 101 C4
Gay Street La RH20 ... 101 A6
Gaywood Wlk RH13 ... 185 D6
Geddes Way GU31..... 68 E4
Gemini Bsns Ctr BN3... 191 B8

Gemini Cl RH11 . . . . 17 E4
Genesis Bsns Ctr RH13 . . . . 36 F3
Genistos The BN6 . . . . . . 128 E4
Genoa BN17 . . . . 205 A6
Geoffrey's Lo 6 RH10 . . . . . 6 A1
George Denyer Cl
GU27 . . . . 27 C7
George Ho PO20 . . . . . . 212 E8
George IV Wlk PO22 . . . . 202 A5
George Pinion Ct RH12 . . . 36 B3
Georges La RH20 . . . . . . 122 C1
George St
Brighton BN2 . . . . 213 B2
Chichester PO19 . . . . . 177 A7
Hove BN3 . . . . 191 B6
Portslade-by-S, Aldrington
BN41 . . . . 190 C7
Portslade-by-S, Fishersgate
BN41 . . . . 190 A7
George V Ave
Lancing BN15 . . . . 188 B5
Worthing BN11 . . . . . . 185 F3
Georgia Ave BN14 . . . . . 186 D4
Georgian Cl RH10 . . . . . . 19 D5
Georgian Gardens Com
Prim Sch BN16 . . . . . . 205 E6
Georgian Gdns BN16 . . . . 205 E6
Gerald Cl RH15 . . . . 109 D3
Gerald Ct RH13 . . . . 36 E2
Gerald Rd BN11 . . . . 185 F2
Gerardes Lo GU27 . . . . . . 27 D8
Gerard St BN1 . . . . 213 B5
Gerrard House Bsns Ctr
BN16 . . . . 205 F6
Gerston Bsns Pk
RH20 . . . . 142 C8
Ghyll Cres RH13 . . . . 58 F8
Ghyll Ct RH13 . . . . 57 F1
Ghyllside BN2 . . . . 170 E1
Gibbon Pl 5 RH11 . . . . . . 18 D8
Gibbons Cl RH10 . . . . . . 19 C3
Giblets La RH12 . . . . 36 E7
Giblets Way RH12 . . . . . . 36 E7
Gibson Rd PO20 . . . . . . 156 C2
Gibson Way PO21 . . . . . 201 D4
Giffards Cl RH19 . . . . 9 F1
Gifford Rd PO18 . . . . . . 175 C7
Gilbert Rd PO19 . . . . . . 176 E8
Gilberts The BN16 . . . . . 205 B3
Giles Cl BN18 . . . . 180 F2
Gilham La RH18 . . . . 23 E2
Gillett Ct RH13 . . . . 37 B4
Gillett Ho RH13 . . . . 37 B4
Gillham's La GU27 . . . . . . 26 A5
Gilligan Cl RH12 . . . . 36 B2
Gilligans The RH15 . . . . . 108 F5
Gillmans Ind Est RH14 . . . 79 D6
Gillway PO20 . . . . 212 G8
Gilmore Rd PO19 . . . . . 177 C6
Gilpin Cl PO19 . . . . 176 B6
Gilwynes PO21 . . . . 200 F2
Gilwynes Ct PO21 . . . . . 200 F2
Ginhams Rd RH11 . . . . . . 18 B6
Girton Rd BN3 . . . . 190 F6
Glade Inf Sch PO21 . . . . 201 A5
Gladepoint RH16 . . . . 87 E5
Glades The RH19 . . . . 10 B1
Glade The
Bognor Regis PO21 . . . 211 A8
Crawley RH10 . . . . 19 A4
Horsham RH13 . . . . 37 A3
Storrington RH20 . . . . . 121 E2
Gladonian Rd BN17 . . . . 204 D7
Gladstone Ct 14 BN2 . . . 192 C8
Gladstone Pl BN2 . . . . . 192 C8
Gladstone Rd
Burgess Hill RH15 . . . . 109 C4
Horsham RH12 . . . . 36 D3
Portslade-by-S BN41 . . . 190 B7
Yapton BN18 . . . . 180 F2
Gladstone Terr
Brighton BN2 . . . . 213 C4
Littlehampton BN17 . . . 204 D7
Gladys Rd BN3 . . . . 190 D8
Glamis Cl PO21 . . . . 201 D3
Glamis St PO21 . . . . 201 D3
Glanville Wlk 7 RH11 . . . . 18 A3
Glaseby La RH20 . . . . . . 143 D4
Glasshouse La GU28,
RH14 . . . . 76 F3
Glass Pavilion BN1 . . . . . 213 B2
Glastonbury Rd BN3 . . . . 190 D6
Glatting La RH20 . . . . . . 117 E1
Glawood Ho BN14 . . . . . 186 E6
Glaziers La GU29 . . . . . . 73 B2
Gleave Cl RH19 . . . . 10 A2
Glebe Cl
Crawley RH10 . . . . 18 E7
Lancing BN15 . . . . 187 E6
Norton PO20 . . . . 157 B1
Southwick BN42 . . . . . 189 F7
Glebe Com Mid Sch
BN42 . . . . 189 D8
Glebefield Rd PO20 . . . . 197 A5
Glebelands
Crawley Down RH10 . . . 21 A7
Loxwood RH14 . . . . 31 F4
Pulborough RH20 . . . . 100 D2
Glebelands Dr BN43 . . . . 189 B8
Glebe Rd
Cuckfield RH17 . . . . 86 F6
Fernhurst GU27 . . . . . . 49 B5
Worthing BN14 . . . . . . 186 A5
Glebeside Ave BN14 . . . . 186 A5
Glebeside Cl BN14 . . . . . 186 B5

Glebe The
Copthorne RH10 . . . . 7 B3
Felbridge RH19 . . . . 9 A4
Horley RH6 . . . . .1 F3
Hurstpierpoint BN6 . . . . 128 A6
Lindfield RH16 . . . . 88 A8
Southwater RH13 . . . . . 189 F8
Tangmere PO20 . . . . . . 156 C1
Glebe Twitten RH17 . . . . . 86 F6
Glebe View RH17 . . . . 41 A1
Glebe Villas
Hove BN3 . . . . 190 D7
Petworth GU28 . . . . 75 F1
Glebe Way
Lancing BN15 . . . . 187 E7
Wisborough Green RH14 . . 78 C8
Glenbarrie Way BN12 . . . 206 E7
Glencathara Rd PO21 . . . 201 B3
Glen Cres PO22 . . . . . . 212 E7
Glen Dale PO9 . . . . 130 E1
Glendale Cl RH12 . . . . . . 37 A6
Glendale Rd
Burgess Hill RH15 . . . . 109 B2
Hove BN3 . . . . 191 D7
Glendon Ho 9 RH10 . . . . 18 D5
Glendor Rd BN3 . . . . . . 190 E6
Glendyne Cl RH19 . . . . . . 23 A8
Glendyne Way RH19 . . . . 23 A8
Glen Eagles RH6 . . . . .2 B2
Gleneagles Ct
Crawley RH10 . . . . 18 D5
13 Haywards Heath
RH16 . . . . 87 E4
Glenelg Cl PO21 . . . . . . 200 F6
Glenfalls Ave BN1 . . . . . 170 A7
Glenfergus 3 RH16 . . . . . 87 E6
Glenfield Cotts RH6 . . . . . 4 D7
Glenfield Ct BN13 . . . . . 185 F6
Glen Gdns BN12 . . . . . . 206 F6
Glen Gordon RH16 . . . . . 87 E6
Glenham Pl RH19 . . . . . . 43 A5
Glenmore Ct 16 BN17 . . . 204 E4
Glen Rise BN1 . . . . 169 B5
Glen Rise BN1 . . . . 169 B5
Glenside 1 RH19 . . . . . . .9 E1
Glen The
Southwater RH13 . . . . . 58 A2
Worthing BN13 . . . . . . 186 A7
Glenview RH10 . . . . 18 F8
Glenville Rd BN16 . . . . . 205 D4
Glen Vue RH19 . . . . .9 E1
Glenway PO22 . . . . 201 D4
Glenwood Ave PO22 . . . . 201 D4
Glenwood Rd PO10 . . . . 152 A1
Glenwood Sch PO10 . . . . 151 B1
Gleton Ave BN3 . . . . . . 168 C2
Globe Pl BN17 . . . . 204 D7
Gloster Dr PO21 . . . . . . 200 B2
Gloucester Cl
East Grinstead RH19 . . . 23 A8
Petersfield GU32 . . . . . . 67 F3
Gloucester Ct
6 Petersfield GU32 . . . . 68 B4
Worthing BN12 . . . . . . 185 F2
Gloucester La BN17 . . . . 204 D5
Gloucester Mews 2
BN1 . . . . 213 B3
Gloucester Pas 4
BN1 . . . . 213 B3
Gloucester Pl
Brighton BN1 . . . . 213 B3
Littlehampton BN17 . . . 204 D5
Gloucester Rd
Bognor Regis PO21 . . . 201 E3
Brighton BN1 . . . . 213 B3
Burgess Hill RH15 . . . . 108 F3
Crawley RH10 . . . . 18 E2
Littlehampton BN17 . . . 204 C5
Gloucester St BN1 . . . . . 213 B3
Gloucester Terr PO18 . . . 175 B4
Gloucester Way PO19 . . . 154 F1
Gloucester Yd 3 BN1 . . . 213 B3
Glovers Field GU27 . . . . . 26 F6
Glovers Ho GU27 . . . . . . 26 F6
Glover's Rd RH6 . . . . 4 D7
Glovers Yd BN1 . . . . . . 169 F1
Glynde Ave
Saltdean BN2 . . . . 194 D2
Worthing BN12 . . . . . . 185 A3
Glyndebourne Ave
BN2 . . . . 194 C2
Glyndebourne Ct 9
BN43 . . . . 188 F7
Glynde Cl BN12 . . . . . . 206 F6
Glynde Cres PO22 . . . . . 202 A5
Glynde Ho
Crawley RH10 . . . . 18 E8
Hove BN3 . . . . 191 D6
Worthing BN11 . . . . . . 186 B1
Glynde Pl 8 RH12 . . . . . . 36 C2
Glynde Rd BN2 . . . . 192 D6
Glyn House Cl PO20 . . . . 212 E7
Glynleigh 18 BN2 . . . . . 213 C3
Goathlands Cvn Pk
PO20 . . . . 212 C8
Gochers Ct BN2 . . . . . . 192 C7
Goda Rd BN17 . . . . 204 E5
Goddard Cl RH10 . . . . . . 19 B3
Goddens The RH19 . . . . . 22 E7
Godman Cl PO21 . . . . . . 200 D2
Godmans Ct RH13 . . . . . 83 E1
Godolphin Rd RH10 . . . . 18 D5
Godstalls La BN44 . . . . . 145 C2
Godwin Cl PO10 . . . . . . 151 A3
Godwin Ct 3 RH12 . . . . . 36 A1
Godwin Rd BN3 . . . . . . 168 D1
Godwin Way
Fishbourne PO18 . . . . . 176 A8

Godwin Way continued
Horsham RH13 . . . . 37 A4
Goepel Ct RH10 . . . . 19 A7
Goffs Cl RH11 . . . . 18 C5
Goffs La RH11 . . . . 18 B6
Goffs Park Rd RH11 . . . . 18 C4
Goldcrest Ave BN17 . . . . 204 C8
Goldcrest Cl RH6 . . . . . . .1 E4
Golden Acre
Bognor Regis PO21 . . . 211 A8
West Kingston BN16 . . . 206 B4
Golden Ave BN16 . . . . . 206 B5
Golden Avenue Cl
BN16 . . . . 206 B4
Goldenfields GU30 . . . . . 25 D3
Goldenfields Cl GU30 . . . . 25 D3
Golden Hill RH15 . . . . . 109 D3
Golden La
Ashurst BN44 . . . . 124 C6
11 Brighton BN1 . . . . . 191 D5
Golden Sands Cvn Pk
BN15 . . . . 188 A4
Golden Sq
Henfield BN5 . . . . 125 E4
Petworth GU28 . . . . 97 F8
Goldfinch Cl
Crawley RH11 . . . . 18 D8
Horsham RH12 . . . . 36 C7
Golding Barn Farm
(Works) BN5 . . . . 146 E2
Golding Cl RH10 . . . . . . 19 C5
Golding La RH13 . . . . . . 59 D7
Goldsmid Mews 10
BN3 . . . . 191 D6
Goldsmid Rd BN3 . . . . . 191 E7
Goldsmith Rd BN14 . . . . 186 E4
Goldstone Cl BN3 . . . . . 169 A2
Goldstone Cres BN3 . . . . 169 B2
Goldstone Ct BN3 . . . . . 169 A3
Goldstone Ho 4 BN3 . . . 191 B7
Goldstone La BN3 . . . . . 191 B8
Goldstone Prim Sch
BN3 . . . . 168 E1
Goldstone Rd BN3 . . . . . 191 B7
Goldstone Ret Pk
BN3 . . . . 191 B8
Goldstone St BN3 . . . . . 191 B7
Goldstone Villas BN3 . . . 191 B7
Goldstone Way BN3 . . . . 169 A2
Golf Club La RH20 . . . . . 120 F7
Golf Dr BN1 . . . . 170 B3
Golfers La BN16 . . . . . . 205 D7
Golf Links La PO20 . . . . 209 E1
Golf Links Rd PO22 . . . . 202 A6
Goodacres
Barnham PO22 . . . . . . 180 C5
Fontwell BN18 . . . . . . 158 B2
Goodhew Cl BN18 . . . . . 181 A3
Goodwin Cl RH11 . . . . . . 17 F3
Goodwins Cl RH19 . . . . . . 9 D3
Goodwood Ave PO22 . . . 201 F5
Goodwood Cl
Crawley RH11 . . . . 19 A3
Midhurst GU29 . . . . 94 A5
Rustington BN16 . . . . . 205 E6
Goodwood Ct
15 Bognor Regis
PO21 . . . . 201 C2
2 Hove BN3 . . . . 191 D7
Selsey PO20 . . . . 212 E8
Southbourne PO10 . . . . 174 A8
Goodwood Ctry Pk★
PO18 . . . . 136 A4
Goodwood Gdns
PO20 . . . . 177 E1
Goodwood Ho★ PO18 . . . 155 F6
Goodwood Rd BN13 . . . . 186 A4
Goodwood Way BN2 . . . . 170 F3
Goose Green Cl RH12 . . . 36 D5
Goosegreen La RH20 . . . 102 C2
Gooserye Ct GU30 . . . . . 25 B3
Gordon Ave
1 Bognor Regis
PO21 . . . . 201 C3
Bognor Regis PO22 . . . 201 D5
Shoreham-by-S BN43 . . . 189 A7
Stockbridge PO19 . . . . 176 E3
Gordon Ave W PO22 . . . 201 D5
Gordon Cl RH16 . . . . 87 E6
Gordon Ho
8 Bognor Regis
PO21 . . . . 201 C3
22 Bognor Regis PO21 . . 201 D3
Burgess Hill RH15 . . . . 109 C4
Gordon Mews 2
BN41 . . . . 190 C7
Gordon Rd
Brighton BN1 . . . . 169 F2
Burgess Hill RH15 . . . . 109 C4
Haywards Heath RH16 . . . 87 E6
Hermitage PO10 . . . . . 173 D8
Horsham RH12 . . . . 36 D4
Lancing BN15 . . . . 187 D6
Portslade-by-S, Aldrington
BN41 . . . . 190 C7
Portslade-by-S, Fishersgate
BN41 . . . . 190 A7
Shoreham-by-S BN43 . . . 189 A7
Worthing BN11 . . . . . . 186 D3
Gordon Terr
Arundel BN18 . . . . 183 C8
Bosham PO18 . . . . 175 A5
Goreside La RH17 . . . . . . 86 F8
Gorham Ave BN2 . . . . . . 194 A2
Gorham Cl BN2 . . . . 194 A2
GORING-BY-SEA 185 C4
Goring-by-Sea CE Fst Sch
BN12 . . . . 185 C3

Goring-by-Sea Sta
BN12 . . . . 185 A4
Goring Chase BN12 . . . . 185 A5
Goring Crossways
BN12 . . . . 185 A5
Goring Ct
Brighton BN1 . . . . 170 F5
Steyning BN44 . . . . . . 145 D2
Goring Hall Hospl
(private) BN12 . . . . . . 185 B2
Goring Rd
Steyning BN44 . . . . . . 145 E2
Worthing BN12 . . . . . . 185 D3
Goring's Mead RH13 . . . . 36 D1
Goring St BN12 . . . . 185 A4
Goring Way
Partridge Green
RH13 . . . . 105 A3
Worthing BN12 . . . . . . 185 A3
Worthing, Goring-by-Sea
BN12 . . . . 185 B4
Gorling Cl RH11 . . . . 17 E5
Gorringe Cl BN43 . . . . . 189 D7
Gorringes Brook RH12 . . . 36 D6
Gorse Ave
Bognor Regis PO22 . . . 202 D6
Kingston Gorse BN16 . . 206 D4
Worthing BN14 . . . . . . 186 B6
Gorse Bank Cl RH20 . . . 122 C3
Gorse Cl
Copthorne RH10 . . . . . . 7 B2
Crawley RH11 . . . . 18 B1
Portslade-by-S BN41 . . . 167 F4
Gorse Cotts GU26 . . . . . 26 C8
Gorse End RH12 . . . . . . 36 D5
Gorse La BN13 . . . . 163 E2
Gorselands RH14 . . . . . . 79 E8
Gorse Rd GU31 . . . . 68 E3
Gorse Terr PO20 . . . . . . 198 D4
Gosden Cl RH10 . . . . . . 19 A5
GOSDEN GREEN 173 E8
Gosden Rd BN17 . . . . . . 204 F6
Gosling Croft Bsns Ctr
BN13 . . . . 162 E1
GOSPEL GREEN 28 E4
Gospond Rd PO22 . . . . . 180 B5
Gosport Ct 11 BN43 . . . . 189 B6
Gossamer La PO21 . . . . 200 D3
Gossops Dr RH11 . . . . . . 18 A5
GOSSOPS GREEN 18 A5
Gossops Green La
RH11 . . . . 18 A5
Gossops Green Prim Sch
RH11 . . . . 18 A5
Gossops Par RH11 . . . . . 17 F5
Gostrode La GU8 . . . . . . 29 A6
Gothic Barns PO18 . . . . 175 F5
Goudhurst Cl RH10 . . . . . 19 E6
Goudhurst Keep RH10 . . . 19 E6
Gower Rd
Haywards Heath RH16 . . . 87 E3
Horley RH6 . . . . .1 E3
Gowers Cl RH17 . . . . 64 B8
Gows Croft BN7 . . . . . . 172 E5
Grace Ct
Hassocks BN6 . . . . 128 E5
Horsham RH13 . . . . 37 A4
Grace Rd RH11 . . . . 18 A1
Graffham Cl
Brighton BN2 . . . . 192 E6
Chichester PO19 . . . . . 155 A3
Crawley RH11 . . . . 18 B8
Graffham Fst Sch
GU28 . . . . 116 B6
Grafton Ave PO22 . . . . . 202 C6
Grafton Cl BN16 . . . . . . 205 C6
Grafton Ct PO20 . . . . . . 212 E6
Grafton Dr BN15 . . . . . . 187 C6
Grafton Gdns BN15 . . . . 187 C6
Grafton Pl 7 BN11 . . . . . 186 D2
Grafton Rd
Selsey PO20 . . . . 212 E6
Worthing BN11 . . . . . . 186 D2
Grafton St BN2 . . . . 213 C1
Graham Ave
Brighton BN1 . . . . 169 F5
Portslade-by-S BN41 . . . 167 F4
Graham Cl BN41 . . . . . . 167 F4
Graham Cres BN41 . . . . 167 F4
Graham Ct
Lancing BN15 . . . . 187 C6
Worthing BN11 . . . . . . 185 F2
Graham Rd
Worthing BN11 . . . . . . 186 D2
Yapton BN18 . . . . 180 F1
Graham's Cotts RH16 . . . 64 B1
Grailands Cl GU27 . . . . . 49 C6
Granary Cl
Horley RH6 . . . . .2 A5
Horsham RH11 . . . . 35 F1
Granary La PO20 . . . . . . 212 D8
Granary The PO18 . . . . . 175 F5
Granary Way
Horsham RH12 . . . . 36 A1
Littlehampton BN17 . . . 204 D8
Grand Ave
Hassocks BN6 . . . . 128 F4
Hove BN3 . . . . 191 C6
Lancing BN15 . . . . 187 E7
Littlehampton BN17 . . . 204 C7
Worthing BN11 . . . . . . 186 A2
Grand Avenue Mans 4
BN3 . . . . 191 C6
Grand Cres BN2 . . . . . . 194 A4
Grand Junction Rd
BN1 . . . . 213 B2
Grand Par
Brighton BN2 . . . . 213 B3

Grand Par continued
Crawley RH10 . . . . 18 D6
Grand Parade Mews
BN2 . . . . 213 B2
Grange Cl
Brighton BN1 . . . . 169 E1
Burgess Hill RH15 . . . . 109 C5
Crawley RH10 . . . . 19 A8
Ferring BN12 . . . . 206 E5
Grange Cres RH10 . . . . . 21 B7
Grange Ct
Bognor Regis PO21 . . . 200 E1
Hove BN3 . . . . 190 F8
7 Middleton-on-S
PO22 . . . . 202 F5
9 Southwick BN42 . . . . 189 E7
Grange Farm Cotts
BN2 . . . . 193 D4
Grange Field Way
PO21 . . . . 200 D2
Grange Ind Est The
BN42 . . . . 189 D7
Grange La PO20 . . . . . . 210 B2
Grange Mus & Art
Gallery★ BN2 . . . . 193 F2
Grange Pk BN12 . . . . . . 206 E5
Grange Rd
Crawley Down RH10 . . . 21 A7
Hove BN3 . . . . 190 E8
Midhurst GU29 . . . . 94 F7
Petersfield GU32 . . . . . . 68 A2
Southwick BN42 . . . . . 189 E7
Grange The
Bognor Regis PO21 . . . 200 E2
Felcourt RH19 . . . . 9 D7
Horley RH6 . . . . .2 A6
New Brighton PO10 . . . 151 B2
Woodmancote PO10 . . . 152 A4
Grange Way RH13 . . . . . 57 F2
Grangeways BN1 . . . . . . 169 E5
Grangeway The BN16 . . . 205 C5
Grangewood 13 PO21 . . . 201 B2
Grangewood Dr PO21 . . . 200 D2
Grant Cl PO20 . . . . 212 D7
Grantham Rd BN1 . . . . . 170 A1
Grantsmead BN15 . . . . . 187 E8
Grant St BN2 . . . . 213 C4
Granville Ct 10 BN3 . . . . 191 B7
Granville Rd
Hove BN3 . . . . 191 E7
Littlehampton BN17 . . . 204 E4
Graperies The 3
BN2 . . . . 192 C5
Grasmere Ave BN15 . . . . 187 B6
Grasmere Ct 1 BN11 . . . 186 C1
Grasmere Gdns RH12 . . . 37 B6
Grasmere RH6 . . . . .2 C4
Grassmere Cl
Bognor Regis PO22 . . . 201 F4
Littlehampton BN17 . . . 205 A7
Grassmere Par PO22 . . . 201 F4
Gratten La BN5,RH17 . . . 106 D3
Grattons Dr RH10 . . . . . . 6 C1
Grattons The RH13 . . . . . 34 E3
Gratwicke Ct RH14 . . . . . 79 D8
Gratwicke Rd BN11 . . . . 186 C2
Gravel La PO19 . . . . 177 C5
Gravelly Cres BN15 . . . . 187 F6
Gravelpit Cnr RH17 . . . . . 39 C1
Gravelye Cl RH16 . . . . . . 88 B5
Gravelye La
Haywards Heath RH16 . . . 88 A4
Walstead RH16 . . . . 88 B6
Graveney Rd RH10 . . . . . 19 C5
Gravett Ct RH15 . . . . . . 108 F2
Gravetye Cl 3 RH10. . . . . 19 A4
Gravits La PO21 . . . . . . 201 B4
Graydon Ave PO19 . . . . 176 E4
Graylingwell Cotts
PO19 . . . . 155 A2
Graylingwell Dr
Chichester PO19 . . . . . 155 B1
Chichester PO19 . . . . . 177 B8
Graylingwell Hospl
PO19 . . . . 155 B1
Grays Cl GU27 . . . . 27 E8
Grayshott Dr PO22 . . . . 201 D6
Grays Wood RH6 . . . . . . .2 C3
Grayswood Ave PO20 . . . 208 B6
Grayswood Pl GU27 . . . . 27 E8
Grayswood Rd GU27 . . . . 27 D8
Great Ballard Sch
PO18 . . . . 157 D7
Great College St BN2 . . . 192 C4
Great Field Pl RH19 . . . . 10 B3
Greatfield Way PO9 . . . . 130 D3
GREATHAM 120 A4
Greatham Ct BN1 . . . . . 169 E6
Greatham Rd
Crawley RH10 . . . . 19 C3
Worthing BN14 . . . . . . 164 A1
Great Hanger GU31 . . . . . 68 D3
Great Heathmead
RH16 . . . . 87 D6
Great House Ct 4
RH19 . . . . 22 F8
Greatlake Ct RH6 . . . . . . .2 B4
Great Lime Kilns RH13 . . . 58 A1
Greatpin Croft RH20 . . . . 99 A3
Great Walstead Sch
RH16 . . . . 88 F6
Great Wilkins BN1 . . . . . 171 B5
Grebe Cl PO10 . . . . 151 D4
Grebe Cres RH13 . . . . . . 37 A1
Greenacre Cl RH20. . . . . 121 D7
Greenacres
Ashington RH20 . . . . . 123 A6
Birdham PO20 . . . . 197 D6

Greenacres *continued*
Brighton BN1 169 F1
Crawley RH10 19 A5
Horsham RH12 36 C4
Shoreham-by-S BN43 188 E8
Steyning BN44 145 D2
Greenacres Ring
BN16 184 A6
Greena Ct 8 BN11 186 C2
Greenbank PO22 180 C5
Greenbank Ave BN2 194 D2
Green Bushes Cl
BN16 205 B4
Green Cl
Southwater RH13 57 F3
4 Southwick BN42 189 E7
Greencourt Dr PO21 201 A5
Green Cross RH17 86 C3
Green Ct
Chichester PO19 177 C6
East Wittering PO20 207 F7
Littlehampton BN17 204 D4
3 Southwick BN42 189 E7
Greenfield RH20 117 F2
Greenfield Cl
Brighton BN1 170 A5
Liphook GU30 25 C5
Green Field Cl BN42 189 E8
Greenfield Cres BN1 169 F5
Green Field La PO18 153 B3
Greenfield Rd RH13 34 D3
Greenfields
Liss GU33 45 C4
Littlehampton BN17 204 B7
Middleton-on-S PO22 202 E5
Nyewood GU31 92 A7
Greenfields Cl
Horley RH6 1 E5
Horsham RH12 37 A6
Nyewood GU31 92 A8
Greenfields Rd
Horley RH6 1 F5
Horsham RH12 37 A5
Greenfields Sch RH18 23 C1
Greenfields Way RH12 37 A6
Greenfield Way RH20 121 E2
Greenfinch Way RH12 36 D7
Greengates GU28 50 D2
Green Hedges Ave
RH19 9 D2
Green Hedges Cl RH19 9 D2
Greenhill Pk RH17 88 A2
Greenhill Way RH17 88 A2
Greenhurst La RH20 121 E4
Green La
Bosham PO18 175 C6
Broadbridge PO18 175 A8
Burstow RH6 6 F6
Chichester PO19 177 B6
Copthorne RH10 7 F4
Crawley, Northgate
RH10 18 E8
Crawley, Worth RH10 19 D6
Cudworth RH5 3 D8
Faygate RH12 15 F4
Kingsley Green GU27 27 B4
Merston PO20 177 F4
Runcton PO20 177 F2
Selsey PO20 212 D6
Sidlesham PO20 209 C8
Street End PO20 198 E6
West Grinstead RH13 104 B8
Woodingdean BN2 193 E6
Greenland Cl BN13 185 E8
Greenland Rd BN13 185 E8
Greenlands Cl RH15 129 B8
Greenlands Dr RH15 129 B8
Greenland Wlk BN13 185 E8
Green Lane Cl BN18 159 F2
Green Lane Terr 11
PO21 201 C4
Green Lawns Cvn Pk
PO20 212 E8
Greenlea Ave PO21 200 B2
Greenleas BN3 168 D2
Greenleaves BN44 145 E1
Green Mdws RH16 88 B8
Greenoaks BN15 187 E8
Green Pk BN12 206 F7
Green Ridge BN1 169 B5
Greens La RH13 59 D7
Greenstede Ave RH19 9 F2
GREEN STREET 81 C2
Green The
Bognor Regis PO21 211 A8
Broadbridge Heath RH12 35 D4
Chichester PO19 177 C7
Copthorne RH10 7 B3
Crawley RH11 18 C7
Dial Post RH13 103 E3
East Lavington GU28 116 E5
Henfield BN5 125 E4
Horsted Keynes RH17 65 C5
Hove BN3 169 C2
Liss GU33 45 A5
Partridge Green RH13 105 A3
Pulborough RH20 100 C4
Rottingdean BN2 193 F2
Rowland's Castle PO9 130 E2
Southwick BN42 189 E7
Storrington RH20 121 F2
Greentree La RH13 105 C5
Greentrees
Lancing BN15 187 C6
5 Worthing BN11 186 B2
Greentrees Cl BN15 187 C6
Greentrees Cres
BN15 187 C6
Green View RH15 108 E3
Greenview The RH11 39 C7
Greenway RH12 36 B3
Green Way PO22 202 F5
Greenway Ct BN2 194 A1
Greenways
Bognor Regis PO21 200 B1
Haywards Heath RH16 87 F6
Henfield BN5 125 D5
Ovingdean BN2 193 D3
Portslade-by-S BN41 168 B1
Southwick BN42 167 F1
Greenway Sch RH12 36 B3
Greenways Cnr BN2 193 D4
Greenways Cres
Ferring BN12 206 F5
Shoreham-by-S BN43 167 A1
Greenways Wlk RH11 18 C1
Greenway The PO10 151 B4
Green Way The BN12 185 B5
Greenwich Cl RH11 18 C2
Green Wlk RH10 18 E8
Greenwood Ave PO22 201 B6
Greenwood Cl PO22 201 B6
Greenwood Ct 2 RH11 18 B1
Greenwood Dr BN16 205 F8
Greenwood Flats RH6 6 F6
Greet Rd BN15 187 D7
Gregory Cl RH10 19 C2
Gregory Ct 2 RH19 9 E1
Gregsons RH12 35 E8
Grendon Cl RH6 1 F5
Grenehurst Way GU31 68 B4
Grenfield Ct PO10 151 B3
Grenville Ave BN12 185 D4
Grenville Cl
Liphook GU30 25 C4
Worthing BN12 185 D4
Grenville Gdns PO19 176 F4
Grenville St BN1 213 A2
Gresham Pl BN5 125 D5
Gresham Wlk RH10 18 E3
Grevatt's La BN17,
BN18 203 B8
Grevatt's La W BN18 202 F8
Greville Gn PO10 151 A3
Grey Alders RH16 88 B6
Greyfriars BN3 191 D8
Greyfriars Cl
Bognor Regis PO21 200 F3
Worthing BN13 186 A6
Greyfriars La RH20 142 C8
Greyhound Slip RH10 19 D7
Greynville Cl PO21 200 C2
Greypoint Ho BN14 163 E6
Greystoke Mews
BN12 206 E6
Greystoke Rd BN12 206 E6
Greystone Ave
Bognor Regis PO21 200 F7
Worthing BN13 185 F6
Gribble La PO20 178 B7
Grier Cl RH11 17 E5
Griffin Cres BN17 204 D8
Griffith's Ave BN15 187 D8
Grinder's La RH13 103 E2
Grinstead Ave BN15 187 E6
Grinstead La
East Grinstead RH19 22 B1
Lancing BN15 187 E6
Sharpthorne RH19 43 C7
Grinstead Mount 4
BN2 192 F5
Grisedale Cl RH11 18 C4
Groombridge Way 4
RH12 35 F1
Grooms Cl BN16 184 A5
Groomsland Dr RH14 79 C6
Grooms The RH10 19 D8
Grosvenor Cl RH6 2 A1
Grosvenor Ct
12 Bognor Regis
PO21 201 C2
Brighton BN1 169 E3
Grosvenor Gdns
PO21 200 C3
Grosvenor Ho RH19 9 E3
Grosvenor Ho 6
BN11 186 D2
Grosvenor Mans 1
BN3 191 B6
Grosvenor Rd
East Grinstead RH19 9 D1
Stockbridge PO19 176 F3
4 Worthing BN11 186 D2
Grosvenor St BN2 213 C2
Grosvenor Way PO21 200 C3
Grouse Rd
Barnsnap RH11, RH13 38 D3
Mannings Heath RH13 59 F7
Grove Bank 9 BN2 213 C3
Grove Cres BN17 204 F6
Grove Ct 12 BN3 191 C6
Grove Hill BN2 213 C3
Grove La
Petworth GU28 98 A6
West Chiltington Common
RH20 121 E5
Grovelands RH6 2 B2
Grovelands Cl RH15 108 F1
Grovelands The BN15 187 E4
Grove Lo BN14 186 C6
Grove Pk PO19 176 D6
Grover Ave BN15 187 D7
Grove Rd
Burgess Hill RH15 109 B3
Chichester PO19 177 B5
Horley RH6 1 F4
Grove Rd *continued*
Selsey PO20 212 E6
Worthing BN14 186 C6
Grove St
Brighton BN2 213 C3
Petworth GU28 97 F7
Grove The
Bognor Regis PO22 202 A4
Crawley RH11 18 C6
Ferring BN12 206 E6
Haywards Heath RH16 88 B3
Horley RH6 2 B2
Liphook GU30 25 B4
Westbourne PO10 151 D3
Grove Villa 3 BN1 213 A4
Guardian Ct BN13 186 A6
Guernsey Cl RH11 18 A2
Guernsey Farm La
PO22 202 D5
Guernsey Rd BN12 206 F4
Guildbourne Ctr The 14
BN11 186 D2
Guilden Rd PO19 177 B6
Guildford Cl
Breach PO10 152 A1
Worthing BN14 186 A3
Guildford Pl PO19 154 F1
Guildford Rd
Brighton BN1 213 A3
Broadbridge Heath RH12 35 B6
Horsham RH12 36 A2
Loxwood RH14 31 F4
Rowhook RH12, RH13 34 C7
Rudgwick RH12 33 C6
Rustington BN16 205 E6
Worthing BN14 186 A3
Guildford St BN1 213 A3
Guildhall Mus* PO19 177 A7
Guildhall St PO19 177 A7
Guillards Oak GU29 94 E7
Guillemot Path 2
RH11 17 D5
Guillods Cotts GU28 116 B7
Guinevere Rd RH11 17 E6
Guinness Ct RH11 18 C2
Gunning Cl RH11 18 A3
Gunns Farm GU30 25 C2
GUNTER'S BRIDGE 75 F4
Gunwin Ct PO21 200 D2
Guyhurst Spinney
RH20 122 A6
Gwydyr Mans 3 BN3 191 D6
Gwynne Gdns RH19 9 C2

H

HABIN 70 B2
Habin Hill GU31 70 B3
Hackenden Cl RH19 9 E3
Hackenden La RH19 9 E3
Haddington Cl BN3 191 B6
Haddington St 11
BN3 191 B7
Hadlands PO21 200 A1
Hadley Ave BN14 186 D6
Hadley Cl PO22 202 E6
Hadlow Cl BN2 192 D6
Hadlow Way BN15 187 F6
Hadmans Cl RH12 36 C1
Hadrian Ave BN42 190 A8
Haglands Copse
RH20 121 D7
Haglands La RH20 121 D7
Haig Ave BN1 170 D6
Haigh Cl BN15 188 B6
Hailsham Ave BN2 194 D3
Hailsham Cl BN16 206 B7
Hailsham Rd BN11 185 F2
Hale Cl PO20 208 B6
HALECOMMON 70 A5
Hales Field GU27 27 C6
Halewick Cl BN15 187 C8
Halewick La BN15 187 C8
Haleybridge Wlk
PO20 156 D1
Halfacres RH10 18 E7
Half Moon Ct 1 BN13 185 F8
Half Moon Hill GU27 27 C6
Half Moon La BN13 185 F8
Halfrey Cl PO18 176 A7
Halfrey Rd PO18, PO19 176 B7
HALFWAY BRIDGE 96 C8
Halfway Sta* BN2 192 C4
Halifax Cl RH10 6 E1
Halifax Dr BN13 185 C7
Halland Cl RH10 19 A7
Halland Rd BN2 170 F4
Hallands The RH15 109 C4
Hall Ave BN14 186 B7
Hall Cl BN14 186 A7
Halleighs RH17 86 E8
Hallett Rd BN2 192 D7
Halley Cl RH11 18 B1
Halley's Ct PO19 177 C6
Halliford Dr PO22 180 C6
Halliwick Gdns PO22 202 B4
Halls Dr RH12 16 F1
Hallsland RH10 21 C8
Hallyburton Rd BN3 190 D8
Halnaker Barn La
PO18 157 B4
Halnaker Gdns PO21 200 C2
Halnaker Wlk 8 RH11 17 F3
Halsbury Cl BN11 186 F3
Halsbury Rd BN11 186 F3
Halsford Croft RH19 9 B3
Halsford Gn RH19 9 B3
Halsford La RH19 9 C3
Halsford Park Prim Sch
RH19 9 C2
Halsford Park Rd RH19 9 C2
Halson Cl PO21 201 C4
Halton Shaws BN6 128 B5
Hamble Ct BN15 187 B6
Hambledon Pl PO21 201 B3
Hamble Gdns BN13 185 C8
Hamble Rd BN15 187 B6
Hambleton Ct RH11 18 C4
Hambleton Hill RH11 18 C4
Hamble Way BN13 185 C8
Ham Bridge Trad Est
BN14 187 A4
Hambrook RH15 109 C1
Hambrook Bsns Ctr
PO18 152 D4
Hambrook Hill N
PO18 152 D3
Hambrook Hill S
PO18 152 D2
Ham Bsns Ctr BN43 189 A7
Ham Cl BN11 187 A4
Hamfield Ave BN43 188 F8
Hamilton Cl
Portslade-by-S BN41 168 A3
Rustington BN16 205 B8
Stedham GU29 71 F1
Worthing BN14 186 E5
Hamilton Ct
Brighton BN2 193 A3
Worthing BN12 185 D5
Hamilton Dr BN16 205 B8
Hamilton Gdns
Bognor Regis PO21 200 D2
Broadbridge PO18 175 C7
Hamilton Lodge Sch
BN2 192 D5
Hamilton Mans 4
BN3 191 B5
Hamilton Mews BN15 187 C6
Hamilton Pl RH6 2 A2
Hamilton Rd
Brighton BN1 213 A4
Horsham RH12 36 B3
Lancing BN15 187 D7
Ham La
Oving PO20 178 D7
Prinsted PO10 173 F7
Scaynes Hill RH17 88 E3
Hamlet The
Bognor Regis PO22 201 C6
Climping BN17 181 D1
Hamlin's Cnr BN6 108 A6
Ham Manor Cl BN16 205 E8
Ham Manor Farm Cotts
BN16 205 D8
Ham Manor Way
BN16 205 E8
HAMMER 26 D5
Hammer Hill
Linchmere GU27 26 C4
Staplefield RH17 62 A3
Hammer La
Chithurst GU29 71 D4
Haslemere GU27, GU30 26 A6
Haslemere, Hammer
GU27 26 C5
Haslemere, Nutcombe GU26,
GU27 26 C8
Hammerpond Rd
Ashfold Crossways
RH13 60 B6
Doomsday Green RH13 59 C8
Horsham RH13 36 F1
HAMMERPOT 183 F8
Hammer Vale GU27 26 B6
Hammerwood Copse
GU27 26 D5
Hammerwood Rd
RH19 23 E6
Hammingden La RH17,
RH19 42 E1
Hammond Cl BN16 206 A8
Hammond Dr BN13 185 E9
Hammond Pl 3 RH20 121 D1
Hammond Rd RH11 39 B8
Hammonds Gdns
RH15 108 F1
Hammonds Ridge
RH15 108 E1
Hammy Cl BN43 189 C8
Hammy La BN43 189 B8
Hammy Way BN43 189 B8
Hampden Cl
Crawley RH10 6 E1
Middleton-on-S PO22 202 F5
Hampden Ct BN11 186 F4
Hampden Pl PO20 156 D2
Hampden Rd BN2 192 C7
Hampers Common Ind Est
GU28 75 F2
Hampers Ct 2 RH13 36 D2
Hampers Gn GU28 75 E2
Hampers La RH20 122 B2
Hamper's La RH13 37 A2
Hampshire Ave PO21 201 B5
Hampshire Ct
Brighton BN2 213 C1
6 Horsham RH12 36 D2
Hampshire Ho GU30 25 B7
Hampstead Rd BN1 169 D1
Hampton Cotts RH13 82 F6
Hampton Ct
Bognor Regis PO21 200 F4
9 Littlehampton BN17 204 D5
8 Worthing BN11 186 F2
Hampton Fields 4
BN17 204 D6
Hampton Lo RH6 2 A2
Hampton Pl BN1 191 E5
Hampton St 24 BN1 191 E5
Hampton Terr 7 BN1 191 E6
Hampton Way RH19 22 F7
Ham Rd
Shoreham-by-S BN43 188 F7
Sidlesham PO20 209 C5
Worthing BN11, BN14 187 A3
Hamsey Cl BN2 192 F5
Hamsey Rd
Saltdean BN2 194 D1
Sharpthorne RH19 43 A6
Hamshire Hill RH17 60 F5
Hamsland RH17 65 C4
Hamstead Mdw PO18 174 E7
Ham Way BN11 187 A4
Hanbury La RH16 88 A5
Hanbury Rd RH11 17 E5
Hanbury Sq GU31 68 C5
Hancock Way BN43 189 B6
Handcross Park Prep Sch
RH17 39 C2
Handcross Prim Sch
RH17 39 C2
Handcross Rd
Balcombe RH17 40 D3
Lower Beeding RH13,
RH17 60 C5
Handford Way RH13 60 D6
Handsworth Ho 8
RH10 18 D5
Hangdown Mead Bsns Pk
RH19 43 B5
Hanger Way GU31 68 D3
Hangleton Cl BN3 168 D2
Hangleton Ct BN11 185 F2
Hangleton Gdns BN3 168 D1
Hangleton Grange
BN12 206 E7
Hangleton Jun & Inf Sch
BN3 168 E2
Hangleton La
Hangleton BN12 206 D8
Portslade-by-S BN41 168 B2
Hangleton Manor Cl
BN3 168 D2
Hangleton Rd BN3 168 E2
Hangleton Valley Dr
BN3 168 D4
Hangleton Way BN3 168 D3
Hanlye La RH17 87 B8
Hannah Sq PO19 176 D7
Hannington Pl BN6 128 A7
Hanover Cl
Bury RH20 140 A7
Crawley RH10 18 F3
Selsey PO20 212 F7
Hanover Cres BN2 213 C4
Hanover Ct
Brighton BN2 213 C4
Haywards Heath RH16 87 D4
1 Horsham RH13 36 F3
Liphook GU30 25 B5
Midhurst GU29 73 A2
Worthing BN14 186 C6
Hanover Gdns RH13 83 E2
Hanover Lofts BN2 213 C3
Hanover Mews BN2 213 C4
Hanover St BN2 213 C4
Hanover Terr BN2 213 C4
Hanover Wlk RH20 121 D1
Harberton Cres PO19 155 A3
Harbolets Rd RH14,
RH20 102 A5
Harborough Cl RH20 121 B8
Harborough Dr RH20 121 B8
Harborough Gorse
RH20 121 B8
Harborough Hill
RH20 121 B8
Harborough Mdw
RH20 121 B8
Harbour Cotts PO18 175 A4
Harbour Ct
Bosham PO18 175 C5
10 Emsworth PO10 173 B8
Southwick BN42 189 F7
Harbour Ho BN43 189 B6
Harbour Rd
Bosham PO18 175 B4
Pagham PO21 210 F6
Harbour View Pk
BN17 204 C4
Harbour View Rd
PO21 211 A8
Harbour Way
Bosham PO18 175 C4
Chidham PO18 174 F5
Emsworth PO10 173 C8
Shoreham-by-S BN43 189 B6
Harcourt Way PO20 212 F8
Hardbarrow Woods
RH20 122 A6
HARDHAM 119 F7
Hardham Cl
Crawley RH11 18 A8
Rustington BN16 205 B4
Hardham Rd PO19 177 B5
Harding Cl PO20 210 A1
Hard's Hill RH13 58 D5
Hard The PO22 203 C5
Hardwick Lo 3 BN11 186 C2

Hardwick Rd BN3 . . . . 168 E3
Hardwick Way BN3 . . . . . . 168 E3
Hardy Ave GU31 . . . . 68 C5
Hardy Cl
  Bognor Regis PO22 . . . . . . 202 D5
  Crawley RH10 . . . . 19 C7
  Horley RH6 . . . . 1 E3
  Horsham RH12 . . . . 36 B4
  Shoreham-by-S BN43 . . . 188 F6
Harebell Cl BN17 . . . . 205 B7
Harebell Dr BN41 . . . . . . 168 A3
Harefield Ave BN13 . . . . . 185 F5
Harefield Gdns PO22 . . . . 202 F5
Harefield Rd PO22 . . . . . . 202 F6
Hare La
  Crawley RH11 . . . . 18 B8
  Selsey PO20. . . . . 212 B8
Haresfield Terr PO20. . . . 156 D1
Haresfoot Ct PO18 . . . . . . 152 F5
Hares La PO18 . . . . 152 E6
Harewood Cl RH10 . . . . . . 6 A1
Harewood Ct 8 BN3 . . . 191 C6
Harfield Ct 6 PO21 . . . . . 201 D3
Harlands Cl RH16 . . . . 87 C6
Harlands Ho RH16 . . . . . . 87 D6
Harlands Prim Sch
  RH16. . . . . 87 D7
Harlands Rd RH16 . . . . . . 87 D6
Harlech Ct BN13 . . . . 185 B6
Harley Ct 6 BN11 . . . . . . 186 B2
Harmans Dr RH19. . . . . . . 10 B1
Harmans Mead RH19 . . . . 10 B1
Harmony Cl RH11 . . . . 17 E4
Harmony Dr PO20. . . . . . 208 B5
Harmsworth Cres
  BN3 . . . . 168 E3
Harold Cl PO21 . . . . 200 F6
Harold Kidd Unit The
  PO19. . . . . 155 A2
Harold Rd
  Crawley RH10 . . . . 19 E5
  Westbourne PO10 . . . . . . 151 D4
Haroldslea RH6. . . . . 2 E2
Haroldslea Cl RH6 . . . . . . 2 C1
Haroldslea Dr RH6. . . . . . . 2 D1
Harold Terr PO10 . . . . . . 151 B1
Harper Dr RH10. . . . . 19 C2
Harrier Cl RH10. . . . . 6 D1
Harrier Ho 6 RH20 . . . . 121 E1
Harrier Way GU31. . . . . . . 68 E2
Harriet Pl 10 BN43 . . . . 189 B6
Harrington Ct BN1 . . . . . . 169 E2
Harrington Mans BN1 . . . 169 E2
Harrington Pl BN1 . . . . . . 170 B2
Harrington Rd BN1 . . . . . 169 E2
Harrington Villas BN1. . . 169 F2
Harriots Cl RH13. . . . . 59 A1
Harriot's Hill RH13. . . . . . 83 A8
Harris Cl RH11 . . . . 18 B3
Harris Ct GU30. . . . . 25 B2
Harris La PO8 . . . . 110 A5
Harrison Ct BN14 . . . . . . 186 E5
Harrison Rd BN14. . . . . . . 186 F5
Harris Path RH11 . . . . 18 B3
Harrow Dr PO20. . . . . . . 207 F7
Harrow Ho RH6. . . . . 2 A3
Harrow La GU32 . . . . 68 B6
Harrow Rd BN11 . . . . 186 B3
Harrowsley Ct RH6. . . . . . . 2 B4
Harrows The GU28 . . . . . . 97 B8
Harsfold Cl BN16 . . . . . . 205 B4
Harsfold Rd BN16 . . . . . . 205 B4
Hartfield Ave BN1. . . . . . 170 A5
Hartfield Rd
  Forest Row RH18. . . . . . . 23 F2
  Saltdean BN2. . . . . 194 D1
Harting Cl BN12 . . . . 185 B5
Harting Ct RH11 . . . . 17 F3
Harting Down GU31. . . . . . 68 D4
*Harting Downs Nature
  Reserve*★ PO18. . . . . . . 112 A7
Harting Rd BN17. . . . . . . 204 D7
Hartings The PO22. . . . . . 202 D6
Hartington Ho 8
  PO21. . . . . 201 B3
Hartington Pl BN2 . . . . . . 192 C8
Hartington Rd BN2 . . . . . 192 C8
Hartington Terr BN2 . . . . 192 C8
Hartington Villas BN3. . . 191 B8
Hartland Ct PO10 . . . . . . 151 F1
Hartley Ct 8 BN1 . . . . . . 213 A4
Harvest Cl RH10. . . . . 88 B7
Harvester Cl PO19 . . . . . 177 C7
Harvesters
  Haywards Heath RH16 . . . 87 D2
  Horsham RH12 . . . . 36 D5
Harvest Hill
  Ansty RH17 . . . . 86 D1
  East Grinstead RH19. . . . 22 E8
Harvest Rd RH10. . . . . . . 19 C4
Harvestside RH6. . . . . 2 C4
Harvey Cl
  Crawley RH11 . . . . 18 A1
  Sayers Common BN6. . . . 107 C1
Harvey Rd BN12 . . . . 185 E2
Harvey Villas GU30. . . . . . 24 D8
Harwarden Cl RH10 . . . . . 21 C8
Harwood Ave BN12 . . . . . 185 D5
Harwood Pk RH1 . . . . 2 A8
Harwood Rd
  Horsham RH12, RH13. . . . 37 A3
  Littlehampton BN17. . . . . 204 C6
Harwood Road Ent Units
  BN17. . . . . 204 C6
Harwoods Cl 3 RH19 . . . 22 F7

HARWOODS GREEN 99 E5
Harwoods Cl RH19. . . . . . 22 F7
Hascombe Ct RH11 . . . . . 18 A5
Hasle Dr GU27 . . . . 27 B6
*Haslemere Educational
  Mus*★ GU27 . . . . 27 D7
Haslemere Gdns
  PO11 . . . . 195 B2
Haslemere Hospl
  GU27. . . . . 27 D7
Haslemere Ind Est
  GU27. . . . . 27 C7
Haslemere Prep Sch
  GU27. . . . . 27 D7
Haslemere Rd
  Breach PO10 . . . . 151 F2
  Fernhurst GU27. . . . . 49 B7
  Kingsley Green GU27. . . . 27 B1
  Liphook GU30 . . . . 25 D4
Haslemere Sta GU27. . . . 27 B6
Hasler's La PO18. . . . . . . 134 E5
Haslett Ave E RH10 . . . . 19 A6
Haslett Ave W RH10. . . . . 18 D5
HASLINGBOURNE 98 A5
Haslingbourne La
  GU28 . . . . 97 F5
Hassocks Ct 3 RH11 . . . 17 F3
Hassocks Inf Sch BN6. . . . 128 F4
Hassocks Lo BN6 . . . . . . 128 F3
Hassocks Rd BN6 . . . . . . 128 B5
Hassocks Sta BN6 . . . . . 128 E4
Haste Hill GU27. . . . . 27 D5
Hastings Cl PO21 . . . . . . 200 F4
Hastings Ct
  9 Shoreham-by-S
    BN43. . . . . 189 B6
  10 Worthing BN11. . . . . 186 A1
Hastings Rd
  Brighton BN2. . . . . 192 C8
  Crawley RH10 . . . . 19 C6
  Worthing BN11 . . . . 186 A1
Hatch Cl GU6. . . . . 11 A3
Hatch End RH18 . . . . 23 F2
Hatches Cotts RH20. . . . 101 E1
Hatchetts Dr GU27. . . . . . 26 D7
Hatchgate RH6 . . . . 1 F2
Hatchgate Ct RH17 . . . . . 87 A6
Hatchgate La RH17. . . . . . 87 A6
Hatch Hill GU27. . . . . 27 B1
Hatch La
  Kingsley Green GU27. . . . 27 B2
  Liss GU33 . . . . 45 E4
Hatchlands
  Cuckfield RH17 . . . . 86 F6
  Horsham RH12 . . . . 37 A7
Hatfield Ct 18 BN3 . . . 191 C6
Hatfield Wlk
  Crawley RH11 . . . . 17 E2
  Worthing BN13 . . . . 185 D6
Hatherleigh Cl PO21 . . . . 201 A5
Hatherleigh Gdns
  PO21. . . . . 201 A5
Hathersham La RH1, RH6 . . 2 F6
Haughton Ho GU27. . . . . . 27 B6
Havant Rd PO10 . . . . 173 A8
Havelock Cl PO22. . . . . . 201 F3
Havelock Rd
  Bognor Regis PO21. . . . . 201 C4
  Brighton BN1 . . . . 169 F1
Haven Cotts 6 PO22 . . . 201 D5
Haven Ct PO20. . . . . 207 F7
Havengate RH12 . . . . 36 F5
Haven Gdns RH10. . . . . . . 8 B1
Haven Rd
  Rudgwick RH12, RH14. . . 33 D3
  South Hayling PO11. . . . . 195 A1
Havenside BN43. . . . . . . 188 E6
Havenstoke Cl PO19 . . . . 155 A1
HAVEN THE 33 D2
Haven The
  Lancing BN15. . . . . 187 F4
  Littlehampton BN17. . . . . 205 A5
Havenwood Pk BN18 . . . . 159 B3
Haversham Cl RH10 . . . . . 18 F6
Haversham Ho RH6 . . . . . . 2 B5
Hawke Cl BN16 . . . . 205 C5
Hawker Cl PO20 . . . . 156 D2
Hawkesbourne Rd
  RH12. . . . . 36 F5
Hawkesmoor Rd RH11 . . . 17 E4
Hawkhurst Pl BN1. . . . . . 170 D6
Hawkhurst Rd BN1. . . . . . 170 D6
Hawkhurst Wlk 2
  RH10 . . . . 19 B4
Hawkins Cl
  Bognor Regis PO21. . . . . 200 B2
  Shoreham-by-S BN43. . . . 167 D1
Hawkins Cres BN43 . . . . 167 D1
Hawkins Rd
  Crawley RH10 . . . . 18 E4
  Shoreham-by-S BN43. . . . 167 D1
Hawkley Rd GU33 . . . . . . 45 A5
Hawkridge RH12. . . . . 12 E1
Hawksfold La E GU27 . . . . 49 A6
Hawksfold La W GU27. . . . 49 A6
Hawkshaw Cl GU30. . . . . . 25 D4
Hawks Mead GU33 . . . . . . 45 A5
Hawks Pl PO22 . . . . 201 B6
Hawley Rd BN16 . . . . 205 B4
Hawmead RH10. . . . . 21 C8
Haworth Rd RH10. . . . . . . 19 C5
Hawth Ave RH10 . . . . 18 F4
Hawth Cl RH10 . . . . 18 E4
Hawthorn Bank BN2 . . . . 170 F4
Hawthorn Cl
  Burgess Hill RH15 . . . . . 109 C5
  Chichester PO19 . . . . . . 176 D7
  Crawley RH11 . . . . 5 C1

Hawthorn Cl *continued*
  Horsham RH12 . . . . 36 C4
  Midhurst GU29 . . . . 94 D6
  6 Rustington BN16 . . . . 205 C4
  Saltdean BN2. . . . . 194 C2
Hawthorn Cres BN14. . . . 186 D6
Hawthorn Ct GU31. . . . . . 68 E3
Hawthorn Gdns BN14 . . . 186 D6
Hawthorn Pl 13 RH16. . . 87 C2
Hawthorn Rd
  Bognor Regis PO21,
    PO22. . . . . 201 B4
  Littlehampton BN17. . . . . 204 D7
  Worthing BN14 . . . . 186 D6
Hawthorns Fst Sch
  BN13. . . . . 185 C6
Hawthorns The
  6 Bognor Regis
    PO21. . . . . 201 C4
  Burgess Hill RH15 . . . . . 109 A5
  West Chiltington Common
    RH20. . . . . 121 E7
Hawthorn Trad Est
  RH13. . . . . 36 E4
Hawthorn Way
  Portslade-by-S BN41. . . . 168 A3
  Storrington RH20. . . . . . 121 D2
Haybarn Dr RH12 . . . . . . 36 E7
Haybourne Cl BN2. . . . . . 192 F5
Haybourne Rd BN2. . . . . . 192 E5
Haydon Cl PO21 . . . . 200 C1
Hayes Cl
  Mid Lavant PO18 . . . . . . 154 E7
  Portslade-by-S BN41. . . . 190 C8
Hayes La RH11 . . . . 34 C2
Hayes Wood Rd RH14 . . . 55 F5
Hayfields RH6 . . . . 2 C4
Hayley Rd BN15. . . . . 187 F7
Hayley's Gdns PO22. . . . 202 A4
Haylind Rd RH10. . . . . . . 88 B5
Hayling Ct RH11 . . . . 18 C3
Hayling Gdns BN13 . . . . . 163 E1
Hayling Rise BN13 . . . . . 163 E1
Haynes Rd BN14 . . . . 186 B4
Haynes Way BN14. . . . . . 186 B4
Hays Rd PO19 . . . . 177 B4
Hays Cotts GU32 . . . . 67 F7
Haystacks GU29 . . . . 115 C8
Hayton Ct BN13. . . . . 185 B6
Haywards RH10. . . . . 6 D1
Haywards Cl PO22 . . . . . . 202 B5
Haywards Heath Rd
  RH17 . . . . 41 A1
Haywards Heath Sta
  RH16. . . . . 87 E6
Haywards Pl PO20 . . . . . . 208 C5
Haywards Rd
  Brighton BN1. . . . . 170 A6
  Haywards Heath RH16 . . . 87 E3
Haywards Villas RH16 . . . 87 F3
Hazel Bank 3 BN2. . . . . 213 C6
Hazelbank Rd
  Liphook GU30 . . . . 25 D4
  Petersfield GU31. . . . . . . 68 D4
Hazelbank Mews GU30. . . 25 D4
Hazel Cl
  Crawley Down RH10 . . . . 21 C8
  Crawley RH11 . . . . 5 C1
  Hove BN41. . . . . 168 C3
  Southwater RH13 . . . . . . 58 A1
Hazel Ct 4 RH12. . . . . . . 36 E4
Hazeldean PO9 . . . . 130 D1
Hazeldean Dr PO9 . . . . . . 130 D1
Hazeldene Meads
  BN1 . . . . 169 D3
Hazeldene Rd GU30. . . . . 24 D4
Hazel Gr
  Arundel BN18 . . . . 159 E2
  Bognor Regis PO22 . . . . . 200 D3
  Burgess Hill RH15 . . . . . 109 B1
Hazelgrove Gdns 8
  RH16. . . . . 87 E4
Hazelgrove Rd RH16 . . . . 87 E4
Hazelholt BN41. . . . . 167 F3
Hazelhurst RH6. . . . . 2 C4
Hazelhurst Cres
  Horsham RH12 . . . . 35 F1
  Worthing BN14 . . . . 163 F3
Hazelhurst Dr RH10. . . . . 19 E6
Hazelmead Dr BN16. . . . . 206 A5
Hazel Rd
  Angmering BN16 . . . . . . 206 A8
  Bognor Regis PO22 . . . . . 201 B6
Hazel Way RH10. . . . . 21 C8
Hazelwick Ave RH10 . . . . 19 B8
Hazelwick Mill La
  RH10 . . . . 19 A8
Hazelwick Rd RH10 . . . . . 19 A7
Hazelwick Sch RH10 . . . . . 19 A8
Hazel Wlk GU31. . . . . 68 B1
Hazelwood
  Brighton BN1. . . . . 169 D3
  Crawley RH11 . . . . 18 A5
Hazelwood Cl
  Crawley Down RH10 . . . . 20 F8
  Heath Common RH20 . . . 122 B2
  Midhurst GU29 . . . . 73 A3
  Worthing BN14 . . . . 186 F4
Hazelwood Cotts GU6. . . . 11 C4
Hazelwood Lo 3
  BN15 . . . . 187 F5
Hazelwood Rd RH13 . . . . 105 A3
Hazelwood Trad Est
  BN14. . . . . 186 F5
Hazleden Cross RH19 . . . 22 B6
Headborough Ct 2
  RH10 . . . . 187 E4

Headborough Gdns 1
  BN15 . . . . 187 E4
Head Down GU31 . . . . . . 68 D3
Headhone Barns
  PO22 . . . . 179 D4
Headley Cl RH10 . . . . 6 D1
Headley Dr PO22. . . . . . . 201 D6
Headley Rd GU30 . . . . 25 B5
Hearn Cl PO20. . . . . 156 C1
Hearnfield Rd BN17. . . . . 204 D8
Heasewood RH16 . . . . . . 87 C3
Heath Bsns Ctr RH1. . . . . . 2 B8
Heath Cl
  Broadbridge Heath
    RH12. . . . . 35 E3
  9 Haywards Heath
    RH16. . . . . 87 E4
  Hunston PO20 . . . . 199 A8
  Mannings Heath RH13. . . 59 D6
  Sayers Common BN6. . . . 107 D1
Heathcote Dr RH19 . . . . . 9 C2
Heathcotes RH10 . . . . 19 D4
Heathcourt BN17 . . . . . . 204 D8
Heath Ct
  Haywards Heath RH16 . . . 87 E5
  Petersfield GU31. . . . . . . 68 D2
HEATH END 97 D2
Heath End GU28 . . . . 97 D2
Heather Bank RH16 . . . . . 87 C5
Heather Cl
  Copthorne RH10 . . . . 7 B2
  Horsham RH12 . . . . 36 D5
  West Ashling PO18 . . . . . 153 C3
Heather Ho BN15 . . . . . . 187 E1
Heather La
  West Chiltington Common
    RH20. . . . . 121 C6
  Worthing BN13 . . . . 163 E2
Heatherlands
  Horley RH6 . . . . 2 B4
  Storrington RH20. . . . . . 121 F2
Heatherlea Ho BN15 . . . . 187 D6
Heatherleigh Ct RH12 . . . 36 C4
Heather Rd GU31. . . . . . . 68 E3
Heathers The BN16 . . . . . 183 F6
Heatherstone Rd
  BN11 . . . . 187 B2
Heatherton Mews
  PO10 . . . . 151 B3
Heatherway RH19. . . . . . . 8 F7
Heather Way RH20. . . . . . 121 F1
Heather Wlk RH11 . . . . . . 18 B3
Heatherwood GU29 . . . . . 94 D8
Heatherwood Ho GU29 . . . 94 D8
Heathfield RH10 . . . . 19 D8
Heathfield Ave
  Angmering BN16 . . . . . . 205 F7
  Saltdean BN2. . . . . 194 D2
Heathfield Cl
  1 Midhurst GU29 . . . . . 94 E7
  Worthing BN13 . . . . 185 F6
Heathfield Copse
  RH20. . . . . 121 C7
Heathfield Cres RH10 . . . 167 F3
Heathfield Dr BN41 . . . . . 167 F4
Heathfield Gate 2
  GU29 . . . . 94 E7
Heathfield Gdns GU29. . . . 94 E7
Heathfield Gn GU29 . . . . . 94 E7
Heathfield Pk GU29 . . . . . 94 E7
Heathfield Rd GU31 . . . . . 68 E3
Heath Hill Ave BN2 . . . . . 170 F1
Heath Lo GU31. . . . . 68 B2
Heath Pl PO22 . . . . 201 D7
Heath Rd
  Haslemere GU27 . . . . 26 D5
  Haywards Heath RH16 . . . 87 E5
  Petersfield GU31. . . . . . . 68 C3
Heath Rd E GU31 . . . . . . 68 D2
Heath Rd W GU31 . . . . . . 68 C2
Heath Sq RH16 . . . . 87 D5
Heathtolt Cotts RH13. . . . 83 A6
Heath Way RH12 . . . . 36 D5
Heaven Farm★ RH17. . . . . 66 B1
Hebe Rd BN43 . . . . 188 E2
Hechle Wood PO21 . . . . . 200 F2
Hectors La RH19 . . . . 23 C7
Hedgecourt Pl RH19 . . . . . 8 E4
Hedge End PO22. . . . . . . 180 C6
Hedgehog La GU27 . . . . . 27 B5
Hedgerow Gdns PO10. . . . 151 B3
Hedgers Hill BN18 . . . . . 158 F2
Hedgeside RH11 . . . . 18 C1
Hedgeway PO22 . . . . 202 D5
Hedingham Cl RH6. . . . . . . 2 C4
Heene CE Fst Sch
  BN11 . . . . 186 C3
Heene Lo BN11 . . . . 186 C1
Heene Pl BN11 . . . . 186 C1
Heene Rd BN11 . . . . 186 B2
Heene Terr BN11 . . . . 186 B1
Heene Way BN11 . . . . 186 B2
Heghbrok Way PO21 . . . . 201 A2
Heights The
  Brighton BN1. . . . . 169 B5
  6 Haywards Heath
    RH16. . . . . 87 E6
  Worthing BN14 . . . . 164 A1
Helena Cl BN14. . . . . 168 C2
Helena Rd BN2 . . . . 171 C1
Helen Ct 7 BN11 . . . . . . 185 F3
Helicon Ho RH11. . . . . . . 18 C5
Hellingly Cl BN2 . . . . 192 F5
Helston Dr PO10 . . . . 151 B3
Helyer's Gn BN17 . . . . . . 204 C6

Hempstead Rd BN2 . . . . . 194 D3
Hemsby Wlk 5 RH10. . . . 19 B4
Hemsleys The RH11 . . . . . 39 B6
Henbane Ct 2 RH11 . . . . 18 B2
Henderson Rd RH11. . . . . 18 B1
Henderson Way RH12 . . . . 57 F8
Henderson Wlk BN44 . . . 145 D4
Hendon Ave BN16. . . . . . 205 A3
Hendon Ho BN16 . . . . . . 205 C6
Hendon St BN2 . . . . 192 D5
Henfield Bsns Pk
  BN5. . . . . 126 A1
Henfield Cl
  Brighton BN2. . . . . 192 F5
  Worthing BN12 . . . . 185 B5
Henfield Common N
  BN5. . . . . 125 F4
Henfield Mus★ BN5. . . . . 125 F4
Henfield Rd
  Albourne Green BN6 . . . . 127 B7
  Upper Beeding BN44,
    BN5. . . . . 146 D3
Henfield Way
  Bognor Regis PO22 . . . . . 202 D6
  Hove BN3. . . . . 168 F3
Henge Way BN41 . . . . . . 168 B2
Hengist Cl RH12 . . . . 36 A1
HENLEY 73 B8
Henley Cl RH10 . . . . 19 D3
HENLEY COMMON 48 F1
Henley Ct
  Brighton BN2. . . . . 192 F4
  Worthing BN11 . . . . 185 F4
Henley Rd BN2 . . . . 192 F4
Henry Ave BN16 . . . . 205 B5
Henry Burt Way RH15 . . . 108 E1
Henry Cl PO19 . . . . 177 D6
Henry Fletcher Cl
  BN16 . . . . 184 A5
Henry St PO21 . . . . 201 D4
Henshaw Cl RH11. . . . . . . 17 F4
Henson Rd RH10. . . . . . . 19 B7
Henty Cl
  Crawley RH11 . . . . 17 E3
  Walberton BN18 . . . . . . 180 E8
  4 Worthing BN14. . . . . 186 C4
Henty Gdns PO19 . . . . . . 176 F6
Henty Rd
  Ferring BN12. . . . . 206 F4
  Worthing BN14 . . . . 186 C4
Henwood Down GU31. . . . 68 C3
Hepplewhite Cl RH11 . . . . 18 B1
Herald Dr PO19 . . . . 177 A5
Herbert Rd
  Brighton BN1. . . . . 169 F2
  North Lancing BN15 . . . . 165 B1
Herbert Shiner Sch
  GU28. . . . . 97 F7
Hercules Pl PO22 . . . . . . 202 D5
Hereford Cl
  Chichester PO19 . . . . . . 154 F1
  Crawley RH10 . . . . 18 E2
Hereford Ct
  15 Brighton BN2. . . . . . 213 C2
  15 Hove BN3. . . . . 191 C7
Hereford Ho BN12 . . . . . 185 A4
Hereford St BN2 . . . . 192 C5
Herington Rd BN18 . . . . . 159 F2
Heritage Lawn RH6. . . . . . 2 C4
Heritage Pl 9 BN16 . . . . 205 C4
Herm Cl RH11 . . . . 18 A2
Hermione Cl BN12 . . . . . 206 E7
Hermitage Cl PO20. . . . . 177 D1
Hermitage La RH19 . . . . . 22 F8
Hermitage Rd RH19 . . . . . 9 D3
Hermitage The PO20. . . . 177 D1
Hermits Rd RH10 . . . . . . 18 F7
Hermit Terr BN14 . . . . . . 163 E6
Hermonger La RH12 . . . . . 12 F2
Herm Rd BN12. . . . . 206 F4
Hernbrook Dr RH13 . . . . . 58 E8
Herne Ct 2 BN16 . . . . . . 205 D6
Herne Gdns BN16 . . . . . . 205 D6
Herne Jun Sch GU31. . . . . 68 C4
Herne La BN16. . . . . 205 D6
Herne Rd GU31 . . . . 68 C4
Heron Cl
  Bognor Regis PO22 . . . . . 201 B7
  Crawley RH11 . . . . 18 C8
  Mid Lavant PO18 . . . . . . 154 E7
Heron Ct
  Chichester PO19 . . . . . . 177 D7
  5 Worthing BN11. . . . . 186 C3
Herondale GU27 . . . . 26 E6
Herondean PO19. . . . . . . 154 F2
Heron La PO20 . . . . 212 B8
Heron Mead PO21 . . . . . . 210 F7
Heron Pl RH19 . . . . 22 F8
Heron Quay PO10 . . . . . . 173 C7
Herons Cl
  Domewood RH10. . . . . . . 8 B5
  Kirdford RH14 . . . . 53 B2
Heron's Court Cl 3
  BN16 . . . . 205 C4
Herons Ct PO22. . . . . 201 C5
Heronsdale Rd BN2 . . . . . 193 F8
Herons Dale Sch
  BN43. . . . . 167 C1
Herons Lea RH10 . . . . 8 A4
Heron's Rye 9 RH20 . . . 100 C2
Herons The
  Lancing BN15. . . . . 187 F4
  Selsey PO20. . . . . 212 D4
  Shoreham-by-S BN43. . . 189 A8
Heron's Tye BN16 . . . . . . 128 F3
Heronswood Ct RH6. . . . . . 2 B4
Herontye Dr RH19 . . . . . . 23 A8

Herontye Ho RH19 22 F7
Heron Way RH13 37 A1
Heron Way Prim Sch
RH13 37 A1
Herrick Cl RH10 19 C8
Herschel Wlk 9 RH11 18 B1
Hersee Way PO20 212 C7
Hertford Cl PO21 200 F3
Hertford Ct 3 BN11 186 D3
Hertford Inf Sch BN1 170 B2
Hertford Jun Sch
BN1 170 C2
Hertford Rd
Brighton BN1 170 B2
Worthing BN11 186 D3
Heston Ave BN1 169 F7
Heston Gr PO21 200 C1
Hett Cl RH17 64 B8
Hevers Ave RH6 2 A4
Hevers Cnr RH6 1 F4
Hewart's La PO21 200 D4
Hewells Ct 4 RH12 36 C2
Hewitts BN5 125 E4
Hewitts End BN5 125 E4
Hewshott Gr GU30 25 E5
Hewshott La
Linchmere GU30 26 A5
Liphook GU30 25 E5
Hexham Cl RH10 19 E6
Heyshott Cl BN15 187 F8
Heyworth Cl BN2 193 F8
Heyworth Prim Sch
RH16 87 F4
Heyworth Ride RH16 87 C3
Hickling Wlk 10 RH10 19 B4
Hickman's Cl RH16 88 B8
Hickmans Ct RH16 88 A7
Hickman's La RH16 88 A8
Hickstead Int Arena★
RH17 107 D4
Hickstead La RH17 107 C5
Hickstead Pk BN6 107 D2
Hide Gdns BN16 205 B6
Higgins La RH13 36 E1
Highams Hill RH11 17 F5
Highbank
9 Bognor Regis
PO22 201 D5
Brighton BN1 169 C5
Haywards Heath RH16 87 C1
High Bank PO20 198 F8
High Bar La RH20 122 A6
Highbarn BN14 163 E7
High Beeches 7
BN11 186 A1
High Beeches Cotts
RH17 39 E2
High Beeches Gdns★
RH17 39 F2
High Beeches La RH17 39 E2
High Beech La RH16 63 F1
Highbirch Cl RH12 37 B5
HIGHBROOK 42 E1
Highbrook Cl BN2 170 D3
Highbrook La RH19 42 F4
Highbury Cotts RH17 61 B8
Highbury Gr GU27 27 C8
High Cl BN41 168 A1
Highclere Way BN13 185 B6
Highcliff Ct BN2 194 A1
Highcroft Ave PO22 201 D5
Highcroft Cl PO22 201 E5
Highcroft Cres PO22 201 E5
Highcroft Dr RH12 12 E1
Highcroft Lo BN1 191 E8
Highcroft Mews BN1 169 D1
Highcroft Rd RH19 43 A6
Highcroft Villas BN1 191 E8
HIGH CROSS 126 F7
Highden 2 BN2 192 C6
Highdown BN42 167 F1
Highdown Ave BN13 186 A5
Highdown Cl
Angmering BN16 184 A5
Ferring BN12 206 E7
Southwick BN42 167 F1
Highdown Ct
Brighton BN1 169 E3
Crawley RH10 19 B3
Highdown Dr BN17 204 D6
Highdown Gdns★
BN12 184 F5
Highdown Rd BN1,
BN3 191 E7
Highdown Way
Ferring BN12 206 E7
Horsham RH12 36 F6
Highercombe Rd GU27 27 E8
Highfield BN17 204 B7
Highfield Cl
Angmering BN16 184 A5
Midhurst GU29 73 A2
Highfield Cotts BN17 204 F7
Highfield Cres BN1 170 A5
Highfield Ct
7 Haywards Heath
RH16 87 E4
Worthing BN14 186 E6
Highfield Dr BN6 128 C5
Highfield Gdns
Bognor Regis PO22 201 D5
Liss GU33 45 D4
1 Rustington BN16 205 B5
Highfield Ho RH11 18 D7
Highfield La
Liphook GU30 25 E3
Oving PO20 178 C7
Highfield Rd
Bognor Regis PO22 201 D5
East Grinstead RH19 9 D3
Petersfield GU32 68 B4
Worthing BN13 186 A6
Highfields
Brighton BN1 170 E5
Forest Row RH18 23 F2
Horsted Keynes RH17 65 C4
Highfield Sch GU30 25 E2
HIGHGATE 23 F1
Highgate Ct RH11 18 C2
Highgate Dr PO21 200 F6
Highgate Rd RH18 23 F1
Highground La PO22 180 B4
Highgrove Gdns
BN11 186 B2
High Hatch La BN6 108 B4
High La GU27 27 C8
Highland Ave PO21 201 B4
Highland Cl PO10 173 A8
Highland Croft BN44 145 D3
Highland Ct RH16 87 E4
Highland Rd
Chichester PO19 155 A2
Emsworth PO10 151 A1
Haywards Heath RH16 87 F3
Highlands Ave RH13 36 E2
Highlands Cl
Keymer BN6 129 A3
Worthing BN13 163 E1
Highlands Cres RH13 36 E2
Highlands Dr RH15 109 A4
Highlands Farm Bsns Pk
RH17 85 D3
Highlands Rd
Horsham RH13 36 F2
Portslade-by-S BN41 168 B1
Highlands The RH17 86 F8
Highleigh 8 BN2 213 C3
Highleigh Rd PO20 198 C2
High Mdw GU29 114 D8
High Oaks RH11 18 B4
High Park Ave BN3 168 E3
High Path GU29 73 A2
High Pines BN11 186 B2
High Point RH16 88 A3
High Ridge Cl BN18 159 F1
HIGH SALVINGTON 163 E1
High Salvington
Windmill★
BN13 163 E2
High Seat Copse RH14 55 D1
High Seat Gdns RH14 55 D1
High Spinney RH20 121 E5
High St
Amberley BN18 140 E7
Angmering BN16 184 A5
Ardingly RH17 64 B8
Arundel BN18 160 B3
Balcombe RH17 40 C5
Billingshurst RH14 55 D1
Bognor Regis PO21 201 D3
Bosham PO18 175 A4
Brighton BN2 213 C2
Chichester PO19 176 F7
Crawley RH10 18 D6
Cuckfield RH17 86 E6
Ditchling BN6 129 D3
East Grinstead RH19 22 F8
Emsworth PO10 173 B8
Findon BN14 163 E6
Handcross RH17 61 C8
Haslemere GU27 27 D7
Henfield BN5 125 F4
Horley RH6 2 B3
Hurstpierpoint BN6 128 A5
Lindfield RH16 88 B8
Littlehampton BN17 204 D5
Loxwood RH14 31 F3
Oving PO20 178 C6
Partridge Green RH13 105 A3
Petersfield GU32 68 B3
Petworth GU28 97 F8
Portslade-by-S BN41 168 A1
Rottingdean BN2 193 F1
Rusper RH12 16 D7
Selsey PO20 212 D7
Shoreham-by-S BN43 188 E7
Steyning BN44 145 D3
Storrington RH20 121 D1
Upper Beeding BN44 146 A2
Worthing BN11 186 E2
Worthing, West Tarring
BN14 186 A5
Highstanding La GU29 95 A6
Highstead La GU28 74 A8
High Titten BN18 140 E5
High Trees
Bognor Regis PO21 200 F2
Bramber BN44 145 F2
Fittleworth RH20 99 A3
Haywards Heath RH16 87 F5
Hunston PO20 177 A1
High Trees Ct RH6 1 A4
Highview BN15 165 D1
High View BN13 163 F1
Highview Ave N BN1 169 E6
Highview Ave S BN1 169 E6
Highview Rd
Brighton BN1 169 E6
Eastergate PO20 179 F7
Highview Way BN1 169 E6
Highway Cl BN2 170 D2
Highways BN41 168 B2
Highway The BN2 170 D3
Highwood Pk RH11 18 C2
Highwoods Ct RH12 35 D3
Hilary Ho PO21 201 B2
Hilary Lo 2 BN2 192 C5
Hilary Rd PO19 176 E7
Hildon Cl BN13 185 D6
Hildon Pk BN13 185 D6
Hilgrove Rd BN2 194 D3
Hilland Rdbt RH14 55 D2
Hillary Cl RH19 10 A3
Hillbank Cl BN41 167 F3
Hillbarn Ave BN15 165 D1
Hillbarn La GU29 114 D6
Hill Barn La BN14 186 C7
Hillbarn Par BN15 187 C8
Hill Brow BN3 169 B3
Hill Brow Cl PO9 130 D1
Hillbrow Rd BN1 169 D4
Hill Brow Rd GU33 45 C3
Hill Cotts GU29 115 C8
Hillcrest
Brighton BN1 169 C5
Horsted Keynes RH17 65 C5
Hill Crest RH19 9 E6
Hillcrest Cl
Ashington RH20 123 A5
Crawley RH10 19 D6
Scaynes Hill RH17 88 F3
Hillcrest Ct BN1 169 C5
Hillcrest Dr RH20 123 A5
Hillcrest La RH17 88 F3
Hillcrest Pk RH20 100 D2
Hillcroft
Haslemere GU27 27 C6
Portslade-by-S BN41 167 F2
Hill Ct GU27 27 B6
Hill Dr BN3 169 B3
Hill Farm Cl GU27 26 F5
Hill Farm La RH20 100 B5
Hill Farm Way BN42 167 E2
Hillfield Rd PO20 212 D6
HILLGROVE 50 E6
Hill House Cl RH10 21 A5
Hill House Hill GU30 25 A6
Hillhouse La RH12 11 F1
Hillingdale RH11 18 C1
Hill La
Barnham PO22 180 C4
South Harting GU31 91 E2
Hillmead RH11 17 F6
Hill Mead RH12 36 B3
Hill Pl RH11 18 C5
Hill Rd
Haslemere GU27 27 C6
Littlehampton BN17 204 F6
Saltdean BN2 194 B1
Hillrise Ave BN15 187 D8
Hills Barns PO20 176 C3
Hillsboro Rd PO21 201 C4
Hills Farm La RH12 35 F1
Hillside
Brighton BN2 170 E2
Crawley Down RH10 21 B8
Forest Row RH18 23 F3
Horsham RH12 36 A2
Portslade-by-S BN41 168 C1
Southwick BN42 167 F1
Hillside Ave BN14 186 B7
Hillside Cl
Crawley RH11 18 B4
East Grinstead RH19 9 E3
Hillside Cotts
Clapham BN13 162 E1
East Marden PO18 112 B1
Hill Brow GU33 45 D2
West Stoke PO18 154 A5
Hillside Cres BN16 184 A5
Hillside La BN5 146 E5
Hillside Pk BN5 146 E5
Hillside Rd
Haslemere GU27 26 F5
Heath Common RH20 122 A2
Lancing BN15 165 C1
Hillside Sch BN41 168 B2
Hillside Scout Camp
BN5 146 E5
Hillside Terr 7 BN44 145 D3
Hillside Way
Brighton BN2 170 E2
Brighton, Westdene
BN1 169 C4
Hillside Wlk
Haywards Heath RH16 87 C6
Heath Common RH20 122 A2
Hills Manor RH12 36 A2
Hills Pl RH12 36 A2
Hills Rd
East Grinstead RH19 9 A3
Steyning BN44 145 C2
Hill Terr BN18 159 F2
Hilltop GU29 114 C6
Hill Top BN1 169 B5
Hilltop Cotts RH6 1 D2
Hilltop Prim Sch RH11 18 C4
Hilltop Rd RH19 42 E6
Hill View
Elsted GU29 92 D4
Small Dole BN5 146 F7
Hillview Cres BN16 206 A6
Hillview Gdns RH11 39 C8
Hillview Rd
Woodingdean BN2 193 B8
Worthing BN14 163 F2
Hillview Rise BN14 163 F1
Hillybarn Rd RH11 4 C1
Hilton Ct
11 Haywards Heath
RH16 87 E4
Horley RH6 2 C4
Hilton Pk PO20 208 A8
Hinde Rd PO22 202 C4
Hindhead Cl RH11 18 C4
Hindhead Rd GU27 26 E7
Hindleap La RH17,
RH18 44 C4
Hindleap Warren Outdoor
Education Ctr RH18 44 D5
Hindle Cl RH20 121 D7
Hinton Cl BN1 170 C2
Hislop Wlk 13 PO21 201 D3
Hither Gn PO10 152 A2
Hoad La RH16 64 D4
Hoadlands GU31 68 D4
Hoadlands Cotts RH17 39 C2
Hoadley's Cnr RH15 109 B2
Hoathly Hill RH19 42 F5
Hobart Cl BN13 185 C8
Hobbs Ind Est RH7 8 D7
Hobbs Rd RH11 18 A2
Hobbs Sq GU31 68 C5
Hobbs Way BN16 205 C5
Hobdens La RH17 64 B7
Hoblands RH16 88 B4
Hobs Acre BN44 146 B1
Hocken Mead RH10 19 D8
Hodgkin Cl RH10 19 C5
Hodshrove La BN2 170 E3
Hodshrove Pl BN2 170 E3
Hodshrove Rd BN2 170 E3
Hoe Ct
Lancing BN15 188 A8
North Lancing BN15 165 F1
Hoefield La GU29 114 C5
Hoe La
Bosham PO18 175 C1
Flansham PO22 202 B7
Walberton BN18 181 C7
Hoelands La GU29 114 C6
Hoewood BN5 146 F7
Hogarth Rd
Crawley RH10 18 F3
Hove BN3 190 F7
Hoggarth Cl GU32 68 C4
Hog La BN18 140 E7
Hogs Edge BN2 171 A2
Hogwood Rd RH14 31 C3
Holbein Rd RH10 18 F3
HOLBROOK 36 E8
Holbrook 16 BN2 192 F5
Holbrook Park Ho
RH12 36 E8
Holbrook Prim Sch
RH12 36 E7
Holbrook School La
RH12 36 E7
Holdens The PO18 175 A5
Holder Rd RH10 19 B3
Holders BN6 127 C6
Holders Cl RH14 55 C1
Holdfast La GU27 27 F7
Holdings The BN7 172 F5
Hole St BN44, BN20 123 B2
Holford Gn PO20 212 F8
Holkham Cotts BN18 181 A3
Holland Cl PO21 200 F5
Holland Mews BN3 191 D5
Holland Rd
Hove BN3 191 D6
Steyning BN44 145 E3
Hollands Ct RH19 10 A4
Hollands Field RH13 35 E4
Hollands La BN5 125 C4
Hollands Rd BN5 125 D5
Holland St BN2 213 C3
Hollands Way
East Grinstead RH19 10 A4
Warnham RH12 35 F8
Hollies Cvn Pk The
PO11 195 A2
Hollies The
Bognor Regis PO21 200 F5
Lancing BN15 187 E6
Hollin Ct RH10 5 E1
Hollingbourne Cres
RH11 39 C8
Hollingbourne Ct 8
BN2 192 E4
HOLLINGBURY 170 B5
Hollingbury Copse
BN1 170 A4
Hollingbury Cres BN1 170 B2
Hollingbury Gdns
BN14 164 A2
Hollingbury Ind Est
BN1 170 C7
Hollingbury Park Ave
BN1 170 A2
Hollingbury Pl BN1 170 B2
Hollingbury Rd BN1 170 B1
Hollingbury Rise BN1 170 B2
Hollingbury Rise W
BN1 170 A3
Hollingbury Terr BN1 170 A2
HOLLINGDEAN 170 B3
Hollingdean La BN1 192 B8
Hollingdean Rd BN2 192 B8
Hollingdean St BN1 170 B1
Hollingdean Terr
BN1 170 B2
Hollist La
Midhurst GU29 72 E2
South Harting GU31 91 F4
Hollow La RH19, RH7 10 D6
Hollow The
Bury RH20 140 A8
Crawley RH11 17 F5
Haywards Heath RH16 88 B5
Washington RH20 143 F8
Hollow The *continued*
West Chiltington RH20 101 D1
West Hoathly RH19 42 F6
Hollyacres BN13 185 D9
Holly Bank 3 BN2 213 C5
Hollybank La PO10 151 B4
Hollybush Bsns Ctr
Copthorne RH6 6 F4
Crawley RH6 6 F4
Hollybush Cl RH10 18 E8
Hollybush Rd RH10 18 E8
Holly Cl
Brighton BN1 169 E3
Crawley RH10 19 A8
Horsham RH12 37 B5
Storrington RH20 121 C1
West Chiltington RH20 101 D1
Worthing BN13 185 C6
Hollycombe Cl GU30 25 C2
Hollycombe Prim Sch
GU30 47 D4
Hollycombe Steam
Collection★ GU30 47 E7
Holly Ct
Bognor Regis PO22 201 C6
Storrington RH20 121 C2
Holly Dr BN17 204 E8
Holly Gate Cactus Gdn★
RH20 123 A8
Holly Ho 2 PO21 201 C4
Hollyhock Way BN17 205 A7
Holly Lo BN14 186 B4
Holly Rd RH16 88 A3
Hollyridge GU27 27 B6
Hollywater Rd GU30,
GU35 24 C8
Hollywood Ct RH16 87 E5
Holman Cl RH11 39 B8
Holmans RH17 64 A8
Holmbury Cl RH11 18 C4
Holmbury Keep RH6 2 C4
Holmbush Cl
Haywards Heath RH16 87 E2
Horsham RH12 36 D6
Shoreham-by-S BN43 167 D2
Holmbush Ct 8 BN43 189 C8
Holmbush Ctr BN43 167 C1
Holmbush Farm World★
RH12 17 B1
Holmbush Fst Sch
BN43 167 D1
Holmbush Ind Est
GU29 94 E6
Holmbush La BN5 147 F8
Holmbush Way
Midhurst GU29 94 E6
Southwick BN42 167 E1
Holmcroft RH10 18 E5
Holmcroft Gdns BN14 163 E6
Holmdale PO20 157 F1
Holmes Ave BN3 168 F1
Holmesdale Rd RH15 109 A1
Holmes Foundation
BN18 160 B2
Holmes La BN16 205 B4
Holmfield Cl BN16 205 B6
Holmgarth BN5 125 F5
Holm Ho RH15 108 F3
Holming End RH12 37 B5
Holm Oak RH20 121 C1
Holm Oaks RH13 83 F1
Holmstead BN2 213 C4
Holmsted Hill RH17 62 A1
Holmwood Cl PO20 196 C1
Holmwood Ct BN6 128 F4
Holt Down GU31 68 D3
Holt Gdns PO9 130 D3
Holt Lo 1 BN2 213 C4
Holton Hill BN2 193 E7
Holt The
Burgess Hill RH15 109 C2
Washington RH20 143 E6
Holtview Rd BN2 193 B8
Holtye Ave RH19 10 A3
Holtye Pl RH19 10 B3
Holtye Rd RH19 10 B3
Holtye Wlk RH10 19 A4
Holy Cross Hospl GU27 26 F7
Holyrood RH19 23 A8
Holy Trinity CE Prim Sch
Cuckfield RH17 86 F6
Lower Beeding RH13 60 A3
Holy Trinity CE Sec Sch
The RH11 18 A4
Homebush Ave
Saltdean BN2 194 D1
Saltdean BN7 194 F3
Home Cl RH10 19 C8
Homecroft Ho 5
PO21 201 B3
Homedrive Ho BN3 191 C8
Home Farm Bsns Ctr
BN1 170 D3
Home Farm Ct
Chiddingfold GU8 29 D5
Horsted Keynes RH17 65 C5
Home Farm Ho 1
RH12 36 C2
Home Farm Rd BN1,
BN2 170 D3
Homefield Ave PO22 202 C6
Homefield Cl RH6 2 B4
Homefield Cotts GU33 45 A5
Homefield Cres BN18 158 D1

Homefield Rd
Westbourne PO10 . . . . . . 151 D4
Worthing BN11 . . . . 186 E3
Homegreen Rd GU27. . . . . 27 A6
Homehaven Ct 2
BN43 . . . . 188 E7
Homelands GU27. . . . . . . 27 B1
Homelands Ave BN16 . . . . 206 A4
Homelands Copse
GU27 . . . . 49 D4
Homelees Ho BN1 . . . . . . 213 A3
Homeleigh BN1. . . . . 169 E5
Homepier Ho 7
BN11 . . . . 186 B2
Home Platt RH19 . . . . 43 A6
Home Rd BN1 . . . . 169 E1
Homeridge Ho BN1. . . . . 194 D1
Homesearle Ho BN12 . . . . 185 C3
Homestall Rd RH19 . . . . . . 23 E8
Homestead Cotts
BN12 . . . . 206 F6
Homestead La RH15 . . . . 109 C6
Homestead The BN16 . . . . 206 A5
Homesteyne Ho 3
BN14 . . . . 186 D4
Homestream Ho RH12. . . . . 36 B1
Homethorne Ho RH11. . . . . 18 C5
Home Way GU31. . . . . 68 E3
Homewood Ho BN12 . . . . 163 E7
Homing Gdns PO22. . . . . . 201 B7
Honer La PO20 . . . . 199 D3
Honeybridge La
Ashurst BN44, RH13 . . . . 124 A6
Dial Post RH13 . . . . 103 E1
**Honeybridge Pk Caravan
& Camping Slte**
RH13. . . . . 103 E1
Honey Croft BN3. . . . . . . 168 D4
Honey La BN16 . . . . 184 A5
Honeysuckle Cl
Horley RH6 . . . . 2 C4
North Lancing BN15 . . . . 165 D1
Rustington BN17 . . . . . . 205 A7
Honeysuckle Dr PO21 . . . 199 F2
Honeysuckle La
Crawley RH11. . . . . 5 C1
Selsey PO20. . . . . 212 C8
Worthing BN13, BN14 . . . 163 C3
Honeysuckle Wlk
RH12 . . . . 36 E4
Honeywood La RH5 . . . . . . 13 F5
Honeywood Rd RH13. . . . . . 37 A4
Hooe Farm Ind Est
BN18. . . . . 158 D2
Hooe The BN17 . . . . 205 A6
Hook Cotts PO20. . . . . . . 179 D5
Hook La
Bognor Regis PO22 . . . . . 201 E4
Bognor Regis, Rose Green
PO21. . . . . 200 B2
Bosham PO18 . . . . 175 F2
West Hoathly RH17,
RH19. . . . . 42 D4
Woodgate PO20. . . . . . . 179 C6
Hooklands La RH13 . . . . . 103 B3
Hook Lane Cl PO21 . . . . . 200 B3
Hooks The BN5 . . . . 125 E4
HOOKSWAY 112 D5
Hope Cotts BN42. . . . . . . 189 E8
Hope Ct RH11 . . . . 18 B1
Hopedene Ct 10 BN1 . . . . 186 C2
Hopewell Cl 3 BN43 . . . . 189 B6
Hop Garden La PO20 . . . . 199 D8
Hopgarton The PO21 . . . . 200 E3
Hop Gdn The GU31. . . . . . 91 D3
Hophurst Cl RH10 . . . . 21 B8
Hophurst Dr RH10 . . . . 21 B8
Hophurst Hill RH19 . . . . . . 8 D2
Hophurst La RH10 . . . . 8 B1
Hopkins Cl RH11. . . . . 18 B1
Horatio Ho BN1. . . . . 213 B3
Horden Ct RH12 . . . . 36 A1
Hordens The RH13. . . . . . . 56 F2
Horizon BN3. . . . . 190 F6
Horizon Ct BN41 . . . . 190 B8
Horley Inf Sch RH6 . . . . . . 2 A3
Horley Lodge La RH1. . . . . 2 A8
Horley Pl BN2 . . . . 192 E6
Horley Rd RH6 . . . . .5 B7
Horley Row RH6 . . . . 2 A4
Horley Sta RH6 . . . . .2 B2
Hormare Cres RH20. . . . . . 121 C2
Hornbeam Cl
Bognor Regis PO21. . . . . 200 F1
Horsham RH13 . . . . 36 F1
Hornbeams The
RH15 . . . . 108 D4
Hornbeam Way GU29 . . . . . 94 D5
Hornbrook Copse
RH13. . . . . 58 F8
Hornbrook Hill RH13. . . . . . 58 F8
Hornby Pl BN2. . . . . 171 A1
Hornby Rd BN2 . . . . 171 A1
Horndean Cl RH10 . . . . 6 D2
Horndean Rd PO10. . . . . . 151 A3
Hornet Rd RH10 . . . . 173 C3
Hornet The PO19 . . . . 177 B6
Horn La BN5. . . . . 126 B1
Hornshill La RH12. . . . . . . 32 F7
Horns La PO21 . . . . 199 F1
Horsebridge Hill RH14 . . . . 77 E2
Horsefield Rd PO20 . . . . . 212 D8
Horse Hill RH6. . . . . .1 B4
HORSEMERE GREEN
. . . . 181 C1

Horsemere Green La
BN17. . . . . 181 D1
Horseshoe Cl
Crawley RH10 . . . . 19 D7
Findon BN14. . . . . 163 E6
Horse Shoe The
PO20 . . . . 212 D7
Horsgate Ho RH17 . . . . 87 A8
Horsgate La RH17. . . . . . . 87 A6
Horsham Cl BN2. . . . . 192 F6
Horsham Hospl RH12 . . . . . 36 C3
Horsham La BN17. . . . . . . 204 F5
Horsham Mus★ RH12. . . . . 36 C1
Horsham Rd
Alfold Crossways GU6,
RH12. . . . . 11 C1
Ashurst BN44 . . . . 145 C7
Cranleigh GU6 . . . . 12 B8
Crawley RH11. . . . . 18 A4
Findon BN14 . . . . 163 D8
Five Oaks RH13, RH14. . . . 56 A6
Handcross RH17 . . . . 61 B7
Kingsfold RH5 . . . . 15 C8
Littlehampton BN17. . . . . 204 F6
Pease Pottage RH11 . . . . . 39 B6
Petworth GU28 . . . . 76 B2
Rowhook RH12, RH5. . . . . 13 D5
Rusper RH12 . . . . 16 B5
Steyning BN44 . . . . 145 C4
Wallis Wood RH5. . . . . . . 13 D8
Horsham Rd W BN17. . . . . 204 F6
Horsham Sta RH13. . . . . . . 36 D2
Horsham Trad Est
RH13. . . . . 36 E4
Horsted Ct BN1. . . . . 213 B4
Horsted Ho 1 RH16 . . . . . . 87 F3
Horsted Keynes Ind Pk
RH17. . . . . 65 B7
Horsted Keynes Sta
RH17. . . . . 65 A7
Horsted La
Danehill RH17 . . . . 66 A4
Sharpthorne RH19. . . . . . . 43 B3
Horton Cl BN11. . . . . 186 F2
Horton Pl BN16 . . . . 206 A8
Horton Rd BN1 . . . . 170 B1
Hoskins Pl RH19 . . . . 10 A4
Hotham Gdns PO22 . . . . . 201 E4
Hotham Way PO21,
PO22 . . . . 201 D4
Houghton Bridge
BN18 . . . . 140 D4
Houghton Cl BN15 . . . . . . 187 F7
Houghton Ho BN17 . . . . . . 204 B7
Houghton La RH20 . . . . . . 140 A6
Houghton Rd RH10. . . . . . . 19 C3
Houndean Rise BN7. . . . . . 172 F8
Housman Way RH19 . . . . . . 8 F4
Hova Villas BN3. . . . . 191 B6
Hove Bsns Ctr BN3. . . . . . 191 B8
Hovedene BN3. . . . . 191 C7
Hove Ent Ctr BN41 . . . . . . 190 C6
Hove Manor 8 BN3. . . . . . 191 A6
Hove Mus & Art Gall★
BN3. . . . . 191 A6
Hove Park Gdns
Hove BN3. . . . . 169 B1
Hove BN3. . . . . 191 B8
Hove Park Rd BN3 . . . . . . 169 C1
**Hove Park Sch & Sixth
Form Ctr**
Hove BN3. . . . . 168 D2
Hove BN3. . . . . 169 A1
Hove Park Villas BN3 . . . . 191 B8
Hove Park Way BN3. . . . . . 169 C1
Hove Pl BN3. . . . . 191 B5
Hove St BN3. . . . . 191 A6
Hove Sta BN3. . . . . 191 B8
Hove Tech Ctr 1
BN3. . . . . 191 A8
Howard Ave
Burgess Hill RH15 . . . . . 108 E4
East Wittering PO20 . . . . 207 D7
Howard Cl BN3 . . . . 169 A2
Howard Ho PO21 . . . . 201 A4
Howard Pl
Brighton BN1. . . . . 213 A4
5 Littlehampton BN17 . . . 204 D5
Howard Rd
Arundel BN18 . . . . 160 A2
Brighton BN2 . . . . 192 C7
Crawley RH11. . . . . 17 D2
Horsham RH13 . . . . 37 A4
Lancing BN15. . . . . 165 D1
Littlehampton BN17. . . . . 204 C5
Howard St BN11 . . . . 186 C3
Howards Way BN16 . . . . . 205 B3
Howard Terr BN1. . . . . . . 213 A4
Howberry Chase GU27 . . . . 27 B6
Hoylake Cl RH11 . . . . 17 D5
HOYLE 95 D1
Hoyle La GU29 . . . . 95 D2
Huddlestones BN16 . . . . . 183 F6
Hudson Dr
Liphook GU30. . . . . 25 C3
Worthing BN13 . . . . 185 D7
Hudson Dr BN16 . . . . 205 E4
Hudson Rd RH10. . . . . 18 E4
Huffwood Trad Est
Billingshurst RH14. . . . . . 79 D7
Partridge Green RH13. . . . 105 A3
Hughes Cl PO21 . . . . 200 F4
Hughes Rd BN2. . . . . 192 B8
Hugo Platt GU31. . . . . 70 A4
Humber Ave BN13 . . . . . . 185 C8
Humber Cl
Littlehampton BN17. . . . . 204 F4
Worthing BN13 . . . . 185 C8

Humphrey Lo RH15 . . . . . 109 D3
Humphrey's Gap
BN43 . . . . 189 A7
Humphrys Rd 5
BN11 . . . . 186 D2
Hundredsteddle La
PO20 . . . . 197 D2
Hungers La GU28 . . . . 97 D6
Hunnisett Cl PO20 . . . . . . 210 A1
Hunstanton Cl 8
RH11 . . . . 17 D5
Hunston Cl BN2. . . . . 193 F7
Hunter Ho RH10 . . . . 18 D3
Hunter Rd
Crawley RH10 . . . . 18 D4
Thorney Island PO10. . . . . 173 C3
Hunters Chase GU30 . . . . . 25 B5
Hunters Cl PO21 . . . . 200 C1
Hunters Lo 8 RH11. . . . . . 17 E5
Hunters Mead RH13. . . . . 105 A3
Hunter's Mead BN6 . . . . . 127 C6
Hunters Mews BN18 . . . . . 158 B3
Hunters Race PO19 . . . . . 154 E3
Hunters Way PO19 . . . . . . 154 F3
Huntingdon Way
RH15. . . . . 109 D4
Huntsbottom La GU33. . . . . 45 D3
Huntscroft Gdns RH13 . . . . 83 E1
Hunt's Gate RH17. . . . . . . 89 E3
Hurley Rd BN15. . . . . 187 F2
Huron Dr GU30 . . . . 25 D3
Hurst Ave
Horsham RH12 . . . . 36 D3
Worthing BN11 . . . . 185 F3
Hurst Cl
Amberley BN18 . . . . 140 E7
Crawley RH11 . . . . 17 F4
Liphook GU30 . . . . 25 A5
Hurst Cotts BN18 . . . . . . 140 E7
Hurst Cres BN41 . . . . 190 B8
Hurst Ct
Brighton BN1. . . . . 169 D1
Horsham RH12 . . . . 36 D3
Hurst Farm Rd RH19 . . . . . 22 D7
Hurstfield BN15. . . . . 187 C5
Hurstfield RH17 . . . . 88 A2
Hurst Gdns BN6 . . . . 127 F7
Hurst Hill BN1 . . . . 170 C5
Hurston Cl
Cootham RH20. . . . . 121 B3
Worthing BN14 . . . . 186 A8
Hurston Gr RH20. . . . . . . 121 B3
Hurston La RH20. . . . . . . 121 B3
Hurstpierpoint Coll
BN6. . . . . 128 B8
Hurst Pk
Horsham RH12 . . . . 36 D3
Midhurst GU29 . . . . 72 D7
Hurst Rd
Hassocks BN6 . . . . 128 D4
Horley RH6 . . . . 1 E4
Horsham RH12 . . . . 36 D3
Rustington BN16 . . . . . . 205 E6
Hurst Wickham Cl
BN6 . . . . 128 C5
Hurstwood Ave PO10. . . . . 152 A1
Hurstwood Cl GU29. . . . . . 94 E5
Hurstwood La
Haywards Heath RH17 . . . . 88 A2
Sharpthorne RH19,
RH19. . . . . 43 D1
Hurstwood Park Hospl
RH17. . . . . 88 A2
Hutchinson Cl 4
BN16. . . . . 205 B7
Hutchins Way RH6. . . . . . . 1 F5
Hutton Rd BN2 . . . . 170 B3
**Huxley's Experience Birds
of Prey Ctr★** RH13 . . . . . 58 F8
Hyde Bsns Pk The
BN2. . . . . 192 F8
Hyde Cl BN7. . . . . 172 E5
Hyde Cotts RH17. . . . . 38 F1
Hyde Dr RH11 . . . . 18 A1
Hyde Heath Ct RH10 . . . . . 19 D8
Hyde La BN4. . . . . 146 B2
Hyde Sq BN44 . . . . 146 B2
Hyde St BN44. . . . . 146 B1
Hyde The RH17 . . . . 38 F1
Hylands Cl RH10 . . . . 19 A5
Hylden Cl BN2. . . . . 193 B8
Hylter's La PO18 . . . . 134 B7
Hylton Rd GU32. . . . . 68 B3
Hyndman Cl RH11. . . . . . . 39 B8
Hyperion Cl RH11 . . . . 17 E4
Hyperion Wlk RH6 . . . . 2 B1
Hythe Cl BN11 . . . . 186 A1
Hythe Rd
Brighton BN1. . . . . 170 A2
Worthing BN11 . . . . 186 A1

I

Icarus Way PO22. . . . . . . 202 C5
Icklesham Ho 9 RH11. . . . . 17 F3
Iden Cl BN2 . . . . 192 E5
Iden Hurst BN6 . . . . 128 A7
Idsworth Cl PO8 . . . . 130 A6
Idsworth Down GU31. . . . . 68 C3
IFIELD 18 A7
Ifield Ave RH11. . . . . 18 A7
Ifield Cl BN2. . . . . 194 E2
Ifield Com Coll RH11. . . . . 18 A7
Ifield Dr RH11 . . . . 18 A7
Ifield Gn RH11 . . . . 5 A1

IFIELD GREEN 5 A1
Ifield Rd
Charlwood RH6 . . . . 4 E5
Crawley, West Green
RH11 . . . . 18 C6
Ifield St RH11 . . . . 17 F8
Ifield Sta RH11 . . . . 18 A6
Ifield Watermill★
RH11. . . . . 17 E5
IFIELDWOOD 4 D1
Ifield Wood RH11 . . . . .4 E1
Ifold Bridge La RH14 . . . . . 31 D4
Ifoldhurst RH14. . . . . 31 C2
**Iford & Kingston CE Prim
Sch** BN7 . . . . 172 F5
Ilex Cl BN16 . . . . 205 C4
Ilex Ct
Portslade-by-S BN42 . . . . 168 A1
Worthing BN13 . . . . 185 B3
Ilex Ho 1 BN16. . . . . 205 C4
Ilex Way
Middleton-on-S PO22. . . . . 202 E6
Worthing BN13 . . . . 185 B3
Image Cross RH19 . . . . . . 43 A5
Imberhorne Bsns Ctr
RH19. . . . . .9 B3
Imberhorne La RH19 . . . . . .9 B2
Imberhorne Lower Sch
RH19. . . . . 9 D3
Imberhorne Sch RH19. . . . . 9 B3
Imberhorne Way RH19 . . . . 9 B3
Imperial Arc BN1 . . . . 213 A2
Imperial Ct PO21. . . . . . . 201 C4
Imperial Ctr RH10 . . . . 6 A3
Independent Bsns Pk The
RH19. . . . . 9 A3
Infirmary Dr RH13 . . . . 57 E6
Infirmary Terr PO19 . . . . . 176 F8
Ingfield Manor Dr
RH14 . . . . 55 F6
Ingfield Manor Sch
RH14. . . . . 55 E6
Ingham Dr BN1 . . . . 170 D6
Inglecroft Ct 4 BN15 . . . . 187 C7
Inglegreen Cl BN12 . . . . . 206 E4
Inglenook RH13. . . . . 81 F7
Ingleside Cres BN15 . . . . . 187 F5
Ingleside Rd BN15 . . . . . . 187 F5
Inglewood Cl PO21. . . . . . 200 C1
Inglewood Dr PO21 . . . . . 200 B1
Ingram Cl
Horsham RH12 . . . . 36 A2
Rustington BN16 . . . . . . 205 B5
Steyning BN44 . . . . 145 D2
Ingram Cres E BN3. . . . . . 190 E8
Ingram Cres W BN3. . . . . . 190 E8
Ingram Ct BN3. . . . . 190 E7
Ingram Rd BN44. . . . . 145 D2
Ingram's Green La
GU29 . . . . 93 C4
Ingrams Ho 4 RH16 . . . . . . 87 F3
Inholmes Cl RH15 . . . . 109 C3
Inholmes Cotts RH17. . . . . 86 E8
Inholmes Park Rd
RH15 . . . . 109 B3
Inkpen La RH18. . . . . 23 F1
Inlands Rd PO18 . . . . 174 B8
Inmans La GU32. . . . . 68 D5
Innerwyke Cl PO22. . . . . . 202 B5
Innerwyke Manor
PO22 . . . . 202 B5
Innes Rd RH12. . . . . 36 F4
Innovation Dr RH15 . . . . . 108 D2
Institute Wlk RH19 . . . . . . .9 C1
**International Coll of
Oriental Medicine The**
RH19. . . . . 9 D2
Inval Hill GU27. . . . . 27 C8
Inverness Rd 4 BN2 . . . . . 192 C8
Inwood Cres BN1 . . . . 169 E1
Inwood Rd GU33. . . . . 45 C3
Iona Cl RH11 . . . . 18 B3
Iona Way 12 RH16 . . . . . . 87 E4
IPING 71 E2
Iping La GU29 . . . . 71 E4
Iping Rd GU29, GU30. . . . . 47 C2
**Iping & Stedham
Commons Nature
Reserve★** GU29. . . . . . . 93 D8
Irene Ave BN15 . . . . 187 D7
Iris Cl BN17 . . . . 205 B7
Ironsbottom RH2, RH6. . . . . 1 A6
Irvine Rd BN17 . . . . 204 E4
Irving Wlk RH10 . . . . 18 E3
Irwin Dr RH12 . . . . 36 A2
Isaac's La RH16, RH15. . . . . 87 A2
Isabel Cres BN3. . . . . 190 E8
Isfield Rd BN1 . . . . 170 C2
ISLAND 67 F8
Island La PO20. . . . . 212 B8
Island Loop PO20 . . . . . . 212 B8
Islington Ho 7 RH11. . . . . . 18 B2
Islingword Pl BN2 . . . . . . 192 C6
Islingword Rd BN2. . . . . . . 192 C7
Islingword St BN2 . . . . . . 213 C3
Itchen Cl GU31. . . . . 68 A2
Itchenor Rd
Shipton Green PO20 . . . . 197 A5
South Hayling PO11 . . . . . 195 B2
Itchingfield Prim Sch
Barns Green RH13. . . . . . 56 F3
Itchingfield RH13. . . . . . . 57 A6
Ithaca Terr PO22. . . . . . . 201 F3
Ivanhoe Cl RH11. . . . . .5 D1
Ivanhoe Pl PO22 . . . . 202 C5
Iveagh Cl RH11 . . . . 18 C1
Ivor Rd BN2 . . . . 171 C1
Ivory Pl BN2 . . . . 213 C3

Ivory Wlk RH11 . . . . 17 E3
Ivy Arch Cl BN14 . . . . 163 F6
Ivy Arch Rd BN14 . . . . 186 D3
Ivy Cl
Ashington RH20. . . . . 123 A5
Southwater RH13 . . . . 57 F1
Westergate PO20 . . . . . . 179 D7
Ivy Cotts RH17 . . . . 86 E8
Ivy Cres PO22. . . . . 201 D5
Ivydale Rd PO21 . . . . 201 A4
Ivydene Ind Est RH19 . . . . 23 D7
Ivy Dene La RH19 . . . . 23 D6
Ivydore Ave BN13 . . . . . . 185 D9
Ivydore Cl BN13. . . . . 185 D8
Ivy La
Ashington RH20. . . . . 123 A6
Bognor Regis PO22 . . . . . 201 D5
Westergate PO20 . . . . . . 179 E7
Ivy Mews 13 BN3. . . . . . . 191 D5
Ivy Pl
Hove BN1, BN3. . . . . 191 D5
Worthing BN11 . . . . 186 B1

J

Jackdaw Cl RH11 . . . . 18 C8
Jackdaw La RH12 . . . . 36 E6
Jacken Cl PO22. . . . . 202 C4
Jacket's Hill RH20. . . . . . . 122 A5
Jackrells La RH13. . . . . . . 58 B2
Jackson Rd RH11 . . . . 39 B8
Jackson St BN2. . . . . 213 C4
Jack Vass Cotts RH16 . . . . 63 C2
Jacobean Cl RH10. . . . . . . 19 C5
Jacobs Ct RH10. . . . . 19 C7
Jacqueline Du Pre Ct 6
BN2. . . . . 192 C5
**James Bradford
Almhouses** RH16 . . . . . . 87 C4
James Cl BN13 . . . . 185 F7
James Pl RH10 . . . . 18 D5
James Searle Ind Est
RH12. . . . . 36 E4
James St PO20 . . . . 212 E6
James Watt Way RH10 . . . . 6 A4
Jane Murray Way BN6,
RH15 . . . . 108 C3
Janes Cl RH15 . . . . 109 C5
Janes La
Burgess Hill RH15 . . . . . 109 D4
River GU28 . . . . 74 E3
Janeston Ct 4 BN3. . . . . . 191 C7
Japonica Cl BN43. . . . . . . 167 B1
Jarvis Cl RH11 . . . . 39 B8
Jarvis Cotts 4 BN44. . . . . 145 D3
Jarvis La BN44. . . . . 145 D3
Jarvis Rd BN18. . . . . 159 F2
Jasmine Cl BN17. . . . . 205 A7
Jasmine Ct
Brighton BN1. . . . . 169 F5
Horsham RH12 . . . . 36 C2
Hove BN3. . . . . 191 D7
Jason Ct BN1 . . . . 186 C1
Javelin Ct RH10. . . . . 6 D1
Javelin Rd PO10 . . . . 173 C3
Jay Cl RH13 . . . . 58 A2
Jays Cl BN17 . . . . 204 D6
Jay's La GU27 . . . . 28 C3
Jays The RH15 . . . . 108 E4
Jay Wlk
9 Chichester PO19. . . . . 177 A6
Turners Hill RH10 . . . . . . 21 C5
Jeans Ct 10 RH11 . . . . 18 B1
Jefferies RH17. . . . . 65 C4
Jefferies La BN12. . . . . . . 185 C2
Jefferis Ho RH11. . . . . .5 A1
Jefferson Ct 4 PO21 . . . . . 201 B2
Jeffreys Ave PO19 . . . . . . 155 A1
Jengers Mead RH14. . . . . . 55 D1
Jengers Pas RH14 . . . . 55 D1
Jenner Rd RH10 . . . . .5 F3
Jennings Way RH6. . . . . . . 2 D3
Jeremy's La RH17. . . . . . . 85 C6
Jerrard Rd PO20 . . . . 156 D2
Jersey Rd
Crawley RH11. . . . . 18 A2
Ferring BN12 . . . . 206 F4
Jersey St BN2. . . . . 213 C3
Jervis Ave BN16 . . . . 205 D5
Jesmond Cl BN3. . . . . 190 E7
Jesmond Rd BN3 . . . . 190 E7
**Jessie Younghusband
Prim Sch** PO19 . . . . 176 F8
Jessop Ho GU27 . . . . 27 A6
Jesters RH16 . . . . 109 C7
Jetty The PO22 . . . . 203 A5
Jevington Cl BN13 . . . . . . 185 B6
Jevington Ct
Shoreham-by-S BN43. . . . . 189 D6
Worthing BN13 . . . . 185 B6
Jevington Dr BN2. . . . . . . 170 D1
Jewel Wlk RH11 . . . . 18 A3
Jew St BN1 . . . . 213 B2
Jib Cl BN17 . . . . 205 A4
Jikack Ind Est BN6. . . . . . 108 B4
Jireh Ct RH16. . . . . 87 E5
Joan Nightingale Ho
RH16 . . . . 87 C4
Jobes RH17 . . . . 40 F1
Job's Cnr BN6 . . . . 107 E5
Job's La BN6, RH17. . . . . . 107 F5
Jobson's La GU27 . . . . 28 D2
Jockey Mead RH12. . . . . . . 36 A1
John Arundel Rd
PO19 . . . . 176 E7

John King Shipyard
  PO10 . . . . 173 C8
John Pounds Ho RH11 . . . 18 D4
Johnson Bank **4**
  BN2 . . . . 192 C7
Johnson Dr RH15 . . . . 109 D3
Johnson Way BN18 . . . . . 181 B2
Johnson Wlk RH10 . . . . . . 18 E3
John St
  Bognor Regis PO21 . . . . . 201 D3
  Brighton BN2 . . . . 213 C3
  Shoreham-by-S BN43 . . . 188 E7
John Whittle Lo BN2 . . . . 170 C1
Jolesfield RH13 . . . . 104 F4
Jolesfield CE Prim Sch
  RH13 . . . . 105 A4
Jolesfield Ct RH11 . . . . . . 17 F3
Jolliffe Ct **13** GU32 . . . . . 68 B3
Jolliffe Rd PO20 . . . . 207 D7
Jones Sq PO20 . . . . 212 E6
Jordan Ct BN3 . . . . 190 E8
Jordans Cl RH11 . . . . 18 D8
Jordans Cres RH11 . . . . . . 5 D1
Jordans The RH19 . . . . . . 22 E8
Joyce Cl BN17 . . . . 204 C7
Joys Croft PO19 . . . . 177 B7
Joys Croft Ct PO19 . . . . . 177 B7
Jubilee Ave BN16 . . . . . . 205 C6
Jubilee Cl RH16 . . . . 88 A4
Jubilee Ct
  Billingshurst RH14 . . . . . . 79 D8
  Brighton BN2 . . . . 170 E2
  Worthing BN11 . . . . 186 B2
Jubilee Ho
  Crockerhill PO18 . . . . 157 B3
  Emsworth PO10 . . . . 151 A1
Jubilee Mews PO10 . . . . . 173 E8
Jubilee Pl PO22 . . . . 201 C5
Jubilee Rd
  Burgess Hill RH15 . . . . . . 108 E2
  Chichester PO19 . . . . 177 A7
  Portslade-by-S BN41 . . . . 190 A4
  Rudgwick RH12 . . . . 33 D8
Jubilee St BN1 . . . . 213 B2
Jubilee Terr
  Chichester PO19 . . . . 177 A7
  Westbourne PO10 . . . . . . 151 D3
Jubilee Way RH20 . . . . . . 121 F3
Jubilee Wlk
  Crawley RH10 . . . . 19 A6
  14 Horsham RH12 . . . . . . 36 C2
Judges Cl RH19 . . . . 22 E8
Judge's Terr RH19 . . . . . . 22 E8
Juggs La RH20 . . . . 101 E1
Juggs The RH20 . . . . 101 E1
Julian Ct **5** BN43 . . . . . 189 C8
Julian Rd BN3 . . . . 191 E7
Junction Cl
  Burgess Hill RH15 . . . . . . 109 C4
  Yapton BN18 . . . . 181 B2
Junction Mews RH15 . . . . 109 B3
Junction Pl GU27 . . . . 26 F6
Junction Rd
  Brighton BN1 . . . . 213 A3
  Burgess Hill RH15 . . . . . . 109 B3
June Cl PO21 . . . . 210 F8
June La GU29 . . . . 94 E8
June Mdws GU29 . . . . 94 D8
June Rise GU29 . . . . 94 E8
Juniper Cl
  Middleton-on-S PO22 . . . 202 E6
  Portslade-by-S BN41 . . . . 168 B3
  Worthing BN13 . . . . 185 C6
Juniper Ct **11** RH16 . . . . 87 C2
Juniper Rd RH11 . . . . 5 C1
Juniper Wlk BN43 . . . . . . 167 C1
Juno Cl BN12 . . . . 185 C4
Jupp's La BN12 . . . . 185 C4
Jura Cl RH11 . . . . 18 B3
Jury La PO20 . . . . 198 D5
Juxon Cl
  Chichester PO19 . . . . 177 A5
  Crawley RH11 . . . . 17 F4

K

Kaithewood Ho RH12 . . . . 37 B5
Kandy Pk BN17 . . . . 204 C4
Karenza Ct BN1 . . . . 192 A8
Katherine's Lo **7**
  BN15 . . . . 187 E5
Kathleen Gdns PO19 . . . . 177 C6
Kearsley Dr BN14 . . . . . . 164 A1
Keaton Ho **2** RH16 . . . . 87 E6
Keats Cl RH12 . . . . 36 F7
Keats Pl RH19 . . . . 9 D1
Keats Wlk PO21 . . . . 201 B3
Kebbell Lo **12** BN2 . . . . 213 C2
Keble Cl
  Bognor Regis PO21 . . . . . 200 F3
  Crawley RH10 . . . . 6 D1
Keelson Way BN17 . . . . . 205 A6
Keenans Cotts GU33 . . . . 45 A5
KEEPER'S CORNER 7 C7
Keepers Wood PO19 . . . . 154 F3
Keir Hardie Ho **7**
  RH11 . . . . 18 B1
Kelly Rd BN3 . . . . 169 D1
Kelmscott Rise RH11 . . . . 39 B8
Kelsey Ave PO10 . . . . 152 A1
Kelsey Cl
  Horley RH6 . . . . 1 F3
  Liss GU33 . . . . 45 C5
Kelsey Ct RH15 . . . . 109 D3
Kelso Cl
  Crawley RH10 . . . . 19 E7
  Lancing BN15 . . . . 187 B7

Kelso Cl continued
  Worthing BN13 . . . . 185 E5
Kelvin Bsns Ctr RH10 . . . . . 5 F1
Kelvin Ho RH10 . . . . 5 F2
Kelvin La RH10 . . . . 5 F2
Kelvin Way RH10 . . . . 5 F2
Kemnal Pk GU27 . . . . 27 D7
Kemp Cl BN2 . . . . 192 E4
Kemps BN7 . . . . 127 F7
Kempshott Mews RH12 . . 36 B4
Kempshott Rd RH12 . . . . . 36 B4
Kemp St BN1 . . . . 213 B3
KEMP TOWN 192 D4
Kemptown Mews **11**
  BN2 . . . . 192 E4
Kemp Town Pl **18**
  BN2 . . . . 192 D4
Kendal Cl BN17 . . . . 205 A7
Kendale Cl RH10 . . . . 19 C2
Kendall Ct RH16 . . . . 87 F2
Kendal Rd
  Hove BN3 . . . . 190 F8
  Lancing BN15 . . . . 187 C6
Kenhurst BN16 . . . . 206 A5
Kenilworth Cl
  Brighton BN2 . . . . 171 A2
  Crawley RH11 . . . . 18 B2
Kenilworth Ho RH14 . . . . 79 C7
Kenilworth Rd PO21 . . . . 201 B4
Kenlegh PO21 . . . . 200 F2
Kenmara Cl RH10 . . . . 6 A1
Kenmara Ct RH10 . . . . 6 A2
Kenmure Ave BN1 . . . . . . 170 A4
Kennard Ct RH18 . . . . 23 E3
Kennedy Ave RH19 . . . . . . 9 D3
Kennedy Rd RH13 . . . . . . 36 D1
Kennel Hill PO18 . . . . 135 E1
Kennel La
  Hookwood RH6 . . . . 1 D2
  Maplehurst RH13 . . . . 82 E2
Kennet Cl
  Crawley RH11 . . . . 17 F5
  Worthing BN13 . . . . 185 D8
Kennet Rd GU31 . . . . 68 A2
Kensett's Cnr RH20 . . . . . 123 A3
Kensington Cl RH20 . . . . . 121 C7
Kensington Gdns BN1 . . . 213 B3
Kensington Pl BN1 . . . . . . 213 B3
Kensington Rd
  Chichester PO19 . . . . 177 D6
  Crawley RH11 . . . . 18 C2
Kensington St BN1 . . . . . 213 B3
Kent Cl BN43 . . . . 189 C7
Kent Ct **4** RH12 . . . . 36 D2
Kent Fields BN7 . . . . 172 E5
Kent Mans **5** BN11 . . . . 186 E2
Kenton Rd BN3 . . . . 190 D7
Kent Rd
  Chichester PO19 . . . . 177 B7
  Littlehampton BN17 . . . . 204 D6
Kents Rd RH16 . . . . 87 F3
Kent St BN5, BN13 . . . . . 106 C6
KENT STREET 106 C7
Kentstreet La RH13 . . . . . 84 C1
Kentwyns Dr RH13 . . . . . 58 E8
Kentwyns Pl RH13 . . . . . . 58 E8
Kenwards BN1 . . . . 170 D7
Kenwood Quay **7**
  BN15 . . . . 187 F5
Kenya Ct
  2 Brighton BN1 . . . . . . 191 E6
  Horley RH6 . . . . 1 F4
Kerrison Mews **7**
  BN3 . . . . 191 D5
Kerry Gdns BN16 . . . . 206 A6
Kerves La RH13 . . . . 58 D6
Kestrel Cl
  Bracklesham PO20 . . . . . 208 A6
  Crawley RH11 . . . . 18 C8
  Horsham RH12 . . . . 36 E5
  Hove BN3 . . . . 191 D8
Kestrel Ct
  Chichester PO19 . . . . 177 D7
  Pagham PO21 . . . . 210 F7
Kestrels The BN43 . . . . . . 189 A8
Kestrel Way RH17 . . . . . . 204 C8
Kestrel Wlk RH10 . . . . . . 21 C5
Keswick Cl
  Crawley RH11 . . . . 17 D4
  Worthing BN12 . . . . 185 D6
Ketche's La RH17, TN22 . . 89 C7
Ketch Rd BN17 . . . . 205 A4
Kevin Gdns BN2 . . . . 193 E8
Kewell's Cnr PO20 . . . . . . 197 C5
Kew Gdns PO21 . . . . 200 F5
Kew St BN1 . . . . 213 A4
Keymer Cres BN12 . . . . . 185 D2
Keymer Ct RH15 . . . . 109 B2
Keymer End RH16 . . . . . . 87 D3
Keymer Gdns RH15 . . . . . 109 B1
Keymer Par RH15 . . . . . . 109 B2
Keymer Pk BN6 . . . . 129 B3
Keymer Rd
  Brighton BN1 . . . . 170 B6
  Burgess Hill RH15 . . . . . . 129 B8
  Crawley RH11 . . . . 18 D4
  Hassocks BN6 . . . . 128 F3
Keymer Way BN12 . . . . . . 185 C2
Keynor Est PO21 . . . . 209 E7
Keynor La PO20 . . . . 209 E8
Keysford La RH14, RH17 . . 64 E3
Keystone Cl BN12 . . . . . . 185 C4
Kidborough Rd RH11 . . . . 17 F5
Kidbrook RH16 . . . . 88 B6
Kidbrooke Rise RH18 . . . . 23 E2
Kidders La BN5 . . . . 125 D8
Kidd Rd PO19 . . . . 155 B1
Kidmans Cl RH12 . . . . 36 F5

Kidworth Cl RH6 . . . . 1 F5
Killinghurst La GU27,
  GU8 . . . . 28 D8
Kilmore Cl BN14 . . . . 163 E6
Kiln Ave GU27 . . . . 27 C8
Kilnbarn Ct RH16 . . . . 87 D2
Kilnbarn Way RH16 . . . . . 87 D2
Kiln Cl RH10 . . . . 21 B7
Kilner Lo RH13 . . . . 57 F1
Kiln Field GU33 . . . . 45 A5
Kilnfield Rd RH12 . . . . 33 D8
Kiln La
  Haywards Heath RH16 . . . 88 B5
  Horley RH6 . . . . 2 A5
Kilnmead RH10 . . . . 18 E7
Kilnmead Cl RH10 . . . . . . 18 E7
Kiln Rd RH10 . . . . 21 B7
Kilnwood Cl PO20 . . . . . . 212 F7
Kilnwood La
  Crawley RH12 . . . . 17 B3
  Faygate RH12 . . . . 16 F3
Kilsham La GU28 . . . . 97 D4
Kilwich Cl PO22 . . . . 202 D6
Kimber Cl BN15 . . . . 187 D5
Kimberley Cl RH6 . . . . 1 E3
Kimberley Ct BN14 . . . . . 186 D6
Kimberley Rd
  Brighton BN2 . . . . 170 D1
  Crawley RH10 . . . . 19 B7
Kimbers GU32 . . . . 68 A4
Kimbridge Pk PO20 . . . . . 208 A6
Kimbridge Rd PO20 . . . . . 208 A6
Kindersley Cl RH19 . . . . . 10 B3
Kinfauns Dr BN13 . . . . . . 163 D2
King Alfred Cl BN44 . . . . 145 D3
King Bsns Ctr BN6 . . . . . 107 C1
King Charles Pl **10**
  BN43 . . . . 189 A6
King Edward Ave
  BN14 . . . . 186 E4
King Edward Cl
  Horsham RH13 . . . . 57 D6
  Worthing BN14 . . . . 186 E4
King Edward Rd RH13 . . . . 57 D6
Kingfisher Cl
  Crawley RH10 . . . . 6 A1
  Red Hill PO9 . . . . 130 D1
  Worthing BN13 . . . . 185 C6
Kingfisher Ct
  Middleton-on-S PO22 . . . 202 F5
  10 Pulborough RH20 . . . 100 C2
  Worthing BN11 . . . . 186 A3
Kingfisher Dr
  Haywards Heath RH16 . . . 87 C1
  Haywards Heath RH16 . . . 87 C1
  Littlehampton BN17 . . . . 204 C8
  Westbourne PO10 . . . . . . 151 D4
Kingfisher La RH10 . . . . . 21 C5
Kingfisher Par PO20 . . . . 207 F7
Kingfisher Rise RH19 . . . . 22 F8
Kingfisher Way RH12 . . . . 36 C5
King George Ave
  East Grinstead RH19 . . . . . 9 C3
  Petersfield GU32 . . . . 68 B4
King George Ct PO21 . . . . 201 B4
King George Gdns
  PO19 . . . . 176 F8
King George Mews **7**
  GU32 . . . . 68 B4
King George Rd
  BN43 . . . . 189 D8
King George VI Ave
  BN3 . . . . 169 A3
King George VI Dr
  BN3 . . . . 169 A4
King George VI Mans
  BN3 . . . . 168 F2
King James's La BN5 . . . . 125 E4
King John Ct **7** BN43 . . . 189 A6
Kingley Ctr PO18 . . . . . . 154 A6
Kingley Vale National
  Nature Reserve★
  PO18 . . . . 133 E2
Kingmere **10** BN17 . . . . 204 E4
King Pl BN1 . . . . 213 A2
King's Arms Hill BN18 . . . 160 B3
King's Ave PO19 . . . . 176 F4
Kings Barn End BN44 . . . 145 F3
King's Barn La BN44 . . . . 145 F4
King's Barn Villas
  BN44 . . . . 145 E3
Kingsbridge Mews
  BN13 . . . . 185 D8
Kingsbury Rd BN1 . . . . . . 213 B4
Kingsbury St BN1 . . . . . . 213 B4
Kings Cl
  Lancing BN15 . . . . 187 F5
  Red Hill PO9 . . . . 130 C1
  Yapton BN18 . . . . 181 A3
Kings Copse **9** RH19 . . . 22 F8
Kingscote Hill RH11 . . . . . 18 B4
Kingscote Lo BN1 . . . . . . 170 F5
Kingscote Sta RH19 . . . . . 21 F4
Kingscote Way BN1 . . . . . 213 B4
Kings Cres BN43 . . . . 188 D5
Kings Ct
  Brighton BN1 . . . . 213 B2
  Horsham RH13 . . . . 36 E3
  Lancing BN15 . . . . 187 F4
  Selsey PO20 . . . . 212 E8
  Shoreham-by-S BN43 . . . 188 D5
King's Ct PO21 . . . . 201 E3
King's Ct PO19 . . . . 177 B5
Kings Dr
  Bognor Regis PO21 . . . . . 211 B8

Kings Dr continued
  Hassocks BN6 . . . . 128 F4
  Midhurst GU29 . . . . 72 E7
  Shoreham-by-S BN43 . . . 188 D5
King's Espl BN3 . . . . 191 A5
Kingsey Ave PO10 . . . . . . 173 A8
Kingsfernsden La
  GU32 . . . . 68 C5
Kingsfield
  Henfield BN5 . . . . 125 E5
  Storrington BN20 . . . . . . 121 E2
Kingsfield Cl BN42 . . . . . 189 E8
Kingsfold **2** BN2 . . . . . 192 F5
Kingsfold Cl RH14 . . . . . . 79 D6
Kingsfold Ct RH12 . . . . . . 15 B5
Kings Gap BN43 . . . . 188 D5
Kings Gate
  Haywards Heath RH16 . . . 87 E6
  Horsham RH12 . . . . 36 B2
  Hove BN3 . . . . 191 C8
King's Gdns BN3 . . . . 191 B5
Kings Hall BN11 . . . . 186 E2
Kingsham Ave PO19 . . . . 177 B5
Kingsham Prim Sch
  PO19 . . . . 177 B4
Kingsham Rd PO19 . . . . . 177 A5
Kings La
  Coldwaltham RH20 . . . . . 119 C6
  Marehill RH20 . . . . 100 F1
  Southwater Street RH13 . . 58 A4
King's La RH13 . . . . 106 B8
Kingsland
  Shoreham-by-S BN43 . . . 189 C7
  Storrington BN20 . . . . . . 121 E2
Kingsland Cotts BN6 . . . . 107 C1
Kingsland Ct RH10 . . . . . . 19 A6
Kingsland Rd BN14 . . . . . 186 D6
Kingslea RH13 . . . . 36 E3
Kingslea Prim Sch
  RH13 . . . . 36 E3
Kingsley Cl
  Horley RH6 . . . . 1 F5
  Worthing BN14 . . . . 186 F4
Kingsley Ct **7** BN1 . . . . 191 E5
Kingsley Mews RH14 . . . . 79 D7
Kingsley Rd
  Brighton BN1 . . . . 169 D1
  Crawley RH11 . . . . 18 A3
  Horley RH6 . . . . 1 F5
King's Manor Com Coll
  BN43 . . . . 189 D8
Kings Mdw PO18 . . . . . . 152 D1
Kingsmead
  Bognor Regis PO22 . . . . . 201 F3
  Littlehampton BN17 . . . . 182 C5
Kingsmead Cl
  Horsham RH12 . . . . 37 B6
  Steyning BN44 . . . . 145 D1
Kingsmead Gdns
  PO22 . . . . 203 A6
Kingsmead Pl RH12 . . . . . 35 C3
Kingsmead Rd
  Ancton PO22 . . . . 203 A5
  Broadbridge Heath RH12 . . 35 D3
Kingsmere BN1 . . . . 169 E2
Kings Mews
  Horsham RH12 . . . . 36 B2
  Hove BN3 . . . . 191 B6
Kingsmill Rd PO22 . . . . . 180 C6
Kings Par BN1 . . . . 170 A2
King's Par PO21 . . . . 201 A2
Kingspit La GU28 . . . . 98 D8
Kings Pl RH13 . . . . 36 E3
Kings Platt RH13 . . . . 103 D8
Kings Rd
  Horley RH6 . . . . 2 A3
  Lancing BN15 . . . . 187 F5
  Petersfield GU32 . . . . 67 F4
  Rudgwick RH12 . . . . 33 D7
  Southwick BN42 . . . . 167 E1
King's Rd
  Brighton BN1, BN3 . . . . . 191 E5
  Emsworth PO10 . . . . 173 A8
  Haslemere GU27 . . . . 27 A6
  Haywards Heath RH16 . . . 87 F3
  Horsham RH13 . . . . 36 E3
Kings Rd Ind Est GU27 . . . 27 A6
Kings Ride RH15 . . . . 109 D1
King's Stone Ave
  BN44 . . . . 145 F3
King St
  Arundel BN18 . . . . 160 A3
  Brighton BN1 . . . . 213 B2
  East Grinstead RH19 . . . . . 9 E1
  Emsworth PO10 . . . . 173 C8
  Westbourne PO10 . . . . . . 151 D3
  Worthing BN14 . . . . 186 D4
King's Terr **6** PO10 . . . . 173 B8
Kingsthorpe Rd BN3 . . . . 190 F8
Kingston Bay Rd
  BN43 . . . . 189 C6
Kingston Broadway
  BN43 . . . . 167 D1
Kingston Buci Fst Sch
  BN43 . . . . 189 C6
KINGSTON BY SEA 189 C7
Kingston Cl
  Brighton BN1 . . . . 170 E6
  Hove BN3 . . . . 168 C2
  Shoreham-by-S BN43 . . . 189 C6
Kingston Ct **17** BN43 . . . 189 C6
Kingston La
  East Preston BN16 . . . . . 206 B5
  Southwick BN42, BN43 . . 189 D7
KINGSTONRIDGE 172 D6
Kingston Ridge BN7 . . . . 172 D6
Kingston Way BN43 . . . . . 167 D1

Kingsway
  Bognor Regis PO21 . . . . . 200 D1
  Hove BN3 . . . . 191 B5
  Selsey PO20 . . . . 212 F6
  Worthing BN12 . . . . 185 F3
Kings Way
  Burgess Hill RH15 . . . . . . 109 D2
  Red Hill PO9 . . . . 130 C1
Kingsway Ct BN3 . . . . 191 C5
Kings Wlk BN43 . . . . 188 D5
Kingswood RH20 . . . . 121 C7
Kingswood Cl RH11 . . . . . 39 C8
Kingswood Flats BN2 . . . 213 C2
Kingswood St BN2 . . . . . 213 B2
King Williams Gate **11**
  GU32 . . . . 68 B3
Kinleside Way BN16 . . . . 206 A8
Kinnell Cl PO10 . . . . 173 B8
Kinrara Ho **10** PO21 . . . 201 C3
Kinsale Ct **5** BN3 . . . . . 191 D7
Kipling Ave
  Woodingdean BN2 . . . . . 193 E7
  Worthing BN14 . . . . 185 A4
Kipling Cl RH10 . . . . 19 C8
Kipling Ct
  3 Haywards Heath
  RH16 . . . . 87 D5
  Horsham RH13 . . . . 37 A4
  Rottingdean BN2 . . . . . . 194 A1
Kipling Way RH19 . . . . 9 C1
Kippens La RH13 . . . . 82 B2
Kirdford Cl
  Burgess Hill RH15 . . . . . . 109 C1
  Crawley RH11 . . . . 18 A4
  4 Rustington BN16 . . . . 205 B4
Kirdford Rd BN18 . . . . . . 160 A2
Kirkby Cl PO18 . . . . 156 D3
Kirkland Cl BN16 . . . . 205 B5
Kites Cl RH11 . . . . 18 C6
Kithurst Cl
  Crawley RH11 . . . . 18 D4
  Littlehampton BN16 . . . . 205 F4
  Worthing BN12 . . . . 185 B5
Kithurst Cres BN12 . . . . . 185 B5
Kithurst Farm Rd
  RH20 . . . . 142 B8
Kithurst La RH20 . . . . 121 C1
Kithurst Pk RH20 . . . . . . 121 B1
Kitilear Ct BN3 . . . . 191 D6
Kitsmead RH10 . . . . 7 A2
Kittiwake Cl RH11 . . . . . . 17 D4
Klada Ct RH20 . . . . 121 E2
Knap La PO20 . . . . 212 D7
Knepp Cl
  Brighton BN2 . . . . 170 F2
  Crawley RH10 . . . . 19 C6
Knepp Ho **7** RH13 . . . . . 36 D1
Knighton Cl RH10 . . . . 6 D2
Knights Cotts PO18 . . . . 153 B3
Knightscroft Ave
  BN16 . . . . 205 C4
Knightscroft Cl **5**
  BN16 . . . . 205 B4
Knightscroft Ho **3**
  BN16 . . . . 205 B4
Knightsfiled **4** GU32 . . . 68 A3
Knights Gate Rd BN1 . . . 171 C7
Knight's Hill PO18 . . . . . 135 E5
Knob Hill RH12 . . . . 15 A1
Knockhundred La
  GU26 . . . . 26 C8
Knockhundred Row
  GU29 . . . . 94 F8
Knole Cl RH10 . . . . 19 D7
Knole Gr RH19 . . . . 9 C3
Knole Rd BN2 . . . . 194 A1
Knoll Bsns Ctr The
  BN3 . . . . 190 D8
Knoll Cl BN3 . . . . 168 D1
Knoll Pl RH16 . . . . 88 B5
Knowle Cl RH10 . . . . 7 C3
Knowle Dr RH10 . . . . 7 B3
Knowle La GU6, RH12 . . . 11 D4
Knowles Cl BN5 . . . . 125 E5
Knowles Mdw GU33 . . . . 45 D1
Knowle The RH17 . . . . . . 86 E7
Knoyle Rd BN1 . . . . 169 D2
Knyveton Ct RH15 . . . . . . 109 B3
Kymer Gdns BN6 . . . . 129 A3
Kynon Gdns PO22 . . . . . . 202 D6
Kyoto Ct PO21 . . . . 201 B3

L

Laburnum Ave BN3 . . . . . 168 E1
Laburnum Cl
  Ferring BN12 . . . . 206 F5
  Lancing BN15 . . . . 187 D4
Laburnum Gr
  Bognor Regis PO22 . . . . . 201 C6
  Brighton BN2 . . . . 170 B3
  Chichester PO19 . . . . 177 A5
Laburnum Grove Jun Sch
  PO22 . . . . 201 C6
Laburnum Lo BN13 . . . . . 185 C6
Laburnum Way RH16 . . . . 88 B4
Laburnum Wlk BN16 . . . . 205 C6
Lackenhurst La RH13 . . . . 81 A6
Lacock Cl PO20 . . . . 208 C3
Lacy Ho PO19 . . . . 176 F5
Ladbroke Rd RH6 . . . . 2 B5
Ladbrooke Cl BN16 . . . . . 205 B4
Ladies Mile BN1 . . . . 170 B7

Ladies Mile Cl BN1.......... 169 F6
Ladies' Mile Ct BN1......... 169 E6
Ladies' Mile Rd BN1........ 169 F6
Lady Bee Marina Ind Est
BN42.......................... 189 E6
Ladydell Rd BN11.......... 186 F3
Lady Margaret Rd
RH11.......................... 18 A7
Lady Margaret Wlk
RH11.......................... 18 A7
Ladymead RH15........... 109 C5
Ladymead Cl RH10........ 19 C3
Ladysmith Rd BN2........ 192 D8
Ladywell Rd BN15......... 187 F7
LAGNESS................... 200 B6
Lagness Rd PO20........ 177 F1
Lagoon Rd PO21.......... 210 F7
Lagwood Cl BN6.......... 128 F3
Laine Cl BN1............... 169 E3
Laines Rd BN44........... 145 C2
Lake Cotts PO22......... 180 D6
Lake La
Barnham BN18, PO22..... 180 D6
Horley, RH6............... 2 C6
Laker Ct RH10............. 19 A6
Lake Rd PO19............. 177 C6
Lakers Lea RH14.......... 31 F1
Lakers Mdw RH14........ 79 D8
Lakeside
Horsham RH12............ 36 C5
Lancing BN15............. 188 B6
Midhurst GU29........... 94 E6
Lakeside Dr RH13........ 58 A1
Lakeview
1 Brighton BN2......... 192 C5
Littlehampton BN17...... 205 A3
Lake View PO21.......... 200 A1
Lake View Rd
Copthorne RH19.......... 8 C4
Dormans Park RH19..... 9 F5
Lamberhurst Wlk
RH10.......................... 19 A5
Lambert's La RH12...... 94 F8
Lamberts Yd GU29...... 114 C8
Lambeth Cl RH11......... 18 B2
Lambeth Wlk RH11...... 18 B2
Lambleys La BN14....... 186 F8
Lambourn Ct RH19....... 9 E3
Lambourne Cl
Brighton BN1............. 170 C2
Crawley RH10............. 18 F4
Lambourne La GU29,
GU30.......................... 47 E2
Lambourne Rd BN1...... 170 C2
Lambs Cres RH12......... 36 F5
Lambs Farm Rd RH12... 37 A4
Lambs Farm Cl RH12.... 37 A5
Lambs Green Rd RH12... 16 F6
Lambs Lease GU33....... 45 D3
Lambyn Croft RH6....... 2 C4
Lammas Cl BN17......... 204 E7
Lamorna Gdns
Ferring BN12.............. 206 F4
Westergate PO20........ 179 D6
Lamorna Gr BN14........ 186 C6
Lampson Ct RH10........ 7 B3
Lanark Cl RH13........... 36 E2
Lanark Ho BN13.......... 185 E8
Lancaster Cl RH10....... 6 D1
Lancaster Ct
Crawley RH10............. 18 F5
12 Hove BN3............ 191 A6
Lancaster Dr RH19....... 10 A3
Lancaster Ho **4**
BN11.......................... 186 A2
Lancaster House Rd
BN1............................ 171 B7
Lancaster Pl PO22....... 201 C6
Lancaster Rd
Brighton BN1............. 213 A4
Worthing BN12........... 185 E3
Lancastrian Grange **5**
PO19.......................... 176 F7
Lancastrian Inf Sch
PO19.......................... 176 F7
Lancelot Cl RH11......... 17 E6
Lancing Bsns Pk
BN15.......................... 187 D4
Lancing Cl
Crawley RH11............. 18 A8
Lancing BN15............. 187 D6
Lancing Coll BN15....... 166 A2
Lancing College Dr
BN15.......................... 166 B1
Lancing Ct
5 Brighton BN2......... 192 F5
Horsham RH12............ 37 A4
Lancing Pk BN15......... 187 D4
Lancing Sta BN15........ 187 E5
Landen Pk RH6............ 1 E5
Landerry Ind Est The
PO20.......................... 212 D8
Lane End Rd PO22....... 203 A6
Lane End Farm Cvn Site
PO22.......................... 203 A6
Lane Ho **1** RH13....... 36 D2
Lanercost Rd RH14...... 31 C4
Lanes The★ BN1.......... 213 B2
Lane The
Chichester PO19......... 155 A2
Ifold RH14.................. 31 C4

Lanfranc Rd BN14........ 186 B4
Langbury Cl RH12........ 206 D7
Langbury La BN12........ 206 E7
Langdale Ave PO19..... 177 C4
Langdale Cl BN15........ 187 C5
Langdale Ct BN3.......... 190 F6
Langdale Gdns BN3..... 190 F6
Langdale Rd
Crawley RH11............. 17 C4
Hove BN3.................. 190 F6
Langham Ct **7** BN11... 186 A2
Langham Gdns BN11.... 186 A2
Langhurst **9** BN2...... 192 E4
Langhurst Cl RH12...... 15 E4
Langhurst La RH12...... 17 A8
Langhurstwood Rd
RH12.......................... 15 D3
LANGLEY..................... 46 B7
Langley Cres BN2........ 171 E1
Langley Ct RH10......... 19 A8
Langley Dr RH11......... 18 D8
Langley Gr PO21......... 200 C1
LANGLEY GREEN......... 5 C2
Langley Green Prim Sch
RH11.......................... 18 C8
Langley La RH11......... 18 A8
Langley Par RH11........ 5 C1
Langley Pl RH11.......... 5 C1
Langley Wlk RH11....... 5 B1
Langmead Cl BN17...... 203 E8
Langridge Dr
East Grinstead RH19.... 22 E8
Portslade-by-S BN41... 168 B3
Langridge Ho **2** RH12. 36 B2
Langridge La RH16...... 88 A5
Langridge Way RH15.... 108 E5
Langrish Prim Sch
GU32.......................... 67 C3
Langshott RH6............ 2 C5
Langshott Inf Sch The
PO18.......................... 174 D8
Langshott La RH6........ 2 C3
Langshott Rd RH6....... 2 C4
Langstone Cl RH10...... 19 C3
Langstone Gdns
PO18.......................... 174 D8
Langton Cl PO20......... 212 D6
Langton Ct **6** BN14... 186 D4
Langton La BN6.......... 127 E7
Langton Pl **9** RH20... 121 D1
Langton Rd
Chichester PO19......... 176 E7
Worthing BN14........... 186 D4
Lanka Ct PO20............ 207 E7
Lansbury Rd RH11...... 18 B1
Lansdown Cl RH12...... 37 B6
Lansdowne Cl
Angmering BN16......... 183 F6
Worthing BN11........... 186 A2
Lansdowne Ct **24**
BN3............................ 191 C6
Lansdowne Ho **16**
PO21.......................... 201 C2
Lansdowne Mans **11**
BN3............................ 191 D6
Lansdowne Mews **7**
BN3............................ 191 D6
Lansdowne Pl
Hove BN3.................. 191 D6
Worthing BN11........... 186 A2
Lansdowne Rd
Angmering BN16......... 183 F6
Hove BN3, BN3.......... 191 D6
Littlehampton BN17.... 204 D7
Worthing BN11........... 186 A2
Lansdowne Sq **1**
BN3............................ 191 D5
Lansdowne St BN3...... 191 D6
Lansdowne Way
BN16.......................... 183 F6
Lansdown Terr PO10.... 151 D5
Lanyards BN17............ 205 A7
Lanyon Cl RH12.......... 37 A6
Lanyon Mews RH12..... 37 A6
Lapwing Cl RH13........ 36 F3
Larch Cl
Bognor Regis PO22..... 201 C4
Chichester PO19......... 154 C4
Liphook GU30............. 25 B3
Rustington BN16......... 205 D5
Woodingdean BN2...... 193 F7
Larch End
Horsham RH12............ 36 B4
West Chiltington Common
RH20.......................... 121 D7
Larches RH19.............. 10 B4
Larches The RH12....... 37 C6
Larches Way RH10...... 21 C8
Larchfield Cl PO21...... 200 D1
Larch Lo BN13............ 185 C6
Larch Way RH16......... 88 A4
Larcombe Rd GU32..... 67 F2
Large Acres PO20....... 212 D7
Larke Cl BN43............. 189 C7
Larkfield Cl BN15........ 187 F5
Larkfield Way BN1....... 170 A4
Larkins Rd RH6........... 5 D7
Lark Rise
Crawley RH11............. 18 C8
Liphook GU30............. 25 A5
Turners Hill RH10........ 21 C5
Lark Rise Lo RH16....... 88 B5
Larksfield RH6............ 2 B4
Larkspur Ct RH17........ 205 A7
Larkspur Way RH13..... 58 A3
Larks View RH14......... 79 C8
Lark Way PO10............ 151 E4
Lashmar Rd BN16........ 206 A6

Lashmere RH10........... 7 D3
Laski Ct RH11.............. 18 B1
Latham Cl BN17........... 204 B6
Latham Rd PO20......... 212 D6
Latimer Cl RH11.......... 5 D1
Latimer Rd BN11......... 185 F2
Laud Dr RH10.............. 19 D5
Lauder Cl PO10.......... 151 F2
Laughton Rd
Horsham RH12............ 36 F5
Woodingdean BN2...... 193 F8
Laundry La RH17......... 44 D1
Laureens Wlk BN2....... 193 F1
Laurel **2** PO21......... 87 D6
Laurel Cl
Burgess Hill RH15....... 109 C5
Crawley RH10............. 19 A3
Worthing BN13........... 185 C6
Laurel Dene RH19....... 9 F1
Laurel Dr PO21............ 199 F2
Laurel Gr PO22............ 201 C6
Laurel Mount RH20..... 100 C2
Laurels Fst Sch The
BN13.......................... 185 B7
Laurels The
4 Brighton BN2....... 213 C5
Crawley RH10............. 6 A1
Henfield BN5.............. 125 E5
Southwater RH13........ 57 F2
Laurel Wlk RH11......... 36 F1
Laurence Gn PO10...... 151 B4
Lauriston Rd RH11...... 169 E2
Lavant CE Prim Sch
PO18.......................... 154 E6
Lavant Cl
Crawley RH11............. 17 F5
Worthing BN12........... 185 A5
Lavant Ct **3** GU32.... 68 A4
Lavant Down Rd
PO18.......................... 154 E7
Lavant House Rosemead
Sch PO18................... 154 E5
Lavant Rd PO18, PO19.. 154 E5
Lavant St GU32........... 68 A3
Lavender Cl PO22....... 202 D4
Lavender Hill BN43..... 167 B1
Lavender Ho BN2........ 213 C1
Lavender Row GU29.... 72 A1
Lavender St BN2......... 213 C1
Lavington Cl RH11...... 18 A8
Lavington Rd BN14..... 186 B6
Lavinia Ct
Bognor Regis PO21..... 200 F4
Worthing BN12........... 185 C4
Lavinia Way BN16....... 206 A5
Lawns Cotts RH12...... 12 A3
Lawns Rd RH12.......... 12 A3
Lawns The
Lancing BN15............. 187 C8
West Kingston BN16.... 206 A4
Lawn The PO21........... 200 E2
Lawrence Ave BN16.... 205 D6
Lawrence Cl
Crawley RH10............. 19 D4
Selsey PO20.............. 212 E6
Lawrence Rd BN3....... 190 F4
Lawrie La RH16.......... 88 B5
Laws Cl RH11............. 17 E5
Lawson-Hunt Ind Pk
RH12.......................... 35 D4
Lawyer's La BN5......... 125 C4
Laxton Mdw PO18...... 153 A5
Laylands Ct BN41....... 190 A4
Laylands Rd BN41...... 190 A4
Layne The PO22......... 203 A5
Lazy Acre PO10.......... 173 F8
Leach Ct BN2.............. 192 C5
Lea Cl RH11................ 17 F5
Leacroft RH19............ 9 D2
Lea Farm La RH20....... 99 C2
Lea Ho PO21............... 201 A6
Leahurst Court Rd
BN1............................ 169 E3
Leahurst Ct **1** BN1.... 169 E3
Leaman Cl PO22......... 202 F5
Leander Rd PO18........ 175 C5
Leas Ct PO22.............. 201 C5
Leas The
Angmering BN16......... 205 E7
Burgess Hill RH15....... 108 F4
Leatherbottle La
PO19.......................... 177 C6
Lechford Rd RH6......... 2 A1
Leconfield Rd BN15..... 187 C5
Ledbury Way PO21...... 200 B2
Ledgers Mdw RH17..... 86 F6
Ledra Dr PO21............. 211 B8
Lee Bank PO21........... 213 C3
Lee Farm Cotts BN13... 142 B1
Leemark Ho **4** BN17.. 204 E4
Lees Cnr BN13............ 205 B5
Leeside RH12.............. 16 C6
Lee St RH6................. 1 E4
Lee's Yd PO20............. 179 D4
Leeward Rd BN13....... 185 F6

Leeward Rd
Littlehampton BN17.... 205 A5
Worthing BN13........... 185 F6
LEGGATT HILL............. 74 B5
Leggs La GU29............ 115 B8
Leggyfield Ct RH12..... 36 B5
Legion Way PO20........ 208 A6
Leicester Ct RH10....... 19 D6
Leicester St BN2......... 213 C2
Leicester Villas BN3.... 190 D7
Leigh Ct PO20............ 208 C4
Leigh Jenkins Way RH6.. 6 B7
Leighlands RH10......... 19 C8
Leigh Rd
Chichester PO19......... 176 F5
Worthing BN14........... 186 D6
Leighton Ave BN14..... 186 E6
Leighton Rd
Horsted Keynes RH17... 65 C5
Hove BN3.................. 191 A8
Leighton Villas RH17... 65 C5
Leinster Gdns PO22.... 202 D4
Leith View Cotts RH12.. 15 B6
Leith View Rd RH12..... 37 A5
Le May Cl RH6............. 2 A4
Lemmington Way
RH12.......................... 37 A7
Lenham Ave BN2........ 194 B1
Lenham Rd E BN2....... 194 B1
Lenham Rd W BN2...... 194 A1
Lenhurst Way BN13.... 185 F5
Lennox Mews **6**
BN14.......................... 186 D3
Lennox Rd
Chichester PO19......... 177 B7
Hove BN3.................. 190 F8
Shoreham-by-S BN43... 189 B8
Worthing BN11........... 186 D3
Lennox St
Bognor Regis PO21..... 201 D2
Brighton BN2............. 213 C2
Leonardslee Ct RH10... 19 B3
Leonardslee Gdns★
Crabtree RH13............ 84 A8
Lower Beeding RH13.... 60 A1
Leonard Way RH13...... 36 F2
Leonora Dr PO21........ 200 B2
Leopold Ct PO22......... 202 A5
Leopold Rd
Brighton BN2............. 213 A3
Crawley RH11............. 18 C6
Lesser Foxholes
BN43.......................... 166 D1
Letchworth Cl BN12.... 206 E5
Letchworth Ct RH11.... 17 E3
Level Mare La PO20.... 157 E2
Leveret La RH11.......... 18 B8
Leverton Ave PO22..... 202 D4
Levine Ct **5** PO22..... 201 D4
Lewes Cl
Bognor Regis PO21..... 200 F4
Crawley RH10............. 19 C6
Saltdean BN2............. 194 E1
Lewes Cres BN2......... 192 E4
Lewes Rd
Ashurst Wood RH19.... 23 C6
Brighton BN1, BN2..... 170 E3
Chelwood Gate RH17... 44 C1
Danehill RH17............ 66 B3
Ditchling BN6............. 129 E2
Forest Row RH18....... 23 E2
Horsted Keynes RH17... 65 C5
Lindfield RH16............ 88 B7
Scaynes Hill RH17...... 88 D4
Lewes St BN2.............. 213 C3
Lewin Cl BN15............. 187 F7
Lewis Ct
6 Brighton BN2....... 192 C5
Worthing BN13........... 185 B6
Lewisham Cl RH11...... 18 C2
Lewis La BN18............ 181 B2
Lewis Rd
Chichester PO19......... 177 B7
Lancing BN15............. 187 D8
New Brighton PO10..... 151 C3
Selsey PO20.............. 212 E7
Leybourne Cl
Brighton BN2............. 171 A1
Crawley RH11............. 18 C1
Leybourne Par BN2..... 171 A1
Leybourne Pl RH19..... 8 F4
Leybourne Rd BN2...... 171 A1
Leyfield BN6............... 127 D5
Leylands Pk RH15....... 109 B5
Leylands Rd RH15...... 109 B4
Ley Rd PO22............... 202 B4
Leys The
Fernhurst GU27.......... 49 A5
Singleton PO18.......... 135 D7
Leyton Ct PO22.......... 202 B4
Leyton Lea RH12........ 86 E6
Library Pl BN11........... 186 E1
Lichfield Ct
10 Brighton BN2...... 192 F5
3 Worthing BN11..... 186 A1
Lichfield Gdns PO21.... 200 E3
Lidsey Cl RH10........... 19 C4
Lidsey Cvn Pk PO22.... 179 D2

Lidsey Rd PO20, PO22.. 179 D4
Lifeboat Way PO20...... 212 E5
Lilac Cl
Middleton-on-S PO22... 202 E6
Rustington BN17........ 205 A4
Worthing BN13........... 185 B6
Lilac Ct BN1............... 169 C4
Lillian Terr BN18........ 183 C8
Lillywhite Cl RH15...... 108 F5
LIMBO...................... 75 D5
Limbourne La RH20.... 99 B3
Limbrick Cl BN12........ 185 C4
Limbrick Cnr BN12..... 185 C5
Limbrick La BN12....... 185 C5
Limbrick Way BN12.... 185 C5
Lime Ave
Horsham RH12............ 37 A4
Woodgate PO20......... 179 E7
Lime Chase RH20....... 121 D2
Lime Cl
Chichester PO19......... 177 B7
Copthorne RH10......... 7 B3
Crawley RH11............. 5 C1
Lime Gr BN16............. 205 F8
Lime Kiln Rd RH13...... 59 D6
Lime Rd BN14............. 163 E6
Limes Ave RH6........... 2 B1
Limes Cl
Bramshott GU30......... 25 C7
Liss GU33.................. 45 B4
Limes The
Dormans Park RH19.... 9 A5
Haslemere GU27......... 27 A6
Rustington BN16......... 205 C6
Worthing BN11........... 186 B3
Yapton BN18.............. 181 A3
Lime Tree Ave BN14... 163 F2
Lime Tree Cl BN16...... 205 F6
Lime Tree Gr RH16...... 88 C7
Limmard Way PO22.... 202 C4
Limmer La PO22......... 202 B4
Limney Rd BN2.......... 192 F2
Linacre Dr GU6, RH12.. 12 C4
Lincett Ave BN13........ 185 F5
Lincett Ct BN13.......... 185 F5
Lincett Dr BN13.......... 185 F4
Linchmere BN2........... 192 F7
Linchmere Ave BN2.... 194 C1
Linchmere Pl RH11..... 18 A7
Linchmere Rd
Haslemere GU27......... 26 C5
Linchmere GU27......... 26 C4
Linch Rd GU29............ 72 B7
Lincoln Ave PO21....... 200 C4
Lincoln Cl
Crawley RH10............. 18 E3
Horley RH6................ 2 A2
Lincoln Cotts BN2...... 213 C3
Lincoln Ct
Hove BN3.................. 191 C8
Liphook GU30............. 25 C4
Lincoln Gn PO19......... 154 F1
Lincoln Ho **10** RH11... 186 B2
Lincoln Rd
Portslade-by-S BN41... 190 B4
Worthing BN13........... 185 F5
Lincoln St BN2............ 213 C4
Lincoln Wood RH16.... 87 C5
Lindale Pl **6** RH20.... 121 D1
Linden Ave RH19........ 9 C2
Linden Cl
Crawley RH10............. 19 A3
Horsham RH12............ 36 E4
Linden Ct
1 Bognor Regis
PO21.......................... 201 C3
Petworth GU28........... 97 E7
Linden Dr GU33.......... 45 B4
Linden Gr RH16.......... 88 B7
Linden Pk BN17.......... 204 C5
Linden Rd
Bognor Regis PO21..... 201 C4
Littlehampton BN17.... 204 C5
Lindens Cl PO10......... 151 B2
Lindens The
4 Brighton BN2....... 213 C4
Copthorne RH10......... 7 B3
Lindfield BN41............ 168 A1
Lindfield Cl BN2......... 194 B2
Lindfield Ct BN1......... 170 C2
Lindfield Ind Est Pk RH16.. 88 C6
Lindfield Prim Sch
RH16.......................... 88 A7
Lindfield Rd RH17...... 64 C6
Lindgren Wlk RH11..... 18 B1
Lindsey Ct PO22......... 202 A6
Lindum Rd BN13........ 185 F6
Lindum Way BN13...... 185 F6
Linemans View **13**
BN43.......................... 188 E7
Lineside Ind Est BN17.. 204 B6
Lineside Way BN17..... 204 B6
Linfield Cl BN16......... 206 A8
Linfield Copse RH20... 121 F6
Linfield Ct PO21......... 201 A2
Linfield La RH20......... 123 A6
Linfield Pl BN13.......... 185 F7
Lingfield Dr RH10....... 19 E7
Lingfield Dr RH19....... 9 D3
Lingfield Way PO20.... 212 F7
Link Dr RH20.............. 100 C2
Link Hill RH20............ 121 B1
Link La RH20.............. 100 C2
Links Ave PO22.......... 201 F4
Links Cl
Portslade-by-S BN41... 190 C8
Red Hill PO9.............. 130 D1
Links La PO9.............. 130 D2

Links Rd
Lancing BN15............187 F6
Portslade-by-S BN41....190 C8
Worthing BN14...........186 A8
Link The RH11............18 D6
Linkway RH6.................6 C7
Link Way PO21............200 A1
Linkway The
Brighton BN1...........170 B1
Worthing BN11..........186 C3
Linnell Cl RH11............39 B8
Linnet Cl
Littlehampton BN17......204 C8
Petersfield GU31........68 E2
Turners Hill RH10.......21 C6
Linton Ho GU28............75 C1
Linton Rd BN3............190 F8
Lintot Ct RH13............57 F1
Lintot Sq RH13............57 F1
Lintott Gdns RH13.........36 E3
Lion Cl GU27...............26 F7
Lion Ct PO21..............200 B2
Lionel Ave PO22..........202 C6
Lion Gn GU27...............26 F6
Lion La
Haslemere GU27........26 F6
Turners Hill RH10.......21 A4
Lion Mead GU27...........26 F6
Lion Mews BN3...........190 F7
Lion Rd PO21..............200 A2
Lions Ct BN2..............192 C5
Lions Dene BN1...........169 D4
Lions Gate BN3...........168 E1
Lions Gdns BN1...........169 D2
Lion St PO19..............177 A6
Liphook CE Jun Sch
GU30...................25 B4
Liphook Cl BN1............170 C1
Liphook Inf Sch GU30...25 B4
Liphook Rd
Haslemere GU27........26 F6
Hollywater GU35.......24 A8
Linchmere GU27.......26 B4
Liphook Sta GU30......25 C2
Lisher Rd BN15...........187 F7
Lisle Way PO10...........151 A3
Lismore Cres RH11.......18 B3
LISS FOREST..............45 C6
Liss Inf Sch GU33........45 C3
Liss Jun Sch GU33.......45 C3
Liss Sta GU33.............45 B4
Lister Ave RH19..........22 F6
Listers RH17...............60 F1
Litten Terr PO19.........177 A7
Little Ashfield GU29......94 E8
Little Babbsham
PO21...................200 E2
Little Barn Pl GU33.......45 D4
Little Bentswood RH16...87 F5
Little Bentswood Cl
RH16...................87 F5
Little Black Hill RH16....88 B7
LITTLE BOGNOR............98 F5
Little Boultons PO20....198 F8
Little Breach PO19.......176 F8
Little Bridges Cl RH13...57 F1
Little Cl RH13..............81 F7
Little Comptons RH13....36 F2
Little Copse Rd BN6.....128 E4
Littlecote GU28............97 F7
Little Court Cl GU29......94 D8
Little Crabtree RH11.....18 C7
Little Cres BN2............194 B1
Littlecroft Cvn Pk
PO20...................197 D2
Little Dipper's RH20.....100 C2
Little Dr BN12.............206 E5
Little Dro BN44...........145 D2
Littledrove Cotts
PO18...................135 D7
Little East St
Billingshurst RH14......55 F5
Brighton BN2..........213 B1
Littlefield Cl PO20........212 C4
Littlefield Rd PO19.......177 B5
Little Finches RH13......105 A3
Little Gables BN13.......185 F7
Little George St BN2....213 B1
Little Grebe RH12.........36 C5
Littlegreen Sch PO18....111 A4
Littlehampton Com Sch
The BN17..............204 E6
Littlehampton Information
Ctr* BN17................204 D3
Littlehampton Mus*
BN17...................204 E5
Littlehampton Rd
Ferring BN12..........206 D7
Worthing BN12, BN13...185 D6
Littlehampton Sta
BN17...................204 C5
Little Hatch RH12........36 F5
LITTLE HAVEN.............36 E5
Littlehaven Inf Sch
RH12...................36 F5
Littlehaven La RH12......36 F5
Littlehaven Sta RH12.....36 F5
Little Hayes Cotts
RH14...................55 F5
LITTLE HEATH............157 F5
Littleheath Rd BN18.....157 E4
Little High St
Shoreham-by-S
BN43...................188 E7
Worthing BN11.........186 D3
Little Hill RH20...........121 C8
Little King St RH19.......9 E1
Little London PO19......177 A6

Little London Mews ......
PO19...................177 A6
Little Oak RH13...........105 A3
Little Paddocks BN12...206 E5
Little Paddocks Way
BN12...................206 F5
Little Park Enterprises
RH6.....................4 E3
LITTLE PARKMINSTER
.......................105 E7
Little Pembrokes
BN11...................186 A3
Little Preston St BN1....191 E5
Littlestone Rd BN13.....185 E7
Little Terr BN1............213 B4
Little Western St ......
BN1....................191 E5
Littleworth Cl BN2.......193 F7
Littleworth La RH13......105 A6
Liverpool Bldgs ......
BN11...................186 D2
Liverpool Gdns BN11....186 D2
Liverpool Rd BN11.......186 D2
Liverpool Terr BN11.....186 D2
Livesay Cres BN14.......186 D4
Livingstone Ho ......
BN3....................191 B7
Livingstone Rd
Burgess Hill BN15......108 F3
Crawley RH10..........18 E4
Horsham RH13.........36 D1
Hove BN3..............191 B7
Livingstone St BN2......192 D5
Lizard Head BN17........205 A6
Llandaff Cl BN11.........186 A2
Lloyd Cl BN3..............191 C8
Lloyd Goring Cl BN16...183 F6
Lloyd Rd BN3.............191 C8
Lloyds Ct RH10............5 E1
Loats La PO21............200 F7
Lobster La PO20.........212 B8
Lobs Wood La RH20.....121 D2
Locke Rd BN15...........187 F7
Lockgate Rd PO20........198 C4
Lockhart Ct RH16.........87 F7
Lockitt Way BN7.........172 E5
Lock La
Birdham PO20..........197 F6
Partridge Green RH13..104 E2
Locksash Cl PO20........196 C2
Locksash La PO18........132 C7
Locks Cres BN41.........168 B1
Locks Ct BN42............189 E7
Locks Cres BN41.........168 B1
Lockwood Cl
Horsham RH12..........37 A5
Woodingdean BN2......193 E7
Lockwood Cres BN2......193 E7
Lockwood Ct RH10.......18 F8
Lockyer Ct GU32..........68 D5
Loddon Cl BN13..........185 C9
Loder Gdns BN14........186 C5
Loder Pl BN1..............169 F2
Loder Rd BN1.............169 F2
Loders RH17...............64 B8
Lodgebury Cl PO10......174 A8
Lodge Cl
Crawley RH11..........18 C6
East Grinstead RH19....9 D1
Middleton-on-S PO22...203 A5
Portslade-by-S BN41....167 F2
Lodge Ct
Bognor Regis PO21.....200 E2
Shoreham-by-S BN43...166 E1
Lodge Hill La BN6.......129 C4
Lodge La
Bolney RH17............85 B3
Keymer BN6............129 A4
Salfords RH1..............1 E8
West Marden PO9......131 F6
Lodgelands RH17..........64 B6
Lodge The BN2...........213 C5
Lodsworth BN2...........192 F7
Lodsworth Cl BN2........192 F7
LODSWORTH COMMON
.......................74 B6
Lodsworth Rd PO21.....200 B3
Lombard St GU28..........97 F8
Lomond Ave BN1.........170 B7
Lond Meadow Villas
RH6......................4 E5
London Fields Ho
RH11...................18 C2
London La RH17...........86 F6
London Meed Com Prim
Sch RH15...............109 A1
London Rd
Albourne Green BN6....127 D5
Arundel BN18..........159 E6
Ashington RH20........123 A5
Balcombe RH17.........40 F2
Bognor Regis PO21.....201 D3
Brighton BN1...........213 B4
Brighton, Withdean
BN1....................169 D4
Burgess Hill RH15......108 F3
Coldwaltham RH20.....119 D6
Crawley RH10...........5 E3
Cuckfield RH17.........86 F2
Danehill RH17..........66 A4
East Grinstead RH19....9 C3
Fontwell BN18.........158 A3
Forest Row RH18.......23 E4
Handcross RH11, RH17...39 C2
Hassocks BN6, RH15....128 E6
Heath Common RH20...125 F6
Henfield BN5...........137 B5
Hill Side GU31, GU33...69 B8
Horsham RH12..........36 C2

London Rd continued
Hurstpierpoint BN6.....127 E2
Liphook GU30..........25 C5
Petersfield GU31.......68 D5
Petworth GU28.........75 D3
Poynings RH45, BN6....148 F7
Pyecombe BN1, BN45...149 C4
Rake GU33..............46 A4
Washington RH20.......143 E7
London Road (Brighton)
Sta BN1................192 A8
London Road Cotts
BN18...................160 A4
London St BN11..........186 C3
London Terr BN1.........213 B4
Lonesome La RH2.........1 D8
Loney Ct BN43...........189 C8
Long Acre
Crawley Down RH10....21 A8
Selsey PO20............212 D6
Longacre Cl GU33........45 C4
Longacre Cres RH17.....86 F8
Longacre La PO20........212 E6
Longacre Pk BN18.......180 F5
Longback Cotts BN15....183 F6
Longbridge Gate RH6....5 E8
Longbridge Rd RH6........1 F1
Longbridge Rdbt RH6....1 E2
Longbridge Way RH6....5 F8
Longbridge Wlk RH6......1 F1
Longbrook PO22..........201 F3
Longchamp Cl RH6........2 C3
Long Cl RH10.............19 D6
Long Copse Cl PO10.....151 B4
Long Copse La PO10.....151 C4
Longcroft BN43...........188 E7
Longdene Rd GU27........27 B6
Long Down GU31.........68 D4
Longfellow Cl RH12.......36 E7
Longfellow Rd BN11.....186 B3
Longfield Rd
Horsham RH12..........36 A1
New Brighton PO10....151 B3
Tower Hill RH12........58 A8
Longford Rd PO21........201 C4
Long Furlong BN13,
BN14...................163 B5
Longfurlong La BN13.....162 E4
Long Hill RH13............83 F9
Longhill Cl BN2............193 E4
Longhill High Sch
BN2....................193 E4
Longhill Rd BN2..........193 E4
Longhurst RH15..........109 D2
Longhurst Rd RH11.......18 A1
Long La
Arundel BN18..........159 D4
East Marden PO18......112 B3
Longland Ave RH20.......121 C2
Longlands BN14..........186 D8
Longlands Glade
BN14...................186 D8
Longlands Rd
East Wittering PO20....207 F6
Southbourne PO10......173 F8
Longlands Spinney
BN14...................186 D8
Longley Ind Est BN1....213 B4
Long Mdw BN14..........164 A3
Longmead GU33..........45 B4
Long Mead BN18.........158 D1
Longmeadow Gdns
PO20...................197 E4
Longmere Rd RH10.......18 D8
Longmoor Dr GU30.......24 D4
Longmoor Rd GU30......24 E4
Long Park Cnr BN6.......129 D2
Longport Rd PO22.......202 B4
Long Rd GU32.............68 C6
Longridge Ave BN2......194 D1
Longships RH17...........205 A6
Longwall RH19.............9 A4
Long Wlk RH16...........88 B4
Longwood View RH10....19 A3
Longyard Ho RH6..........2 B5
Looes Barn Cl BN2.......194 D3
Loop The PO22...........202 C4
Loose La BN15...........187 B6
Loppets Rd RH10.........18 F3
Lordings La RH20........121 D7
Lordings Rd RH14........79 A4
Loriners RH10.............18 D3
Loriners Ct BN3..........190 D8
Lorna Rd BN3.............191 D7
Lorne Rd BN1.............213 B5
Lorraine Ct
Hove BN3...............191 B6
Hove BN3...............191 E7
Lotts La BN15.............187 C6
Loudoun Rd BN17........204 C5
Lourier Ct BN14..........186 D4
Lovegrove Ct BN3........190 E8
Love La
Petersfield GU31.......68 C4
Petersfield GU31.......68 D4
Storrington RH20.......121 D2
Loveletts RH11............18 A5
Lovell Path RH11.........17 E5
Lovells Cl PO21...........200 B2
Lover's Wlk BN1..........191 F8
Lover's Wlk Cotts
BN1....................191 F8
Lovett Ct BN12...........185 C5
Loveys Rd BN18..........180 F2
Lowdells Cl RH19..........9 C4
Lowdells Dr RH19.........9 D4
Lowdells La RH19.........9 C3
Lowe Cl RH11.............39 B8

Lower Barn Cl RH12......36 F5
Lower Beach Rd
BN43...................188 F6
Lower Bevendean Ave
BN2....................170 E1
Lower Bognor Rd PO20,
PO21...................200 D5
Lower Chalvington Pl
BN2....................192 E5
Lower Church Rd
BN15...................108 F3
LOWER COKEHAM 187 C5
Lower Dene RH19.........10 A1
Lower Dr BN42...........167 E1
Lower Faircox BN5.......125 D3
LOWER FITTLEWORTH
.......................99 A2
Lower Forecourt RH6....6 D7
Lower Hanger GU27......26 D6
Lower Heyshott GU31....68 E3
Lower Hone La PO18....175 A2
LOWER HORNCROFT
.......................118 C8
Lower Market St ......
BN3....................191 D5
Lower Mead GU31........68 D3
Lower Mere RH19.........22 F8
Lower Rd
East Lavant PO18......155 A5
Forest Row RH18.......23 A5
Lower Rock Gdns
BN2....................213 C1
Lower Roedale Cotts
BN1....................170 B3
Lower Sq RH18...........23 F3
Lower St
Fittleworth RH20.......99 A2
Haslemere GU27........27 C6
Pulborough RH20......100 C2
LOWER STANDEAN.......150 A3
Lower Station Rd
Billingshurst RH14......79 D6
Henfield BN5...........137 B5
Lower Tanbridge Way ......
RH12...................36 B2
Lower Village RH16......87 C2
Lower Village St RH16...87 C1
Lower Wardown GU31...68 D4
Lowestoft Wlk RH10.....19 B4
LOWFIELD HEATH........5 E4
Lowfield Heath Ind Est
RH11....................5 E5
Lowfield Heath Rd RH6...4 F5
Lowfield Heath Windmill*
RH6.....................4 C6
Lowfield Rd
Haywards Heath RH16...87 C4
Slinfold RH13...........34 D3
Lowfield Way RH11........5 E5
LOW HEATH...............98 C7
Lowlands Rd RH15........109 B5
Lowther Rd
Brighton BN1...........170 A2
Worthing BN11.........185 F8
Loxdale (The Swedish
Folk High Sch)
BN41...................168 B1
Loxley Gdns BN14........186 C4
Loxmeadows RH14........31 D3
Loxwood
East Preston BN16......206 B7
Lancing BN15...........187 D5
Loxwood Ave BN14......186 B5
Loxwood Farm Pl
RH14...................31 F3
Loxwood Prim Sch
RH14...................32 A4
Loxwood Rd
Alfold Crossways GU6...11 A3
Loxwood, Alfold Bars GU6,
RH14...................31 F8
Loxwood RH12, RH14...32 D4
Plaistow RH14..........31 A2
Rudgwick RH12.........33 A6
Loxwood Wlk RH11......18 A8
Loyal Par BN1............169 C5
Lucas RH17...............65 D5
Lucas Cl
Crawley RH10...........19 C3
East Grinstead RH19....10 A1
Lucas Field GU27.........26 E6
Lucas Grange RH16......87 D5
Lucas Rd RH12............35 F8
Lucastes Ave RH16.......87 C6
Lucastes La RH16.........87 C5
Lucastes Rd RH16........87 C5
Lucas Way RH16..........87 C5
Lucerne Cl BN41.........168 B1
Lucerne Cl PO21.........200 E2
Lucerne Dr RH10.........19 D4
Lucerne Rd BN1..........170 A1
Lucking La PO22.........202 F5
Lucksfield Way BN16....184 A5
Lucraft Rd BN2...........170 F5
Ludlow Cl PO21...........200 E2
Ludlow Ct BN42..........186 F2
Ludlow Rise BN2.........171 A1
Luffs Mdw GU28..........51 A7
Luggs Cl RH14.............79 D8
Luker Dr GU31.............68 C5
Lullington Ave BN3.......190 F8
Lulworth Cl RH11..........18 B3
Lumley Cl RH6.............2 A4
Lumley Gdns PO10.......173 C8
Lumley Path PO10........173 C8
Lumley Rd
Horley RH6..............2 A3
Lumley PO10...........151 C1

Lumley Terr PO10........151 C1
Lunce's Hill RH16,
RH17...................109 F8
Lund Ho GU28.............97 F7
Lundy Cl
Crawley RH11..........18 C3
Littlehampton BN17....205 A6
Lupin Cl BN17............205 A7
Lurgashall RH15.........109 C1
Lustrells Cl BN2..........194 B2
Lustrells Cres BN2.......194 A2
Lustrells Rd BN2.........194 A2
Lustrells Vale BN2.......194 C2
Lutener Rd GU29.........73 A1
Luther Mews BN2........192 C7
Luther St BN2............192 C7
Luth The
Wisborough Green
RH14...................54 B1
Wisborough Green RH14...78 A8
Lutman St PO10.........151 A4
Lutyens Cl RH11..........17 E4
Luxford Cl RH12..........36 F5
Luxford Rd RH16.........88 B7
Luxford's La RH19.........23 B6
Luxford Way RH14........79 C7
Lychgates The BN18....180 F4
Lychpole Wlk BN12.....185 B4
Lydon Ho RH11............5 D1
LYMINSTER...............182 D6
Lyminster Ave BN1.......170 A5
Lyminster Gate BN17....204 D8
Lyminster Inf Sch
BN17...................204 D7
Lyminster Rd
Crossbush BN18.........160 D1
Littlehampton BN17,
BN18...................182 D6
Lynchborough Rd
GU30...................24 D8
Lynch Down PO18.......153 A6
Lynchet Cl BN1...........170 C2
Lynchet Down BN1.......170 C2
Lynchets Cres BN3.......168 D3
Lynchette The BN43.....166 F1
Lynchet Wlk BN1..........170 C2
Lynchmere Ave BN15....187 D8
Lynchmere Ct PO18......175 C2
Lynden Ct BN1...........169 E2
Lyndhurst Cl RH11........18 D5
Lyndhurst Ct
Bognor Regis
PO21...................201 B2
Hove BN3...............191 D7
Lyndhurst Farm Cl
RH19.....................8 D4
Lyndhurst Fst Sch
BN11...................186 F3
Lyndhurst Rd
Chichester PO19.......177 B5
Hove BN3...............191 D7
Worthing BN11.........186 F3
Lyndons The GU30........24 D8
Lyndum Cl GU32..........68 B4
Lyne Ho RH5...............3 A1
Lyn Rd BN13..............185 C7
Lynton Cl
East Grinstead RH19....10 A2
Hurstpierpoint BN6....128 B5
Lynton Park Ave RH19...10 A2
Lynton Rd GU32...........68 A4
Lyntons RH20.............100 A2
Lynton St BN2............192 C7
Lynwick St
Rudgwick, Cox Green
RH12...................12 D1
Rudgwick RH12.........33 C8
Lynwood Ct RH12.........36 C3
Lyon Cl
Crawley RH10...........19 C2
Hove BN3...............191 D7
Lyon Ct
Bognor Regis
PO21...................201 D3
Horsham RH13..........36 E2
Lyon St W PO21..........201 D3
Lyons Cl RH13.............34 D3
Lyons Rd RH13............34 E3
Lyon St PO21.............201 D3
Lyons Way BN14.........186 E2
Lyoth La RH16.............88 C4
Lyoth Villas RH16.........88 C4
Lyric Cl RH10.............19 D4
Lysander Ho RH20........121 E1
Lysander Way PO20.....156 D1
Lyss Ct GU33..............45 B4
Lytham RH6.................2 B2
Lythe La GU32.............67 C5
Lytton Dr RH10...........19 D7

M
McGechie Ho RH19.........9 D3
McIndoe Rd RH19..........9 D3
McIver Cl RH19.............8 F4
Mackenzie Ho RH19.......9 A4
McKerchar Cl BN15.......187 F7
Mackerel Cl PO20........212 B8
Mackie Ave
Brighton BN1...........170 A2
Keymer BN6............129 A5
Mackley's Ind Est
BN5....................146 F6

Macklin Rd PO22.......**201** E4
Macleod Rd RH13.........**36** F1
McNair Cl PO20.........**212** D8
McNair Ct BN3...........**190** E7
McRae Ct **2** PO20......**212** D7
McWilliam Rd BN2......**171** C1
Maddox Dr RH10.........**19** E5
MADEHURST..........**139** B1
Madehurst Cl
  Brighton BN2.........**192** D5
  Littlehampton BN16...**205** F4
Madehurst Ct
  Crawley RH11.........**17** F3
  6 Littlehampton BN17...**204** D5
Madehurst Way BN17...**204** D6
Madeira Ave
  Bognor Regis PO22....**201** E5
  Horsham RH12.........**36** C2
  Worthing BN11........**186** E2
Madeira Dr BN2.........**192** C4
Madeira Par PO22.......**201** E5
Madeira Pl BN2.........**213** C1
Madeline Rd GU31......**68** B4
Madgwick La PO18......**155** D1
Mafeking Rd BN2........**170** D1
Magdalene Terr RH10...**6** A2
Magellan Ter BN1.......**169** D4
Magnolia Cl BN13.......**185** B6
Magnolia Ct
  Bognor Regis PO21....**201** C4
  Horley RH6...........**2** A3
Magnus Pl **14** BN43....**188** E7
Magpie Cotts PO8......**130** E4
Magpie La PO20.........**209** C1
Magpie Rd PO8..........**130** E5
Magpie Wlk RH10.......**18** F8
MAIDENBOWER........**19** C4
Maidenbower Bsns Pk
  RH10................**19** E4
Maidenbower Dr RH10...**19** D4
Maidenbower Jun & Inf
  Schs RH10...........**19** C4
Maidenbower La RH10...**19** C4
Maidenbower Pl RH10...**19** C4
Maidenbower Sq RH10...**19** C4
Maiden La RH11.........**18** C8
Maidment Ct BN5.......**125** F6
Main Dr **3** PO22.......**202** F5
Maines Farm Rd
  BN44................**146** C1
Mainline Bsns Ctr
  GU33................**45** B4
Main Rd
  Birdham PO20........**197** E4
  Broadbridge PO18....**175** D7
  East Dean PO18......**136** C6
  Hermitage PO10......**173** E8
  Nutbourne PO10, PO18..**174** C7
  Yapton BN18.........**180** F3
Mainstone Rd **1** BN3...**190** F7
Maizecroft RH6.........**2** C4
Major Cl BN1...........**170** B1
Major's Hill RH10......**20** C5
Malcolm Cl BN12.......**206** E5
Malcolm Gdns RH6......**1** D1
Malcolm Rd PO20........**156** C2
Malden Pl **4** RH20....**121** D1
Malden Way PO20........**212** D7
Maldon Rd BN1.........**169** D2
Malham Cl RH10........**19** C3
Malin Rd BN17.........**205** A5
Mallard Cl
  Haslemere GU27......**26** E6
  Horley RH6...........**2** A5
  Horsham RH12.........**36** C5
Mallard Cres PO21......**210** F7
Mallard Rd PO9........**130** D1
Mallards La PO20.......**212** B8
Mallard Way
  Henfield BN5.........**125** E6
  Westbourne PO10......**151** E4
Mallion's La RH17.......**61** E2
Mallon Dene BN16......**205** D4
Mallory Rd BN3.........**169** C2
Mallow Cl RH12.........**36** E6
Malmayne Ct PO21......**200** E3
Malthouse Cl
  Arundel BN18........**160** A2
  Lancing BN15.........**187** B7
Malthouse Cotts
  Bignor RH20.........**118** A1
  Cocking GU29........**114** D7
  West Wittering PO20...**196** D3
  Worthing BN12.......**185** C2
Malthouse Ct
  14 Brighton BN2.....**213** C2
  Liphook GU30........**25** C4
Malthouse La
  Brighton BN2.........**213** C3
  Burgess Hill BN6, RH15..**108** C2
  Burgess Hill RH15....**108** A4
  West Ashling PO18....**153** B3
Malthouse Mdws GU30...**25** C4
Malthouse Pas **3**
  BN17................**204** D6
Malthouse Rd
  Crawley RH10........**18** D4
  Selsey PO20..........**212** E7
Malt House Trad Est
  BN43................**189** B7
Maltings Gn BN44......**145** D2
Maltings The
  Billingshurst RH14....**55** D1
  Burgess Hill RH15....**108** D4

Maltings The continued
  Chichester PO19......**176** F6
  Liphook GU30........**25** D4
  Petersfield GU31......**68** B3
Maltravers Ct **2**
  BN17................**204** E4
Maltravers Dr BN17....**204** E4
Maltravers Rd BN17....**204** E4
Maltravers St BN18....**160** B3
Malvern Cl BN11.......**187** B3
Malvern Mews PO10....**151** B1
Malvern Rd
  Crawley RH11........**18** C5
  Hill Brow GU33.......**45** D2
Malvern St **12** BN3....**191** B7
Malvern Way PO21......**200** B1
Manaton Cl RH16.......**87** F4
Manchester St BN2.....**213** B1
Manchester Terr
  PO10................**151** D4
Mandalay Ct BN1.......**169** D4
Manet Sq PO22.........**201** B6
Manhattan Ct BN1......**169** D3
Manhood Com Coll
  PO20................**212** D8
Manhood Cotts PO20...**208** F7
Manhood La PO20.......**209** F8
Manitoba Way BN13....**185** C7
Manley's Hill RH20....**121** E1
Mann Cl RH11..........**39** B8
Manning Ct RH19.......**9** D2
Mannings **8** BN43....**188** F7
Mannings Cl RH10......**6** D1
Mannock Rd PO20......**156** B1
Manor Ave BN6.........**129** A5
Manor Cl
  Bognor Regis PO22....**202** A4
  Brighton BN2.........**192** E5
  Burgess Hill RH15....**109** D4
  East Preston BN16....**205** F5
  Haslemere GU27......**26** E6
  Henfield BN5.........**125** F5
  Horley RH6...........**1** F3
  Lancing BN15.........**187** F7
  Southwick BN42......**190** A8
  Stockbridge PO19....**176** A3
  Storrington RH20.....**121** D1
  Worthing BN11........**186** B2
Manor Cotts BN6.......**127** F6
Manor Cres
  Brighton BN2.........**192** E5
  Haslemere GU27......**26** E6
Manor Ct
  Elmer PO22..........**203** B5
  Horsham RH12.........**37** A5
  Lancing BN15.........**187** D8
  Rustington BN16......**205** B6
  Southwick BN42......**190** A7
  7 Storrington RH20...**121** D1
  Worthing BN11........**186** B1
Manor Dr
  Cuckfield RH17.......**86** E7
  Horley RH6...........**1** F3
Manor Farm Bsns Ctr
  BN45................**148** C5
Manor Farm Cl PO20...**212** E8
Manor Farm Ct
  Elmer PO22..........**203** B5
  Selsey PO20..........**212** E8
Manor Field Ct BN14...**186** D5
Manorfield Prim Sch
  RH6.................**1** F3
Manor Field Prim Sch
  RH15................**109** C4
Manorfields RH11......**17** D2
Manor Fields
  Horsham RH12, RH13...**37** A4
  Liphook GU30........**25** D4
Manor Gdns
  Breach PO10.........**151** F1
  Brighton BN2.........**192** E5
  Hurstpierpoint BN6...**127** F6
  Rustington BN16......**205** B5
Manor Gn BN2..........**192** E5
Manor Green Coll
  RH11................**18** A7
Manor Green Prim Sch
  RH11................**18** A7
Manor Hall Fst Sch
  BN42................**189** F7
Manor Hall Mid Sch
  BN42................**189** F8
Manor Hall Rd BN42....**189** F8
Manor Hill BN2........**192** E6
Manor Ho
  Horsham RH12.........**36** C1
  Worthing BN11........**186** B2
Manor House Pl BN15...**187** F8
Manor La
  Doomsday Green RH13..**59** B8
  Selsey PO20..........**212** F8
  South Mundham PO20..**199** D6
Manor Lea
  Haslemere GU27......**26** E6
  Worthing BN11........**186** B1
Manor Lodge Rd PO9...**130** C1
Manor Paddock BN2....**192** E4
Manor Par
  Littlehampton BN17....**204** D5
  Worthing BN13.......**185** D8
Manor Pk
  Bognor Regis PO21....**200** A1
Manor Pl
  Bognor Regis PO21....**201** C2
  Brighton BN2.........**192** E4

Manor Rd continued
  Burgess Hill RH15....**109** D4
  East Grinstead RH19...**9** C2
  Horsham RH12.........**37** A5
  Hurstpierpoint BN6...**127** F6
  Lancing BN15.........**187** E8
  Portslade-by-S BN41...**168** B1
  Rustington BN16......**205** B6
  Selsey PO20..........**212** E7
  Upper Beeding BN44...**146** B2
  West Kingston BN16...**206** A4
  Worthing BN11........**186** B2
MANOR ROYAL.......**5** F2
Manor Royal BN2.......**5** E1
Manor Royal Ind Est
  RH10................**5** E2
Manor The **3** BN11...**186** B6
Manor View Ct BN14...**186** D5
Manor Villas PO18.....**175** C5
Manor Way
  Bognor Regis PO21....**200** C1
  Breach PO10.........**151** F1
  Brighton BN2.........**192** E5
  Elmer PO22..........**203** B5
  Henfield BN5.........**125** F6
  Lancing BN15.........**187** F7
Mansbergh Rd PO19....**155** B1
Mansell Ct RH15.......**109** B3
Mansell Rd BN43.......**189** B8
Manser Rd BN18........**158** F1
Mansfield Cl BN11.....**187** A4
Mansfield Cotts PO18...**174** D7
Mansfield Rd
  Bognor Regis PO22....**201** B6
  Hove BN3............**190** E7
  Worthing BN11........**187** A4
Mansion Cl RH15.......**109** D3
Mant Cl
  Climping BN17........**181** D1
  Storrington RH20.....**121** D1
Mantell Ho **2** BN2....**213** C2
Mantelmas Cotts RH10..**21** A4
Mantling Rd BN17......**204** D5
Manton Cl PO20........**208** C5
Manton Rd BN2.........**170** E1
Mant Rd GU28..........**97** F7
Mants Farm Ct PO21...**200** C3
Maple Cl
  Billingshurst RH14....**55** C1
  Burgess Hill RH15....**109** B5
  Crawley RH11........**5** C1
  Haywards Heath RH16...**88** B3
  Horsham RH12.........**37** A5
  Middleton-on-S PO22..**202** E6
  New Brighton PO10....**151** B2
  Woodingdean BN2.....**193** E7
  Worthing BN13.......**163** E1
Maple Ct **5** BN11.....**185** F3
Mapledown Cl RH13....**57** F2
Maple Dr
  Burgess Hill RH15....**109** A5
  East Grinstead RH19...**10** A1
Maple Gdns
  Bognor Regis PO22....**201** C7
  Hove BN3............**168** F1
Maplegreen RH11.......**18** C5
Maple Ho RH12.........**185** A6
Maplehurst Ct RH14....**79** E7
Maplehurst Rd
  Chichester PO19......**155** B2
  Maplehurst RH13.....**83** A3
  Portslade-by-S BN41...**168** A1
Maple Leaf RH20.......**119** D6
Maple Par BN18........**180** E8
Maple Rd
  Billingshurst RH14....**79** D7
  Walberton BN18......**180** E8
Maples The
  3 Bognor Regis
    PO21.............**201** B3
  Ferring BN12........**206** F4
Maple Wlk
  Lancing BN15.........**187** B7
  Petersfield GU31......**68** B1
  Rustington BN16......**205** C6
Maplewood **4** BN1....**169** E3
Mapsons La PO20.......**198** B3
Marama Gdns BN16.....**205** B3
Marchants Cl BN6......**128** A6
Marchants Rd BN6......**128** A6
Marchants Way RH15...**108** F5
March CE Prim Sch The
  PO18................**155** E1
March Cl PO21.........**200** C3
Marches Rd RH12......**14** E4
Marches The
  Fernhurst GU27.......**49** B5
  Kingsfold RH12.......**15** B5
March Ho BN43.........**169** B1
March Sq PO19.........**155** A3
Marchwell Ind Unit
  PO19................**155** B1
Marchwood PO19.......**155** A3
Marchwood Gate
  PO19................**155** A3
Marcuse Fields PO18...**175** B6
Mardale Rd BN13......**185** E7
Marden Ave PO19......**176** E3
Marden Cl BN2.........**171** E1
Marden Ho
  Barnham PO22........**180** C6
  Littlehampton BN17....**204** B7
Mardens The RH11.....**18** A8
Marden Way GU31......**68** C3
Mardyke BN43.........**188** D6
Mare Hill Rd RH20....**100** D1
Maresfield Rd BN2.....**192** E5

Margaret Cl PO21......**200** E3
Margaret Cotts RH13...**83** E2
Margaret Ho PO22......**201** E4
Margaret St BN2.......**213** C1
Margary Cl PO19.......**176** B7
Margery Rd BN3........**190** D8
Marianne Way PO21....**201** E3
Marigolds Lo **2** BN16..**205** B4
Marigolds (Park Homes)
  PO22................**179** D1
Marik Mews **5** BN11...**186** F2
Marina Ct PO10........**173** C7
Marina Ct BN15........**188** C5
Marina Way BN2........**192** F3
Marine Ave BN3........**190** E6
Marine Cl
  East Wittering PO20...**207** E6
  Saltdean BN2........**194** B1
  Worthing BN11........**186** A1
Marine Cres BN12......**185** D2
Marine Ct
  Littlehampton BN17....**204** E4
  Rottingdean BN2......**194** A1
  Selsey PO20..........**212** F7
  Worthing BN12.......**185** B1
Marine Dr
  East Wittering PO20...**207** E7
  Rottingdean BN2......**193** C2
  Selsey PO20..........**212** D5
Marine Dr W
  Bognor Regis PO21....**201** A2
  East Wittering PO20...**207** D7
Marine Gdns
  Brighton BN2.........**213** C1
  Selsey PO20..........**212** D5
Marine Par
  Bognor Regis PO21....**201** B2
  Brighton BN2.........**192** C4
  Worthing BN11........**186** D1
Marine Park Ho PO21...**201** B2
Marine Pk **3** PO21....**201** B2
Marine Pl BN11........**186** D1
Marine Point **14**
  BN11................**186** A1
Mariners Cl BN43......**188** D5
Mariners Quay
  Brighton BN2.........**192** F3
  Littlehampton BN17....**204** C5
Mariners Terr PO18....**175** B4
Mariners The BN15....**187** D3
Mariners Wlk BN16....**205** D4
Marineside PO20.......**208** B5
Marine Terrace Mews **7**
  BN2.................**192** C4
Marine View **3** BN2...**213** C2
Marion Rd RH10.......**19** B3
Marisfield Pl PO20....**212** F8
Marjoram Pl BN43.....**167** B1
Market Ave PO19......**177** A5
Market Cl PO22........**180** B6
Market Field BN44.....**145** E3
Market Pl
  Haywards Heath RH16...**87** D6
  Worthing BN13.......**186** A4
Market Place Sh Ctr
  RH15................**109** A2
Market Rd PO19........**177** A6
Market Sq
  9 Horsham RH12.....**36** C2
  Midhurst GU29.......**94** F7
  Petworth GU28.......**97** F8
Market St
  Bognor Regis PO21....**201** C2
  Brighton BN1.........**213** B2
  13 Worthing BN11....**186** D2
Markfield PO22........**201** B6
MARK STREET.......**66** F3
Markwick Mews
  BN11................**186** E3
Marlborough Bsns Ctr
  BN15................**187** C4
Marlborough Cl
  Chichester PO19......**177** D6
  Crawley RH11........**18** C2
  5 Horsham RH12.....**36** D5
Marlborough Ct
  Bognor Regis PO21....**200** F5
  Burgess Hill RH15....**108** E3
  1 Hove BN3.........**191** C6
Marlborough Dr
  RH15................**109** C2
Marlborough Ho **6**
  PO21................**201** B2
Marlborough Mews
  BN1.................**213** A2
Marlborough Pl
  6 Brighton BN1,
    BN2.............**213** B3
  Horsham RH12.........**36** C3
Marlborough Rd
  Lancing BN15.........**187** D4
  Worthing BN12.......**185** D3
Marlborough St BN1....**213** A5
Marlborough Way
  BN12................**185** D3
Marle Ave RH15........**109** A4
Marles La
  Five Oaks RH14......**55** C8
  Rudgwick RH14......**33** C1
Marley Combe Rd
  GU27................**26** F4
Marley Hanger GU27...**27** A3
MARLEY HEIGHTS....**27** A1
Marley La GU27........**26** E4
Marley Way RH20......**121** E2
Marlin Cl BN15........**187** F4
Marline Ct BN43.......**188** E7

Marlinespike The
  BN43................**189** A6
Marlings The RH16.....**87** C3
Marlipins Mus *
  BN43................**188** E7
Marlow Ct
  Brighton BN2.........**213** C4
  Crawley RH10........**18** D7
Marlow Dr RH16.......**88** C4
Marlowe Ct PO22......**202** E6
Marlowe Rd BN14......**186** E5
Marlow Rd BN2.........**192** F4
Marlpit Cl RH19.......**9** E4
Marlpit La
  Oving PO20..........**178** B7
  Woodmancote PO10,
    PO18............**152** C4
Marlpit Rd RH19.......**43** A6
Marlpost Rd RH13.....**57** C3
Marmion Rd BN3.......**190** F7
Marquis Way PO21.....**200** E1
Marringdean Rd RH14..**79** E4
Marshall Ave
  Bognor Regis PO22....**201** B4
  Worthing BN14.......**163** F3
Marshall Cl PO22......**180** B5
Marshall Rd RH10......**19** C4
Marshalls Row BN1....**213** B4
Marshall Way BN3.....**168** F1
Marsh Barns PO20.....**177** F2
Marsh Cl RH11.........**18** B1
Marsh Ho **3** BN42....**189** D7
Marsh La
  Chidham PO18........**174** C4
  Crockerhill PO18......**157** A2
  Merston PO20........**178** A2
  Mid Lavant PO18......**154** F6
  Tangmere PO18.......**156** F2
Marston Ct **10** BN3...**191** E7
Marston Rd BN14......**186** E4
Martello Ent Ctr
  BN17................**204** C8
Martha Gunn Rd BN2...**170** E1
Martin Cl RH11........**18** D8
Martineau Cl PO21.....**200** E3
Martin Rd BN3.........**168** D1
Martins La PO20.......**197** F5
Martins The RH10.....**21** C8
Martlet Cl PO19.......**177** A5
Martlet Cnr RH12.....**33** D7
Martlet Ct **5** BN2....**192** C5
Martlet Ho BN1........**192** A8
Martlet Rd GU28.......**97** F7
Martlets RH20.........**121** D8
Martlets Cl RH12......**36** C5
Martlets Ct BN18......**160** B2
Martlets Sh Ctr The
  RH15................**109** A3
Martlets The
  Crawley RH10........**18** E6
  Lancing BN15.........**187** C6
  Littlehampton BN16....**205** A4
  Shoreham-by-S BN43...**188** F8
Martlets Trad Est
  BN12................**185** C4
Martlets Way BN12....**185** C4
Martlet The BN3.......**169** D1
Martlet Way PO21.....**210** F7
Marts The RH12........**33** D7
Martyn Cl BN5.........**125** E5
Martyn's Cl BN2.......**193** E4
Martyns Pl RH19.......**23** A8
Martyrs Ave
  Crawley RH11........**5** C1
  Crawley RH11........**5** D1
Marvell Cl RH10.......**19** C8
Marylands RH16.......**87** F5
Marylands Cres PO22...**201** E5
Masefield Rd RH11.....**17** E3
Mash Barn La BN15....**188** A7
Mason Cl RH19.........**9** E2
Mason Rd RH10........**18** E4
Masons Field RH13....**59** C6
Masons Way RH20.....**100** D5
Massetts Rd RH6.......**2** A2
Matform Bsns Ctr
  PO19................**176** E5
Matlock Rd BN1.......**169** D2
Matthew Ho **14** BN3...**191** A6
Matthews Dr RH10.....**19** C3
Matthey Pl RH10......**6** D1
Maudlin La BN44......**145** E1
Maudlyn Cl BN44......**145** E1
Maudlyn Parkway
  BN44................**145** D1
Maudlyn Pk BN44......**145** D1
Mauldmare Cl PO21....**200** F2
Maunsell Ct RH16.....**87** F3
Maunsell Pk RH10.....**19** B6
Maxton Wlk RH11.....**18** B2
Maxwell Rd
  Arundel BN18........**159** F1
  Littlehampton BN17....**204** C5
Maxwell Way RH10.....**6** A1
Maybridge Cres BN12...**185** C4
Maybridge Sq BN12....**185** C5
Maybush Dr PO18......**174** D7
May Cl
  Bognor Regis PO22....**201** D1
  Climping BN17........**181** D1
  Sidlesham PO20......**209** F8
  Worthing BN12.......**185** C5
Maydwell Ave RH13....**34** C5
Mayes Cl RH10.........**19** C5
Mayes La RH12........**14** F3
Mayes Lane Cotts
  RH12................**14** F2
Mayfair Ct PO19.......**176** F7

Mayfield
Crawley RH10 19 D6
East Preston BN16 206 B7
Mayfield Cl
Bognor Regis PO21 200 B3
Brighton BN1 170 A5
Worthing BN14 164 A1
Mayfield Cres BN1 169 F5
Mayfield Ct
Burgess Hill RH15 109 B3
Saltdean BN2 194 C2
Mayfield Ho RH17 86 F8
Mayfield Rd PO21 201 A4
Mayfields RH17 85 C4
Mayflower Cl RH10 19 D5
Mayflower Ct
Haywards Heath RH16 87 F4
11 Shoreham-by-S BN43 189 A6
Mayflower Rd RH16 87 F4
Mayflower Sq BN1 213 B4
Mayflower Way BN16 206 A7
Mayhouse Rd RH15 108 F1
Maynard Cl RH10 7 C4
Mayo Ct 5 BN2 192 B8
Mayo Rd BN2 192 B8
Maypole Rd
Ashurst Wood RH19 23 E6
East Grinstead RH19 9 D2
May Rd BN2 192 D7
Mayridge PO20 212 B8
May Tree Ave BN14 163 F3
Maytree Cl
Angmering BN16 205 F8
Lancing BN15 187 B6
May Tree Cl BN3 190 D8
May Tree Wlk BN3 168 E1
Mead Cotts GU31 91 D4
Mead Ct 15 PO22 201 D4
Mead Ho The RH13 57 F1
Mead La
Bognor Regis PO22 201 E4
Storrington RH20 121 E2
Meadow App RH10 7 A3
Meadowbank RH14 78 B8
Meadow Brook Ind Ctr RH10 6 A1
Meadow Cl
Balcombe RH17 41 A1
Copthorne RH10 7 A3
Horsham RH12 37 A5
Hove BN3 169 B3
Hunston PO20 199 A8
Liphook GU30 25 C4
Portslade-by-S BN41 168 B2
Rottingdean BN2 193 F3
Southwick BN42 190 A8
Worthing BN11 187 B3
Meadow Court Est 4 BN11 187 B3
Meadow Cres BN11 187 A3
Meadowcroft Cl
Crawley RH11 17 F5
East Grinstead RH19 9 C2
Meadow Croft Cl RH6 6 C8
Meadow Ct
East Grinstead RH19 9 E2
4 Emsworth PO10 173 B8
Middleton-on-S PO22 202 D6
Meadow Dr RH16 88 B6
Meadow End GU30 25 C5
Meadow Farm La RH12 36 F7
Meadowfield Dr PO19 177 B7
Meadowgate RH12 36 F7
Meadow La
Burgess Hill RH15 108 F1
Lancing BN15 187 E5
Lindfield RH16 88 B6
West Wittering PO20 196 D1
Meadowland PO20 212 D6
Meadowlands
Crawley RH11 18 C6
Rowland's Castle PO9 130 E3
Meadow Lands GU32 68 A2
Meadow Par BN2 193 F3
Meadow Pk BN16 206 B5
Meadow Rd BN11 187 B3
Meadow Road Ind Est BN11 187 B4
Meadows BN6 128 F5
Meadowside
Angmering BN16 184 A6
Horley RH6 2 B4
Storrington RH20 121 D1
Meadowside Ct BN12 185 A3
Meadowside Wlk PO20 156 D2
Meadows Rd PO20 208 A7
Meadows The
East Preston BN16 206 A5
Hove BN3 168 C3
Stockbridge PO19 176 E3
Walberton BN18 180 E8
Meadow Sweet Cl BN13 185 A6
Meadow Terr RH17 41 A1
Meadow The RH10 7 A3
Meadow Vale
Haslemere GU27 27 A6
Ovingdean BN2 193 E5
Meadowview BN2 170 E1
Meadow View BN6 107 C1
Meadowview Rd BN15 187 D8
Meadow Way
Bognor Regis, North Bersted PO22 201 A6
Bognor Regis PO21 200 B1
Meadow Way *continued*
Ferring BN12 206 E6
Liphook GU30 25 C5
Littlehampton BN17 204 F5
Petworth GU28 97 E7
Tangmere PO20 156 D2
Westergate PO20 179 D6
Meadow Wlk
Liss GU33 45 B4
Middleton-on-S PO22 203 A5
Mead Rd RH10 18 F7
Meads Ave BN3 168 C3
Meads Cl BN3 168 C3
Meads Prim Sch RH19 22 E7
Meads The
Brighton BN1 170 D5
Burgess Hill RH15 108 F3
East Grinstead RH19 22 E7
Fulking BN5 147 F4
Haslemere GU27 26 F6
Meadsway BN18 158 D4
Mead The
Liphook GU30 25 B5
Liss GU33 45 B4
Petersfield GU32 67 F2
Meadvale RH12 35 F2
Meadway
Haslemere GU27 26 F6
Rustington BN16 205 D5
Mead Way GU29 94 E6
Meadway Cres BN3 168 F2
Meadway Ct
Southwick BN42 189 D8
Worthing BN13 185 E5
Meadway The
Brighton BN2 192 F5
Horley RH6 2 C3
Shoreham-by-S BN43 189 A6
Measham Cl BN12 206 F5
MEATH GREEN 1 F5
Meath Green Ave RH6 1 F5
Meath Green Inf Sch RH6 1 F5
Meath Green Jun Sch RH6 1 F5
Meath Green La RH1, RH6 1 E6
Mechanical Music & Doll Mus★ PO19 177 D7
Medina Pl BN3 191 B6
Medina Terr BN3 191 B5
Medina Villas BN3 191 B6
Medlar Cl RH11 5 C1
Medmerry PO20 212 A8
Medmerry Ct 1 PO20 212 D7
Medmerry Hill BN2 170 E2
Medmerry Prim Sch PO20 212 D7
Medway RH10 21 A5
Medway Cl BN13 185 D8
Medway Cotts BN18 180 F2
Medway Ct RH12 37 B5
Medway Dr RH19 22 D6
Medway Rd RH11 17 F5
Medwin Wlk 5 RH12 36 C2
Meeds Rd RH15 109 A2
Meeting House La BN1 213 B2
Meiros Way RH20 122 F5
Melanie's Gdns 12 PO21 201 D4
Melbourne Ave BN12 185 C3
Melbourne Rd
Chichester PO19 177 B7
Worthing BN12 185 D3
Melbourne St BN2 192 C8
Melbourne Way
Horsham RH12 36 F5
Worthing BN12 185 C3
Melchbourne Villas RH19 42 E6
Melksham Cl RH13 36 E1
Melrose Ave
Portslade-by-S BN41 168 A1
Worthing BN13 185 E5
Melrose Cl
Brighton BN1 170 C2
Worthing BN13 185 E5
Melrose Pl RH20 122 C3
Melton Ave RH20 121 D3
Melton Cl RH20 121 E3
Melton Dr RH20 121 E3
Melville Rd BN3 191 E7
Melville Way BN12 185 C5
Mendip Cl BN16 206 A6
Mendip Cres BN13 185 E8
Mendip Ct 1 BN16 205 C6
Mendip Rd BN13 185 E8
Mendip Wlk RH11 18 B6
Meon Cl GU32 68 A4
Mercer Cl RH10 19 C3
Mercer Rd RH12 36 C8
Mercers Mead RH13 83 E1
Merchant St PO21 201 C3
Mercury Cl RH11 17 E3
Mere Cl PO20 208 B5
Meredith Rd BN14 186 F4
Merevale BN1 170 B2
Mereworth Dr RH10 19 D8
Meridian Cl RH11 17 F3
Meridian Gr RH6 2 C4
Meridian Way RH19 9 F3
Merle Court Gdns PO20 198 F8
Merle Way GU27 49 A6
Merlin Cl
Crawley RH11 17 E6
Merlin Cl *continued*
Hove BN3 191 D8
Merlin Ct BN13 185 F7
Merlin Ctr RH11 5 D2
Merlin Way
East Grinstead RH19 10 A3
Middleton-on-S PO22 202 D6
Merrion Ave PO21, PO22 201 B5
Merrivale Ct PO10 151 F1
Merry End PO22 202 D5
Merryfield Cres BN16 184 A6
Merryfield Dr
Horsham RH12 36 A3
Selsey PO20 212 F7
Merryfield Rd
Petersfield GU31 68 D4
Storrington RH20 121 D2
Merryfield Way RH20 121 D2
Merry Hills La RH14 32 A5
Merryweather Rd PO18 175 B5
Merrywood Ho RH20 122 B3
Merrywood La RH20 122 B4
Mersey Cl BN13 185 C8
Mersey Rd BN13 185 C8
Mersham Gdns BN12 185 C3
Merston Cl BN2 193 E6
Merton Ave BN16 205 D4
Merton Cl PO21 200 E4
Merton Ct BN2 193 A3
Merton Dr 1 BN17 204 D6
Merton Rd
Crawley RH11 39 B8
Worthing BN11 186 F2
Merton Terr BN11 186 F2
Messenger Cl RH11 18 A8
Metcalf Way RH11 5 D2
Meteor Rd PO10 173 C3
Metropole Ct 12 BN1 191 E5
Mews Ct RH19 22 F6
Mews The
14 Bognor Regis PO21 201 C3
Bognor Regis PO22 201 E4
Brighton BN1 169 E2
Brighton, Preston BN1 169 F2
Broadbridge Heath RH12 35 D4
Littlehampton BN17 204 F5
Petersfield GU31 68 B4
Petworth GU28 97 F8
Pulborough RH20 100 D2
Meyers Wood RH13 105 A2
Meyners Cl BN3 168 C3
Michael Ayres Jun Sch PO21 201 A5
Michael Cres RH6 2 A1
Michael Fields RH18 23 E2
Michael Hall Sch RH18 23 D1
Michelbourne Cl RH15 108 E1
Michel Gr BN16 205 F5
Michelgrove Cotts BN13 162 C5
Michell Cl RH12 36 A2
Micklam Cl PO21 200 C2
Mid Acre Cl PO22 202 A6
Middlefield
Horley RH6 2 C4
West Wittering PO20 196 C1
Middlefield La PO18 155 C7
Middle Mdw GU33 45 C4
Middle Mead
Littlehampton BN17 205 A5
Steyning BN44 145 D4
Middle Onslow Cl BN12 206 E7
Middle Rd
Brighton BN1 169 E1
Lancing BN15 187 D5
Partridge Green RH13 105 A3
Shoreham-by-S BN43 189 B7
Middle Row 1 RH19 22 F8
Middle St
Brighton BN1 213 A2
Falmer BN1 171 C6
7 Horsham RH12 36 C2
Petworth GU28 97 F8
Portslade-by-S BN41 190 B6
Shoreham-by-S BN43 188 F7
Middle Street Prim Sch BN1 213 A2
Middleton Ave BN3 190 D6
Middleton Bsns Pk PO22 202 F6
Middleton Cl PO20 208 B6
Middleton Ct 6 PO22 202 F5
Middleton Gdns PO20 156 D2
Middleton Pl PO22 202 E5
Middleton Rd
Horsham RH12 36 A2
Middleton-on-S PO22 202 D5
Middleton Rise BN1 170 E5
Middleton Way RH11 17 E5
Middle Tyne BN13 185 D6
Middle Village RH16 87 C2
Middle Way
Burgess Hill RH15 109 B3
Kingston Gorse BN16 206 D4
Midfields Cl RH15 109 B3
Midfields Dr RH15 109 B3
Midfields Wlk RH15 109 B4
Midgley Rd RH10 18 F8
Midholme BN16 205 F5
Midhurst CE Prim Sch GU29 94 E7
Midhurst Cl
Crawley RH11 18 A7
Ferring BN12 206 F6
Midhurst Com Hospl GU29 72 F1
Midhurst Dr BN12 185 A3
Midhurst Gram Sch GU29 94 F8
Midhurst Intermediate Sch GU29 73 A2
Midhurst Rd
Fernhurst GU27 49 A4
Haslemere GU27 27 B5
Liphook GU30 25 C2
Mid Lavant PO18 154 E7
Midhurst Rise BN1 170 B6
Midhurst Wlk BN3 168 F3
Midway Rd BN2 193 C8
Midway The PO22 202 A4
Mighell St BN2 213 C2
Milborne Rd RH10 19 C2
Milbury Cl 7 BN12 206 F4
Milcote Ave BN3 190 F8
Mile End Cotts BN1 169 E6
Mile End La PO20 176 C2
MILE OAK 167 F4
Mile Oak Cres BN42 167 F1
Mile Oak Gdns BN41 168 A1
Mile Oak Prim Sch BN41 167 F3
Mile Oak Rd
Portslade-by-S BN41 167 F3
Southwick BN42 167 F1
Miles Cl BN18 181 B2
Miles Cotts PO18 175 C5
Miles Wlk BN3 191 B6
Milford Ct BN15 187 D3
Millais RH13 37 A3
Millais Cl RH11 17 F2
Millais Ct RH13 37 A4
Millais Sch RH13 36 F2
Milland La GU30 47 A5
Millars Ct PO21 200 B1
Mill Ave BN43 166 F1
Millbank RH15 109 B4
Millbank The RH11 17 F6
Mill Bay La RH12 36 B1
Millbrook Cl GU33 45 C4
Millbrook Ct GU29 94 F8
Mill Cl
Burgess Hill RH15 109 B4
Crabtree RH13 84 A7
East Grinstead RH19 22 E7
Fishbourne PO19 176 B6
Haslemere GU27 26 E6
Horley RH6 1 E4
Portslade-by-S BN41 168 C1
Poynings BN45 148 C5
Rustington BN16 205 D6
Mill Copse Rd GU27 27 B4
Mill Cotts
East Grinstead RH19 22 E7
Rudgwick RH12 33 D5
Millcroft BN1 169 C5
Millcroft Ave BN42 167 E1
Millcroft Gdns BN42 167 E1
Millcross Rd BN41 168 B1
Mill Ct
Burgess Hill RH15 109 B2
Poynings BN45 148 C5
Worthing BN11 186 B2
Mill Dr
Henfield BN5 125 F4
Hove BN3 169 A3
Mill End
Henfield BN5 125 E4
Hermitage PO10 173 D8
West Chiltington Common RH20 121 C8
Millennium Cl BN15 188 B6
Millennium Ho RH11 17 F3
Millennium Seedbank★ RH17 41 F4
Miller Pl BN41 168 A3
Millers Cl
Burgess Hill RH15 109 A4
Rustington BN16 205 D6
Millers Gate RH12 36 D6
Miller's Rd BN1 169 E1
Millers The BN18 180 F2
Millers Way RH15 109 B4
Millfarm Dr PO21 200 A2
Mill Farm (Park Home Est) PO21 199 F2
Mill Farm Rd RH13 37 A4
Millfield
Lancing BN15 187 C7
Southwater RH13 82 A7
Upper Beeding BN44 146 A2
Millfield Cl
Chichester PO19 177 C8
Rustington BN16 205 B3
Millfield Cotts 8 BN2 192 D4
Millfield Ct BN17 204 C8
Mill Field Lo 9 BN11 186 A2
Millfields Cres RH6 4 D6
Mill Gdns PO20 207 F7
Mill Green Ind Est RH16 87 E6
Mill Green Rd RH16 87 E6
Millhaven Ct RH15 109 B3
MILL HILL 166 E1
Mill Hill BN43 166 E3
Mill Hill Cl
Haywards Heath RH16 87 E7
Shoreham-by-S BN43 166 E1
Mill Hill Dr BN43 166 E1
Mill Hill Gdns BN43 166 E1
Mill Ho
21 Bognor Regis PO21 201 B2
6 Worthing BN11 187 B3
Mill House Gdns BN11 186 A2
Milliers Ct BN16 205 F6
Millington Dr PO20 209 F1
Mill La
Amberley BN18 140 E6
Arundel BN18 160 B3
Ashington RH20 122 F4
Balcombe RH17 41 C1
Clayton BN6, BN45 149 E7
Cocking GU29 114 D8
Coolham RH13 80 D3
Copthorne RH10 7 E3
Crabtree RH13 84 B7
Crawley RH11 18 A8
Dormansland RH7 9 F8
Dumpford GU31 92 F8
Felbridge RH19 8 E5
Fishbourne PO19 176 B6
Goddards' Green BN6 108 A3
Heyshott Green GU29 95 A2
Hookwood RH6 1 D3
Kingsley Green GU27 27 C3
Littlehampton BN17 182 D5
Littleworth RH13 104 F5
Petersfield GU32 68 E5
Portslade-by-S BN41 168 B1
Poynings BN45 148 C5
Runcton PO20 177 E1
Rustington BN16 205 D6
Sayers Common BN6 107 E2
Selsey PO20 212 C7
Shoreham-by-S BN43 188 F8
Sidlesham PO20 209 F7
Slindon BN18 158 C6
South Harting GU31 91 D4
Stedham GU29 72 A2
Steep GU32 68 A8
Storrington RH20 121 D2
Trotton GU31 71 A1
Walberton BN18 158 D1
Westbourne PO10 151 D2
West Chiltington Common RH20 121 C8
Worthing BN13 163 F1
Mill Lo PO21 200 A2
Mill Mead RH20 123 A4
Mill Park Rd PO21 200 B2
Mill Pk RH15 109 B3
Mill Pond La PO18 153 B3
Mill Pond Way BN16 205 F6
Mill Prim Sch The RH11 18 A6
Mill Quay PO10 173 C7
Mill Race BN6 128 E8
Mill Rd
Angmering BN16 183 F5
Arundel BN18 160 C3
Brighton BN1 169 C6
Burgess Hill RH15 109 B3
Crawley RH10 19 B7
Lancing BN15 187 E8
Liss GU33 45 C4
Portslade-by-S BN41 190 B7
Steyning BN44 145 C3
Walberton BN18 158 D3
West Ashling PO18 153 A3
Westbourne PO10 151 D4
West Chiltington Common RH20 121 C8
Worthing BN11 186 A2
Mill Rd Ind Est BN41 190 B7
Mill Rise BN1 169 C5
Mill Road Ave BN16 183 F5
Mill Row BN1 213 A3
Mills Cl RH13 36 F1
Mill St BN1 171 C7
Mill Straight RH13 81 F8
Mill Stream Mdw RH16 87 D7
Millstream The GU27 26 E5
Millthorpe Rd RH12 36 F4
Mill Vale Mdws GU30 47 B3
Millview Cl PO21 200 A2
Mill View Hospl BN3 168 E1
Mill View Rd BN18 180 F2
Mill Way
Billingshurst RH14 55 D1
East Grinstead RH19 22 E7
Millwood RH10 21 E5
Mill Wood RH15 109 B3
Millyard Cres BN2 193 D7
Milne Cl RH11 17 E3
Milner Flats BN2 213 C2
Milner Rd BN2 170 D1
Milnthorpe Rd BN3 190 F8
Milnwood Rd RH12 36 C3
Milton Ave BN16 205 B5
Milton Cl
Lancing BN15 187 F5
Rustington BN16 205 B5
Milton Cres RH19 22 C8
Milton Ct
6 Haywards Heath RH16 87 D5
4 Worthing BN11 186 C1
Milton Dr BN42 189 F8
Milton Mount RH10 6 D1
Milton Mount Ave RH10 19 D8

Milton Mount Prim Sch
RH10 . . . . 19 C8
Milton Rd
Brighton BN2 . . . . 213 C4
Crawley RH10 . . . . 19 C7
Haywards Heath RH16 . . . . 87 D6
Horsham RH12 . . . . 36 C3
Worthing BN11 . . . . 186 C1
Milton St BN11 . . . . 186 C1
Milward Ct 3 BN43 . . . . . . 189 C8
Milwood Ct PO19 . . . . 176 F7
Mimmack Cl BN44 . . . . . . 145 D4
Mimosa Ct BN1 . . . . 170 B3
Mindelheim Ave RH19 . . . . 10 B2
Minnels The BN6 . . . . 129 A3
MINSTED 93 E6
Minsted Rd GU29 . . . . 93 F7
Minster Ct BN17 . . . . 204 C8
Minton Rd PO22 . . . . 202 B4
Mint Rd GU33 . . . . 45 D6
MINT THE 45 D6
Mint The GU31, GU32 . . . . 68 B2
Miranda Wlk RH11 . . . . . . 17 E4
Mistley Gdns RH11 . . . . . . 1 D2
Mitchell Ct RH6 . . . . 2 A2
Mitchell Gdns BN13 . . . . . 34 E3
Mitchells Rd RH10 . . . . . . 18 F6
Mitchmere Cotts
PO18 . . . . 132 F2
Mitford Wlk 10 RH11 . . . . 18 A3
Mitre Ct 10 RH12 . . . . 36 B2
Mitre Ho 23 BN1 . . . . 191 E5
Mixon Cl PO20 . . . . 212 E6
Moatfield La RH13 . . . . . . 106 A8
Moat La RH20 . . . . 100 D2
Moat Rd RH19 . . . . 9 E2
Moat The RH20 . . . . 100 C2
Moat Way BN12 . . . . 185 E2
Moat Wlk RH10 . . . . 19 C7
Mocatta Way RH15 . . . . . 108 D5
Modena Rd BN3 . . . . 190 F7
Modern Moulds Bsns Ctr
Lancing BN15 . . . . 187 C4
Littlehampton BN17 . . . . . . 204 C6
Moggs Mead GU31 . . . . . . 68 C3
Mole Cl RH11 . . . . 18 B8
Molecomb Broadwalk
PO18 . . . . 136 A2
Molesworth St BN3 . . . . . 190 F8
Mole The BN17 . . . . 205 A5
Molineux Pl RH16 . . . . 87 D5
Molins Ct 4 RH11 . . . . 18 A3
Monarch Cl RH11 . . . . 18 A3
Monarchs View RH41 . . . . 167 F2
Monastery La RH20 . . . . . 121 C1
Monckton Way BN7 . . . . . 172 E5
Monk Cl BN1 . . . . 170 E6
Monkmead Copse
RH20 . . . . 121 C6
Monkmead La RH20 . . . . . 121 B6
Monks Ave BN15 . . . . 187 F6
Monks Cl BN15 . . . . 187 F6
Monks Ct 2 BN15 . . . . . . 187 E6
Monksfield RH10 . . . . 18 F7
Monk's Hill PO10 . . . . 151 C5
Monks La RH5 . . . . 13 F5
Monks Manor RH5 . . . . . . 13 F5
Monks Orch GU32 . . . . 68 B5
Monks Wlk BN44 . . . . 146 B2
Monks Wood GU32 . . . . . . 68 B5
Mons Ave PO21 . . . . 201 B5
Montacute Rd BN7 . . . . . . 172 F8
Montague Cl BN43 . . . . . . 189 D7
Montague Ct
6 Brighton BN2 . . . . 192 C4
Lancing BN15 . . . . 187 B7
2 Shoreham-by-S
BN43 . . . . 189 D7
Montague Ctr 10
BN11 . . . . 186 D2
Montague Gdns GU31 . . . . 68 D3
Montague Ho BN11 . . . . . 186 A3
Montague Pl
Brighton BN2 . . . . 192 C4
Worthing BN11 . . . . 186 D1
Montague Rd GU29 . . . . . 73 A2
Montague St
4 Brighton BN2 . . . . 192 C4
Worthing BN11 . . . . 186 D1
Montagu Ho PO18 . . . . . . 155 E1
Montagu Rd PO19 . . . . . . 176 E8
Montalan Cres PO20 . . . . 212 B8
Montefiore Rd BN3 . . . . . 191 E7
Monterey Ct BN1 . . . . 169 E3
Monterey Gdns PO21 . . . . 201 A4
Monterey Pines PO22 . . . 202 A5
Montes Hill RH16 . . . . 88 F8
Monteswood La RH16,
RH17 . . . . 89 B8
Montford Cl BN43 . . . . . . 189 D8
Montfort Rise RH1 . . . . 1 F8
Montgomeri Dr BN16 . . . . 205 B7
Montgomery Dr PO22 . . . 202 B6
Montgomery St BN3 . . . . 191 A7
Montgomery Terr 2
BN3 . . . . 191 A7
Montpelier Cotts
RH20 . . . . 143 E8
Montpelier Cres BN1 . . . . 191 E6
Montpelier Gdns
RH20 . . . . 143 E8
Montpelier Lo 9 BN1 . . . 191 E6
Montpelier Pl BN1 . . . . . . 191 E6
Montpelier Rd
Brighton BN1 . . . . 191 E5

Montpelier Rd continued
East Preston BN16 . . . . 206 A5
Montpelier St BN1 . . . . . . 191 E6
Montpelier Terr BN1 . . . . 191 E6
Montpelier Villas
BN1 . . . . 191 E6
Montpellier Apartments 25
BN1 . . . . 191 E5
Montreal Rd BN2 . . . . 213 C3
Montreal Way BN13 . . . . 185 C7
Montreal Wlk GU30 . . . . . 25 C3
Montreux Ct RH11 . . . . . . 18 B6
Montrose Cl BN12 . . . . . . 185 C3
Montrose Ct BN12 . . . . . . 185 C4
Monument La PO18 . . . . . 152 B7
Monument View BN2 . . . . 192 D6
Moonhill Pl RH17 . . . . 86 E1
Moonsgate 5 RH13 . . . . . 36 E1
Moons La RH13 . . . . 36 E1
Moon's La RH7 . . . . 10 E8
Moorcroft Cl RH11 . . . . . . 18 B7
Moore Cl BN13 . . . . 185 B7
Moore Ct RH12 . . . . 36 A1
Moore Pl 4 PO21 . . . . 201 C4
Moor Farm GU29 . . . . 95 E7
Moorfield GU27 . . . . 26 F5
Moorfoot Rd RH15 . . . . . . 185 F8
Moorhead Rd RH12 . . . . . 37 B5
Moorhen Way PO22 . . . . . 201 B6
Moorhouse La GU29 . . . . . 71 D6
Moorings The
East Grinstead RH19 . . . . . . 9 A3
Lancing BN15 . . . . 187 F8
5 Littlehampton BN17 . . 205 A6
Shoreham-by-S BN43 . . . . 189 C6
Moorland Rd RH10 . . . . . . 19 C3
Moor Park Cres RH11 . . . . 17 D5
Moor Pl RH6 . . . . 2 B4
Moor Pl RH11 . . . . 9 D2
Moor Rd GU27 . . . . 26 C5
Morants Ct PO19 . . . . 177 C8
Mora Soomaree 11
BN11 . . . . 186 B2
Moraunt Dr PO22 . . . . . . 202 E6
Morecambe Cl RH11 . . . . . 17 F4
Morecambe Rd BN1 . . . . . 170 A6
Moreton Rd PO18 . . . . . . 175 B5
Morgan Ho 1 RH10 . . . . . 19 B6
Morland Ave BN14 . . . . . 186 E7
Morley Lo BN2 . . . . 213 C4
Morleys RH20 . . . . 123 A4
Morley St BN2 . . . . 213 C4
Mornington Cres
Bognor Regis PO22 . . . . . . 202 A5
Hove BN3 . . . . 190 D7
Mornington Mans 5
BN3 . . . . 190 D7
Morrell Ave RH12 . . . . 36 F6
Morris Dr RH14 . . . . 79 C7
Morrison Ct 5 RH11 . . . . . 18 B1
Morris Way RH20 . . . . 121 C7
Morth Gdns 3 RH12 . . . . . 36 C1
Mortimer Ho BN14 . . . . . 186 E6
Mortimer Mews BN3 . . . . 191 A8
Mortimer Rd BN3 . . . . 190 F8
Morton Cl RH11 . . . . 39 B8
Morton Ct BN41 . . . . 190 B8
Morton Rd RH19 . . . . 22 E7
Mosdell Rd PO10 . . . . 174 A8
Mosford Cl RH6 . . . . 1 F1
Moss Cl GU33 . . . . 45 C4
Mosse Gdns PO19 . . . . . . 176 B7
MOULSECOOMB 170 E2
Moulsecoomb Prim Sch
BN2 . . . . 170 E3
Moulsecoomb Sta
BN2 . . . . 170 D2
Moulsecoomb Way
BN2 . . . . 170 F4
Mountain Ash Ct 1
RH12 . . . . 36 F4
Mountbatten Cl RH11 . . . . 18 C2
Mountbatten Ct
Bognor Regis PO21 . . . . . . 201 D2
Hove BN3 . . . . 190 E8
7 Littlehampton BN17 . . 205 A6
Mount Cl RH10 . . . . 19 D7
Mount Ct PO20 . . . . 212 E7
Mount Dr BN2 . . . . 194 D2
Mountfields BN1 . . . . 170 C2
Mount La
Chichester PO19 . . . . 176 F6
Turners Hill RH10 . . . . 21 A4
Mount Noddy
Ansty RH17 . . . . 86 C3
Crawley RH10 . . . . 20 C2
Mount Pk BN44 . . . . 145 D1
Mount Pleasant
Arundel BN18 . . . . 160 A3
Brighton BN2 . . . . 213 C4
Henfield BN5 . . . . 125 E4
Mount The
Rusper RH1, RH12 . . . . 4 B1
Rusper RH17 . . . . 17 B8
Mountview Rd BN15 . . . . 165 C1
Mount Way BN15 . . . . . . 165 E1
Mountwood Rd
Breach PO10 . . . . 151 F1
Selsey PO20 . . . . 212 F8
Mount Zion Pl BN1 . . . . . 213 A3
Mouse La BN44 . . . . 144 E6
Mouthey's La PO18 . . . . . 153 E2
Mowbray Dr RH11 . . . . . . 17 F4
Mowden Sch BN3 . . . . . . 169 D1
Moyne Cl BN3 . . . . 168 E1
Moyne Rd RH11 . . . . 18 C2
M'tongue Ave PO18 . . . . 175 D7
Mudberry La PO18 . . . . . 175 A8

Muggeridge's Hill RH12,
RH5 . . . . 15 E8
Muir Cl BN14 . . . . 186 D5
Muirfield Cl
Crawley RH11 . . . . 17 D5
Worthing BN13 . . . . 185 E7
Muirfield Ct 16 RH16 . . . . 87 E4
Muirfield Rd BN13 . . . . . . 185 E7
Mulberry Cl
Brighton BN1 . . . . 169 F3
Ferring BN12 . . . . 206 E6
Horsham RH12 . . . . 36 C5
Lancing BN15 . . . . 187 E6
Shoreham-by-S BN43 . . . . 167 D1
Worthing BN12 . . . . 185 C4
Mulberry Ct
Bognor Regis PO21 . . . . . . 211 A7
Petworth GU28 . . . . 97 E7
Selsey PO20 . . . . 212 D7
Worthing BN12 . . . . 185 C3
Mulberry Gdns BN12 . . . . 185 C3
Mulberry Hollow
BN16 . . . . 205 D8
Mulberry La
Ditchling BN6 . . . . 129 D3
Worthing BN12 . . . . 185 C3
Mulberry Rd RH11 . . . . 5 B1
Mullein Wlk RH11 . . . . . . 18 A2
Mumford Pl PO19 . . . . . . 177 B4
Munmere Way 3
BN16 . . . . 205 E6
Munnion Rd RH17 . . . . 64 B7
Munns Dr RH15 . . . . 109 B4
Muntham Dr RH13 . . . . . . 56 F3
Muntham House Sch
RH13 . . . . 56 E4
Muntham House School
Flats 56 E4
Muriel Ho BN3 . . . . 190 E8
Murina Ave PO21 . . . . . . 201 C5
Murray Ct
Crawley RH11 . . . . 18 A1
Horsham RH13 . . . . 37 B4
Murray Rd PO20 . . . . 212 D6
Museum Hill GU27 . . . . . . 27 D6
Mushroom Field BN7 . . . . 172 E5
Mustang Cl BN18 . . . . 181 B2
Muster Ct RH16 . . . . 87 D4
Muster Gn N RH16 . . . . . . 87 D4
Muster Gn S RH16 . . . . . . 87 D4
Mutton Hill RH7 . . . . 10 B7
Mutton's La RH20 . . . . . . 122 D3
Myrtle Cres BN15 . . . . . . 187 D5
Myrtle Gr
Clapham BN13 . . . . 162 E5
East Preston BN16 . . . . . . 205 F5
Myrtle La RH14 . . . . 79 D7
Myrtle Rd BN15 . . . . 187 D5
Mytchett Ho 1 PO19 . . . 155 A2
Mytten Bank RH17 . . . . . . 86 F6
Mytten Cl RH17 . . . . 86 F6

N

Nab Tower La PO20 . . . . 212 B8
Nab Wlk PO20 . . . . 207 F6
Nagels Cl PO20 . . . . 208 A6
Naiad Gdns PO22 . . . . . . 202 D5
Naldrett Cl RH12 . . . . 36 F4
Naldretts La RH12 . . . . . . 33 D5
Namrik Mews BN3 . . . . . . 191 A6
Nan Kemp's Grave
BN7 . . . . 172 E6
Nansen Cotts PO20 . . . . . 177 A1
Nanson Rd BN1 . . . . 170 D6
Napier Ho 3 BN2 . . . . . . 192 C7
Napier Way RH10 . . . . 6 A1
Nappers Wood GU27 . . . . 49 A6
Nash La RH17 . . . . 89 B4
Nash Rd RH10 . . . . 18 E3
Nash Way BN18 . . . . 158 D1
Natal Rd BN2 . . . . 170 D1
Natts La RH14 . . . . 79 D6
Naunton Rd PO19 . . . . . . 155 A2
Nautilus BN11 . . . . 186 D1
Navarino Rd BN11 . . . . . . 187 A2
Neale Cl RH19 . . . . 9 B3
Needlemakers PO19 . . . . 177 B6
Needles Cl RH12 . . . . 36 B1
Need's Hill RH13 . . . . 104 F6
Nell Ball RH14 . . . . 30 E2
Nelson Cl
Crawley RH10 . . . . 19 C5
Hermitage PO10 . . . . 173 C8
Lancing BN15 . . . . 187 D8
Tangmere PO20 . . . . 156 D2
Nelson Ct
Chichester PO19 . . . . 177 D7
Shoreham-by-S BN43 . . . . 188 D5
Nelson Dr GU31 . . . . 68 C5
Nelson Pl 17 BN2 . . . . . . 213 C3
Nelson Rd
Bognor Regis PO21 . . . . . . 201 A3
Horsham RH12 . . . . 36 C3
Worthing BN12 . . . . 185 D5
Nelson Row
Brighton BN2 . . . . 213 C2
Ford BN18 . . . . 181 E3
Nep Cl BN5 . . . . 125 E4
Nepcote BN14 . . . . 163 F5
Nepcote La BN14 . . . . . . 163 E6
Nepcote Par BN14 . . . . . . 163 E6
Nepfield Cl BN14 . . . . 163 F5
NEP TOWN 125 E4
Nep Town Rd BN5 . . . . . . 125 E4
Neptune Cl RH11 . . . . 17 E4

Neptune Ct
Bognor Regis PO22 . . . . . . 202 D4
Brighton BN2 . . . . 192 F3
Horsham RH12 . . . . 36 B4
Neptune Way BN17 . . . . . 205 A4
Nesbit Ct RH11 . . . . 17 E3
Nesbitt Rd BN2 . . . . 170 D1
Nestor Ct BN1 . . . . 191 E8
Netherfield Gn BN2 . . . . . 193 F8
Netherton Cl
Selsey PO20 . . . . 212 E7
Southwater RH13 . . . . 57 F4
Netherwood RH11 . . . . . . 18 B4
Netley Cl RH11 . . . . 39 C8
Netley Ct BN17 . . . . 204 D5
Nettleton Ave PO20 . . . . 156 C2
Nettleton Ct BN1 . . . . 170 B1
Nevile Cl RH11 . . . . 18 A3
Nevill Ave BN3 . . . . 168 F1
Nevill Cl BN3 . . . . 169 A2
Nevill Cotts BN6 . . . . 129 D2
Nevill Ct BN3 . . . . 169 A1
Neville Gdns PO10 . . . . . 151 A3
Neville Rd
Bognor Regis PO22 . . . . . . 201 D4
Chichester PO19 . . . . 176 D7
Nevill Gdns BN3 . . . . 169 A2
Nevill Pl BN3 . . . . 169 A2
Nevill Rd
Hove BN3 . . . . 169 A2
Rottingdean BN2 . . . . 193 F1
Nevill Way BN3 . . . . 169 A2
Newark Pl BN2 . . . . 213 C3
Newark Rd RH10 . . . . 18 F8
New Barn RH14 . . . . 53 A2
New Barn Cl
Portslade-by-S BN41 . . . . 168 B2
Shoreham-by-S BN43 . . . . 167 B1
New Barn Hill PO18 . . . . . 156 B7
Newbarn La
Bognor Regis PO21 . . . . . . 200 F6
Henfield BN5 . . . . 125 F2
Walderton PO18 . . . . 152 B8
New Barn La
Bognor Regis, Felpham
PO22 . . . . 202 B6
West Chiltington Common
RH20 . . . . 121 B8
New Barn Rd
Amberley BN18 . . . . 140 D5
Rottingdean BN2 . . . . 193 F3
Shoreham-by-S BN43 . . . . 167 B1
Newbridge Cl RH12 . . . . . 35 C3
Newbridge Rd E RH14 . . . 79 B8
New Brighton Rd
PO10 . . . . 151 B2
New Broadway BN14 . . . . 186 A3
Newbury La RH17 . . . . 86 E5
Newbury Rd RH10 . . . . 19 D6
New Church Rd BN3 . . . . . 190 E7
New Cotts
Angmering BN16 . . . . 183 E5
Conford GU30 . . . . 24 E8
Partridge Green RH13 . . . . 105 A3
Scaynes Hill RH17 . . . . 88 F1
Turners Hill RH10 . . . . 21 A4
Washington RH20 . . . . 143 C6
New Courtwick La
BN17 . . . . 204 C8
Newcroft Cotts RH17 . . . . 42 A2
New Cut BN18 . . . . 160 B3
Newdigate Rd RH12 . . . . . 16 C8
New Dorset St BN1 . . . . . 213 A3
Newells Cl BN2 . . . . 171 E1
Newells La
Broadbridge PO18 . . . . . . 175 A7
Monk's Gate RH13 . . . . 59 D2
West Ashling PO18 . . . . . . 152 F1
NEW ENGLAND 40 B2
New England Ho BN1 . . . . 213 B4
New England Rd
Brighton BN1 . . . . 213 A4
Haywards Heath RH16 . . . 87 F4
New England Rise
BN41 . . . . 168 A4
New England St BN1 . . . . 213 B4
New Farthingdale RH7 . . . 10 B8
Newfield Rd
Liss GU33 . . . . 45 C6
Selsey PO20 . . . . 212 G8
New Gdns BN15 . . . . 186 F7
Newhall Cl PO21 . . . . 200 F3
New Hall La RH5 . . . . 146 E2
Newham Cl BN44 . . . . 145 C3
Newham La BN44 . . . . . . 145 C2
Newhaven St BN2 . . . . . . 213 C3
Newhouse Bsns Ctr
RH12 . . . . 37 C7
Newhouse La
East Dean PO18 . . . . 136 D8
Heath Common RH20 . . . . 122 C3
New House La RH1 . . . . 2 E8
Newick House Sch
RH15 . . . . 109 C1
Newick Rd BN1 . . . . 170 E4
New La GU31 . . . . 91 D2
Newland Rd
Upper Beeding BN44 . . . . 146 B2
Worthing BN11 . . . . 186 D3
Newlands RH17 . . . . 40 F1
Newlands Cl
Horley RH6 . . . . 1 F5
Keymer BN6 . . . . 129 B3
Newlands Cres RH19 . . . . 9 D2
Newlands La PO19 . . . . . . 176 D8
Newlands Pk RH10 . . . . . . 7 A3
Newlands Rd BN18 . . . . . . 23 D7

Newlands Rd
Crawley RH11 . . . . 18 C5
Horsham RH12 . . . . 36 C4
Rottingdean BN2 . . . . 194 A1
Newland St BN11 . . . . 186 D3
New Larchwood BN1 . . . . 170 D6
Newling Way BN1 . . . . . . 163 E6
Newman Cl RH10 . . . . 19 C4
Newman's Gdns BN15 . . . 187 D3
Newmarket Rd
Brighton BN2 . . . . 192 C8
Crawley RH10 . . . . 19 A4
Newmarket Terr 12
BN2 . . . . 192 C8
New Moorhead Dr
RH12 . . . . 37 C6
New Par
East Wittering PO20 . . . . . 207 E2
Selsey PO20 . . . . 212 D7
Worthing BN11 . . . . 186 F2
New Park Ct PO19 . . . . . . 177 B6
New Park Rd PO19 . . . . . . 177 A7
New Place Rd BN20 . . . . . 100 C3
Newport 4 BN43 . . . . 189 B6
Newport Dr PO19 . . . . . . 176 B7
Newport Mews BN11 . . . . 187 B3
Newport Rd RH15 . . . . . . 108 F3
Newport St BN2 . . . . 213 C4
Newpound RH14 . . . . 54 E3
NEWPOUND COMMON
. . . . 54 E2
Newpound La RH14 . . . . . 54 D1
New Rd
Angmering BN16 . . . . 205 E7
Billingshurst RH14 . . . . 56 B2
Brighton BN1 . . . . 213 B2
East Dean PO18 . . . . 136 D8
Haslemere GU27 . . . . 26 F5
Keymer BN6 . . . . 129 B2
Littlehampton BN17 . . . . . 204 D4
Midhurst GU29 . . . . 94 E6
Shoreham-by-S BN43 . . . . 188 F7
South Ambersham GU29 . . 95 E4
Southbourne PO10 . . . . . . 174 A8
Southwater RH13 . . . . 57 F4
Upper Beeding BN44 . . . . 146 B1
Upperton GU28 . . . . 75 A2
Westbourne PO10 . . . . . . 151 D3
Westerton PO18 . . . . 155 D4
Worthing BN13 . . . . 185 C8
New Row BN44 . . . . 145 C3
New Salts Farm Rd
BN43 . . . . 188 C6
New St
Crawley RH10 . . . . 19 A7
Horsham RH12 . . . . 36 D2
Petworth GU28 . . . . 97 F8
2 Worthing BN11 . . . . . . 186 D1
Newstead BN1 . . . . 213 A4
Newstead Hall RH6 . . . . . . 2 D1
New Steine BN2 . . . . 213 C1
New Steine Mews
BN2 . . . . 213 C2
New Terr BN18 . . . . 183 C8
Newtimber Ave BN12 . . . 185 B4
Newtimber Dr BN41 . . . . 168 A1
Newtimber Gdns
BN43 . . . . 166 F1
Newton Ave RH19 . . . . . . 22 F6
Newton Cl RH16 . . . . 88 B7
Newton Ct RH16 . . . . 87 E5
Newton Rd
Crawley RH10 . . . . 5 F2
Lindfield RH16 . . . . 88 C7
NEWTOWN 25 B3
NEW TOWN 58 E8
New Town
14 Chichester PO19 . . . . 177 A6
Copthorne RH10 . . . . 7 B3
Newtown Ave PO21 . . . . . 201 A4
New Town Cotts
RH20 . . . . 121 B1
Newtown Ct 1 RH13 . . . . 36 E1
Newtown Rd
Hove BN3 . . . . 191 B8
Liphook GU30 . . . . 25 C3
New Town Rd RH20 . . . . . 121 B1
New Way La BN6 . . . . 128 B2
Nicholsfield RH14 . . . . 31 F4
Nicolson Cl PO20 . . . . . . 156 C2
Nicolson Dr BN43 . . . . . . 189 A8
Nightingale Cl
Crawley RH11 . . . . 18 C8
East Grinstead RH19 . . . . . 22 D7
Fernhurst GU27 . . . . 49 A6
Haywards Heath RH16 . . . 87 F4
Red Hill PO9 . . . . 130 C1
Storrington RH20 . . . . 121 C1
Nightingale Ct
Middleton-on-S PO22 . . . . 202 F5
Westbourne PO10 . . . . . . 151 D4
Nightingale Ind Est
RH12 . . . . 36 D3
Nightingale La
Burgess Hill RH15 . . . . . . 128 F8
Hambrook PO18 . . . . 152 D3
Storrington RH20 . . . . 121 E1
Turners Hill RH10 . . . . 21 C5
Nightingale Pk RH20 . . . . 121 E1
Nightingale Pl GU27 . . . . . 27 C6
Nightingale Rd
Horsham RH12 . . . . 36 D3
Petersfield GU31 . . . . 68 A2
Nightingales
Findon BN14 . . . . 163 E7
West Chiltington Common
RH20 . . . . 121 D7
Nightingales Cl RH13 . . . . 36 F2

Nightingale Wlk RH14.... 79 E8
Nile St
  Brighton BN1...........213 B2
  Emsworth PO10.........173 B8
Nimbus Cl BN17 ....205 A6
Nimrod Ct RH10 .... 6 D1
Nimrod Ho 🖪 RH20 ....121 E1
Nine Acres GU29...... 94 D8
Nineveh Shipyard
  BN18...............160 B3
Ninfield Ct RH11 ...... 17 F2
Ninfield Pl
  Brighton BN2...........192 E6
  Brighton BN2...........192 E7
Nini-hi Cvn Site
  BN17...............181 D1
Niven Cl RH10 .... 19 D5
Nizells Ave BN3........191 E7
Noahs Ark La RH16 .... 88 C7
Noble Ct BN3..........190 E7
Noel Gn RH15 ....109 B4
Noel Rise RH15 ....109 B4
Nolan Rd BN2 ....193 E7
Nonnington La GU28.... 96 B1
Nook Cvn Pk The
  PO20...............212 C8
Nookery The BN16......206 A5
Norbury Cl BN15.......187 F8
Norbury Dr BN15.......187 F8
Nordseter Lo 🖪 BN16...205 B4
Nore Down Way
  PO18...............132 A8
Noreuil Rd GU32....... 67 F3
Nore Wood La BN18....158 C7
Norfolk Bldgs 🖪 BN1 ...191 E5
Norfolk Cl
  🈲 Bognor Regis
  PO21...............201 C2
  Crawley RH11 .... 17 E2
  Horley RH6 .... 2 A2
Norfolk Cotts
  Bury RH20 ....140 A7
  🖪 Steyning BN44 .....145 D3
Norfolk Ct
  🔟 Bognor Regis
  PO21...............201 C2
  🖪 Brighton BN1 ....191 E5
  🖪 Rustington BN16 ....205 B4
  🈂 Worthing BN11......186 C3
Norfolk Gdns BN17.....204 F4
Norfolk Ho PO22........201 F4
Norfolk Mews
  🖪 Brighton BN1 ....191 E5
  🖪 Littlehampton BN17...204 F4
Norfolk Pl
  🖪 Brighton BN1 ....191 E5
  🖪 Littlehampton BN17...204 F4
Norfolk Rd
  Brighton BN1...........191 E6
  Horsham RH12........ 36 D2
  Littlehampton BN17....204 F4
Norfolk Sq
  Bognor Regis PO21......201 C2
  Brighton BN1...........191 E5
Norfolk St
  Bognor Regis PO21.....201 C2
  Brighton BN1...........191 E5
  Worthing BN11........186 C3
Norfolk Terr
  Brighton BN1...........191 E6
  🈂 Horsham RH12...... 36 D2
Norfolk Way PO22 ......203 B5
Norman Cl
  Billingshurst RH14..... 55 E1
  Littlehampton BN17.....204 F5
Norman Cres 🖪 BN43 ...166 F1
Normandy RH12 .... 36 C1
Normandy Cl
  Crawley RH10 .... 19 C4
  🈂 East Grinstead RH19 ... 22 F8
Normandy Ct
  Chichester PO19 ......177 B7
  🈂 Worthing BN11......186 B1
Normandy Dr BN16 .....206 A4
Normandy Gdns 🈳
  RH12...............36 C1
Normandy Ho 🖪 BN3 ...191 C6
Normandy La RH10 .....206 A4
Normandy Rd BN14.....186 C4
Normanhurst
  🔟 Brighton BN2.......213 C3
  🈳 Shoreham-by-S
  BN43...............188 F7
Normanhurst Cl
  Crawley RH10 .... 18 F6
  Rustington BN16 ......205 C4
Norman Rd
  Burgess Hill RH15.......109 A3
  Hove BN3.............190 E6
Normanscourt 🖪
  BN43...............166 F1
Norman's Dr PO22 ......202 B6
Normanton Ave PO21 ...201 B3
Normanton St 🖪 BN2 ...192 C7
Norman Way
  Middleton-on-S PO22.....202 F5
  Steyning BN44.........145 D4
North Ash 🖪 RH12..... 36 C4
North Ave
  Middleton-on-S PO22.....202 F5
  Worthing BN14........185 E2
North Ave E PO22......203 A5
North Ave S PO22......203 A5
North Bank BN6........128 E4
North Bay PO10........173 C3

NORTH BERSTED 201 A7
North Bersted St
  PO22...............201 A7
Northbourne Cl BN43 ...188 F8
Northbrook Bsns Pk
  BN14...............186 E6
Northbrook Cl BN14 ....186 E6
Northbrook Coll
  Horsham RH14........ 36 C4
  Worthing, Goring-by-Sea
  BN12...............185 B5
  Worthing, West Worthing
  BN11...............186 D2
Northbrook Coll
  (Broadwater Campus)
  BN14...............186 D5
Northbrook Farm Cvn Pk
  BN13...............185 B7
Northbrook Rd BN14....186 E6
Northbrook Trad Est
  BN14...............186 E6
Northchapel Com Prim
  Sch GU28............ 51 A7
North Cl
  Chichester PO19 ......177 A7
  Crawley RH10 .... 18 F7
  Portslade-by-S BN41...168 A2
Northcliffe Rd PO22.....201 E4
Northcommon Farm Ctr★
  PO20...............209 E2
Northcote Gdns PO10 ...174 A8
Northcote Rd PO21 .....201 A4
Northcourt BN16 ....205 E6
Northcourt Mews
  BN14...............186 C4
Northcourt Rd BN14.....186 C4
Northcroft BN5 ....125 E5
North Ct BN6..........128 E4
Northdown Cl RH12..... 36 F4
Northdown Terr RH19.... 9 D3
North Dr
  Angmering BN16 ......205 F8
  Brighton BN2..........192 C6
  Dormansland RH19 ..... 10 B6
Northease Cl BN3......168 D2
Northease Dr BN3 .....168 E3
Northease Gdns BN3....168 E3
North End BN6.........129 D4
Northend Cl GU28..... 75 F1
North End Cotts BN14...163 E8
Northend La BN6.......107 F3
North End Rd BN18.....180 F4
Northerlea BN14.......168 A1
Northern Breach RH17... 86 F6
Northern Cres PO20....207 F7
North Farm Cotts
  Findon RH20 ....143 D2
  Portslade-by-S BN41...168 A2
North Farm Ct 🖪
  BN15...............187 E6
North Farm Rd BN15....187 F6
Northfield PO20 ....212 F7
Northfield Rd BN13 ....186 A6
Northfield Rise
  Hove BN3.............168 D4
  Rottingdean BN2......194 A2
Northfields La PO20....157 D1
Northfield Way BN1.....170 A4
NORTHGATE 18 F7
Northgate PO19 ....177 A7
Northgate Ave RH10 .... 18 F7
Northgate Cl
  Lancing BN15.........187 C6
  Rottingdean BN2......193 F2
Northgate Pl RH10 ..... 18 E7
Northgate Prim Sch
  RH10...............18 E7
Northgate Rd
  Crawley, Gatwick Airport
  RH6...............5 F8
  Crawley RH10 .... 18 D6
North Gdns BN1........213 A3
North Ham Rd BN17....204 D6
NORTH HEATH 100 F7
North Heath Cl RH12.... 36 D5
North Heath Com Prim
  Sch RH12............ 36 D5
North Heath La RH12.... 36 E6
North Heath Lane Ind Est
  RH12...............36 D6
North Ho PO19 ....177 A7
North Holmes Cl RH12 ... 37 B5
North La
  Buriton GU31......... 90 A5
  Charlton PO18........136 A8
  East Preston BN16 .....206 B6
  Littlehampton BN16.....205 B6
  Portslade-by-S BN41...168 A3
  South Harting GU31.... 91 D4
  West Hoathly RH19 .... 42 E6
  Wiston BN44.........123 C2
North Lancing Fst & Mid
  Sch BN15............187 E8
Northlands Ave RH16 .... 88 B4
Northlands Bsns Pk
  RH12...............14 C4
Northlands Cotts RH12 ... 14 D4
Northlands Ho RH19 ....154 B1
Northlands La RH20....121 E4
Northlands Rd
  Horsham RH12........ 36 E7
  Warnham RH12....... 14 D2
Northlands Wood Com
  Prim Sch RH16....... 88 B4
North Lo PO21.........200 A2
North Lodge Ind Pk
  GU30...............25 D1

North Lodge Mans 🖪
  BN11...............186 D2
NORTH MARDEN 112 B5
Northmead GU28 ...... 75 F1
North Mead
  Crawley RH10 .... 18 E8
  Henfield BN5 ....125 E6
Northmoor Ct 🈲
  PO21...............201 B2
NORTH MOULSECOOMB
  ....170 E4
North Mundham Prim Sch
  PO20...............177 D1
Northolmes Jun Sch
  RH12...............37 A4
North Pallant PO19 .....177 A6
North Par RH12........ 36 C3
North Pk BN17.........204 C5
North Pl
  Brighton BN1..........213 B2
  🈳 Littlehampton BN17...204 E4
North Point 🈲 BN43 ...189 A6
North Pound BN18.....158 D1
North Rd
  Brighton BN1..........213 B3
  Brighton, Preston BN1 ...169 E1
  Broadbridge PO18.....175 C7
  Crawley RH10 .... 18 F7
  Haywards Heath RH16 ... 88 A4
  Lancing BN15.........187 E6
  Petersfield GU32...... 68 B4
  Portslade-by-S BN41...168 A2
  Selsey PO20..........212 E5
North St Quadrant
  BN1...............213 A2
Northside PO18........154 E7
North-South Rd BN1 ...171 B7
North St
  Brighton BN1..........213 B2
  Chichester PO19 ......177 A7
  Emsworth PO10.......151 B1
  Horsham RH12, RH13 ... 36 D3
  Midhurst GU29 .... 94 F8
  Petworth GU28 .... 75 F1
  Shoreham-by-S BN43...188 C7
  Storrington RH20......121 D1
  Turners Hill RH10 ..... 21 A4
  Westbourne PO10......151 D4
  Worthing BN11........186 D3
NORTH STOKE 140 C2
North Stroud La GU32... 67 A3
North Terminal App
  RH6...............5 F8
North View BN5 ....126 E5
Northview Terr BN14....163 E6
North Walls PO19 ......176 F6
Northway
  Burgess Hill RH15......109 C4
  Crawley RH6 .... 5 F8
North Way
  Bognor Regis PO22.....201 F4
  Petworth GU28 .... 97 E7
Northway Rd BN17......204 D8
Northwood Ave BN2 ....194 E1
Northwood Ct BN14.....186 C6
Northwood Pk RH10 .... 6 A2
Northwyke Cl PO22......202 C5
Northwyke Rd PO22.....202 C5
Norton Cl BN3.........191 B6
Norton Dr BN2.........171 E1
Norton La PO20........157 B1
Norton Rd
  Hove BN3.............191 B6
  Lancing BN15.........187 D5
Norway La BN17 ....204 F7
Norway St BN41.......190 C7
Norwich Cl PO20.......171 A2
Norwich Cres BN2......170 F2
Norwich Dr BN2.......170 F2
Norwich House Rd
  BN1...............171 B7
Norwich Rd
  Chichester PO19 ......154 F1
  Crawley RH10 .... 19 B5
Norwood BN1..........170 A4
Norwoodhill Rd RH6 ..... 4 E8
Norwood La GU28.......116 C6
Norwood La GU28.......116 E5
Nowhurst La RH12...... 35 A5
Nuffield Cl PO21 ....200 D1
Nuffield Hospl Brighton
  BN2...............193 C8
Nunnington Farm Cvn Pk
  PO20...............196 D2
Nurseries The
  Balcombe RH10........ 41 A1
  Bognor Regis PO21......200 C3
Nursery Cl
  Barnham PO22.........180 B6
  Haywards Heath RH16 ... 87 D5
  Hurstpierpoint BN6 .....127 F7
  Lancing BN15.........187 D7
  New Brighton PO10.....151 B3
  Portslade-by-S BN41...167 E4
  Shoreham-by-S BN43.....189 B8
  West Kingston BN16....206 A4
Nursery Cres PO22 .....180 C6
Nursery Field GU33 .... 45 A3
Nursery Gdns
  Chichester PO19 ......177 B5
  Littlehampton BN17.....204 D7
Nursery La
  Fishbourne PO19.......176 B7
  Hookwood RH6 .... 1 D2
  Worthing BN11........186 C1
Nurserylands RH11 ..... 18 A6

Nursery Rd BN16 ......206 A8
Nursery The RH15 .....109 C4
NURSTED 90 E7
Nutbourne Ct 🖪 RH12... 36 D5
Nutbourne Halt PO18 ...174 D8
Nutbourne La BN20 ....101 A4
Nutbourne Pk PO18 ....174 B7
Nutbourne Rd
  Nutbourne Common
  RH20...............101 A1
  South Hayling PO11....195 A1
  Worthing BN14........186 B4
Nutbourne Vineyards★
  RH20...............101 C2
Nutcombe La GU26,
  GU27...............26 E8
Nutcroft RH20 ....100 C3
Nutham La RH13....... 58 A1
Nuthatch Cl PO9.......130 D1
Nuthatch Way
  Horsham RH12........ 36 D7
  Turners Hill RH10 ..... 21 C5
Nuthurst Cl
  Brighton BN2..........192 F6
  Crawley RH11 .... 18 A7
Nuthurst Pl BN2........192 F5
Nuthurst Rd
  Maplehurst RH13...... 82 F6
  Monk's Gate RH13...... 59 B3
Nuthurst St RH13...... 59 A2
Nutley Ave
  Saltdean BN2..........194 C1
  Worthing BN12........185 C2
Nutley Cl
  Hove BN3.............168 F3
  Worthing BN12........185 C2
Nutley Cres BN12 ......185 C2
Nutley Dr BN12........185 C2
Nye La
  Ditchling BN6.........129 D1
  Westmeston BN6......150 D8
Nye Rd RH15 ....109 C3
Nyes Cl BN5 ....125 F5
Nye's Hill RH17 .... 84 E1
Nyes La RH13......... 57 F3
NYETIMBER 200 A1
Nyetimber Cl PO21......200 B2
Nyetimber Copse
  RH20...............121 C6
Nyetimber Cres PO21 ...200 B2
Nyetimber Hill BN2 ....170 F2
Nyetimber La
  Bognor Regis PO21.....200 B2
  West Chiltington Common
  RH20...............121 C7
Nyetimber Mill PO21 ...200 A2
Nyetimbers The PO21 ...200 A2
Nyewood CE Inf Sch
  PO21...............201 A4
Nyewood CE Jun Sch
  PO21...............201 A3
Nyewood Gdns 🈳
  PO21...............201 B3
Nyewood La PO21.......201 B3
Nyewood Pl PO21.......201 B2
Nymans Cl RH12....... 37 A7
Nymans Cotts
  Handcross RH17 .... 61 C7
  Henfield BN5 ....105 E1
Nymans Ct RH10 ...... 19 B3
NYTON 179 D8
Nyton Rd PO20 ....179 C8

O

Oakapple Cl RH11......18 B1
Oak Apple Cl RH13.....83 E1
Oakapple Rd BN42.....167 E1
Oak Ave
  Chichester PO19 ......176 E7
  Heath Common RH20 ...122 B3
Oak Bank RH16 .... 87 F7
Oak Cl
  Bognor Regis PO22.....201 C6
  Brighton BN1..........169 E3
  Chichester PO19 ......176 E7
  Copthorne RH10 ...... 7 A3
  Southwater RH13...... 81 F7
  Storrington RH20......121 F2
  Worthing BN13........163 E1
Oak Cotts GU27....... 26 E6
Oak Croft RH19 .... 23 A8
Oakcroft Gdns BN17....204 F7
Oak Ct RH10.......... 5 D2
Oakdale Rd RH16 ..... 87 F3
Oak Dell RH16 .... 19 C7
Oakdene RH16........ 87 D5
Oakdene Ave BN41.....167 E3
Oakdene Cl BN41......167 E3
Oakdene Cres BN41....167 E3
Oakdene Gdns BN41....167 E3
Oakdene Rise BN41.....167 E4
Oakdene Way BN41.....167 E4
Oak Dr GU31.......... 68 A1
Oak End
  Arundel BN18 ....159 E2
  West Chiltington Common
  RH20...............121 D8
Oakendene BN2 ....170 D4
Oakendene Ind Est
  RH13...............84 B1
Oakenfield RH15.......109 A5
Oak Farm Pl RH19 ..... 8 E7
Oakfield
  Lodsworth GU28 ...... 74 B3
  Plaistow RH14........ 30 D1
Oakfield Ave PO20......207 F7

Oakfield Cl RH16...... 88 A7
Oakfield Cotts RH13.... 83 E1
Oakfield Mid Sch
  BN17...............187 E7
Oakfield Rd
  Cowfold RH13........ 83 F1
  East Wittering PO20 ...207 F7
Oakfields
  Crawley RH10 .... 19 D7
  Wallis Wood RH5........ 13 D8
Oakfield Way RH19 ..... 9 F3
Oak Gr
  Bognor Regis PO22.....201 C6
  Loxwood RH14........ 32 A4
Oak Grove Coll BN13...185 E6
Oak Hall Pk RH15......109 B1
Oakhaven RH10........ 18 D4
OAKHILL 36 E1
Oakhill Chase RH10 .... 19 D7
Oakhill Rd RH13 ...... 36 E2
Oakhurst
  Haywards Heath RH16 ... 87 D8
  Henfield BN5 ....125 F6
  Midhurst GU29 .... 94 D7
  Sayers Common BN6.....107 D2
Oakhurst Bsns Pk
  RH13...............58 A4
Oakhurst Gdns
  East Grinstead RH19 .... 9 C2
  Rustington BN16 ......205 E6
Oakhurst La
  Haywards Heath RH16 ... 87 D8
  Loxwood RH14........ 31 A5
Oakhurst Mews RH12 ... 37 A4
Oak La RH12.......... 35 E3
Oakland Ct
  Bognor Regis, Felpham
  PO22...............202 A4
  Bognor Regis, Nyetimber
  PO21...............200 A1
  🈲 Littlehampton BN17...204 E4
  🈳 Shoreham-by-S
  BN43...............188 F7
  Worthing, Goring-by-Sea
  BN12...............185 A3
  🈳 Worthing, West Worthing
  BN11...............186 C2
Oaklands
  Ardingly RH17 .... 64 B8
  Billingshurst RH14..... 79 D7
  Haslemere GU27...... 27 C7
  Horley RH6 .... 2 C3
  Horsham, Oakhill RH13 ... 36 E2
  Horsham RH12........ 36 B5
  🈲 Lancing BN15.......187 F5
Oaklands Ave BN2 .....194 D1
Oaklands Bsns Ctr
  BN11...............185 F4
Oaklands Cl RH13...... 58 E8
Oaklands Ct PO19......177 A8
Oaklands La GU29 ..... 94 F5
Oaklands Rd
  Haywards Heath RH16 ... 87 D5
  Petersfield GU32...... 68 A4
Oaklands Way PO19....177 A7
Oakleigh Cl BN11 ......187 A4
Oakleigh Ct
  🈳 Bognor Regis
  PO21...............201 B2
  Worthing BN11........187 A4
Oakleigh Rd
  Horsham RH12........ 36 F4
  Worthing BN11........187 A4
Oakley Cl RH19 .... 23 B7
Oakley Cotts
  Ashurst Wood RH19 .... 23 C7
  Handcross RH17 .... 61 C8
Oakley Gdns BN16 .....206 A5
Oakley Ho BN2 ....213 C2
Oak Mdw PO20 ....197 E5
Oakmeadow Cl PO10...151 C3
Oakmead Rd RH15 .....108 F1
Oakmeeds Com Coll
  RH15...............109 A2
Oak Rd
  Crawley RH11 .... 18 C5
  Southwater RH13...... 57 F1
Oakroyd Cl RH15.......109 D5
Oaks Cl
  Fernhurst GU27....... 49 A6
  Horsham RH12........ 37 B6
  Westergate PO20......179 D6
Oakside Ct RH6........ 2 C4
Oakside La RH6........ 2 C4
Oaks Mews PO21.......200 E3
Oaks Prim Sch The
  RH10...............18 F3
Oaks The
  Bognor Regis PO21.....200 E3
  Burgess Hill RH15......108 D4
  East Grinstead RH19 ... 23 B8
  Haywards Heath RH16 ... 88 A4
  Haywards Heath RH16 ... 88 A4
  Rustington BN16 ......205 E5
  Small Dole BN5 ....146 E6
  Southwater RH13...... 57 F2
Oaktree Cl PO21 ....199 F2
Oak Tree Cl RH13 ..... 9 C3
Oaktree Cotts BN18....180 C8
Oak Tree Cotts
  Burgess Hill RH15......109 B3
  Danehill RH17........ 66 A4
Oak Tree Ct GU29......94 E6
Oak Tree Dr
  Liss GU33............ 45 C4

Oak Tree Dr continued
New Brighton PO10......151 B4
Oak Tree Farm PO18......152 D1
Oak Tree La
Haslemere GU27.........26 D6
Woodgate PO20.........179 D5
Oak Tree Way RH13......36 F4
Oakvale RH20.........121 C7
Oak View PO20........198 F7
Oakway RH13..........59 C6
Oak Way
Crawley RH10...........18 E8
Ifold RH14..............31 D2
Oakwood
Haywards Heath RH16....87 D4
Partridge Green RH13....105 A3
Oakwood Cl
Burgess Hill RH15.......109 B2
Midhurst GU29..........94 E7
Tangmere PO20.........156 D2
Oakwood Ct
3 Bognor Regis
PO21...............201 C4
Crawley RH11...........39 B8
Petworth GU28..........97 E7
Oakwood Dr BN16......206 A8
Oakwood Gdns PO21....201 C4
OAKWOODHILL 14 A7
Oakwood Ind Pk RH10....6 A2
Oakwood Pk RH18.......23 F2
Oakwood Rd
Burgess Hill RH15.......109 B2
Haywards Heath RH16....87 D4
Horley RH6..............2 B4
Oakwood Sch
East Ashling PO18.......153 F2
Horley RH6..............2 C3
Oates Wlk RH10.........18 F3
Oathall Ave RH16.......87 F6
Oathall Com Coll RH16...87 F6
Oathall Rd RH16........87 E5
Oatlands
Crawley RH11...........18 A5
Horley RH6..............2 C1
Oberon Way RH11.......17 E3
Observer Ct RH12.......36 C1
Ocean Bldg The BN1.....213 A3
Ocean Cl BN12.........206 E4
Ocean Dr BN12.........206 E4
Ocean Par BN12........206 E4
Ocean Reach BN2.......194 A1
Ockenden La RH17.......86 E6
Ockenden Way BN6......128 E3
Ockley Ct PO21.........201 C3
Ockley Hill BN6, RH15...129 B6
Ockley La
Burgess Hill RH15.......129 B7
Keymer BN6............129 B4
Ockley Rd PO21.........201 C3
Ockley Way BN6........129 A5
Octagon The BN2.......192 F3
OFFHAM 160 D6
Offington Ave BN14.....186 B6
Offington Cnr BN13,
BN14................186 A8
Offington Ct BN14......186 C6
Offington Dr BN14......186 A6
Offington Gdns BN14....186 A6
Offington La BN13,
BN14................186 A7
Ognells Flats GU29......94 F8
Okehurst La RH14.......55 D4
Okehurst Rd
Five Oaks RH14.........55 A6
Rudgwick RH14.........33 C1
Old Arundel Rd PO18....155 F2
Old Bakery Gdns
PO19...............177 B5
Old Bakery Mews
PO20...............212 E7
Old Barn Cl PO21.......200 A2
Old Barn Ct
East Wittering PO20......207 F6
Haywards Heath RH16....87 D2
Old Barns BN16.........183 F5
Old Barn The GU31......69 C4
Old Barn Way BN42.....190 A7
Old Blendworth PO8.....130 B8
Old Boat Cnr BN1.......170 D8
Old Boat Wlk BN1.......170 B7
Old Boundary La
RH20...............121 B8
Old Bridge Rd PO18.....175 C7
Old Brighton Rd N
RH11................39 C7
Old Brighton Rd S
Crawley RH11...........5 E5
Pease Pottage RH11.....39 B6
Old Broyle Rd PO19.....154 D2
OLD BUDDINGTON 72 E3
Old Buddington La
GU29................72 E3
Oldbury Cl RH12.........37 A7
Old Canal (park homes)
The PO18.............179 D3
Old Church Ho The
PO21...............201 A6
Old Coach Ho The
BN11................186 B3
Old Coastguard Cotts
PO20...............212 C7
Old Coastguards
PO22...............201 F3
Old College Ho BN2.....213 C4

Old Control Tower Rd
RH6.................5 D6
Old Convent The RH19....9 E2
Old Cottage Cl PO20....156 C1
Old Cotts BN14.........163 E7
Old Court Cl BN1.......169 F4
Old Courthouse The **3**
BN44................145 D3
Old Crawley Rd RH12.....37 C7
Old Dairy Workshops
PO10...............151 D3
Old Denne Gdns **6**
RH12................36 C1
Olde Place Ct BN2......193 F1
Olde Place Mews
BN2.................193 F1
OLDER HILL 48 B2
Older Way BN16........183 F6
Old Farm Cl
Bognor Regis PO21......200 D2
Bracklesham PO20......208 B5
Haywards Heath RH17....88 A2
Old Farm Ct BN43.......188 C6
Old Farm Dr PO20......179 D7
Old Farm La PO10......151 E3
Old Farm Rd
Brighton BN1...........169 F5
Selsey PO20............212 C8
Oldfield Cl RH6...........1 F1
Oldfield Cres BN42......189 E8
Oldfield Rd RH6..........1 F1
Old Forge Cl RH12.......16 F1
Old Fort Rd BN43.......189 B6
Old Glebe GU27..........49 B6
Old Granary The
PO18...............156 D4
Old Guildford Rd RH12...35 E4
Old Haslemere Rd
GU27................27 C5
Old Holbrook RH12......15 F1
Old Hollow RH10.........19 F7
Old Horsham Rd RH11....18 B4
Old Hospital The RH17....86 F8
Oldhouse La
Balls Green RH14,
RH13................80 B2
Broadford Bridge RH14,
RH20...............102 A7
Sidlesham PO20........209 C7
West Marden PO9,
PO18...............132 A6
Old House La RH13.......81 B6
Oldlands Ave
Balcombe RH17.........41 A1
Keymer BN6............129 A4
Oldlands Way PO22......201 E7
Old London Rd
Brighton BN1...........169 E6
Coldwaltham RH20......119 D6
Washington RH20.......143 E8
Old Manor Cl RH11......18 A8
Old Manor Ct RH11......18 A8
Old Manor House Gdns
PO22...............202 B5
Old Manor Rd BN16.....205 B6
Old Market Ave **13**
PO19...............177 A6
Old Market Cotts **17**
BN3.................191 D5
Old Market Sq BN44.....145 E3
Old Martyrs RH11.........5 D1
Oldmeadow Rd RH11....18 D6
Old Mead Rd BN17......182 C5
Old Mill Cl
Brighton BN1...........169 E5
Portslade-by-S BN41.....190 A7
Old Mill Dr RH20........121 D1
Old Mill La GU31........68 D5
Old Millmeads RH12.....36 C5
Old Mill Mews BN1......191 E8
Old Mill Pl
Haslemere GU27........26 F7
Pulborough RH20.......100 D1
Old Mill Sq RH20.......121 D1
Old Mill The
Arundel BN18...........160 B3
Bognor Regis PO22......201 F3
Chichester PO19........177 A7
Old Moat Cl PO22.......179 C1
Old Mus Ct GU27........27 D6
Old Orchards RH10......19 E6
Old Parish La BN2......193 C8
Old Park Cl RH17........87 A6
Old Park La
Bosham PO18..........175 D2
Fishbourne PO18........175 E5
Old Patcham Mews
BN1.................169 E6
Old Pl PO21............200 E3
Old Place La PO18......155 D1
Old Point PO22.........202 E4
Old Quarry The GU27....26 F4
Old Rd RH19.............9 F1
Old Rectory Cl PO10....151 D3
Old Rectory Dr PO20....179 E7
Old Rectory Flats
PO22...............202 A4
Old Rectory Gdns
Bognor Regis PO22......202 A4
Southwick BN42........189 D8
Old Rectory The
PO22...............202 A4
Old Rowfant Cotts
RH10................20 B8
Old Salts Farm Rd
BN15................188 A5
Old School Cl PO20......197 E4
Old School Ct RH16......88 B7

Old School Mews
PO22...............202 A5
Old School Pl
Burgess Hill RH15.......108 F2
Portslade-by-S BN3......168 D1
Woodgate PO20........179 D6
Old School Rd GU33......45 B4
Old School The
Cocking GU29..........114 D8
Fittleworth RH20.........99 A2
OLD SHOREHAM 188 E8
Old Shoreham Rd
Lancing BN15...........188 A8
Portslade-by-S BN3,
BN41...............190 C8
Shoreham-by-S BN43....188 E8
Southwick BN42........167 E1
Old Slipway The
BN18................160 B2
Old Stables The PO22....201 F4
Old Station Cl RH10......21 B7
Old Steine BN1.........213 B2
Old Stocks Oak GU33....45 A5
Old Surgery The **4**
RH19.................9 F2
Old Sussex Stud The
RH13................82 B1
Old Viaduct Ct **10**
BN2.................192 C8
Old Warehouse Mews **3**
BN17................204 F4
Old Wickham La RH16....87 E7
Old Wickhurst La
RH12................35 D2
Oldwick Mdws PO18....154 F5
Old Worthing Rd
BN16................206 B7
Old Yard Cl RH13.......105 A3
Olive Rd BN3...........190 D8
Oliver Ho **5** BN3.......191 B5
Oliver Rd RH12...........36 A1
Olivers Mdw PO20......179 D7
Oliver Whitby Rd
PO19...............176 E7
Olivia Ct PO21.........201 B3
Olivier Cl BN2.........192 C5
Olivier Ct PO21........201 A6
Olivier Rd RH10.........19 D5
Onslow Ct
2 Crawley RH10........6 A1
9 Worthing BN11.....187 B3
Onslow Cvn Pk BN12....206 E6
Onslow Dr BN12........206 E6
Onslow Rd BN3.........169 C2
Ontario Cl BN13........185 C7
Ontario Gdns BN13.....185 C7
Ontario Way GU30.......25 C3
Open Univ (South East)
The RH19..............9 E1
Ophir Rd BN11.........187 A3
Orange Row
Brighton BN1...........213 B2
Emsworth PO10........173 B8
Orchard Ave
Chichester PO19........176 F7
Hove BN3..............169 A1
Lancing BN15...........187 E7
Selsey PO20............212 E6
Worthing BN14.........186 B5
Orchard Bsns Ctr The
RH1..................2 A8
Orchard Bsns Pk
BN18................180 F4
Orchard Cl
East Harting GU31........92 A4
Elsted GU29.............92 D4
Ferring BN12............206 E7
Haslemere GU27.........26 F5
Haywards Heath RH16....87 D8
Horley RH6..............1 F4
Petworth GU28..........97 F7
Scaynes Hill RH17........88 F3
Shoreham-by-S BN43....188 E8
Small Dole BN5.........146 F6
Southwick BN42........189 F8
Worthing BN14.........186 B5
Orchard Cl The PO21....201 B3
Orchard Cnr RH16........88 B5
Orchard Cott RH17.......86 F6
Orchard Cotts
Charlwood RH6...........4 F7
Fishbourne PO18........176 A8
Woodgate PO20........179 D5
Orchard Cres BN18.....158 A3
Orchard Croft PO20.....177 D1
Orchard Ct BN11.......186 A3
Orchard Cvn Pk PO21...200 E7
Orchard Dell PO20......101 E2
Orchard Farm Pk RH1....2 E8
Orchard Gdns
Chichester PO19........176 F7
Hove BN3..............169 B1
Rustington BN16........205 D6
Woodgate PO20........179 D5
Orchard Ho RH12........33 C7
Orchard Ho
Crawley RH10............5 D1
Hove BN3..............169 B1
Lancing BN15...........187 E6
Orchard La
Ditchling BN6..........129 D4
Hassocks BN6..........128 F4
Hermitage PO10.........173 D4
West Itchenor PO20......197 A7
Orchard Par PO20......212 F8
Orchard Pk BN16.......205 B7
Orchard Pl BN18.......160 B3

Orchard Rd
Burgess Hill RH15.......108 E3
East Preston BN16......206 A6
Horsham RH13...........36 E2
Hove BN3..............169 B1
Orchard Side PO20......199 A8
Orchards Mid Sch The
BN12................185 D5
Orchards Sh Ctr RH16....87 E4
Orchard St
Chichester PO19........176 F7
Crawley RH10, RH11.....18 D6
Orchards The
Brighton BN2...........170 E3
4 Crawley RH11.......17 D5
Horsham RH12..........36 F5
Orchard The
Bognor Regis PO21......200 C1
Broadbridge Heath RH12...35 D3
Hassocks BN6..........128 C3
Horley RH6..............2 A3
Horsham RH12..........37 B4
Shoreham-by-S BN43....167 C1
Orchard Villas BN18.....180 E8
Orchard Way
Barnham PO22.........180 B6
Bognor Regis PO22......201 C5
Bolney RH17.............85 D8
Burgess Hill RH15.......108 F3
East Grinstead RH19......9 E1
Fontwell BN18..........158 A3
Haywards Heath RH16....87 D8
Hurstpierpoint BN6......127 F6
Lancing BN15...........187 E7
Midhurst GU29..........94 F8
Petersfield GU31........68 B1
Pulborough RH20.......100 C3
Orchid Pk RH16.........88 C4
Orchid View BN1........170 C6
Orde Cl RH10............6 D1
Oriel Cl
Barnham PO22.........180 B6
Crawley RH10............6 C1
Oriel High Sch RH10.....19 C4
Oriental Pl BN1.........191 E5
Orient Rd BN15.........188 C5
Orion Ct
Crawley RH11...........17 D4
Horsham RH12..........36 B3
Orion Par BN6..........128 F3
Orkney Ct BN13........185 B6
Orlando Ho BN1........192 A8
Orltons La RH12..........3 F2
Orme Cotts BN16.......183 F6
Orme Rd BN11.........186 C3
Ormerod Ct RH16........87 E5
Ormesby Wlk **6** RH10...19 B4
Ormonde Ave PO19.....177 B6
Ormonde Way BN43.....188 D6
Orpen Pl PO20.........212 F7
Orpen Rd BN3..........169 D1
Orwell Rd GU31..........68 A2
Osborn Cl
Littlehampton BN17......204 C6
Sayers Common BN6....107 D1
Osborn Cres PO19......155 A1
Osborne Cl BN15.......187 C6
Osborne Cres PO19......177 D6
Osborne Ct
8 Crawley RH11........18 B2
7 Shoreham-by-S
BN43...............189 C8
Osborne Dr BN15.......187 C6
Osborne Mews RH16....87 D4
Osborne Rd
Brighton BN1...........170 A2
Petersfield GU32........68 B4
Osborne Villas BN3......191 B6
Osier Rd GU31...........67 F2
Osmonde Cl BN14......186 C4
Osmonde Ct **3** BN14...186 C4
Osmond Gdns BN3......191 E7
Osmond Rd BN3........191 E7
Osmunda Bank RH19.....9 E6
Osmund Cl RH10........19 E6
Osney Cl RH11..........18 C5
Osprey Ct BN17........204 D8
Osprey Gdns PO22.....201 C7
Osprey Ho **18** BN1.....191 E5
Osprey Quay PO10......173 C7
Osterley Ho **5** RH12....36 F4
Ostlers View RH14.......79 C7
Otard Cl PO20..........212 E7
Otford Cl RH11..........39 C8
Otmers Quay BN18......160 B2
Ottafield Ct RH16........87 F6
Ottawa Dr BN10.........25 C3
Otterbourne Pl RH19......9 B1
Otter Cl PO19..........176 E8
Otway Cl RH11...........17 F4
Otway Rd PO19.........155 A2
Oulton Wlk **9** RH10.....19 B4
Our Lady of Lourdes RC
Prim Sch BN2.........193 F1
Our Lady of Sion Sch
(Juniors) BN11........186 D2
Our Lady of Sion Sch
(Seniors) BN11........186 C2
Our Lady Queen of Heaven
RC Sch RH11...........18 B8
Outerwyke Ave PO22....202 A6
Outerwyke Gdns
PO22...............202 B6
Outerwyke Rd PO22.....202 B6
Outram Ho PO22........201 F3
Outram Rd PO22........201 F3
Outram Way PO20......177 A1

Oval La PO20..........212 E5
Oval The
Findon BN14...........163 E7
Liss GU33..............45 B4
Worthing BN13.........186 A5
Oval Waye BN12........206 E4
Overdene Dr RH11.......18 A6
Overdown Rd PO22......202 B5
Overdown Rise BN41....167 E4
Overhill BN42...........167 E1
Overhill Dr BN1.........169 E5
Overhill Gdns BN1......169 E5
Overhill Way BN1.......169 E6
Overmead BN43........188 E8
Over St BN1............213 B3
Overstrand Ave BN16....205 C4
Overton Ct **4** RH19......9 E1
Overton Rd PO10.......152 A1
Overton Shaw RH19......9 E4
Ovingdean Cl BN2......193 D5
Ovingdean Hall Sch
BN2.................193 D4
Ovingdean Rd BN2......193 D5
Oving Rd
Chichester PO19........177 C6
Oving PO20............178 B7
Oving Terr PO19........177 C6
Owen Cl RH15..........108 F1
Owers Cl RH13..........36 E2
Owers Way PO20.......207 E2
Owlbeech Ct RH13......37 B4
Owlbeech Lo RH13......37 B4
Owlbeech Pl RH13......37 B4
Owlbeech Way RH13.....37 B4
Owletts RH10...........19 D7
Owlscastle Cl RH12......36 D5
Oxen Ave BN43.........188 F8
Oxen Ct BN43..........188 F8
Oxford Cl PO20........207 F7
Oxford Ct
Brighton BN1...........213 B4
7 Midhurst GU29......94 E7
Oxford Dr PO21........200 F3
Oxford Mews BN3......191 C7
Oxford Pl BN1..........213 B4
Oxford Rd
Crawley RH10...........18 F2
Horsham RH13...........36 E2
Worthing BN11.........186 C3
Oxford St
Bognor Regis PO21......201 B2
Brighton BN1...........213 B4
Oxford Terr **8** BN44....145 D3
Oyster Mews **7** PO10...173 B8

P

Pacific Ct **3** BN43......188 F6
Pacific Ho **11** BN16.....205 B4
Pacific Way PO20.......212 E6
Packer Ct RH19..........10 A3
Packham Way RH15.....108 F4
Pack House Cotts
RH14................53 B3
Paddock Cl GU27........49 A5
Paddock Ct BN41.......167 F3
Paddock Field BN1......171 B5
Paddock Gdns RH19......22 E7
Paddock Gn BN26......205 E6
Paddockhall Rd RH16....87 D5
Paddockhurst La RH17...41 D3
Paddockhurst Rd
Crawley, Gossops Green
RH11...............18 A5
Crawley RH10...........20 C2
Paddock La PO20.......212 D8
Paddocks PO22........180 B6
Paddocks The
Haywards Heath RH16....87 C3
Lancing BN15...........187 F5
Upper Beeding BN44.....146 B3
Paddock The
Bognor Regis PO22......201 C5
Crawley RH10...........19 D7
Haslemere GU27.........27 A8
Hove BN3..............169 C1
Littlehampton BN17......182 C6
Shoreham-by-S BN43....166 D1
Paddock Way
Findon BN14...........163 E6
Liphook GU30...........25 C5
Petersfield GU32........67 F2
Padstow Wlk RH11......17 F4
Padua Ho BN2..........193 F8
Padua House Flats
BN2.................193 F8
Padwick Rd RH13........37 A2
Padwicks Field RH20......99 A3
Page Ct RH13...........36 D1
Pages Cnr BN11........187 A3
Pages La BN11.........187 A4
Paget Ct RH13...........58 E8
PAGEWOOD 4 D7
Pagewood Ct RH10......19 D4
Pagham Beach Est
PO21...............210 F6
Pagham Cl PO10.......173 C8
Pagham Gdns PO11.....195 B2
Pagham Harbour Nature
Reserve★ PO20,
PO21...............210 C6
Pagham Harbour Nature
Reserve Visitor Ctr★
PO20...............209 F6
Pagham Ho BN17.......204 B7
Pagham Rd PO20,
PO21...............200 A3

Pain's Flat RH15,
RH17 . . . . 108 D8
Palace Pier★ BN2 . . . . . . 213 B1
Palace Pl BN1 . . . . 213 B2
Palace Yd PO19 . . . . 176 F6
Palatine Rd BN12 . . . . . . 185 D5
Palatine Sch BN12 . . . . . . 185 D6
Palings Way GU27 . . . . . 49 A5
Pallant The BN12 . . . . . . 185 B5
Pallingham Dr RH10 . . . 19 C3
Pallingham La RH14 . . . 77 F2
Palm Court Cotts 12
BN16 . . . . 206 A4
Palm Ct
2 Hove BN3 . . . . 191 D6
Worthing BN3 . . . . 185 E8
Palm Dr BN2 . . . . 192 F3
Palmeira Ave BN3 . . . . . 191 D6
Palmeira Avenue Mans 25
BN3 . . . . 191 C6
Palmeira Ct BN3 . . . . 191 C6
Palmeira Grande 9
BN3 . . . . 191 D6
Palmeira Ho 6 BN3 . . . . 191 D7
Palmeira Mans 22
BN3 . . . . 191 C6
Palmeira Pl BN3 . . . . 191 D7
Palmeira Sq BN3 . . . . 191 C6
Palmer Cl
Horley RH6 . . . . 1 F5
Storrington RH20 . . . . . . 121 F2
Palmer Pl PO20 . . . . 177 D1
Palmer Rd
Angmering BN16 . . . . . . 183 F7
Crawley RH10 . . . . 19 C3
Palmers Field Ave
PO19 . . . . 155 B1
Palmer's Rd PO10 . . . . . . 151 B1
Palmers Rd Ind Est
PO10 . . . . 151 B1
Palmerston Ave BN12 . . . 185 C3
Palmers Way BN13 . . . . . 163 D1
Pangdean La BN6,
RH15 . . . . 108 C4
Pangdene Cl RH15 . . . . . . 108 F1
Pankhurst Ave BN2 . . . . 192 D6
Pankhurst Ct 11 RH11 . . . 18 B1
Pannell Cl RH11 . . . . 9 D1
Pannells Ash RH14 . . . . . . 31 C3
Pannett RH15 . . . . 108 E4
Pantiles The BN12 . . . . . 206 E5
Panton Cl PO10 . . . . 151 A3
Parade Mans 8
BN16 . . . . 206 A4
Parade The
Bognor Regis PO21 . . . . . 211 A7
Brighton BN1 . . . . 169 B4
Crawley RH10 . . . . 18 E7
East Wittering PO20 . . . . 207 F7
Hove BN3 . . . . 168 E2
5 Lancing BN15 . . . . . . 187 C7
Loxwood RH14 . . . . 31 F4
Nepcote BN14 . . . . 163 E5
7 West Kingston
BN16 . . . . 206 A4
Paradise La PO10 . . . . . . 151 D4
PARBROOK 79 C7
Parchment St PO19 . . . . . 176 F7
Parham Cl
Brighton BN2 . . . . 192 D5
Chichester PO19 . . . . . . 177 C5
Littlehampton, Wick
BN17 . . . . 204 D6
Rustington BN16 . . . . . . 205 B4
Worthing BN14 . . . . 163 F1
Parham Ct 6 BN1 . . . . . . 186 A2
Parham Ho 13 BN3 . . . . . 191 D7
Parham House & Gdns★
RH20 . . . . 120 D1
Parham Rd
Crawley RH11 . . . . 17 F7
Worthing BN14 . . . . 163 F1
Parish Ho 6 RH11 . . . . . . 18 D5
Parish La RH10, RH11 . . 39 E6
Park Aparments The
BN1 . . . . 169 D4
Park Ave
Hove BN3 . . . . 190 E7
Keymer BN6 . . . . 129 A2
Selsey PO20 . . . . 212 F7
Shoreham-by-S BN43 . . . 189 A8
Worthing BN11 . . . . 186 E3
Park Cl
Brighton BN1 . . . . 170 E5
Burgess Hill RH15 . . . . . 108 F4
Hove BN3 . . . . 168 E3
Hurstpierpoint BN6 . . . . 128 A6
Portslade-by-S BN41 . . . 168 B1
Worthing BN14 . . . . 186 A7
Park Copse PO20 . . . . . . 210 C1
Park Cotts BN6 . . . . 127 F6
Park Cres
Brighton BN2 . . . . 213 C4
Emsworth PO10 . . . . 151 A1
Midhurst GU29 . . . . 94 E8
Portslade-by-S BN41 . . . 190 A8
Rottingdean BN2 . . . . . . 193 F1
Selsey PO20 . . . . 212 G8
Worthing BN11 . . . . 186 C2
Park Crescent Pl BN2 . . 213 C4
Park Crescent Rd
BN2 . . . . 213 C4
Park Crescent Terr
BN2 . . . . 213 C4
Park Ct
11 Brighton BN2 . . . . . . 192 C6
Brighton, Patcham BN1 . . 169 E6
Brighton, Preston BN1 . . . 169 F1

Park Ct continued
Burgess Hill RH15 . . . . . 109 A3
4 Haywards Heath
RH16 . . . . 87 E4
Hove BN3 . . . . 191 D7
2 Petersfield GU32 . . . . 68 B3
Park Dr
Bognor Regis PO22 . . . . . 202 D5
Ferring BN12 . . . . 206 F6
Rustington BN16 . . . . . . 205 D6
Yapton BN18 . . . . 181 A2
Park E RH16 . . . . 87 F2
Parker Cl RH10 . . . . 19 D5
Parker Ct BN41 . . . . 168 B2
Parkers RH13 . . . . 56 F3
Parker's Cotts PO18 . . . . 155 A6
Park Farm Cl RH12 . . . . . 36 D7
Park Farm Cotts
BN18 . . . . 159 E3
Park Farm Rd RH12 . . . . 36 D7
Parkfield RH12 . . . . 36 C3
Parkfield Ave PO21 . . . . . 200 D3
Parkfield Cl RH11 . . . . . . 17 F6
Parkfield Ct BN13 . . . . . . 186 A4
Parkfield Rd BN13 . . . . . 186 A4
Parkfield Way RH16 . . . . 87 C3
Park Gate
4 Brighton BN1 . . . . . . 191 F8
Hove BN3 . . . . 191 D6
Parkhaven Ct 7
BN15 . . . . 187 E6
Park Hill BN2 . . . . 213 C2
Park Ho
Burstow RH6 . . . . 6 F6
5 Worthing BN11 . . . . . 187 B3
Parkhurst Gr RH6 . . . . 1 F4
Parkhurst Rd RH6 . . . . . . 1 E4
Park La
Aldingbourne PO20 . . . . . 179 B7
Ashurst Wood RH19 . . . . 23 D6
Fernhurst GU27 . . . . 49 B6
Halnaker PO18 . . . . 156 C5
Heath Common RH20 . . . 122 D5
Lindfield RH16 . . . . 64 D2
Maplehurst RH13 . . . . . . 83 B6
Selsey PO20 . . . . 210 A1
Slindon BN18 . . . . 158 C4
Southwick BN42 . . . . 189 D7
Westbourne PO10,
PO18 . . . . 151 E8
West Grinstead RH13 . . . 104 D8
Parkland Bsns Ctr
BN15 . . . . 187 D4
Parklands BN43 . . . . 189 C8
Parklands Ave
Bognor Regis PO21 . . . . . 201 B4
Worthing BN12 . . . . 185 D2
Parklands Com Prim Sch
PO19 . . . . 176 E7
Parklands Ct BN12 . . . . . 185 D3
Parklands Rd
Chichester PO19 . . . . . . 176 F7
Hassocks BN6 . . . . 128 F3
Parklawn Ave RH6 . . . . . . 1 F5
Park Lo BN1 . . . . 191 D8
Park Manor BN1 . . . . 169 D3
Parkmead BN2 . . . . 213 C4
Parkmore Terr BN1 . . . . . 213 A5
Park Par RH16 . . . . 87 E4
Park Pl
Arundel BN18 . . . . 160 A3
1 Horsham RH12 . . . . . 36 C1
Park Rd
Barnham PO22 . . . . 180 D6
Bognor Regis PO21 . . . . . 201 B2
Breach PO10 . . . . 151 F1
Brighton BN1 . . . . 170 E5
Burgess Hill RH15 . . . . . 109 A3
Burstow RH9 . . . . 7 C8
Dormans Park RH19 . . . . 9 F6
East Grinstead RH19 . . . . 9 D1
Faygate RH12 . . . . 16 F1
Forest Row RH18 . . . . . . 23 F2
Goodwood Park PO18 . . . 155 F6
Handcross RH17 . . . . 61 B6
Haslemere GU27 . . . . . . 27 C5
Henfield BN5 . . . . 125 E4
3 Petersfield GU31 . . . . 68 B3
Petworth GU28 . . . . 97 F8
Rottingdean BN2 . . . . . . 193 F1
Selsey PO20 . . . . 212 G8
Shoreham-by-S BN43 . . . 189 A8
Worthing BN11 . . . . 186 E3
Yapton BN18 . . . . 181 A2
Park Rise
Horsham RH12 . . . . 36 B4
Hove BN3 . . . . 168 E3
Petworth GU28 . . . . 97 E7
Park Road Terr 4
BN2 . . . . 213 C2
Park Royal BN1 . . . . 191 E6
Parkside
10 Bognor Regis
PO21 . . . . 201 D4
Burgess Hill RH15 . . . . . 108 F4
Crawley RH10 . . . . 18 E6
East Grinstead RH19 . . . . 9 C1
Keymer BN6 . . . . 129 A4
Shoreham-by-S BN43 . . . 167 A1
Worthing BN11 . . . . 186 E3
Parkside Ave BN17 . . . . . 204 F5
Parkside Ct BN17 . . . . . . 204 F5
Parkside Mews RH12 . . . 36 D2
Park Sq BN2 . . . . 192 F3
Park St
Brighton BN2 . . . . 213 C2

Park St continued
Falmer BN1 . . . . 171 C6
Horsham RH12 . . . . 36 D2
Tillington GU28 . . . . 75 C1
Parks The BN41 . . . . 168 B3
PARK STREET 34 C4
Park Terr
Bognor Regis PO21 . . . . . 201 B2
Rottingdean BN2 . . . . . . 193 F1
Tillington GU28 . . . . 75 C1
Park Terr E RH13 . . . . 36 D1
Park Terr W RH13 . . . . . . 36 D1
Parkview BN6 . . . . 128 A5
Park View
Brighton BN2 . . . . 192 C6
Brighton, Preston BN1 . . . 191 E8
Crawley RH11 . . . . 18 B2
Haywards Heath RH16 . . 87 E6
Horley RH6 . . . . 2 A3
Park View Ct BN16 . . . . . 205 C6
Park View Rd BN3 . . . . . . 169 B1
Park View Terr BN1 . . . . . 191 E8
Park Village Rd BN1 . . . . 171 B8
Park Village The BN1 . . . 171 A8
Park W RH16 . . . . 87 F2
Parkway
Bognor Regis PO21 . . . . . 201 A3
Crawley RH10 . . . . 19 C7
Parkway Ho 2 RH12 . . . . 36 C1
Parkway The BN15 . . . . . 205 D5
Parnell Cl RH10 . . . . 19 D4
Parnell Ct 3 BN2 . . . . . . 191 B6
Parochial Terr BN2 . . . . . 213 B2
Parry Cl RH13 . . . . 37 C4
Parry Dr BN16 . . . . 205 B5
Parsonage Bsns Pk
RH13 . . . . 36 E4
Parsonage Cl GU32 . . . . . 68 D5
Parsonage Est GU31 . . . . 70 B4
Parsonage Rd
Henfield BN5 . . . . 125 E6
Horsham RH12, RH13 . . . 36 E4
Parsonage Way RH12 . . . 36 E4
Parsons Cl
Angmering BN16 . . . . . . 206 A8
Haslemere GU27 . . . . . . 27 C5
Horley RH6 . . . . 1 E4
Parsons Gn GU27 . . . . . . 27 C8
Parson's Hill BN18 . . . . . 160 B3
Parsons Wlk
Horsham RH12 . . . . 57 F8
Walberton BN18 . . . . . . 180 E8
Parthings La RH12,
RH13 . . . . 57 F8
Partridge Green Rd
RH13 . . . . 105 C3
Partridge La RH5, RH12 . . 3 F3
Partridge Pl RH10 . . . . . . 21 C6
Pascoe Ct 2 PO19 . . . . . . 176 F7
Pashley Ct 10 BN43 . . . . 188 F7
Passfield Ent Ctr GU30 . . 24 D8
Passfield Rd GU30 . . . . . . 24 E8
Paston Ho 5 BN1 . . . . . . 191 F8
Paston Pl BN2 . . . . 192 D4
Pasture Hill Rd RH16 . . . 87 D6
Pasture The RH10 . . . . . . 19 C6
Patcham By-Pass
BN1 . . . . 169 E6
Patcham Grange BN1 . . . 169 E5
Patcham High Sch
BN1 . . . . 169 F6
Patcham House Special
Sch BN1 . . . . 169 E6
Patcham Inf Sch BN1 . . . 169 E6
Patcham Jun Sch
BN1 . . . . 169 F5
Patchdean BN1 . . . . 169 F5
Patching Cl
Crawley RH11 . . . . 17 F7
Worthing BN12 . . . . 185 B5
Patchings RH13 . . . . 36 F3
Paterson Wilson Rd
BN17 . . . . 204 E6
Pathfield Cl RH12 . . . . . . 33 D7
Pathfield Rd RH12 . . . . . . 33 D7
Pathfields GU27 . . . . 27 C7
Pathfields Cl GU27 . . . . . 27 C7
Path Link PO10 . . . . 18 E7
Patricia Ave BN12 . . . . . . 185 D2
Patricia Cl BN12 . . . . 185 D2
Patrick's Cl GU33 . . . . . . 45 C4
Patrick's Copse Rd
GU33 . . . . 45 C4
Patrington Cl RH11 . . . . . 18 A3
Patterdale Cl RH11 . . . . . 18 C4
Paulus Ct 1 PO19 . . . . . . 176 F7
Pavement The RH10 . . . . 18 E6
Pavilion Bldgs BN1 . . . . . 213 B2
Pavilion Cl BN6 . . . . 128 E5
Pavilion Ct
15 Brighton BN1 . . . . . . 191 E7
Brighton BN1 . . . . 213 B2
Pavilion Ho BN14 . . . . . . 186 B3
Pavilion Mews BN1 . . . . 213 B2
Pavilion Par BN2 . . . . . . 213 B2
Pavilion Rd
Falmer BN1 . . . . 171 C7
Worthing BN14 . . . . 186 B3
Pavilion Ret Pk BN2 . . . . 170 C1
Pavilion St BN2 . . . . 213 B2
Pavilions The RH11 . . . . . 39 C6

Pavilion Way RH19 . . . . . 22 E8
Pax Cl RH11 . . . . 17 E4
Paxmead Cres BN14 . . . . 186 F6
Pay Gate RH20 . . . . 143 E7
Payne Ave BN3 . . . . 190 F8
Payne Cl
Bognor Regis PO21 . . . . . 211 A8
Crawley RH10 . . . . 19 D8
Payne Ho RH15 . . . . 109 D3
Paynesfield RH17 . . . . . . 85 C3
PAYNES GREEN 14 D8
Paynes Green Cotts
RH5 . . . . 14 D7
Payne Terr BN1 . . . . 170 B1
Paythorne Cl BN42 . . . . . 167 D1
Paythorne Dro BN5 . . . . 147 D4
Payton Dr RH15 . . . . 108 F2
Payton Ho RH15 . . . . 109 D3
Peace Cl BN1 . . . . 170 C1
Peacemaker Cl RH11 . . . 17 E4
Peace Rd GU29 . . . . 95 A2
Peacheries The PO19 . . . 177 C5
Peachey Ho GU29 . . . . . . 94 E7
Peachey Rd PO20 . . . . . . 212 D6
Peacock Cl PO19 . . . . 155 C1
Peacock Ind Est BN3 . . . 191 D7
Peacock La BN1 . . . . 169 E4
Peacocks RH13 . . . . 105 A3
Peacocks La RH20 . . . . . 102 C1
Peacock's Hill RH13 . . . . 83 D6
Peacock Wlk 8 RH11 . . . 18 A3
Peak La BN16 . . . . 206 C4
Peak The PO9 . . . . 130 E2
Pearman Ct PO18 . . . . . . 135 D7
Pears Gr PO10 . . . . 173 F8
Pearson Rd
Arundel BN18 . . . . 159 F2
Crawley RH10 . . . . 19 C6
Pearsons Retreat 10
BN11 . . . . 187 B3
Peartree Cl RH15 . . . . . . 108 E3
Peartree Cnr RH13 . . . . . 83 C2
Pear Tree Hill RH1 . . . . . 2 A8
Peary Cl RH12 . . . . 36 D6
Pease Croft GU31 . . . . . . 91 D3
Pease Pottage Hill
RH11 . . . . 18 D1
Pebble Cotts PO21 . . . . . 200 B2
Pebble Ct PO22 . . . . 201 E5
Pebble Wlk BN17 . . . . . . 205 A7
Peckhams Copse La
PO20 . . . . 177 D3
Peeks Brook La
Crawley RH6 . . . . 6 E7
Horley RH6 . . . . 2 F2
Peel Cl BN17 . . . . 204 C6
Peel Rd BN2 . . . . 192 F4
Peerley Cl PO20 . . . . 208 A6
Peerley Rd PO20 . . . . 208 A6
Pegasus Cl GU27 . . . . . . 26 D5
Pegasus Ct
Chichester PO19 . . . . . . 176 F6
Crawley RH11 . . . . 17 E4
Rustington BN16 . . . . . . 205 C5
11 Worthing BN11 . . . . 186 C2
Pegasus Pl RH10 . . . . 6 A1
Pegasus Way RH19 . . . . . 10 B3
Pegler Way RH11 . . . . . . 18 D6
Pegwell Cl RH11 . . . . 17 F4
Pelham Ct
2 Brighton BN2 . . . . . . 170 C1
5 Horsham RH12 . . . . . 36 B2
6 Worthing BN13 . . . . . 186 A5
Pelham Ct Bsns Ctr
RH11 . . . . 18 B2
Pelham Dr RH11 . . . . 18 A2
Pelham Pl RH11 . . . . 18 B2
Pelham Place Cotts
RH16 . . . . 88 A7
Pelham Rd
Lindfield RH16 . . . . 88 A6
Worthing BN13 . . . . 186 A5
Pelham Sq BN1 . . . . 213 B3
Pelham St BN1 . . . . 213 B3
Pelham Terr
1 Brighton BN2 . . . . . . 170 C1
Emsworth PO10 . . . . 173 C8
Pelleys La PO20 . . . . 176 F1
Pemberton Cl BN15 . . . . 187 E7
Pembley Gn RH10 . . . . . . 7 C7
Pembroke Ave
Hove BN3 . . . . 191 A7
Worthing BN13 . . . . 185 F3
Pembroke Cres BN3 . . . . 191 A7
Pembroke Ct 2 BN3 . . . . 191 A6
Pembroke Gdns BN3 . . . 191 A6
Pembroke Rd RH10 . . . . . 6 C1
Pembroke Way PO21 . . . 200 E4
Pembury Cl
Haywards Heath RH16 . . 88 B3
Worthing BN14 . . . . 186 A4
Pembury Rd BN14 . . . . . . 186 A4
Penarth Gdns BN17 . . . . 182 C5
Pendean RH15 . . . . 109 C1
Pende Cl BN15 . . . . 187 D8
Pendine Ave BN11 . . . . . 187 A3
Pendragon Ct BN3 . . . . . 191 A8
Penfold La BN16 . . . . 205 D4
Penfold Manor GU27 . . . 27 D6
Penfold Rd
Crawley RH10 . . . . 19 B2
Worthing BN14 . . . . 186 E5
Penfolds Pl BN18 . . . . . . 160 A2
Penfold Way BN44 . . . . . 145 D2
Penhill Ct 4 BN15 . . . . . 187 F5
Penhill Rd BN15 . . . . 187 F5
Penhurst Ct
Worthing BN13 . . . . 185 B6

Penhurst Ct continued
Worthing, Broadwater
BN14 . . . . 186 C6
Penhurst Pl BN2 . . . . 192 F6
Penland Cl RH16 . . . . 87 D7
Penland Ct BN44 . . . . 145 D2
Penland Rd RH16 . . . . . . 87 D7
Penland's Ct BN44 . . . . . 145 D2
Penlands Rise BN44 . . . . 145 C2
Penlands Vale BN44 . . . . 145 C2
Penlands Way BN44 . . . . 145 D2
Penleigh Cl BN15 . . . . . . 187 F5
Penn Cl
Crawley RH11 . . . . 5 D1
Middleton-on-S PO22 . . . 202 E5
Penn Cres RH16 . . . . 88 A5
Pennells Cl GU30 . . . . . . 47 B2
Pennett Ho RH16 . . . . . . 87 D2
Penn Gdns RH20 . . . . 122 E5
Pennine Cl RH11 . . . . 18 B6
Pennington Ho RH16 . . . 88 A3
Penns Cl BN44 . . . . 145 C4
Penns Pl GU31 . . . . 68 F3
Penns Rd GU32 . . . . 68 A4
Pennthorpe Sch RH12 . . 33 D7
Penny Cl 5 GU32 . . . . 68 B3
Pennycord Cl PO20 . . . . . 212 E5
Pennycress Ave BN13 . . 185 A6
Pennyfields PO22 . . . . . . 202 C5
Penny La PO10 . . . . 173 D8
Penrith Ct BN14 . . . . 186 D5
Pensfold RH12 . . . . 33 E5
Penshurst Cl RH10 . . . . . 19 D7
Penstone Cl BN15 . . . . . . 187 D6
Penstone Ct 4 BN43 . . . . 189 C8
Penstone Pk BN15 . . . . . 187 E6
Pentland Rd BN13 . . . . . 185 E8
Penwarden Way
PO18 . . . . 175 C7
Penwith Dr GU27 . . . . . . 26 E5
Peperham Cotts GU27 . . 27 C7
Peperham Ho GU27 . . . . 27 C7
Peperham Rd GU27 . . . . 27 C8
Peppard Rd RH10 . . . . . . 19 D3
Pepper Ct BN17 . . . . 204 C5
Pepper Dr RH15 . . . . 108 F1
Peppering La BN18 . . . . . 161 A7
Pepperscoombe La
BN44 . . . . 146 B2
Peppersgate RH13 . . . . . 84 A7
Pepper's La BN44 . . . . . . 124 C5
Perche Cl GU29 . . . . 94 D6
Perching Dro BN5 . . . . . . 147 E4
Percival Mans 20
BN2 . . . . 192 D4
Percival Terr 14 BN2 . . . 192 D4
Percy Cotts RH17 . . . . . . 86 F8
Percy Rd RH12 . . . . 36 B3
Percy Terr GU28 . . . . 97 F8
Percy & Wagner
Almshouses 5 BN2 . . . 213 C4
Peregrine Rd BN17 . . . . . 204 F6
Perimeter Rd E RH6 . . . . 6 B6
Perimeter Rd N RH6 . . . . 5 D8
Perimeter Rd S RH6,
RH11 . . . . 5 E5
Perkstead Ct 6 RH11 . . . 18 A3
Perrots La BN44 . . . . 145 C2
Perry Ave RH19 . . . . 9 E3
Perryfield Ho 7 RH10 . . 18 D5
Perryfield La RH13 . . . . . 84 C6
Perryfield Rd RH11 . . . . . 18 D5
Perryfields RH15 . . . . 108 E4
Perry Hill BN2 . . . . 194 D4
Perrylands RH6 . . . . 4 F7
Perrylands La RH6 . . . . . . 2 F1
Perryman's La RH17 . . . . 66 D3
Perrymount Rd RH16 . . . 87 E5
Perth Cl RH11 . . . . 5 D1
Perth Ho GU29 . . . . 94 E6
Perth Way RH12 . . . . 36 F4
Pescott's Cl PO20 . . . . . . 197 E5
Peskett Cl RH13 . . . . 56 F3
Peterborough Rd RH10 . . 18 E2
Peter Gladwin Prim Sch
BN41 . . . . 168 B2
Peterhouse Cl PO21 . . . . 200 F4
Peterhouse Par RH10 . . . 6 C1
Peterlee Wlk RH11 . . . . . 17 E2
Peter Rd BN15 . . . . 187 C4
Peters Cl RH13 . . . . 82 A8
Petersfield Bsns Pk
GU32 . . . . 67 F3
Petersfield Hospl
GU32 . . . . 68 A3
Petersfield Inf Sch
GU32 . . . . 68 B3
Petersfield Mus★
GU32 . . . . 68 B3
Petersfield Rd GU29 . . . . 94 E8
Petersfield Sch The
GU32 . . . . 68 A2
Petersfield Sta GU32 . . . 68 A4
Peter's La PO20 . . . . 212 A8
Peter's Pl PO20 . . . . 212 A8
Peter Weston Pl
PO19 . . . . 177 B6
Petlands Gdns RH16 . . . 87 F3
Petlands Rd RH16 . . . . . . 87 E3
Pett Cl BN2 . . . . 192 F6
Petts Cl PO20 . . . . 209 C1
Petworth Ave BN12 . . . . 185 C1
Petworth CE Prim Sch
GU28 . . . . 97 F7

Petworth Cottage Mus★
GU28. . . . . .97 F8
Petworth Ct
Billingshurst RH14. . . . . . . .79 D7
Crawley RH11 . . . . .17 F3
Haslemere GU27 . . . . .27 D6
5 Rustington BN16 . . . .205 B3
Petworth Dr
Burgess Hill RH15 . . . . . . .109 A4
Horsham RH12 . . . . .36 F2
Petworth Ho **14** BN3 . . . .191 D7
Petworth Ho★ GU28 . . . . .97 F7
Petworth Park★ GU28 . . .75 D2
Petworth Rd
Ansteadbrook GU27 . . . . . .28 B6
Brighton BN1. . . . . .170 B6
Chiddingfold GU8. . . . . .29 A8
Wisborough Green RH14. . .78 B8
Pevensey Cl RH10. . . . . . .19 C5
Pevensey Gdn BN11. . . .186 A1
Pevensey Gdn
Bognor Regis PO21 . . . . . .201 A4
7 Brighton BN2. . . . . . .192 C8
Southwater RH13 . . . . .58 A2
Worthing BN11 . . . . .186 A1
Peverel Ct GU30 . . . . . . .25 B5
Peverel Rd
Crawley RH11 . . . . .17 E5
Worthing BN14 . . . . .186 A4
Peverill Cl BN15. . . . . . . .187 B6
Peveril Dr BN15. . . . . . . .187 B6
Pharos Quay BN17 . . . . .204 C5
Pheasant Cotts PO18. . .134 F6
Philip Ct
Bognor Regis PO21. . . . . . .200 C3
8 Hove BN3. . . . . .191 C7
Phillips Cl RH10 . . . . .19 C2
Philliswood La PO18. . . .112 D3
PHILPOTS. 42 C5
Philpots Manor Sch
RH19. . . . . .42 C5
Phoenix Brewery Halls
BN2 . . . . .213 C4
Phoenix Bsns Ctr
PO19. . . . . .177 C5
Phoenix Cl
Chichester PO19 . . . . .177 A5
Littlehampton BN17. . . . . .204 B7
Phoenix Cres BN42. . . . .189 D8
Phoenix Ct PO21. . . . . . .201 C3
Phoenix Ho **7** BN14 . . . .186 D3
Phoenix La RH19. . . . . . . .23 E6
Phoenix Pl BN2. . . . . . . .213 C3
Phoenix Rise BN2. . . . . .213 C3
Phoenix Terr RH19. . . . . .23 E6
Phoenix Way BN42. . . . .189 D8
Phrosso Rd BN11 . . . . . .185 F2
Pickers Gn RH16. . . . . . . .88 A8
PICKETTS. 2 C8
Picketts La RH1. . . . . .2 C8
PICKHURST. 100 A6
Pickhurst La RH20 . . . . .100 B6
Pickhurst Rd GU8. . . . . . .29 D8
Pickwell La RH17 . . . . . . .85 F4
Picton St BN2 . . . . .192 C7
Picts Hill RH13. . . . . .58 A7
Picts La RH13. . . . . .84 A4
Pierces La **7** RH16. . . . . .87 C2
Pier Five Rd E RH6. . . . . . .5 E8
Pier Four Rd N RH6. . . . . . .5 F5
Pierpoint Cl BN6. . . . . . .127 F6
Pier Rd BN17 . . . . .204 D4
Piers Secombe Cl
RH20. . . . . .119 D5
Pigbush La RH14. . . . . . . .32 A4
Pigeonhouse La BN16. . .205 E4
Pigeon Pass RH10. . . . . . .21 C5
Piggery Hall La PO20. . .196 F1
Pike The RH20. . . . . .143 F7
Pilgrim Ct PO19. . . . . . . .177 B7
Pilgrims Cl **1** BN14 . . . . .186 B3
Pilgrims Terr BN13 . . . . .186 A3
Pilgrims Way PO21. . . . .200 B1
Pilgrims Wlk BN13. . . . . .186 A3
Pilot Ho **1** BN2. . . . . . . .213 C2
Piltdown Rd BN2. . . . . . .192 F6
Pine Cl
Billingshurst RH14. . . . . . . .55 C1
Crawley RH11 . . . . .5 C1
Heath Common RH20 . . . .122 B3
Midhurst GU29. . . . . .94 C7
Pine Cotts GU33 . . . . .45 C7
Pine Ct PO10. . . . . .151 B4
Pine Gdns RH6. . . . . .2 A2
Pine Gr
Chichester PO19 . . . . .154 C1
East Grinstead RH19 . . . . . . .9 B3
Pineham Copse RH16. . . .87 F4
Pinehurst
Burgess Hill RH15. . . . . . . .109 A1
Horsham RH12 . . . . .36 C4
Pinehurst Pk PO21. . . . . .200 D4
Pines Ave BN14. . . . . . . .186 D7
Pine Shaw RH10. . . . . . . .19 D7
Pine Rd GU30. . . . . .24 E4
Pines The
Angmering BN16 . . . . .205 F8
2 Brighton BN2. . . . . . .213 C4
Crawley RH10 . . . . .19 D6
Haywards Heath RH16 . . . .88 B4
Horsham RH12 . . . . .37 C5
Hove BN3. . . . . .191 E6
Hurstpierpoint BN6. . . . . .127 F7
Littlehampton BN17. . . . . .204 D6
Yapton BN18 . . . . .180 F3

Pine Tree Cl BN6 . . . . . . .128 B5
Pine Trees BN6. . . . . .128 D4
Pinetrees Cl RH10 . . . . .7 B3
Pine Trees Cl BN16 . . . . .183 F7
Pine Trees Cl BN6 . . . . . .128 D4
Pine View Cl GU27 . . . . . .27 C8
Pine Way Cl RH19. . . . . . .22 E7
Pine Wlk
Bognor Regis PO21. . . . . . .200 D4
Liss GU33 . . . . .45 C6
Pinewood **5** BN1. . . . . . .169 E3
Pinewood Cl
Brighton BN1. . . . . .169 D2
Broadbridge Heath RH12 . . .35 D3
East Preston BN16 . . . . . . .206 A6
Pinewood Ct
Haywards Heath RH16 . . . .87 D2
West Lavington GU29 . . . . .95 A6
Pinewood Gdns PO21. . . .201 A3
Pinewood Ho PO19 . . . . .155 B1
Pinewood Way
Haywards Heath RH16 . . . .87 D2
Midhurst GU29. . . . . .94 E5
Pinfold **4** RH16. . . . . .87 D6
Pinfold Cl BN2. . . . . .193 E6
Pinkhurst La RH13 . . . . . . .35 A2
Pinks La PO20 . . . . .197 D3
Pinland Rd RH13. . . . . . . .104 F1
Pipers Cl
Hove BN3. . . . . .168 C3
Southwater RH13 . . . . .57 F1
Pipers End RH13. . . . . . . .34 E3
Pipers La
Balls Cross GU28. . . . . .52 A4
Northchapel GU28. . . . . . . .51 A7
Pipers Mead PO20 . . . . . .197 D3
Piries Pl RH12 . . . . .36 C2
Pitcroft La GU31. . . . . .90 B5
Pitcroft The PO19. . . . . . .177 C8
Pitfold Ave GU27. . . . . . . .26 D6
Pitfold Cl GU27. . . . . .26 E6
Pit La BN1. . . . . .128 A5
Pitsham La GU29. . . . . .94 D5
Pitsham Wood GU29 . . . . .94 D6
Pitt Ct BN6. . . . . .128 A5
Pitt Gdns BN2 . . . . .193 D7
Place St Maur Des Fosses
PO21. . . . . .201 D2
Plainfields Ave BN1. . . . .170 A7
Plainwood Cl PO19 . . . . .154 F2
Plaistow Cl BN2 . . . . .192 F6
Plaistow & Kirdford Prim
Sch RH14 . . . . .30 F3
Plaistow The
Chiddingfold GU8. . . . . .29 D6
Dunsfold GU8. . . . . .30 B7
Ifold RH14. . . . . .31 D1
Kirdford RH14 . . . . .53 B5
Plantain Cres RH11 . . . . . .18 A2
Plantation Cl **2** BN13 . . .185 F8
Plantation Rd GU33. . . . . .45 D2
Plantation Rise BN13. . . .186 A7
Plantation The
Cootham RH20. . . . . .121 B1
East Preston BN16 . . . . . . .206 A5
Horne RH7. . . . . .8 C7
Worthing BN13 . . . . .186 A7
Plantation Way
Storrington RH20. . . . . . . .121 C1
3 Worthing BN13. . . . . .185 F8
Plat The RH12 . . . . .36 A3
Platts Mdw RH14 . . . . .79 C8
Platts Rdbt RH14. . . . . . . .79 C8
Platt The
Dormansland RH7. . . . . . . .10 A8
Handcross RH17 . . . . .61 C8
Haywards Heath RH16 . . . .88 B5
Plaw Hatch La RH18,
RH19 . . . . .43 E5
Playden Cl **1** BN2 . . . . . .192 E4
Playden Cl **3** RH11 . . . . . .18 A3
Playing Field Cl GU27 . . . .27 C8
Plaza Ct BN11 . . . . .186 C1
Pleasant La PO10 . . . . . . .173 F1
Plough Cl RH11. . . . . .17 F8
Plough La RH12. . . . . .36 E5
Plover Cl
Bognor Regis PO22 . . . . . .201 C7
Bracklesham PO20 . . . . . .208 A6
Crawley RH11 . . . . .18 C8
Plovers Rd RH13 . . . . .36 F3
Plovers The BN15. . . . . . .188 A5
Plummerden La RH16. . . . .64 F7
Plumpton Rd BN2. . . . . . .192 D6
Plum Pudding Cnr
GU28. . . . . .98 D6
Plumtree Cross RH13 . . . .57 A5
Plumtree Cross La
RH13. . . . . .57 A5
Plymouth Ave BN2 . . . . . .170 F1
Poels Ct RH19. . . . . .9 E2
Polecat La RH13 . . . . .82 C8
Poles La RH11 . . . . .5 C3
Polestub La RH17. . . . . . . .86 F7
Policemans La BN6 . . . . .127 F5
POLING. 183 B6
Poling Cl RH11. . . . . .18 A3
POLING CORNER. 183 A8
Poling St BN18. . . . . .183 B7
Pollard Ct BN11. . . . . .186 A3
Pollards RH11. . . . . .18 A5
Pollards Dr RH13 . . . . .36 F2
Pollard's Hill RH13. . . . . . .82 A6
POLLINGFOLD. 12 E5
Polperro Cl BN12 . . . . . . .206 E5
Pomper La BN6. . . . . .108 A2
Pompeys Terr BN44. . . . .145 C4

Pond Cl
Billingshurst RH14. . . . . . . .79 C8
Loxwood RH14. . . . . .32 A4
Pond Copse La RH14. . . . .31 F5
Pondcroft Rd RH16 . . . . . .88 B7
Pond Farm Cl RH13 . . . . . .57 F3
Pondfield Rd RH12. . . . . . .33 E8
Pond La BN13. . . . . .185 D8
Pond Mews BN13 . . . . . . .185 D8
Pond Rd
Bracklesham PO20 . . . . . .208 B6
Shoreham-by-S BN43. . . . .188 F7
Pond Rise RH20. . . . . .101 E1
Pondside RH16. . . . . .87 C3
Pondtail Cl RH12. . . . . .36 D6
Pondtail Copse RH12. . . . .36 D6
Pondtail Dr RH12 . . . . .36 D7
Pondtail Pk RH12. . . . . . . .36 D6
Pondtail Rd RH12. . . . . . . .36 D6
Pond Way RH19. . . . . .10 B1
Pond Wood Rd RH10 . . . . .19 A8
Pony Farm BN14. . . . . . . .163 F6
Pookbourne La BN6. . . . .107 E4
Pook La PO18 . . . . .155 A5
Pool Pas BN1. . . . . .213 B1
Pool Valley BN2 . . . . .213 B1
Popes Ct BN2. . . . . .170 B1
Popes Mead GU27 . . . . . .27 C7
Poplar Ave BN3. . . . . .168 E3
Poplar Cl
Brighton BN1. . . . . .169 F2
Crawley RH11 . . . . .5 C1
Hove BN3. . . . . .168 E3
Poplar Ct
Pulborough RH20. . . . . . . .100 A2
Worthing BN13 . . . . .185 C6
Poplar Mews
12 Haywards Heath
RH16. . . . . .87 C2
Selsey PO20. . . . . .212 E8
Poplar Rd BN13. . . . . .185 C6
Poplars Cl RH15. . . . . .108 E3
Poplars The
Cudworth RH5. . . . . .3 E8
Ferring BN12 . . . . .206 E4
Horsham RH13 . . . . .36 E3
Keymer BN6. . . . . .129 A3
Littlehampton BN17. . . . . .204 F7
Yapton BN18 . . . . .181 A3
Poplar Way GU29 . . . . .94 E5
Poplar Wlk GU31. . . . . .68 A1
Poppy Cl
Rustington BN17 . . . . .205 A7
Southwater Street RH13 . . .58 A3
Porchester Cl RH13 . . . . . .58 A2
PORTFIELD. 177 D6
Portfield Ave BN1. . . . . . . .170 A6
Portfield Com Prim Sch
PO19. . . . . .177 C7
Portfield Pl PO19. . . . . . . .177 D7
Portfield Ret Pk
PO19. . . . . .177 D7
Portfield Trad Ctr
PO19. . . . . .177 D5
Portfield Way PO19 . . . . .177 D8
Port Hall Ave BN1. . . . . . .191 E8
Port Hall Mews BN1 . . . . .191 E8
Port Hall Pl BN1 . . . . .191 E8
Port Hall Rd BN1 . . . . .191 E8
Port Hall St BN1 . . . . .191 E8
Portland Ave BN3. . . . . . .190 E7
Portland Bsns Pk
BN3. . . . . .190 E8
Portland Cl BN17 . . . . . . .205 A6
Portland Ho **5** RH19. . . . .22 F8
Portland La BN3. . . . . .190 D7
Portland Mews **19**
BN2. . . . . .192 C4
Portland Pl **18** BN2. . . . .192 C4
Portland Rd
Burgess Hill RH15. . . . . . . .108 F3
East Grinstead RH19 . . . . . .22 F8
Hove BN3. . . . . .190 E7
Worthing BN11 . . . . .186 D2
Portland Road Trad Est
BN3. . . . . .190 D8
Portland's Cl GU32. . . . . . .68 D5
Portland Sq
Liss GU33 . . . . .45 B4
Worthing BN11 . . . . .186 D2
Portland St BN1. . . . . .213 A2
Portland Villas BN3. . . . . .190 D7
Portside BN2 . . . . .192 F3
Portslade Com Coll
BN41. . . . . .168 A1
Portslade Com Coll
(Lower) BN41. . . . . .168 A3
Portslade Inf Sch
BN41. . . . . .190 B8
Portslade Sta BN3. . . . . . . .190 C8
Portsmouth La RH16. . . . . .87 F8
Portsmouth Rd
Bramshott GU26, GU30. . . .25 E6
Liphook GU30. . . . . .25 B2
Portsmouth Wood
RH16. . . . . .87 F8
Portsmouth Wood Cl
RH16. . . . . .87 F8
Portsmouth Wood Dr
RH16. . . . . .87 F8
Portway BN44. . . . . .145 C2
Posthorses RH20. . . . . . . .123 A4
Post Office La PO20. . . . .177 D1
Post View RH20. . . . . .142 E8
Pot La BN13. . . . . .184 E7
Potnore PO18 . . . . .154 E7
Potters Cnr PO18. . . . . . . .152 C1
Potters Croft RH13. . . . . . .36 E2

Pottersfield RH10. . . . . . . .18 D7
Potters Field GU33. . . . . . .45 C4
Potters Gn RH13. . . . . .83 E2
Potters La RH15 . . . . .108 F1
Potters Mead BN17 . . . . .204 C7
Potters Pl RH12. . . . . .36 C2
Pottery La PO18. . . . . .174 D8
Poulner Cl PO22 . . . . .202 A5
Poulter's Cnr BN14 . . . . .186 A6
Poulter's La BN14. . . . . . .186 B6
Pound Cl
Loxwood RH14. . . . . .31 F5
Petworth GU28 . . . . .97 F7
Pound Cnr
Shipley RH13. . . . . .103 D7
Warnham RH12 . . . . .14 E2
Pound Cotts GU29. . . . . . . .73 A1
Pound Farm Rd PO19 . . . .177 C6
Poundfield La RH14. . . . . . .31 B3
Pound Gate BN6. . . . . . . .128 D3
POUND HILL. 19 C8
Pound Hill Jun & Inf Schs
RH10. . . . . .19 C7
Pound Hill Par RH10 . . . . .19 C7
Pound Hill Pl RH10. . . . . . .19 C6
Pound La
Mannings Heath RH13. . . . .59 C6
Shipley RH13. . . . . .81 D1
Upper Beeding BN44. . . . .146 B2
Pound Rd
Walberton BN18 . . . . .158 D1
West Wittering PO20. . . . .196 B2
Pound St GU28 . . . . .97 F8
Pound The
Bognor Regis PO21. . . . . . .200 E2
Burgess Hill RH15 . . . . . . .108 F4
Pound Way BN16. . . . . . . .184 A5
POVEY CROSS. 1 D1
Povey Cross Rd RH6. . . . . . .1 E1
Poveys Cl RH15. . . . . .108 D3
Powell Rd RH6. . . . . .1 E4
Powis Gr BN1. . . . . .213 A3
Powis Rd BN1 . . . . .191 E6
Powis Sq BN1. . . . . .191 E6
Powis Villas BN1. . . . . . . .213 A3
Poynes Rd RH6. . . . . .1 E5
Poynings Crossways
BN6. . . . . .127 B1
Poynings Dr BN3 . . . . . . .168 F3
Poynings Rd
Crawley RH11 . . . . .17 E5
Poynings BN45 . . . . .148 C6
Poynter Rd BN3 . . . . .191 A8
Poyntz Ct PO19 . . . . .176 F3
Pratton Ave BN15. . . . . . .187 D7
Prawn Cl PO20. . . . . .212 C8
Prebendal Sch The
PO19. . . . . .176 F6
Precinct The PO21. . . . . . .200 F4
Prescott Gdns RH15. . . . .109 A3
PRESTON. 169 F1
Preston Ave BN16. . . . . . .205 D5
Preston Cir BN1. . . . . .213 B4
Preston Dro BN1. . . . . . . .169 F2
Preston Grange BN1 . . . .169 E1
Preston Hall BN16 . . . . . .205 F6
Preston Manor Mus★
BN1. . . . . .169 E1
Preston Mans **3** BN1 . . . .191 F8
Preston Paddock
BN16. . . . . .205 E5
Preston Park Ave
BN1. . . . . .169 F1
Preston Park Sta
BN1. . . . . .169 D2
Preston Rd BN1. . . . . .191 F8
Preston St BN1 . . . . .191 E5
Preston Village Mews
BN1. . . . . .169 E1
Prestonville Ct **2**
BN1. . . . . .191 E7
Prestonville Rd BN1 . . . . .213 A4
Prestwick Cl RH11 . . . . . . .17 D5
Prestwood Cl RH11 . . . . . . .5 B1
Prestwood La RH11 . . . . . .4 C3
Pretoria Ave GU29 . . . . . . .94 E7
Pretoria Rd **4** GU29 . . . . .94 E7
Priceholme RH17. . . . . .64 E7
Price Way RH17. . . . . .64 B7
Priest Croft Cl RH11. . . . . .18 A6
Priest House (Mus) The★
RH19. . . . . .42 E6
Priestlands Cl RH6. . . . . . . .1 F4
Priestley Way
Crawley RH10 . . . . .6 A3
Middleton-on-S PO22. . . . .202 D5
Prime Cl BN18. . . . . .180 E8
Primrose Ave RH6. . . . . . . .2 B1
Primrose Cl
Burgess Hill RH15. . . . . . . .108 D4
Crawley RH11 . . . . .18 B3
Rustington BN17 . . . . .205 A7
Primrose Copse RH12. . . . .36 E7
Primrose Ct BN44. . . . . . .145 D2
Primrose La GU33 . . . . .45 F4
Prince Albert St BN1. . . . .213 B2
Prince Ave BN15. . . . . . . .188 B5
Prince Charles Cl
BN42. . . . . .168 A1
Prince Of Wales Ct
BN3. . . . . .190 F6
Prince Regent's Cl
BN2. . . . . .192 E4
Prince Regent's Ct **2**
BN2. . . . . .192 E4
Princes Ave BN3. . . . . . . .191 A6
Princes Cres BN3. . . . . . . .191 A6
Prince's Cres BN2 . . . . . . .213 C5

Princes Croft PO21 . . . . . .200 A1
Princes Ct
6 Hove BN3. . . . . .191 A6
Shoreham-by-S BN43. . . . .188 D6
Prince's Dr PO18 . . . . .135 E1
Princes Gate BN11. . . . . . .185 F3
Prince's Ho BN1. . . . . .213 B2
Princes Rd GU32. . . . . .67 F4
Prince's Rd BN2 . . . . .192 B8
Princess Anne Rd
RH12. . . . . .33 D7
Princess Ave
Bognor Regis PO21 . . . . . .201 A2
Worthing BN13 . . . . .185 F5
Princess Ct
Haywards Heath RH16 . . . .87 F6
Worthing BN13 . . . . .185 F4
Princess Ho **20** PO21 . . . .201 D3
Princess Margaret Rd
RH12. . . . . .33 D7
Princes Sq BN3. . . . . .191 A6
Princess Rd RH11 . . . . .18 C6
Princess Royal Hospl RH16,
RH17. . . . . .88 A3
Prince's St BN2. . . . . .213 B2
Prince's Terr BN2 . . . . . . .192 C4
Prince William Cl
BN14. . . . . .186 A8
Prince William Ct **4**
PO21 . . . . .201 D3
Prings La RH13 . . . . .83 C8
Prinsep Rd BN3. . . . . .191 A8
Prinsted La PO10 . . . . . . .173 F7
Prior Pl PO19 . . . . .177 C8
Priors Acre PO18 . . . . .156 D7
Priors Cl
Breach PO10. . . . . .152 A1
Upper Beeding BN44. . . . .146 A2
Priors Leaze La PO18 . . . .152 C1
Priors Waye PO21. . . . . . .200 A2
Priors Wlk RH10 . . . . .18 F6
Priors Wood
Haslemere GU27 . . . . .26 F6
Kingsfold RH12 . . . . .15 B6
Priory Cl
Bognor Regis PO21 . . . . . .211 B8
Boxgrove PO18 . . . . .156 D3
Horley RH6. . . . . .1 F4
Lancing BN15. . . . . .187 B3
Worthing BN14 . . . . .186 A4
Priory Ct
17 Bognor Regis
PO21. . . . . .201 D3
Brighton BN1. . . . . .191 F8
7 Haywards Heath
RH16. . . . . .87 C2
Priory Field BN44. . . . . . .146 A2
Priory Flats GU29 . . . . .73 B1
Priory Gate **1** BN15. . . . .187 E6
Priory La PO19 . . . . .177 A7
Priory Rd
Arundel BN18 . . . . .159 F2
Burgess Hill RH15 . . . . . . .109 A1
Chichester PO19 . . . . .177 A7
Forest Row RH18. . . . . .23 D2
Hassocks BN6 . . . . .128 C5
Littlehampton BN16. . . . . .205 B6
Priory The
Brighton BN1. . . . . .169 D5
2 Hove BN3. . . . . .191 B5
Priory Way RH16. . . . . .87 F4
Proctor Cl RH10. . . . . .19 C4
Promenade PO21 . . . . . . .201 A2
Promenade The
Emsworth PO10. . . . . .173 B7
Littlehampton BN17. . . . . .204 E3
Pronger's Cnr RH13. . . . . .59 C2
Prospect Pl
Crawley RH11 . . . . .18 C6
3 Worthing BN11. . . . . .186 D1
Providence Pl
Brighton BN1. . . . . .213 B4
7 Chichester PO19 . . . .176 F7
Providence Terr
BN11. . . . . .186 E2
Providence The **6**
PO19. . . . . .176 F7
Pruetts La GU31, GU33 . . . .45 B1
Pryors Gn PO21 . . . . .200 C2
Pryors La PO21. . . . . .200 C1
Puckshott Way GU27. . . . .27 D8
Pudding La RH6. . . . . .4 E7
Puffin Hill RH10. . . . . .21 C5
Puffin Rd RH11. . . . . .17 D5
Pulborough Brooks Nature
Reserve★ RH20. . . . . .120 D7
Pulborough Cl BN2 . . . . . .192 F7
Pulborough Rd BN12. . . . .121 B2
Pulborough Sta RH20. . . . .100 A2
Pulborough Way
PO22. . . . . .202 D6
Pulens Cres GU31. . . . . . . .68 E4
Pulens La GU31. . . . . .68 D4
Pump Ho The BN3. . . . . . .190 D8
Punch Copse Rd RH10 . . . .18 F7
Punches La PO20 . . . . . . .199 D5
Punnetts Ct RH11. . . . . . . .17 F2
Purbeck Ho BN2 . . . . .213 C2
Purbeck Pl BN17. . . . . . . .204 C5
Purcell Rd RH11 . . . . .17 F3
Purley Cl RH10. . . . . .19 D3
Purrocks The GU32. . . . . . .68 D5
Purton Rd RH12. . . . . .36 B4
Putmans La GU31. . . . . . . .91 B7
Puttick Cl RH20. . . . . .121 E2
Puttocks Cl GU27. . . . . . . .26 D5

Pyecombe Ct **4** RH11.... 17 F3
Pyecombe St BN45..... 149 A6
Pyrford Cl PO21 .... 200 B2

Q

Quadrangle The
 2 Horley RH6............ 2 B3
 Nepcote BN14........... 163 E4
Quadrant The
 Keymer BN6........... 129 A4
 Worthing BN12.........185 C4
Quail Cl RH12............ 36 D7
Quakers La RH16 .... 88 A5
QUAKER'S PLATT 10 A8
Quantock Cl
 Crawley RH11 .... 18 B6
 Worthing BN13.........185 F9
Quantock Rd BN13......185 F8
Quantocks **2** BN17 .... 204 D6
Quarries The RH13........ 59 D6
Quarry Bank Rd BN1 ... 170 B2
Quarry Cl
 Burgess Hill RH15......109 D3
 Horsham RH12 .... 36 F6
Quarry Hill RH16........ 87 C6
Quarry La PO19.........177 C5
Quarry Lane Ind Est
 PO19.................177 C5
Quarry Rise RH19 .... 10 A3
Quarry Way RH13 .... 57 F2
Quarterbrass Farm Rd
 RH12................. 36 D7
Quarterdeck The
 PO21.................201 A2
Quarter Mile The
 RH13................. 57 D5
Quashetts The
 Worthing BN14........186 D4
 Worthing, Broadwater
 BN14................186 D5
Quay Ct BN43...........189 B6
Quayside BN17 ....204 B5
Quayside Bldgs BN41...190 D6
Quay The **5** BN43........189 A6
Quebec GU31........... 91 C7
Quebec Cl GU30 .... 25 C3
Quebec St BN2 ....213 C3
Queen Alexandra Ave
 BN3.................169 A3
Queen Caroline Cl
 BN3.................169 A3
Queen Elizabeth Ave
 RH15................109 A2
Queen Elizabeth II Silver
 Jubilee Sch RH13...... 36 F1
Queen Elizabeth Rd
 RH12................. 33 D7
Queen Mary Ave BN3 ...169 A3
Queen's Ave PO19 ......176 E4
Queensborough Ct **5**
 BN11................186 A3
Queensbury Mews
 BN1.................191 E5
QUEEN'S CORNER 71 E8
Queens Cres RH15 ......109 A2
Queens Ct RH13 .... 36 D1
Queen's Ct
 Haywards Heath RH16 .... 87 F6
 Horley RH6 .... 2 A3
Queensdown School Rd
 BN1, BN2.............170 D2
Queens Dr BN6 ....128 F4
Queens Fields E PO21 ... 200 F4
Queens Fields W
 PO21.................200 F4
Queens Fields Wlk
 PO21.................200 F4
Queens Gate RH6 .... 6 A8
Queen's Gdns
 Brighton BN1..........213 B3
 Hove BN3.............191 C6
 Stockbridge PO19 ......176 F4
Queen's Mans **2**
 BN11................186 C1
Queensmead
 Bognor Regis PO21 .....210 F8
 Worthing BN13.........185 E7
Queen's Par BN3 ....168 E2
Queen's Par BN15 ......187 E6
Queens Park Mews
 BN2.................192 C6
Queen's Park Prim Sch
 BN2.................192 C5
Queen's Park Rd BN2 ...192 C6
Queen's Park Rise
 BN2.................192 C6
Queen's Park Terr
 BN2.................192 C6
Queen's Pl
 Brighton BN1..........213 B4
 Hove BN3.............191 C6
 Shoreham-by-S BN43.....188 F7
Queen Sq BN1..........213 A2
Queens Rd
 Griggs Green GU30 ...... 24 C3
 Haywards Heath RH16 .... 87 E6
 Lancing BN15.........187 F5
 Petersfield GU32....... 67 F4
 Southwick BN42.......167 E1
Queen's Rd
 Brighton BN1..........213 A3
 East Grinstead RH19..... 9 E1
 Horley RH6 .... 2 A2
 Worthing BN11.........186 C1
Queens Sq RH10 .... 18 D6

Queen's Sq PO21 ....201 D3
Queens St GU29 .... 72 A2
Queen St
 Arundel BN18 ....160 B2
 Emsworth PO10........173 C8
 Horsham RH13 .... 36 D1
 Littlehampton BN17.....204 D5
 Worthing BN14.........186 C4
Queensway
 Bognor Regis, Aldwick
 PO21................200 E1
 Bognor Regis PO21.....201 C3
 Brighton BN2..........192 D6
 Crawley RH10 .... 18 E6
 East Grinstead RH19..... 9 E1
 Horsham RH13 .... 36 C1
 Lancing BN15.........187 E6
Queensway Ho **7**
 PO21.................201 C3
Queen's Wlk RH19 ....9 E1
Queen Victoria Ave
 BN3.................169 A3
Queen Victoria Hospl The
 RH19..................9 F3
Quell Farm Ind Est
 RH20................119 E4
Querneby Cl BN43......189 D7
Quest Cl PO19 ....177 B6
Quinta Carmen **10**
 BN11................186 B1
Quinton Fields PO10 ....151 C3

R

Racecourse Rd RH6 ...... 6 A8
Racecourse Way RH6 ......5 F8
Rackfield GU27 .... 26 D7
Rackham Cl
 Crawley RH11 .... 18 D4
 Worthing BN13.........185 F6
Rackham Rd
 Amberley BN18 ....140 F7
 3 Rustington BN16 .....205 B3
 Worthing BN13.........185 F6
Rackham St
 Amberley BN18,
 RH20................141 A8
 Rackham RH20 ....141 C8
Racton Rd PO10 ....151 C3
Radbone Cl BN14 ....186 E6
Radford Rd
 Bognor Regis PO21,
 PO22................201 B5
 Crawley RH6, RH10 ..... 6 C4
Radinden Dr BN3 ....169 D1
Radinden Manor Rd
 BN3.................191 D8
Radnor Cl BN13.........185 F5
Radnor Ho RH16 .... 87 D6
Radnor Rd BN13........185 F5
Raglan Ave BN13 ....185 E6
Raglan Ct
 Brighton BN1..........213 A2
 5 Worthing BN11........186 A2
Raglan Terr PO10 ....151 C1
Railey Rd RH10 .... 18 E7
Railway App
 East Grinstead RH19..... 9 E1
 Worthing BN11.........186 D3
Railway Cotts
 East Grinstead RH19..... 21 F3
 Horsted Keynes RH17.... 65 A8
Railway St BN1 ....213 A3
Railway Terr GU29 ...... 94 D7
Rainbow Way RH20 .....121 F3
Rake Bsns Pk GU33 ..... 46 B4
Rake CE Fst Sch GU33 ... 46 B5
RAKE HANGER 45 E2
Rake Rd
 Liss GU33 .... 45 D4
 Milland GU30.......... 47 A2
Rakers Ridge RH12 ..... 36 D5
Raleigh Cl BN43.........188 F6
Raleigh Cres BN12 .....185 D4
Raleigh Rd RH10 .... 6 A3
Raleigh Rd PO21........200 C3
Raleigh Way BN12 .....185 C4
Raleigh Wlk RH10....... 18 E1
Rambledown La
 RH20................121 C6
Ramblers Ct RH12 ...... 35 E3
Ramblers The **13**
 BN16................206 A4
Ramblers Way RH11 .... 39 B8
Ramilles Gdns PO22....202 C5
Ramsdean Rd GU32 ..... 67 B2
Ramsey Cl
 Horley RH6 ....1 F3
 Horsham RH12 .... 36 D5
Ramsey Ct **18** RH11 .... 18 B1
Ramshill Cl GU32....... 68 C4
Ramshill GU31..........68 C4
RAMSNEST COMMON
 ....29 A6
Rams Wlk GU32.........68 B3
Randall Scofield Ct
 RH10................. 19 A7
Randiddles Cl BN6 .....128 B4
Ranelagh Villas BN3 ...191 B8
Rangers Lo RH13 .... 36 E2
Ranmore Ct RH11....... 39 C8
Ransome Cl RH11.......17 E3
Ranville Cl GU28........97 E7
Ranworth Cl PO22 .....201 F5
Rapeland Hill RH12 .... 15 F2
Raphael Rd BN3 ....190 F7
Rapley Ave RH20.......121 B2

Rascals Cl RH13 .... 81 F7
Rastrick Cl RH15........108 F1
Ratham La
 Broadbridge PO18......175 C8
 West Ashling PO18......153 C1
Rathbone Ho RH11..... 18 B1
Rathlin Rd RH11 .... 18 B3
Raughmere Ct PO18 ....154 F4
Raughmere Dr PO18 ....154 F4
Raven Cl
 Horsham RH12 .... 36 E6
 Turners Hill RH10 ...... 21 C5
Raven La RH11.......... 18 C8
Ravensbourne Ave
 BN43................166 F1
Ravensbourne Cl **11**
 BN43................166 F1
Ravensbourne Ct
 BN2.................193 D8
Ravenscroft PO20......142 D8
Ravens Croft **7** BN16 ...205 C4
Ravenscroft RH12 ...... 36 C3
Raven's Rd BN43........188 F7
Ravens Way PO22......201 B6
Ravenswood BN6 ....128 C4
Ravenswood Ct BN13 ...186 A4
Ravenswood Dr BN2 ...193 F6
Ravenswood Rd RH15 ...109 B3
Ravenwood Ct PO21 ....200 E2
Rawlinson Rd RH10 ..... 19 D4
Raworth Cl RH10....... 19 C4
Rawson Ct **10** BN16 .....205 B4
Rawson Villas BN16.....205 C6
Ray Cl GU31 .... 68 C5
Raycroft Cl PO21.......200 A4
Rayden Cl BN17.........204 E5
Raylands Park Cvn Site
 RH13................. 58 B2
Raymede Ho BN11 ......186 B3
Raymer Wlk RH6........ 2 C4
Rayner Ct BN5.........125 E4
Reading Rd BN2 ....192 F4
Readon Cl GU31 .... 68 C4
Readon Ho GU31........ 68 C4
Reapers Cl RH12....... 36 D5
Record Rd PO10 ....151 A1
Rectory Cl
 Ashington RH20........123 A5
 Hove BN3.............190 D7
 Pulborough RH20.......100 C2
 Shoreham-by-S BN43....189 D7
 Storrington RH20.......121 D1
Rectory Cotts **1**
 RH20................121 D1
Rectory Ct **15** BN43.....189 C8
Rectory Farm Rd
 BN15................187 B7
Rectory Gdns BN14.....186 C5
Rectory La
 Angmering BN16 ......183 F5
 Ashington RH20........122 E6
 Bramshott GU30....... 25 D7
 Charlwood RH6 .... 4 D7
 Church Norton PO20.....210 B3
 Crawley RH11 .... 17 F8
 Pulborough RH20.......100 C2
 Rusper RH11............4 F1
Rectory Mews **1**
 BN14................186 A5
Rectory Pl RH20 ....122 F5
Rectory Rd
 Shoreham-by-S BN43....189 D7
 Storrington RH20.......121 D1
 Worthing BN13, BN14...186 A5
Rectory Wlk
 Lancing BN15.........187 C7
 Storrington RH20.......121 D1
Red Acre Ct PO21.......201 D4
Red Admiral St RH12....36 E5
Redcotts **1** BN11......186 B2
Redcross St BN1........213 B3
Red Deer CI RH13....... 37 B4
Redditch Cl RH11 ...... 17 E2
Redehall Ind Pk RH6..... 7 C7
Redehall Rd RH6........ 7 C8
REDFORD 48 A1
Redford Ave RH12 ...... 36 B4
Redgarth Ct RH19.......9 B3
Redgrave Dr RH10 ..... 19 D5
Redhill Cl BN1..........169 C5
Redhill Distribution Ctr
 RH1.................. 2 A8
Redhill Dr BN1.........169 C5
Redhill Rd PO9 ....130 D1
Red Ho BN13 ....186 A4
Red House Cl GU31..... 70 B4
Red House Farm BN6 ...148 F7
Red House Farm Camping
 & Cvn Site PO20......208 D8
Redhouse Mews GU30 ... 25 C2
Redkiln Cl RH13 .... 36 F4
Redkiln Close Trad Est
 RH13................. 36 F3
Redkiln Way RH13 ...... 36 F3
Red La RH13............ 81 D1
Redlands La
 New Brighton PO10.....151 B4
 Shipton Green PO20 ....196 F3
Red Lion St GU29 ...... 94 F7
Red Oak Ct GU29 ...... 73 A2
Red Ridges PO21.......201 A2
Red River Ct RH12 ..... 36 B5
Redshank Ct **5** RH11 ... 17 D5
Red Square Ret Pk
 BN14................186 E7
Redvers Rd BN2 ....170 D1

Pye–Riv 243

Richmond Villas
 PO22................201 F3
Richmond Way RH19 ... 22 F8
Rickfield RH19.......... 18 A5
Rickman's La
 Kirdford RH14 .... 53 B8
 Plaistow RH14 .... 30 F2
Rickwood RH6..........2 B4
Riddens The RH12 ..... 33 A6
Ride The
 Brighton BN1..........169 F1
 Ifold RH14............ 31 C2
Ridge Cl BN41 ....168 A4
Ridge Common La
 GU32................. 67 E6
Ridgedale RH10........ 21 B8
Ridgehurst Dr RH12..... 35 F1
Ridge Rd BN1 ....171 C7
Ridgeside RH10........ 18 F6
Ridgeside Ave BN1.....169 E5
Ridge The RH12........ 33 B8
Ridge Top La
 Froxfield Green GU32 ... 67 B7
 Froxfield Green GU32 ... 67 C7
Ridge View BN1 ....170 E5
Ridgeway
 East Grinstead RH19 ... 22 E7
 Southwick BN41, BN42 ...167 F1
Ridge Way RH17 ...... 88 B2
Ridgeway Cl BN42......167 F1
Ridgeway Gdns BN2 ...193 E7
Ridgeway Ho RH6...... 2 A1
Ridgeway Office Pk
 GU31................. 67 F2
Ridgeway The
 Burgess Hill RH15......109 B4
 Chichester PO19 ......176 E7
 Fernhurst GU27....... 49 B6
 Horley RH6 .... 2 A1
 Horsham RH12 .... 36 B4
Ridgewood Ave BN2 ...194 C3
Ridgway Cl BN2 ....193 D8
Ridgway Paddock
 BN7.................172 E6
Ridgway The
 Bognor Regis PO22.....202 A4
 Woodingdean BN2......193 D8
Ridings The
 Bognor Regis PO21.....200 C1
 Burgess Hill RH15......109 C2
 Crawley RH10 .... 19 D7
 Fontwell BN18 ....158 A2
 Liss GU33 .... 45 D4
 Littlehampton BN16.....205 F4
 Ovingdean BN2........193 C4
 Steyning BN44.........145 D1
Ridley Ct RH10......... 19 D8
Ridleys RH19 .... 42 E6
Rife La PO20...........212 B8
Rifeside Gdns BN12.....206 E7
Rife Way
 Bognor Regis PO22.....201 F4
 Ferring BN12..........206 E6
Rigden Rd BN3 ....169 C1
Rikkyo Sch-in-England
 RH14................. 32 D8
Riley Rd BN2 ....170 C1
Rillside RH10.......... 19 A3
Rill Wlk RH11 .... 10 B1
Rimmer Cl RH11....... 39 B8
Ringley Ave RH6 .... 2 A2
Ringley Oak RH12....... 36 F4
Ringley Rd RH12 ...... 36 E4
Ringmer Cl BN1 ....170 F4
Ringmer Dr BN1 ....170 F4
Ringmer Rd
 Brighton BN1..........170 E4
 Worthing BN13 ....185 E6
Ring Rd BN15...........165 F1
Ring Rd N RH6......... 6 C8
Ring Rd S RH6.......... 6 C7
Ringwood Cl RH10 ..... 18 E4
Ripley Rd BN11 ....185 F4
Ripon Gdns PO21 ......200 E3
Rise The
 Crawley RH10 .... 19 D6
 East Grinstead RH19 ... 22 F8
 Haywards Heath RH16 ... 88 B5
 Partridge Green RH13 ...105 A4
 Portslade-by-S BN41 ...167 F2
Rissom Ct BN1.........169 E2
Ritchie Cl RH10 .... 19 C2
Rival Moor Rd GU31.... 68 E2
Riverbank Bsns Ctr
 BN43................188 E7
River Cl BN43 ....188 E6
RIVERHILL 98 E7
Riverhill La GU28, RH20 ...98 E7
River La
 River GU28 .... 74 E3
 Watersfield RH20 ......119 B4
Rivermead RH20........100 D1
River Mead
 Crawley RH11 .... 5 A1
 Horsham RH12 .... 36 B1
Rivermead Ct PO10 ....151 C3
River Rd
 Arundel BN18 ....160 B2
 Littlehampton BN17.....204 C5
Riverside
 Chichester PO19 ......177 B7
 Forest Row RH18.......23 E3
 Horley RH6 .... 2 A1
 Horsham RH12 .... 36 A2
 Littlehampton BN17.....204 C4

Redwing Cl
 Horsham RH13 .... 36 F3
 Littlehampton BN17.....204 C8
Redwood Cl
 Crawley RH10 .... 18 E8
 Worthing BN13 ....185 C6
Redwood Ct BN17......204 F5
Redwood Dr RH16 ..... 87 D3
Redwood Manor GU27 ... 27 C7
Redwood Pl PO21.......200 E2
Reed Cl
 Hunston PO20.........199 A8
 Storrington RH20.......121 C1
Readings RH11 .... 17 D4
Reed Pond Wlk RH16 ... 88 A4
Reeds La
 Liss GU33 .... 45 F6
 Southwater Street RH13 ...58 B3
Reed's La BN6..........127 B8
Reef Cl BN17 ....204 F4
Rees Cl BN13 ....185 B7
Reeves Hill BN1........170 D5
Reeves Ho **2** RH16 .... 19 B6
Refectory Rd BN1......171 B7
Regal Dr **10** RH19 ..... 22 F8
Regency Ct
 Brighton BN1..........169 D3
 Ferring BN12..........206 F6
 Worthing BN13 ....186 A6
Regency Mews **15**
 BN1.................191 E5
Regency Rd BN1 ....213 A2
Regency Sq BN1........191 E5
Regency Way BN2 .....193 E8
Regent Arc BN1 ....213 B2
Regent Bsns Pk RH15 ...108 E2
Regent Cl BN15.........188 B6
Regent Hill BN1 ....213 A2
Regent Mews
 11 Bognor Regis
 PO21................201 B2
 Petersfield GU32....... 67 F4
Regent Row BN1 ....213 A2
Regents Cl RH11....... 18 C2
Regents Mews RH6 ..... 2 A3
Regent St BN1 ....213 B2
Regents Way PO21.....200 F4
Regis Ave PO21........211 B8
Regis Bsns Ctr PO22 ...201 D6
Regis Ct
 Bognor Regis PO21.....201 D3
 Worthing BN11.........186 A1
Regisgate **10** PO21......201 C4
Regis Ho **17** PO21.....201 C3
Regnum Ct PO19.......177 A7
Reigate Cl RH10........ 6 D1
Reigate Ct BN11 ....185 F3
Reigate Rd
 Brighton BN1..........169 D1
 Hookwood RH2, RH6 .... 1 C6
 Worthing BN11.........185 F4
Renfields RH16 .... 87 C3
Renoir Ct PO22.........201 A6
Renoir Mews PO22.....201 A6
Renton Cl RH14....... 79 D8
Reservoir La GU32 ..... 68 B6
Retreat The RH14 ...... 31 F5
REWELL HILL 159 A7
Rew La PO19 ....154 F3
Rex Ct GU27 .... 26 F6
Reydon Ho BN11.......186 F3
Reynard Cl RH12....... 37 B5
Reynolds La BN18......158 D4
Reynolds Pl RH11 ...... 18 C7
Reynolds Rd
 Crawley RH10 .... 18 C7
 Hove BN3.............190 F7
Rhodes Way RH10 ..... 18 F3
Ribbetts Cotts BN6.....128 A5
Ribbetts Ho BN6 ....128 A5
Rices Hill RH19 ....9 E1
Richard Allen Ct BN2 ...170 C1
Richard Ho **6** PO21.....201 C2
Richardson Ct
 17 Crawley RH11 ..... 18 B1
 5 Hove BN3..........190 F7
Richardson Rd BN3 ....190 F7
Richborough Ct RH11 ...18 C6
Richmond Ave
 Bognor Regis PO21.....201 B2
 Chichester PO19 ......155 A1
Richmond Ave W
 PO21................201 A3
Richmond Cl **1** BN16 ...205 E6
Richmond Ct
 Crawley RH10 .... 18 E5
 9 Hove BN3..........191 E7
 3 Rustington BN16 .....205 B5
 Worthing BN11.........186 C2
Richmond Gdns **2**
 BN2.................213 C3
Richmond Ho **11**
 PO21................201 C3
Richmond Hts **12**
 BN2.................213 C3
Richmond Par BN2 ....213 C3
Richmond Pl BN2.......213 B3
Richmond Rd
 16 Bognor Regis
 PO21................201 C3
 Brighton BN2..........192 B8
 Horsham RH12 .... 36 D4
 Westerton PO18 ......155 F3
 Worthing BN11.........186 D2
Richmond Rd N **6**
 PO21................201 D4
Richmond Sq RH19 .... 9 D2
Richmond St BN2 ......213 C3
Richmond Terr BN2....213 C4

Riverside *continued*
Shoreham-by-S BN43..... 188 F6
Southwick BN42 .... 189 E7
Storrington RH20........ 121 D2
Upper Beeding BN44..... 146 A2
Riverside Bsns Ctr
BN43.................. 189 A7
Riverside Caravan Pk
BN44.................. 146 A2
Riverside CI GU33....... 45 B4
Riverside Ct RH20....... 100 A1
Riverside Ho BN43...... 188 E6
Riverside Ind Est
BN17.................. 204 B5
Riverside Rd BN43...... 188 F6
Riverside Terr 3
PO10.................. 173 C8
Riverside Wlk GU31..... 68 D3
River's Rd RH16........ 63 D3
River St PO10......... 151 D4
River Terr BN18........ 160 B2
Rivoli Ct BN11......... 186 D3
Rixons CI RH17......... 65 C5
Rixons Orch RH17...... 65 C5
Robell Way RH20....... 121 F3
Robert Lo BN2......... 192 F4
Roberts CI RH13....... 57 F4
Roberts Marine Mans
BN11................. 185 F2
Robertson Rd BN1..... 169 D1
Roberts Rd BN15...... 187 E4
Robert St BN1......... 213 B3
Robert Way RH12...... 36 F7
Robin CI
Crawley RH11 .... 18 C8
1 East Grinstead RH19....9 F2
Littlehampton BN17..... 204 C8
Southwater RH13....... 58 A2
Robin Davis CI BN2..... 170 E1
Robin Dene BN2....... 192 E4
Robin Hood La RH12.... 35 F5
Robinia Lo BN1........ 169 E2
Robin Rd RH15........ 108 D2
Robin Rise RH16....... 87 F3
Robin Row RH10....... 21 C5
ROBINS.............. 71 D7
Robin's CI PO20....... 212 E8
Robins Dr PO20........ 200 D3
Robins La GU29........ 71 D7
Robinson CI
4 Lancing BN15....... 187 E6
Selsey PO20........... 212 E8
Robinson Ho RH10..... 18 D5
Robinson Way PO20... 208 B6
Robins Row BN14..... 168 A1
Robinswood Ct RH12... 36 F4
Robson Ct BN12....... 185 E4
Robson Rd BN12....... 185 E3
Rochester CI
Chichester PO19 ...... 154 F1
5 Hove BN3.......... 191 D6
Worthing BN13......... 185 B6
Rochester Ct 4 BN3... 191 D6
Rochester Gdns BN3... 191 D6
Rochester St BN2...... 192 D5
Rochester Way PO21... 200 E3
ROCK................ 143 E8
Rockall CI BN17....... 205 A7
Rockall Way PO18..... 175 D7
Rock CI 12 BN42...... 189 E7
Rockdene CI RH19..... 10 A1
Rockeries The 11 GU29.. 94 E7
Rock Gdns PO21....... 201 C2
Rock Gr BN2.......... 192 E4
Rockingham CI BN13... 185 E7
Rockingham Ct BN13... 185 E7
Rock La RH20......... 122 E1
Rockpit Cotts GU33.... 45 D4
Rock PI BN2.......... 213 C1
Rock Rd RH20......... 122 C2
Rocksacre Cotts
BN15................. 186 F7
Rocks La RH17........ 40 F1
Rock St BN2.......... 192 E4
Rocks The RH19....... 23 D6
Rockwood Ct PO10..... 151 B1
Rodgate La GU27...... 28 E5
Rodmell Ave BN2...... 194 D1
Rodmell PI BN1....... 170 A6
Rodmell Rd BN13...... 185 E6
Rodney CI PO21....... 200 C3
Rodney Cres BN18..... 181 D4
Roebuck CI RH13...... 37 B4
Roedale Ct 1 BN1..... 170 B1
Roedale Rd BN1....... 170 B1
ROEDEAN............ 193 B4
Roedean Cres BN2..... 193 A4
Roedean Ct BN2....... 192 F4
Roedean Hts BN2...... 193 A4
Roedean Path BN2..... 193 A3
Roedean Rd
Brighton BN2.......... 192 F4
Worthing BN13......... 185 E2
Roedean Sch BN2...... 193 C3
Roedean Terr BN2..... 193 B3
Roedean Vale BN2..... 193 B3
Roedean Way BN2..... 193 B3
Roedeer Copse GU27... 26 E6
ROFFEY.............. 37 A5
Roffey CI RH6..........1 F3
Roffey Cnr RH12....... 37 B4
Roffey's CI RH10........7 A4
Roffye Ct RH12........ 37 A4

Rogate CE Prim Sch
GU31................. 70 B4
Rogate CI
Lancing BN15......... 187 B7
Worthing BN13........ 186 A6
Rogate Rd BN13...... 186 A6
Roger's La BN14...... 163 E4
Rokewood Dr RH11......5 A1
Rolfe Dr RH15........ 109 D3
Rollaston Pk BN18..... 181 C2
Rolston Rd GU27...... 26 F6
Romaine CI RH15...... 109 C5
Roman Acre BN17..... 204 C6
Roman Ave BN16...... 206 A8
Roman Cres BN42..... 189 E8
Roman Ct RH15....... 109 A3
Roman Fields PO21.... 201 A4
Roman Landing PO20.. 196 B2
Roman Rd
Bramber BN44......... 145 E3
Hove BN3............. 190 D6
Southwick BN42....... 189 E8
Roman Way
Billingshurst RH14...... 55 D1
Fishbourne PO19....... 176 B6
Southwick BN42....... 189 E8
Roman Wlk BN15...... 187 B7
Romany CI BN41...... 190 B8
Romany Rd BN13..... 185 B6
Romney Broadwalk
PO22................ 201 B6
Romney Ct BN11...... 185 F2
Romney Garth PO20... 212 F7
Romney Rd
Rottingdean BN2....... 194 A1
Worthing BN11........ 185 E2
Romsey CI BN1....... 170 C2
Rona CI RH11......... 18 B3
Rookcross La RH13.... 104 A4
Rookery CI BN11...... 169 E1
Rookery La PO20..... 209 F8
Rookery The
Lumley PO10.......... 151 C1
Selsey PO20.......... 212 F8
Rookery Way RH16.... 87 E1
Rookes Mews GU31.... 68 C4
Rook Way RH12....... 36 F6
Rookwood La PO20... 196 D4
Rookwood Pk RH12.... 35 F3
Rookwood Rd PO20... 196 C2
Ropeland Way RH12... 36 E7
Ropes La GU27....... 49 C5
Ropetackle BN43...... 188 E7
Rope Wlk
Littlehampton BN17.... 204 C4
Shoreham-by-S BN43... 188 E7
Rosamund Rd RH10... 19 B3
Rosary Ct RH15....... 109 B2
Rosary The RH13..... 104 F3
Rose Ave PO22....... 202 F5
Rosebarn CI RH15.... 109 C1
Rosebery Ave
Woodingdean BN2..... 193 C8
Worthing BN12........ 185 E3
Rose Cottage La RH17.. 62 A5
Rose Cotts
Danehill RH17......... 66 A4
Forest Row RH18...... 23 E3
Handcross RH17....... 61 C8
Horsham RH12......... 37 D7
Rosecroft CI BN15..... 187 E5
Rose Ct
Bognor Regis PO21..... 200 D3
Chichester PO19....... 177 A4
Hassocks BN6......... 128 E4
8 Littlehampton BN17.. 204 D5
2 Worthing BN11..... 187 B3
Rosedale CI RH11..... 18 A4
Rosedene CI BN2..... 193 E6
Rose Garden The★
PO20................ 176 C3
ROSE GREEN......... 200 C2
Rose Green Inf Sch
PO21................ 200 C2
Rose Green Jun Sch
PO21................ 200 C3
Rose Green Rd
Bognor Regis PO21..... 200 C3
Bognor Regis PO21..... 200 D3
Rosehill RH14........ 55 D1
Rose Hill BN2........ 213 C4
Rose Hill CI BN1...... 213 B4
Rose Hill Ct BN1...... 213 B4
Rose Hill Terr BN1.... 213 B4
Roseleigh Gdns RH17.. 88 F3
Rosemary Ave BN44... 145 E4
Rosemary CI
Bognor Regis PO21..... 200 C3
Bramber BN44......... 145 E4
Haywards Heath RH16... 87 B6
Petworth GU28........ 97 F8
Rosemary Ct
Haslemere GU27....... 27 C7
Horley RH6........... 1 E4
Rosemary Dr BN43.... 167 C1
Rosemary Ho 4 RH10... 6 A1
Rosemary La
Alfold GU6........... 31 E8
Charlwood RH6......... 4 E7
Horley RH6............ 2 B3
Petworth GU28........ 97 F8
Rosemarys Ctyd GU29.. 94 F8
Rosemead BN17...... 204 C5
Rosemead Gdns RH10.. 18 E5
Rose PI BN17......... 205 B7
Rose Terr PO22...... 180 D6

Rose Wlk
Burgess Hill RH15...... 109 C7
Worthing BN12........ 185 C2
Rosewood GU27....... 27 C5
Rosier Commercial Ctr
RH14................. 79 F7
Rosier Way RH14...... 79 E6
Roslan Ct RH6..........2 B2
Rossalyn CI PO21..... 200 B3
Ross CI
Bognor Regis PO21..... 200 B2
Crawley RH10......... 18 F3
Ross Ct 5 RH6..........2 B3
Rossiter Rd BN15..... 187 E8
Rosslyn Ave BN43..... 189 A7
Rosslyn Ct BN43...... 188 F7
Rosslyn Rd BN43..... 188 F7
Rossmore CI RH10......6 D2
Rostock Ct PO20..... 208 B6
Rosvara Ave PO20.... 179 D7
Rotary Ho BN15...... 187 E4
Rotary Lo
Brighton BN1......... 170 E6
Worthing BN11........ 186 B3
Rotary Point BN41.... 168 B1
Rothbury Rd BN3..... 190 D7
Rotherbank Farm La
GU33................ 45 C6
Rotherbridge La GU28.. 97 E5
Rotherbrook Ct GU31... 67 F2
Rother CI
Petersfield GU31...... 68 E4
Storrington RH20...... 121 F3
Rothercombe La GU32.. 67 C4
Rother Cres RH11..... 17 F5
Rotherfield CI BN1..... 170 B6
Rotherfield Cres BN1.. 170 B5
Rother Ho GU33....... 45 B3
Rother La GU31........ 71 A1
Rotherley 1 GU32..... 68 A4
Rothermead GU28..... 97 E7
Rothervale RH6..........1 F5
Rothesay CI BN13..... 185 E5
Rothley Chase RH16... 87 F4
Rotten Row PO20..... 198 B3
Rottingdean PI BN2.... 193 H4
Rotyngs The BN2..... 193 F2
Rough Field RH19.......9 D4
Rough Way RH12...... 36 F5
Roundabout Copse
RH20................ 121 D5
Roundabout Cotts
RH12................ 33 C5
Roundabout La RH20.. 121 D6
Roundabouts The
GU33................ 45 C5
ROUND HILL.......... 192 B8
Round Hill Cres BN2... 192 B8
Round Hill Rd 2 BN2.. 192 B8
Round Hill St 3 BN2.. 192 B8
Roundhouse Mdw
PO10................ 173 C7
Roundle Ave PO22.... 202 C6
Roundle Rd PO22..... 202 C5
Roundle Sq PO22..... 202 B5
Roundle Square Rd
PO22................ 202 B5
Round Piece La PO20... 212 B8
Roundstone By-Pass Rd
BN16................ 206 A7
Roundstone Cres
BN16................ 206 A6
Roundstone Dr BN16... 206 A6
Roundstone House Cvn Pk
BN16................ 206 A7
Roundstone La BN16... 206 A8
Roundstone Pk RH13... 57 F3
Roundstone Way
PO20................ 212 F8
ROUNDSTREET COMMON
.... 54 C6
Roundway
Brighton BN1......... 170 E5
Haywards Heath RH16... 87 C1
Roundway Ct 2 RH10.. 18 D8
Roundway The BN16... 205 D4
Roundwood BN13..... 185 F9
Roundwood La RH16... 87 F8
Rowan Ave BN3...... 168 E1
Rowan CI
Crawley RH10......... 18 F6
Haywards Heath RH16... 88 B4
Horsham RH12......... 37 B5
Portslade-by-S BN41... 168 A1
Storrington RH20...... 121 F2
Rowan Ct
Billingshurst RH14..... 55 D1
Brighton BN1......... 169 E1
Rowan Dr RH14....... 55 D1
Rowan Ho
6 Brighton BN2...... 213 C4
1 Rustington BN16... 205 C5
Worthing BN12........ 185 A5
Rowans BN43......... 188 E8
Rowans The
Burgess Hill RH15..... 108 D4
Hurstpierpoint BN6.... 128 A7
Worthing BN11........ 186 A2
Rowan Tree CI GU33... 45 C4
Rowan Way
Angmering BN16....... 206 A8
Bognor Regis PO22..... 201 C7
Horsham RH12......... 37 C5
Ovingdean BN2........ 193 E4
Rowan Wlk RH10..... 21 C8
Rowena Ct 4 RH12.... 36 A1
Rowfant Bsns Ctr
RH10................ 20 E6

Rowfant CI RH10...... 19 E6
Row Hill La RH17...... 62 E7
Rowhook Hill RH12.... 34 F8
Rowhook Rd
Rowhook RH12......... 13 E1
Slinfold RH12......... 35 A8
Rowland CI RH10........7 E5
Rowlands Castle Rd
Blendworth PO8....... 130 B6
Blendworth PO8....... 130 B7
Rowlands Castle Sta
PO9................. 130 E2
Rowlands Ct BN11.... 186 C1
Rowlands Rd
Horsham RH12......... 37 A6
Worthing BN11........ 186 B1
Rowner Rd RH14...... 55 A2
Rowplatt CI RH19.......8 E4
Rowplatt La RH19.......8 E4
Roxburgh CI BN13.... 185 F8
Royal Alexandra Children's
Hospl BN2............ 192 D4
Royal Arc BN11....... 186 C1
Royal Arms Ho 10
PO19................ 177 A6
Royal Bay Ct PO21.... 200 D1
Royal Bldgs BN15..... 187 C4
Royal CI PO19........ 177 C6
Royal Cres BN2....... 192 C4
Royal Crescent Mans 10
BN2................. 192 C4
Royal Crescent Mews 8
BN2................. 192 C4
Royal Gdns PO9...... 130 C1
Royal George Ct
RH15................ 108 F3
Royal George Par
BN43................ 167 C1
Royal George Rd
RH15................ 108 E3
Royal Oak Cotts BN45.. 148 C5
Royal Oak Ho RH10... 21 B7
Royal Par PO21....... 201 A6
Royal Pavilion★ BN1.. 213 B2
Royal Sussex Cty Hospl
BN2................. 192 D4
Royce CI PO20........ 196 C1
Royce Rd RH10..........6 A3
Royce Way PO20..... 196 C1
Royles CI BN2........ 194 A2
Royston CI RH10........6 A2
Roystons The BN16.... 205 F4
Ruckmans La RH5..... 14 B7
Rucrofts CI PO21...... 200 F3
Rudd Ho BN13....... 185 E8
Rudford Ind Est BN18.. 181 D2
Rudge Ho 2 RH19.......9 F1
Rudgwick Ave BN12... 185 A3
Rudgwick CI BN16.... 205 B4
Rudgwick Keep RH6.....2 C4
Rudgwick Prim Sch
RH12................ 33 D7
Rudgwick Rd RH11.... 17 F7
Rudkin PI PO19...... 176 A8
Rudwick's CI PO22.... 202 C4
Rudwick Way PO22... 202 C4
Rudyard CI BN2...... 193 E8
Rudyard Kipling Prim Sch
BN2................. 193 E7
Rudyard Rd BN2...... 193 E8
Rufwood RH10....... 21 A8
Rugby CI
5 Brighton BN2...... 192 E4
3 Worthing BN11.... 186 A3
Rugby PI BN2........ 192 E4
Rugby Rd
Brighton BN1......... 170 A1
Worthing BN11........ 186 A3
Ruislip Gdns PO21.... 200 C2
Rumbolds CI PO19.... 177 C5
Rumbolds Hill GU29... 94 F7
Rumbolds La RH16.... 87 D2
Rumboldswyke CE Inf Sch
PO19................ 177 C5
Rummers The PO19... 154 F2
Runcorn CI RH11...... 17 E2
Runcton La PO20..... 199 E7
Runnymede Ct PO21.. 200 F5
Runshooke Ct 9 RH11.. 18 A3
Rusbridge CI PO21.... 200 D4
Rushams Rd RH12.... 36 B3
Rushes Ct GU32...... 68 A4
Rushes Farm GU32.... 68 A4
Rushes Rd GU32...... 68 A4
Rushes The RH16..... 88 C4
Rushetts PI RH11.......5 C1
Rushetts Rd RH11.......5 B1
Rushfield Rd GU33.... 45 B3
Rushlake CI BN1...... 170 E5
Rushlake Rd BN1..... 170 E5
Rushwood CI RH16.... 88 B4
Ruskin CI
Crawley RH10..........6 C1
Selsey PO20.......... 212 F7
Ruskin PI BN3........ 190 F7
Ruskin Rd
Hove BN3............. 190 F8
Worthing BN14........ 186 F4
Rusper Prim Sch RH12.. 16 C7
Rusper Rd
Brighton BN1......... 170 D6
Crawley RH11......... 17 D7
Faygate RH12......... 16 A1
Horsham RH12......... 36 F6
Kingsfold RH5........ 15 E8
Newdigate RH12, RH5....3 C4
Worthing BN13........ 185 E4
Rusper Rd S BN13.... 185 F6

Ruspers RH15........ 109 D2
Ruspers Keep RH11.... 17 F7
Russell CI BN14...... 186 E5
Russell Cres 1 BN1... 213 A4
Russell Ct
5 Lancing BN15...... 187 E5
10 Midhurst GU29.... 94 E7
Russell Ho 9 GU29.... 94 E7
Russell Mews 14 BN1.. 191 E5
Russell PI
7 Bognor Regis
PO21................ 201 D3
Brighton BN1......... 213 A2
Russell Rd
Brighton BN1......... 213 A2
East Wittering PO20... 207 E2
Russell's CI BN16..... 206 B6
Russells Cres RH6.......2 A2
Russells Dr BN15..... 187 E5
Russell Sq BN1....... 213 A2
Russell St PO19...... 177 C6
Russell Way
Crawley RH10......... 19 A5
Petersfield GU31...... 68 C2
Russet CI RH6..........2 C3
Russet Gdns PO10.... 173 D8
Russett Ct
Fernhurst GU27....... 49 E5
Horsham RH12......... 37 A4
Russett PI RH14...... 53 A3
Russ Hill RH6..........4 C5
Russ Hill Cotts RH6....4 C6
Russ Hill Rd RH6.......4 C6
Rustington Com Prim Sch
BN16................ 205 B6
Rustington Rd BN1.... 170 A5
Rustington Retail Pk
BN16................ 205 D7
Rustington Trad Est
BN16................ 205 D7
Rustlings CI RH16..... 88 B5
Ruston Ave BN16..... 205 D5
Ruston CI RH10...... 19 C3
Ruston Pk BN16...... 205 E5
Rutherford Way RH10...6 A3
Rutherford Way Ind Est
RH10.................6 A3
Rutherwick CI RH6......1 F3
Ruthven CI RH17...... 86 F7
Rutland Ct BN3...... 190 F6
Rutland Gdns BN3.... 190 F7
Rutland Rd BN3...... 191 A7
Rutland Way PO19... 177 D8
Rydal CI
Crawley RH11......... 17 D4
Littlehampton BN17.... 205 A4
Ryde Ct BN3......... 168 D1
Ryde Rd BN2......... 192 D7
Ryders Way RH12..... 36 F7
Rydon Com Coll
RH20................ 122 A2
Rye Ash RH10........ 19 A7
Ryebank Cvn Site
BN18................ 202 F7
Rye CI
Saltdean BN2......... 194 F2
Worthing BN11........ 186 A1
Ryecroft
12 Brighton BN2..... 192 F5
Haywards Heath RH16... 87 E3
Ryecroft CI BN12..... 185 C2
Ryecroft Ct BN15.... 187 E5
Ryecroft Dr RH12..... 36 A3
Ryecroft Gdns BN12... 185 C3
Ryecroft La RH20..... 121 D1
Ryecroft Mdw RH13... 59 C6
Ryecroft Rd RH17..... 85 C3
Rye Farm La RH13.... 57 A2
Ryefield CI GU31..... 68 E3
Ryelands
Crawley RH11......... 18 A5
Horley RH6............2 C4
Ryelands Dr BN2..... 170 D3

S

Sabey Ct 16 PO21..... 201 D3
Sabre Rd PO10....... 173 C2
Sack La PO22........ 179 E2
Sackville CI RH19........9 C3
Sackville Coll★ RH19....9 F1
Sackville Cres BN14... 186 E4
Sackville Ct 3 RH19... 22 F8
Sackville Gdns
East Grinstead RH19.....9 C3
Hove BN3............. 190 F6
Sackville La RH19.......9 C3
Sackville Rd
Hove BN3............. 191 A7
Worthing BN14........ 186 E4
Sackville Sch RH19.... 10 A1
Sackville Trad Est
BN3................. 191 B8
Sackville Way BN14... 186 E4
Saddle La PO20...... 212 D8
Saddler Row RH10.... 18 D3
Saddlers CI
Billingshurst RH14..... 79 C8
Burgess Hill RH15..... 109 D1
Saddler's Row GU28... 97 F8
SADDLESCOMBE...... 148 E3
Saddlescombe Rd
BN45................ 148 D4
Sadler St PO21....... 201 C2
Sadlers The PO18..... 155 D1
Sadlers Wlk
6 Chichester PO19... 177 A6

Sadlers Wlk continued
Hermitage PO10 . . . . 173 C8
Sadler Way BN2 . . . . 192 F6
Saffron Cl
  Crawley RH11 . . . . 18 A3
  Shoreham-by-S BN43. . . . 167 C1
Saffron Ct 8 PO21. . . . . . 201 C4
Saffron Gate BN3 . . . . . . 191 C7
Saffrons Ct BN13 . . . . . . 186 A3
Saffrons The RH15 . . . . . . 108 F5
Sage Ho 3 RH10. . . . . 6 A1
St Agnes Pl PO19 . . . . . . 177 B6
St Agnes Rd RH19. . . . . 9 E2
St Andrews RH6 . . . . 2 B2
St Andrew's CE High Sch
  for Boys BN14 . . . . 186 E4
St Andrew's CE Prim Sch
  Crawley RH10 . . . . 19 A4
  Hove BN3. . . . . 191 B7
  Nuthurst RH13. . . . . 59 A1
  Steyning BN44 . . . . 145 D4
St Andrew's Cl
  Ferring BN12. . . . . 206 E6
  Oving PO20 . . . . 178 C4
St Andrews Ct BN11. . . . . 186 C2
St Andrew's Gdns
  BN13 . . . . 186 A4
St Andrews La PO20 . . . . 156 C1
St Andrews Rd
  Burgess Hill RH15 . . . . . 109 C4
  Crawley RH11 . . . . 17 D5
St Andrew's Rd
  Brighton BN1. . . . . 170 A1
  Portslade-by-S BN41. . . . 190 C7
  Worthing BN13 . . . . 185 F5
St Anne's Ct
  5 Brighton BN1 . . . . . . 213 A4
  9 Brighton, Kemp Town
  BN2. . . . . 192 C4
  East Wittering PO20 . . . . 207 F7
St Anne's Gdns BN6. . . . . 129 A3
St Anne's Ho 6 BN1 . . . . 213 A4
St Anne's Rd RH10 . . . . 6 C2
St Annes Well Ho 6
  BN3 . . . . 191 D6
St Ann's Ct BN3. . . . . 191 D7
St Ann's Hill GU29 . . . . 94 F7
St Anns Mans 5 BN1 . . . . 191 E7
St Anselm's Rd BN14. . . . 186 B4
St Anthony's Sch
  PO19. . . . . 176 F8
St Anthony's Way 1
  BN16 . . . . 205 D6
St Anthony's Wlk
  PO21 . . . . 200 D3
St Aubin Cl RH11 . . . . 17 F2
St Aubins Ct 1 BN12. . . . 206 F4
St Aubins Rd 3 BN12 . . . 206 F4
St Aubyns BN3. . . . . 191 B6
St Aubyn's Cres BN41 . . . 190 B7
St Aubyn's Gdns 13
  BN3 . . . . 191 A6
St Aubyns Mans BN3 . . . . 191 A5
St Aubyn's Mead BN2 . . . 194 A1
St Aubyn's Rd
  Portslade-by-S, Aldrington
  BN41. . . . . 190 C7
  Portslade-by-S, Fishersgate
  BN41. . . . . 190 A7
St Aubyns S BN3. . . . . . . 191 A5
St Aubyns St BN2 . . . . . . 193 F1
St Augustine Rd 12
  BN17 . . . . 204 E4
St Augustine's CE Prim
  Sch RH17 . . . . 88 F3
St Augustines Ct RH17 . . . 88 F3
St Barnabas Ct RH10 . . . . 19 C7
St Bartholomew's CE Prim
  Sch
  Brighton BN1. . . . . 213 B4
  Haslemere GU27. . . . . . . 27 C7
St Bartholomews Cl
  PO19 . . . . 176 E6
St Bernadette's RC Prim
  Sch BN1 . . . . 169 E2
St Bernards Ct BN15 . . . . 187 E5
St Blaises Rd PO18. . . . . . 156 C4
St Botolphs Ct 2
  BN11 . . . . 186 B3
St Botolph's Rd BN11 . . . 186 B3
St Brelades Rd RH11 . . . . 17 F2
St Catherines Ct
  BN17 . . . . 204 D4
St Catherine's Ct RH19 . . . 9 D2
St Catherine's RC Prim
  Sch BN17 . . . . 204 D6
St Catherines Rd RH10 . . . 6 D1
St Catherine's Rd
  BN17 . . . . 204 D4
St Catherines Terr
  PO22 . . . . 201 F3
St Catherine's Terr 1
  BN3 . . . . 191 B5
St Christophers Cl 5
  RH12 . . . . 36 C4
St Christopher's Cl
  Chichester PO19 . . . . . . 176 C6
  Haslemere GU27. . . . . . . 27 A6
St Christopher's Gn
  GU27 . . . . 27 A6
St Christopher's Rd
  Haslemere GU27. . . . . . . 27 A6
  Hurstpierpoint BN6. . . . . 128 A6
St Christopher's Sch
  BN3. . . . . 191 A6
St Clare's Gdns PO21. . . . 201 A6
St Clare's Mews PO22. . . 201 F4

St Clement Rd RH11 . . . . 17 F2
St Cuthmans Cl BN2 . . . . 192 F6
St Cuthman's Rd
  BN44 . . . . 145 D4
St Cyriacs PO19. . . . . 177 A7
St David's Gate 4
  BN15 . . . . 187 D6
St Dunstan's Rd BN13 . . . 186 A3
St Edmunds Cl RH11 . . . . 5 D1
St Edmund's Rd RH16 . . . 87 F3
St Edward's Cl RH19 . . . . 9 C1
St Elmo Rd BN14. . . . . . . 186 B4
St Flora's Cl BN17 . . . . . . 204 F5
St Flora's Rd BN17. . . . . . 204 F5
St Francis Cl RH16 . . . . . . 87 F2
St Francis Gdns RH10 . . . . 7 C4
St Francis of Assisi RC
  Prim Sch RH10 . . . . 18 E4
St Francis Wlk RH11 . . . . 17 E4
St Gabriels Rd BN14 . . . . 79 E8
St Georges RH6. . . . . 2 B2
St Georges Cl RH6 . . . . 2 B3
St George's Cl PO20 . . . . 212 F8
St Georges Ct
  Chichester PO19 . . . . . . 177 B5
  Crawley RH10 . . . . 18 D8
  East Grinstead RH19. . . . . 9 C3
St George's Dr PO19 . . . . 176 F3
St George's Gdns
  Horsham RH13 . . . . 36 E4
  1 Worthing BN11. . . . . . 186 E4
St George's Ho BN6. . . . . 128 B5
St George's La BN6 . . . . . 128 B5
St George's Mews
  BN1 . . . . 213 B3
St George's Pl
  Brighton BN1. . . . . 213 B3
  Hurstpierpoint BN6. . . . . 128 B5
St Georges Rd RH13 . . . . 105 A3
St George's Rd
  Brighton BN2. . . . . 192 D4
  Worthing BN11 . . . . 186 F2
St George's Terr 5
  BN2 . . . . 192 C4
St Georges Wlk PO20 . . . 179 F7
St Georges Wood
  GU27 . . . . 27 D8
St Giles CE Prim Sch
  RH17. . . . . 65 C6
St Giles Cl BN43 . . . . 189 B8
St Helen's Cres BN3 . . . . 168 D3
St Helen's Dr BN3 . . . . . . 168 D3
St Helen's Rd BN3 . . . . . . 192 D7
St Helier Cl RH11 . . . . . . 18 A2
St Helier Ct 2 BN12 . . . . 206 F4
St Helier Rd BN12. . . . . . 206 F4
St Heliers Ave BN3. . . . . . 190 E7
St Hilda's Cl
  Crawley RH10 . . . . 6 C1
  Horley RH6 . . . . 2 B3
  Selsey PO20. . . . . 212 D6
Saint Hill Grn RH19 . . . . . 22 D4
Saint Hill Manor*
  RH19. . . . . 22 C4
Saint Hill Rd RH19 . . . . . 22 C5
St Hugh's Cl RH10 . . . . 6 C1
St Itha Cl PO20 . . . . 212 E7
St Itha Rd PO20 . . . . 212 E6
St Ives Cl RH10 . . . . 19 C7
St Ives Sch GU27 . . . . 27 E8
St James Ave BN15 . . . . 187 E8
St James CE Prim Sch
  PO10. . . . . 151 B2
St James' CE Prim Sch
  RH20. . . . . 119 C6
St James Cotts RH17 . . . . 41 A1
St James Ct
  Chichester PO19 . . . . . . 177 B7
  East Grinstead RH19. . . . . 9 E1
St James' Ho 13 BN2 . . . 213 C2
St James' Ind Est
  PO19. . . . . 177 C7
St James' Rd
  Chichester PO19 . . . . . . 177 C7
  Emsworth PO10. . . . . . . 151 B1
St James's Ave BN2. . . . . 213 C2
St James's Cl PO20 . . . . . 197 E5
St James's Pl BN2 . . . . . . 213 B2
St James's Sq PO19 . . . . 177 C7
St James's St BN2 . . . . . . 213 C2
St James's Street Mews
  BN2 . . . . 213 C2
St James Wlk RH11 . . . . . 18 C2
St Joan Cl RH11 . . . . 5 D1
St John Cl RH13 . . . . 36 E1
St John's Ave
  Burgess Hill RH15 . . . . . 108 F4
  Worthing BN12 . . . . 185 D2
St Johns Cl PO20 . . . . . . 179 D5
St John's Cl
  Bognor Regis PO21. . . . . 200 F4
  East Grinstead RH19. . . . . 9 F2
  Midhurst GU29 . . . . 94 E7
  Worthing BN12 . . . . 185 D2
St John's Coll BN2. . . . . . 192 D5
ST JOHN'S COMMON
  . . . . 108 E4
St John's Cres RH12 . . . . 35 E3
St Johns Ct RH15 . . . . . . 109 A3
St John's Ct 5 BN15 . . . . 187 D6
St John's Mews Cotts 7
  BN43 . . . . 188 E7
St John's Mount 8
  BN2 . . . . 213 C2
St John's Pl
  Brighton BN2. . . . . 213 C2
  23 Hove BN3. . . . . 191 C6

St John's RC Prim Sch
  RH12. . . . . 36 A1
St Johns Rd RH15. . . . . . 109 A3
St John's Rd
  Breach PO10 . . . . 151 F1
  Crawley RH11 . . . . 18 C6
  East Grinstead RH19. . . . . 9 E2
  Haywards Heath RH16 . . . 87 E2
  Hove BN3. . . . . 191 C5
St John's Sch BN2 . . . . . . 192 D5
St John The Baptist CE
  Prim Sch BN14 . . . . 163 E6
St John the Baptist RC
  Sch BN2 . . . . 192 D5
St Josephs Abbey
  BN20 . . . . 142 D8
St Josephs Bsns Pk 2
  BN3. . . . . 191 A8
St Joseph's Cl BN3. . . . . . 191 A8
St Joseph's Mews
  BN20 . . . . 142 D8
St Joseph's RC Prim Sch
  Brighton BN2. . . . . 170 C1
  Haywards Heath RH16 . . . 87 E4
St Joseph's Trad Est 3
  BN3. . . . . 191 A8
St Josephs Way RH16 . . . 87 E4
St Julian 5 RH19 . . . . 9 F2
St Julians Ct BN43 . . . . . 189 C7
St Julian's La BN43 . . . . . 189 D7
St Keyna Ave BN3. . . . . . 190 D6
St Lawrence Ave
  BN14 . . . . 186 B4
St Lawrence CE Prim Sch
  BN6. . . . . 128 A6
St Lawrence Ct BN14. . . . 186 B4
St Lawrence Way
  BN6 . . . . 128 A7
St Leodegar's Way
  PO20 . . . . 177 A1
St Leonards RH12. . . . . . . 36 F4
St Leonard's Ave BN3 . . . 190 C7
St Leonards Dr RH10 . . . . 19 A4
St Leonard's Gdns
  BN3 . . . . 190 D7
St Leonard's Park Ho
  RH13 . . . . 37 C3
St Leonards Pk RH19. . . . . 9 E1
St Leonards Rd RH13. . . . 37 A1
St Leonard's Rd
  9 Brighton BN2 . . . . . . 192 C8
  Hove BN3. . . . . 190 C7
St Louie Cl BN42. . . . . . . 190 A8
St Luke's Cl BN15 . . . . . . 187 B4
St Lukes Ct RH15 . . . . . . 109 A3
St Luke's Inf Sch BN2 . . . 192 C6
St Luke's Jun Sch
  BN2. . . . . 192 C6
St Luke's Rd BN2 . . . . . . 192 C6
St Luke's Terr BN2 . . . . . . 192 C6
St Malo Cl BN2. . . . . 206 F4
St Malo Ct 4 BN12. . . . . 206 F4
St Margarets BN2. . . . . . 194 A1
St Margaret's Rd RH19 . . . 9 F6
St Margaret's CE Prim Sch
  Angmering BN16 . . . . . . 183 F7
  Crawley RH11 . . . . 18 B7
  Rottingdean BN2. . . . . . 194 A2
St Margaret's Cotts
  GU27 . . . . 49 B6
St Margarets Ct RH12 . . . 35 F7
St Margaret's Ct
  BN16 . . . . 183 F6
St Margaret's Pl BN1. . . . 213 A2
St Margaret's Rd RH19 . . . 9 F3
St Margaret's Sch
  GU29. . . . . 94 E8
St Mark's CE Prim Sch
  Brighton BN2. . . . . 192 E5
  Staplefield RH17 . . . . 61 F5
St Mark's Cres BN15 . . . . 187 B4
St Mark's La RH12 . . . . . . 36 E6
St Mark's Mews 13
  BN2 . . . . 192 E4
St Mark's St BN2. . . . . . . 192 E4
St Martin Cl RH17 . . . . . . 61 B7
St Martins CE Prim Sch
  BN2. . . . . 192 C6
St Martin's Ct 6 BN2 . . . 213 C5
St Martin's Flats 6
  BN2 . . . . 192 C7
St Martin's La 11
  BN17 . . . . 204 D5
St Martin's Pl BN2 . . . . . . 192 C7
St Martins Rd BN17 . . . . 204 D5
St Martin's Sq PO19 . . . . 177 A7
St Martin's St
  Brighton BN2. . . . . 213 C5
  Chichester PO19 . . . . . . 177 A6
St Mary Magdalene St
  BN2 . . . . 213 C5
St Mary Magdalen RC
  Prim Sch BN1 . . . . 191 C5
St Mary's 12 RH20. . . . . . 100 C2
St Mary's Abbey GU27. . . 26 D7
St Mary & St Paul CE Fst
  Sch GU31 . . . . 91 D3
St Mary's CE Fst Sch
  RH20. . . . . 143 D4
St Mary's CE Prim Sch
  Climping BN17 . . . . 203 E8
  Horsham RH12 . . . . 36 C1
  Pulborough RH20. . . . . . 100 C3
St Mary's CE Sch RH19 . . . 9 D2
St Marys Cl
  Bognor Regis PO22 . . . . 201 D5
  Lancing BN15. . . . . 187 B7

St Mary's Cl
  Billingshurst RH14. . . . . . 79 D8
  Littlehampton BN17. . . . 204 E5
  Mid Lavant PO18 . . . . . . 154 F7
  Pulborough RH20. . . . . . 100 C2
  Shoreham-by-S BN43. . . . 188 F7
St Mary's Ct
  Bramber BN44. . . . . 145 F2
  6 Littlehampton BN17 . . 204 E5
  Worthing BN13 . . . . 185 D7
St Mary's Ctyd PO22 . . . . 201 F4
St Mary's Ctyd PO19 . . . . 177 A6
St Mary's Dr
  Crawley RH10 . . . . 19 B8
  Rustington BN16 . . . . . . 205 F5
St Mary's Gdn PO19. . . . 177 A6
St Mary's Gdns
  Horsham RH12 . . . . 36 C1
  1 Littlehampton BN17. . . 204 E5
St Mary's Ho 5 RH12 . . . . 36 C1
St Mary's Ho & Gdns*
  BN44. . . . . 145 F2
St Mary's Lo 1 PO19 . . . . 177 A6
St Marys Mdw BN18. . . . . 180 F4
St Mary's Mews PO22 . . . 201 F4
St Marys Pl 3 BN43. . . . . 189 A6
St Mary's Pl BN2. . . . . . . 213 C2
St Mary's RC Prim Sch
  Bognor Regis PO21 . . . . 201 D3
  Portslade-by-S BN41 . . . . 190 B7
  Worthing BN11 . . . . 186 C3
St Mary's Rd
  Boxgrove PO18 . . . . 156 C4
  Burgess Hill RH15 . . . . . 108 F4
  Liss GU33 . . . . 45 B4
  Shoreham-by-S BN43. . . . 188 F7
St Mary's Slindon CE Prim
  Sch BN18 . . . . 158 D3
St Mary's Sq 1 BN2. . . . . 192 D4
St Mary's Terr 6
  BN43 . . . . 188 E7
St Mary's Way BN17. . . . 204 E5
St Matthews Ct BN2. . . . . 192 C5
St Matthew's Rd
  BN11 . . . . 186 C3
St Maur's Rd BN11 . . . . . 186 C3
St Michaels Cl GU28 . . . . 51 A7
St Michaels Cotts 11
  BN44 . . . . 145 D3
St Michael's Ct 7
  BN15 . . . . 187 D5
St Michael's Ct BN11. . . . 186 B2
St Michael's Pl BN1 . . . . 191 E6
St Michaels Rd RH19 . . . . 9 E2
St Michael's Rd
  Portslade-by-S BN41 . . . . 190 B7
  Worthing BN11 . . . . 186 B2
St Michaels Way
  RH13 . . . . 105 A3
St Nicholas' CE Jun Sch
  BN41 . . . . 190 B8
St Nicholas Ct
  Crawley RH10 . . . . 19 C7
  Lindfield RH16 . . . . 88 A6
  8 Middleton-on-S
  PO22 . . . . 202 F5
St Nicholas' Ct 3
  BN15 . . . . 187 D6
St Nicholas La 5
  BN43 . . . . 189 A6
St Nicholas Lo BN1 . . . . . 213 A2
St Nicholas Pl 2
  BN43 . . . . 189 A6
St Nicholas Rd
  Brighton BN1. . . . . 213 A3
  Mid Lavant PO18 . . . . . . 154 E6
  Portslade-by-S BN41 . . . . 190 B7
St Nicolas Ct BN43 . . . . 188 D8
St Nicolas La BN43 . . . . 188 D8
St Nicolas & St Mary CE
  Fst & Mid Sch BN43. . . 189 A8
St Osmund Rd BN12. . . . 206 E6
St Pancras PO19 . . . . . . 177 B7
St Pancras Ct PO19 . . . . 177 B6
St Pancras Gn BN7. . . . . 172 E5
St Patrick's La GU33 . . . . 45 F5
St Patrick's Rd BN3 . . . . 191 A7
St Paul's Ave BN15. . . . . 187 B4
St Paul's CE Prim Sch
  Ardingly RH17 . . . . 64 A8
  Cowfold RH13 . . . . 83 E2
  Henfield BN5. . . . . 125 D5
St Peters Cl PO21. . . . . . 200 E4
St Peter's Cl
  Cowfold RH13 . . . . 83 E1
  Hove BN3. . . . . 168 F2
St Peter's Com Inf Sch
  BN41. . . . . 190 B7
St Peter's Cres PO20 . . . . 212 E8
St Peters Ct 1 PO10 . . . . 173 C8
St Peter's Ct GU32 . . . . . 68 B3
St Peter's Gn BN44. . . . . 146 A2
St Peter's Ho BN1 . . . . . 213 B3
St Peter's Pl
  Brighton BN1, BN2 . . . . 213 B3
  Lancing BN15. . . . . 187 C4
St Peter's RC Prim Sch
  BN43. . . . . 189 A8

St Peter's RC Sch RH19 . . . 9 C1
St Peters Rd RH15 . . . . . 109 A4
St Peter's Rd
  Crawley RH11 . . . . 18 C6
  Petersfield GU32. . . . . . . 68 B3
  Portslade-by-S BN41 . . . . 190 B7
St Peter's Sq 9 PO10 . . . 173 B8
St Peter's St BN1 . . . . . . 213 B4
St Peters View BN5 . . . . 125 E6
St Philip Howard RC High
  Sch The PO22. . . . . 180 A6
St Philip's Ct BN17 . . . . . 204 D7
St Philips Mews 3
  BN3 . . . . 190 F7
St Philip's RC Prim Sch
  BN18. . . . . 160 A3
St Raphael Rd BN11. . . . . 185 F3
St Richards Cl BN12. . . . . 185 C4
St Richards Cotts
  Codmore Hill RH20 . . . . 100 D6
  Cootham RH20. . . . . . . 121 A1
  Fittleworth RH20. . . . . . . 99 A2
St Richard's Cotts
  GU31 . . . . 92 A4
St Richard's Ct BN3 . . . . 168 D1
St Richard's Dr PO21. . . . 200 D3
St Richards Flats GU29 . . 94 D8
St Richard's Flats
  BN41 . . . . 190 B7
St Richard's Hospl
  PO19. . . . . 177 B8
St Richard's RC Prim Sch
  PO19. . . . . 177 A5
St Richards Rd PO20 . . . . 179 E7
St Richard's Rd BN41 . . . 190 B7
St Richard's Way
  PO21. . . . . 200 D3
St Richard's Wlk
  PO19. . . . . 176 F6
St Robert's Lo 1
  BN15 . . . . 187 E5
St Robert Southwell RC
  Prim Sch RH12 . . . . 37 A6
St Roche's Cl PO18 . . . . . 154 F7
St Sampson Rd RH11. . . . 17 F2
St Saviours Ct 1 BN1 . . . 192 B8
St Stephen Cl RH11 . . . . . 5 D1
St Stephen's Cl GU27 . . . . 26 F6
St Swithun's Cl RH19. . . . . 9 F1
St Thomas Ct PO21 . . . . 211 A8
St Thomas Dr PO21. . . . . 210 F8
St Thomas's Ct BN14. . . . 186 B4
St Thomas's Rd BN14 . . . 186 B4
St Valerie Rd BN11. . . . . 186 A1
St Vincent Cl RH10. . . . . . 19 D5
St Vincent's Ct BN2 . . . . 193 A3
St Wilfred Ho BN15 . . . . 187 C5
St Wilfreds Ct PO20 . . . . 212 G8
St Wilfred's Ct 5 RH16. . . 87 E4
St Wilfred's Rd BN14. . . . 186 D4
St Wilfrid Rd PO19 . . . . . 176 F7
St Wilfrid's CE Prim Sch
  RH16. . . . . 87 F3
St Wilfrids Cl RH15 . . . . 109 B4
St Wilfrids Flat's BN2 . . . 192 C7
St Wilfrid's RC Comp Sch
  RH11. . . . . 18 B5
St Wilfrid's RC Prim Sch
  BN16. . . . . 183 F6
St Wilfrids Rd RH15 . . . . 109 B4
St Wilfrids View
  PO20. . . . . 212 C6
St Wilfrid's Way RH16. . . 87 E4
St Winefride's Rd
  BN17 . . . . 204 E4
St Winifred's Cl PO21 . . . 201 B2
Sake Ride La BN5. . . . . . 106 C1
Salbrook Rd RH1 . . . . 2 A8
Salehurst Rd RH10. . . . . . 19 C6
Salisbury Ct
  19 Hove BN3. . . . . 191 C6
  Southwater RH13 . . . . . . 58 A2
Salisbury Ho BN12 . . . . . 185 A4
Salisbury Rd
  Crawley RH10 . . . . 18 E2
  Hove BN3. . . . . 191 C6
  Tower Hill RH13. . . . . . . 58 A8
  Worthing BN11 . . . . 186 D2
Salisbury Way PO19. . . . . 154 F1
Salt Box Cl RH13. . . . . . . 56 F2
Saltdean Cl RH10 . . . . . . 18 D3
Saltdean Dr BN2 . . . . . . 194 B1
Saltdean Park Rd
  BN2 . . . . 194 C1
Saltdean Prim Sch
  BN2. . . . . 194 C2
Saltdean Vale BN2 . . . . . 194 D2
Salterns Rd RH10 . . . . . . 19 C3
Saltham La PO20. . . . . . . 177 E1
Salthill La PO19. . . . . 176 C8
Salthill Rd PO19 . . . . 176 B7
Saltings The
  Birdham PO20. . . . . 197 E4
  Lancing BN15. . . . . 187 F5
  Littlehampton BN17. . . . 205 A6
  Shoreham-by-S BN43. . . . 188 D6
Saltings Way BN44 . . . . . 146 A2
SALVINGTON 186 A7
Salvington Cl BN13 . . . . . 185 D8
Salvington Ct BN13 . . . . 163 F2
Salvington Gdns
  BN13 . . . . 185 F7
SALVINGTON HILL 163 E2

Salvington Hill BN13 . . . . 163 E1
Salvington Rd
　Crawley RH11 . . . . 17 F3
　Worthing BN13 . . . . 185 E8
Samaritan Cl RH11 . . . . 17 E4
Samphire Cl RH11 . . . . 18 A3
Samphire Dr BN13 . . . . . . 185 A6
Sampsons Dr PO20 . . . . . 178 C7
Sanctuary La RH20 . . . . . 122 C1
Sandbrook BN6 . . . . 128 F3
Sandcroft PO20 . . . . 179 D7
Sandeman Way RH13 . . . . 58 F8
Sanders Ho BN3 . . . . 190 E8
Sanderstead **1** BN2 . . . . . 192 F5
Sandfield Ave BN17 . . . . . 204 D8
Sandgate La RH20 . . . . . . 122 A2
Sandgate Rd BN1 . . . . 170 A2
Sandhawes Hill RH19 . . . . 10 A4
Sandhill La
　Crawley Down RH10 . . . . . 21 B7
　Washington RH20 . . . . . . 143 E7
Sandhills Rd RH13 . . . . . . 56 F3
Sandhurst Ave BN2 . . . . . 171 D1
Sandhurst Sch BN1 . . . . . 186 F2
Sandown Ave BN12 . . . . . 185 C2
Sandown Cl BN12 . . . . . . 185 C2
Sandown Ct
　Crawley RH10 . . . . 19 D6
　Hove BN3 . . . . 168 D1
　3 Worthing BN11 . . . . . 186 C1
Sandown Rd
　Brighton BN2 . . . . 192 D7
　Southwick BN42 . . . . 189 E8
Sandpiper Cl RH11 . . . . . . 17 D4
Sandpiper Ct PO20 . . . . . 208 A6
Sandridge La RH16 . . . . . . 63 F1
Sandringham Cl
　Bracklesham PO20 . . . . . 208 B5
　East Grinstead RH19 . . . . 23 A8
　Hove BN3 . . . . 169 A3
Sandringham Ct **6**
　BN15 . . . . 187 F5
Sandringham Dr BN3 . . . 169 A3
Sandringham Lo **17**
　BN3 . . . . 191 C6
Sandringham Mews
　Worthing BN14 . . . . 186 D6
　Worthing, Durrington
　BN13 . . . . 185 D8
Sandringham Rd
　Chichester PO19 . . . . . . 177 C6
　Crawley RH10 . . . . 18 B2
　Petersfield GU32 . . . . 68 B4
Sandringham Way
　PO21 . . . . 201 B4
Sandrock
　Haslemere GU27 . . . . 27 C6
　Midhurst GU29 . . . . 94 D8
Sandrock Cotts GU28 . . . 51 A7
Sandrocks Way RH16 . . . . 87 E2
Sandsbury La GU32 . . . . . 67 E5
Sands La BN5 . . . . 146 F6
Sands The RH20 . . . . 123 A5
Sandwich Rd BN11 . . . . . 185 F2
Sandy Beach Est
　PO11 . . . . 195 B1
Sandy Cl GU31 . . . . 68 E3
Sandy Cotts RH10 . . . . . . 21 A8
Sandygate La RH13 . . . . . 59 F3
Sandy La
　Chelwood Gate RH17 . . . . 66 C8
　Crawley Down RH10 . . . . . 21 A8
　East Ashling PO18 . . . . . 153 D4
　East Grinstead RH19 . . . . . 9 F1
　Fittleworth RH20 . . . . 99 A2
　Haslemere GU26, GU27 . . . 26 C7
　Heath Common RH20 . . . 122 C1
　Henfield BN5 . . . . 125 D4
　Midhurst GU29 . . . . 94 D8
　Rake GU33 . . . . 46 A4
　Steep GU32 . . . . 68 D8
　Watersfield RH20 . . . . . . 119 A5
　West Hoathly RH19 . . . . . 42 E6
Sandymount Ave
　PO22 . . . . 201 B5
Sandymount Cl PO22 . . . 201 C6
Sandy Point Ct BN12 . . . 212 B8
Sandy Point La PO20 . . . 212 B8
Sandy Point Rd PO11 . . . 195 A1
Sandy Rd PO21 . . . . 211 A7
Sandy Vale RH16 . . . . 87 E2
San Feliu Ct PO18 . . . . . . 10 B2
Sangers Dr RH6 . . . . 1 F3
Sanyhills La BN1 . . . . 169 F7
Sapex Bldgs PO19 . . . . . 177 C7
Sarel Way RH6 . . . . 2 B5
Sargent Cl RH10 . . . . 18 F2
Sarisbury Cl PO22 . . . . . . 202 A5
Sark Cl RH11 . . . . 18 A2
Sark Gdns BN12 . . . . 206 F4
Satellite Bsns Village The
　RH10 . . . . 5 E2
Satinwood Cl PO22 . . . . . 202 E6
Saturn Cl RH11 . . . . 17 E4
Saucelands La RH13 . . . . 102 E7
Saunders Cl RH10 . . . . . . 19 B7
Saunders Hill BN1 . . . . . 170 D7
Saunders Park Ho **2**
　BN2 . . . . 192 C8
Saunders Park Rise
　BN2 . . . . 170 C1
Saunders Park View
　BN2 . . . . 170 C1
Savernake Wlk RH10 . . . . 18 F3
Saville Ct RH14 . . . . 79 D7

Saville Gdns RH14 . . . . . . 79 D7
Savill Rd RH16 . . . . 88 A8
Sawyers Cl RH15 . . . . 109 D1
Saxby Cl PO22 . . . . 180 B5
Saxby Ct PO22 . . . . 180 B5
Saxby Rd RH15 . . . . 108 D4
Saxifrage Way BN13 . . . . 185 A6
Saxley RH6 . . . . 2 C4
Saxley Ct RH6 . . . . 2 C4
Saxonbury **16** BN2 . . . . . 213 C3
Saxon Cl
　Billingshurst RH14 . . . . . . 55 D1
　East Preston BN16 . . . . . 206 B7
　Pagham PO21 . . . . 210 B5
　Saltdean BN2 . . . . 194 C2
Saxon Cres RH12 . . . . 36 B4
Saxon Ct BN3 . . . . 190 D6
Saxon Mdw PO20 . . . . . . 156 C1
Saxon Rd
　Bramber BN44 . . . . 145 F3
　Crawley RH10 . . . . 19 E5
　Hove BN3 . . . . 190 D6
Saxons BN43 . . . . 166 F1
Saxony Rd BN14 . . . . 186 C4
Sayers Cl RH13 . . . . 36 E2
Sayers The **5** RH19 . . . . . 9 C1
Scallows Cl RH10 . . . . 19 A7
Scallows Rd RH10 . . . . . . 19 A7
Scamps Hill RH16 . . . . . . 88 C6
Scant Cl RH10 . . . . 152 F2
Scant Rd W PO18 . . . . . . 152 E2
Scarborough Rd BN1 . . . 169 D1
Sceptre BN1 . . . . 169 E2
Schaffer Ho RH10 . . . . . . 19 C4
Scholars Ct RH10 . . . . 21 A8
Scholar's Row PO22 . . . . 180 C5
School Cl
　Burgess Hill RH15 . . . . . 108 F2
　Fittleworth RH20 . . . . 99 A3
　Horsham RH12 . . . . 37 A6
　1 Southwick BN42 . . . 189 E7
School Ct RH14 . . . . 53 B2
School Dell PO18 . . . . . . 153 A3
School Hill
　Findon BN14 . . . . 163 E6
　Slindon BN18 . . . . 158 C5
　Storrington RH20 . . . . . . 121 E1
　Warnham RH12 . . . . 35 F8
School La
　Arundel BN18 . . . . 160 A2
　Ashurst BN44 . . . . 124 D5
　Ashurst Wood RH19 . . . . 23 E6
　Billingshurst RH14 . . . . . . 79 C7
　Bosham PO18 . . . . 175 C5
　Compton PO18 . . . . 111 B2
　Danehill RH17 . . . . 66 B5
　Eastergate PO20 . . . . . . 179 F7
　Emsworth PO10 . . . . 173 B8
　Fittleworth RH20 . . . . 99 A3
　Forest Row RH18 . . . . . . 23 F2
　Lindfield RH16 . . . . 88 B7
　Liss GU33 . . . . 45 B4
　Lodsworth GU28 . . . . 74 A7
　North Mundham PO20 . . . 177 D2
　Nutbourne PO18 . . . . . . 174 B7
　Petersfield GU32 . . . . 68 B4
　Pyecombe BN45 . . . . . . 149 C6
　Saltdean BN2 . . . . 194 C2
　Selsey PO20 . . . . 212 D8
　Shipley RH13 . . . . 81 C1
　Stedham GU29 . . . . 71 F1
　Steyning BN44 . . . . 145 D3
　Storrington RH20 . . . . . . 121 C1
　Sutton RH20 . . . . 117 F4
　Washington RH20 . . . . . 143 E6
　Westbourne PO10 . . . . . 151 D5
School Rd
　Amberley BN18 . . . . 140 E7
　Haslemere GU27 . . . . 26 F5
　Hove BN3 . . . . 190 F8
　Upper Beeding BN44 . . . 146 B2
　Wisborough Green RH14 . . 78 C8
School Rise BN2 . . . . 192 E6
Schooner Ct **3** BN17 . . 205 A6
Science Park Rd BN1 . . . 171 B7
Science Park Sq BN1 . . . 171 B6
Scolliers Crossways
　RH13 . . . . 81 B3
Scory Cl RH11 . . . . 18 A3
Scotland La GU27 . . . . 27 C5
Scotlands Cl GU27 . . . . . . 27 B5
Scotlands Dr GU27 . . . . . . 27 C5
Scotland St BN2 . . . . 213 C3
Scotney Cl BN13 . . . . 185 B6
Scott Cl PO21 . . . . 201 C2
Scott Lo **1** BN17 . . . . . 204 D5
Scott Rd
　Crawley RH10 . . . . 18 F3
　Hove BN3 . . . . 190 F7
Scotts Farm Cvn Pk
　PO20 . . . . 207 E8
Scott St PO21 . . . . 201 C2
Scrace Hill Terr RH16 . . . 109 F8
Scrase Lo RH15 . . . . 109 D3
Scratchings La GU28 . . . . 52 C5
Sculpture at Goodwood★
　PO18 . . . . 156 C8
Sea Ave BN16 . . . . 205 D5
Seabright **11** BN11 . . . . . 186 B1
Seabrook Cl PO21 . . . . . 200 D3
Seabrook Ct **5** BN15 . . 187 E4
Sea Cl
　Middleton-on-S PO22 . . . 202 E5
　Worthing BN12 . . . . 185 E3
Seacourt Cl PO21 . . . . . . 200 D2
Seacroft BN16 . . . . 205 F5
Seadown Par BN15 . . . . . 187 C5

Sea Dr
　Bognor Regis PO22 . . . . 202 D4
　Ferring BN12 . . . . 206 F4
Seafarers Wlk PO11 . . . . 195 B1
Seafield Ave BN12 . . . . . 185 D2
Seafield Cl
　East Wittering PO20 . . . . 208 A6
　Littlehampton BN16 . . . . 205 C4
Seafield Rd
　Hove BN3 . . . . 191 B6
　Littlehampton BN16 . . . . 205 C4
　West Kingston BN16 . . . . 206 A4
Seafields
　Bracklesham PO20 . . . . . 208 C5
　Emsworth PO10 . . . . 173 B8
　Shoreham-by-S BN43 . . . 188 F8
Seafield Terr **5** PO21 . . 201 B2
Seafield Way PO20 . . . . . 208 A6
Seaford Ave **8** BN43 . . . 189 B6
Seaford Coll GU28 . . . . . 116 E5
Seaford Rd
　Crawley RH11 . . . . 18 A2
　Chichester PO19 . . . . . . 155 A3
　Crawley RH11 . . . . 18 A7
Seaford Rd
　Crawley RH11 . . . . 18 A2
Seagate Ct PO20 . . . . . . 207 E6
Seagate Wlk **1** BN17 . . 205 A4
Sea Gr BN20 . . . . 212 C6
Seagull Ct PO10 . . . . 151 B1
Seagull Ct PO10 . . . . 151 B1
Seagull La PO10 . . . . 151 B1
Seahaven Gdns BN43 . . . 188 D5
Sea Ho **14** BN42 . . . . . . 189 E7
Sea La
　Ferring BN12 . . . . 206 F6
　Kingston Gorse BN16 . . . 206 D4
　Littlehampton BN16 . . . . 205 F4
　Middleton-on-S PO22 . . . 202 E5
　Pagham PO21 . . . . 210 F7
　Rustington BN16 . . . . . . 205 B4
　Worthing BN12 . . . . 185 C2
Sea Lane Cl
　East Preston BN16 . . . . . 205 F5
　Ferring BN12 . . . . 206 F6
Sea Lane Gdns BN12 . . . 206 F5
Seal Ct PO20 . . . . 212 D7
Seal Prim Sch PO20 . . . . 212 E7
Seal Rd PO20 . . . . 212 D5
Seal Sq PO20 . . . . 212 D5
Seamill Cl **7** BN11 . . . . 187 B3
Seamill Park Ave
　BN11 . . . . 187 B3
Seamill Park Cres
　BN11 . . . . 187 B3
Seamill Way BN11 . . . . . 187 B3
Sea Pl BN12 . . . . 185 E2
Sea Rd
　Bognor Regis PO22 . . . . 201 F3
　Littlehampton BN16,
　BN17 . . . . 205 A3
　West Kingston BN16 . . . . 206 A5
Searle's View RH12 . . . . . 36 E5
Sea-Saw Way BN2 . . . . . 192 F7
Seaside Ave BN15 . . . . . 187 F5
Seaside Cl BN15 . . . . 187 F5
Seaside Rd BN15 . . . . . . 187 F5
Sea Spray Ave BN43 . . . . 189 B6
Seaton Cl BN17 . . . . 204 D8
Seaton La BN17 . . . . 204 D8
Seaton Park Cotts
　BN17 . . . . 204 D8
Seaton Pk BN17 . . . . 204 D8
Seaton Rd BN17 . . . . 204 D8
Seaview Ave
　Kingston Gorse BN16 . . . 206 D4
　West Kingston BN16 . . . . 206 A4
Sea View Cotts PO10 . . . 173 B8
Seaview Ct
　2 Bognor Regis
　PO21 . . . . 201 C2
　Lancing BN15 . . . . 187 D4
　Selsey PO20 . . . . 212 D6
　4 Worthing BN11 . . . . 186 B1
Seaview Est BN42 . . . . . 189 F7
Seaview Gdns **5**
　BN16 . . . . 205 C4
Seaview Rd
　West Kingston BN16 . . . . 206 A4
　Woodingdean BN2 . . . . . 193 B8
Sea View Rd BN11 . . . . . 186 B1
Sea View Way BN2 . . . . . 171 D1
Seaward Ct **6** PO21 . . . 201 C3
Seaward Dr PO20 . . . . . . 196 C1
Seawaves Cl BN16 . . . . . 206 A5
Sea Way
　Bognor Regis PO21 . . . . 210 F8
　Elmer PO22 . . . . 203 B5
　Middleton-on-S PO22 . . . 202 E4
Seawood Ho PO20 . . . . . 207 F7
Second Ave
　Almodington PO20 . . . . . 197 F1
　Bognor Regis PO22 . . . . 202 B4
　Bracklesham PO20 . . . . . 208 B5
　Hove BN3 . . . . 191 C6
　Lancing BN15 . . . . 187 E7
　Southbourne PO10 . . . . 173 F8
　Worthing BN14 . . . . 186 D7
Sedbury Rd BN15 . . . . . . 187 C8
Seddon Cl PO19 . . . . 177 C8
Seddon Ct RH11 . . . . 18 B1
Sedgefield Cl RH10 . . . . . 19 E7
Sedgewick Cl RH10 . . . . . 19 C6
Sedgwick La RH13 . . . . . . 58 F5
Sefter Rd PO21 . . . . 200 B3
Sefton Ave PO21 . . . . . . 200 D3
Sefton Cl BN13 . . . . 185 D5
Sefton Rd BN41 . . . . 167 F3
Selba Dr BN2 . . . . 170 E3
Selborne Cl GU32 . . . . . . 68 C5

Selborne Pl
　Hove BN3 . . . . 191 C7
　Littlehampton BN17 . . . . 204 E4
Selborne Rd
　Hove BN3 . . . . 191 C6
　Littlehampton BN17 . . . . 204 E4
　Worthing BN11 . . . . 186 F3
Selborne Way BN16 . . . . 205 F4
Selbourne Cl RH10 . . . . . . 6 D2
Selby Ct RH16 . . . . 87 E3
Selden La
　Selden BN13 . . . . 162 B1
　Worthing BN13 . . . . 186 F2
Selden Mews **3**
　BN11 . . . . 186 F2
Selden Par **4** BN13 . . . . 185 F8
Selden Rd BN11 . . . . 186 F2
Selden's Mews BN13 . . . 185 F7
Selden's Way BN13 . . . . 185 F8
Sele Gdns BN44 . . . . 146 B2
Selham Cl
　Brighton BN1 . . . . 170 D6
　Chichester PO19 . . . . . . 155 A3
　Crawley RH11 . . . . 18 A7
Selham Dr BN1 . . . . 170 D6
Selham Pl BN1 . . . . 170 D6
Selham Rd GU29 . . . . 95 C6
Selhurst Cl BN15 . . . . . . 205 F5
Selhurstpark Rd
　PO18 . . . . 137 B4
Selhurst Rd BN2 . . . . 193 E6
Selkirk Cl BN13 . . . . 185 E5
Selmeston Pl BN2 . . . . . 192 F6
Selsey Ave PO21 . . . . . . 201 C3
Selsey Bsns Ctr **3**
　PO20 . . . . 212 D7
Selsey Cl
　Brighton BN1 . . . . 170 E6
　South Hayling PO11 . . . . 195 B2
　Worthing BN13 . . . . 185 F6
Selsey Ct
　3 Crawley RH11 . . . . . 18 B2
　7 Rustington BN16 . . . 205 B4
Selsey Cvn Site
　PO20 . . . . 212 D6
Selsey Lifeboat Mus★
　PO20 . . . . 212 F6
Selsey Rd
　Crawley RH11 . . . . 18 A2
　Sidlesham PO20 . . . . . . 209 F7
　Stockbridge PO19 . . . . . 176 E3
　Street End PO20 . . . . . . 198 D7
　Street End PO20 . . . . . . 198 F6
SELSFIELD COMMON . . . 21 B1
Selsfield Dr BN2 . . . . 170 D3
Selsfield Rd
　Little London RH17,
　RH19 . . . . 42 A4
　Turners Hill RH10, RH19 . . 21 A2
　West Hoathly RH19 . . . . . 42 C7
Selway La RH10 . . . . 204 F6
Selwyn Ave BN17 . . . . . . 204 D7
Selwyn Ct
　Bognor Regis PO21 . . . . 200 A3
　Crawley RH10 . . . . 6 C1
Semley Lo BN6 . . . . 128 E4
Semley Rd
　Brighton BN1 . . . . 170 A1
　Hassocks BN6 . . . . 128 E4
Senator Gdns PO19 . . . . 176 B7
Sequoia Pk RH11 . . . . 18 D4
Sergeant Cl RH16 . . . . . . 87 C5
Sergison Cl RH16 . . . . 87 C5
Sergison Rd RH16 . . . . . . 87 D5
Serrin Way RH12 . . . . 36 E5
Service Rd RH6 . . . . 5 F8
Servite Cl PO21 . . . . 201 B4
Servite Ho PO21 . . . . 201 B4
Sett The BN41 . . . . 168 B2
Sevelands Cl BN2 . . . . . . 192 F7
Seven Dials BN1 . . . . 213 A4
Sevenfields RH15 . . . . . . 108 D4
Seventh Ave BN15 . . . . . 187 E8
Severals Rd GU29 . . . . . . 94 C7
Severn Rd RH10 . . . . 19 C5
Seville St BN2 . . . . 192 C7
Sewill Cl RH6 . . . . 4 F7
Sextant Ct **6** BN17 . . . . 205 A6
Seymore Pl **12** PO21 . . 201 C3
Seymour Ho **5** BN2 . . . 192 D4
Seymour Prim Sch
　RH11 . . . . 18 B2
Seymour Rd RH11 . . . . . . 18 B2
Seymour Sq **3** BN2 . . . 192 D4
Seymour St **4** BN2 . . . . 192 D4
Shackleton Rd RH10 . . . . 18 F3
Shadwells Cl BN15 . . . . . 187 F7
Shadwells Ct BN15 . . . . . 187 F7
Shadwells Rd BN15 . . . . 187 F7
Shaftesbury Ave BN12,
　BN13 . . . . 185 E4
Shaftesbury Ct **4**
　BN16 . . . . 205 C4
Shaftesbury Pl
　Brighton BN1 . . . . 192 A8
　Rustington BN16 . . . . . . 205 C4
Shaftesbury Rd
　Brighton BN1 . . . . 213 B5
　Crawley RH10 . . . . 19 D4
　Littlehampton BN16 . . . . 205 C4
Shakespeare Ct BN11 . . . 186 C1
Shakespeare Ho **12**
　BN11 . . . . 186 C2
Shakespeare Rd
　BN11 . . . . 186 C3
Shakespeare St BN3 . . . . 191 A8
Shalbourne Cres
　PO20 . . . . 208 C5
Shalesbrook La RH18 . . . 23 F1

Shamrock Cl
　Bosham PO19 . . . . 175 C5
　Chichester PO19 . . . . . . 177 B8
Shandon Gdns BN14 . . . 186 D6
Shandon Rd BN14 . . . . . 186 D6
Shandon Way BN14 . . . . 186 D6
Shands BN6 . . . . 128 F3
Shandys Cl RH12 . . . . 36 A1
Shanklin Ct
　11 Brighton BN2 . . . . . 192 C8
　Hove BN3 . . . . 168 D1
Shanklin Rd BN2 . . . . . . 192 C8
Shannon Cl BN17 . . . . . . 205 A4
Shardeloes Rd BN16 . . . 183 F6
Sharon Cl **2** RH10 . . . . . 19 A4
Sharpthorne Cl RH11 . . . 17 F6
Sharpthorne Cres
　BN41 . . . . 168 C1
Sharpthorne Ct BN1 . . . . 213 B4
Sharrow Cl RH16 . . . . 87 E5
Shaves Wood La BN6 . . . 127 A2
Shaw Cl **1** PO22 . . . . . . 202 F5
Shawcross Ho **5** BN1 . . 169 E2
Shaw's La RH13 . . . . 57 D1
Shaws Rd RH10 . . . . 18 F7
Shear Hill GU31 . . . . 68 D5
Shearwater Ct **6**
　RH11 . . . . 17 D5
Shearwater Dr PO22 . . . . 201 C6
Sheddingdean Bsns Ctr
　RH15 . . . . 108 F5
Sheddingdean Cl
　RH15 . . . . 109 A4
Sheddingdean Com Prim
　Sch RH15 . . . . 109 A5
Sheddingdean Ct
　RH15 . . . . 108 F4
Sheddingdean
　Neighbourhood Ctr
　RH15 . . . . 109 A5
Sheepbell Cl BN41 . . . . . 168 B3
Sheepcote Valley Cvn Site
　BN2 . . . . 193 A5
Sheepdown Cl GU28 . . . . 98 A7
Sheepdown Dr GU28 . . . . 98 A7
Sheep Fold Ave BN16 . . . 205 C6
Sheep La GU29 . . . . 94 F8
Sheep Pen La BN44 . . . . 145 D3
Sheep St GU32 . . . . 68 B3
Sheepwash La
　East Lavant PO18 . . . . . 154 F5
　Shipton Green PO20 . . . 196 E4
Sheep Wlk BN2 . . . . 193 F1
SHEET 68 D6
Sheet Prim Sch GU32 . . . 68 D6
Sheffield Cl RH10 . . . . . . 19 B4
Sheffield Ct BN1 . . . . 213 B4
Sheffield Mews RH16 . . . 87 D5
Shelby Rd BN13 . . . . 185 C7
Sheldon Cl RH10 . . . . 19 D5
Sheldon Ct BN11 . . . . . . 186 B1
Shelhurst Forest Wlk★
　PO18 . . . . 137 B4
Shellbridge Rd BN18 . . . 158 E4
Shelldale Ave BN41 . . . . 190 B7
Shelldale Cres BN41 . . . . 190 B7
Shelldale Rd BN41 . . . . . 190 B8
Shelley Cl RH10 . . . . 19 C4
Shelley Ct **4** RH16 . . . . 87 D5
Shelley Dr RH12 . . . . 35 C3
Shelley Ho **7** RH12 . . . . 36 B2
Shelley Lo BN17 . . . . 204 F4
Shelley Prim Sch RH12 . . 35 E3
Shelley Rd
　Bognor Regis PO21 . . . . 201 B3
　East Grinstead RH19 . . . . 9 D1
　Horsham RH12 . . . . 36 B3
　Hove BN3 . . . . 190 F7
　Worthing BN11 . . . . 186 C2
Shelleys Ct RH13 . . . . 37 A3
Shelley Wood RH15 . . . . 108 D4
Shell La RH17 . . . . 41 C1
Shenfield Way BN1 . . . . . 170 B3
Shenstone RH16 . . . . 88 B8
Shepham Ave BN2 . . . . . 194 D2
Shepherd Cl RH10 . . . . . . 18 E3
Shepherds Cl PO18 . . . . . 152 D2
Shepherds Croft
　Brighton BN1 . . . . 169 C4
　Findon BN14 . . . . 163 E6
Shepherdsgrove La
　RH19 . . . . 10 F5
SHEPHERD'S HILL 27 C6
Shepherd's Hill GU27 . . . 27 C6
Shepherd's Hill Bglws
　GU27 . . . . 27 C6
Shepherds La GU28 . . . . 74 B3
Shepherds Mead
　RH15 . . . . 108 F4
Shepherd's Mead
　BN14 . . . . 164 A2
Shepherds Way
　Horsham RH12 . . . . 37 A5
　Liphook GU30 . . . . 25 D3
Shepherds Wlk BN6 . . . . 128 F3
Sheppard Way BN41 . . . . 168 A3
Sheppey Cl RH11 . . . . 18 C3
Sheppeys RH16 . . . . 87 D2
Sheraton Ct **12** BN11 . . 186 B1
Sheraton Wlk **13** RH11 . . 18 B1
Sherborne Rd PO19 . . . . 176 E7
Sherbourne Cl BN3 . . . . 168 D3
Sherbourne La PO20 . . . 212 B8
Sherbourne Rd BN3 . . . . 168 D3
Sherbourne Way BN3 . . . 168 D3
Sherbrooke Cl BN13 . . . . 185 D7
Sheridan Ho BN3 . . . . . . 191 D6

Sheridan Mans BN3 . . . . . .191 A8
Sheridan Pl RH19 . . . . 9 C1
Sheridan Rd BN14 . . . . . .186 E5
Sheridan Terr BN3 . . . . . .191 A8
Sherlock Ave PO19 . . . . .176 E7
SHERMANBURY 105 D3
Shermanbury Ct
  Horsham RH12 . . . . .36 D4
  Lancing BN15. . . . . .187 C5
Shermanbury Dr
  RH20 . . . . .121 C2
Shermanbury Grange
  RH13 . . . . .105 C3
Shermanbury Rd
  Partridge Green
  RH13. . . . . .105 B3
  Worthing BN14 . . . . .186 B4
Sherrington Mews [1]
  PO20 . . . . .212 F8
Sherrington Rd BN2 . . . .193 F8
Sherston Cl RH20 . . . . . .121 E2
Sherwood Cl
  Bognor Regis PO22 . . . . .201 B6
  Liss GU33 . . . . .45 C7
Sherwood Dr RH16. . . . . . .87 C5
Sherwood Rd PO22 . . . . .201 B6
Sherwood Wlk RH10 . . . . .18 F3
Shetland Cl RH10 . . . . . . .19 E7
Shetland Ct BN13 . . . . . .185 B6
Shillinglee Rd RH14. . . . . .30 B4
Shimmings GU28 . . . . .98 B8
Shingle Rd BN43 . . . . . . .189 A6
Shingle Wlk PO20 . . . . . .207 F6
Shinwell Wlk [3] RH11 . . . . .18 B1
Shipfield PO21. . . . . .200 F2
SHIPLEY BRIDGE 6 F6
Shipley Bridge La RH6,
  RH10 . . . . .6 F4
Shipley CE Prim Sch
  RH13. . . . . .81 B1
Shipley Ct GU30 . . . . .25 C3
Shipley Paygate RH13 . . . . .81 E2
Shipley Rd
  Crawley RH11 . . . . .18 A6
  Southwater RH13 . . . . . . .81 E5
  Woodingdean BN2. . . . . .193 E7
Shipley Windmill★
  RH13. . . . . .103 C8
Shippen Ho [5] PO19 . . . . .177 A6
Ship St
  Brighton BN1. . . . . .213 A2
  East Grinstead RH19. . . . . .22 E8
  Shoreham-by-S BN43. . . .188 E7
Ship Street Gdns
  BN1 . . . . .213 A2
Shipton Green La
  PO20 . . . . .197 B4
Shire Par RH10 . . . . .19 D7
Shire Pl RH10. . . . . .19 D7
Shirlands Ct [3] BN16. . . . .205 D6
Shirley Ave BN3 . . . . . . .169 B3
Shirley Cl
  Bognor Regis PO21 . . . . .211 A8
  Crawley RH11 . . . . .17 E2
  Rustington BN16 . . . . . . .205 D4
  Shoreham-by-S BN43. . . .189 D8
  Worthing BN14 . . . . .186 B7
Shirley Dr
  Bognor Regis PO22 . . . . .202 A6
  Hove BN3. . . . . .169 C2
  Worthing BN14 . . . . .186 B6
Shirley Mews BN3 . . . . . .191 B7
Shirley Rd BN3 . . . . .191 C8
Shirleys BN6 . . . . .129 E2
Shirleys Gdn PO22 . . . . . .202 B5
Shirley St BN3 . . . . .191 B7
Shooting Field BN44 . . . .145 D4
Shopfield Cl BN16 . . . . . .205 C6
Shop La PO18 . . . . .155 A5
Shopsdam Rd BN15 . . . . .187 F4
Shopwhyke Ind Ctr
  PO20. . . . . .177 D7
Shopwhyke Rd PO20 . . . .177 E7
Shorecroft PO21. . . . . . . .200 F1
Shoreham Airport BN15,
  BN43. . . . . .188 C8
SHOREHAM BEACH 189 A6
Shoreham Beach Com Fst
  Sch BN43. . . . . .189 A6
Shoreham By-Pass BN41,
  BN43 . . . . .167 D2
Shoreham-by-Sea Sta
  BN43. . . . . .188 F7
Shoreham Coll BN43. . . . .189 D7
Shoreham Ct BN43. . . . . .188 F8
Shoreham Fst Sch
  BN43. . . . . .188 F8
Shoreham Rd
  Crawley RH10 . . . . .19 C3
  Small Dole BN5 . . . . .146 F8
  Upper Beeding BN44. . . . .166 B7
Shore Ho PO20 . . . . .212 D5
Shore Rd
  Bosham PO18 . . . . .175 B3
  East Wittering PO20 . . . . .207 E7
Shoreside Wlk PO20 . . . . .207 F7
Short Cl RH11 . . . . .18 D8
Short Furlong BN17 . . . . .204 F5
Short Gallop RH10 . . . . . .19 D7
Shortgate Rd BN2 . . . . . .170 F4
Shorts Cl RH6 . . . . .87 E3
Shortsfield Cl RH12 . . . . . .36 C5
Shotford PO20. . . . . .209 F8
Shotterfield Terr GU33 . . . .45 B4
SHOTTERMILL 26 F6
Shottermill RH12 . . . . .37 A7
Shottermill Inf Sch
  GU27. . . . . .26 F7

Shottermill Jun sch
  GU27. . . . . .26 F7
Shottermill Pk GU27 . . . . . .26 E5
Shottermill Rd GU27 . . . . . .26 E5
Shotters RH15 . . . . .108 E1
Shovelstrode La RH19. . . . . .23 D8
Shrewsbury Ct [6]
  BN11 . . . . .186 B1
Shripney La PO22 . . . . . .179 C1
Shripney Rd
  Bognor Regis PO22 . . . . .201 D5
  Bognor Regis PO22 . . . . .201 E7
Shripney Trad Pk
  PO21. . . . . .201 E6
Shrubbs Dr PO22 . . . . . . .202 F5
Sickle Mill Ct GU27 . . . . . .26 F6
Sickle Rd GU27 . . . . .27 A5
Sidehill Dr BN41. . . . . . . .167 F2
Sidengreen La PO18 . . . . .155 F2
Sideways La RH6 . . . . .1 D2
Sidings The RH12 . . . . .33 D7
Sidlesham Cl PO11. . . . . .195 B2
Sidlesham La PO20 . . . . .198 A4
Sidlesham Prim Sch
  PO20. . . . . .209 D8
Sidney Tidy Ho [5]
  BN2 . . . . .192 C6
Siena Dr RH10 . . . . .6 C2
Silchester Dr RH11 . . . . . . .18 B4
Silkin Wlk [8] RH11 . . . . . . .18 B1
Sillwood Ct [19] BN1 . . . . .191 E5
Sillwood Hall [20] BN1 . . . .191 E5
Sillwood Pl [17] BN1 . . . . .191 E5
Sillwood Rd BN1. . . . . . . .191 E5
Sillwood St BN1 . . . . .191 E5
Sillwood Terr [22] BN1 . . . .191 E5
Silver Birch Ct GU33 . . . . . .45 C4
Silver Birch Dr
  Middleton-on-S PO22. . . .202 E6
  Worthing BN13 . . . . .185 C6
Silver Birches
  Brighton BN1. . . . . .169 E1
  Haywards Heath RH16 . . . .88 A4
  Small Dole BN5 . . . . .146 F7
Silver Birch Ho RH11 . . . . . .18 C1
Silver Ct RH19 . . . . .9 B2
Silverdale
  Coldwaltham RH20 . . . . .119 C5
  Keymer BN6. . . . . .129 B3
Silverdale Ave BN3 . . . . . .191 D7
Silverdale Cl PO21 . . . . . .211 A8
Silverdale Dr BN15. . . . . .187 C5
Silverdale Ind Est
  BN11. . . . . .187 B3
Silverdale Rd
  Burgess Hill RH15 . . . . . .109 B2
  Hove BN3. . . . . .191 D7
Silver Glade BN20. . . . . . .121 E6
Silver La RH14 . . . . .79 D8
Silver Lakes Mobil Home
  Pk PO20 . . . . .178 A4
Silverlea Gdns RH6 . . . . . . .2 C2
Silverlock Cl PO19 . . . . . .177 C8
Silverlock Pl PO10 . . . . . .151 D5
Silverston Ave PO21 . . . . .201 A2
Silvertrees PO10. . . . . . . .151 B2
Silver Way PO20 . . . . . . .208 C4
Silverwood RH20 . . . . . . .121 B7
Silverwood Copse
  RH20 . . . . .121 B7
Silverwood Ct [10]
  BN16 . . . . .205 C5
Simon Ct [13] PO21. . . . . .201 C3
Sinclair Cl RH10 . . . . .19 C4
Sinclair Wlk BN1 . . . . . . .213 B4
Sincox La RH13. . . . . .102 C6
Singleton CE Prim Sch
  PO18. . . . . .135 D7
Singleton Cl
  Bognor Regis PO21 . . . . .200 C1
  Ferring BN12. . . . . .206 F7
Singleton Cres BN12 . . . . .206 F6
Singleton Ho BN17. . . . . .204 B7
Singleton Rd
  Brighton BN1. . . . . .170 A6
  Broadbridge Heath RH12 . . .35 D3
Singleton Way RH15 . . . . .109 C1
Sinnocks PO21 . . . . .101 E1
Sir George's Pl BN44. . . . .145 C3
Sir Robert Peel Ct [14]
  PO21 . . . . .201 D4
Siskin Ave RH10 . . . . .21 C5
Siskin Cl RH12 . . . . .36 E5
Sissinghurst Cl RH10. . . . . .19 D7
Siward Ho [1] GU32. . . . . . .68 A3
Six Acres RH13 . . . . .34 D2
Six Acres Cl RH13. . . . . . . .56 F2
Skelmersdale Wlk
  RH11 . . . . .17 E2
Skeyne Dr [4] RH20. . . . . .100 C2
Skiff La
  Kirdford RH14 . . . . .53 F5
  Loxwood RH14 . . . . .32 A1
Skipton Way RH6 . . . . .2 B5
Skylarks RH14 . . . . .79 C7
Skylark View RH12 . . . . . . .36 D7
Slade La GU31 . . . . .69 F5
Slattsfield Cl PO20 . . . . . .212 F7
SLAUGHAM 61 B5
Slaugham Ct RH11 . . . . . . .17 F3
Slaugham La RH17 . . . . . . .61 A2
Sleets Rd RH12 . . . . .35 E3
Slider's La
  Furner's Green TN22 . . . . .66 B1
  Scaynes Hill TN22 . . . . . . .89 F6
Slimbridge Rd RH15 . . . . .108 F3
Slindon Bottom Rd
  BN18 . . . . .158 A4

Slindon Cl BN14 . . . . . . .186 D6
Slindon Coll BN18 . . . . . .158 B5
Slindon La BN14. . . . . . . .186 D6
Slinfold CE Prim Sch
  RH13. . . . . .34 D4
Slinfold Cl BN2 . . . . .192 D5
Slinfold Wlk RH11 . . . . . . .18 A6
Slipe The BN18 . . . . .160 B2
Slipper Cvn Pk PO10 . . . .173 C8
Slipper Rd PO10 . . . . . . .173 C8
Sloane Ct [4] BN2 . . . . . .192 C5
Sloe Cl PO19 . . . . .177 C7
Slonk Hill Rd BN43. . . . . .167 A1
Sloop La RH17 . . . . .89 D5
Sloughbrook Cl RH12 . . . . .36 F6
Sloughgreen La RH17 . . . . .61 E1
Slugwash La RH17 . . . . . . .88 D2
Small Cl RH15 . . . . .68 C5
Smallcroft Cl BN17. . . . . .204 C5
Smallcutts Ave PO10 . . . .151 F1
Smallfield Rd RH6 . . . . .2 D3
Smallmead RH6 . . . . .2 B3
Small's La RH11 . . . . .18 C6
Smalls Mead RH11 . . . . . . .18 C6
Smeeds Cl RH19 . . . . .10 A3
Smithbarn RH13 . . . . .37 A2
Smithbarn Cl RH6. . . . . . . .2 B4
SMITHBROOK 74 B4
Smith Cl RH10 . . . . .18 D3
Smithers Cotts RH12 . . . . . .33 F7
Smithers Hill La RH13. . . . . .81 B2
Smithfields Ho RH13 . . . . . .57 F1
Smith La PO10. . . . . .173 F1
Smith's Cross RH13 . . . . . .84 C3
Smithy The RH13 . . . . .83 E1
SMOCK ALLEY 121 D7
Smock Alley PO20 . . . . . .121 E7
Smokejack Hill RH5. . . . . . .13 D7
Smokyhouse La GU28 . . . . .96 B5
Smolletts RH19 . . . . .22 C8
Smugglers End RH17. . . . . .61 C8
Smugglers La BN44 . . . . .146 B2
Smugglers' La
  Barns Green RH13. . . . . . .56 D3
  Barns Green RH13. . . . . . .56 F3
Smuggler's La PO18 . . . . .175 B1
Smugglers' La RH5 . . . . . . .14 E7
Smugglers Way RH13 . . . . .56 F2
Smugglers Wlk BN12. . . . .185 E2
Snapes Rd RH20 . . . . . . .121 F3
Snednore BN7. . . . . .172 F5
Snell Hatch RH11 . . . . .18 B6
Snipe La GU27. . . . . .27 A1
Snowdrop Cl
  Crawley RH11 . . . . .18 A2
  Rustington BN17 . . . . . . .205 B7
Snowdrop La RH16. . . . . . .88 C4
Snowflakes La RH16 . . . . . .88 D6
SNOW HILL 8 A4
Snow Hill
  Copthorne RH10 . . . . .7 F3
  Domewood RH10 . . . . .7 F5
Snow Hill Bsns Ctr
  RH10. . . . . .8 A4
Snow Hill Cvn Site
  PO20 . . . . .196 B1
Snowhill La RH10 . . . . .7 F3
Soalwood La GU32. . . . . . .67 A8
Soames Ct RH15 . . . . . . .108 F4
Soane Cl RH11. . . . . .17 E4
Sobell Ct BN5 . . . . .125 E5
Soberton Dr GU31 . . . . . . .68 C5
Solent Cl BN17 . . . . .205 A7
Solent Rd PO20 . . . . .207 F6
Solent Way PO20 . . . . . . .212 C5
Solway Ave BN1 . . . . .169 F7
Solway Cl BN17 . . . . .205 A5
Somergate RH12. . . . . .35 F2
Somerhill Ave BN3 . . . . . .191 D7
Somerhill Ct [10] BN3 . . . .191 D7
Somerhill Jun Sch
  BN3. . . . . .191 D6
Somerhill Lo BN3 . . . . . . .191 D6
Somerhill Rd BN3. . . . . . .191 D6
Somerley La PO20 . . . . . .197 E1
Somersbury La GU6,
  RH12 . . . . .12 F7
Somerset Cl BN13 . . . . . .186 A5
Somerset Ct [3] BN3. . . . .191 C7
Somerset Gdns PO21. . . . .201 C5
Somerset Hospl GU28 . . . . .97 F8
Somerset Point [1]
  BN2 . . . . .192 C4
Somerset Rd
  East Preston BN16 . . . . . .206 B6
  Ferring BN12. . . . . .206 F4
Somerset St BN2 . . . . . . .192 C5
Somerstown PO19 . . . . . .176 F8
Somerton Gn PO22. . . . . .201 F5
Somerville Dr RH10 . . . . . . .6 C1
SOMPTING 187 B7
Sompting Abbotts Sch
  BN15. . . . . .187 A8
Sompting Ave BN14 . . . . .186 D5
Sompting By-Pass
  BN14 . . . . .186 E2
Sompting Cl BN2 . . . . . . .192 F7
Sompting Ct
  Brighton BN2. . . . . .192 F7
  [3] Shoreham-by-S
  BN43. . . . . .189 B8
Sompting Lo [5] BN15 . . . .187 D5
Sompting Rd
  Lancing BN15. . . . . .187 B5
  Worthing BN14 . . . . .186 E6
Sopers La BN44. . . . . .165 C7
Sorlings Reach [6]
  BN43. . . . . .189 B6

Sorrel Cl RH11. . . . . .18 A2
Sorrel Rd BN2 . . . . .36 E5
South Acre GU31 . . . . .91 D3
Southall Ave BN2 . . . . . . .170 D2
Southampton St BN2. . . . .213 C3
South Ash BN44 . . . . .145 A3
South Ave
  Bognor Regis PO21 . . . . .200 F3
  Brighton BN2. . . . . .192 C5
  Hurstpierpoint BN6 . . . . .128 A5
  Worthing BN12 . . . . .185 E2
South Bank
  Hassocks BN6 . . . . .128 E3
  Stockbridge PO19 . . . . . .176 F4
South Bank Ct PO19 . . . .176 F4
South Bank Ct BN15 . . . . .188 A4
South Bay PO10. . . . . . . .173 C3
South Beach [6] BN43 . . . .188 F6
SOUTH BERSTED 201 D6
South Bersted CE Prim
  Sch PO22 . . . . .201 C5
South Bersted Ind Est
  PO22. . . . . .201 D6
Southbourne Ave
  PO10 . . . . .173 D8
Southbourne Halt
  PO10. . . . . .174 A8
Southbourne Jun & Inf
  Schs PO10. . . . . .174 A8
Southbrook RH11 . . . . .18 C1
Southbrook Rd
  West Ashling PO18 . . . . .153 B3
  West Ashling PO18 . . . . .153 C3
South Cl
  Burgess Hill RH15 . . . . . .108 E3
  Crawley RH10 . . . . .18 F7
Southcote Ave PO20 . . . . .207 F2
Southcourt Cl BN16. . . . . .205 E6
Southcourt Rd BN14 . . . . .186 C3
Southdean Cl [2]
  PO22. . . . . .202 F5
Southdean Dr PO22 . . . . .202 F5
Southdown Ave
  Brighton BN1. . . . . .170 A1
  Portslade-by-S BN41. . . . .190 C8
Southdown Bldgs
  PO19. . . . . .176 F5
Southdown Cl
  Chichester PO19 . . . . . . .177 C8
  Haywards Heath RH16 . . . .87 D2
  Horsham RH13 . . . . .37 A5
  Midhurst GU29 . . . . .94 D6
Southdown Ct
  [8] Bognor Regis
  PO22. . . . . .201 D5
  East Wittering PO20 . . . . .208 A7
Southdown Cvn Pk
  BN5. . . . . .146 D2
Southdown Ho BN12. . . . .185 D3
Southdown Mews
  BN2 . . . . .192 C5
Southdown Pl BN1. . . . . . .170 A1
Southdown Rd
  Bognor Regis PO21 . . . . .201 C3
  Brighton BN1. . . . . .170 A1
  Portslade-by-S BN41. . . . .168 A2
  Shoreham-by-S BN43. . . .188 F7
  Southwick BN42 . . . . . . .189 E7
Southdowns Ct BN2. . . . .194 C2
South Downs
  Planetarium★
  PO19. . . . . .177 A4
Southdown Terr
  BN44 . . . . .145 E3
Southdown View Cl
  BN14 . . . . .186 F5
Southdownview Rd
  BN14 . . . . .186 F5
Southdown View Way
  BN14 . . . . .186 E6
Southdown Way
  RH20 . . . . .121 F3
South Dr
  Angmering BN16 . . . . . . .205 E7
  Bognor Regis PO22 . . . . .202 C5
  Burgess Hill RH15 . . . . . .108 E3
  Ferring BN12. . . . . .206 E4
Southease [18] BN2 . . . . . .192 F5
SOUTHERN CROSS 190 A8
Southern Cross BN4 . . . . .190 B8
Southern Cross Ind Est
  PO22. . . . . .201 E2
Southern Gate PO19 . . . . .176 F5
Southern Rd PO20 . . . . . .212 E6
Southern Ring Rd
  BN1. . . . . .171 B6
Southey Rd BN11 . . . . . . .186 C1
South Farm Cotts
  BN14 . . . . .186 C5
South Farm Inds
  BN14. . . . . .186 C5
South Farm Rd BN14. . . . .186 C5
Southfield Ind Pk
  PO18. . . . . .175 B6
Southfield Rd BN14 . . . . .186 D5
Southfields Cl PO19. . . . . .176 F3
Southfields Rd BN17,
  BN16 . . . . .204 F5
SOUTHGATE 18 C4
Southgate PO19 . . . . .176 F5
Southgate Ave BN14 . . . . . .18 E4
Southgate Dr RH10 . . . . . . .18 E4
Southgate Par RH10 . . . . . .18 E4
Southgate Prim Sch
  RH10. . . . . .18 D4
Southgate Rd RH10 . . . . . .18 D4
South Gr
  Horsham RH13 . . . . .36 D1

South Gr continued
  Petworth GU28 . . . . .97 F7
South Holmes Rd
  RH13. . . . . .37 B4
South La
  Breach PO10 . . . . .152 A2
  Houghton BN18 . . . . . . .140 B3
  Tillington GU28 . . . . .96 F7
  Woodmancote PO10 . . . .152 A3
SOUTH LANCING 187 E4
Southlands
  East Grinstead RH19. . . . .22 E7
  Horley RH6 . . . . .1 F3
Southlands Ave RH6 . . . . . .2 A4
Southlands Ct
  RH16. . . . . .87 E6
Southlands Ct
  [5] Haywards Heath
  RH16. . . . . .87 E6
  [14] Littlehampton BN17. . .204 E4
  [1] Shoreham-by-S
  BN43. . . . . .189 B8
Southlands Hospl
  BN43. . . . . .167 B1
Southlands La RH20. . . . . .121 E8
Southlands Pk GU29 . . . . . .94 E5
South Leas RH13. . . . . .83 E1
Southleigh Rd PO10,
  PO9 . . . . .151 B3
South Lo
  Bognor Regis PO21 . . . . .200 A2
  [9] Brighton BN2 . . . . . . .192 F5
  [3] Lancing BN15. . . . . . .187 C7
South Lodge Cl RH15. . . . .108 F4
Southmount BN1 . . . . . . .170 B1
Southon BN41. . . . . .167 F3
Southon View BN15. . . . . .187 C3
Southover Pl BN2. . . . . . . .213 C4
Southover Rd PO21 . . . . . .201 C3
Southover St BN2. . . . . . . .213 C3
Southover Way PO20. . . . .177 A1
South Pallant PO19 . . . . . .177 A6
South Par RH6. . . . . .1 F4
South Pas BN17. . . . . .204 F4
South Perimeter Tk
  RH11 . . . . .5 B5
South Pier Rd RH6. . . . . . . .6 B7
South Point [9] BN43 . . . . .189 A6
South Rd
  Bognor Regis PO22 . . . . .201 F5
  Brighton BN1. . . . . .169 E1
  Haywards Heath RH16 . . . .87 E4
  Liphook GU30 . . . . .25 D1
South Rd Mews BN1 . . . . .169 E1
Southsea Ave BN12 . . . . . .185 E2
Southside BN20. . . . . .100 D2
South St
  Brighton BN1. . . . . .213 A2
  Chichester PO19 . . . . . . .177 A6
  Cuckfield RH17 . . . . .86 E6
  Ditchling BN6. . . . . .129 D3
  Emsworth PO10. . . . . . . .173 B8
  Falmer BN1 . . . . .171 C6
  Horsham RH12 . . . . .36 C2
  Lancing BN15. . . . . .187 E4
  Midhurst GU29 . . . . .94 F7
  Partridge Green RH13. . . .105 A3
  Portslade-by-S BN41. . . . .168 A1
  Worthing BN11 . . . . .186 D1
  Worthing, West Tarring BN11,
  BN13, BN14 . . . . .186 A4
SOUTH STOKE 160 D8
South Strand BN16. . . . . .206 A4
South Strand Par [6]
  BN16 . . . . .206 A4
South Terr
  [5] Bognor Regis
  PO22. . . . . .201 D5
  Littlehampton BN17. . . . .204 E4
Southview
  Scaynes Hill RH17 . . . . . . .88 F3
  Small Dole BN5 . . . . .146 F6
South View
  Ditchling BN6. . . . . .129 E5
  West Kingston BN16 . . . . .206 B4
Southview Cl
  Shoreham-by-S BN43. . . .189 C7
  Southwick BN42 . . . . . . .167 E1
South View Cl RH10 . . . . . . .7 E3
Southview Dr BN11 . . . . . .186 A2
Southview Gdns
  BN11 . . . . .186 A2
South View Lo [8]
  BN15 . . . . .187 E5
Southview Rd
  Bognor Regis PO22 . . . . .202 B4
  Findon BN14 . . . . .163 G6
  Southwick BN42 . . . . . . .189 E8
South View Terr BN5. . . . .125 E4
Southwark Cl RH11 . . . . . . .18 B2
Southwark Wlk PO21. . . . .200 E4
Southwater Bsns Pk
  RH13. . . . . .57 F1
Southwater Cl
  Brighton BN2. . . . . .192 D6
  Crawley RH11 . . . . .18 A6
  Worthing BN12 . . . . .185 B4
Southwater Ctry Pk★
  RH13. . . . . .81 F8
Southwater Inf Sch
  RH13. . . . . .57 F2
Southwater Jun Sch
  RH13. . . . . .57 F2
Southwater St RH13 . . . . . .58 A4
Southway
  Burgess Hill RH15 . . . . . .108 D3

Southway continued
Littlehampton BN17......204 F4
South Way PO21..........201 A5
Southway Jun Sch
RH15................108 D3
Southways Ave BN14....186 E6
Southways Pk RH10......5 D3
Southwick Cl RH19........9 D2
Southwick Ho RH19........9 D2
Southwick Sq BN42......189 E7
Southwick St BN42.......189 E8
Southwick Sta BN42......189 E7
South Wlk PO22..........202 E5
Southwold Cl BN13.......163 E1
South Woodlands
BN1................169 E5
Southwood Rd PO11.....195 A1
Sovereign Bsns Pk
RH15................108 E2
Sovereign Ct
21 Bognor Regis
PO21..............201 D3
Brighton BN2.........193 A3
Sovereign Ctr RH15......108 E2
Spa Ct 11 BN3...........191 B5
Spain Bldgs 3 GU32......68 A3
Spain The GU32..........68 A3
Spanish Ct RH15.........109 B4
Sparks Ct BN17..........204 D5
Spark's La RH17..........62 E2
Sparrows La RH20.......123 A5
Sparrow Way RH15.......108 D3
Sparshott Rd PO20......212 E5
Spartan Cl PO10.........173 C3
Spartan Way RH11........5 A1
Spatham La BN6..........129 F4
Spear Hill RH20..........123 A7
Spears Wlk BN2..........193 D8
Speedwell Cl BN3........185 A6
Speedwell Way RH12......36 E5
Spencer Ave BN3.........168 D3
Spencer Rd
Lancing BN15..........187 D5
New Brighton PO10.....151 A4
Spencers La RH6..........1 A2
Spencers Pl RH12.........36 B4
Spencers Rd RH11........18 D5
Spencer's Rd RH12........36 B3
Spencer St PO21..........201 D4
Spey Cl BN13.............185 C9
Spicers Cl RH15..........108 F5
Spierbridge Rd RH20.....121 C2
Spiers Way RH6...........2 B1
Spindle Way RH10........18 F5
Spinnaker Ct RH17........205 A5
Spinnals Gr BN42.........189 D7
Spinney Cl
Crawley Down RH10......21 C8
Horsham RH12..........37 B6
Hurstpierpoint BN6.....128 C5
Selsey PO20............212 D8
Spinney La
West Chiltington Common
RH20................121 D5
West Itchenor PO20....197 A6
Spinney N RH20..........100 D2
Spinney The
Bognor Regis PO21......200 E3
Burgess Hill RH15......109 B5
Crawley RH11..........18 A4
Haslemere GU27........27 C8
Hassocks BN6..........128 F5
Haywards Heath, Franklands
Village RH16..........87 F3
Haywards Heath RH16...87 D8
Horley RH6.............2 A5
Hove BN3..............169 C3
Pulborough RH20.......100 D2
West Itchenor PO20....197 A5
West Kingston BN16....206 A4
Spinney Wlk PO22........180 B6
Spinningfield Ho 1
GU32................68 B4
Spiro Cl RH20............100 B2
Spitalfield La PO19.......177 B7
Spitfire Ct PO20.........156 D2
Spithandle La BN44.......124 B3
Spooners Rd RH12........37 A4
Springate Rd BN42.......189 F8
Springbank PO19.........154 F1
Spring Cl 11 RH11........18 D5
Spring Copse
Copthorne RH10........7 C3
East Grinstead RH19.....9 D3
Spring Copse Bsns Pk
RH13................34 C3
Spring Cotts RH20.......121 C1
Spring Ct BN1...........186 C3
Springfarm Rd GU27......26 E5
Springfield
Bognor Regis PO21......200 A2
East Grinstead RH19.....9 D4
Liss GU33.............45 B4
Springfield Cl
Birdham PO20..........197 F5
Bolney RH17...........85 C4
Mid Lavant PO18.......154 F7
Rustington BN16.......205 E5
Springfield Cotts RH17...85 C4
Springfield Cres RH12.....36 B2
Springfield
Crawley RH11..........18 D5
2 Horsham RH12........36 C2

Springfield Fst Sch
BN14................186 E4
Springfield Gdns
BN13................186 A7
Springfield La RH12......38 B5
Springfield Park Ho
RH12................36 C3
Springfield Park Rd
RH12................36 B2
Springfield Rd
Brighton BN1..........192 A8
Crawley RH11..........18 D5
Horsham RH12.........36 C2
Springfields Farm Ind Est
RH17................109 F5
Spring Gdns
Brighton BN1..........213 B2
Copthorne RH10........7 C3
Emsworth PO10.........173 C8
Heath Common RH20....122 E2
Horsham RH12.........36 C3
6 Southwick BN42.......189 E7
SPRINGHEAD..........26 E5
Springhills BN5..........125 E4
Spring La
Clayton BN6...........149 E8
Lindfield RH16.........64 B1
Slinfold RH13..........34 C3
Spring Mdw RH18.........23 F1
Spring Mdws GU29........94 E6
Springmead Ct GU27......26 D5
Spring Plat RH10.........19 C6
Spring Plat Ct RH10......19 C6
Spring St BN1............191 E5
Spring Way RH19.........10 A4
Spronkett's La RH17......84 E3
Sproule Cl BN18.........181 B2
Sproutes La RH13........102 D8
Sprucefield Ct RH11......18 B6
Spruce Pl RH19..........10 A3
Spurgeon Pl RH11........18 C7
Spur Rd PO19............177 D5
Spy La RH14.............32 A4
Squadron Dr BN13.......185 B7
Square Dr
Fernhurst GU27........49 B7
Kingsley Green GU27....27 B1
Square The
Barnham PO22.........180 B5
Brighton BN1..........169 E6
Compton PO18.........111 B2
Crawley RH10..........18 D6
Findon BN14...........163 E6
Liphook GU30..........25 B4
Petersfield GU32.......68 B3
Prinsted PO10.........173 F7
South Harting GU31.....91 D4
Storrington RH20.......121 D1
Washington RH20.......143 C3
Westbourne PO10......151 D3
Squires Cl RH10..........21 A8
Squires Cotts RH20.......140 A7
Squires The RH11.........39 B6
Squire Way BN5..........125 E4
Squirrel Cl RH11..........5 B1
Squirrels Copse
RH20................122 C3
Stable Cl RH10...........19 D3
Stable Cotts
Crawley RH11..........39 A4
Shopwyke PO20........177 F7
Stable Field PO22........203 B5
Stable La
Findon BN14..........163 E6
7 Petersfield GU31......68 B3
Stable View BN15........188 A5
Stace Way RH10..........19 E8
Stackfield Rd RH11........17 E5
Stafford Cl BN2..........213 C2
Stafford Ho BN6.........129 A3
Stafford Rd
Brighton BN1..........191 E8
Crawley RH11..........5 B1
Petersfield GU32.......68 B5
Staffords Cl BN16........205 B6
Staffords Pl RH6..........2 B2
Stafford Way BN6.........129 A3
Stag Cl BN5..............125 E6
Stagelands RH11..........18 C8
Stagelands Ct RH11.......18 C8
Stairbridge La RH17......107 E7
Stakers La
Southwater RH13........58 A1
Southwater RH13........82 A8
Stalham Way PO22.......202 A6
Stallard Cl PO10.........151 A1
Stallhouse La RH20......101 A7
Stamford 6 RH16.........87 D6
Stamford Lo 2 BN1......169 E2
Stammerham Bsns Ctr
RH12................15 E8
Stammers Hill BN5.......147 F3
Stanbridge Cl RH11.......17 E6
Stanbridge Way RH17......64 B7
Stanbrok Cl PO21........200 B3
Stanbury Cl PO18........175 C7
Standean Cl BN1.........170 D6
Standen Cl RH19..........9 A4
Standen Ct BN44.........146 B2
Standen Ho* RH19.........22 D4
Standen Pl RH12..........37 A7
Standgrove Rd RH17......64 A6
Standinghall La RH10......20 A3
Stane St
Billingshurst RH14,
RH20................79 A4
Codmore Hill RH20......100 D6
Five Oaks RH14........55 E4

Stane St continued
Slinfold RH13..........34 C4
Strettington RH18......156 B3
Westhampnett PO18....155 E1
Wisborough Green RH14,
RH20................78 F1
Stane Street Cl RH20.....100 C4
Stanford Ave
Brighton BN6..........170 A1
Hassocks BN6..........128 E4
Stanford Cl
Bognor Regis PO22.....201 E5
Hassocks BN6..........128 E4
Hove BN3.............169 C1
Stanford Ct
1 Brighton BN1........191 F8
Crawley RH10..........19 C4
Stanford Inf Sch BN1.....191 E8
Stanford Jun Sch
BN1................191 F8
Stanford Orch RH12......35 F8
Stanford Rd BN1.........191 F8
Stanford Sq 2 BN11......186 E2
Stanford Terr BN6........128 E4
Stanford Way RH12.......35 D3
Stan Hill RH6.............4 D8
Stanhope Rd
Littlehampton BN17.....204 E5
Worthing BN11.........186 D3
Stanier Cl RH10..........19 B5
Stanley Ave BN41........167 F3
Stanley Ave S BN41......167 F3
Stanley Cl
Bognor Regis PO21.....201 D4
Crawley RH10..........18 E4
Stanley Ct 3 BN2.........192 A8
Stanley Ctr RH10..........5 F2
Stanley Rd
Brighton BN1..........213 B4
Emsworth PO10........173 C8
Littlehampton BN17.....204 D7
Portslade-by-S BN41....190 A8
Worthing BN11.........186 D3
Stanley St BN2...........213 C3
Stanley Wlk 8 RH13.......36 D2
Stanmer BN1.............170 F8
Stanmer Ave BN2.........194 D3
Stanmer Ct BN1..........170 A2
Stanmer Ho BN1.........170 B2
Stanmer Park Rd
BN1................170 B2
Stanmer St BN1..........170 B2
Stanmer Villas BN1.......170 B2
Stanmore Gdns PO21.....200 E2
Stanmore Ho
Billingshurst RH14......79 D8
5 Storrington RH20.....121 C1
Stanover La PO22........202 A7
Stansfield Ct BN16.......205 D6
Stanstead Cres BN2......193 F6
Stansted Cl RH10.........19 C4
Stansted Ho* PO9........131 E1
Stan's Way 10 RH12.......36 C2
Stanton Dr PO19.........155 A3
Stanton Rd GU32..........68 A4
Stanwater La GU29.......71 F3
Staplecross Ct 1
RH11................18 A3
Staplefield Ct RH17.......61 F6
Staplefield Dr RH17.......170 F3
Staplefield Rd
Cuckfield RH17.........86 C8
Staplefield RH17.......61 E4
Staple La PO18..........154 F8
Staples Barn BN5.........125 D5
Staples Barn La BN5......125 D5
STAPLES HILL...........52 F3
Staples Hill RH13.........104 F4
Stapleton Ct PO21.......200 D2
Stapley Ct BN3...........190 B8
Stapley Rd BN3..........168 D1
Starboard Ct BN2........192 F3
Starboard Wlk BN17.....204 F4
Starborough Cotts RH7....9 F7
Star Cl RH13.............37 A4
Starling Cl RH15.........108 C3
Star Rd RH13............105 A2
Star Road Trad Est
RH13................105 A2
Station App
Chichester PO19.......176 F5
Falmer BN1...........171 B6
Faygate RH12..........16 F1
Haslemere GU27.......27 B6
Hassocks BN6.........128 F4
Horley RH6.............2 B2
Horsted Keynes RH17...65 A7
Hove BN3.............191 B8
Pulborough RH20.......100 A2
Station App E BN6........128 E4
Station Approach Ind Est
RH20................100 A2
Station Approach Rd
RH6.................6 B7
Station App W BN6.......128 E4
Station Cl RH13...........36 D2
Station Cotts
Hassocks BN6.........128 E4
Horsham RH13.........57 D7
Station Hill RH16.........19 B7
Station Par
2 Lancing BN15........187 E5
1 Rustington BN16.....205 E6
1 Worthing BN11.......186 A3
Station Rd
Angmering BN16.......205 F8
Baynards RH12.........12 C3
Billingshurst RH14......79 D7

Station Rd continued
15 Bognor Regis PO21....201 C3
Brighton BN1..........169 D3
Broadbridge PO18......175 C7
Burgess Hill RH15......109 B2
Cowfold RH13..........83 B2
Crawley Down RH10.....21 B8
Crawley RH10, RH11.....18 D5
Crossbush BN18........160 C1
East Grinstead RH19.....9 D1
East Preston BN16......205 F6
Ford BN18............181 E4
Forest Row RH18........23 F3
Henfield RH15.........125 D5
Horley RH6.............2 B3
Horsham RH13..........36 D2
Horsted Keynes RH17....65 C5
Itchingfield RH13........57 D7
Liphook GU30...........25 C2
Liss GU33.............45 B4
Loxwood RH14..........32 A3
Midhurst GU29..........94 D7
Petersfield GU31, GU32...68 A4
Petworth GU28.........97 E5
Portslade-by-S BN3,
BN41................190 C7
Pulborough RH20.......100 A2
Rudgwick RH12.........33 D7
Sharpthorne RH19.......43 A6
7 Southwick BN42.......189 E7
Steyning BN44.........145 E3
Warnham RH12.........36 B8
Worthing BN11.........186 E3
Station Road N RH13......57 F1
Station Road S RH13......57 F1
Station St BN1...........213 B3
Station Villas RH20.......100 A2
Station Way RH11,
RH11................18 D5
Staunton Cntry Pk*
PO9.................130 A2
Stavely Gdns PO19.......154 F3
Stean Furlong BN17......204 C7
Stedham Hall GU29........72 A2
Stedham La GU29.........72 A3
Stedham Prim Sch
GU29................71 F1
Steeds Cnr RH13..........82 D6
Steele Cl RH10...........101 E1
Steels La PO18..........174 E5
Steep CE Prim Sch
GU32................68 B7
Steep Cl BN14...........163 E5
Steepdown Rd BN15......187 C8
Steep La BN14...........163 E5
Steeple View RH13.......186 A5
Steeres Hill RH12.........16 C6
Steers La RH10...........6 C4
Steine Gdns BN2.........213 B2
Steine St BN2...........213 B1
Stein Rd PO10...........151 F2
Stemp Dr RH14...........79 C8
Stempswood Way
PO22................180 C6
Stennings The RH19........9 C3
Stephens Cl PO19........177 C7
Stephenson Dr RH19......22 F7
Stephenson Pl RH10......19 B6
Stephenson Way RH10....19 B6
Stephens Rd BN1.........170 B2
Stepney Cl RH10.........19 C4
Stepney Rd BN1..........213 B4
Sterling Bldgs 6 RH12.....36 C2
Sterling Par 3 BN16......205 C5
Sterling Pk RH10..........6 B3
Sternway BN17...........205 A5
Stetson The BN17........204 D4
Stevenage Rd RH11........17 E3
Stevens Cl BN3..........190 E7
Stevenson Rd BN2.......192 C5
Stewards Rise BN18......159 F1
Steyne Gdns BN11.......186 E2
Steyne Hall 4 PO21......201 C2
Steyne St PO21..........201 C2
Steyne The
Bognor Regis PO21.....201 C2
Worthing BN11.........186 E2
Steyning 2 BN15........187 D5
Steyning Ave BN3........168 F3
Steyning By-Pass
BN44................145 E3
Steyning Cl
Crawley RH10..........18 E8
Lancing BN15.........187 D8
Worthing BN12........185 B4
Steyning Cres RH20.......121 C2
Steyning Ct 7 BN3.......191 B7
Steyning Gram Lower Sch
BN44................145 D4
Steyning Gram Upper Sch
BN44................145 D4
Steyning Ho 1 BN14......186 D5
Steyning Mus* BN44.....145 D3
Steyning Rd
Rottingdean BN2.......194 A1
Shoreham-by-S BN43,
BN44................166 C4
Shoreham-by-S, Mill Hill
BN43................166 D1
West Grinstead RH13...104 C7
Steyning Way PO22......201 E7
Stildon Mews RH19........9 C3
Stile Gdns GU27.........26 F6
Stipenhoke BN5..........125 C1
Stirling Cl
Burgess Hill RH15......109 C4
Crawley RH10..........19 C5

Stirling Court Rd
RH15................109 C4
Stirling Ct 5 BN3.........191 C7
Stirling Pl BN3...........191 A6
Stirling Rd PO19.........177 A5
Stirling Way
Bognor Regis PO21.....200 E2
East Grinstead RH19....10 B3
Horsham RH13.........36 E3
Stirrup Way RH10.........19 D7
Stoatley Hollow GU27.....27 A8
Stoatley Rise GU27.......27 A8
Stockbridge Gdns
PO19................176 E4
Stockbridge Pl PO19......176 F4
Stockbridge Rd PO19....176 F4
Stockcroft Rd RH17.......41 A1
Stockfield RH6............2 B4
Stockham Cl BN15........187 A7
Stocklands Cl RH17.......86 F8
Stocks Cl RH6.............2 B2
Stock Ho BN15...........187 A7
Stock's Field BN44.......123 D1
Stock's Hill BN44........123 D1
Stocks La
Bracklesham PO20......208 A6
Chichester PO18, PO19...155 C3
Stocks Mead RH20.......143 E6
Stockwell Ct
Burgess Hill RH15......108 F3
1 Haywards Heath
RH16................87 E3
Stockwell Ctr RH10........19 A6
Stockwell Rd RH19........22 E6
Stodham La
Hill Side GU33.........45 C2
Liss GU33.............45 B1
Stoke Abbott Ct 2
BN1................186 D2
Stoke Abbott Rd
BN11................186 D2
Stoke Brunswick Sch
RH19................23 E7
Stoke Cl BN11...........186 B1
Stoke Rd BN18...........140 D3
Stokers Cl RH6............5 E7
Stokes Cl RH10...........19 C4
Stoneage Cl PO22........201 C7
Stonebridge Ct
Crawley RH11..........18 C2
Horsham RH12..........36 A2
Stonechat GU31..........68 E2
Stone Cl BN13...........185 F7
Stone Cotts RH10.........20 B1
Stonecourt Cl RH6.........2 C3
Stonecourt Cotts RH17....62 A5
Stonecroft BN44.........145 D3
Stonecroft BN3..........168 E4
Stonecrop Cl RH11.......18 B3
Stone Cross RH16........64 D3
Stonecross La RH16.......64 E3
Stonecross Rd BN2.......170 F4
Stone Ct
Crawley RH10..........19 D5
Midhurst GU29.........94 D8
Stonefield Cl RH10,
RH11................18 D5
Stonefields BN16........205 D5
Stonefield Way RH15.....108 F5
Stonehall La RH17........63 C6
Stoneham Cl GU32........67 F4
Stoneham Pk GU32.......67 F4
Stoneham Rd BN3........190 F7
Stone Hatch GU6.........11 A3
Stonehill Cres PO21......200 B3
Stonehouse La RH13......83 B1
Stonehouse Rd GU30......25 D4
Stonehurst Ct 10 BN2....192 C6
Stonehurst Rd RH13......186 A5
Stone La BN13...........185 F7
Stoneleigh Ave BN1......169 F6
Stoneleigh Cl
Brighton BN1..........169 F6
East Grinstead RH19.....9 F1
Stonepit La BN5..........125 C5
Stonepound Crossroads
BN6.................128 D3
Stonepound Rd BN6.....128 E4
Stonepound Ridge
BN6.................128 D4
STONEQUARRY..........10 A3
Stone Quarry Rd RH17....66 D7
Stonery Cl BN41.........168 A2
Stonery Rd BN41.........168 A2
Stone St BN1............191 E5
Stonewall Cotts RH14.....53 A3
Stoneybrook 1 RH12......35 F1
Stoneycroft Wlk 3
RH11................17 D5
Stoneyfield Cotts
PO20................158 B1
Stoney La
Balcombe Lane RH17.....41 B5
Bracklesham PO20......208 D4
Shoreham-by-S BN43....189 C8
Stoney Stile Cl PO21.....200 C2
Stoney Stile La PO21.....200 C1
Stoneywish Nature
Reserve* BN6..........129 E3
STOPHAM...............99 D3
Stopham Cl BN14........186 A5
Stopham Rd
Crawley RH10..........19 C3
Pulborough RH20.......99 E1
Stor Mdw RH20..........121 D2
Storrington Cl
Fishbourne PO19.......176 B7
Hove BN3.............168 E2

Storrington Ct RH11 . . . . . 18 A7
Storrington & District
Mus★ RH20 . . . . 121 D1
Storrington Fst Sch
RH20. . . . . 121 C2
Storrington Rd
Heath Common RH20 . . . . 122 A5
Washington RH20 . . . . . . 143 C8
Storrington Rise
BN14 . . . . 163 F4
Story Rd PO19 . . . . 177 C7
Stour Cl
Petersfield GU31 . . . . 68 A2
Worthing BN13 . . . . 185 C9
Stour Rd BN13 . . . . 185 C9
Strachey Ct 10 RH11 . . . . . . 18 B1
Strand Cl RH11 . . . . 19 D4
Strand Ct
Rustington BN16 . . . . 205 B3
11 West Kingston
BN16 . . . . 206 A4
Strand Par BN12 . . . . 185 E4
Strand The
Brighton BN2 . . . . 193 A3
Ferring BN12 . . . . 206 E4
Worthing BN12 . . . . 185 C4
Strand Way PO22 . . . . 202 B4
Strange Gdn PO21 . . . . . . 200 E1
Stratford Ct BN11 . . . . 186 C2
Strathfield Cl RH16 . . . . 87 F4
Strathmoor Gdns GU29 . . . . 72 F1
Strathmore Ct BN13 . . . . . 185 E5
Strathmore Rd
Crawley RH11 . . . . 5 A1
Worthing BN13 . . . . 185 E5
Stratton Ct PO22 . . . . 201 E5
Strawberry Field
RH20 . . . . 100 D3
Strawberry La RH20 . . . . . 122 B5
Strawson Ct RH6 . . . . 1 F4
Stream Cl PO18 . . . . 175 B5
Stream La RH20 . . . . 101 B1
Stream Pk RH19 . . . . 9 A3
Streathleigh Ct PO21 . . . . 201 A2
Streel's La GU28 . . . . 51 F5
Street Barn BN15 . . . . 187 A4
Streete Ct 12 PO21 . . . . . . 201 B2
Street End La RH20 . . . . . . 198 E3
Street End Rd PO20 . . . . . 198 E3
Streetfield Rd RH13 . . . . 34 E3
Street Hill RH10 . . . . 19 E5
Street La RH17 . . . . 64 A8
Street The
Albourne Green BN6 . . . . . 127 C6
Bolney RH17 . . . . 85 C3
Boxgrove PO18 . . . . 156 D4
Bramber BN44 . . . . 145 F2
Bury RH20 . . . . 140 A7
Charlwood RH6 . . . . 4 E7
Clapham BN13 . . . . 162 E1
Cowfold RH13 . . . . 83 E2
East Preston BN16 . . . . . . 205 F6
Kingston near Lewes
BN7 . . . . 172 E5
Lancing BN15 . . . . 187 F8
Nutbourne RH20 . . . . 101 A2
Patching BN13 . . . . 162 D2
Plaistow RH14 . . . . 30 E2
Rustington BN16 . . . . 205 C5
Shoreham-by-S BN43 . . . . 166 E1
Slinfold RH13 . . . . 34 D4
South Harting GU31 . . . . . . 91 C3
Stedham GU29 . . . . 72 A1
Thakeham RH20 . . . . 122 B7
Walberton BN18 . . . . 158 D1
Warninglid RH17 . . . . 84 F8
Washington RH20 . . . . . . 143 D6
West Itchenor PO20 . . . . . 196 F7
Westmeston BN6 . . . . 150 F8
Stretch Hill RH20 . . . . 99 A5
Stretham Farm BN5 . . . . . . 146 C8
Stretham La BN5 . . . . 146 E8
Strettington La RH14 . . . . . 156 A3
Stretton Ct 6 BN3 . . . . . . 190 F7
Strettons Copse GU30 . . . . . 47 B2
Strickland Ct 4 RH11 . . . . . 17 E5
Stride Cl PO19 . . . . 177 C6
Stringer Way BN1 . . . . 169 F3
Strone Ct BN11 . . . . 185 F2
STROOD GREEN 35 A6
Strood La RH12 . . . . 35 C7
Stroud End GU32 . . . . 67 D4
Stroud Green Dr
PO21 . . . . 200 F5
Stroudley Cl RH10 . . . . 19 B5
Stroudley Ct BN16 . . . . . . 205 E6
Stroudley Rd BN1 . . . . 213 B4
Strouds La PO21 . . . . 200 F5
Strudgate Cl 1 RH10 . . . . . 19 B4
Strudwick Ho BN11 . . . . . 187 A3
Stuart Cl
Crawley RH10 . . . . 19 D5
Worthing BN11 . . . . 186 F4
Stuart Ho 5 RH11 . . . . 36 F3
Stuarts Mdw GU28 . . . . . . 116 C8
Stuart Way RH19 . . . . 22 F7
Stubbermere PO9 . . . . 151 B8
Stubcroft La PO20 . . . . . . 208 B7
Stubfield RH12 . . . . 36 A3
Stubpond La RH7 . . . . 8 C8
Stumblemead RH17 . . . . . . 41 A1
Stumblets RH10 . . . . 19 C7
Stumps End PO18 . . . . . . 175 C4
Stumps La PO18 . . . . 175 C6
Sturges Rd PO21 . . . . 201 C3
Sturt Ave GU27 . . . . 26 F5
Sturt Rd GU27 . . . . 26 F5
Sudbury Cl PO21 . . . . 200 C1

Sudeley Pl BN2 . . . . 192 D4
Sudeley St BN2 . . . . 192 D4
Sudeley Terr 6 BN2 . . . . . 192 D4
Sudley Gdns PO21 . . . . . . 201 D3
Sudley Rd PO21 . . . . 201 D3
Sudley Terr 23 PO21 . . . . . 201 D3
Suffolk Cl RH16 . . . . 2 A2
Suffolk St BN3 . . . . 190 F8
Sugar La RH17 . . . . 65 C4
Sugden Rd BN11 . . . . 186 F3
Sugworth Cl RH16 . . . . 87 D7
SULLINGTON 142 F7
Sullington Cl BN2 . . . . 170 F4
Sullington Copse
RH20 . . . . 121 F2
Sullington Gdns BN14 . . . . 163 F3
Sullington Hill RH11 . . . . . . 18 D4
Sullington La RH20 . . . . . . 142 F7
Sullington Mead RH12 . . . . 35 E3
Sullington Way BN43 . . . . 189 A8
Sullivan Dr RH11 . . . . 17 E3
Sultan Rd PO10 . . . . 151 B1
Summer Cl BN41 . . . . 190 A4
Summerdale Rd BN3 . . . . . 168 D2
Summerdown Cl
BN13 . . . . 185 B6
Summerdown Ct
BN13 . . . . 185 B6
Summerfield Rd
PO20 . . . . 196 C2
Summerfields BN14 . . . . . 163 E6
Summerfold RH12 . . . . 33 E8
Summerhill Cl
Bognor Regis PO22 . . . . . 202 C6
Haywards Heath RH16 . . . . 87 F7
Summerhill Dr
Bognor Regis PO22 . . . . . 202 C6
Lindfield RH16 . . . . 88 A7
Summerhill Grange
RH16 . . . . 87 F7
Summerhill La RH16 . . . . . . 87 F7
Summer Ho RH11 . . . . 18 C5
Summer La PO21 . . . . 199 F1
Summerlea Ct BN16 . . . . . 205 B8
Summerlea Com Prim Sch
BN16 . . . . 205 B7
Summerlea Gdns 5
BN17 . . . . 204 E5
Summerley La PO22 . . . . . 202 B5
Summers Cl BN16 . . . . 205 C4
SUMMERSDALE 155 B2
Summersdale Ct
PO19 . . . . 154 F3
Summersdale Rd
PO19 . . . . 155 A1
Summersdeane BN42 . . . . 167 F4
Summersfield GU33 . . . . . . 45 B4
Summers Ho PO22 . . . . 94 D6
Summersvere Cl RH10 . . . . . 6 A1
Sumners RH17 . . . . 64 B7
Sun Brow GU27 . . . . 27 A5
Sun Ct 11 BN1 . . . . 186 A1
Sundale La PO22 . . . . 202 E5
Sunderland Cl PO20 . . . . . 156 D2
Sundew Cl RH11 . . . . 18 A2
Sunflower Cl BN17 . . . . . . 205 B7
Sunleigh Ct RH6 . . . . 127 F6
Sunningdale RH6 . . . . 2 B2
Sunningdale Ct
Crawley RH10 . . . . 18 D4
Worthing BN12 . . . . 185 C4
Sunningdale Gdns
Bognor Regis PO22 . . . . . 201 B7
East Wittering PO20 . . . . . 207 D7
Sunningdale Rd BN13 . . . . 185 E2
Sunninghill Ave BN3 . . . . . 168 F2
Sunninghill Cl BN3 . . . . . . 168 F2
Sunny Ave RH10 . . . . 21 A8
Sunnybox La BN18 . . . . . . 158 E4
Sunny Cl BN12 . . . . 185 E2
Sunnycroft Cl RH17 . . . . . . 88 E2
Sunnydale Ave BN1 . . . . . 170 A6
Sunnydale Cl BN1 . . . . 170 A6
Sunnydown Ct BN16 . . . . . 205 A3
Sunnyhill Cl RH10 . . . . 21 A8
Sunnymead RH11 . . . . 18 D6
Sunnymead Cl
Ancton PO22 . . . . 203 A6
Selsey PO20 . . . . 212 E6
Sunnymead Dr PO20 . . . . 212 E6
SUNNYSIDE 22 E7
Sunnyside Cl BN16 . . . . . . 206 A8
Sunnyside Cotts
RH20 . . . . 121 D1
Sunny Way PO18 . . . . 175 B5
Sunnywood Cl RH16 . . . . . 87 D3
Sunnywood Dr RH16 . . . . . 87 D3
Sun Park Ct PO21 . . . . 201 A6
Sunset La RH20 . . . . 121 C5
Sunte Ave RH16 . . . . 87 E7
Sunte Cl RH16 . . . . 87 E7
Sunvale Ave GU27 . . . . 26 D6
Sunvale Cl GU27 . . . . 26 D6
Surrenden Cl BN1 . . . . 169 F4
Surrenden Cres BN1 . . . . . 169 E4
Surrenden Holt BN1 . . . . . 169 F3
Surrenden Lo BN1 . . . . . . 169 F2
Surrenden Pk BN1 . . . . . . 170 A4
Surrenden Rd BN1 . . . . . . 169 F3
Surrenden Rise RH11 . . . . . 39 C8
Surrey Cott 6 BN17 . . . . . 204 F4
Surrey Ct 5 RH11 . . . . 36 D2
Surrey Ho 12 BN2 . . . . . . 192 D4
Surrey St
Arundel BN18 . . . . 160 A2
Brighton BN1 . . . . 213 A4
Littlehampton BN17 . . . . . 204 D5
Worthing BN11 . . . . 186 C1

Surrey Wharf BN18 . . . . . . 160 B2
Surry St BN43 . . . . 188 F7
Sussex Aquatic & Falconry
Ctr★ PO20 . . . . 198 C7
Sussex Bsns Village The
PO22 . . . . 180 E6
Sussex Cotts RH19 . . . . 43 A6
Sussex Ct
Billingshurst RH14 . . . . 79 D7
7 Bognor Regis PO21 . . . . 201 B2
Elmer PO22 . . . . 203 B5
Findon BN14 . . . . 163 E6
2 Haywards Heath
RH16 . . . . 87 E3
2 Horsham RH13 . . . . . . 36 E1
15 Hove BN3 . . . . 191 A7
4 Shoreham-by-S
BN43 . . . . 189 A6
Worthing BN11 . . . . 186 C2
Sussex Cty Cricket Gd
BN3 . . . . 191 C7
Sussex Dr PO21 . . . . 200 A1
Sussex Eye Hospl
BN2 . . . . 192 D4
Sussex Gdns
Haywards Heath RH17 . . . . 88 B3
Petersfield GU31 . . . . 68 B2
Rustington BN16 . . . . 205 C6
Sussex Gr PO20 . . . . 208 C5
Sussex House Bsns Pk
BN3 . . . . 190 F8
Sussex Hts 13 BN1 . . . . . . 191 E5
Sussex Lo RH12 . . . . 36 C4
Sussex Manor Bsns Pk
RH10 . . . . 6 A2
Sussex Mews 4 BN2 . . . . 192 E4
Sussex Pl BN2 . . . . 213 C3
Sussex Rd
Haywards Heath RH16 . . . . 87 E3
Hove BN3 . . . . 191 B5
Lancing BN15 . . . . 188 C5
Petersfield GU31 . . . . 68 D1
Worthing BN11 . . . . 186 D3
Sussex Sq
Brighton BN2 . . . . 192 E4
17 Haywards Heath
RH16 . . . . 87 E4
Sussex Square Mews 16
BN2 . . . . 192 E4
Sussex St
Bognor Regis PO21 . . . . . 201 D3
Brighton BN2 . . . . 213 C2
Littlehampton BN17 . . . . . 204 D6
Sussex Terr
Brighton BN2 . . . . 213 C3
3 Midhurst GU29 . . . . . . 94 E7
Sussex View BN1 . . . . 191 D7
Sussex Village PO22 . . . . 203 B5
Sussex Way RH15 . . . . 108 E5
Sussex Wharf BN43 . . . . . 189 B6
Sutherland Cl
Bognor Regis PO22 . . . . . 201 C3
Rustington BN16 . . . . 205 B5
Sutherland Ct 4
PO21 . . . . 201 C3
Sutherland Rd BN2 . . . . . . 192 C5
Sutton Ave BN16 . . . . 205 C4
Sutton Cl
Bognor Regis PO22 . . . . . 201 F6
Woodingdean BN2 . . . . . 171 E1
SUTTON END 118 A5
Sutton Tye RH16 . . . . 87 F6
Suva Ct RH19 . . . . 9 C3
Swainsthorpe Cl RH16 . . . . 87 F3
Swaledale Cl RH11 . . . . . . 18 C3
Swallowfield Cl RH15 . . . . . 59 C5
Swallow Field Copse
RH13 . . . . 58 A3
Swallow Rd RH11 . . . . 18 C8
Swallow Rest RH15 . . . . . 108 C3
Swallows Cl 3 BN15 . . . . . 188 C5
Swallows Green Dr
BN13 . . . . 185 C6
Swallows La RH13 . . . . . . 103 F6
Swallow St RH10 . . . . 21 C5
Swallows The BN17 . . . . . 204 D4
Swallowtail Rd RH12 . . . . . 36 E6
Swan Barn Rd GU27 . . . . . 27 D6
Swanborough Ct 7
BN43 . . . . 188 F7
Swanborough Dr BN2 . . . . 192 F4
Swanborough Dro
BN7 . . . . 172 F4
Swanborough Pl BN2 . . . . 192 F7
Swanborough BN15 . . . . . 187 F8
Swanbourne Rd
BN17 . . . . 204 D7
Swan Cl
Emsworth PO10 . . . . 173 C8
Southwater RH13 . . . . 58 A2
Storrington RH20 . . . . 121 C2
Swan Cnr RH20 . . . . 100 B2
Swandean Cl BN13 . . . . . . 185 E9
Swan Dene PO21 . . . . 210 F7
Swanfield Dr PO19 . . . . . . 177 C8
Swan La RH6 . . . . 4 F7
Swan Lo 6 BN15 . . . . 187 F5
Swann Cl RH15 . . . . 109 D3
Swann Way RH12 . . . . 35 E3
Swansea Gdns PO21 . . . . 201 B2
Swans Ghyll RH18 . . . . 23 E3
Swan Sq RH12 . . . . 36 C2
Swan St GU32 . . . . 68 A3
Swan View RH20 . . . . 100 C1
Swan Wlk RH12 . . . . 36 C2
Sweda Ct 13 BN2 . . . . 192 D4
Sweetlands BN6 . . . . 129 B5

Swift Cl RH15 . . . . 108 D3
Swift La RH11 . . . . 18 C8
Swift Rd PO10 . . . . 173 C3
Swift Way BN17 . . . . 204 C8
Swillage La BN16,
BN13 . . . . 184 A8
Swindon Rd RH12 . . . . 36 B4
Swiss Gdns BN43 . . . . 188 F7
Swissland Hill RH19, RH7 . . . 9 E7
Sycamore Ave RH12 . . . . . 37 C6
Sycamore Cl
Angmering BN16 . . . . 205 F8
Crawley RH11 . . . . 5 C1
Hove BN41 . . . . 168 C3
Woodingdean BN2 . . . . . 193 E8
Sycamore Ct
Brighton BN2 . . . . 192 D8
Nepcote BN14 . . . . 163 E6
Sycamore Dr RH19 . . . . . . 10 A3
Sycamore Rd PO22 . . . . . 201 C2
Sycamores The
Chichester PO19 . . . . 177 A7
Sayers Common BN6 . . . . 107 C3
Sycamore Wlk GU31 . . . . . 68 A1
Sydenham Terr PO10 . . . . 151 D5
Sydney Rd RH16 . . . . 87 E6
Sydney St BN1 . . . . 213 B3
Syers Cl GU33 . . . . 45 B4
Syers Rd GU33 . . . . 45 A4
Syke Cluan Cl PO22 . . . . . 180 B6
Sylvan Cl RH16 . . . . 88 A4
Sylvan Rd
Crawley RH10 . . . . 19 A4
Lancing BN15 . . . . 187 B6
Sylvan Way PO21 . . . . 201 B3
Sylvester Way BN3 . . . . . . 168 C3
Sylvia Cl PO21 . . . . 200 A1
Symbister Rd BN41 . . . . . . 190 C7
Syresham Gdns RH16 . . . . 87 F4

T

Tabard Gate PO21 . . . . . . 200 B1
Tacklee Rd BN18 . . . . 180 F3
Talbot Cres BN1 . . . . 170 D6
Talbot La RH12 . . . . 36 C1
Talbot Rd BN17 . . . . 204 C5
Taldua Pl 22 PO21 . . . . . . 201 B2
Tallis Cl RH11 . . . . 17 F3
Tall Oaks RH16 . . . . 88 B5
Talman Cl RH11 . . . . 17 E5
Tamar Ave BN13 . . . . 185 C8
Tamar Cl
Crawley RH10 . . . . 19 C5
Worthing BN13 . . . . 185 C8
Tamarisk Cl PO22 . . . . . . 201 C6
Tamarisk Way
Ferring BN12 . . . . 206 F5
Littlehampton BN16 . . . . . 205 F4
Tamarisk Wlk PO20 . . . . . 207 F6
Tamar Way PO20 . . . . 156 D2
Tamplin Terr BN2 . . . . 213 C3
Tamworth Rd BN3 . . . . . . 190 F7
Tanbridge Ho RH12 . . . . . . 36 B1
Tanbridge House Sch
RH12 . . . . 35 F2
Tanbridge Pk RH12 . . . . . . 36 B1
Tanbridge Pl RH12 . . . . . . 36 B1
Tanbridge Ret Pk
RH12 . . . . 36 B1
Tandridge Rd BN3 . . . . . . 190 E6
Tanfield Ct 4 RH12 . . . . . . 36 B2
Tangle Oak RH19 . . . . 8 E4
Tangmere Ct 8 BN16 . . . . 205 C4
Tangmere Gdns PO20 . . . 200 D2
Tangmere Military
Aviation Mus★
PO20 . . . . 156 D4
Tangmere Prim Sch
PO20 . . . . 156 D2
Tangmere Rd
Brighton BN1 . . . . 170 A6
Crawley RH11 . . . . 17 F6
Oving PO20 . . . . 178 B8
Tankerdale La
Liss GU33 . . . . 45 A1
Steep GU33 . . . . 68 F8
Tanners Cross 1 RH16 . . . . 87 C2
Tanners Ct GU27 . . . . 27 C7
Tanners La GU27 . . . . 27 C7
Tanners Mead RH17 . . . . . 61 F5
Tannery Cl
Chichester PO19 . . . . 176 E6
Slinfold RH13 . . . . 34 D3
Tannery Ct 5 RH13 . . . . . . 36 D1
Tansy Mead RH20 . . . . . . 121 B2
Tanyard Ave RH19 . . . . . . 23 A8
Tanyard Cl
Crawley RH10 . . . . 19 C5
Horsham RH13 . . . . 36 E1
Tanyard Cotts BN44 . . . . . 145 C3
Tanyard La
Chelwood Common RH17,
TN22 . . . . 66 C4
Steyning BN44 . . . . 145 D3
Tanyard Way RH6 . . . . 2 B4
Tarham Cl RH11 . . . . 1 E5
Tarmount La BN43 . . . . . . 188 F7
Tarner Rd BN2 . . . . 213 C4
Tarragon Way BN43 . . . . . 167 C1
Tarrant St BN18 . . . . 160 B2
Tarrant Wharf BN18 . . . . . 160 B2
Tarring Gate BN14 . . . . . . 186 A4
Tarring Rd BN11 . . . . 186 B3
Tasman Cl BN16 . . . . 205 D4
Tasman Way BN13 . . . . . . 185 C7
Tatchells GU29 . . . . 94 D6

Tate Cres RH15 . . . . 108 F5
Tate's Way RH12 . . . . 33 D7
Tatham Ct RH11 . . . . 19 E6
Taunton Cl RH10 . . . . 19 E6
Taunton Gr BN2 . . . . 171 A1
Taunton Pl BN2 . . . . 171 A1
Taunton Rd BN2 . . . . 170 F1
Taunton Way BN2 . . . . . . 171 A1
Tavern Ct GU27 . . . . 49 B6
Taverner Pl PO19 . . . . . . 177 B5
Tavistock Down BN1 . . . . 170 C2
Tavistock & Summerhill
Sch RH16 . . . . 87 F7
Tavy Cl BN13 . . . . 185 C7
Tavy Rd BN13 . . . . 185 C7
Taw Cl BN13 . . . . 185 D8
Taylor Cl 9 BN16 . . . . 205 B7
Taylors Field GU29 . . . . . . 94 E6
Taylor's La PO18 . . . . 175 C4
Taylors Rise GU29 . . . . . . 94 E6
Taylor Wlk RH11 . . . . 18 C6
Taymor Ct BN1 . . . . 186 A1
Teachers Terr GU33 . . . . . 45 B4
Teal Cl RH11 . . . . 18 B3
Teal Ct RH12 . . . . 36 C5
Teal La PO20 . . . . 212 C8
Teasel Cl RH11 . . . . 18 B3
Teazle Cl GU31 . . . . 68 C2
Teesdale RH11 . . . . 18 C3
Teg Cl BN41 . . . . 168 C4
Teg Down GU31 . . . . 68 D4
Teign Wlk BN13 . . . . 185 C9
Teknol Ho RH15 . . . . 108 C3
Telegraph La GU31 . . . . . . 92 A3
Telegraph St 12 BN2 . . . . 192 C5
Telford Pl RH10 . . . . 18 E5
Telgarth Rd BN12 . . . . . . 206 F4
Telham Ct 5 RH11 . . . . . . 17 F3
Templars Cl PO22 . . . . . . 202 D6
Templars Fst Sch
BN15 . . . . 187 B6
Templars Mews BN15 . . . 187 B6
Templars The BN14 . . . . . 186 E7
Temple Bar Bsns Pk
PO18 . . . . 156 A3
Temple Cl RH10 . . . . 19 D5
Temple Ct 2 BN17 . . . . . . 204 E5
Temple Gdns BN1 . . . . . . 191 E6
Temple Gr RH15 . . . . 108 D4
Temple Hts 14 BN1 . . . . . 191 E6
Temple Rd GU33 . . . . 45 C6
Templesheen Rd
PO22 . . . . 203 B5
Temple St BN1 . . . . 191 E6
Ten Acres BN11 . . . . 187 E4
Tenantry Down Rd
BN2 . . . . 192 E8
Tenantry Rd BN2 . . . . 192 D8
Tennis Rd BN3 . . . . 190 E6
Tennyson Ave BN16 . . . . . 205 B5
Tennyson Cl
Crawley RH10 . . . . 19 B8
Horsham RH13 . . . . 36 E6
Tennyson Ct
5 Haywards Heath
RH16 . . . . 87 D5
3 Hove BN3 . . . . 191 A7
Tennyson Ho 4 BN11 . . . . 186 C2
Tennyson Rd
Bognor Regis PO21 . . . . . 201 B3
Worthing BN11 . . . . 186 C2
Tennyson Rise RH19 . . . . . 22 C8
Tennyson's La GU27 . . . . . 27 E4
Tennysons Ridge GU27 . . . 27 E5
Terminus Mill PO19 . . . . . 176 F5
Terminus Pl
7 Brighton BN1 . . . . 213 A4
Littlehampton BN17 . . . . . 204 D5
Terminus Rd
Brighton BN1 . . . . 213 A4
Chichester PO19 . . . . 176 E5
Littlehampton BN17 . . . . . 204 C5
Terminus Road Ind Est
PO19 . . . . 176 E5
Terminus St BN1 . . . . 213 A3
Tern Rd RH11 . . . . 17 D5
Terraces The BN2 . . . . . . 213 C1
Terrace The
Crossbush BN18 . . . . 160 E1
Lancing BN15 . . . . 187 E4
Sidlesham PO20 . . . . 209 F7
Worthing BN12 . . . . 185 F6
Terringes Ave BN13 . . . . . 185 F6
Terry Rd RH11 . . . . 18 B1
Terry's Cross BN5 . . . . . . 126 C2
TERWICK COMMON 70 D6
Terwick La GU31 . . . . 93 A8
Terwick Rise GU31 . . . . . . 70 D6
Test Cl GU31 . . . . 68 A2
Testers Cl RH13 . . . . 82 A7
Test Rd BN15 . . . . 187 B6
Teville Gate BN11 . . . . . . 186 D3
Teville Inds BN14 . . . . . . 186 F5
Teville Pl BN11 . . . . 186 C3
Teville Rd BN11 . . . . 186 D3
Thackeray Rd BN14 . . . . . 186 F4
Thakeham Cl
East Preston BN16 . . . . . . 206 B7
Worthing BN12 . . . . 185 A3
Thakeham Copse
RH20 . . . . 122 B3
Thakeham Dr BN13 . . . . . 185 A3
Thakeham Fst Sch
RH20 . . . . 122 B7
Thakeham Rd RH20 . . . . . 121 F2

Thalassa Rd BN11......187 B3
Thames Cl
  Brighton BN2.........213 C2
  Littlehampton BN17...205 A4
Thames Way BN13.....185 D8
Thatch Cl RH10.........18 D3
Thatcher Cl RH10......18 D3
Thatchers Cl
  Burgess Hill RH15....109 D1
  Horley RH6............2 B5
  Horsham RH12........36 E4
Thatchers Lo **2**
  BN17...............204 D5
Thatchway Cl BN17....204 D6
Thatchway The
  Angmering BN16......183 E5
  Rustington BN16......205 D4
Theatre La PO19.......177 A6
Theatre Pl **12** PO19...177 A6
Thelton Ave RH12.......35 D3
Theobald Ho **1** BN1...213 B3
Theobalds Rd RH15....109 D6
Thesiger Cl BN11......187 A4
Thesiger Rd BN11.....187 A4
Thetford Wlk RH11.....17 E2
Theydon Cl RH10.......19 A4
Thicket La PO18......157 B5
Third Ave
  Almodington PO20....208 E8
  Bognor Regis PO22...202 B4
  Bracklesham PO20....208 B5
  Hove BN3............191 B6
  Lancing BN15.......187 E7
  Worthing BN13......186 D7
Thirlmere Cres BN15...187 B5
Thirlmere Rd RH11.....17 D4
Thirlmere Way PO22...202 B6
Thistledowne Gdns
  PO10...............173 D8
Thistledown Vale
  RH14...............31 D3
Thistle Way RH13......58 A3
Thomas A Becket Fst Sch
  BN13...............186 A5
Thomas A Becket Mid Sch
  BN14...............186 A5
Thomas Bennett Com Coll
  RH10...............18 D2
Thomas Rd GU31.......68 C5
Thompson Rd
  Brighton BN1........170 C1
  Middleton-on-S PO22..202 F5
Thompson's Hospl
  GU28...............75 F1
Thomson Cl BN3......185 B7
Thomson Ct **16** RH11...18 B1
Thorgate Rd BN17.....204 B7
Thorlands GU27........27 A7
Thornberry Middle Sch
  BN15...............187 F5
Thornbush Cres BN41..168 B3
Thorn Cl GU31.........68 E2
Thorncroft Rd BN17....204 F6
Thorndean Rd RH7.....85 D7
Thorndean Rd BN2.....170 D3
Thornden RH3.........83 E2
Thorndene Ave PO21...201 B4
Thorndyke Cl RH10.....19 D5
Thorney Dr PO20......212 C7
Thorney Island Com Prim
  Sch PO10............173 C3
Thorney Old Pk PO10..173 F1
Thorney Rd PO10......173 D6
Thornham La PO10.....173 D6
Thornham Marina
  PO10...............173 E6
Thornhill RH11........18 B4
Thornhill Ave BN1.....170 A7
Thornhill Cl BN3......168 E2
Thornhill Rise BN41....168 A4
Thornhill Way BN41....168 A3
Thornhurst RH15......109 C1
Thornlea Pk BN17.....182 C5
Thorn Rd BN11........186 C1
Thornscroft BN44.....145 D4
Thornsdale **5** BN2....213 C3
Thornton Cl RH6.......1 E3
Thornton Ct **2** BN16..205 E4
Thornton Mdw RH14...78 B8
Thornton Pl RH6.......1 F3
Threals Copse RH20...121 E5
Threal's La RH20......121 E6
Three Acres RH12......36 A1
THREE BRIDGES......19 A8
Three Bridges Inf Sch
  RH10...............19 A7
Three Bridges Jun Sch
  RH10...............18 F6
Three Bridges Rd
  RH10...............19 A6
Three Bridges Sta
  RH10...............19 B6
Three Gates GU27......27 E8
Threestile Cnr RH12....14 E1
Threestile Rd RH12....14 F1
Thrusloes PO21.......200 F3
Thurlow Rd BN11......186 F3
Thurne Way RH12......33 D7
Thyme Cl BN43........167 C1
Thyme Ho **5** RH12.....6 A1
Ticehurst Cl RH10.....19 E6
Ticehurst Rd BN2......192 F5
Tichborne Cotts RH15..88 C6
Tichborne St BN1......213 B2
Tideway BN17.........205 A4

Tide Way PO20........208 C5
Tideys Mill RH13......104 F3
Tidy St BN1...........213 B3
Tilbury Pl BN2........213 C2
Tilbury Way BN2......213 C3
Tilebarn Ct RH16......87 E2
Tile Barn Est PO20....197 C1
Tile Barn La PO20.....197 C1
Tilemakers Cl PO18....155 E1
Tilers Cl RH15........109 D3
Tilford Dr PO22.......201 E6
TILGATE............18 E2
Tilgate Cl BN2........192 D6
Tilgate Dr RH10, RH11..18 E2
Tilgate Forest Bsns Ctr
  RH11...............18 D1
TILGATE FOREST ROW
  ....39 C5
Tilgate Forest Row
  RH11...............39 C5
Tilgate Mans RH10.....18 E3
Tilgate Par RH10......18 E3
Tilgate Park Ctry Pk★
  RH10...............18 F1
Tilgate Pl RH10........18 E3
Tilgate Way RH10......18 E3
Tilletts La RH12........35 E8
Tillinghurst La RH17...42 A2
Tillington BN2.........192 F7
Tillington Cotts BN18..180 F3
Tillington Rd GU28.....97 C7
Tillotson Cl RH10......19 D5
Tillstone Cl BN2......170 D2
Tillstone St BN2.......213 C2
Tilmore Gdns GU32....68 B5
Tilmore Rd GU32......68 B5
Tilsmore **17** BN2.....192 F5
Tiltwood Dr RH10......21 C8
Timber Cl BN13.......185 C6
Timber Ct RH12........36 C3
Timberham Farm Rd
  RH6................5 D8
Timberham Ho RH6.....5 E8
Timberham Way RH6....5 E8
Timberlaine Ind Est
  PO19...............177 C5
Timberlaine Trad Est
  BN14...............186 F5
Timberlands
  14 Crawley RH11....18 B1
  Storrington RH20.....121 E2
Timberlea Cl BN20....123 A5
Timberleys **1** BN17...205 A6
Timber Mill RH13......57 F2
Timbermill Ct GU27....26 F6
Timbers The
  East Grinstead RH19...9 C2
  Mannings Heath RH13..59 C6
Tindal Cl RH15........109 D3
Tinghall PO21........200 E3
Tinsley Cl RH10........6 A1
Tinsley Gn RH10.......6 B4
TINSLEY GREEN......6 C4
Tinsley La RH10........6 A1
Tinsley La N RH10......6 B3
Tinsley La S RH10......19 A8
Tintagel Ct
  Horsham RH13........36 D1
  Hove BN3...........191 A8
  6 Shoreham-by-S
  BN43...............188 F7
Tintern Cl BN1........170 B1
Tintern Rd RH11.......18 A4
Tinwood La
  Crockerhill PO18.....157 A4
  Halnaker PO18......156 E5
Tipper La GU31........91 D3
Tiree Path RH11........18 B3
Tisbury Rd BN3.......191 C6
TISMAN'S COMMON.....33 A6
Titchfield Cl RH15.....109 D1
Titch Hill BN15.......165 A3
Tithe Barn RH15......187 E8
Tithe Barn Chalets
  PO20...............212 B8
Tithe Barn Cl PO21....200 C1
Tithe Barn Ct PO21....211 B8
Tithe Barn Way PO21..200 B1
Tithe Gn BN16........205 B5
Tithe Orch RH19........8 C4
Tithe The RH11........5 A1
Titian Rd BN3........190 F7
Titmus Dr RH10.......18 F2
Titnore La BN12, BN13.185 A7
Titnore Way BN12,
  BN13...............185 A4
Tivoli BN1............169 E2
Tivoli Cres BN1.......169 D1
Tivoli Cres N BN1.....169 D2
Tivoli Pl BN1.........169 D2
Tivoli Rd BN1.........169 D2
Toat Hill RH13.........56 E8
Toat La RH20.........100 A8
Tobias Sch of Art
  RH19...............22 E6
TODDINGTON.......204 E8
Toddington La BN17...204 E8
Toddington Pk BN17...204 E7
Todds Cl RH6...........1 C5
Toftwood Cl RH10......19 C5
Tollbridge Ho BN43...188 D8
Tollgate RH16.........88 B8
Tollgate Hill RH11......18 C1
Tollgate La RH17.......86 E8
Tollgate Pl **12** RH19...22 E8
Tollhouse Cl PO19....176 F6
Tompset's Bank RH18..23 F1
Tomtit Cres RH10......21 C5

Tomtits La RH18.......23 E1
Tongdean Ave BN3....169 C2
Tongdean La BN1.....169 C4
Tongdean Pl BN3......169 C3
Tongdean Rd BN3.....169 C3
Tongdean Rise BN1...169 C4
Top Hill Cl BN41......167 F2
TOPLEIGH...........95 F2
Top Rd
  Sharpthorne RH19....43 B5
  Slindon BN18........158 C5
Top St RH17...........85 C4
Torberry Dr GU31......68 D2
Torcross Cl BN2.......170 E1
Toronto Cl BN13......185 D7
Toronto Terr BN2.....192 C6
Torrance Cl BN3.......168 F1
Torridge Cl BN13.....185 C8
Tortington Manor,
  Arundel Wing The
  BN18...............181 E7
Tortington manor,
  Goodwood Wing The
  BN18...............181 E7
Tortington Manor, Manor
  Ho The BN18........181 E7
Tortington ManorNew
  England Wing The
  BN18...............181 E7
Tortington Manor,
  Norfolk Wing The
  BN18...............181 E7
Tortington Manor, Stable
  Ctyd The BN18......181 E7
Torton Hill Rd BN18...159 F2
Tor Way GU31.........68 C3
TOTE HILL...........72 A4
Tote La GU29..........72 A5
Totland Rd BN2.......192 D7
Tott Hill BN6.........128 B5
Tottington Dr BN5....146 F6
Tottington Way BN43..167 B1
Tower Approach Rd
  RH6................5 E6
Tower Cl
  Chichester PO19.....176 F7
  East Grinstead RH19...9 E2
  Horley RH6...........1 F3
  Liphook GU30........25 B4
  Tower Hill RH13......58 A8
Tower Ct RH19.........9 E2
Towergate BN1.......169 E2
Tower Hill RH13.......58 A8
Tower Ho
  Brighton BN1........169 E2
  Burgess Hill RH15....109 B2
Tower House Cl RH17...86 E7
Tower House Gdns
  BN18...............160 B3
Tower Pl PO20........207 F7
Tower Rd
  Brighton BN2........192 C6
  Colgate RH12........38 A7
  Faygate RH12........37 F8
  Lancing BN15.......187 D5
  Liphook GU30........25 B4
  Worthing BN11......186 E3
Tower Rd Flats **6**
  BN15...............187 D5
Towers Convent Sch The
  BN44...............146 B1
Towers Rd BN44......146 B2
Tower St
  Chichester PO19.....176 F6
  Emsworth PO10.....173 C8
Town Barn Rd RH11....18 C7
Town Cross Ave
  PO21...............201 C4
Townfield RH14........53 B2
Town La
  Petersfield GU32.....68 D5
  Singleton PO18......135 C4
Town Mead RH11......18 D7
Town Place Farm Cotts
  RH17...............89 C7
Town Quay BN43.....188 E6
Town Quay Appartments
  BN43...............188 E6
Townsend Cres RH17..204 F6
Townsend Way RH10...19 D4
Tozer Cl BN41.........190 B7
Tozer Way PO19......177 B6
Trafalgar Cl PO10.....173 F8
Trafalgar Com Inf Sch
  RH12...............36 B4
Trafalgar Ct
  14 Bognor Regis
  PO21...............201 B2
  Brighton BN1........213 B3
  3 Rustington BN16..205 C6
Trafalgar Gate BN2...192 F3
Trafalgar Gdns **1**
  RH10...............19 B7
Trafalgar La BN1.....213 B3
Trafalgar Pl BN1.....213 B3
Trafalgar Rd
  Horsham RH12........36 C4
  Portslade-by-S BN41..190 B8
Trafalgar St BN1......213 B3
Trafalgar Terr BN1....213 B3
Trafalgar View BN1...213 B3
Tramway Cl PO20.....198 F8
Treadcroft Dr RH12....36 E5
Treadwheel Rd PO8...130 D6
Tredcroft Rd BN3....169 C2
Treemans Rd (Lewes Rd)
  RH17...............65 B2

Trees Ct PO20........212 E8
Treeview RH11........81 F7
Treetops Cl RH12.....193 E8
Treeview RH11........18 C1
Trefoil Ct RH12........36 E5
Trefoil Cres RH11......18 A2
Tregarth Rd PO19....155 A2
Tregenna Ho GU30....25 B5
Treharne Cl RH13.....185 D8
Treloar Rd PO11......195 B1
Tremola Ave BN2.....194 C2
Trendle Gn PO21.....200 F2
Trenear Cl RH13.......36 E2
Trent Cl
  Crawley RH11........17 F4
  Lancing BN15.......187 C6
Trent Ho **3** BN14....186 A5
Trent Rd BN12.......185 E3
Tretawn Gdns PO22..212 F6
Trevanne Plat RH10....19 D7
Trevelyan Pl RH16......87 E5
Treveor Cl BN11......186 C1
TREYFORD..........92 F2
Treyford Cl
  Crawley RH11........17 F6
  Woodingdean BN2....171 E1
Triangle Bsns Ctr
  BN15...............187 C4
Triangle Ho **4** RH16..87 F3
Triangle Rd RH16......87 E3
Triangle The BN15....187 C4
Triangle Way RH15...108 D5
Trident Bsns Pk PO20..210 A3
Trinity Cl RH10........19 C8
Trinity Ct
  Horsham RH12........36 C3
  Hurstpierpoint BN6...128 B5
Trinity Rd BN6.......128 A6
Trinity St BN2........213 C4
Trinity Way
  Bognor Regis PO21...200 F4
  Littlehampton BN17...204 F4
Tripp Hill RH20.......118 F7
Tristan Cl RH15......187 B7
Tristram Cl BN15.....187 B7
Trist Way RH11........18 A8
Triton Pl PO22.......202 C5
Tritton Pl RH20.......121 B2
Troon RH6............2 B2
Troon Cl RH11........17 D5
Troon Ct RH16........87 E4
Trotten Marsh.......70 E7
Trotton Rd GU29, GU31..93 A7
Trotyn Croft PO21....200 F2
Trout La RH13.........81 A7
Trout Rd GU27........26 E6
Troymede RH17........41 A1
True Blue Prec BN17..204 D7
Truggers RH17........61 C8
Truggers Ct RH17.....61 C8
Truleigh Cl BN2......193 F7
Truleigh Cl BN44.....146 B2
Truleigh Dr BN41.....168 A4
Truleigh Hill YH
  BN43...............147 A2
Truleigh Rd BN44.....146 B2
Truleigh Way BN43...167 A1
Trumpkins BN6......128 A5
Trumps Alley GU28....97 F8
Trundle Cl PO18......154 E6
Trundle Mead RH12....36 C5
Trundle View Cl PO22..180 B6
Truro Cl PO19........154 F1
Truro Cres PO21......200 E3
Trusler's Hill La BN15..126 F6
Tryndel Way PO22....202 B4
Tudor Bldgs PO21....200 E2
Tudor Cl
  Chichester PO19.....154 F2
  Crawley RH10........19 D5
  East Grinstead RH19...22 F8
  Findon BN14........163 E6
  Hove BN3...........168 F2
  Lancing BN15.......188 B6
  Marehill RH20.......100 F1
  Middleton-on-S PO22..202 D5
  Rottingdean BN2.....194 A2
Tudor Ct
  11 Bognor Regis
  PO21...............201 D4
  Haslemere GU27.....27 C7
Tudor Dr
  Upper Beeding BN44..146 A3
  Westergate PO20.....179 D8
Tudor Gdns RH15.....108 F4
Tudor Ho **2** RH13....36 F3
Tudor View BN17.....204 C4
Tudor Village RH20...122 C3
Tuff's Hard PO18.....197 C7
Tufts Field GU29......94 D6
Tufts Mdw GU29......94 E6
Tuggles Plat RH12.....35 E7
Tulip Ct RH12.........36 C4
Tullett Rd RH10.......19 B2
Tulleys Farm★ RH10...20 D4
Tumulus Rd BN2.....194 C3
Tunbridge Cres GU30..25 B5
Tunbridge La GU30....25 B6
Tunnel Rd RH6.........5 F8
Tunnmeade **7** RH11..17 E5
Tunsgate **5** BN44...145 D3
Tuppen Ho BN7.......172 E5
Tuppenny La PO10....173 E8
TURKEY ISLAND.....91 F3
Turkey La RH15......109 B3

Turnberry Ct **14** RH16..87 E4
Turnbull Rd PO19.....177 B7
Turner Ave BN14.......79 C6
Turner Ct RH19.......10 A3
Turner Dumbrell
  Workshops BN6......129 D4
Turner Ho **3** BN41...190 C7
Turner Rd BN14......186 E6
Turners Cl RH13.......82 A8
Turners Hill CE Sch
  RH10...............21 A3
TURNERS HILL PARK..21 C5
Turners Hill Rd
  Copthorne RH10......7 F2
  Crawley Down RH10...21 A7
  Crawley RH10........20 C5
  Turners Hill RH10....20 F5
Turner's Hill Rd RH19..22 B6
Turners Mead RH20...121 B2
Turners Mill Cl RH16...87 D7
Turners Mill Rd RH16...87 D6
Turners Way RH15....108 F4
Turner Way PO20.....212 F7
Turner Wlk RH10......18 F3
Turnpike Cl PO19.....176 F2
Turnpike Cl RH17.....64 B8
Turnpike Ho RH13.....57 F1
Turnpike Piece BN1...171 B6
Turnpike Pl RH11......18 D8
Turnpike Rd BN18....140 F6
Turnpike Way RH20...123 A5
Turret Ct RH19........9 C3
Turtledove Ave RH10..21 C5
Turton Cl BN2........192 D5
Tuscan Ave PO22.....202 F5
Tuscany Gdns RH10....18 E8
Tushmore Ave RH10....5 E1
Tushmore Cres RH10...5 E1
Tushmore Ct RH10.....18 E8
Tushmore La RH10.....18 E8
Tushmore Rdbt RH11...18 D8
Tussock Cl RH11......18 A4
Tuxford Cl RH10......19 C4
Tweed La RH11.........4 F1
Twineham CE Prim Sch
  RH17...............107 A4
Twineham Cl BN2.....192 F7
TWINEHAM GREEN...107 B6
Twineham La BN6,
  RH17...............107 A3
Twitten Cl **2** BN42...189 E7
Twitten La RH19.......8 E4
Twittenside BN44.....145 D2
Twitten The
  Albourne Green BN6..127 C6
  Burgess Hill RH15....109 B4
  Crawley RH11........18 C6
  Ditchling BN6.......129 D3
  Southwick BN42.....189 E7
Twitten Way BN14....186 A4
Two Barns La PO18...154 D6
Two Mile Ash Rd
  Barns Green RH13....56 F3
  Two Mile Ash RH13...57 D3
Two Ways RH11........32 A4
Twyford Cl BN13.....185 E7
Twyford Gdns BN13..185 E7
Twyford Rd
  Brighton BN1........170 E6
  Worthing BN13......185 E7
Twyhurst Ct RH19......9 D3
Twyne Cl RH11........17 F4
Twyner Cl RH6.........2 D4
Tye La BN18.........158 E1
Tylden Way RH12......36 F6
Tyler Rd RH10........18 D3
Tyler's Gn RH16, RH17..87 B4
Tylston Mdw GU30....25 B5
Tymperley Ct RH13....36 E3
Tyne Cl
  Crawley RH11........19 C5
  Worthing BN13......185 C4
Tyne Way PO21......200 D4
Tynings The BN15....187 E5
Tyson Pl **9** BN2.....213 C2
Tythe Barn RH17......85 C3
Tythe Barn Rd PO20..212 E6

U

Uckfield Cl BN2......192 F6
Ullswater Dr BN17...205 A7
Ullswater Gr PO22....202 B6
Ullswater Rd BN15...187 B5
Underdown Rd BN42..189 E8
Underhill La
  Clayton BN6........149 E8
  Westmeston BN6.....150 C8
Undermill Rd BN44...146 B2
Underwood Cl RH10...21 B8
Underwood Rd GU27...26 F6
Unicorn Trad Est The
  GU27...............27 B7
Unifax BN12.........185 C4
Union Pl BN11.......186 D2
Union Rd BN2........213 C4
Union St BN1........213 B2
Unita Ho **5** BN1....186 B1
Univ of Brighton
  Brighton BN1........213 B2
  Falmer BN1.........171 B6
Univ of Brighton
  (Cockcroft/Watts
  Annexes) BN2......170 D2
Univ of Brighton (St
  Peter's Ho) BN2.....213 B3

Univ of Chichester
(Bishop Otter Campus)
PO19 ....177 A8
Univ of Chichester Bognor
Regis Campus PO21 ...201 E4
Univ of Sussex BN1 .....171 A4
Updown Hill RH16 .....87 C2
Upfield RH6 ....2 A1
Upfield Cl RH6 ....2 A1
Upfield Villas RH14 ....54 C2
Uphill Way PO22 ....199 A8
Uplands Ave BN13 .....185 F9
Uplands Cl GU27 ....27 D8
Uplands Rd
  Brighton BN1 ....170 C2
  Rowland's Castle PO9 ..130 C2
UP MARDEN 111 F1
Uppark★ GU31 ....111 B8
Uppark Gdns RH12 .....36 F6
Uppark Way PO22 ......202 D7
Upper Abbey Rd BN2 ..192 D4
Upper Bedford St
  BN2 ....192 C4
Upper Beeding Prim Sch
  BN44 ....146 A2
Upper Bevendean Ave
  BN2 ....170 E1
Upper Bognor Rd
  3 Bognor Regis
  PO21 ....201 D4
  Bognor Regis PO21 ...201 E4
Upper Boundstone La
  Lancing, North Lancing
  BN15 ....187 D8
  Lancing, Upper Cokeham
  BN15 ....187 D7
Upper Brighton Rd
  Lancing BN15 ....187 C8
  Worthing BN14 ....186 D7
Upper Chalvington Pl
  BN2 ....192 E5
Upper Cl RH18 ....23 F2
UPPER COKEHAM 187 C7
Upper Dr BN16 ....206 B4
Upper Dr The BN3 .....191 D8
Upperfield GU29 ....72 F2
Upper Forecourt RH6 ...6 B7
Upper Gardner St
  BN1 ....213 B3
Upper Gloucester Rd
  BN1 ....213 A3
Upper Hamilton Rd
  BN1 ....213 A5
Upper Heyshott GU31 ..68 C3
Upper High St BN11 ...186 E3
Upper Hollingdean Rd
  BN1 ....170 B1
UPPER IFOLD 30 F7
Upper Kingston La BN42,
  BN43 ....167 D1
Upper Lewes Rd BN2...213 C4
Upper Lodges BN1 .....170 D8
Upper Market St 5
  BN3 ....191 D5
Upper Mount GU33 ....45 A3
Upper North St BN1 ...213 A2
UPPER NORWOOD 116 D8
Upper Park Pl 7 BN2..213 C2
Upper Rock Gdns
  BN2 ....213 C2
Upper Roedale Cotts
  ....170 B4
Upper St James's St
  BN2 ....213 C1
Upper St Johns Rd
  RH15 ....109 A4
Upper School Dr GU27 ..26 F5
Upper Shoreham Rd
  BN43 ....167 B1
Upper Sq RH18 ....23 F3
Upper St RH20 ....99 A3
Upper Stables RH16 ....87 C3
Upper Station Rd
  BN5 ....125 C5
Upper Sudeley St 7
  BN2 ....192 D4
Upperton Rd GU28 .....75 C1
Upperton's Barn Visitors
  Ctr★ RH20 ....120 D5
UPPER WARDLEY 47 C6
Upper Wardown GU31 ..68 D4
Upper Wellington Rd 5
  BN2 ....192 C7
Upper West Dr BN12 ..206 E5
Upper West La BN15 ...187 E8
Upper Winfield Ave
  BN1 ....169 F6
Upton Ave BN42 ....167 E1
Upton Cl BN13 ....185 F4
Upton Gdns BN13 ......185 F5
Upton Rd
  Stockbridge PO19 ....176 F4
  Worthing BN13 ....185 F5
UPWALTHAM 137 E8
Upways Cl PO20 ....209 F1
Ursa Cl 14 BN2 ....192 C8
Ursula Ave PO20 ....212 D6
Ursula Ave N PO20 .....212 D6
Ursula Sq PO20 ....212 D5

V

Vachery La GU6 ....11 E7
Valdoe Yd PO18 ....155 D4
Vale Ave
  Brighton BN1 ....169 E7
  Worthing BN14 ....163 F2

Valebridge Cl RH15 ....109 C6
Valebridge Cres RH15 ..109 C6
Valebridge Rd RH15 ...109 C6
Vale Ct BN41 ....190 B7
Vale Dr
  Horsham RH12 ....36 B3
  Worthing BN14 ....163 F2
Vale Fst & Mid Sch
  BN14 ....163 F2
Vale Gdns BN41 ....190 B7
Valencia Rd BN11 ......186 A3
Valentine Cl
  Shoreham-by-S BN43..166 D1
  Worthing BN14 ....186 D7
Valentine Ct 14 BN3...191 C7
Valentine Dr RH15 .....108 E4
Valentines Gdns
  PO21 ....201 C7
Valentines Lea GU28 ...51 A8
Vale Rd
  Haywards Heath RH16 ..87 E2
  Portslade-by-S BN41..190 C7
  Saltdean BN2 ....194 D3
Valerie Cl BN41 ....168 C2
Vale The
  Ovingdean BN2 ....193 E5
  Petersfield GU32 .....68 D6
Valetta Pk PO10 ....173 E6
Valetta Rd PO10 ....173 F1
Vale Wlk BN14 ....163 F1
Valewood Cl RH13 .....56 D1
Valewood La RH13 .....56 D1
Valewood Rd GU27 ....27 C4
Valiant Rd PO10 ....173 F1
Vallance By-ways RH6 ..4 F1
Vallance Cl RH15 ....108 E4
Vallance Ct 7 BN3 .....191 A6
Vallance Gdns BN3 ....191 A6
Vallance Rd BN3 ....191 A6
Vallensdean Cotts
  BN41 ....168 C2
Valley Cl BN1 ....169 C4
Valley Dr BN1 ....169 C4
Valley Farm Bsns Pk
  BN6 ....107 B1
Valley Gdns BN14 .....164 A1
Valley Rd
  Lancing BN15 ....187 C8
  Portslade-by-S BN41..168 A2
Valley Side GU30 ....25 B5
Valverde Rd 13 BN3...191 C7
Van Alen Bldg The
  BN2 ....213 C1
Van Alen Mews BN2...213 C1
Vanbrugh Cl RH11 .....17 E3
Vanbrugh Ct 21 BN3...191 C7
Vancouver Cl BN13 ....185 D7
Vancouver Dr RH10,
  RH11 ....5 D1
Vancouver Rd BN13 ...185 D7
Van Dyck Pl PO22 .....201 A6
Van Gogh Pl PO22 .....201 B6
Vann Bridge Cl GU27 ..49 A6
Vanners RH10 ....18 E7
Vann Rd GU27 ....49 A6
Vanzell Rd GU29 ....73 A1
Varey Rd BN13 ....185 B7
Varndean Cl BN1 ......169 E3
Varndean Coll BN1 ....169 E3
Varndean Dr BN1 ......169 E3
Varndean Gdns BN1...169 E3
Varndean Holt BN1 ....169 E3
Varndean Rd BN1 .....169 E3
Varndean Sch BN1 ....170 A3
Varsity Rd RH19 ....173 F1
Vauxhall Way GU32 ...68 A3
Velyn Ave PO19 ....177 B6
Velyn Ct PO19 ....177 B6
Ventnor Villas BN3 ....191 B6
Venus La PO21 ....210 E7
Veras Wlk RH19 ....122 C1
Verbania Way RH19 ...10 B1
Verdley Cotts GU27 ...49 C3
Verdley Pl GU27 ....49 C3
Vere Rd BN1 ....213 B5
Veric 12 BN3 ....191 C7
Verica Ct PO19 ....176 B7
Vermont Dr BN16 ......206 A5
Vermont Way BN16 ...206 A5
Verner Ho 7 BN3 ......191 B5
Vernon Ave BN2 ....193 C8
Vernon Cl
  Horsham RH12 ....37 A4
  Rustington BN16 .....205 C5
Vernon Ct 3 BN1 ......191 E6
Vernon Terr BN1 ....191 E7
Veronica Cl BN16 ......206 A4
Veronica Way BN2 ....213 C1
Viaduct Rd BN1 ....213 B4
Via Ravenna PO19 ....176 E5
Vicarage Fields BN13..185 D8
Vicarage Hill RH14 ....32 A2
Vicarage La
  Bognor Regis PO22...202 A4
  East Preston BN16 ...205 F5
  Haslemere GU27 .....26 F6
  Horley RH6 ....1 F4
  Lodsworth GU28 .....74 B2
  Rottingdean BN2 .....193 F1
  Scaynes Hill RH17 ...88 F3
  Steyning BN44 ....145 D3
Vicarage Rd RH10 .....21 A8
Vicarage Terr RH19 ...193 F1
Vicarage The RH12 ....38 C6
Vicars Cl 11 PO19 .....177 A6
Viceroy Ct BN12 ......206 E5
Viceroy Lo 10 BN3 ....191 A6

Victor Ct RH10 ....6 D1
Victoria Ave
  Burgess Hill RH15 ...108 E3
  Midhurst GU29 ....73 A1
Victoria Bldgs BN11...186 E2
Victoria Bsns Ctr
  RH15 ....108 E2
Victoria Cl
  Burgess Hill RH15 ...108 E2
  Horley RH6 ....2 A3
  5 Midhurst GU29 .....94 E7
Victoria Cottage Hospl
  PO10 ....173 B8
Victoria Cotts 9 BN3..191 B5
Victoria Ct
  10 Bognor Regis
  PO21 ....201 B2
  9 Horsham RH13 .....36 D2
  6 Hove BN3 ....191 C6
  10 Lancing BN15 .....187 E4
  Portslade-by-S BN41..190 C8
  3 Shoreham-by-S
  BN43 ....188 E7
  3 Worthing BN11 ....186 C3
  10 Worthing BN11 ...186 C3
Victoria Dr PO21 ....201 B3
Victoria Gdns
  Burgess Hill RH15 ...108 F2
  Westergate PO20 ....179 D7
Victoria Gr 7 BN3 .....191 C6
Victoria Ind Est RH15 ..108 E2
Victoria Lo 7 BN11 ....186 C3
Victoria Mews
  Crawley RH11 ....18 D6
  Rottingdean BN2 .....193 F1
Victorian Bsns Ctr
  BN18 ....181 D4
Victoria Park Gdns
  Portslade-by-S BN41..190 C8
  2 Worthing BN11 ....186 C3
Victoria Pl
  Balcombe RH17 ......41 A1
  Bognor Regis PO21 ..201 B2
  Brighton BN1 ....191 E6
  Burgess Hill RH15 ...108 E2
  Chichester PO19 .....177 C7
  Crawley RH11 ....18 C6
  Emsworth PO10 .....151 A4
  Haywards Heath RH16..88 A3
  Horley RH6 ....2 B2
  Portslade-by-S BN41..190 C8
  Shoreham-by-S BN43..188 E7
  Southwick BN42 .....189 D7
  Worthing BN11 ....186 C3
Victoria Rd S PO21 ....201 B2
Victoria Road Trad Est
  BN41 ....190 C8
Victoria St
  Brighton BN1 ....191 E6
  Horsham RH13 ....36 D2
Victoria Terr
  Bognor Regis PO22...201 F3
  6 Hove BN3 ....191 B5
  Lumley PO10 ....151 C1
  Prinsted PO10 ....173 E8
  Westbourne PO10 ...151 D3
Victoria Villas BN18...181 A3
Victoria Way
  Burgess Hill RH15 ...108 F2
  East Grinstead RH19..22 F7
  Liphook GU30 ....25 B4
Victor Rd PO10 ....173 F1
Victory Ct 15 PO21 ...201 B2
Victory Mews BN2 .....193 A3
Victory Rd RH12 ....36 B3
Views Path RH16 ......88 B4
View Terr RH7 ....10 A8
View The PO21 ....211 A8
Viking Terr BN17 ......204 D4
Viking Way PO18 ......175 B5
Village Barn The BN1..169 E7
Village Cl BN41 ....168 B2
Village St GU32 ....68 D6
Village Way BN1 ....171 C6
Villa Plage PO22 ....203 A5
Villiers Cl BN2 ....193 E8
Villiers Ct BN1 ....213 B3
Vinall Gdns RH12 ......35 D4
Vinalls Bsns Ctr BN5 ..125 E4
Vincent Cl
  Horsham RH13 ....36 F2
  Lancing BN15 ....187 D6
Vincent Rd PO20 ....212 C6
Vine Pl BN1 ....213 A3
Vineries Cl BN13 ....186 A6
Vineries The
  Burgess Hill RH15 ...109 D3
  Hove BN3 ....191 E6
Vinery Ct BN13 ....186 A6
Vinery The BN18 ....183 C8
Vines Cross Rd BN2 ...192 F7
Vine St BN1 ....213 B3
Viney Cl RH20 ....122 F5
Vinnetrow Farm Bsns Ctr
  PO20 ....177 E3
Vinnetrow Rd PO20 ...177 E3
Vinols Cross RH19 .....42 F6
Vinson Rd GU33 ....45 C4
Visage 17 BN3 ....191 D7
Viscount Dr PO21 .....211 B8
Vivienne Cl RH11 ......5 D1
Volks Electric Rly★ BN1,
  BN2 ....192 C4

Vowels Forest Wlk★
  RH19 ....21 E3
Vowels La RH19 ....21 E3
Vulcan Cl RH11 ....18 C2
Vulcan Ho 4 RH20 ....121 E1
Vulcan Rd PO10 ....173 F1

W

Waddington Cl RH11...18 A3
Wade Ct RH18 ....23 F2
Wade End PO20 ....212 C8
Wadeway Cvn Site
  PO20 ....212 C8
Wadeway The PO20 ..212 C8
Wadeys The RH14 ....79 C8
Wadham Cl RH10 .....6 C1
Wadhurst Cl PO21 ....201 B4
Wadhurst Ct BN13 ...186 A3
Wadhurst Dr BN12 ...185 B3
Wadhurst Rise BN2 ..192 F5
Wadlands Brook Rd
  RH19 ....9 D5
Wad The PO20 ....196 B1
Wagg Cl RH19 ....10 A1
Wagtail Cl RH12 ......36 D7
Wain End RH12 ....36 D5
Wainwrights RH10 ....18 D3
Wakefield Ct 3 RH12..36 D2
Wakefield Rd BN2 ....213 C5
Wakefield Way PO21 ..200 D8
Wakehams Green Dr
  RH10 ....6 D1
Wakehurst Ct BN11...186 F3
Wakehurst Dr RH10 ..18 D3
Wakehurst La RH17 ..64 A8
Wakehurst Mews RH12..35 F1
Wakehurst Pl BN16 ..205 C6
Wakehurst Place (Royal
  Bot Gdn)★ RH17 ...41 F3
Wakestone La RH20 ..77 A2
Walberton & Binstead CE
  Prim Sch BN18 ....158 E1
Walberton Cl PO22 ...202 B5
Walberton Ct BN11 ..185 F2
Walberton Pk BN18 ..180 E8
Waldby Ct RH11 ......18 A3
Waldegrave Ct BN2 ..194 D3
Waldegrave Rd BN1...170 A1
Walders Rd BN16 .....205 B6
Waldron Ave BN1 ....170 D6
Waldron Pl BN1 ......170 D6
Walesbeech RH10 ....19 A5
Walhatch Cl RH18 ....23 F2
Walker Rd RH10 ......19 C4
Walkway The BN16 ..206 A8
Wallace Ave BN11 ...185 F2
Wallace Ct 10 BN11..185 F3
Wallace Par 4 BN11..185 F3
Wallace Rd BN16 .....205 C6
Wallage La RH10 .....20 D6
Walled Gdn The RH14..31 F7
Wallfield PO21 ....200 F2
Wall Hill Rd RH18,
  RH19 ....23 E5
Wallis Ct RH10 ....5 F2
Wallis Ho RH19 ....9 E1
Wallis Way
  Burgess Hill RH15 ...108 E4
  Horsham RH13 ....37 A4
Wallner Cres PO22 ...202 C5
Wallrock Wlk PO10 ..151 B4
Walmer Cl
  Brighton BN2 ....171 B1
  Southwater RH13 ...58 A2
Walmer Cres BN2 ....171 B1
Walmsleys Way PO20..208 C5
Walnut Ave
  Chichester PO19 .....176 F8
  Rustington BN16 .....205 B5
Walnut Cl BN1 ....169 E3
Walnut Ct
  Horsham RH13 ....36 C1
  Worthing BN14 ....186 A6
Walnut La RH11 ......5 B1
Walnut Lo BN16 ......186 C4
Walnut Pk RH16 ......88 B4
Walnuts The RH12 ...36 C4
Walnut Tree Cotts
  RH14 ....79 A3
Walnut Tree Cvn Pk
  PO20 ....196 C2
Walnut Tree Dr PO10..152 A3
Walnut Tree Way
  BN13 ....185 B6
Walpole Ave BN12 ...185 D3
Walpole Rd BN2 ......192 D5
Walpole Terr BN2 ....192 D5
Walsham Cl PO22 ....201 F6
Walsingham Rd BN11..190 F6
Walstead Ct 2 RH10..18 D5
Walter May Ho 14
  BN2 ....192 F5
Walters Gn BN17 .....182 C5
Waltham Park Rd
  RH20 ....119 B6
Walton Ave PO21 ....201 B3
Walton Bank BN1 ....170 D6
Walton Cl BN13 ......185 F7
Walton Dr BN13 .....37 C4
Walton Heath RH10 ..19 D8
Walton Ho PO10 .....175 C7
Walton La PO18 .....175 C5
Walton Lo PO18 .....175 C5
Walton Rd PO21 ....201 B3
Walwyn Cl PO20 .....197 E5
Wanderdown Cl BN2..193 E4

Uni-War 251

Wanderdown Dr BN2..193 E4
Wanderdown Rd BN2..193 D4
Wanderdown Way
  BN2 ....193 E4
Wandle Cl RH10 ......19 C5
Wandleys Cl PO20 ...157 F1
Wandleys Dr PO20 ...157 F1
Wandleys La BN18,
  PO20 ....158 A2
Wandleys Lane Cvn Site
  PO20 ....157 F1
Wansford Way PO22..202 C4
Wantage Cl RH10 ....19 C3
Wantley Hill Est BN5..125 F6
Wantley La RH20 .....121 E2
Wantley Rd BN14 ....164 A1
Warble Heath Cl
  PO18 ....154 F6
Warblers Way PO22..201 B7
Warbleton Cl BN2 ...192 E5
Warbleton Ho 6 RH11..17 F3
Warblington Rd PO10..173 A8
Warborough Ct RH11..18 A3
Warburton Cl RH19 ..23 A8
Ward Cres PO10 .....151 C3
Warden Ct RH17 .....87 A6
Warden Park Sch
  RH17 ....87 A5
WARDLEY 47 C4
Wardley Cotts GU30..47 D4
Ware Ct RH15 ....109 D3
Wareland Ho 3 RH19..9 E1
Warelands RH15 .....108 F1
Warenne Rd BN3 ....168 C4
Warleigh Rd BN1 ....213 B6
Warltersville Way RH6..2 C1
Warmdene Ave BN1..169 F6
Warmdene Cl BN1 ...169 F5
Warmdene Rd BN1 ..169 F6
Warmdene Way BN1..169 F6
War Meml Hospl
  PO22 ....201 C5
WARMINGHURST 122 D6
Warminghurst Cl
  RH20 ....122 F5
Warminghurst Ct 4
  RH12 ....36 D2
Warner Cl RH10 ......19 C2
Warner Ct RH15 .....109 A3
Warner Rd
  Selsey PO20 ....212 C6
  Worthing BN14 ....186 F4
Warner's La PO20 ....212 C8
Warners Par BN11 ...186 C3
Warnes BN11 ....186 E1
Warnham CE Prim Sch
  RH12 ....35 F8
Warnham Cl BN12 ..185 D2
Warnham Ct
  Hove BN3 ....191 C5
  Lancing BN15 ....187 D4
  Warnham RH12 ......35 F7
Warnham Manor RH12..35 C7
Warnham Nature
  Reserve★ RH12 .....36 B6
Warnham Rd
  Broadbridge Heath
  RH12 ....35 D4
  Crawley RH10 ....19 B4
  Horsham RH12 ....36 B5
  Worthing BN12 ....185 D3
Warnham Rise BN1 ..170 A5
Warnham Sta RH12 ..36 C8
Warninglid La RH13,
  RH17 ....60 D2
Warninglid Prim Sch
  RH17 ....61 A2
Warren Ave BN2 .....193 C8
Warren Chase RH20..121 E2
Warren Cl
  Felbridge RH19 ......8 E3
  Woodingdean BN2...193 B8
  Worthing BN14 ....186 B7
Warren Cotts
  Handcross RH17 .....61 B8
  West Dean PO18 .....134 F6
Warren Cres BN16 ..206 A6
Warren Croft RH20 ..121 B1
Warren Ct
  Lancing BN15 ....187 D5
  Southwick BN42 .....167 E1
  Worthing BN14 ....186 B7
Warren Dr
  Crawley RH11 ....18 A8
  Southwater Street RH13..58 A3
Warren Farm La
  PO19 ....154 F2
Warren Farm Pl
  BN14 ....186 A8
Warren Gdns BN14...186 B7
Warren Rd
  Liss GU33 ....45 E7
  Woodingdean BN2...193 B8
  Worthing BN14 ....186 B7
Warren Rise BN2 .....193 B8
Warren Side GU31 ...91 D3
Warren The
  Ashfold Crossways
  RH17 ....60 E6
  Burgess Hill RH15 ...109 C1
  Conford GU30 ....24 C8
  Ferring BN12 ....206 F4
  West Dean PO18 .....134 F6
Warren Way
  Barnham PO22 ....180 B6

Warren Way *continued*
Woodingdean BN2......**193** D8
Warrington Cl RH11.....**17** E2
Warrior Cl RH11.......**168** B2
Warrs Hill La BN8.......**89** E1
Warwick Cl PO21.......**200** B2
Warwick Ct
Arundel BN18..........**160** A2
5 Emsworth PO10...**173** B8
8 Hove BN3..........**191** E7
Warwick Gdns BN11....**186** E2
Warwick La 1 BN11....**186** E2
Warwick Mount 2
BN2.................**192** C4
Warwick Pl
Bognor Regis PO22.....**202** D5
Worthing BN11.........**186** E2
Warwick Rd BN11......**186** E2
Warwick St BN11......**186** E2
Warwick Wlk 3 BN43...**166** F1
Washbrooks Farm Pk★
BN6.................**127** F5
Washington Bostal
RH20................**143** D5
Washington Cotts
RH20................**143** D8
Washington Rd
Buncton BN44.........**144** E8
Crawley RH11..........**17** E3
Emsworth PO10........**151** B1
Haywards Heath RH16....**88** A5
Storrington RH20......**121** F1
Washington RH20......**143** A8
Washington St
Brighton BN2.........**213** C4
Chichester PO19.......**176** F4
Washington Towers Cvn &
Camping Pk RH20.....**143** E7
Wassand Cl RH10......**19** A6
Waterbury Hill RH17...**65** B5
Watercress Pl 6 RH13..**36** F3
Waterdyke Ave BN42...**189** E7
Waterfield Cl RH13.....**36** E3
Waterfield Gdns RH11...**17** E4
Waterfield Prim Sch
RH11................**17** E4
Waterford Gdns BN17...**181** E1
Waterfront BN2........**192** F3
Waterhall Rd BN1......**169** C6
Water La
Angmering BN16.......**183** F3
Buncton BN44.........**144** C8
Littlehampton BN17....**204** D6
Selden BN16, BN13.....**184** C7
Storrington RH20......**121** F2
Waterlands La RH12....**13** E1
Water Lane Ind Est
RH20................**121** E3
Waterlea RH10.........**19** A5
Waterloo Ct 1 PO21....**201** C2
Waterloo Ho 9 BN3....**191** D5
Waterloo Pl 1 BN1.....**213** C3
Waterloo Rd PO22......**202** A4
Waterloo Sq PO21......**201** C2
Waterloo St BN3.......**191** D5
Waterplat The PO19....**177** C8
Waters Edge
Bognor Regis PO21.....**200** E1
Pulborough RH20......**100** A1
13 Shoreham-by-S
BN43................**189** A6
Watersedge Gdns
PO20................**207** E6
Waters Edge Gdns
PO10................**173** B8
Watersfield Rd BN14...**186** B5
Waterside
East Grinstead RH19....**10** B1
Horley RH6............**2** A5
Waterside Cl RH11.....**17** E4
Waterside Dr PO19.....**176** F4
Waterside The BN17...**204** C5
Watersmead Bsns Pk
BN17................**204** F8
Watersmead Cl BN17...**205** A7
Watersmead Dr BN17...**205** A7
Waterstone Cl PO20....**197** A7
Water View RH6........**2** C3
Waterworks Cl RH18....**23** F3
Waterworks Cotts
Hove BN3............**169** A2
Worthing BN11........**186** C7
Waterworks Rd GU32...**68** C6
Watery La
Chichester PO19......**177** A4
Funtington PO18......**153** A4
Watling Cl 5 BN42.....**189** E7
Watling Ct 8 BN42.....**189** E7
Watling Rd BN42......**189** E7
Watney Cotts RH17.....**42** E1
Watson Cl RH10........**19** C3
Watson Way PO20......**179** E2
Wattlehurst Dr RH12....**15** B7
Watts Cnr RH12.........**33** C7
Watts Lo RH15........**109** D3
Waveney Wlk 7 RH10...**19** B4
Waverley Cres BN1.....**170** C1
Waverley Ct
6 Horsham RH12......**36** B2
7 Worthing BN11......**186** B1
Waverley Rd
Bognor Regis PO21.....**201** A4
Rustington BN16......**205** D5
Wavertree Ct RH6.......**1** F2
Wavertree Rd BN12....**185** D4

Wayfield Ave BN3......**168** F1
Wayfield Cl BN3.......**168** F1
Wayland Ave BN1......**169** C3
Wayland Hts BN1......**169** C4
Wayside
Brighton BN1.........**169** D6
Crawley RH11..........**17** E4
Lancing BN15.........**187** C5
Wayside Ave BN13.....**185** D8
Wayside Cotts GU6......**12** F4
Wayside Rd BN16......**206** A8
Way The BN16.........**206** A4
Weald Ave BN3........**190** F8
Weald Cl
Horsham RH13.........**58** E8
Hurstpierpoint BN6....**127** F6
Weald Ct RH14.........**79** D7
Weald Day Hospl The
RH11................**18** C6
Weald & Downland Open
Air Mus★ PO18.....**135** C6
Weald Dr RH10........**19** A4
Weald Dyke BN15......**188** F6
Wealden Way RH16......**87** D4
Wealdon Cl RH13.......**81** F7
Weald Rd RH15.......**108** E3
Weald Rise RH16.......**87** E1
Weald Sch The RH14....**79** D7
Weald The RH19........**9** F4
Wear Cl BN13.........**185** C8
Wear Rd BN13.........**185** C8
Weatherhill Cl RH6......**2** F3
Weaver Cl 5 RH11......**17** E5
Weavers Cl
Burgess Hill BN15.....**109** D1
Midhurst GU29........**72** F2
Weavers Ct 10 BN43....**188** E2
Weavers Hill BN16.....**184** A5
Weavers Mead 6
RH16................**87** C2
Weavers Mead Cotts
BN16................**184** A6
Weavers Ring BN16....**184** A5
Webb Cl
Bognor Regis PO21....**211** A7
Crawley RH11.........**18** B1
Weddell Rd RH10.......**19** A3
Wedges The RH13......**56** D5
Wedgwood Rd PO22....**202** A4
Weirbrook RH10........**19** A3
Weir Wood Resr Nature
Reserve★ RH19......**22** D1
Welbeck Ave BN3......**190** E6
Welbeck Cl RH15......**109** D4
Welbeck Ct BN3.......**190** E6
Welbeck Dr RH15......**109** D5
Welbeck Mans BN3.....**190** E6
Welesmere Rd BN2....**194** A3
Welkin The RH16.......**88** B8
Welland Cl BN13......**185** D9
Welland Rd BN13......**185** D9
Wellcroft Cotts BN6...**127** C5
Wellend Villas 2
BN1.................**191** F8
Weller Cl RH10.........**19** D5
Wellesey Ct BN11......**185** F2
Wellesley Ave BN12....**185** D3
Wellesley Ct 8 BN17...**204** E4
Wellfield RH19.........**23** C7
Wellfield Cotts GU31....**91** D3
Wellgreen La BN7......**172** F5
Wellhouse La RH15....**129** C7
Well House Rd RH20....**123** A5
Wellingham La BN13...**163** E1
Wellingham Way RH12...**17** C1
Wellington Cl RH10......**6** E1
Wellington Ct
Brighton BN2.........**193** A3
1 Worthing BN11.....**186** A2
Wellington Gdns
PO20................**212** E8
Wellington Ho BN41....**190** C6
Wellingtonia Ct 8
BN1.................**169** E3
Wellington Rd
Bognor Regis PO21....**201** B3
Brighton BN2.........**213** C4
Chichester PO19......**155** A1
Horsham RH12.........**36** D2
Portslade-by-S BN41...**190** B6
Wellington St BN2.....**192** C7
Wellington Town Rd
RH19................**9** D2
Wellington Way RH6.....**1** F5
Well La
Haslemere GU27.......**27** D6
Midhurst GU29........**94** E4
Well Lo PO21..........**200** A2
Well Rd PO21.........**210** F7
Wellsbourne BN2......**192** F5
Wells Cl RH12.........**35** F2
Wells Cres
Bognor Regis PO21....**200** E4
Chichester PO19......**154** F1
Wellsfield PO20.......**196** C1
Wells Ho GU29.........**94** E6
Wells Lea RH19.........**9** D3
Wells Mdw RH19........**9** D3
Wells Rd RH10.........**18** E2
Wells The GU27........**27** C6
Wellswood RH16.......**87** F3
Wellswood Gdns PO9..**130** E3
Wellsworth La PO9....**130** E3
Wellwood Cl RH13.....**37** B4
Welwyn Cl RH11........**17** E2
Wembley Ave BN15....**187** D6

Wembley Gdns BN15...**187** D6
Wenban Mews 5
BN14................**186** D3
Wenban Rd BN11......**186** D3
Wenceling Cotts 4
BN15................**188** C5
Wendover Grange 3
BN3.................**191** A6
Wendy Ridge BN16....**205** B6
Wenlock Cl RH11........**18** A4
Wensleydale RH11......**18** C3
Wensley Gdns PO10...**151** B3
Wentworth RH6.........**2** B2
Wentworth Cl
Barnham PO22........**180** B7
Worthing BN13.......**185** F9
Wentworth Ct
1 West Kingston
BN16................**206** A4
8 Worthing BN11.....**186** A2
Wentworth Dr
Breach PO10.........**152** A2
Crawley RH10.........**19** D7
Wentworth St BN2....**213** C1
Weppons 2 BN43......**188** F7
Wesley Cl
Crawley RH11.........**17** E3
Horley RH6............**2** A5
Wessex Ave
Bognor Regis PO21....**201** B2
East Wittering PO20...**208** A7
Wessex Cl BN12......**186** C2
Wessex Wlk 1 BN43...**166** F1
West Ashling Rd
PO18................**152** C3
West Ave
Bognor Regis PO21....**200** F3
Crawley RH10..........**19** A8
Lancing BN15.........**188** A5
Middleton-on-S PO22..**202** F6
Worthing BN11.......**186** A2
West Bank BN18.......**181** A5
West Beach Rd BN43...**188** D5
WEST BLATCHINGTON
..................**168** F1
West Blatchington Inf Sch
BN3.................**168** A4
West Blatchington Jun
Sch BN3............**168** A4
West Blatchington
Windmill★ BN3......**168** F2
West Bldgs BN11......**186** D1
Westbourne Ave
New Brighton BN16....**151** C2
Worthing BN14.......**186** D4
Westbourne Cl PO10...**151** C2
Westbourne Gdns
BN3.................**191** A7
Westbourne Gr BN3....**191** A7
Westbourne House Sch
PO20................**177** F7
Westbourne Pl BN3....**191** A6
Westbourne Prim Sch
PO10................**151** D4
Westbourne Rd PO10...**151** C3
Westbourne St BN3....**191** A7
Westbourne Villas
BN3.................**190** F6
West Bracklesham Dr
PO20................**208** A6
Westbrook
Forest Row RH18......**23** E3
Saltdean BN2.........**194** C2
Westbrook Cl PO18....**175** A5
Westbrooke BN11......**186** D2
Westbrooke Ct 12
BN11................**186** D2
Westbrook Field
PO18................**175** A5
Westbrook Way BN42...**189** F7
West Broyle Dr PO19...**154** C2
West Burton La RH20...**139** E8
West Burton Rd RH20..**139** D8
Westbury Ct 4 BN11...**186** B2
Westbury Lo BN18.....**160** B2
West Chiltington Com Fst
Sch RH20...........**101** E1
West Chiltington La
Balls Green RH14......**79** F2
Coneyhurst RH14, RH13..**80** C6
West Chiltington Rd
West Chiltington Common
RH20................**121** D5
West Chiltington RH20..**102** A2
West Cl
Bognor Regis PO22....**202** B4
Fernhurst GU27........**49** B6
Middleton-on-S PO22..**202** D5
Westcombe 1 BN1.....**191** E7
West Comm RH16.......**87** F6
West Common Dr
RH16................**88** A7
Westcott Cl RH11......**39** C8
Westcott Keep RH6......**2** C4
Westcourt Pl BN14....**186** C3
Westcourt Rd BN14....**186** C4
West Ct 8 BN43.......**188** E7
West Dean CE Prim Sch
PO18................**134** F5
West Dean Coll PO18...**135** A6
West Dean Gdns★
PO18................**135** A6
Westdean Rd BN14....**186** B5
WESTDENE...........**169** C5
Westdene Dr BN1......**169** C5
Westdene Prim Sch
BN1.................**169** C5

Westdown Ct 2
BN11................**186** A3
West Dr
Angmering BN16......**205** D8
Bognor Regis PO21....**200** B1
Brighton BN2.........**192** C6
Ferring BN12.........**206** E4
Middleton-on-S PO22..**203** A5
West Durrington Sh Ctr
BN13................**185** C7
WEST END...........**125** C5
West End La
Ansteadbrook GU27,
GU8.................**28** D8
Henfield BN5.........**125** B5
West End Way BN15...**187** D3
Westergate Bsns Ctr
BN2.................**170** E4
Westergate Cl BN12...**206** F6
Westergate Com Sch
PO20................**179** E7
Westergate Mews
PO20................**179** D8
Westergate Rd BN2....**170** E4
Westergate St PO20...**179** D6
Westerley Gdns PO20..**208** B6
Western Ave PO10....**173** A8
Western Cl BN15......**187** C4
Western Concourse
BN2.................**192** F3
Western Espl BN41....**190** D6
Western Lo BN15......**187** C4
Western Par PO10.....**173** A7
Western Pl BN11......**186** C1
Western Rd
Burgess Hill BN15.....**108** E3
Haywards Heath RH16...**87** F4
Hove BN1, BN3........**191** C6
Hurstpierpoint BN6....**127** F6
Lancing BN15.........**187** C4
Liss GU33.............**45** B4
Littlehampton BN17...**204** F4
Selsey PO20..........**212** E6
Shoreham-by-S BN43...**188** F7
Western Rd N BN15...**187** C6
Western Row BN16.....**186** C1
Western St BN1.......**191** D5
Western Terr
21 Brighton BN1......**191** E5
Worthing BN15.......**186** F9
Westfield PO22.......**201** B7
Westfield Ave
Saltdean BN2.........**194** D3
West Kingston BN16...**206** A4
Westfield Ave N BN2..**194** D3
Westfield Ave S BN2..**194** D3
Westfield Cl BN1......**170** A4
Westfield Cres BN1....**170** A5
Westfield Ct 1 BN17...**204** F4
Westfield Rd RH11......**18** B6
Westfield Rise BN2....**194** E3
West Front Rd PO21...**210** F2
West Furlong Ct BN6..**128** A5
West Furlong La BN6..**128** A5
Westgate PO19........**176** E6
Westgate Ct BN12....**185** B3
WEST GREEN.........**18** C6
West Green Dr RH11....**18** C6
West Green Prim Sch
RH11................**18** C7
Westgrove Gdns 11
PO10................**173** B8
West Gun Copse RH13..**57** D5
Westham 13 BN42.....**192** F5
Westhampnett Rd
PO19................**177** C7
WEST HARTING.......**91** D7
West Head BN17......**204** F4
WEST HILL...........**41** D1
West Hill
Ardingly RH17.........**63** E8
Dormans Park RH19....**9** E6
East Grinstead RH19...**22** D8
West Hill Cl BN13.....**163** E2
Westhill Dr RH15.....**108** E3
West Hill Pl BN1......**213** A3
West Hill Rd BN1......**213** A3
West Hill St BN1......**213** A4
West Hoathly CE Prim Sch
RH19................**42** E6
West Hoathly Rd RH19..**22** D4
West Hove Inf & Jun Schs
BN3.................**190** F7
Westingway PO21.....**201** A3
West La
East Grinstead RH19...**22** D8
Lancing BN15.........**187** E7
Westlake BN13.......**185** E6
Westlake Gdns BN13...**185** F6
Westland Ave BN14....**186** A4
Westland Ct BN41.....**190** D8
WESTLANDS..........**197** D6
Westlands
Ferring BN12.........**206** E5
Horsham RH13.........**36** E3
Littlehampton BN17...**205** A6
Westland's Copse La
GU28................**75** A4
Westlands La PO20....**197** D5
Westlands Rd
Haywards Heath RH16...**88** B5
Hunston PO20........**199** A8

Westloats Gdns PO21..**201** A5
Westloats La PO21....**201** B5
West Mallion BN16......**87** F3
West Mans BN11......**186** B1
West Mare La RH20....**100** F1
West Mead BN16......**205** A4
West Meade GU30......**47** B2
Westmead Gdns
BN11................**185** F3
Westmead Rd PO19....**176** C6
Westmeads RH6........**2** C3
West Meads Dr PO21..**200** F4
Westmeston Ave BN2..**194** B2
Westminster Ct 9
BN11................**186** F2
Westminster Dr PO21..**200** E3
Westminster Rd RH10..**19** C5
Westmoreland Wlk 2
BN43................**166** F1
Westmorland Ct 16
BN1.................**191** E7
Westmorland Dr
PO22................**202** B6
Westmount 3 BN2....**192** C6
Westmount Cl BN42...**189** D8
West Mount Cvn Pk
PO20................**212** D8
Weston La PO18.......**152** F5
Weston Rd GU31.......**68** C3
Westons Cl RH12.......**36** D7
Westons Hill RH13......**57** B6
West Onslow Cl BN12..**206** E7
Westout Cotts BN14...**186** F7
West Pallant PO19.....**177** A6
West Par
Horsham RH12.........**36** C4
Worthing BN11.......**186** A1
West Park CE Fst & Mid
Sch BN12...........**185** D3
West Park Cres RH15..**108** D4
Westpark La BN12.....**185** E3
West Park Rd
Domewood RH10, RH7...**7** F5
Handcross RH17........**61** B7
Horne RH7.............**8** B7
West Point 8 BN43....**189** A6
West Preston Manor
BN16................**205** E5
West Preston Mews
BN16................**205** E5
West Rd
Emsworth PO10.......**173** A8
Portslade-by-S BN41...**190** A7
Poynings BN45, BN6...**148** E7
West Ridings BN16....**205** F4
West Sands Holiday Pk
PO20................**212** B8
West Sands La PO20...**212** B7
West Side GU28.......**97** B8
West St
Billingshurst RH14.....**79** C8
Bognor Regis PO21....**201** C2
Brighton BN1.........**213** A2
Burgess Hill RH15.....**108** E4
Chichester PO19......**176** F6
Crawley RH11.........**18** D5
Ditchling BN6........**129** D3
Dormansland RH7......**10** A8
East Grinstead RH19...**22** E8
Emsworth PO10.......**173** B8
Haslemere GU27........**27** C6
Horsham RH12.........**36** C2
Lancing BN15.........**187** B7
Midhurst GU29.........**94** F7
Portslade-by-S BN41...**190** C7
Rogate GU31..........**70** B4
Rottingdean BN2......**193** F1
Selsey PO20..........**212** C7
Shoreham-by-S BN43...**188** C4
Storrington RH20......**121** D1
Worthing BN11.......**186** C1
West Stoke Rd PO19...**154** C3
West Strand PO20.....**207** B8
WEST TARRING......**186** A4
WEST TOWN.........**127** E6
West Tyne BN13......**185** D6
Westup Rd RH17.......**40** E2
West View
Fishbourne PO19......**176** B6
Hove BN3............**191** C8
Lindfield RH16.........**88** B6
West View Cotts
Breach PO10.........**152** A2
Lindfield RH16.........**88** B6
West View Ct 9
BN11................**186** B2
West View Dr BN18...**180** F2
West View Gdns
East Grinstead RH19...**22** E8
Yapton BN18.........**180** F1
Westview Terr BN14...**163** E6
West Walberton La
BN18................**158** C2
Westward Cl PO18....**175** C5
Westward Ho PO19....**176** C6
Westward La RH20....**121** C6
Westway
Bognor Regis PO22....**201** D5
Copthorne RH10.......**7** A3
Crawley RH6...........**6** B7
Littlehampton BN17...**204** C7
West Way
Chichester PO19......**154** C2
Crawley RH10..........**19** A7
Hove BN3............**168** D2
Lancing BN15.........**188** B5
Slinfold RH13.........**34** D3
Worthing BN13.......**163** D1

Westway Cl BN41 . . . . 167 E4
Westway Gdns BN41 . . . . . 167 E4
West Wittering Parochial
  CE Sch PO20 . . . . 196 B1
Westwood Cl PO10 . . . . . . 151 C3
WEST WORTHING 186 A1
West Worthing Sta
  BN13 . . . . 186 A3
Wetherdown GU31 . . . . 68 C3
Weycombe Rd GU27 . . . . . . 27 C8
Weydown Ct GU27 . . . . 27 B7
Weydown Ind Est
  GU27 . . . . 27 B7
Weydown Rd GU27 . . . . 27 B7
Wey Gdns GU27 . . . . 26 F5
Weyhill GU27 . . . . 27 A6
Weyland Cl GU30 . . . . 25 C5
Wey Lodge Cl GU30 . . . . . . 25 D4
Weysprings GU27 . . . . 27 A6
Whapple The 8 BN17 . . . 204 F4
Wharf Ho PO19 . . . . 176 F5
Wharf Rd
  Hove BN3 . . . . 190 D6
  Littlehampton BN17 . . . . . 204 C5
Wharf The GU29 . . . . 94 F7
Wheatcroft BN17 . . . . 204 C7
Wheatear Dr GU31 . . . . 68 C2
Wheatfield Rd PO20 . . . . . 212 F8
Wheatfield Way
  Brighton BN2 . . . . 170 F3
  Horley RH6 . . . . 2 C4
Wheat Ho BN44 . . . . 145 D2
Wheatlands Ave
  PO11 . . . . 195 A1
Wheatlands Cres
  PO11 . . . . 195 A1
Wheatsheaf Cl
  Burgess Hill RH15 . . . . . . 108 E5
  Horsham RH12 . . . . 36 E5
Wheatsheaf La RH17 . . . . . 87 A6
Wheatsheaf Rd
  Henfield BN5 . . . . 126 A8
  Wineham BN5 . . . . 106 C1
Wheatstone Cl RH10 . . . . . . 6 B3
Wheelbarrow Castle
  GU29 . . . . 73 A2
Wheeler Cl RH16 . . . . 87 F2
Wheeler Rd RH10 . . . . 19 B4
Wheelers Way RH19 . . . . . . .8 E3
Wheelwright La RH15 . . . . 109 D1
Wheelwrights RH20 . . . . . 101 E1
Wheelwrights Cl
  Arundel BN18 . . . . 160 A2
  Fernhurst GU27 . . . . 49 B6
Wheelwrights Lo 6
  BN15 . . . . 187 C7
Whichelo Pl BN2 . . . . 192 C6
Whippingham Rd
  BN2 . . . . 192 C7
Whippingham St BN2 . . . . 192 C8
Whipping Post La
  BN2 . . . . 193 F1
Whistler Ave PO19 . . . . . . 155 A1
Whistler Cl RH10 . . . . 18 F3
Whistler Ct BN1 . . . . 169 F1
Whitaker Pl PO20 . . . . 178 B7
White Acre BN17 . . . . 204 C7
Whitebeam Ct 9 RH16 . . . 87 C2
Whitebeam Mews 8
  RH16 . . . . 87 C2
Whitebeam Rd BN13 . . . . 185 C6
Whitebeam Way
  Middleton-on-S PO22. . . . 202 E6
  Tangmere PO20 . . . . 156 D1
Whitechimney Row
  PO10 . . . . 151 D3
White City GU29 . . . . 94 E7
Whitecroft
  Horley RH6 . . . . 2 B4
  7 Littlehampton BN17 . . 205 C5
Whitecross St BN1 . . . . . . 213 B3
Whitehall Dr RH11 . . . . 17 E6
White Hart Ct RH12 . . . . . . 36 C4
White Hart Mews
  GU30 . . . . 25 B2
WHITEHAWK 192 E5
Whitehawk Cl BN2 . . . . . . 192 E5
Whitehawk Cres BN2 . . . . 192 E5
Whitehawk Hill Rd
  BN2 . . . . 192 D5
Whitehawk Prim Sch
  BN2 . . . . 192 E6
Whitehawk Rd
  Brighton BN2 . . . . 192 E6
  Brighton BN2 . . . . 192 F5
Whitehawk Way BN2 . . . . 192 F6
Whitehill Pk GU35 . . . . 24 A8
White Horse Cnr
  PO20 . . . . 179 A8
White Horse Ct 2
  RH20 . . . . 121 D1
White Horse Cvn Pk
  PO20 . . . . 212 D8
Whitehorse Rd RH12 . . . . . 37 B6
White Horse Sq BN44 . . . 145 D3
White Horses Way
  BN17 . . . . 205 A5
White Horse Yd RH20 . . . 121 D1
White House Gdns
  GU32 . . . . 68 A5
White House Pl BN13 . . . . 185 E9
Whitelands PO22 . . . . 202 A6
Whitelea Rd BN17 . . . . . . 204 D6
White Lion Ct 5
  BN43 . . . . 188 E7
White Lo
  Hove BN3. . . . . 191 C8

White Lo continued
  4 Littlehampton BN17 . . 204 E5
Whitelot Cl BN42 . . . . 167 E2
Whitelot Way BN42 . . . . . 167 E2
Whitely Hill RH10 . . . . 19 F1
Whiteman's Cl RH17 . . . . . . 86 E8
Whitemans Gn RH17 . . . . . 86 E8
WHITEMANS GREEN 86 E7
Whiterock Pl BN42 . . . . . . 189 E7
White's Cl BN6 . . . . 128 A7
WHITE'S GREEN 74 F7
Whiteside Cl PO19 . . . . . . 177 B7
Whites La GU27 . . . . 48 E3
White St BN2 . . . . 213 C2
White Styles Mid Sch
  BN15 . . . . 187 B6
White Styles Rd BN15 . . . 187 B7
White Styles Terr
  BN15 . . . . 187 B7
Whitethorn Dr BN1 . . . . . . 169 B4
Whitethroat La RH17 . . . . . 62 D6
Whiteway La BN2 . . . . 194 A2
Whiteways PO22 . . . . 201 A6
Whiteways Cl
  Bognor Regis PO22 . . . . . 201 A6
  Littlehampton BN17 . . . . . 204 D6
Whitfield Cl
  Angmering BN16 . . . . 206 A8
  Bognor Regis PO22 . . . . . 201 E5
Whitfield Rd GU27 . . . . 27 C8
Whitgift Wlk RH10 . . . . 18 D3
Whitley Cl PO10 . . . . 151 D5
Whitmore Way RH6 . . . . 1 E3
Whittingehame Gdns
  BN1 . . . . 169 F3
Whittington Coll
  (Almshouses) RH19 . . . . . 9 A4
Whittington Ct 1
  PO10 . . . . 173 B8
Whittington Rd RH10. . . . . 18 E3
Whittle Way RH10 . . . . 6 A3
Whitwell Hatch GU27 . . . . 27 D5
Whitworth Ho 3
  BN11 . . . . 186 B3
Whitworth Rd RH11 . . . . 5 D2
WHYKE 177 B5
Whyke Cl PO19 . . . . 177 B4
Whyke Ct PO19 . . . . 177 B4
Whyke La PO19 . . . . 177 B5
Whyke Rd PO19. . . . . 177 B5
Whylands Ave BN13 . . . . . 185 D9
Whylands Cl BN13 . . . . . . 185 D9
Whylands Cres BN13 . . . . 185 D9
Whytemead Fst Sch
  BN14 . . . . 186 E5
Whytings RH13 . . . . 59 C6
WICK 204 D8
Wickbourne Ho BN17 . . . 204 C6
Wickbourne Inf Sch
  BN17 . . . . 204 C6
Wick Cl PO22 . . . . 202 B5
Wick Ct BN17 . . . . 204 B7
Wickens Ct 2 RH16 . . . . . 87 C2
Wickens The RH13 . . . . 57 F1
Wickets The RH15 . . . . . . 108 F5
Wick Farm Rd BN17 . . . . . 204 C6
Wick Hall BN3 . . . . 191 D6
Wickham Bsns Ctr
  BN17 . . . . 204 C6
Wickham Cl
  Haywards Heath RH16 . . . 87 E7
  Horley RH6 . . . . 1 F4
Wickham Dr BN6 . . . . 128 C5
Wickham Hill BN6 . . . . . . 128 C4
Wickham Way RH16 . . . . . . 87 E7
Wickhurst Cl BN41 . . . . . . 167 F2
Wickhurst Gdns RH12 . . . . 35 E3
Wickhurst La RH12 . . . . . . 35 E3
Wickhurst Rd BN41 . . . . . 168 A2
Wickhurst Rise BN41 . . . . 167 F3
Wick La
  Bognor Regis PO22 . . . . . 202 B5
  Midhurst GU29 . . . . 73 B4
Wickland Ct RH10 . . . . 18 D3
Wicklands Ave BN2 . . . . . 194 D1
Wickor Cl PO10 . . . . 151 C2
Wickor Way PO10 . . . . . . 151 C2
Wick Par BN17 . . . . 204 D7
Wicks Cotts BN18 . . . . . . 181 C4
Wicks Farm Cvn Pk
  PO20 . . . . 196 F3
Wicks Rd RH14 . . . . 79 C8
Wick St BN17 . . . . 204 D7
Widdicombe Way
  BN2 . . . . 170 E2
Widewater Cl 1
  BN15 . . . . 188 C5
Widewater Ct 7
  BN43 . . . . 188 C5
Widgeon La PO20 . . . . . . 212 B8
Widgeon Way RH12 . . . . . . 36 C5
Widworthy Mews 7
  PO21 . . . . 201 B3
Wight Ct BN17 . . . . 204 D4
Wight Way PO20 . . . . 212 E5
Wigmore Cl BN1 . . . . 170 B1
Wigmore Rd BN14 . . . . . . 186 D6
Wigmore Trad Est
  BN14 . . . . 186 F5
Wilberforce Cl RH11 . . . . . 39 C8
Wilberforce Way RH13 . . . 58 A4
Wilbury Ave BN3 . . . . 191 C8
Wilbury Cres BN3 . . . . 191 D7
Wilbury Gdns BN3 . . . . . . 191 C7
Wilbury Gr BN3 . . . . 191 C6
Wilbury Grange 9
  BN3 . . . . 191 C6
Wilbury Lo 13 BN3 . . . . . 191 C6

Wilbury Mans BN3 . . . . . . 191 D8
Wilbury Rd BN3. . . . . 191 C6
Wilbury Villas BN3. . . . . . . 191 C7
Wilby Ave BN42 . . . . 167 E1
Wildacre Rd RH14 . . . . 31 D3
Wildbrooks Cl RH20 . . . . . 100 D2
Wilderness Rd BN6 . . . . . 128 A6
Wilderness Rise RH19 . . . . 10 A6
Wilderness The RH16 . . . . . 88 B8
Wilderwick Rd RH19 . . . . . 10 A5
Wildgoose Dr RH12 . . . . . . 35 F3
Wild Orchid Way RH13 . . . 58 A3
Wild Park Cl BN2 . . . . 170 E3
Wild Park Nature Trail *
  BN2 . . . . 170 D5
Wildwood La GU6 . . . . 11 C5
Wilfrid Rd BN3 . . . . 168 D1
Wilfs Copse PO20 . . . . . . 177 B1
Wiliamson Cott Homes
  BN3 . . . . 191 A7
Wilkinson Cl
  Angmering BN16 . . . . 184 A5
  Rottingdean BN2 . . . . 193 F3
Wilkinson Ct 4 RH11 . . . . 18 B1
Willard Way
  Ashington RH20 . . . . 122 F5
  East Grinstead RH19 . . . . . 9 A3
Willett Cl GU28 . . . . 117 B7
Willetts Way RH14 . . . . 31 F3
William Allen La RH16 . . . . 88 B6
William Cawley Mews 3
  PO19 . . . . 177 A8
William Morris Ct
  BN14 . . . . 186 F4
William Morris Way
  RH11 . . . . 39 C8
William Olders Rd
  BN16 . . . . 206 A8
William Penn Sch
  RH13 . . . . 80 E2
William Rd RH10 . . . . 177 D6
Williams Rd
  Broadbridge PO18 . . . . . . 175 C7
  Shoreham-by-S BN43. . . . 189 C8
William St
  Bognor Regis PO21 . . . . . 201 D3
  Brighton BN2 . . . . 213 B2
  Portslade-by-S BN41 . . . . 190 B7
William Street Trad Est
  BN41 . . . . 190 A7
William Sutton Ho
  BN1 . . . . 213 B2
Williams Way RH10 . . . . . . 19 B6
Willingdon Rd BN2. . . . . . 170 E1
Willmington Ct 2
  BN11 . . . . 186 B1
Willoughby Ho BN12 . . . . 185 C3
Willow Ave BN16 . . . . 205 E5
Willowbed Ave PO19 . . . . 177 C4
Willowbed Dr PO19 . . . . . 177 C4
Willow Brean RH6 . . . . 1 E5
Willow Brook
  Littlehampton BN17 . . . . . 204 C7
  Middleton-on-S PO22 . . . 203 A5
Willowbrook Ct BN15 . . . 187 F4
Willowbrook Park Cvn Pk
  BN15 . . . . 188 A5
Willowbrook Pk
  BN15 . . . . 188 A5
Willowbrook Rd
  BN14 . . . . 187 A4
Willowbrook Way
  BN6 . . . . 129 A3
Willow Cl
  Crawley RH10 . . . . 18 E8
  East Grinstead RH19 . . . . . 9 D3
  Hurstpierpoint BN6 . . . . . 127 F7
  2 Lancing BN15 . . . . 188 C5
  Liphook GU30 . . . . 25 D3
  Steyning BN44 . . . . 145 D4
  West Chiltington Common
  RH20. . . . . 121 E6
  Woodingdean BN2 . . . . . 193 E8
Willow Cnr RH6. . . . . 4 F7
Willow Cres BN13 . . . . . . 185 C6
Willow Ct
  Chichester PO19 . . . . 176 D6
  Horley RH6 . . . . 2 B6
  4 Hove BN3 . . . . 191 D7
  Worthing BN12 . . . . 186 A3
Willowdale Cl GU32 . . . . . . 67 C4
Willow Dr
  Billingshurst RH14 . . . . . . 79 D8
  Petersfield GU31 . . . . 68 B1
Willowfield 4 RH11 . . . . . 18 D5
Willow Gdns
  Hurstpierpoint BN6 . . . . . 128 A7
  Liphook GU30 . . . . 25 D3
  Westbourne PO10 . . . . . . 151 D4
Willowhale Ave PO21 . . . . 200 D2
Willowhale Gn PO21 . . . . 200 C2
Willowhayne Ave
  BN16 . . . . 206 A4
Willowhayne Cl 4
  BN16 . . . . 206 A4
Willowhayne Cres 5
  BN16 . . . . 206 A4
Willowhayne Ct 9
  BN16 . . . . 206 A4
Willow Ho
  Hassocks BN6 . . . . 128 E5
  Worthing BN12 . . . . 185 A5
Willow Mead 8 RH19 . . . . 22 F8
Willowmead Cl PO20 . . . . 177 E1
Willow Pk RH16. . . . . 88 B4
Willow Rd
  Horsham RH12 . . . . 37 B5
  Liss GU33 . . . . 45 B4

Willow Ridge RH10 . . . . . . 21 A3
Willows Cvn Pk PO20 . . . 179 E4
Willows Cvn Pk The
  PO11 . . . . 195 A2
Willows Fst Sch The
  BN15 . . . . 187 E7
Willows The
  Billingshurst RH14 . . . . . . 79 C7
  5 Bognor Regis PO21 . . . 201 C4
  2 Brighton BN2 . . . . 213 C5
  Burgess Hill RH15 . . . . . . 109 B5
  Findon BN14 . . . . 163 E6
  Ford BN18 . . . . 181 E5
  Hassocks BN6 . . . . 128 E4
  Horsham RH12 . . . . 36 D5
  4 Lancing BN15 . . . . 187 E5
  Pulborough RH20 . . . . . . 100 A1
  Rustington BN16 . . . . 205 D5
  Selsey PO20. . . . . 212 E8
  Storrington RH20 . . . . 121 C1
Willow Way
  Ashington RH20 . . . . 123 A4
  Bognor Regis PO21 . . . . . 200 B1
  Hurstpierpoint BN6 . . . . . 127 F8
Willow Wlk GU30 . . . . 97 E7
Willowwood Cl BN16 . . . . 206 A8
Wills Cl BN18 . . . . 181 B2
Wilman Gdns PO21 . . . . . 200 D2
Wilmington Cl
  Brighton BN1 . . . . 170 A5
  Crawley RH11 . . . . 18 C1
  Hassocks BN6 . . . . 128 C4
Wilmington Par BN1 . . . . 169 F5
Wilmington Way
  Brighton BN1 . . . . 170 A5
  Haywards Heath RH16 . . . 88 A5
Wilmot Ct 6 BN43 . . . . . . 189 C8
Wilmot Rd BN43 . . . . 189 C8
Wilson Ave BN2 . . . . 192 F6
Wilson Cl
  Chichester PO19 . . . . 176 D7
  Crawley RH10 . . . . 19 D3
Wilson Ct BN18 . . . . 181 B2
Wilton 1 RH16 . . . . 87 D6
Wilton Ct
  Bracklesham PO20 . . . . . 208 C5
  Partridge Green RH13 . . . 105 A3
  Rustington BN16 . . . . 205 B7
Wilton Dr BN16 . . . . 205 B7
Wilton Villas BN17 . . . . . . 41 A1
Wiltshire Croft Ct
  PO20 . . . . 212 D7
Wiltshire Ho 16 BN2. . . . . 213 C2
Wimbledon Ct BN14 . . . . 186 D5
Wimblehurst Ct 4
  RH12 . . . . 36 C4
Wimblehurst Rd RH12. . . . 36 C4
Wimborne Ct BN11 . . . . . 185 F3
Wimbourne Ho RH11 . . . . . 18 C6
Wimland Hill RH12 . . . . . . 16 D2
Wimland Rd
  Faygate RH12 . . . . 16 D1
  Rusper RH12 . . . . 16 C4
Wimlands La RH12 . . . . . . 16 E3
Wincanton Ct RH10 . . . . . . 19 D6
Winchelsea Ct 9
  BN11 . . . . 186 A1
Winchelsea Gdns
  BN11 . . . . 186 A1
Winchester Ct
  Southwater RH13 . . . . 58 A2
  Worthing BN11 . . . . 186 B2
Winchester Dr PO19 . . . . 176 F8
Winchester Ho
  Petersfield GU32 . . . . 68 A4
  Worthing BN12 . . . . 185 A4
Winchester Rd
  Crawley RH10 . . . . 18 E2
  Rustington BN16 . . . . 205 E6
  Stroud GU32 . . . . 67 D4
  Worthing BN11 . . . . 186 C2
Winchester St BN1 . . . . . . 213 B5
Wincombe Rd BN1 . . . . . . 169 D1
Winden Ave PO19 . . . . . . 177 B6
Windermere 2 BN16 . . . . 205 C5
Windermere Cres
  BN12 . . . . 185 D6
Windermere Ct
  9 Brighton BN2 . . . . 192 C6
  Worthing BN12 . . . . 185 B3
Windermere Rd RH16 . . . . 87 F4
Windlesham Ave BN1 . . . 191 E6
Windlesham Cl BN41 . . . . 168 A1
Windlesham Ct
  14 Brighton BN1 . . . . 191 E7
  Littlehampton BN17 . . . . . 204 D7
  5 Worthing BN11 . . . . . . 186 A1
Windlesham Gdns
  Brighton BN1, BN3 . . . . . 191 E7
  East Preston BN16 . . . . . 206 A6
  Shoreham-by-S BN43. . . . 188 F6
Windlesham Hall 18
  BN1 . . . . 191 E6
Windlesham Ho 15
  BN1 . . . . 191 E6
Windlesham House Sch
  RH20. . . . . 143 D3
Windlesham Mans 17
  BN3 . . . . 191 E7
Windlesham Rd
  Brighton BN1 . . . . 191 E6
  Shoreham-by-S BN43. . . . 188 F8
Windlesham Sch BN1 . . . 191 E8
Windmill Ave BN6 . . . . . . 128 D5
Windmill Cl
  Angmering BN16 . . . . 206 A8
  Ashington RH20 . . . . 123 A5
  Bognor Regis PO21 . . . . . 200 B1

Windmill Cl continued
  Horley RH6 . . . . 2 B3
  Horsham RH13 . . . . 37 A4
  Hove BN3. . . . . 168 F2
  Upper Beeding BN44 . . . . 146 B2
Windmill Copse RH20 . . . 121 E2
Windmill Ct
  Barnham PO22 . . . . 180 B5
  Crawley RH10 . . . . 18 D8
  East Wittering PO20 . . . . 207 F7
  Tangmere PO20 . . . . 156 D1
Windmill Dr
  Brighton BN1 . . . . 169 C6
  Burgess Hill RH15 . . . . . . 109 A6
  Rustington BN16 . . . . 205 D6
Windmill Field PO18 . . . . 175 A5
Windmill La
  Ashurst Wood RH19 . . . . . 23 C7
  East Grinstead RH19 . . . . . 9 D3
  Henfield BN5 . . . . 125 E4
Windmill Par
  Rustington BN16 . . . . 205 C6
  Southwick BN42 . . . . 167 E1
Windmill Platt RH17 . . . . . 61 C8
Windmill Rd
  Littlehampton BN17 . . . . . 204 D4
  Southwick BN42 . . . . 167 E1
Windmills Jun Sch The
  BN6 . . . . 129 A3
Windmill St BN2 . . . . 213 C3
Windmill Terr 20 BN2 . . . 213 C3
Windmill View BN1 . . . . . 170 B7
Windrum Cl RH12 . . . . 57 F8
Windrush Cl
  Crawley RH11 . . . . 17 F4
  Worthing BN13 . . . . 185 C9
Windsor Cl
  Bognor Regis PO21 . . . . . 200 E4
  Crawley RH11 . . . . 18 C2
  Haywards Heath RH16 . . . 87 E2
  Hove BN3. . . . . 169 A3
  5 Rustington BN16 . . . . . 205 B7
  Southwater RH13 . . . . 58 A1
Windsor Ct
  Brighton BN1. . . . . 213 A2
  Brighton, Withdean
  BN1. . . . . 169 D4
  3 Horsham RH13. . . . . . . 36 F3
  Worthing BN11 . . . . 187 A2
Windsor Dr
  East Wittering PO20 . . . . 207 F7
  Rustington BN16 . . . . 205 B7
Windsor Lo 5 BN3 . . . . . . 191 B6
Windsor Pl RH10. . . . . .5 F2
Windsor Pl RH19. . . . . 23 A8
Windsor Rd
  Chichester PO19 . . . . 177 D6
  Petersfield GU32 . . . . 68 B4
  Selsey PO20. . . . . 212 E6
  Worthing BN11 . . . . 186 F3
Windsor St BN1. . . . . 213 A2
Windsor Way BN15 . . . . . 188 B6
Windward Cl BN17 . . . . . . 205 A5
Windyridge RH11 . . . . 18 A5
Wineham La BN5,
  RH17 . . . . 106 D5
Winfield Ave BN1 . . . . 169 F6
Winfield Cl
  Brighton BN1. . . . . 169 F5
  Portslade-by-S BN41. . . . 168 A3
Winfield Way PO10 . . . . . 151 B4
Wingle Tye Rd RH15 . . . . 129 A8
Winguard Way PO19 . . . . 177 A5
Winkfield Ct RH16 . . . . 87 D5
Winkhurst Way RH15. . . . . 109 D1
Winnals Pk RH16 . . . . 87 D5
Winner Way RH6 . . . . 5 D6
Winnet Way RH13 . . . . 58 A2
Winnipeg Cl GU30 . . . . 25 C3
Winston Bsns Ctr
  BN15. . . . . 187 C5
Winston Cl PO21. . . . . 200 F6
Winston Cres PO21 . . . . . 200 F6
Winston Ct PO19. . . . . 154 F3
Winston Rd BN15 . . . . 187 D4
Winterbourne RH12. . . . . . 36 F7
Winterbourne Cl
  BN13 . . . . 185 B6
Winterbourne Ct
  BN13 . . . . 185 B6
Winterbourne Rd
  PO19 . . . . 155 A2
Winterbourne Way
  BN13 . . . . 185 B6
Winterfold RH10. . . . . 19 A3
Winter Gdns RH11 . . . . 18 C5
Winter Knoll The
  BN17 . . . . 204 F5
Winterpit Cl RH13. . . . . 59 D6
Winterpit La RH13 . . . . 59 E6
Winters Cotts 8 GU29 . . . 94 E7
Winterton Ct RH13 . . . . 36 D2
Winterton Lo BN17. . . . . . 204 E5
Winterton Way BN43 . . . . 189 B6
Winton Ave BN2 . . . . 194 C3
Winton Ct 1 GU32 . . . . . . 68 B3
Winton Lo BN15 . . . . 185 D8
Winton Pl BN11 . . . . 186 D3
Winton Rd GU32. . . . . 68 B4
Wire Mill La RH7. . . . . .8 F8
Wisborough Ct
  Crawley RH11 . . . . 17 F3
  Worthing BN13 . . . . 185 F7

Wisborough Gdns
RH14 . . . . 78 D8
Wisborough Green Prim
Sch RH14 . . . . 54 C1
Wisborough La RH20 . . . 121 E1
Wisden Ave RH15 . . . . . . 108 E5
Wisden Ct BN14 . . . . 186 A8
Wish Ct BN3 . . . . 190 E8
Wish Rd BN3 . . . . 190 E6
Wisley Ct BN11 . . . . 186 A2
Wisteria Pl RH13 . . . . 80 E2
Wiston Ave
Stockbridge PO19 . . . . . 176 E4
Worthing BN14 . . . . 186 B5
Wiston Bsns Pk RH20 . . . 122 E2
Wiston Cl BN14 . . . . 186 B5
Wiston Ct
Crawley RH11 . . . . 17 F3
1 Horsham RH12 . . . . . 36 D5
12 Shoreham-by-S
BN43 . . . . 189 C8
Wiston Rd BN2 . . . . 192 F6
Wiston Way BN2 . . . . . . 192 F7
WITHDEAN 169 F4
WITHDEAN 169 F4
Withdean Ave
Brighton BN1 . . . . 169 D2
Worthing BN13 . . . . 185 B1
Withdean Cl BN1 . . . . . . 169 D3
Withdean Court Ave
BN1 . . . . 169 D3
Withdean Cres BN1 . . . . 169 E3
Withdean Ct **7** BN1 . . . 169 E3
Withdean Hall 9
BN1 . . . . 169 E3
Withdean Rd BN1 . . . . . . 169 D3
Withdean Rise BN1 . . . . 169 D3
Withdean Stad (Brighton
& Hove Albion FC)
BN1 . . . . 169 D3
Wither Dale RH6 . . . . 1 E4
Withey Brook RH6 . . . . 1 D1
Withey Mdws RH6 . . . . 1 D1
Withy Bush RH15 . . . . . . 108 E5
Witham Ave BN2 . . . . . . 194 C3
Withylands View RH17 . . . 64 B8
Withy Patch Cvn Pk
BN15 . . . . 188 B8
WITHYPITTS 21 A3
Withypitts RH10 . . . . 21 A3
Withypitts E RH10 . . . . . . 21 A3
Wittering Rd PO11 . . . . . 195 B2
WIVELSFIELD 109 F6
Wivelsfield Prim Sch
RH17 . . . . 109 F6
Wivelsfield Rd
Haywards Heath RH16 . . . 87 E2
Saltdean BN2 . . . . 194 C3
Wivelsfield Sta RH15 . . . 109 C4
Woburn Ct BN11 . . . . . . 186 C1
Woburn Pl BN1 . . . . 170 F5
Woburn Rd RH11 . . . . 18 A4
Woelfs Cl RH20 . . . . 123 A5
Woking Ct BN16 . . . . 205 E6
Wold Cl RH11 . . . . 17 F4
WOLDHURST 199 E8
Woldhurst Ct PO20 . . . . . 199 E8
Woldhurstlea Cl RH11 . . . 18 A4
Wolfe Cl PO19 . . . . 154 F1
Wolseley Rd
Brighton BN1 . . . . 170 D6
Portslade-by-S BN41 . . . 190 A8
Wolsey Cl PO21 . . . . 200 B1
Wolsey Pl BN11 . . . . 186 A2
Wolstead Lo **3** RH16 . . . 87 F3
Wolstenbury Rd
BN16 . . . . 205 C7
Wolstonbury Cl
Crawley RH11 . . . . 18 C4
Hurstpierpoint BN6 . . . . 128 B4
Wolstonbury Ct RH15 . . . 109 B2
Wolstonbury Rd BN3 . . . 191 E7
Wolstonbury Way
RH15 . . . . 109 B2
Wolstonbury Wlk 7
BN43 . . . . 166 F1
Wolverstone Dr BN1 . . . 170 C4
Wolverton Cl RH6 . . . . 1 F1
Wolverton Gdns RH6 . . . . 1 F2
Wood Acre Ct 9
PO21 . . . . 201 D4
Woodard Mews BN5 . . . 125 E5
Woodard Rd BN15 . . . . . 187 F7
Woodards View BN43 . . . 188 D5
Woodbanke La 5
RH16 . . . . 87 C2
Woodberry Ho GU28 . . . . 97 D2
Woodberry La
Rowland's Castle PO9 . . . 130 F1
Stubbermere PO10,
PO9 . . . . 151 B7
Woodbine Ct **8** PO21 . . . 201 D4
Woodborough Cl
PO20 . . . . 208 C5
Woodbourne Ave
BN1 . . . . 170 A4
Woodbourne Cl GU33 . . . 45 C4
Woodbridge Cl RH12 . . . . 37 A5
Woodbridge Pk BN16 . . . 206 A5
Woodbury Ave
East Grinstead RH19 . . . . 10 B1
Petersfield GU32 . . . . 68 A5
Woodbury Cl RH19 . . . . . 23 B8
Wood Cl RH1 . . . . 2 A8
Woodcock Hill RH19 . . . . . 8 F6
Woodcote RH6 . . . . 2 C4

Woodcote Cotts
GU28 . . . . 116 A8
Woodcote Ho **3** RH16 . . . 87 C2
Woodcote La
Fittleworth RH20 . . . . 99 D5
Littlehampton RH17 . . . . 182 D5
Woodcote Rd RH18 . . . . . 23 F2
Woodcourt RH11 . . . . 18 C1
Woodcrest Rd RH15 . . . . 108 E5
Woodcroft RH15 . . . . 108 F5
Woodcroft Rd RH11 . . . . . 17 D4
Woodcutters RH17 . . . . . . 88 F3
Wooddale La RH14 . . . . . . 56 A2
Woodend
Bognor Regis PO21 . . . . 201 A4
West Ashling PO18 . . . . 153 C5
Wood End RH12 . . . . 37 C5
Woodend Cl RH10 . . . . . . 19 A8
Woodfield RH13 . . . . 57 F1
Woodfield Cl
Bognor Regis PO21 . . . . 211 A7
Crawley RH10 . . . . 18 E7
Tangmere PO20 . . . . 156 D1
Woodfield Lo RH10 . . . . . 19 A8
Woodfield Park Rd
PO10 . . . . 173 D8
Woodfield Rd
Crawley RH10 . . . . 18 F7
Rudgwick RH12 . . . . 33 D7
Woodfield Terr RH13 . . . . 83 E1
Woodgate RH10 . . . . 36 F3
Woodgate Pk PO20 . . . . . 179 D5
Woodgate Rd PO20 . . . . . 179 D5
Woodgates CI RH13 . . . . . 36 F3
Woodhall Cl RH17 . . . . . . 86 F7
Woodhatch RH13 . . . . 57 F2
Woodhayes RH6 . . . . 2 B4
Woodhorn Cotts
PO20 . . . . 178 E6
Woodhorn La PO20 . . . . . 178 D6
Woodhouse Cl BN3 . . . . 190 E7
Woodhouse La PO8,
PO9 . . . . 130 E4
Woodhouse Rd
Blendworth PO8 . . . . 130 C7
Hove BN3 . . . . 190 E7
Woodingdean Bsns Pk
BN2 . . . . 171 D1
Woodingdean Prim Sch
BN2 . . . . 193 C8
Wooding Gr **15** RH11 . . . 18 F1
Wood La BN5 . . . . 146 F7
Woodland Ave
Burgess Hill RH15 . . . . . 109 C4
Hove BN3 . . . . 169 B3
Worthing BN13 . . . . 163 F1
Woodland Cl
Burgess Hill RH15 . . . . . 109 C4
Five Oaks RH14 . . . . 55 E6
Horsham RH13 . . . . 37 B4
Hove BN3 . . . . 169 B2
Woodland Cotts
RH20 . . . . 122 A7
Woodland Cres RH15 . . . 109 C4
Woodland Ct BN3 . . . . . . 169 B4
Woodland Dr
Crawley Down RH10 . . . . 21 B8
Hove BN3 . . . . 169 B3
Woodland La RH13 . . . . . 38 C3
Woodland Par BN3 . . . . . 169 B3
Woodland Pl PO19 . . . . . 155 A3
Woodland Rd PO20 . . . . . 212 D6
Woodlands
Crawley RH10 . . . . 19 D8
Horley RH6 . . . . 2 D4
Hove BN3 . . . . 169 C2
Woodlands Ave
New Brighton PO10 . . . . 151 B3
Rustington BN16 . . . . . . 205 C6
Woodlands Cl
Angmering BN16 . . . . . . 184 A7
Clapham BN13 . . . . 162 F1
Crawley Down RH10 . . . . 21 B7
Rustington BN16 . . . . . . 205 C6
Woodlands Cotts
BN16 . . . . 205 C6
Woodlands Ctr
(Rustington Heritage
Exhibition Ctr)★
BN16 . . . . 205 C6
Woodlands La
Chichester PO19 . . . . . . 176 F8
Haslemere GU27 . . . . 26 F7
Heath Common RH20 . . . 122 C3
Liss GU33 . . . . 45 D3
Walderton PO18 . . . . 132 B2
Woodlands Pk BN18 . . . 180 F3
Woodlands Rd
Bognor Regis PO22 . . . . 201 B6
East Grinstead RH19 . . . . 10 A4
Haywards Heath RH16 . . . 87 F4
Littlehampton BN17 . . . . 204 E4
Woodlands The BN1 . . . . 169 E5
Woodlands Way
Billingshurst RH14 . . . . . 79 E6
Southwater RH13 . . . . . . 81 E8
Woodlands Wlk RH13 . . . 59 C5
Woodland View RH13 . . . 81 A7
Woodland Villas
PO20 . . . . 157 F1
Woodland Way
Brighton BN1 . . . . 169 F4
Horsham RH13 . . . . 37 B4
Woodland Wlk BN2 . . . . 193 D4
Woodlark Gdns GU31 . . . 68 E3
Wood Lea Cotts RH12 . . . 34 F7
Woodlea Rd BN13 . . . . . 186 A4
Woodleigh Rd RH15 . . . . 109 C4

Woodmancote Ct 6
RH12 . . . . 36 D5
Woodmancote La PO10,
PO18 . . . . 152 B4
Woodmancote Rd
BN14 . . . . 186 B4
WOODMANSGREEN 48 A3
Woodmans Hill RH11 . . . . 18 C2
Woodpecker Cres
RH15 . . . . 108 D3
Woodpecker Ct GU28 . . . 97 F7
Woodpecker La RH20 . . . 121 E1
Woodpecker Rd GU28 . . . 97 E7
Woodpeckers RH13 . . . . . 57 F3
Woodpecker Way
Turners Hill RH10 . . . . . . 21 C5
Worthing BN13 . . . . 185 C6
Wood Ride RH16 . . . . 87 D3
Woodridge Cl RH16 . . . . . 88 A3
Woodroffe Benton Ho
RH11 . . . . 17 F6
Woodroffe Wlk PO10 . . . 151 B4
Woodroyd Ave RH6 . . . . . . 1 F1
Woodroyd Gdns RH6 . . . . 1 F1
Woodruff Bsns Ctr The
PO19 . . . . 176 E5
Woodsdale Ct BN14 . . . . 186 E5
Woods Hill Cl RH19 . . . . . 23 D6
Woods Hill La RH19 . . . . . 23 D6
Woods Ho
Hove BN3 . . . . 191 A8
3 Petersfield GU32 . . . 68 B4
Woodside
Barnham PO22 . . . . 180 B6
Horsham RH13 . . . . 37 B4
Woodside Ave BN1 . . . . . 169 D2
Woodside Cl
Partridge Green
RH13 . . . . 105 D4
Storrington RH20 . . . . . . 121 E2
Woodside Ct **6** BN17 . . . 204 E4
Woodside Lo RH11 . . . . . 169 D2
Woodside Rd
Crawley RH10 . . . . 18 F8
Worthing BN14 . . . . 186 B4
Woodside Road (Worthing
FC) BN14 . . . . 186 B4
Woodsland Cl BN6 . . . . . 128 F4
Woodsland Cross
RH16 . . . . 64 E3
Woodsland Rd BN6 . . . . . 128 F4
Woodsmill Cl BN5 . . . . . 146 E6
Wood's Mill Countryside
Ctr★ BN5 . . . . 146 F8
Wood St
Bognor Regis PO21 . . . . 201 B2
East Grinstead RH19 . . . . . 9 D1
Woodstock RH19 . . . . 9 C2
Woodstock Ct RH12 . . . . . 36 D5
Woodstock Gdns
PO21 . . . . 200 F2
Woods Way BN12 . . . . . . 185 C4
Woodview BN43 . . . . 166 F1
Wood View BN18 . . . . . . 160 A2
Woodview Cl BN1 . . . . . 170 D6
Woodview Ct **13** BN43 . . . 166 F1
Woodwards RH11 . . . . 18 C1
Woodwards Cl RH15 . . . . 109 B1
WOOLBEDING 72 C2
Woolbeding La GU29 . . . . 72 B4
Woolborough Cl RH10 . . . 18 E7
Woolborough La
Crawley RH10 . . . . 5 F1
Crawley, Three Bridges
RH10 . . . . 19 A8
Salfords RH1 . . . . 2 F8
Woolborough Rd RH10 . . . 18 E7
Wooldridge Wlk
BN17 . . . . 181 D1
Wool La GU29 . . . . 94 F7
WOOLMER HILL 26 D7
Woolmer Hill Ho GU27 . . 26 C6
Woolmer Hill Rd GU27 . . 26 D7
Woolmer Hill Tech Coll
GU27 . . . . 26 D7
Woolmer La GU30 . . . . . . 25 C8
Woolmer St PO19 . . . . . . 151 A4
Woolner Ave GU32 . . . . . . 68 B4
Woolstaplers The
PO19 . . . . 176 F5
Woolven Cl BN15 . . . . . . 108 E1
Woolven Row BN5 . . . . . 125 F5
Wophams La PO20 . . . . . 198 D7
Worcester Ct PO21 . . . . . 200 E3
Worcester Ct **1** BN3 . . . 191 E6
Worcester Rd
Chichester PO19 . . . . . . 154 F1
Crawley RH10 . . . . 18 E2
Worcester Villas BN3 . . . 190 C7
Wordsworth Cl RH10 . . . . 19 B8
Wordsworth Gdns
PO22 . . . . 202 D6
Wordsworth Pl RH12 . . . . 36 E7
Wordsworth Rd BN11 . . . 186 C1
Wordsworth Rise 6
RH19 . . . . 9 C1
Wordsworth St BN3 . . . . 191 A7
WORLD'S END 109 D4
Worms La PO22 . . . . 202 D4
Worsted La RH19 . . . . . . 23 B8
WORTH 19 E6
Worth Abbey★ RH10 . . . 20 B1
Worthing Coll BN11 . . . . 185 E4
Worthing High Sch
BN14 . . . . 186 C4
Worthing Hospl BN11 . . . 186 E3

Worthing Mus & Art
Gallery★ BN11 . . . . 186 D2
Worthing Rd
Dial Post RH13 . . . . 103 E3
East Preston BN16 . . . . . 205 F6
Horsham RH12 . . . . 36 B1
Littlehampton BN16,
BN17 . . . . 205 F4
Littlehampton BN17 . . . . 204 E7
Southwater RH13 . . . . . . 57 F2
Tower Hill RH12, RH13 . . 58 A7
West Grinstead RH13 . . . 104 A6
Worthing Sta BN11 . . . . 186 C3
Worth Park Ave RH10 . . . 19 C7
Worth Rd RH10 . . . . 19 C6
Worth Sch RH10 . . . . 20 B1
Worth Way RH10 . . . . 19 E5
Wray Cl RH19 . . . . 23 D6
WRAYS 1 B5
Wraysbury Gdns
BN15 . . . . 187 E7
Wraysbury Park Dr
PO10 . . . . 151 B4
Wren Cl
Burgess Hill RH15 . . . . . 108 D3
Horsham RH12 . . . . 36 D7
Pulborough RH20 . . . . . 100 B2
Wren Cres PO22 . . . . 201 B6
Wren Ct RH10 . . . . 18 E5
Wren Ctr The PO10 . . . . . 151 C3
Wrenfield Pl **9** PO21 . . . 201 C2
Wren St RH10 . . . . 21 C5
Wrentham Ho RH15 . . . . 109 B3
Wright Cl RH10 . . . . 19 C2
Wroxham Way PO22 . . . . 201 F6
Wroxham Wlk **8** RH10 . . 19 B4
Wr Twr Bldgs 3
PO21 . . . . 201 D3
Wyatt Cl RH14 . . . . 54 B1
Wyatt Ct PO20 . . . . 207 F7
Wyatts La RH17 . . . . 65 D5
Wyberlye Rd RH15 . . . . . 109 A4
Wyberton Ho PO19 . . . . 155 A3
Wychache RH10 . . . . 121 B8
Wychcroft 4 BN17 . . . . 204 D5
WYCH CROSS 44 C5
Wychperry Rd RH16 . . . . 87 D5
Wychwood RH14 . . . . 31 D3
Wychwood Ct PO21 . . . . 200 E1
Wychwood Gdns
BN11 . . . . 187 B3
Wychwood Wlk PO21 . . . 200 E1
Wyck Ct BN41 . . . . 190 A7
Wycliffe Ct
Crawley RH11 . . . . 17 E3
15 Worthing BN11 . . . 186 A1
Wyde Feld PO21 . . . . 200 E2
Wye Cl RH11 . . . . 39 C8
Wye Ho BN11 . . . . 186 B2
Wyke Ave **6** BN11 . . . . 186 E2
Wykeham Cl BN44 . . . . . 145 D3
Wykeham Ct BN11 . . . . . 186 C2
Wykeham Rd BN11 . . . . . 186 C2
Wykeham Terr BN1 . . . . . 213 A2
Wykeham Way RH15 . . . . 109 C2
Wyke La N PO22 . . . . . . 202 C6
Wykwood GU30 . . . . 25 D4
Wyld Green La GU33 . . . . 45 D5
Wyncombe Cl RH20 . . . . . 99 B3
Wyndham Bsns Pk
GU29 . . . . 94 D7
Wyndham Lea RH20 . . . . 121 D6
Wyndham Rd GU28 . . . . . 97 F7
Wyndham St BN1 . . . . . . 213 C1
Wynlea Cl RH10 . . . . 21 A8
Wynnes Mews BN3 . . . . 191 A7
Wynnstay RH15 . . . . 109 B2
Wysemead RH6 . . . . 2 C4
Wyshe The BN45 . . . . . . 149 C6
Wythering Cl PO21 . . . . . 210 F7
Wythwood RH6 . . . . 87 E1
Wyvern Cl PO20 . . . . 156 E1
Wyvern Ct **6** BN11 . . . . 186 C1
Wyvern Pl RH12 . . . . 35 F8
Wyvern Way RH15 . . . . . 109 C3

Y

Yachtsmens Cotts
PO18 . . . . 175 C5
Yapton CE Prim Sch
BN18 . . . . 180 F4
Yapton La BN18 . . . . 180 F7
Yapton Rd
Barnham BN18, PO22 . . . 180 D4
Climping BN17, BN18 . . . 181 C1
Middleton-on-S BN18,
PO22 . . . . 202 E7
Yarborough Terr GU29 . . . 72 A1
Yarbrook PO18 . . . . 154 E7
Yardlea Cl PO9 . . . . 130 D1
Yardley St BN1 . . . . 213 B5
Yarmouth Cl RH10 . . . . . . 19 A4
Yarrow Cl RH12 . . . . 36 E5
Yattendon Rd RH6 . . . . . . 2 B3
Yattendon Sch RH6 . . . . . 2 A4
Yeoman Gate BN13 . . . . 185 B5
Yeoman Rd BN13 . . . . . . 185 B6
Yeomans Acre PO21 . . . . 200 F3
Yeomans Field PO18 . . . 152 D1
Yeomans La GU30 . . . . . . 25 A4
Yeoman Way BN13 . . . . . 185 B5
Yew Ct
Crawley RH11 . . . . 18 D5
1 East Grinstead RH19 . . 9 D2
Yew La RH19 . . . . 9 B3
Yewlands Wlk RH11 . . . . 17 D4

Yew Tree Cl
Bognor Regis PO22 . . . . 201 B6
Cowfold RH13 . . . . 83 E2
Horley RH6 . . . . 2 A4
Lancing BN15 . . . . 187 E5
Yew Tree Cotts
Burgess Hill RH15 . . . . . 109 B3
5 Worthing BN14 . . . . 186 D5
Yew Tree Ct RH17 . . . . . . 86 F6
Yew Tree Pl GU33 . . . . . . 45 C4
Yew Tree Rd RH6 . . . . 4 E7
York Ave
East Grinstead RH19 . . . . 23 A8
Hove BN3 . . . . 191 E6
York Chase PO19 . . . . . . 154 F1
York Cl
Horsham RH13 . . . . 36 E5
Petersfield GU32 . . . . 67 F3
Southwater RH13 . . . . . . 58 A1
York Ct **13** BN3 . . . . 191 E7
York Gdns BN17 . . . . 204 D5
York Gr BN1 . . . . 213 A4
York Hill BN1 . . . . 213 B4
York Ho
Portslade-by-S BN41 . . . 190 B8
Worthing BN11 . . . . 187 A3
Yorkhurst Hill PO18 . . . . 114 F1
Yorklands BN3 . . . . 169 B4
York Lo **11** BN11 . . . . . 186 C3
York Mansions E 13
BN3 . . . . 191 E6
York Mansions W 12
BN3 . . . . 191 E6
York Pl
Brighton BN1 . . . . 213 A4
Hove BN3 . . . . 191 E6
York Rd
Bognor Regis PO21 . . . . 201 D3
Burgess Hill RH15 . . . . . 108 D2
Chichester PO19 . . . . . . 177 C5
Crawley RH10 . . . . 18 E2
Hove, Brighton BN1, BN3 191 E6
Littlehampton BN17 . . . . 204 D5
Selsey PO20 . . . . 212 E5
Worthing BN11 . . . . 186 E2
York Villas BN1 . . . . 213 A4
Yorkwood GU33 . . . . 45 B4
Youngsmere Cl BN1 . . . . 170 B6
Young St **4** PO19 . . . . . 155 A2

Z

Zachary Merton Com
Hospl BN16 . . . . 205 D4
Zion Gdns BN1 . . . . 213 A2

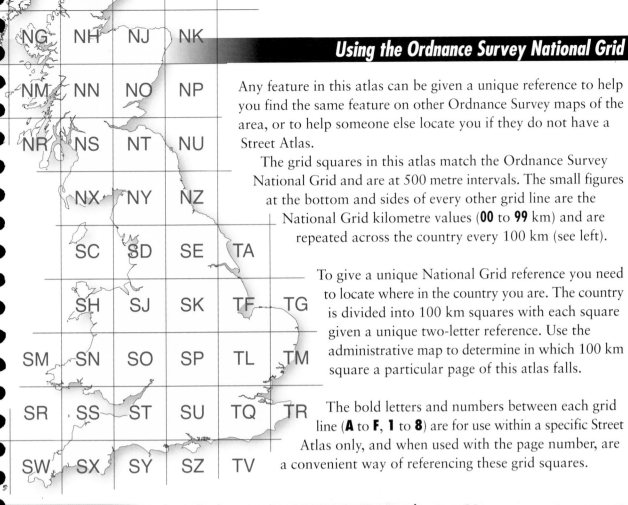

Using the Ordnance Survey National Grid

Any feature in this atlas can be given a unique reference to help you find the same feature on other Ordnance Survey maps of the area, or to help someone else locate you if they do not have a Street Atlas.

The grid squares in this atlas match the Ordnance Survey National Grid and are at 500 metre intervals. The small figures at the bottom and sides of every other grid line are the National Grid kilometre values (**00** to **99** km) and are repeated across the country every 100 km (see left).

To give a unique National Grid reference you need to locate where in the country you are. The country is divided into 100 km squares with each square given a unique two-letter reference. Use the administrative map to determine in which 100 km square a particular page of this atlas falls.

The bold letters and numbers between each grid line (**A** to **F**, **1** to **8**) are for use within a specific Street Atlas only, and when used with the page number, are a convenient way of referencing these grid squares.

Example   The railway bridge over DARLEY GREEN RD in grid square B1

Step 1: Identify the two-letter reference, in this example the page is in **SP**

Step 2: Identify the 1 km square in which the railway bridge falls. Use the figures in the southwest corner of this square: Eastings **17**, Northings **74**. This gives a unique reference: **SP 17 74**, accurate to 1 km.

Step 3: To give a more precise reference accurate to 100 m you need to estimate how many tenths along and how many tenths up this 1 km square the feature is (to help with this the 1 km square is divided into four 500 m squares). This makes the bridge about **8** tenths along and about **1** tenth up from the southwest corner.

This gives a unique reference: **SP 178 741**, accurate to 100 m.

Eastings (read from left to right along the bottom) come before Northings (read from bottom to top). If you have trouble remembering say to yourself "Along the hall, THEN up the stairs"!

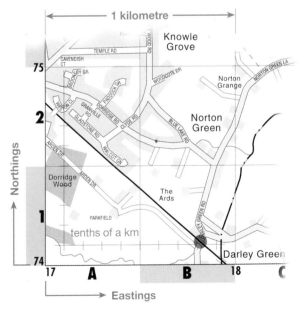

PHILIP'S MAPS

the Gold Standard for drivers

◆ **Philip's street atlases cover every county in England, Wales, Northern Ireland and much of Scotland**

- ◆ Every named street is shown, including alleys, lanes and walkways
- ◆ Thousands of additional features marked: stations, public buildings, car parks, places of interest
- ◆ Route-planning maps to get you close to your destination
- ◆ Postcodes on the maps and in the index
- ◆ Widely used by the emergency services, transport companies and local authorities

For national mapping, choose **Philip's Navigator Britain** the most detailed road atlas available of England, Wales and Scotland. Hailed by Auto Express as 'the ultimate road atlas', the atlas shows every road and lane in Britain.

Street atlases currently available

England
Bedfordshire and Luton
Berkshire
Birmingham and West Midlands
Bristol and Bath
Buckinghamshire and Milton Keynes
Cambridgeshire and Peterborough
Cheshire
Cornwall
Cumbria
Derbyshire
Devon
Dorset
County Durham and Teesside
Essex
North Essex
South Essex
Gloucestershire and Bristol
Hampshire
North Hampshire
South Hampshire
Herefordshire Monmouthshire
Hertfordshire
Isle of Wight
Kent
East Kent
West Kent
Lancashire
Leicestershire and Rutland
Lincolnshire
Liverpool and Merseyside
London
Greater Manchester
Norfolk
Northamptonshire
Northumberland
Nottinghamshire
Oxfordshire
Shropshire
Somerset
Staffordshire
Suffolk

Surrey
East Sussex
West Sussex
Tyne and Wear
Warwickshire and Coventry
Wiltshire and Swindon
Worcestershire
East Yorkshire Northern Lincolnshire
North Yorkshire
South Yorkshire
West Yorkshire

Wales
Anglesey, Conwy and Gwynedd
Cardiff, Swansea and The Valleys
Carmarthenshire, Pembrokeshire and Swansea
Ceredigion and South Gwynedd
Denbighshire, Flintshire, Wrexham
Herefordshire Monmouthshire
Powys

Scotland
Aberdeenshire
Ayrshire
Dumfries and Galloway
Edinburgh and East Central Scotland
Fife and Tayside
Glasgow and West Central Scotland
Inverness and Moray
Lanarkshire
Scottish Borders

Northern Ireland
County Antrim and County Londonderry
County Armagh and County Down
Belfast
County Tyrone and County Fermanagh